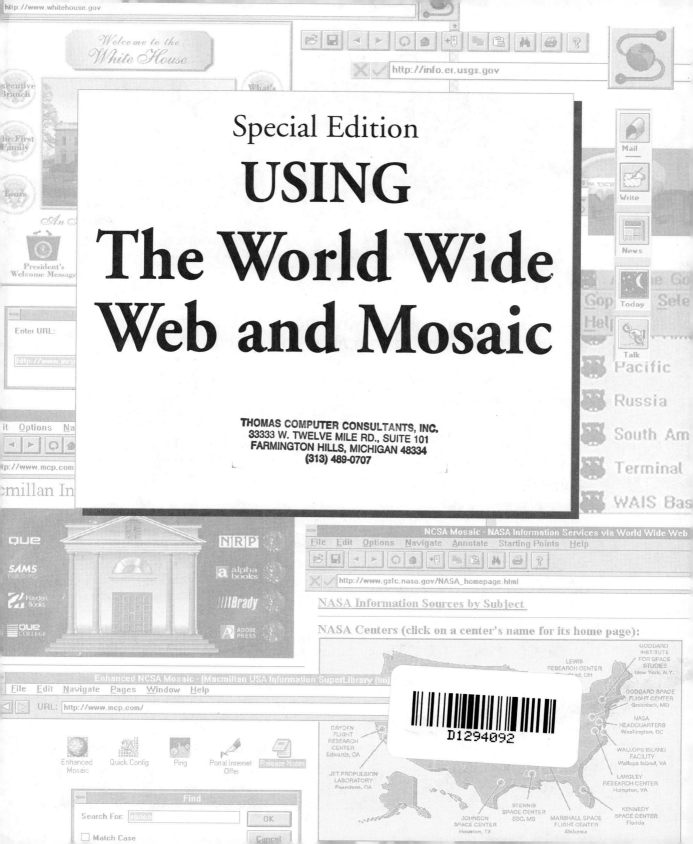

Special Edition
USING
The World Wide Web and Mosaic

THOMAS COMPUTER CONSULTANTS, INC.
33333 W. TWELVE MILE RD., SUITE 101
FARMINGTON HILLS, MICHIGAN 48334
(313) 489-0707

PLUG YOURSELF INTO...

THE MACMILLAN INFORMATION SUPERLIBRARY™

Free information and vast computer resources from the world's leading computer book publisher—online!

FIND THE BOOKS THAT ARE RIGHT FOR YOU!

A complete online catalog, plus sample chapters and tables of contents give you an in-depth look at *all* of our books, including hard-to-find titles. It's the best way to find the books you need!

- **STAY INFORMED** with the latest computer industry news through our online newsletter, press releases, and customized Information SuperLibrary Reports.

- **GET FAST ANSWERS** to your questions about MCP books and software.

- **VISIT** our online bookstore for the latest information and editions!

- **COMMUNICATE** with our expert authors through e-mail and conferences.

- **DOWNLOAD SOFTWARE** from the immense MCP library:
  - Source code and files from MCP books
  - The best shareware, freeware, and demos

- **DISCOVER HOT SPOTS** on other parts of the Internet.

- **WIN BOOKS** in ongoing contests and giveaways!

TO PLUG INTO MCP: ➜ WORLD WIDE WEB: **http://www.mcp.com**

GOPHER: gopher.mcp.com

FTP: ftp.mcp.com

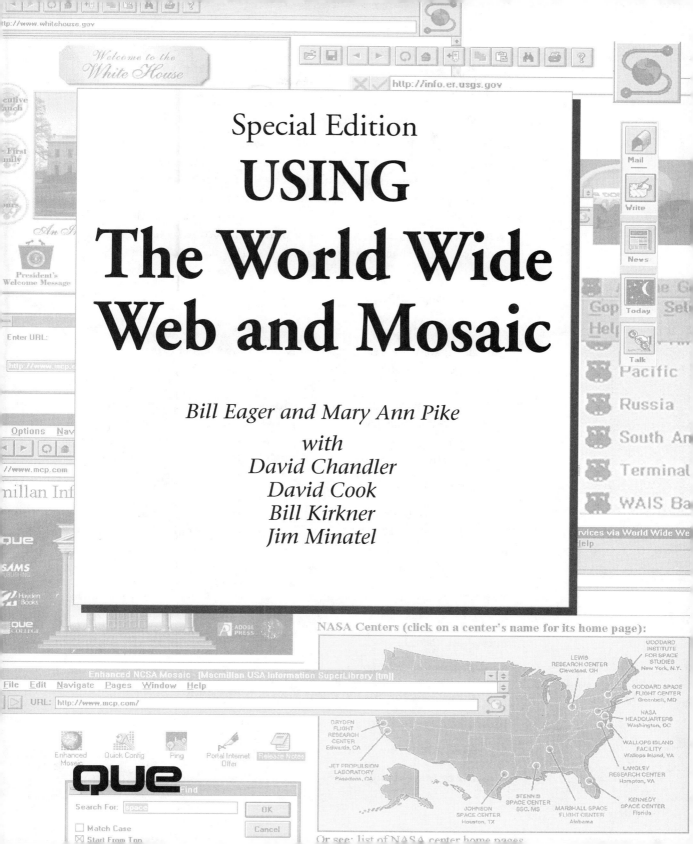

Special Edition

USING
The World Wide
Web and Mosaic

Bill Eager and Mary Ann Pike

with
David Chandler
David Cook
Bill Kirkner
Jim Minatel

Special Edition Using the World Wide Web and Mosaic

Library of Congress Catalog No.: 95-67674

ISBN: 0-78970-250-9

98 97 96 95   6 5 4 3 2 1

Interpretation of the printing code: the rightmost double-digit number is the year of the book's printing; the rightmost single-digit number, the number of the book's printing. For example, a printing code of 95-1 shows that the first printing of the book occurred in 1995.

Screen reproductions in this book were created using Collage Plus from Inner Media, Inc., Hollis, NH.

Publisher: Roland Elgey

Associate Publisher: Stacy Hiquet

Publishing Director: Brad R. Koch

Director of Product Series: Charles O. Stewart III

Managing Editor: Sandy Doell

Director of Marketing: Lynn E. Zingraf

Credits

Acquisitions Editor
Cheryl D. Willoughby

Product Director
Jim Minatel

Production Editor
Chris Nelson

Editors
Danielle Bird
Geneil Breeze
Kelli M. Brooks
Barb Colter
Kezia Endsley
Noelle Gasco
Lisa M. Gebken
Thomas F. Hayes
Theresa Mathias
Linda Seifert
Kathy Simpson
Heather Kaufman Urschel

Technical Editors
Alp Berker
Don Doherty

Figure Specialist
Cari Ohm

Book Designer
Sandra Schroeder

Cover Designer
Dan Armstrong

Acquisitions Assistant
Ruth Slates

Editorial Assistant
Andrea Duvall

Production Team
Stephen Adams
Angela D. Bannan
Claudia Bell
Amy Cornwell
Chad Dressler
DiMonique Ford
Karen Gregor
Dennis Clay Hager
Aren Howell
John Hulse
Daryl Kessler
Bob LaRoche
Donna Martin
Bobbi Satterfield
Clair Schweinler
Kris Simmons
Michael Thomas
Elaine Voci-Reed
Jody York

Indexer
Rebecca Mayfield

Composed in *Stone Serif* and *MCPdigital* by Que Corporation

About the Authors

Bill Eager lives in Conifer, Colorado. With more than 12 years of communications technology experience, Mr. Eager designs, writes, and speaks about electronic communications. While Manager for the Corporate Communications Department at BASF Corporation, Mr. Eager proposed and helped develop a system that distributes hypertext-based multimedia to thousands of employees at sites across the country. Mr. Eager has been an editor of several national trade magazines including *ComSat Technology* and *Communications Technology*. His book *The Information Payoff*, by Prentice Hall, details how companies and businesses use electronic communication to improve productivity, enhance training, and become more competitive. Among Mr. Eager's other Que titles are *Information Superhighway Illustrated*, which uses vivid color drawings and photographs to explore cutting-edge technology and applications of the info highway, and *Using the Internet*, which provides an excellent starting point for people who are just gearing up to use the Internet. Mr. Eager is President of the Colorado Chapter of the International Interactive Communications Society (IICS). In addition to computers, he enjoys photography, hiking, and skiing. You can reach him electronically at **BILLE2000** (America Online), **74010,1511** (CompuServe) or **Eager@sosi.com** (Internet).

Mary Ann Pike has a B.S. in electrical engineering and an M.A. in professional writing from Carnegie-Mellon University. She has experience in software design and development, and is currently working as a technical writer at the Software Engineering Institute at Carnegie-Mellon University. She has authored several other Que Internet books, including *Special Edition Using the Internet*, Second Edition, and *Using Mosaic*.

David Chandler is a World Wide Web enthusiast in Cedar Rapids, Iowa. He currently runs Internet at Work, an eastern Iowa Internet service provider also offering leased server space nationwide. Chandler previously managed Web servers for the Collins Avionics and Communications Division of Rockwell International. He has programmed computers since 1982 when he received a TI-99/4A as a gift. As a hobbyist, he enjoys learning new computer languages and building PCs. Chandler holds a degree in electrical engineering from the University of Kansas and worked as a signal processing engineer in GPS before moving into the information systems field. When he's not at his computer, Chandler enjoys the mountains and flying as a private pilot. He can be reached via e-mail at **73143,3110@compuserve.com** and is available for Internet training and consulting. You can find Chandler on the Web at **http://www.infonet.net/showcase/chandler**.

David Cook has worked in the computing industry since 1980 for a variety of organizations including NASA, CDI, and Truevision. He is currently president of Cookware, which was started in 1990 to provide high-end computing solutions in graphics, VR, interactive networking, and the World Wide Web. David was a contributor to Que's *Special Edition Using the Internet*, Second Edition.

Bill Kirkner first learned how to use a computer at the Boys' Latin School of Maryland on a set of spiffy TRS-80 Color computers at a time when 64K was considered a lot of RAM and an external 5 1/4-inch floppy drive was a quantum leap forward in technology. He first learned how to use the Internet as a consultant for the Academic Computing Service of Loyola College in Maryland, and he fondly remembers the days when you could still print a map of all of the nodes on the Internet and post it on one wall. He has since earned his J.D. from the Georgetown University Law Center and now works as a Technical Specialist for Walcoff and Associates, an information and technology transfer contractor based in Fairfax, Virginia. Bill was a contributor to Que's *Special Edition Using the Internet*, Second Edition. He currently lives in the Dupont Circle neighborhood of Washington, D.C.

Jim Minatel is a Product Development Specialist working for Que. His areas of expertise include computer graphics, the Internet, and multimedia. Before coming to Que, he developed college math texts and earned an M.S. in mathematics from Chicago State University, in addition to a B.A. in mathematics and physics from Wabash College. Jim was a contributor to Que's *Special Edition Using the Internet*, Second Edition.

Acknowledgments

To my family and friends, the many people at Que who put in thousands of hours to get an incredible book project like this from the idea stage into bookstores—and to you, the reader, who as an active Internet surfer will continue to explore and push the envelope on what can be done with this great medium.

Bill Eager

I would like to thank all of those who contributed to the success of this project: the Internet users who volunteer their efforts to make the Internet community what it is; and the staff at Que who put a lot of hard work into this project, including Jim Minatel and Chris Nelson.

Mary Ann Pike

Trademarks

Contents at a Glance

Finding Web Resources

WebCD

Contents

6 Navigating with Mosaic — 99

7 Mosaic Shortcuts and Tips — 125

III Netscape and Other World Wide Web Browsers   205

11 Netscape   207

IV Creating Web Pages and Web Sites   317

14 Creating Home Pages with HTML   319

23 Education   591

24 Government   653

25 Health and Medicine 691

26 History and Geography 719

27 International Web Resources 739

28 Issues, Politics, Religion, and World Events   775

29 Publications: News, Periodicals, and Books   805

30 Science   837

31 Shopping 871

32 Sports, Games, Hobbies, Travel, Cooking, and Recreation 903

33 Hot FTP and Gopher Sites   941

VII WebCD   969

34 What's on WebCD   971

Introduction

The Internet—the global network of networks, referred to by users as simply the *Net*—continues to receive tremendous publicity. Magazines, newspapers, television networks, and radio stations all produce stories about the Internet. In successive weeks, *BusinessWeek* featured a cover story called "The Information Revolution: How Digital Technology Is Changing the Way We Work and Live," and the cover of *Time* magazine pronounced, "The Strange New World of the Internet: Battles on the Frontiers of Cyberspace." Furthermore, many major periodicals now have regular columns for online topics.

The technology and applications of the Internet now extend beyond the realm of computer techies and industry trade publications. The Internet receives this extensive attention because it is an exciting communications medium, business tool, and commercial outlet, much as television and radio were 50 and 100 years ago, respectively. Now, with its simple interface and multimedia applications, the World Wide Web makes the Internet accessible to millions of people who previously stayed away because of the difficult technical command language and the dull appearance of the system.

One indication that the Internet has evolved from technical experiment to widespread acceptance is the fact that jokes are beginning to surface. Some of the more than 20 million Internet users have posted suggestions for new books about the Internet, including the following:

- *The Internet User's Guide to Internet User Guides*

- *Confessions of an Internet Guide Reader*

- *The Lost Guides of the Internet*

- *A Guide to Getting Coffee on the Internet*

The suggestions, of course, poke fun at the phenomenal growth of books and guides about the Internet. Some bookstores devote entire sections to the subject. Why are publishers and authors madly creating new titles for the Internet?

It Keeps on Growing

The Internet has doubled in size every 10 months for the past six years. This growth occurs in both the physical aspects of the Net—the host computers and the connections between computers—as well as the number of people who use the system. In 1985, the Internet had about 1,961 host computers, or *nodes*. These mainframes, minicomputers, and microcomputers can provide access to the services of the Internet to hundreds of thousands of people. Today, the number of hosts exceeds 2-1/2 million.

Two years ago, the Internet was used almost exclusively by scientists, academics, and students as a vehicle for sharing information about work and research projects. Today, all demographic groups use the Internet: lawyers, teachers, homeowners, business professionals, and so on. The number of users continues to increase at the phenomenal rate of two million new logins each month—the equivalent of four new users every minute.

The Internet is not only growing in terms of size, but also expanding in terms of the types of services that are available. The application that was responsible for the initial growth of the Internet is electronic mail, known as *e-mail*. E-mail represents a cost-effective mechanism for people to share messages and send files to friends and colleagues around the world. Other popular Internet applications include File Transfer Protocol (FTP) and Telnet. FTP enables users to download files and even software programs from computers around the world; and Telnet enables users to log in to remote computers and to run programs. The Internet also has applications that search for information, and the latest Internet application—the World Wide Web—lets you view documents from around the world. Understanding how these applications work makes using the Internet easier.

Most people want to use technology to accomplish a task: provide entertainment, retrieve information, or assist with research. They don't want to spend time and energy making the technology work. Telephones, radios, and television sets use standard, user-friendly technology; you push keys to operate the telephone, turn a dial on the radio, and press buttons on a remote-control for the television. People want the Internet to be just as simple to use as these common household communication devices.

Until recently, however, both connecting to and using the Internet were complex processes. There are several reasons for this:

- Rather than being created by a commercial foundation, the system was born from a U.S. government-sponsored research program.

- Many types of computers can connect to the Internet, ranging from 286-based PCs to Pentium machines, Macintoshes, and terminals. These computers can use a variety of connections and connection speeds. Users can have dial-in, SLIP, or PPP accounts or direct access lines; and communication speeds range from 2,400 bytes per second to 1.544M (megabytes) per second.

- Many software programs—running under UNIX, DOS, Windows, and Macintosh, for example— are used as interfaces to the resources of the Internet and the World Wide Web.

Today, national and local service providers eliminate many of these choices and technical obstacles by offering services that include connection and installation of interface programs. Also, the new software programs and interfaces are extremely easy to use, with point-and-click operation and simple icons that represent functions, such as searching.

The World Wide Web: A New Paradigm

The ultimate in user-friendly interfaces is the World Wide Web, also called WWW, W3, or the Web. The WWW is part of the Internet; globally, it represents all the computers (*servers*) that offer users access to hypermedia-based information and documentation. Hypermedia enables users to navigate the Internet, moving with point-and-click ease from one location or one document to another. The Web eliminates unfriendly computer commands. In addition, the resources of the WWW include graphic images, photographs, audio, and full-motion video—elements that make locating and using information fun and useful.

The WWW is an interactive medium. Unlike television, the Web doesn't make you wait for a predetermined schedule to get the information you want, and programming is not defined by a small group of producers. When you use the resources of the Web, you are in control. You decide what you want and when you want it.

This empowerment extends to the creation of information. In the 1400s, the Gutenberg press gave a kick-start to the widespread distribution of knowledge through printed material such as books and newsletters. A modern-day version of the printing press is a WWW/Internet resource known appropriately as "Project Gutenberg." This is a computer database that consists of the full text of more than 100 public domain books ranging from titles by Charles Dickens to Mark Twain. You can either read these famous works online, or download them to your computer to view at your leisure.

Indeed, the WWW enables anyone who has a computer and the proper Internet connection to be a multimedia publisher. In a few minutes, you can create a message or a document that the entire world can access. When you travel the WWW, you'll find electronic books, magazines, and journals. Authors live and write in countries around the world.

Combining global connectivity and individual empowerment, the Internet and WWW represent a form of electronic democracy. No single government, organization, company, or person controls the technical infrastructure, the computer systems, the applications, or the information that comprise this electronic communications system. The democratic nature of the Internet and WWW is exemplified by the tremendous variety of information that is available—everything from technical studies of astrophysics to reports on rock-and-roll bands. Information and messages fly from country to country in seconds. The speed of information delivery promotes political democracy as uncensored, unpackaged news and information move freely around the world.

Reports, personal messages, and fund-raising requests were sent through the Internet during the Chinese military crackdown in Tiananmen Square, the 1991 coup attempt in the Soviet Union, and the recent war in Croatia. The widespread dissemination of information is not limited to personal correspondence. For example, the complete text of the North American Free Trade Agreement (NAFTA) is maintained as a WWW document by *The Tech*, MIT's oldest newspaper. In addition, the news-service company VOGON operates a Web server that provides *UK News*, a compilation of hypertext-based stories received from the BBC; and the *San Francisco Chronicle* and the *San Francisco Examiner* maintain Web computers that enable users to access news articles.

Finding the Needle in the Haystack

Because it is easy to use, combines multiple forms of media, and provides access to unlimited information, the Web contributes to the explosive growth of the Internet. The most widely used Web interface is Mosaic, a free, public-domain software program partly developed under a U.S. government grant.

In a six-month period, more than two million people downloaded Mosaic from the host computer at the National Center for Supercomputer Applications (NCSA) site.

Universities, government agencies, companies, and individual users are fervently developing hypermedia documents and starting W3 servers. This volume of development creates a good news/bad news situation. The good news is that every subject known to humankind can be found through the Web. The bad news is that navigating that mountain of information is difficult.

One of the best-selling national periodicals is *TV Guide*, a publication that informs viewers what programs are available and lists air time and channel location. With the growth of cable television, *TV Guide* and other publications cater to people who don't want to spend an hour to locate a good 30-minute television program.

If 40 channels of television programming create confusion, imagine how difficult it is to locate a specific topic, service, resource, or company on a global computer system with two million hosts. Also, although radio and broadcast-television programming are free, you have to pay monthly or hourly charges to wander through the resources of the World Wide Web.

What This Book Is

This book is intended to provide a comprehensive overview of the World Wide Web. The Web and the Internet services with which it interfaces are discussed.

The World Wide Web has a wealth of resources available for those who can find them. This book tells you how to get access to the Internet and the World Wide Web, and gives you a complete overview of Mosaic, the most popular interface to the WWW. Some of the newer Web browsers are examined, including one that interfaces Microsoft Word to the Web. You are introduced to HTML, the language of the Web, and shown how to create your own Web documents for others to access. Finally, you get a look at some of the most interesting places and documents to visit on the Web, and see how to use the software on the CD included with this book to get the information you need.

This Book Is a Guide

Despite the jokes about new Internet publications, this book firmly stands as a guide. It is a guide that provides an overview of the principal applications of the World Wide Web. It is a guide to the various connections and interfaces that provide access to the Web. And it is a guide that provides a basic tutorial on procedures for writing home pages—the starting point for each of the resources on the WWW—and multimedia documents for publication on the Web.

Here is a brief glimpse at the contents of the book, with short descriptions of each chapter.

- Chapter 1, "Introduction to the World Wide Web," teaches you the techniques and terminology you need to know to navigate successfully through the Internet and the World Wide Web.

- Chapter 2, "Connecting to the World Wide Web," tells you how you can get access to the exciting online world that's waiting for you.

- Chapter 3, "Browsers in Brief," introduces you to the applications that let you access the multimedia information of the WWW.

- Chapter 4, "Getting Mosaic Running in Windows," introduces you to Mosaic, one of the first and most popular WWW browsers, and tells you how to get Mosaic running under Windows.

- Chapter 5, "Multimedia—Using Viewers," tells you what you need to do to get full access to the multimedia documents you find on the Web.

- Chapter 6, "Navigating with Mosaic," explains the basic features of Mosaic that let you move from one WWW site to another.

- Chapter 7, "Mosaic Shortcuts and Tips," explains how to use Mosaic to keep track of your favorite places on the Web.

- Chapter 8, "FTP and Mosaic," shows you how to use Mosaic as a friendly interface to one of the Internet's oldest applications.

- Chapter 9, "Gopher and Mosaic," shows you how to explore Gopherspace with the Mosaic interface.

- Chapter 10, "Using Mosaic to Access Other Internet Services," shows you how easy it is to access Internet applications such as WAIS, Telnet, and UseNet with Mosaic.

■ Chapter 11, "Netscape," gives you a comprehensive overview of the hottest new WWW navigator.

■ Chapter 12, "Luckman Interactive Enhanced Mosaic," introduces you to an easy-to-use Web browser (included on WebCD with this book) for those who may be overwhelmed by other browsers.

■ Chapter 13, "Microsoft Internet Assistant," introduces you to the first application that integrates a word processor, WWW authoring tool, and WWW browser into one application.

■ Chapter 14, "Creating Home Pages with HTML," gives you a lesson on how to develop a home page of your own. You learn how to write HTML (Hypertext Markup Language), the programming language for the WWW.

■ Chapter 15, "Advanced HTML," tells you how to create documents containing some of the more complicated HTML features, such as forms and tables.

■ Chapter 16, "HTML Editors and Filters," introduces you to some applications that make writing in HTML a breeze and let you translate other document formats to HTML.

■ Chapter 17, "Setting Up a Web Site," tells you what you need to do to make your WWW documents available to millions of people around the globe.

■ Chapter 18, "The Future of the Web," looks at where this explosion of information availability will lead us.

■ Chapter 19, "Web Searching," introduces you to some of the applications that exist today to help you find the needle in the electronic haystack.

■ Chapters 20–32, broken down by subject area, are a reference guide to Web sites around the world. The listings give you the URL (Uniform Resource Locator) address for home pages of each Web resource. In addition to a brief review of the resource that highlights the information and the links to other resources and multimedia, each chapter includes figures that depict many of the home pages. Chapters also include detailed descriptions of the most popular Web resources for a specific category. For example, in the chapter on science resources, there is a comprehensive review of NASA's Web site, which offers connections to hundreds of scientific, educational, and space-related organizations and multimedia documents. Be forewarned—you may never go home again!

- Chapter 33, "Hot FTP and Gopher Sites," is included because you can use Mosaic to access FTP and Gopher archives. The listings can help you find the most useful FTP and Gopher sites.

- Chapter 34, "What's on WebCD," is a detailed overview of the contents of the CD-ROM that accompanies this book and instructions on how to use it.

With its point-and-click interfaces, the Web encourages exploration. One link quickly leads to a new area or topic. The listings in this book facilitate exploration as they provide a starting point for jumping into the vast resources of the World Wide Web. Enjoy—and don't worry about getting lost. Home is only a click away.

WebCD: Your One-Stop Web Resource

If all of this sounds like a good deal, hold onto your socks—there's more. This book includes an incredible CD-ROM called WebCD (just inside the back cover). What makes it incredible is that it contains such a tremendous variety of Internet and Web-based software programs for the Microsoft Windows environment—everything from a popular e-mail program to a Web browser and HTML authoring tools. Combined with the text-files that are on WebCD, these resources will help you become a "Webmaster" in no time.

You'll see the WebCD icon (shown beside this paragraph) throughout the book in the margins. Whenever you see this icon, the text is discussing software or a document on WebCD.

Conventions Used in This Book

This book uses various conventions designed to make it easier to use. That way, you can quickly and easily learn to use the Web and locate the resources you want.

With most programs, you can use the mouse or keyboard to perform operations. The keyboard procedures may include shortcut key combinations or *mnemonic* keys. In this book, key combinations are joined with plus signs (+). For example, Ctrl+X means hold down the Ctrl key, press the X key, and then release both keys. Some menu and dialog box options have underlined or highlighted characters that indicate mnemonic keys. To choose such an option using the mnemonic key, you press the Alt key and then press the indicated mnemonic key. In this book, mnemonic keys are set in bold: for example, **F**ile.

The book uses several other typeface enhancements to indicate special text, as indicated in the following table.

Typeface	Meaning
Italic	Italic is used to indicate variables in commands or addresses, and also terms used for the first time.
Bold	Bold is used for text you type and also to indicate actual Internet addresses: World Wide Web pages, FTP sites, newsgroups, mailing lists, and more.
`Computer type`	This special type is used for on-screen messages and for commands (such as the DOS COPY or UNIX cp command).

Note

Notes provide additional information that may help you avoid problems or offer advice or general information related to the topic at hand.

Tip
Tips suggest easier or alternative methods of executing a procedure.

Caution

Cautions warn you of hazardous procedures and situations that can lead to unexpected or unpredictable results, including data loss or system damage.

Troubleshooting

Troubleshooting sections anticipate common problems...

...and then provide you with practical suggestions for solving those problems.

Margin cross-references direct you to related information in other parts of the book. Right-facing triangles indicate later chapters, and left-facing triangles point you back to information earlier in the book.

▶ See "How Does the World Wide Web Relate to the Internet?" p. 14

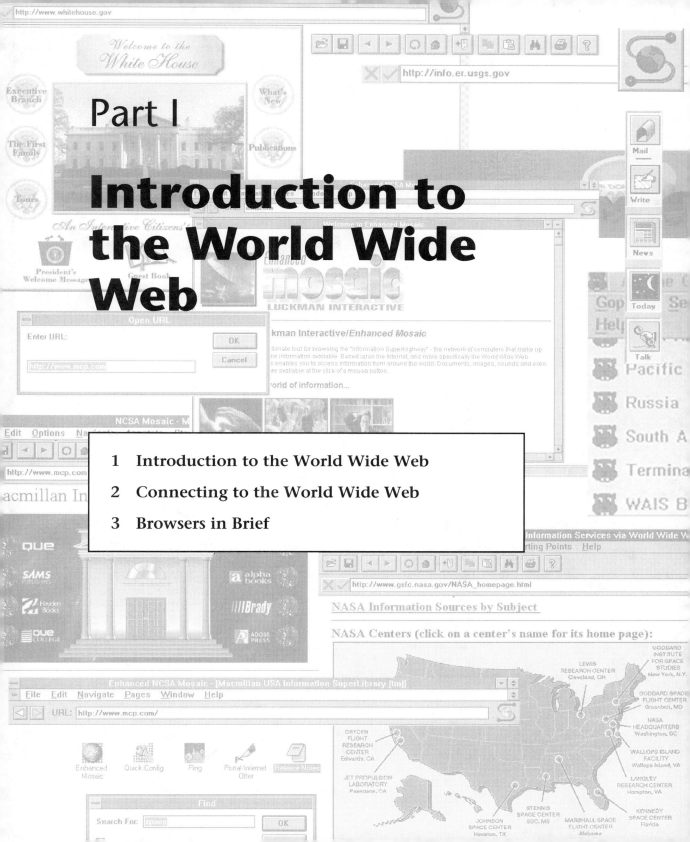

Part I

Introduction to the World Wide Web

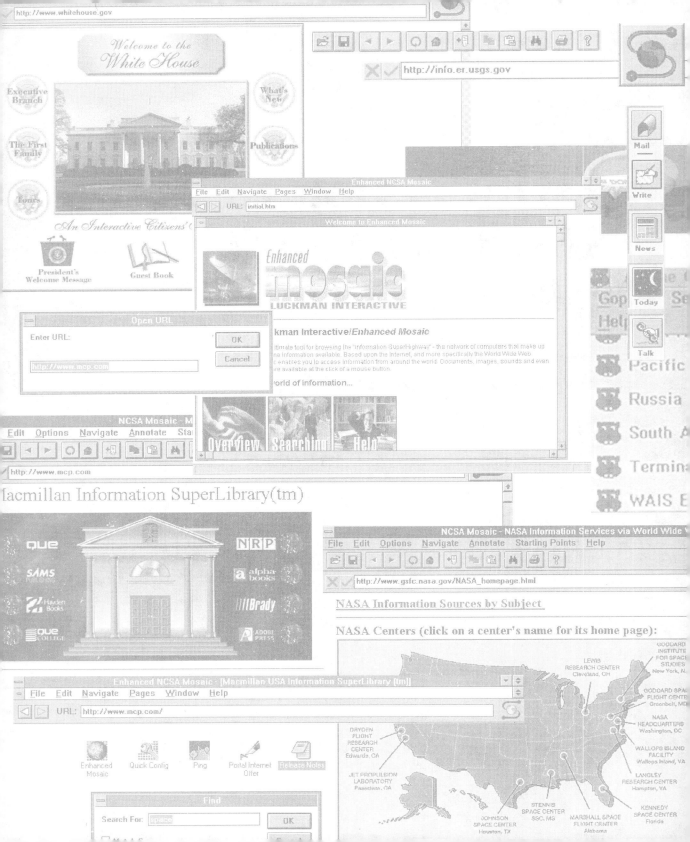

Chapter 1

Introduction to the World Wide Web

by Bill Eager

World Wide Web is a simple, catchy phrase that contains tremendous meaning. Activities that occur around the globe affect the lives of millions of people. In the realm of finance, stock-market activity in Europe, the Far East, or South America directly affects financial institutions and economies around the world. Environmental activities also interconnect. A volcanic explosion in the United States emits debris that affects weather in China; and man-made disasters, such as oil spills and nuclear accidents, don't stop at the borders of the countries in which they occur.

The notion of an integrated world has evolved in this century. R. Buckminster Fuller, the inventor of the geodesic dome, referred to the world as Spaceship Earth, a single entity in which the relationship between ecological forces is always delicate. In the 1960s, Marshall McLuhan, then director of the Center for Culture and Technology at the University of Toronto, spoke and wrote about the concept of a global village: a world in which electronic media enable people of all nations to share their thoughts and experiences.

Communication technology facilitates global connectivity, and the World Wide Web provides a functional means for people around the world to locate information and share knowledge. The World Wide Web, alternatively known as simply the Web or WWW, is:

- An Internet-based navigational system

- An information-distribution and management system

- A dynamic format for mass and personal communications

In this chapter, you'll look at some important background information about the World Wide Web. In particular, this chapter tells you:

■ What the World Wide Web is

■ Some important historical information about the Web

■ How the Web works

■ What you can do with the Web

How Does the World Wide Web Relate to the Internet?

It's impossible to understand or take full advantage of the Web without a basic knowledge of the Internet. Why? Two good reasons. First, the Web is part of the Internet. Web computers, or servers, send multimedia information and files to your PC by way of the Internet system of computers and communication lines. Second, you can use the Web to access a treasure chest of other Internet applications and resources that are not on Web computers.

The next few sections in this chapter provide a mini-tour of the Internet applications which you are most likely to use via the Web. These include:

■ File transfers

■ Gopher

■ UseNet newsgroups

> **Note**
>
> Chapter 8, "FTP and Mosaic," and Chapter 9, "Gopher and Mosaic," provide step-by-step instructions on how to use the Mosaic browser for FTP and Gopher applications. Chapter 11, "Netscape," shows how to use the Netscape browser to view newsgroup articles.

File Transfer Protocol

One of the first Internet services that was developed—the *file transfer protocol* (*FTP*) service—allows users to move files from one place to another. You can use FTP to access files that reside on remote computers and transfer them directly to your computer. This capability is particularly useful when you don't want to spend much online time scanning through a large text file; when using the file requires special tools, such as a spreadsheet program; or, when you simply want to have a copy of the file, such as a shareware database program or a game. *Files* can be documents, digital images, sound files, or programs. File transfer protocol is the application that enables you to send and receive files between distant computers.

> **Note**
>
> For more information on FTP, see Chapter 8, "FTP and Mosaic."

The FTP is an example of a *client-server system*. In this kind of system, you use a program on your local computer (called a *client*) to talk to a program on a remote computer (called a *server*). In the case of FTP, the server on the remote computer is designed to let you download and upload files.

To connect to a computer system using an FTP program, the system must have an FTP server running on it. This server must be set up by the administrators of the machine, and the administrators decide which files and information are made available on the FTP server.

One common type of FTP server is an *anonymous* FTP server. This server allows you to connect and download files without having an account on the machine. If an FTP server is not anonymous, you have to provide a user name and password when you connect to the server, just as if you were logging into the machine. On an anonymous FTP server, you use the special user name "anonymous" when you connect. This "anonymous" user name lets you log in by entering any password you want.

Using anonymous FTP servers is one of the primary methods of distributing software and information across the Internet. There is a large amount of software available on anonymous FTP servers, and this software is often provided free of charge. Software is available for many different types of computer systems, such as UNIX, IBM PC, and Macintosh systems.

Locate Files at FTP Sites

Using FTP to browse for files can be a challenge, because FTP doesn't allow you to look at a file's contents. Therefore, file names and extensions provide the best indication of what a file might contain—but they might be misleading. A file with the name diamond.txt, for example, could be a document

Tip

When you use the Web browser Mosaic to access anonymous FTP sites, you don't actually need to log in to the site—Mosaic does it for you.

that contains information about the precious gem. But it could just as easily be a short story about baseball. If you know generally what information resides on a particular computer, you will have a better idea about the information in individual files.

On some machines (especially the very large archive sites), the site maintainers keep an index of available files with brief descriptions of what the files contain. This is very useful, and makes finding useful files much easier. When you enter a directory, you should look for a file called INDEX (either in uppercase or lowercase). You should also look for a file called README (or perhaps readme, or read.me). These README files are generally descriptions of the contents of the directories, or information about the server system. You should always download the README files and read the contents—the files are put there for a reason.

> **Caution**
>
> Sometimes downloaded files (especially programs) are infected with viruses. You should use a virus scanning program before running downloaded files.

Retrieve Information with Gopher

Gopher is another information distribution service within the Internet. Sites on the Internet that want to distribute information through the Gopher system set up and run Gopher servers that allow people with Gopher clients to display and download files and directories. The Internet has more than 5,000 Gopher servers. It is a very popular information storage and retrieval system, and many of the Web sites have links to Gopher servers.

> **Note**
>
> For more information on Gopher, see Chapter 9, "Gopher and Mosaic."

In addition to displaying and retrieving directories and files, Gopher can connect you to other Internet services. You use Gopher to search and navigate the Internet by making menu-based choices. Gopher menus have a hierarchical structure. You begin with a main menu that offers a broad category listing. One of several things may happen when you choose a menu item:

- A new menu appears, providing a further breakdown of the subject area.

- The text of a document appears.

- A connection is made to a different Internet computer, which may display new Gopher menus.

The ability to link Gopher sites together makes it very easy to examine available files at one site and then move to other interesting sites. All Gopher servers are at some point interconnected—this network of Gopher servers is known as *Gopherspace*. When a new Gopher site becomes available on the Internet, the administrators send a mail message to the maintainers of the Gopher software (at the University of Minnesota) to have their site included in the master list of all Gopher sites worldwide. Many organizations run Gopher servers—universities and colleges, companies, and government agencies all have information available through Gopher.

Get the News with Newsgroups

Although it may not fit the scientific definition of life, the Internet is a living entity. More than any other communications medium, the Internet represents communication *among* people. Electronic newsgroups, also known as *NetNews*, represent a significant vehicle for global interpersonal communications.

Need to find out what type of flowers grow well at high altitudes? Want to share some favorite scuba-diving locations? Need tips about what clothes to bring on a trip to Indonesia? Have an urge to discuss the latest proposal for health care? Newsgroups are an ideal place to do these things. Newsgroups are global forums in which people with common interests share information, discuss topics, and ask questions.

A *newsgroup* is a database of messages focused on one subject. Borrowing publishing terminology, newsgroup messages are called *articles*, and articles are open-ended. For example, someone in Egypt may post a message about cat behavior. A cat lover in Florida reads the message and adds a new message that talks about the effect of hot weather on cats. Next, a veterinarian in Australia provides some useful tips about cat care...and the stream goes on.

Every day thousands of new articles appear on more than 9,000 different newsgroups. You don't have to be a math genius to realize that there are a lot of interesting newsgroup articles out there on the Internet. Many World Wide Web documents have links that take you directly to newsgroup articles.

The name of a newsgroup describes the subject on which the articles focus. One newsgroup, for example, is called **alt.politics.usa.constitution**. It doesn't take much imagination to realize that this newsgroup focuses on politics in relation to the U.S. Constitution with articles about topics that include free speech and the right to bear arms. Newsgroups are organized in a hierarchy that identifies the information that can be found in articles. Newsgroup names contain several subcategories, separated by periods. The broad, top-level category name is on the left side; the most specific identification category is on the right. The following table lists the major top-level categories for newsgroups.

Top-Level Category	Description
alt	alternative system
biz	business
comp	computer-related
k12	education (kindergarten through 12th grade)
misc	miscellaneous
rec	recreation
sci	science
soc	social issues
talk	controversial subjects

You view newsgroup articles by using software called a *newsreader*. The CD-ROM that comes with this book includes several newsreader programs. You can also use one of the Web browser programs (like Mosaic, InternetWorks, or Netscape) to read and respond to newsgroup messages. When you're "cruising the Web," it doesn't take long to realize that it's a very versatile system which can, with the click of a mouse, help you download a file from an FTP site, search Gopherspace, or read and respond to newsgroup articles. With its combination of useful applications, the Internet is the epitome of electronic one-stop shopping.

The Web Ties It All Together

The Web links many different resources that exist on the Internet. For users, the Web is easier and more exciting than the other Internet navigation and information systems. This is because the Web seamlessly integrates different forms of information: still images, text, audio, and video. When you use the World Wide Web, you jump effortlessly among locations (the thousands of computer hosts), system applications (FTP, Gopher, newsgroups), and information formats (files and documents).

The multimedia aspects of the Web transform the Internet from a clerical operation to an exciting voyage. You become an adventurer as you jump from topic to topic and place to place. Leap to Canada to join Canadian Broadcasting Corporation Radio's "Quirks and Quarks," an acclaimed science program that covers topics including ozone updates, DNA fingerprinting, and chimpanzees that diagnose and treat themselves. Click an icon, and you can listen to a 10-minute broadcast in which endocrinologist Dr. Jerilyn Prior of the Department of Medicine at the University of British Columbia explains why giving women estrogen helps slow bone loss from osteoporosis.

Alternatively, you can jump to a NASA computer and view photographs of Jupiter that show fragments of the comet Shoemaker-Levy 9 smashing into the planet's atmosphere. These amazing images were transmitted from the Hubble Space Telescope to NASA, and then shipped around the world via the Internet and WWW. This live coverage of an event that occurred some 390 million miles from Earth created enough excitement that in one week more than a million people (that's 1,000,000) accessed the NASA Web computer that stores pictures of the collision. Today, no other medium can beat the Internet/Web for the timely creation and delivery of news. The NASA home page, URL address **http://www.gsfc.nasa.gov/NASA_homepage.html**, is shown in figure 1.1.

The images and applications on the Web are not all about scientific subjects; you can just as easily get pictures of music's great Muddy Waters, the Eiffel Tower, or rare Chinese art. If you'd rather entertainment, connect with the Web server at the Massachusetts Institute of Technology lab for computer science, whose Telemedia, Networks, and Systems Group stores video clips from the Indiana Jones movies, *Star Trek*, CNN Headline News, and *The Nightly Business Report*.

Not tired yet? Visit J.P. Morgan & Company's Web site and delve into information about financial investments; book a nice hotel room through the Hyatt site; catch up on world events with publications on Time Inc.'s Web server; tour the White House site and sign the electronic guest book; or browse through the collection of artifacts at the Vatican digital museum. Teachers, students, artists, business people—everyone can find something of interest on the Web.

Fig. 1.1
NASA's site appears on the World Wide Web, from which you can jump to a wealth of information about the U.S. Space Program.

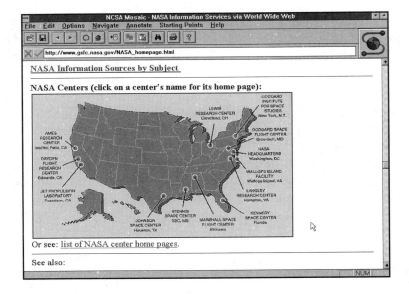

This is just a small sample of the diverse multimedia information and applications available via the Web. The Web is a constantly changing repository of information that helps people learn about subjects ranging from medical breakthroughs to scientific exploration and business news. The Web is knowledge that organizations, companies, and individual users passionately develop and format to share with other people. The Web is global, interactive, multimedia communications.

Where Did the Web Come From?

The Web began at the European Particle Physics Laboratory, known as CERN, an organization comprised of European high-energy-physics researchers. Funded jointly by the 12-nation European Community, CERN is a meeting place for physicists from around the world to collaborate on complex physics, engineering, and information-handling projects. The facility straddles the Swiss–French border near Geneva, Switzerland.

In 1989, CERN physicist Tim Berners-Lee proposed the concept of the Web as a system for transferring ideas and research among scientists in the high-energy-physics community. Effective communication was critical for this group of scientists located around the world. The proposal defined a simple system that would use *hypertext*—a way of presenting and relating information that uses links rather than linear sequences—to transmit documents and other communications over computer networks. Initially, the system was not intended to transmit images or to include sound or video.

By the end of 1990, the first Web software was introduced on Steven Job's NeXT computer system. The NeXT software provided the capability to view and transmit hypertext documents over the Internet and enabled users to edit hypertext documents. Demonstrations of this system were presented to CERN committees and attendees at the Hypertext '91 conference.

During 1992, CERN began publicizing the WWW project. People saw what a great idea this was, and began creating their own WWW servers to make their information available to Internet users. A few people also began working on WWW clients or browsers, which are software programs that help you access the wonderful multimedia that's on the Web. By the end of 1993, browsers had been developed for many different computer systems, including X Windows, Apple Macintosh, and PC/Windows.

How Fast Is It Growing?

By the summer of 1994, the World Wide Web had become one of the most popular ways to access Internet resources. While it's amazing that the Internet doubles in size every 10 months, the Web grows even faster—at an annual rate of 3,000 percent. In 1993, fewer than 100 Web servers existed; today, the Web has more than 12,000 servers (see figs. 1.2 – 1.4).

Now 12,000 may not seem like a very big number. However, the scope of the Web starts to expand quickly when you consider that these servers represent in excess of 1 million Web documents and Internet resources. The real significance of the Web can be measured by the number of people that are out there visiting Web sites. Many of the servers run programs that log the number of connections to their site on a daily and weekly basis.

The National Center for Supercomputing Applications (NCSA) is one of the popular Web sites. In addition to having great samples of multimedia documents, this site offers (at no charge) one of the software programs (NCSA Mosaic) which enables you to use the advanced features of the Web. As figure 1.3 shows, the number of people who visit this site has increased from 100,000 a week in mid-1993 to more than 3 million per week today.

Fig. 1.2
World Wide Web server use has grown tremendously since mid-1993.

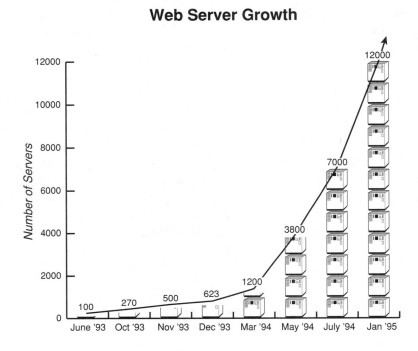

Web Server Growth

Fig. 1.3
Statistics from NCSA Web site show amazing growth in the number of weekly connections to the NCSA Web site, URL address **http://www.ncsa.uiuc.edu/SDG/Presentations/Stats**.

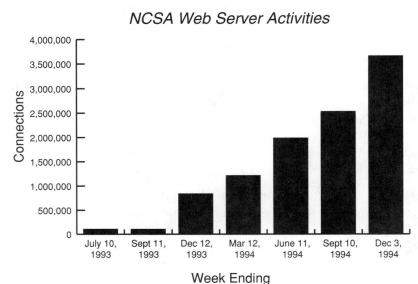

NCSA Web Server Activities

Mar 89	Initial project proposal written and circulated for comment at CERN.
Nov 90	World Wide Web prototype developed on the NeXT computer system.
Mar 91	Web line mode browser released to limited audience on priam vax, rs6000, sun4.
May 91	General release of WWW on central CERN machines
June 91	CERN conducts a computer seminar about WWW.
Oct 91	VMS/HELP and WAIS gateways created. Two Internet mailing lists, www-interest (now www-announce) and www-talk@info.cern.ch, begin. Anonymous Telnet service lets new users test the Web.
Jul 92	Distribution of WWW through CernLib, including Viola, and WWW library code ported to DECnet.
Jan 93	CERN Mac Browser and XMosaic released in alpha version. Around 50 known HTTP servers.
Feb 93	NCSA releases first alpha version of Marc Andreessen's "Mosaic for X."
Mar 93	WWW (Port 80 HTTP) traffic measures 0.1% of the NSF backbone traffic
Sep 93	WWW (port 80 http) traffic measures 1% of the NSF backbone traffic. NCSA releases working versions of Mosaic several computer platforms including X, PC/Windows, and Macintosh.
Oct 93	There are 500 HTTP servers.
Dec 93	The Web rates 11th of all network services in terms of sheer byte traffic - one year earlier it was 127th.
Jan 94	Spry announces the commercial "Internet In A Box" browser, an advanced version of Mosaic.
Mar 94	Marc Andressen and several colleagues leave NCSA to form Netscape Communications Corp. (formerly Mosaic Communications Corp.).
May 94	The first international WWW conference is held in CERN, Geneva.
Jul 94	MIT/CERN agreement to start W3 Organization is announced.
Aug 94	More than 7,000 Web servers on line.
Dec 94	Estimates as high as 800,000 Web pages on the Internet.
May 95	The second international WWW conference held in Frankfurt, Germany, organized by the Fraunhofer Gesellschaft and CERN.

Fig. 1.4
WWW Timeline shows important events in the brief life of the Web.

Introduction to the WWW

Hypertext and Hypermedia Concepts

When we sleep, dreams carry us effortlessly from one location or subject to the next. Images, sounds, and scenes move quickly and sometimes irrationally in an unending stream-of-consciousness pattern. This process is similar to navigating through information on the World Wide Web. The computer-based information programs that make WWW navigation possible are hypertext and hypermedia.

Hypertext, a subset of hypermedia, refers specifically to computer-based documents in which readers move from one place in a document to another or between documents in a nonlinear or nonsequential manner. This means that you don't access information in a traditional beginning-to-end fashion. With a book, for example, you normally begin reading at page one and move page by page, chapter by chapter to the end. In a nonlinear computer document, you move randomly through the document. Words, phrases, and icons in the document become links that enable you to jump at will to a new location in the document or even to a new document.

Hypertext has several advantages over normal text:

- Eases navigation in very large documents. Northern Telecom, the world's leading supplier of digital telecommunications switching equipment, provides customers this type of electronic documentation for telecommunications switches. Because the hard-copy, multivolume manuals can exceed 100,000 pages, it is much easier for readers to click a subject and instantly hop to that topic in the hypertext document than to locate the right volume and find the proper page in the hard-copy version of the manual.

- Helps readers explore new ideas and locate additional sources of information as they jump from place to place. For example, an article about the Civil War might mention Abraham Lincoln, whose name links to a biography that in turn links to a guidebook on Illinois.

- Brings depth—a type of third dimension—to the written word. Readers become explorers and make navigational decisions about the topics that they want to investigate. Hypertext enables users—not documents or computer-system administrators—to decide exactly what information is most important at any moment.

Hypermedia is a natural extension of hypertext. In hypermedia, links connect to visuals such as graphics or photographs, audio messages, or video, as well as to text (see fig. 1.5). Hypermedia brings documents to life, and the personal computer becomes a multimedia device that can have far more appeal and impact than radio or television. An electronic auto-repair manual, for example, could have a section that describes how to adjust a carburetor. Click an icon, and a short movie shows the proper procedure. Later, the text may say, "Adjust until it sounds smooth." You don't know what smooth sounds like, so you click an audio link that plays a recording of a smoothly running carburetor.

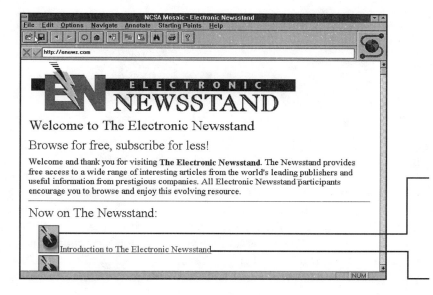

Fig. 1.5
A sample Web page shows graphical and textual hypertext links. (This one's at **http://enews.com**.)

A graphical hypertext link is an image with a box around it. If you have a color screen, the box will be blue.

Textual links are underlined. On color screens, the links are usually colored blue and underlined.

The home page of the U.S. Geological Survey (USGS) WWW server (**http://www.usgs.gov/**) provides an excellent example of the electronic combination of different media (see fig. 1.6). The page opens with several Graphic Interchange Format (GIF) images of covers of USGS literature. These images link to additional menus for USGS activities. The home page also contains an icon that links to an audio welcome message.

The resources of the Internet and World Wide Web are vast. At least 3 million document files are available on the Internet, and more than 12,000 Web host computers support interactive hypermedia information. The Web is a distributed system—its bits and pieces are located on different Web servers worldwide, each of which uses electronic pointers, or links, to connect information and resources on other Web servers. As a result, you can leap among documents and media sources located on thousands of computers in more than 80 countries.

Fig. 1.6

The USGS home page shows effective use of different types of media.

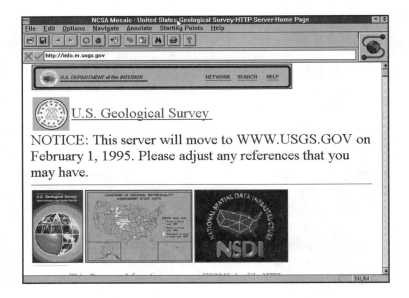

In addition to opening and displaying documents, photographs, and audio, WWW links can perform other functions. For example, a link can open an FTP site where you can find and download a software program, or it can open a form where you enter a keyword to begin an information search using the Gopher system. Traveling through the Web gives new meaning to the term *channel surfing*. When you surf your television set, you flip channels because you're not happy with the programs that appear. When you surf the Web, you change channels every few seconds, and you click because every link opens new avenues for exploration.

The documents and information on the Web frequently are linked by different authors. The process is similar to placing a footnote in a document; the footnote can automatically open the resource to which it refers. Hypermedia authors use a special software language known as *HyperText Markup Language* (*HTML*) to create hypertext and hypermedia links. Chapter 14, "Creating Home Pages with HTML," highlights the application of this language and the creation of hypermedia. Look to this chapter to learn how to develop your own Web document.

Hypertext and hypermedia are the engines that make it possible to maneuver easily through the immense resources available on Web servers. They facilitate the seamless connection of different types of information—text, visuals, audio, and video—in a type of electronic dreaming.

What Happens When You Connect to the Web?

The computers that maintain Web information are Web servers. Using the HyperText Transport Protocol (HTTP), these servers enable you to access hypertext and hypermedia information on your computer (known as a *client*), which sends requests to the server.

A significant difference exists between what occurs when you connect to a remote computer with File Transfer Protocol and with a Web browser such as Mosaic. With FTP, the connection to the remote computer is continuous. You open a line and continue to use the connection until you finish; and while you are online, nobody else can use the connection.

Mosaic and other Web browsers, on the other hand, are *stateless* programs— that is, they open a connection to a remote computer, retrieve the initial information, and then quickly close the connection. The connection briefly reopens when more information needs to be transmitted to your computer, or when you click a link that in turn requests more information from the server. Because the connection with a remote host occurs for only a fraction of a second, the process minimizes the impact on the limited resources (the amount of lines and bandwidth for the number of users) of the Internet.

The first information that you get from a remote Web server is known as a *home page.* The home page is an initial interface to a series of other documents, files, and resources that reside on that computer or on other Web servers around the world. The concept of the home page extends to your own computer. You can create and save a personal home page that has links to the resources and servers on the Web. Chapter 9, "Gopher and Mosaic," explains this process.

Links and URLs Transport You from Place to Place

One of the defining features of any hypertext documents are *links* (also known as *hyperlinks*). Links are simply references to other documents. But they aren't just stated references like, "See pages 2-3 for more information." They're actual live links, where you can activate the link and cause what it references to appear on your screen. When someone writes a hypertext document, he or she can insert links to other documents that have information relevant to the text in the document. WWW documents are all hypertext documents.

The links in Web documents use hidden addresses to connect with the resources to which they point. For example, a Web document about the speed of light may include the phrase, "Einstein was a great scientist," with the word *Einstein* highlighted to indicate a link, possibly to a picture of Einstein. Here the word Einstein is a hyperlink. When you click it with your mouse, the picture of Einstein appears. The address (the location of the computer and file) of the photograph of Einstein, however, is encoded behind the link. Other Web documents may have pictures or parts of the screen which are links.

These hidden addresses, called *Uniform Resource Locators* (URLs for short), can represent a link to almost every document, file, and resource on the Internet. If you know the URL address for a document or a server, you can enter the address in a browser and jump to that resource. Following is the URL address for an interactive Web dinosaur exhibit located on a server at Honolulu Community College:

http://www.hcc.hawaii.edu/dinos/dinos.1.html

The U.S. Senate maintains a Gopher server that offers information about the Senate as well as documents distributed by Senate members and committees. The URL address that gets you to this site is the following:

gopher://gopher.senate.gov

Tip

Even if you are retrieving files from a server that is running on a PC, you must use a slash (/) to indicate a sub-directory, not a backslash.

The first portion of the URL address, on the left side of the colon, refers to the method of access or protocol used to retrieve a resource. Notice that the dinosaur exhibit is an HTTP resource and that the Senate URL indicates a connection to a Gopher server. The information between the first set of double forward slashes (//) and the next single forward slash (/) refers to the specific computer host on which the information resides and to which your connection will go. The remaining portion of the address details the path on the computer to the specific resource that you want. You type a URL as a single, unbroken line (no spaces).

The URL address can be referenced as an easy-to-remember name. Thus, **http://nearnet.gnn.com/wic/med.11.html** can be referenced as CancerNet (the NCI International Cancer Information Center).

Obviously, it is much easier to remember a plain-English name for a Web resource than it is to remember the URL, which can be quite complex and long. Mosaic and other Web browsers, however, require the URL address to make a connection, because your local Internet host computer initially must look up the address of the computer to which you are trying to connect. The good news is that after you enter or save a URL address and its plain-English equivalent in the Web browser software, you can simply click the name during future sessions.

Key WWW Developments: A Recipe for Success

In addition to the tremendous contributions of CERN, Tim Berners-Lee, and others involved with the creation of the Web, several factors played a role in the phenomenal growth of the WWW. The expansion of the Internet as a global communications network set the stage for the application of a system that links resources all over the world. Two software developments also are responsible for igniting the explosion of the Web. The first development is the software that enables people who are not computer geniuses to author Web documents with hypertext links. The second development is the software programs (known as *browsers*) that help users navigate the links of the Web.

Today, multimedia technology is found in offices and homes around the world. Businesses quickly embraced the concept of multimedia for employee training (usually with stand-alone, computer-based training stations) and for the distribution of electronic documents. Using their own private computer networks, companies can send electronic news, phone directories, manuals, and product information to employees around the world. Divisions, departments, and work groups share data, status reports, and details about specific projects. Hypertext software links this information.

Interactive information kiosks and CD-ROM applications enhance consumer awareness of multimedia. More than 5,000 CD-ROM titles currently are available. Sponsored by Interval Research Corporation, the Electric Carnival is a traveling road show of interactive digital multimedia. The Carnival tours with the Lollapalooza concerts and shows hundreds of thousands of concertgoers, mostly people in their 20s, how to create and send poems, art, and music via the Internet.

The Internet represents functional anarchy—a multitude of networks that successfully connect but don't have one designated owner or overseeing organization. The Web is a close cousin because no single person, company, or organization owns the Web; it is a distributed system with millions of users and, potentially, an equal number of document/multimedia authors who can become information providers to the world in a few keystrokes. Authors are holders of Ph.D. degrees, students ranging from grade-school age through college, marketing professionals, lawyers, musicians, gardeners, and so on—all types of people.

When multimedia information moves into this enormous computer network, a universally accessible database of knowledge begins to form. So many people contribute to the electronic warehouse that the database contains all sorts of information and knowledge. The applications of this global database range from entertainment to education to business communication. The Web links this smorgasbord-like collection of human thought.

An initial challenge arose, however: how do you navigate these endless links easily? The solution was the development of software interfaces known as browsers that make using the Web a simple and exciting experience.

The first Web browsers were text-based programs whose simple keyboard commands enabled users to follow the links of the Web. These browsers can operate at modem speeds of 2,400 bps (bits per second) and up; they don't require direct-access connections to the Internet (such as SLIP or PPP); and they remain easy-to-use interfaces to the Web. These browsers do not, however, enable users to access the most exciting aspect of the Web: multimedia.

► See "Where to Get the Basic Mosaic Software," p. 65

The National Center for Supercomputing Applications (NCSA) helps the scientific-research community by developing and distributing non-proprietary software and by investigating new technologies that may be transferred to the private sector for commercial application. Beginning in 1991, Marc Andreessen and a team of programmers at NCSA, known as the Software Design Group, used NSF funds to write a program which has become the de facto graphical-interface browser for the Web—NCSA Mosaic. (See Chapter 4, "Getting Mosaic Running in Windows," for information on how to get NCSA Mosaic via anonymous FTP.)

NCSA Mosaic was one of the first browsers; it continues to be a free, public-domain program, and there is nothing quite as enticing in the world of computers as free software. Mosaic is available at many FTP host computers on the Internet, including the NCSA FTP site where approximately 100,000 people download the program each month.

Who Uses the Web?

Millions of people use the Internet and the Web. What are the demographics of the people who use these resources? Stanford Research Institute (SRI International) compiles statistics about use of the Internet and the World Wide Web. A comparison of hosts at government, research, education, and corporate Web sites shows that the people who use the Web are similar to the people who use the Internet, with an emphasis on users in the educational sector.

Table 1.1 breaks down Web use by domain and compares use to the approximate percentage of Internet hosts that these domains maintain.

Table 1.1   Organizational Use of the WWW

Domain	% of Web Traffic	% of Internet Hosts
U.S. educational	49	27
U.S. commercial	20	26
U.S. government	9	6
Other countries	22	41 and domains

*Statistics available by anonymous FTP from **nic.merit.edu**.*

In 1994, James Pitkow and Mimi Recker of the Georgia Institute of Technology conducted a survey to identify traits of Web users. (As the Web evolves, becoming more accessible to a broader cross section of the world's population, these demographics are likely to change.) The 1,300 responses to the study indicate the following facts about Web users:

■ 56 percent are between the ages of 21 and 30.

■ 94 percent are male.

- 69 percent are located in North America.

- 45 percent are professionals.

- 22 percent are graduate students.

A Good Cause: Lynx, Mosaic, and WWW Assist People with Disabilities

In the United States alone, 49 million people have disabilities; around the world, millions more do. Computer technology has greatly helped people with disabilities improve their lives and communicate more successfully.

One notable case is physicist Dr. Stephen Hawking, author of *A Brief History of Time*; Hawking suffers from Lou Gehrig's disease and uses a computer to write and communicate. Hawking and other people with disabilities take advantage of devices that translate ASCII text to a synthesized computer voice, display the text as extra-large letters on a monitor, or create Braille output. With millions of ASCII documents being stored and transmitted as e-mail, newsgroup articles, FTP files, Gopher documents, and now Web pages, an inexhaustible supply of information is available to people with disabilities.

Web pages use ASCII text. The Lynx Web browser can isolate this text and then enable people who are blind or visually impaired to "read" the pages. The Lynx browser (for both UNIX and DOS platforms) works with speech synthesis and Braille display systems. Disabled users must purchase a speech synthesizer or Braille display unit. Speech synthesizers with screen-reading software range in price from about $400 to $1,600, depending on the quality of the computerized voice. Braille displays range in price from around $3,000 to $12,000, depending on the number of characters that the display can accommodate.

For people with disabilities, Web navigation is similar to the process used by people who have full use of their vision. The user finds links and then activates them by keystrokes. The challenge for disabled people is to find the link, move the cursor to the link, and then activate the link.

Internet Devices for the Disabled

Dr. Lawrence A. Scadden is senior program director for the Programs for Persons with Disabilities at the National Science Foundation (NSF). Dr. Scadden provides some insight into the value of the Internet and the Web for the disabled.

"The Internet is providing people with disabilities the highest level of independent access to information ever known. This is especially true for blind and visually impaired individuals, who can read material available on the Internet by using computers equipped with access devices: speech synthesizers and screen-reading software, Braille devices, or large-character generators for people with low vision. People who cannot turn print pages usually cannot use keyboards, either, but they can use a variety of alternative data-entry systems: breath-activated Morse code, cursor activation on visually displayed virtual keyboards, or speech-recognition systems.

"The Web and its multimedia information resources can expand the level of independent information access for people with a variety of disabilities, but problems of usability must be met before this statement rings true. The graphical user interface of information displays is unfriendly, if not unusable, for most blind people, because speech systems will not respond unless the ASCII-based information buried within a system can be accessed.

"Screen-reading software used with speech synthesizers also must be configured so that the synthesizers will detect and announce only highlighted menu bars or links when desired. This is a trivial matter for power users of computers, but the majority of computer users find this task to be overwhelming.

"The NSF has awarded funds to the National Center on Supercomputing Applications (NCSA) for work on making Mosaic accessible. It is too early in the process to indicate the NCSA's approach, but that organization will be providing character-based information, where needed, to augment pictorial displays. The NCSA will be providing guidance to NSF and other organizations that will be developing home pages for Mosaic-based Web sites, so that those sites can be used by people who use alternative access technologies.

"NSF is also funding the University of Delaware in a project with the developers of Lynx at the University of Kansas to improve interaction with the Web in future generations of Lynx. The NSF believes that as other Web browsers emerge (as they undoubtedly will), developers will learn how to make good Web documents from the experiences of making Lynx and Mosaic usable to people with disabilities."

Finding What You Want on the Web

Like Gopher, the Web is a tool that helps you locate information. The Web is similar to Gopher because it is a client-server information system that runs over the Internet. One important distinction exists, however—the Web delivers all information (documents, menus, and indexes) as hypertext and hypermedia.

You can travel through the Web in two ways: click and then follow a link, or send a search to the Web server to which you link. The search option is part of a Web document; this option appears as a search box in which you enter your search term and then click a search button. Not every Web document or server includes the searching function.

Not only does the Web deliver all information in a standard format, but almost every information system on the Internet can be represented in a Web document. This arrangement means that you can use the Web to access Gopher information, as well as menus and files from FTP servers, and you can use the Web to perform a Gopher search for specific resources. Gopher menus on the Web are lists of items containing icons that link to other Gopher resources.

When you use a Web browser to retrieve files with FTP, you again get this same visually easy-to-use interface that makes the Web an all-encompassing Internet navigator. Chapter 7, "Mosaic Shortcuts and Tips," and Chapter 8, "FTP and Mosaic," explain in detail how you can use the NCSA Mosaic browser to connect to FTP and Gopher sites.

The following table identifies some of the protocols and applications that you can access with the proper URL address. The protocol becomes the first part of the URL address. For example, the URL address for the Gopher site of the Bryn Mawr Classical Review, a review of classical literature distributed over the Internet, is:

gopher://gopher.lib.Virginia.EDU:70/11/alpha/bmcr

Protocol	Application
gopher	Starts a Gopher session.
ftp	Starts an FTP session.
file	Gets a file on your local disk if followed by ///**c**|; or, equivalent to ftp if followed by //. Any local disk may be specified, and it must be followed by the bar character rather than a colon, because the colon has a special significance in a URL.

Protocol	Application
wais	Accesses a WAIS server.
news	Reads UseNet newsgroups.
telnet	Starts a Telnet session.

Robots on the Web

Even with browsers and guidebooks, quickly getting all the information you want on one subject via the Web remains a challenge. To make this task easier, research is being done on electronic robots called *knowbots*, computer programs that search the Web for you. You tell the knowbot exactly what you are looking for, and it weaves its way through the networks and host computers to find the information or resources that meet your needs.

For commercial applications, a knowbot can do price-comparison shopping. The knowbot first searches for all vendors that carry a specific product; it then accumulates specific details about the product, checks prices, and brings back a report to help you make your purchasing decision.

▶ See "Finding the Elusive Resource: Web Searchers," p. 450

Knowbot companies face some technical challenges, however, including issues related to the security of individual computers (a knowbot could spread a computer virus) and system traffic (millions of knowbots weaving through the network could really slow traffic).

Some first-generation knowbots already are running around on the Internet and the Web. Alternately known as web crawlers, searchers, and digital agents, these software applications look for and report on information related to Web servers and information resources. Chapter 19, "Web Searching," provides details on how you can use these searchers to find specific resources on the Web. MIT's Matthew Gray developed a program named The World Wide Web Wanderer. This program travels through links in the Web to find the number of sites that provide specific information and the quantity of hypertext documents that are available.

The WebCrawler is another knowbot. Developed by Brian Pinkerton at the University of Washington, the WebCrawler program focuses on accumulating information about the specific documents that reside on Web servers. The program creates indices of the documents that it locates on the Web, and it enables users to keyword-search these indices.

Functionally, the WebCrawler begins with a set of one or more documents; it then locates the outbound links in the document and visits those links. The WebCrawler database compiles a list of all these documents, visited and unvisited, and establishes an index based on the content of visited documents. Each document link points to a specific host that, if visited, lists pointers to other documents. The program uses CERN's Web library to locate the necessary URL and then retrieves the document to the database in which it indexes.

The WebCrawler typically operates with 5 to 10 knowbots simultaneously. Figure 1.7 shows the mechanics of the WebCrawler process. Refer to Chapter 19 for more information on using WebCrawler.

Fig. 1.7

A schematic diagram shows the WebCrawler process. The UI, or user interface, is your window into the process. The search engine employs agents to comb the databases and libraries on the Web, eventually compiling a collection of relevant Web pages for your perusal.

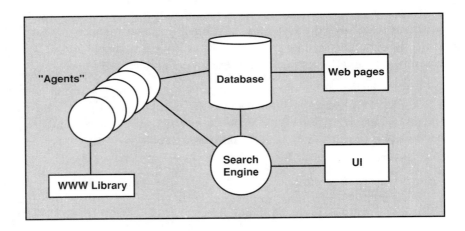

In the WebCrawler home page, Pinkerton notes:

The WebCrawler tries hard to be a good citizen. Its main approach involves the order in which it searches the Web. Some Web robots have been known to operate in a depth-first fashion, retrieving file after file from a single site. This kind of traversal is bad. The WebCrawler searches the Web in a breadth-first fashion. When building its index of the Web, the WebCrawler will access a site at most a few times a day.

Is the Web Electronic Nirvana?

With all these capabilities, the Web may seem to be perfect. A downside exists, however. One disadvantage is that multimedia information—pictures, graphics, and sound—consumes a tremendous amount of digital space. If you have a modem with less than 14.4 Kbps speed, transmitting this information to your computer will take an intolerable amount of time.

In addition, many people who write Web documents are not professional multimedia developers. As a result, many documents with which you connect contain as many as 20 graphic images, and you can't access any of the links on the home page until all the graphics download to your computer.

As with Gopher or WAIS, a link can connect you to a resource that doesn't meet your needs. Web users rely on document and server authors to update their information. When these authors don't update their material, you can link to information that is out-of-date or the link might point to an offline server.

Although these complications become frustrating at times, they are a small price to pay for access to the knowledge databases of humankind.

From Here...

This chapter is your first step into the rich world of the Web. From here you can continue your journey by referring to the following chapters:

- Chapter 2, "Connecting to the World Wide Web," details the procedures and systems that get you on this system.

- Chapter 4, "Getting Mosaic Running in Windows," tells you how to obtain and use the NCSA Mosaic Web browser.

- Chapter 18, "The Future of the Web," provides some insight into how the Web is developing.

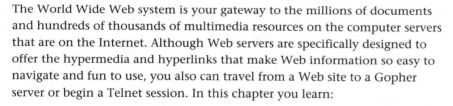

Chapter 2

Connecting to the World Wide Web

by Bill Eager

The World Wide Web system is your gateway to the millions of documents and hundreds of thousands of multimedia resources on the computer servers that are on the Internet. Although Web servers are specifically designed to offer the hypermedia and hyperlinks that make Web information so easy to navigate and fun to use, you also can travel from a Web site to a Gopher server or begin a Telnet session. In this chapter you learn:

- The pros and cons of different types of Internet accounts.

- How IBM and Microsoft are helping customers get onto the Internet/ Web with new software programs.

- How to find Internet service providers that offer local and national access accounts.

- What the commercial online services are doing to get their customers onto the Internet.

To access and use the World Wide Web you must connect with a computer that speaks the Internet's computer language. All of the computers on the Internet communicate with each other using a set of protocols known as TCP/IP—or Transmission Control Protocol and Internet Protocol. This *suite* of protocols enables Internet computers to connect, send, and receive mail and files, and check and correct errors in information.

Large businesses, educational organizations, and government agencies normally purchase a direct—or *dedicated*—Internet connection. A dedicated connection enables these organizations to operate a computer that speaks the

TCP/IP language, allowing users to link to other Internet hosts directly. Dedicated connections use high-speed lines (56 kilobits per second (kbps) to 1.544 megabits per second (mbps)) and provide full-time access. These features make this type of connection attractive to organizations that have many employees and to students who need to use the Internet. In fact, the number of users allowed to connect through a dedicated line has no specified limit. Therefore, a business or university may have a computer in each department linked to the Internet through a local network.

High-speed access is important for applications such as scientific research projects and business communications (video conferencing), which require extremely fast transmissions of large amounts of data. A full-time connection has two benefits: it enables people in an organization to use the Internet; and it enables companies, schools, and government agencies to make their computers WWW servers. Dedicated connections are great, but annual fees can exceed $10,000.

The benefits of dedicated connectivity for businesses and organizations are:

- File and information transfers over dedicated lines take much less time than with other types of connectivity; transfer speeds range from 56 kbps to T3—45 mbps.

- Multiple users (for example, students in a classroom or business people in an office) can share one dedicated line simultaneously.

- Dedicated connections enable companies and educational institutions to operate servers that are available to other Internet users 24 hours a day. As a result, organizations can start Web servers to offer information to the outside world.

Account Types

People who want to connect to the Internet and WWW usually don't need dedicated access. A home-based user can use a modem to link his PC to a service provider's computer, which is known as a *local host*. A local host contains application software that uses the TCP/IP protocols to communicate with other Internet host computers directly. This type of access is appropriately called a *dial-up account*.

▶ See "Text-Only Connection (Terminal Emulation)," p. 53

Three main types of dial-up accounts exist. One type is *dial-up terminal emulation,* in which your computer acts as a "dumb" terminal that connects to the local host (you choose a terminal-emulation protocol in your communications software). Terminal emulation requires minimal software investment and perhaps none at all. In this type of dial-up account, the local host manages all Internet activity, including file and document storage.

A second type of dial-up account, sometimes called *client software access*, places client software on your computer. You then can perform some Internet functions, such as accessing electronic mail and newsgroups, on your computer. The Internet provider normally supplies the client software as part of the service. These programs (Windows or Macintosh-based) provide a graphical interface—toolbars and on-screen buttons—that makes navigating the Internet/Web a point-and-click procedure.

The third type of account is *dial-up IP*, a variation on a direct connection. In dial-up IP, your computer becomes a physical part of the Internet—it receives a host name and an Internet Protocol (IP) address. You still contract for access with a service provider, but when you connect to the provider's computer, you transmit TCP/IP packets between machines. While your connection remains open, your PC is on the Net.

To communicate with other Internet computers directly, you load a software program that enables your computer to use the TCP/IP language. You have two choices: *SLIP* (Serial Line Internet Protocol) and *PPP* (Point-to-Point Protocol). Besides being low-cost alternatives to direct access, SLIP and PPP provide full peer access to the Internet. As a result, you can load and run software programs that reside on other Internet computers. You don't need to shuttle files between the local host and your PC; other PCs in a small local network can connect through your PC to the Internet, and you can use all the functions of a WWW multimedia browser.

SLIP and PPP are serial protocols that are used when two computers and their modems connect by a telephone circuit. SLIP (sometimes called Serial Line IP) was developed first. SLIP doesn't provide error correction or data compression, but it works well for home and small-business applications.

To address SLIP's error-correcting weakness, Point-to-Point Protocol (PPP) was developed as an Internet standard. PPP checks incoming data and asks the sending computer to retransmit when it detects an error in an IP packet. Modern modems, which use advanced error-correction schemes, can be used very effectively with SLIP.

Because you connect to the Internet directly when you use SLIP or PPP, you need an IP (Internet Protocol) address. Your Internet access provider assigns this address each time you start a dial-up session. You can receive a permanent IP address, which is necessary if you have a registered host name. You also need a modem with a minimum speed of 9600 bps (14.4 kbps is desirable) when you use a SLIP or PPP connection.

The benefits of a dial-up SLIP/PPP account for individual users include:

- Connection costs are relatively low (usually a per-hour fee), and you pay only for what you use.

- You have direct access to the resources of the Internet (you are on the Net).

- You can use WWW browsers that have graphical interfaces.

- You can transfer files directly from other remote hosts (*servers*) to your computer.

- SLIP/PPP dial-up connections are available from many national, state, and local commercial Internet service providers.

Windows 95 and OS/2 Internet Applications

In their battle for the hearts and pocketbooks of PC users who plan or need to purchase new operating software in 1995, both Microsoft and IBM include Internet access and application programs in their new systems. Microsoft's Windows NT 3.5 currently offers point-and-click SLIP/PPP connectivity. Microsoft's new version of Windows, known as Windows 95 (available to the public in late 1995), includes a 32-bit TCP/IP stack to speak the language of the Internet. The system also supports SLIP/PPP and dial-in connectivity. Windows 95 supports Internet and Web software, including programs such as Mosaic, WinWAIS, and WinGopher. Built-in utilities enable users to take advantage of Telnet and FTP. Windows 95 also has a built-in link to the Microsoft Network, an online service operated by Microsoft which is likely to let users access the Internet. (See Chapter 13, "Microsoft Internet Assistant," for more information.)

IBM incorporates the Internet Connection in its latest version of OS/2, known as Warp. To begin surfing the Internet, you click the Internet folder, which initiates a one-time registration process and connects you with the IBM Global Network via a SLIP connection. IBM thus becomes not only your software provider, but also your service provider. The IBM Global Network is managed by Advantis, a partnership formed by IBM and Sears, Roebuck and Company. This network offers local dial-up access in more than 100 different cities across the U.S. These local access connections are known as *points of presence* or POPs. You have the option of using Warp to connect to the Internet through other service providers.

Warp includes custom-designed applications for Telnet, Gopher, and FTP. UltiMail Lite is a built-in e-mail program that supports the Internet's SMTP and MIME e-mail standards. SMTP, short for *Simple Mail Transfer Protocol*, is the set of protocols that enable e-mail to travel from one Internet computer to another. MIME, short for *Multipurpose Internet Mail Extensions*, enables e-mail messages to incorporate pictures, sound, and video as well as plain old text. IBM also has a custom Web browser: the IBM WebExplorer. In addition, as a nice forethought, IBM includes multimedia viewers that play video and sound files.

Figure 2.1 shows the OS/2 Warp Internet interface.

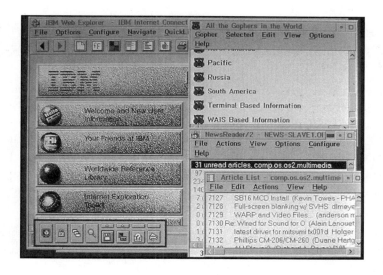

Fig. 2.1
IBM's OS/2 Warp has built-in Internet access and application programs.

The battle between computer-industry leaders Microsoft and IBM is guaranteed to benefit the end user: you!

Service Providers and More Service Providers

In our supply-and-demand economy, service providers have been popping up across the country, in large cities and small towns, to fill the increasing need for Internet access. National service providers offer nationwide access; some providers have toll-free numbers that users can use to dial in to the services. In addition, local service providers offer Internet access to a region, state, or even just a city.

Even long-distance carriers are leaping into the Internet-access business. MCI now offers a service appropriately called internetMCI. This service is a package that includes access, a Web browser (Netscape), communications software, and electronic mail. Other options—including FTP, Gopher, and Telnet—are available. To make its package one-stop shopping, MCI also maintains an electronic shopping mall on the Web. To find out more, call MCI toll-free at (800) 955-6505 or connect to the company's Web site at the URL address **http://www.mci.com**.

Prices and services vary widely among vendors. Some service providers simply sell access to the Internet; these companies don't provide the software programs that you need to take advantage of the Internet or Web (many of these programs are on the CD-ROM included with this book). Other service providers do include these programs.

The best advice is to spend a day shopping around; make a few phone calls, and compare providers' services and fees. You can find a comprehensive list of service providers on the CD-ROM that comes with this book.

Several text files (.txt) on the CD-ROM contain lists of providers around the world. The lists were created by the InterNIC (short for the Internet Network Information Center), which was established by the National Science Foundation in 1993. InterNIC is a collaborative effort of three organizations that offer a variety of services, including providing information about how to access and use the Internet and how to locate people and companies that have Internet addresses. The term *InterNIC* comes from the cooperative effort among Network Information Centers (NICs).

On the CD-ROM, the text files that contain lists of service providers are located in the directory docs/lists/provider. If you installed the files on your hard drive, you can go to the subdirectory in which the files are located. The following table lists the files and the corresponding countries and areas of the world that the files cover:

Country/Region	File Name
Africa	africa.txt
Asia	asia.txt
Australia	australia.txt
Canada	canada.txt
Commonwealth of Independent States (former USSR)	commonwe.txt
Eastern Europe	eastern-.txt

Country/Region	File Name
Germany	germany.txt
Latin America	latin-am.txt
Middle East	middle-e.txt
United States	internic.txt
Western Europe	western-.txt

Service Providers with Custom Internet and Web Interfaces

Several national service providers offer their own Windows-based software programs that make using Internet and Web applications easy. Based in New York City, The Pipeline offers a program that comes on one disk and that incorporates all the software you need to connect to the provider's computer and get on the Internet. If you don't happen to live in Manhattan, you may be able to dial into The Pipeline through a SprintNet access number in your area.

The Pipeline eliminates the need to worry about (or bother with) SLIP setup procedures. You don't need to load or use a separate Windows Sockets program to manage the TCP/IP packets between your computer and the provider's. Figure 2.2 shows what access to the Web looks like with The Pipeline software.

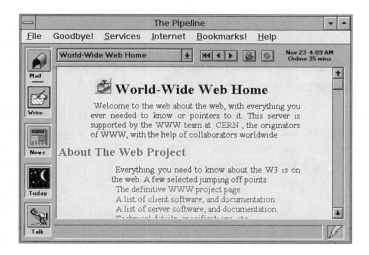

Fig. 2.2
The Pipeline is a national service provider that offers a custom interface for cruising the Web.

For more information, contact The Pipeline at:

150 Broadway

New York, NY 10038

Phone: (212) 267-3636

Dial-up: (212) 267-6432

Telnet: **pipeline.com**

e-mail: **info@pipeline.com**

NETCOM is another national Internet service provider that has a custom interface. The company offers dial-up access up to 14.4 kbps using their custom software program called NetCruiser. When you use NetCruiser to access the Web, you can start your journey with NETCOM's own home page, which offers links to all sorts of interesting locations, organized by category. NetCruiser allows you to save as many as 500 bookmarks that enable you to return to your favorite Web sites quickly.

For more information, contact NETCOM at:

3031 Tisch Way

San Jose, CA 95128

Phone: (800) 501-8649

Telnet: **netcom.com**

Web: **http://www.netcom.com**

e-mail: **personal@netcom.com**

Connect to the Web through a Commercial Online Service

Not to be left out of the action, the commercial online services now offer extensive Internet access and services. America Online and CompuServe have a combined subscriber base that approaches 4 million users, bringing a lot of new people to the Internet party.

America Online

In 1992, America Online had 181,000 subscribers; today, the number exceeds 1,500,000. This rapid success can be attributed partially to the service's simple graphic user interface. When you first connect with AOL, you recognize how easy this service is to use; the main screen contains buttons for operations such as electronic mail, news, and talking with other members.

America Online scores big points for aggressively expanding the Internet services that it offers. From AOL, you can send e-mail, read newsgroups, join mailing lists, search and retrieve information from Gopher and WAIS databases, and access the World Wide Web (during 1995).

You get to the AOL Internet Connection from a link in the main (welcome) screen or by following these steps:

1. Open the **G**o To menu and choose **K**eyword. The Go to Keyword dialog box appears.

2. Type **internet** (upper- or lowercase; it doesn't matter).

3. Choose OK. The Internet Connection screen appears.

The Internet Connection screen has two areas: a scroll-down area that lists the names of folders and files, and an area that contains buttons. You click the buttons to open screens that provide access to specific Internet applications, including the following:

Mail Gateway

Mailing Lists

Newsgroups

Gopher & WAIS Databases

The World Wide Web

Expert Connection

To find out more about America Online contact:

8619 Westwood Center Drive

Vienna, Virginia 22182

Phone: (800) 827-6364

e-mail: **aolhotline@aol.com**

CompuServe

Headquartered in Columbus, Ohio, CompuServe is owned by H&R Block. The service began operation in 1979. Today, gaining new members at the rate of 80,000 every month, CompuServe has the largest membership of any commercial online service. CompuServe also offers extensive Internet access and service. Follow these steps:

1. In the toolbar, click the green-stoplight icon. A GO to Service dialog box appears.

2. Type **internet** (upper- or lowercase).

3. Choose OK.

A new on-screen box appears. From here, click and jump to two Internet forums (the Internet New Users Forum and the Internet Resources Forum) that offer utility programs, useful documents, and messages; UseNet newsgroups; FTP; and (if not now, soon) the Web. Figure 2.3 shows these choices.

Fig. 2.3
CompuServe provides point-and-click access to many Internet applications. This is the Internet New Users Forum area.

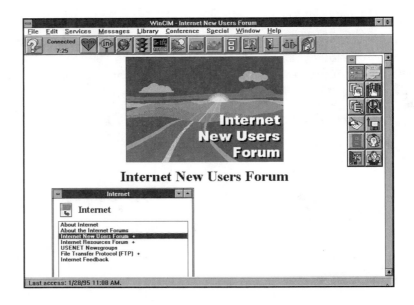

In another Web-related business move, CompuServe is working with Spry (the developer of the Air Mosaic Web browser) to help companies design and set up commercial presences on the World Wide Web.

CompuServe currently supports 14.4 kbps dial-up access; and is planning to offer 28.8 kbps modem access and high-speed Integrated Services Digital Network (ISDN) lines that offer speeds of 64 kbps over phone lines.

To find out more about CompuServe contact:

PO Box 20212

Columbus, Ohio 43220

Phone: (800) 554-4067 or (800) 848-8199

World Wide Web: **http://www.compuserve.com**

Computer Hardware and Software Requirements

Obviously, you need to have a computer to connect to the Internet and Web. But what kind of computer do you need? The cost of high-powered personal computers continues to decline. You can buy hard drives with storage capacity between 350M and 600M for less than $1 per megabyte. RAM memory chips also are inexpensive, going for less than $50 per megabyte. Simultaneously, computer processor speeds continue to increase.

▶ See "Basic System Requirements," p. 62

But where there is good news, there also is bad: to use the sophisticated, memory-eating WWW browsers and to have access to the multimedia resources of the Web, you need a powerful PC. Mosaic software files, for example, take up more than 5M of hard disk space. To run under Windows, Mosaic requires at least a 386DX machine with 4M of RAM; if you have anything less, the application simply won't work.

▶ See "Read, Listen, and Watch: Multimedia Is Here," p. 82

The multimedia information that you link with or download also consumes digital space. The home pages on the WWW often contain many graphic images that temporarily download to RAM, and multimedia information takes even more space. For example, digital photographs (commonly in JPEG file format) can exceed 150K, and a 10-second audio clip requires about 3M of space.

▶ See "Multimedia Browsers," p. 56

▶ See "Obtaining Auxiliary Software for Mosaic," p. 68

Beyond the issue of memory, you must have software and hardware that can run the multimedia information on the Web. Audio files, for example, require a digital-to-analog conversion chip, which you get with an audio card.

But don't throw away your old computer just yet—you can use WWW browsers that don't require as much system memory and that can jump from one Web server to another without downloading every multimedia file. Consider a television analogy. A few people still own small black-and-white television sets and don't subscribe to cable, whereas other people own room-size, cable-ready color televisions and subscribe to every movie channel available. All these people, however, can turn on their TVs and watch the NBC Nightly News. Like television, the Web is a form of media; you need certain hardware configurations to take full advantage of its resources.

From Here...

Just as there is more than one way to skin a cat, there is more than one way to get onto the Internet/Web (and more every day). To learn more about what you can do when you get on the Internet/Web, refer to these chapters:

■ Chapter 3, "Browsers in Brief," provides more in-depth coverage of the different browsers or software programs you can use to navigate through the Web.

■ Chapter 7, "Mosaic Shortcuts and Tips," offers some time-saving procedures that make it easier to access Web information with the NCSA browser.

Chapter 3

Browsers in Brief

by Bill Eager

The software programs that you use to access the Web and navigate from site to site are known as *browsers*. Browsers isn't a bad name, because you use these applications to browse through documents, files, sights, and sounds.

All Web browsers take advantage of *hypertext*—the interactive links that enable you to jump from one document or server to another. Additionally, all Web browsers use *URL (Uniform Resource Locator) addresses* to identify and load Web pages to your screen.

◄ See "Links and URLs Transport You from Place to Place," p. 27

In this chapter, you will learn about the three types of Web browsers including:

- *Line-mode browser.* Provides WWW access to anyone who has a "dumb" terminal; operates as a general-purpose retrieval tool.

- *Full-screen browser.* A hypertext browser for systems that use terminal emulation.

- *Multimedia browsers.* A hypertext and hypermedia browser that lets you access the pictures, sound, and video resources of the Web.

The following sections examine two of the text-based software programs that help you navigate the World Wide Web. These applications use the client/server technique to bring information from a remote computer to your PC. A multimedia browser (like Mosaic, InternetWorks, Netscape, and so on) installs and becomes a client on your PC. The overview of each type of browser will give you a good understanding of the major functions and operational procedures. You can obtain more details from the reference sites and documents mentioned in the text.

Dumb-Terminal Connection

The most inexpensive way to access the WWW is to use a line-mode browser. The CERN Line Mode Browser was the first browser developed for the Web. A UNIX-based server, this simple WWW browser works with any terminal and provides access for people who use PCs or Macs that emulate a dumb terminal. (Communications software programs provide terminal-emulation options.)

The CERN Line Mode Browser (see example of display in fig. 3.1) enables you to find information by following references or by searching for keywords. The program uses HTML hypertext links, enabling you to follow a link to display text. Reference numbers help you navigate a page; to follow a link, type a number and press Enter. Table 3.1 shows specific keyboard commands for the Line Mode Browser. To try this WWW interface, Telnet to **telnet.W3.org**, and log in as **WWW**, if you are asked for a user name.

Fig. 3.1
This figure illustrates the CERN Line Mode Browser interface. Links to other documents appear as numbers in the text.

Table 3.1 CERN Line Mode Browser Commands

Function/Command	Description
Help, ?	Provides a list of available commands, based on the context, the version number of the WWW program, and the hypertext address (or UDI) of the document that you are reading
Enter	Displays the next page (if any) of the current document

Function/Command	Description
Top, Bottom	Goes to the top or bottom of the current document
Up, Down	Scrolls up or down one page in the current document
Load a Document *number*	Follows the corresponding reference number from the currently displayed document
Back	Returns to the document that you were reading before
Next, Previous	Goes to the following or preceding document in the list of pointers
Go *address*	Goes to the document represented by the hypertext address
Home	Goes back to the first document that you were reading
Find, Keywords *keywords*	Queries the current index with keywords (separated by blanks)
Recall	Displays a numbered list of the documents that you have visited
Quit, Exit	Leaves the application

Text-Only Connection (Terminal Emulation)

Lynx is a WWW browser that fills a niche between line-mode browsers and multimedia browsers (see fig. 3.2). Lynx was designed by Lou Montulli, Charles Rezac, and Michael Grobe of Academic Computing Services at the University of Kansas as part of an effort to build a campus wide information system. Initial efforts produced a user-friendly hypertext interface for multiuser systems that were UNIX- and VMS-based. Lynx evolved from its initial hypertext language to the current use of HTML.

You can use Lynx from dial-up access, a dedicated connection, or Telnet. PCs need to run VT100 terminal emulation for presentation. When you start Lynx, it opens a default file—or *home page*—that usually is selected by your Internet service provider. When Lynx displays WWW documents, the connections to other resources appear as highlighted text. You use simple keyboard commands (detailed in table 3.2) to navigate through documents

▶ See "Under-standing HTTP and HTML: The Languages of the WWW," p. 321

Tip
If you get stuck or just want more information, you can find a World Wide Web Lynx user's guide at **http://www.cc.ukans.edu/lynx_help/Lynx_users_guide.html**.

with Lynx. To select a particular link on-screen, for example, press the up-arrow or down-arrow key until the link is highlighted; then press the right-arrow or Enter key to view the information. Lynx keeps a list of each file that you visit; this list is a *history list*. Pressing the Backspace or Delete key displays the history list and enables you to recall any of those documents.

Fig. 3.2

With the Lynx browser, the connections to other resources appear as high-lighted text. Here, Lynx is being used with the Terminal program of Microsoft Windows.

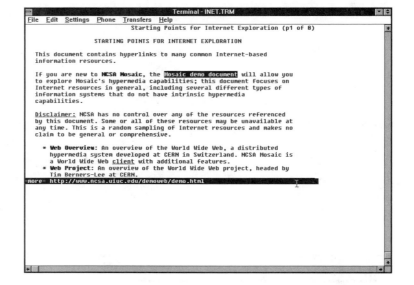

Table 3.2 Summary of Key Commands for Lynx	
Key	**Action**
\	Displays the original source of an HTML document.
/	Activates searching within a document. The search type depends on options set by the system administrator.
? or H	Displays online help. A list of help topics is provided.
Ctrl+L	Refreshes (or *wipes*) screen to remove or correct operating-system errors.
Ctrl+W	Refreshes (or *wipes*) screen to remove or correct operating-system errors.
Ctrl+R	Reloads the current file.
Delete	Displays the history list.
Space bar	Moves to the next page.

Key	Action
=	Shows information about the current document and the currently selected link (if any). Displays the file, URL, title, owner, and type.
a	Creates a bookmark. You will be asked whether you want to Save Document, Link to Bookmark File, or Cancel. Answer by typing **d** to save a link to the document that you are currently viewing or **l** to save the link that is currently selected on the page. Select **c** to cancel without saving anything to your bookmark file.
c	Mails a message to the owner of the current document, if the author has specified ownership. If no ownership is specified, comments are disabled. The system prompts you for information. End the message with a single period (.) in a line.
d	Downloads a file. Lynx transfers the file to a temporary location and presents a list of options. The default option is Save File to Disk.
e	Enables you to edit a file.
g	Displays a URL. A prompt asks you to enter the URL that you want to view.
i	Displays an index of documents.
m	Returns to the starting document.
o	Opens the Lynx Options menu, which you use to configure Lynx.
p	Displays a menu of print options.
q	Quits Lynx.
s	Activates searching. The s option enables you to search index documents from an index server.
v	Displays a list of saved bookmarks. While viewing the bookmark list, you can select a bookmark as you would any other link.
z	Halts the connection or data-transfer process. Lynx supports completely interruptible I/O processes. If any data was transferred before the interrupt, that data is displayed.

Multimedia Browsers

▶ See "Where to Get Mosaic for Windows and Associated Software," p. 64

American essayist Ralphæ Waldo Emerson wrote, "Invention breeds invention." In the world of the Web, it might be said that browsers breed new browsers. Two years ago, one multimedia browser was available: NCSA Mosaic. Today, many multimedia browsers are available for all computer platforms, and many of these browsers are direct descendants of NCSA Mosaic.

Figure 3.3 shows how the latest version of NCSA Mosaic displays Web documents.

Fig. 3.3
NCSA Mosaic is the granddaddy of browsers. This is the home page for the White House.

NCSA Mosaic is such a popular browser that many commercial Web browsers use the source code for Mosaic as the basis for their applications. At least eight companies have licenses to use NCSA Mosaic, and four have rights to sublicense it. Spyglass, Inc., formed in 1990 to enhance and commercialize technology from NCSA, creates new tools and upgrades for commercial versions of Mosaic. Spyglass took over master licensing of Mosaic from NCSA in August 1994; the company develops custom versions of Mosaic (known as Enhanced Mosaic) for corporations that want to distribute the product. Spyglass has licensed 10 million copies of Enhanced Mosaic. A large percentage of this market is companies such as AT&T, IBM, and NEC, which have site licenses to use the product.

The most recent round of multimedia browsers are extremely easy to use. These programs offer toolbars, point-and-click access to features, and options that enable you to configure the appearance of Web documents on your monitor. The browsers provide access to the multimedia elements—pictures, sounds, and movies—that make the Web such a popular communications medium. You can download and use some of these multimedia browsers from Internet sites without charge. Commercial Web browsers (such as Spry's Air Mosaic, which comes with the Internet-In-A-Box package) are available for purchase at computer software stores.

Noticeable differences exist among browser programs. Some Web browsers offer a feature that enables you to enter text and other information in a form and then send the form back to a Web site; others don't. Some Web browsers allow you to access UseNet newsgroups or send electronic mail; others won't. Some Web browsers enable you to take advantage of advanced Windows features such as OLE (object linking and embedding); others can't.

From Here...

In this chapter, you learned about the three different types of Web browsers. For most people, the thrill of using the Web comes from seeing and hearing the multimedia information that's on Web pages. The focus of the following chapters is on the multimedia browsers that let you use multiple senses as you "cruise the Web."

- Chapter 4, "Getting Mosaic Running in Windows," introduces you to the NCSA Mosaic browser.

- Chapter 5, "Multimedia—Using Viewers," shows you how to attach media viewer programs to Mosaic.

- Chapter 11, "Netscape," provides an overview of the browser by Netscape Communications.

- Chapter 12, "Luckman Interactive Enhanced Mosaic," highlights the Luckman Web browser.

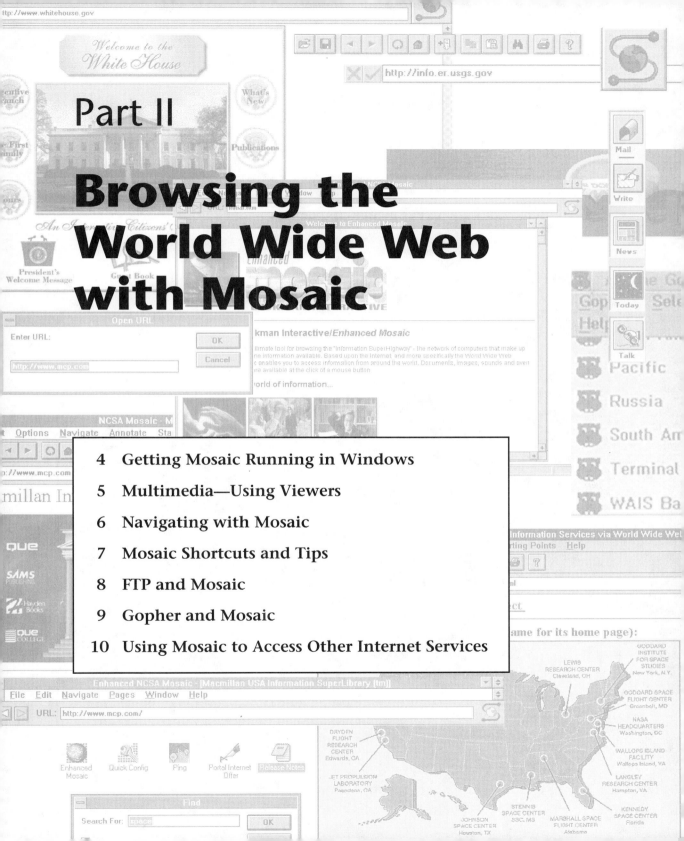

Part II

Browsing the World Wide Web with Mosaic

Chapter 4

Getting Mosaic Running in Windows

by Mary Ann Pike

Depending on how your system is set up, getting Mosaic for Windows to run can be as easy as just loading the software. If your system is not already connected to the Internet, however, getting Mosaic for Windows running requires you to do some extra work.

In this chapter, you learn the following:

- Whether your computer system can run Mosaic for Windows, and what additional hardware and software you might need

- Where to get a copy of Mosaic for Windows, and any additional software you might need to run it

- How to set up Mosaic for Windows on your system

- What the Mosaic for Windows interface looks like and how you interact with it

Can Your Computer System Run Mosaic for Windows?

Before you can get Mosaic for Windows running on your personal computer, you must make sure that your computer system is capable of running the software. While this might seem fairly basic, it is disappointing (not to mention annoying) to spend a number of hours getting software and setting it up only to discover that your system does not have enough memory to run Mosaic for Windows, or that the software runs so slowly that you can't effectively use it.

This section, then, outlines what type of hardware and software you must have on your computer to run Mosaic for Windows.

Basic System Requirements

First of all, your computer system must be capable of running Microsoft Windows version 3.1 or a later version of Windows (for example, Windows NT or Windows for Workgroups). If you don't already have Windows 3.1 or later, you'll have to purchase and install this software before you can run Mosaic.

Mosaic for Windows version 2.0a9 is a 32-bit application and requires the Windows 32-bit extension software. (This extension software is not necessary for Windows NT or Windows 95, which are both 32-bit operating systems.) The Windows extension software (Win32s) is available at FTP sites on the Internet, and is included on WebCD that comes with this book.

In addition, Mosaic for Windows requires at least 4M of main memory and an Intel 80386 processor. This means that most older systems cannot run Mosaic for Windows, and many newer systems may need additional memory to run Mosaic properly.

> **Note**
>
> Although these are minimum system requirements recommended by the Mosaic developers, you will probably find anything less than 8M on a 33MHz i486 to be frustratingly slow.

The basic Mosaic for Windows configuration requires around 7M of disk space for the Mosaic software and documentation and the Win32s libraries. You also need some temporary disk space to hold the compressed Mosaic and Win32s files while you're unpacking them (about 3M for both files). In addition to this basic disk space requirement, Mosaic requires some disk space to hold temporary files while it is running, disk space for documents you want to store locally, and disk space for any viewers that you need to display movies, image files, sound files, and so on.

If your system has a minimal configuration to run Mosaic for Windows, you can add additional hardware capacity to make Mosaic more effective and pleasant to use. A fast 80486 or Pentium system runs Mosaic much better than a slower 80386-based system. Adding more memory to a system also greatly improves the performance of Mosaic (and the rest of the system for that matter).

Network Requirements

In addition to these system requirements, Mosaic for Windows requires a direct connection to the Internet, either through an Ethernet card in your system, or through some kind of modem connection. The best configuration is with an Ethernet card that is directly connected to a local network— this provides the best Mosaic performance and requires the least additional software.

If your system does not have a direct Ethernet connection, you'll have to get an account from an Internet provider to connect to the Internet. You have to obtain software that enables your system to run the *Serial Line Internet Protocol* (SLIP) or *Point-to-Point Protocol* (PPP). This software allows you to connect to the Internet through a modem on your system.

There are a number of different options available for obtaining the software you need to connect to your Internet account. Many service providers will supply you with the software as part of your account startup. Some shareware that lets you connect to SLIP and PPP accounts is available on WebCD that comes with this book (the most popular being the Trumpet Winsock). Or, you can buy commercially available connection software (such as NetManage Chameleon).

> **Note**
>
> You do not need SLIP or PPP software if you are using Windows NT 3.5 (it is built into the operating system).

Other Software Requirements

After Mosaic is running on your system, you may want to extend its capabilities by adding software to handle more types of documents. Mosaic for Windows comes with software that lets you display some types of images, but you may want to get software to process sound files, animation files, and additional picture formats. Obtaining and setting up these additional programs are discussed in more detail in Chapter 5, "Multimedia—Using Viewers."

II

Browsing with Mosaic

Where to Get Mosaic for Windows and Associated Software

One of the best features of Mosaic for Windows is that the basic software is free for anyone to use. The software, which is written and maintained at the National Center for Supercomputer Applications (NCSA) at the University of Illinois, is available through anonymous FTP. This section discusses exactly how to get this software and any additional software you will need to run Mosaic for Windows.

Obtaining Network Software

If your system has an Ethernet card that allows you to be directly connected to a local network, the card vendor should have provided all the software necessary for your system to use the TCP/IP protocol suite that is required by Mosaic for Windows. You may have to consult your local network administrator to get information that is required by the Ethernet software (such as your host name and number), but this network configuration is beyond the scope of this book. (Another Que book, *Special Edition Using the Internet,* Second Edition, discusses TCP/IP network configuration.) If the Ethernet software is running on your system (that is, you can run FTP and Telnet), Mosaic for Windows should work correctly.

Mosaic for Windows uses the Winsock (Windows socket) standard to talk to the network. Your Ethernet card vendor should have provided a version of the Winsock libraries for your system. If the vendor hasn't, contact this person to determine what Winsock library is suitable for use with the vendor's Ethernet software.

> **Note**
>
> Windows NT 3.5 and all later versions of Windows will have Winsock built into the operating system.

Several publicly available SLIP software packages are included on WebCD that comes with this book. One of the most popular packages is the Trumpet Software International Winsock (Trumpet Winsock for short). If you want to pick up this software directly from the Internet, there are several places where you can find it. You can get a shareware version of the Trumpet SLIP software via anonymous FTP to the machine **ftp.ncsa.uiuc.edu**. The file you want to retrieve is /Web/Mosaic/Windows/sockets/winsock.zip. This shareware version of SLIP comes with the Winsock libraries that Mosaic for Windows 2.0a9 requires.

After you have obtained the software for running SLIP (or PPP) on your computer system, you have to configure the software for your network. You have to set up your SLIP software with the proper phone number for your Internet provider, and might have to set up your host name, address, and other network information. Read the installation instructions that came with your SLIP software carefully. You may have to contact your Internet provider for some of the information that is needed by the software.

Where to Get the Basic Mosaic Software

The basic Mosaic for Windows software is available through anonymous FTP at the machine **ftp.ncsa.uiuc.edu**. This site has versions of Mosaic for several different machine types, but you are interested in the Mosaic software for PC machines running Windows found in the file mos20a9.exe. The latest version of Mosaic for Windows (as of the writing of this book) is version 2.0a9 which, although fairly stable, is still under development.

> **Note**
>
> The "a" in this version number indicates that this is an "alpha" version. Alpha versions are the early testing, pre-release versions of software. Be aware that these versions still have *bugs,* or features that don't work.

Mosaic for Windows version 2.0a9 also requires the Windows 32-bit extension software. This software is available on WebCD included with this book in the directory \win32s. It also can be found in the same FTP directory as the Mosaic software itself. If you already run a 32-bit version of Windows (such as Windows NT), you do not need this software. These two packages (Mosaic and Win32s) make up the basic Mosaic for Windows software.

> **Note**
>
> The Alpha 9 version of Mosaic requires Win32s version 1.2 to work properly. Earlier versions of Mosaic worked with the 1.1.5 version of Win32s. If you're currently running an older version of Mosaic, you can download both the 2.0a9 version of Mosaic and the 1.2 version of the Win32s software from the NCSA Windows Mosaic home page.

If you have a Windows-based FTP program, such as WS_FTP (included on WebCD that comes with this book), and you want to retrieve the Mosaic and Win32s software from the Internet, follow these steps:

Tip
When you download Mosaic, be sure to see if there is a more recent version. If there is, it may run better and have fewer problems.

WebCD

II

Browsing with Mosaic

1. Connect to your Internet provider.

2. Start the FTP program.

3. Click Connect and enter the address of the site you want to retrieve the files from (usually in a text box called something like "Host" or "Host Name"). Enter **anonymous** as the **U**ser ID and your e-mail address as the Password (see fig. 4.1).

Fig. 4.1
The WS_FTP Session Profile dialog box lets you enter the information you need to connect to the anonymous FTP site.

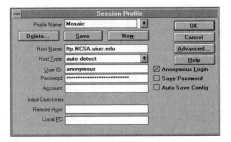

4. Navigate to the directory that contains the files you want to transfer (see fig. 4.2).

Double-click here to
move to that directory

Fig. 4.2
WS_FTP lets you navigate through directories by double-clicking the directory names in the top section of the Remote System window.

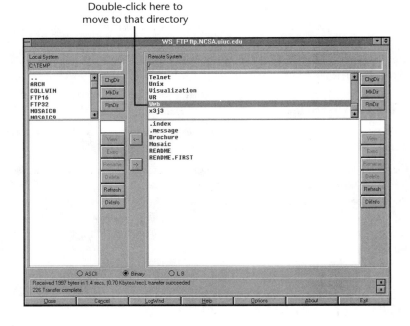

5. When you're at the correct directory, select the mos20a9.exe and
w32sOLE.exe file to transfer and initiate the transfer to your machine
(see fig. 4.3).

> **Note**
>
> Transferred files are saved in the directory in the Local System window in the
> upper-left corner of the screen. To change this directory, click the desired
> directory.

Fig. 4.3
Click the left arrow
to transfer the files
you selected in the
lower portion of
the Remote System
window to your
local hard drive.

Click to transfer
selected files

Browsing with Mosaic

6. After transferring all the files you need, click **C**lose and E**x**it to close
your FTP connection and exit FTP.

> **Note**
>
> The size of the Win32s EXE file is more than 2M. This can take quite a while to
> transfer, even with a relatively fast modem.

There is one problem you may encounter in obtaining the Mosaic and
Win32s software. Because this software is so popular, the NCSA site is often
very busy. There are limits to the number of users that can connect to it at
once; at busy times, you may not be able to connect. If this happens, be patient and try again. If you still can't get connected, don't despair. Many other

FTP sites have copies of the Mosaic and Win32s ZIP files. Table 4.1 lists a couple alternate anonymous FTP sites and the directories in which to look for the software.

Table 4.1 Alternate FTP Sites for Mosaic and Win32	
Site Address	**Directory**
nic.switch.ch	/mirror/WWW/NCSA/Mosaic/Windows
ftp.mcp.com	/pub/que/net-cd
ftp.cac.psu.edu	/pub/access/test

Another thing to keep in mind when looking for this software is that just as you move files around on your computer, the system administrators of the FTP sites may occasionally move files or rename directories. If you can't find the files you're looking for, look in another directory. They may be somewhere else.

Obtaining Auxiliary Software for Mosaic

Besides the standard software necessary to run Mosaic for Windows, there is some additional software which you may need to either set up Mosaic or allow Mosaic to handle certain documents.

ZIP Utilities

WebCD

Tip
You can associate either PKUNZIP or WinZIP with the ZIP file extension so that when you double-click a file with that extension from the Windows File Manager, the unpacking application is automatically invoked.

First of all, because many of the viewers that can be used with Mosaic are packed in ZIP file format, you will need an application that allows you to unpack these files. A copy of WinZIP is included on the WebCD that comes with this book. You can also use the PKZIP package, available through anonymous FTP at the same site you found Mosaic (**ftp.ncsa.uiuc.edu**) in the directory /PC/Windows/Contrib. Retrieve the file pkz204g.exe from this directory. (Make sure that the version of PKZIP that you get is 2.04 or later.)

> **Note**
>
> If you unpack the pkz204g.exe file in a directory that is found in the PATH statement of your autoexec.bat file (like the DOS directory), you can just enter the commands **pkzip** and **pkunzip** at the DOS prompt. Alternatively, you can unpack the file in any directory that you want and add that directory to the PATH statement of your autoexec.bat file.

After you have retrieved the file, you have to run it to unpack it. Either enter the command **pkz204g** at the DOS prompt, or open the **F**ile menu and choose **R**un.

Table 4.2 lists alternative sites where you can find the PKZIP software.

Table 4.2 Alternate FTP Sites for PKZIP	
Site Address	**Directory**
oak.oakland.edu	/pub/msdos/zip
ftp.cica.indiana.edu	/pub/pc/starter
ftp.uu.net	/systems/ibmpc/msdos/simtel/zip

Multimedia Viewers

Although Mosaic for Windows displays normal Web documents, you may want to obtain additional software to allow Mosaic to handle things such as pictures, sounds, and animations (movies). Chapter 5, "Multimedia—Using Viewers," discusses how to get, install, and use viewers.

Setting Up Mosaic for Windows on Your System

After you have obtained all of the files that you need to run Mosaic for Windows on your PC, you can go through the process of getting the software ready to run. This section covers the steps necessary to set up the basic Mosaic for Windows software and discusses how to set up any auxiliary software you have retrieved to use with Mosaic.

Setting up the basic Mosaic for Windows software consists of unpacking and installing the Windows 32-bit libraries and the Mosaic software itself. The first step is to install the Windows 32-bit libraries into your Microsoft Windows directories.

Installing the Windows 32-bit Libraries

The Windows 32-bit libraries, written by Microsoft, come with the standard Windows setup utility to do the installation. This makes the process of installing these libraries simple and almost foolproof. The following are the steps necessary to install these libraries:

1. Move the w32sOLE.exe file you retrieved from the FTP site to a temporary directory on your hard drive.

   Or, if you are using the version of the Win32s software that is included on WebCD, find the win32s directory and go to step 4.

2. Execute this file. Simply enter the file name as a DOS command, or double-click the file name from the Windows File Manager.

Tip

If you double-click the EXE file from the File Manager to execute it, press F5 to refresh the file display so that you can see the unpacked files.

3. The temporary directory now contains the original archive file and several other files. One of these files is another archive file (w32spack.exe) which contains the actual Windows libraries. Execute the file install.bat to unpack the libraries. Simply enter the file name as a DOS command, or double-click the file name from the Windows File Manager.

4. The temporary directory now contains three directories called disk1, disk2, and disk3 that hold the Windows 32-bit library distribution files.

5. Start Microsoft Windows (you must do the setup in Windows).

6. Open the **F**ile menu and choose **R**un.

Tip

You can also double-click setup.exe from the File Manager to execute it.

7. If the temporary directory you used is called C:\temp, type the command **C:\Ptemp\disk1\setup** in the Run dialog box. Choose OK to run the setup program.

8. Choose **C**ontinue in the Microsoft Win32s Setup dialog box, shown in figure 4.4, to start the installation process.

Fig. 4.4

The initial Microsoft Win32s Setup dialog reminds you to close other applications and save your data before starting the installation.

You may get the dialog box shown in figure 4.5 informing you that you need to have file sharing enabled.

> **Note**
>
> You should put the statement `c:\dos\share.exe` in your autoexec.bat file. You may want to use the /F switch to increase the size of the file that keeps track of the sharing information (default is 2048 bytes), and the /L switch to set the number of files that can be locked at one time (default is 20).

Fig. 4.5
File sharing must
be enabled on
your computer for
the OLE features of
this version of the
Win32s software
to work properly.

9. The dialog box shown in figure 4.6 appears asking you to confirm your standard Windows System Directory. Choose Continue to load the libraries.

Fig. 4.6
Correct the
Windows System
directory name if
necessary in this
dialog box.

II

Browsing with Mosaic

10. The dialog box shown in figure 4.7 appears after setup has loaded the 32-bit libraries. Choose OK to continue.

Fig. 4.7
Win32s tells you
when the library
installation has
completed
successfully.

11. The dialog box shown in figure 4.8 appears, asking if you want to load a 32-bit version of the game Freecell to test that the libraries were loaded correctly. (This dialog does not appear if you are doing a minor upgrade of the Win32s software.) If you have enough disk space to do this (less than 1M of space is required), you should choose Continue to load this software; it allows you to make sure that the 32-bit libraries are running correctly. If you don't want to install Freecell, choose Exit.

Fig. 4.8
You can install the
Freecell game to
test your Win32s
libraries.

12. A final dialog box, shown in figure 4.9, asks if you want to exit the setup program. If you are installing a major Win32s upgrade (or installing the software for the first time), it asks you if you want to restart Windows. Choose **C**ontinue to exit. The 32-bit libraries should be completely loaded.

Fig. 4.9
Once the Win32s libraries are loaded, the installation program exits and returns you to Windows.

13. You can remove the files from the temporary directory, since they are no longer needed.

This completes the process of loading the Windows 32-bit library software. You can now proceed with loading the Mosaic for Windows software.

> ### Note
>
> The Win32s add-ins enable Windows to run 32-bit programs such as Mosaic. 32-bit programs run faster than their 16-bit counterparts. The down side of this is that some users have complained that Win32s is not 100 percent stable. There have been complaints that it is buggy and won't work reliably with many existing applications. So, many Windows users have been reluctant to upgrade to Win32s.
>
> Most software vendors whose programs have had trouble under Win32s have released updates and fixes so that their programs work in Win32s. Microsoft also has released several updated versions of Win32s that have dramatically reduced the problems with Win32s incompatibilities.
>
> The authors and development staff of this book all have worked using the latest version of Mosaic, which is a 32-bit version. We have not experienced any problems with Win32s—with only one exception, noted later in this section. The best advice we can give you is to back up your Windows directory and subdirectory before installing Win32s. That way, if you have problems, you can restore from your backup.

Installing Win32s with a LaserMaster Printer

If you have a LaserMaster printer or printer accessory, you may have a little work to do before you can install Win32s. For years, LaserMaster has used the term *Winspool* for their printer ports. For example, if you have a WinJet800—

a modification that makes a LaserJet III print at 800 dots per inch—you have a print driver that is named *LM WinJet 800 PS on WINSPOOL*. The term WINSPOOL, then, is a protected one—after you've started Windows, you cannot create a file called WINSPOOL, in the same way that you cannot create a file in DOS called LPT1 or COM1.

Unfortunately, Microsoft picked the name winspool.drv for one of the Win32s files. So if you have installed a LaserMaster product, when you try to install your Win32s system, the setup program locks up when it tries to copy and extract the winspool.dr_ file off the disk.

That's if you have the Win32s files on a disk, of course—if you're getting the ZIP file off the Internet and are trying to extract the archived files out of the ZIP file, you won't even be able to get as far as the installation procedure. You'll be able to extract all of the files out of the ZIP file except for one—winspool.dr_.

Luckily, the fix is fairly easy. Just follow these steps:

1. At the File Manager or Program Manager, open the **F**ile menu and choose **R**un. Type **sysedit** and press Enter. The Windows System Configuration Editor appears. This contains several document windows, one of which contains the system.ini file.

2. Maximize the system.ini document window.

3. In the system.ini file, find these lines:

   ```
   device=LMHAROLD.386
   device=LMCAP.386
   device=LMMI.386
   ```

4. Place a semicolon (;) at the beginning of each line (;device-LMHAROLD.386, for example).

5. Exit Windows.

6. Restart Windows.

7. Now you can continue. If you got the Win32s files off the Internet, extract them from the ZIP file into the directory you created for that purpose, and run the installation program.

8. After you've finished installing the Win32s system, go back to the system.ini and remove the colons that you placed. The next time you open Windows, you'll be able to use both your 32-bit Mosaic *and* your LaserMaster printer.

Uninstalling the Win32s Software

If for some reason you decide you want to uninstall the Win32s software (if it is causing a problem with one of your other applications, for example) follow these steps:

1. Edit your system.ini file in your /windows directory.

2. In the [386enh] section, remove the line

   `device=C:\WINDOWS\SYSTEM\WIN32S\W32S.386`

3. Delete the \windows\system\win32s directory and everything in it.

4. Delete win32s.ini, win32s16.dll, and win32sys.dll files from the \windows\system directory.

Tip

If you're just testing the change, you can just put a ; at the beginning of the line in your system.ini file, and rename the files and directories that need to be removed.

Installing the Mosaic for Windows Software

After you have loaded the 32-bit libraries, loading the Mosaic for Windows software is very straightforward. To set up the software, follow these steps:

1. Move the Mosaic for Windows file (mos20a9.exe) you retrieved from the FTP site into a temporary directory.

2. Execute this file. Simply enter the file name as a DOS command, or double-click the file name from the Windows File Manager.

3. Open the **F**ile menu and choose **R**un.

4. If the temporary directory you used is called c:\temp, type the command **c:\temp\setup** in the Run dialog box. Choose OK to run the setup program.

5. Choose **C**ontinue in the first installation screen (see fig. 4.10).

Tip

You can also double-click setup.exe from the File Manager to execute it.

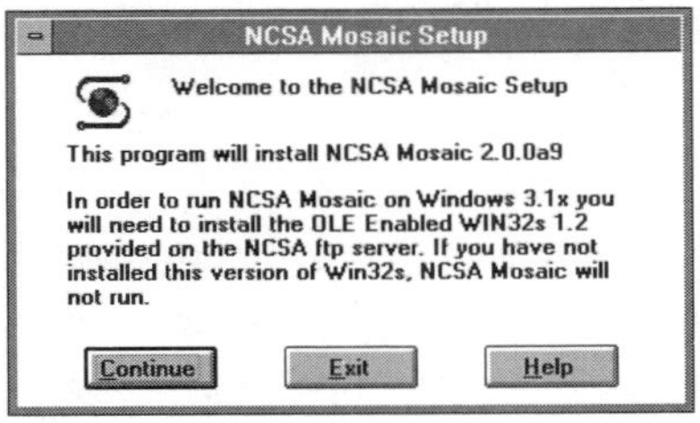

Fig. 4.10

The initial Mosaic Setup dialog box reminds you to install the Win32s version 1.2 OLE libraries.

NCSA Mosaic Setup

Welcome to the NCSA Mosaic Setup

This program will install NCSA Mosaic 2.0.0a9

In order to run NCSA Mosaic on Windows 3.1x you will need to install the OLE Enabled WIN32s 1.2 provided on the NCSA ftp server. If you have not installed this version of Win32s, NCSA Mosaic will not run.

[Continue]   [Exit]   [Help]

6. The next screen asks where you want to install your Mosaic software (see fig. 4.11). Change the default path that is shown, if necessary. Then choose **C**ontinue to install Mosaic and create a program group for it.

Fig. 4.11
You can install the Mosaic software anywhere on your hard disk.

7. A screen providing information about the new Mosaic features appears briefly during the installation (see fig. 4.12). The progress of the installation is shown on a linear graph.

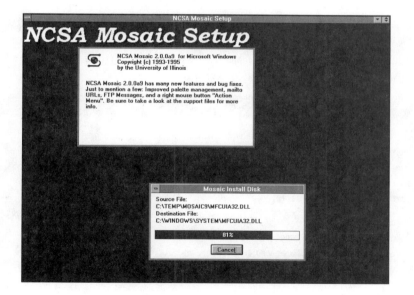

Fig. 4.12
This installation screen tells you that Mosaic version 2.0a9 has improved palette management, among other new features.

After the installation is complete, the Mosaic program group shown in figure 4.13 appears open on your screen. If you already had a Mosaic program group, it simply adds the icon for the new version to that program group.

Fig. 4.13
You can shrink the Mosaic program group to a more appropriate size after the installation is complete.

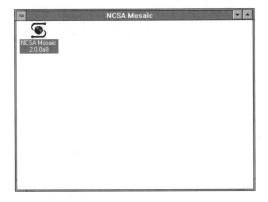

8. The setup of the Mosaic for Windows software is now complete. You can remove the temporary directory where you unpacked the Mosaic files if you want—it's no longer needed.

While there are some customizations that can be done to the Mosaic for Windows software to personalize it to your needs, you can run Mosaic without any further work. Of course, you need to set up your software to connect to the Internet before using Mosaic for Windows.

> **Note**
>
> After you have unpacked the Mosaic software, there's a file you might want to read before installing the software. The file readme.wri gives important installation information and contains a copy of the Mosaic FAQ (Frequently Asked Questions) document, which answers some common questions about Mosaic, and also contains some installation information.
>
> After you have installed Mosaic, there's a release notes file (relnotes.htm) in HTML format (readable by Mosaic) that contains Mosaic configuration information, and talks about the new features, enhancements, and bug fixes in this release.

Using the Mosaic Interface

After you have installed all of the software that you need to run Mosaic, you can connect to your Internet provider and start Mosaic. Mosaic is a very powerful application, and because it's graphically oriented, it's not difficult to use once you become familiar with all of its features.

Starting Mosaic

Before starting Mosaic, you should first be connected to the Internet. If your Internet connection is via your LAN, be sure you are logged onto your network. If you're connected to the Internet by a modem, start your TCP/IP software and log in to your account.

After you have established your Internet connection, open the Mosaic program group (or whatever program group you put Mosaic in), and double-click the Mosaic icon. You're now ready to explore the Internet with Mosaic.

The Mosaic Window

When Mosaic starts, it loads the document that is specified as the home page in your mosaic.ini file. Unless you have specified a personal home page, your window should look like the one shown in figure 4.14. The full URL for the default home page (which is the Mosaic home page) is the following:

**http://www.ncsa.uiuc.edu/SDG/Software/Mosaic/
NCSAMosaicHome.html**

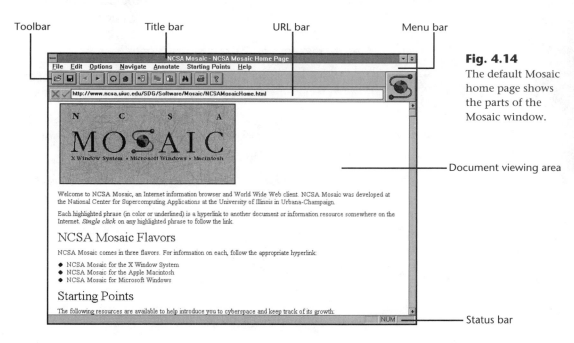

Toolbar   Title bar   URL bar   Menu bar

Document viewing area

Status bar

Fig. 4.14
The default Mosaic home page shows the parts of the Mosaic window.

A brief description of each window part is given in the remainder of this chapter. Each window function is discussed in more depth in Chapter 6, "Navigating with Mosaic," and Chapter 7, "Mosaic Shortcuts and Tips."

Caution

Although the current version of Mosaic is very powerful, it is an application that is still under development. Some of the features shown in the menus and toolbar are not yet implemented. Features (words or icons that you would select) that are not available are dimmed. The developers intend to implement these features as soon as possible.

- The title bar contains the usual window function buttons (control menu box, and maximize and minimize buttons). In addition, it has the name of the application (NCSA Mosaic) and the name of the WWW document that you're viewing.

- The menu bar gives access to all of the functions you need to use Mosaic. You can retrieve documents to view, print documents, customize the look of your Mosaic window, navigate between documents, annotate documents, save files, and access Mosaic's online help.

- The URL bar shows the URL of the current document. When you open a document, its URL is displayed, and the Mosaic logo on the right side of the URL bar spins while the document is being retrieved.

- The document viewing area is the area of the window in which you see the text of a document and any inline images it may contain.

- The status bar serves two functions. While Mosaic is loading your document, it shows the progress of the different files that are being loaded. When you're viewing a document, it shows the URL of the hyperlink that's under your cursor. The three boxes on the right side of the status bar show the state of your Caps Lock, Num Lock, and Scroll Lock keys on your keyboard.

- The toolbar gives you quick access to some of the most used features in Mosaic (see fig. 4.15).

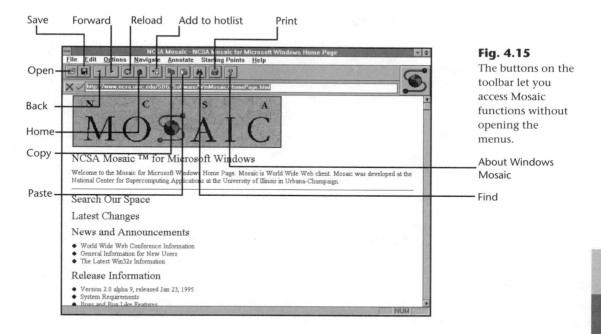

Fig. 4.15
The buttons on the toolbar let you access Mosaic functions without opening the menus.

The following list gives basic descriptions of these buttons:

- *Open* opens a URL.

- *Save/Save As* saves the current document to disk.

- *Back* displays the previous document in the history list.

- *Forward* displays the next document in the history list.

- *Reload* reloads the current document.

- *Home* goes to the default home page.

- *Add to Hotlist* adds the URL of the current document to one of your hotlists.

- *Copy* copies the current selection to the Clipboard.

- *Paste* pastes the contents of the Clipboard to the active window.

- *Find* locates a text string in the current document.

- *Print* prints the current document.

- *About Windows Mosaic* shows the About Windows Mosaic window.

Tip
If you place your cursor over a toolbar button for a few seconds, the button name appears.

II

Browsing with Mosaic

From Here...

To learn more about using Mosaic and to find interesting WWW documents, refer to these chapters:

- Chapter 5, "Multimedia—Using Viewers," shows you how to attach media viewer programs to Mosaic.

- Chapter 6, "Navigating with Mosaic," tells you how to use Mosaic to find and view documents on the WWW.

- Chapter 7, "Mosaic Shortcuts and Tips," tells you how to become an expert WWW navigator.

- Chapter 19, "Web Searching," discusses how to use automated software to find some of the most interesting collections of WWW documents.

Chapter 5

Multimedia—Using Viewers

by Mary Ann Pike

Everyone has experienced multimedia. On any given day, we exercise all our senses to process a variety of information. That information is packaged in different forms: text and pictures in the morning newspaper, highway bill-boards, the reports that we read at work, music and news on the radio, and video and graphics on the television set. The WWW offers access to a wealth of information, much of it stored as multimedia documents.

The public-domain (free) browsers, such as NCSA Mosaic and Cello, require that you download and install special viewer software and drivers to see images or play movies. These external viewer programs allow you to display files in standard multimedia formats: JPEG image files, WAV audio files, and MPEG movie files. When you have the different viewers installed on your PC, getting them to work with Mosaic and other browsers is a straightforward process.

In this chapter, you learn the following:

- What you can expect to find in multimedia documents

- Where to get different viewers that can be used with Mosaic and other browsers

- How to install viewers on your PC

- How to set up Mosaic to use your installed viewers

After you read this chapter, you should be able to set up viewers and config-ure Mosaic to use them.

Read, Listen, and Watch: Multimedia Is Here

Computer technology enhances the utility of multimedia. You can convert all kinds of information to digital data and then place that data on computer hard drives and other media (floppy disks and CD-ROMs). You can search and access this digital information rapidly, deciding what information you want and when you want it.

◀ See "File Transfer Protocol,"
p. 14

▶ See "FTP and Mosaic," p. 147

> **Note**
>
> To use the public-domain browsers, such as NCSA Mosaic and Cello, you must download and install special viewer software and drivers to see images or play movies. The section "How to Find Multimedia Viewers" later in this chapter lists the Internet sites, directories, and files where you can use anonymous FTP to acquire public-domain and shareware multimedia viewers. If you don't want to deal with this aspect of getting multimedia on your PC, consider purchasing one of the commercial browsers that have viewers bundled with them.

Graphics Galore: Images on the Web

If you enjoy thumbing through illustrated books or watching slide shows, you'll love the digital-image resources on the Web. Perhaps you're a history buff. Take a trip to the University of Georgia library's server, and examine a collection of photographs that chronicle the various Works Progress Administration (WPA) projects that were built in Georgia, including streets, airports, and schools. Fascinated by the world of insects? The Gillette Entomology Club at Colorado State University offers a large collection of insect slides for sale; take a peek at slide 281: a close-up of *Vanessa cardui* (painted lady butterfly). The On-Line Images from the History of Medicine service provides access to nearly 60,000 color and black-and-white images, including a photograph of a Greek vase from the 4th century B.C. that shows a bandaging scene, and a picture of Abraham Lincoln visiting soldiers' graves at Bull Run.

You encounter two types of images on the WWW. The first type consists of images embedded directly in the various Web home pages and documents. These *inline images* appear when you link to those documents (through the URL address). One example is the graphic icon or seal that many universities include at the top of their home page. You can see these inline images, but you can't manipulate them or store them on your computer.

Two image-file formats—GIF (Graphics Interchange Format) and XBM (X Bitmap)—display inline images in Web home pages and documents. GIF (pronounced "jif") was introduced by CompuServe in 1987 as a medium for exchanging pictures over that commercial service. GIF files can hold images that contain up to 256 distinct colors, from a palette of about 16 million.

GIF files are compressed to save space and transmission time. When you connect to a home page (load a URL address into your browser), the WWW document begins to transmit to your computer. You should be aware that your computer and the remote host don't have an exclusive, uninterrupted link. After all, it would waste valuable transmission-line time to have your computer linked to a remote host in Japan while your PC processes a graphic image or you go to the kitchen for a glass of water. Normally, your computer (the client) and the remote server communicate several times before an entire home page appears. If the page contains more than one inline GIF or XBM image, the images are downloaded to your PC individually and then decoded or decompressed.

The second type of Web image that you will encounter is one that you ask to view or download to your PC. Housed in a database, these images usually are in a graphic-file format that provides higher image resolution than GIF or XBM, such as JPEG. The JPEG (Joint Photographic Experts Group) format is an industry standard for compressing 24-bit and 8-bit color and gray-image files. GIF images take up less space than JPEG images, but they represent only 8-bit images and 256 colors, whereas JPEG supports 24-bit images and 16.7 million colors. Table 5.1 lists some of the most common image formats.

Table 5.1 Some Graphic File Formats	
File Type	**Description**
GIF	Graphics Interchange Format (bit-mapped)
JPEG	Joint Photographic Experts Group
PCX	Bit-mapped file format
PICT	Macintosh image format
PostScript, Encapsulated PostScript	Intermediate print format
TIFF	Tagged image-file format
XBM (X Windows Bitmap)	UNIX bitmap image

At the Paramount Web site for their new show, *Star Trek: Voyager*, you can view images of all the ship's personnel. When you click the word Photo on any of the personnel pages, a GIF file is transmitted to your computer and GIF viewer, as shown in figure 5.1.

Fig. 5.1
This GIF image (viewed with Lview from Mosaic) of the holographic doctor from the new *Star Trek: Voyager* TV series is available at the **voyager. paramount.com** Web site.

There are at least 15 graphic-file formats, each of which requires the use of image-display software. *Image-display software*—known as viewer software—processes and presents images on your monitor. Public-domain browsers (such as Cello and Mosaic) display inline images in home pages, but they don't have built-in viewers for display of other types of graphic-file formats, notably JPEG.

You must, therefore, install and load a graphics viewer, either a commercial product or a shareware or freeware viewer to see, manipulate, and store these images (table 5.2 lists some of the publicly available viewers). In Mosaic, after you click and download an image file, Mosaic automatically launches the appropriate viewer application (such as LView), but you must have that program resident on your computer. Public-domain and shareware viewers, such as LView for Windows, are available on the Net (and on WebCD, which accompanies this book). Commercial browsers, such as Internet In A Box, are bundled with viewers.

Table 5.2 NCSA-Recommended Viewers	
Medium Type	**PC**
GIF/JPEG images	LViewPro
PostScript files	GhostScript
Adobe PDF	Adobe Acrobat Reader
TIFF images	LViewPro

Graphics and photographs add spice to computer-based information; unfortunately, downloading and processing images can take a long time. Some WWW home pages take more than two minutes to appear, even at 14.4 Kbps. To prevent temporary insanity—when you may want to throw your keyboard through the monitor—multimedia Web browsers do have options that allow you to disable the presentation of images. These options speed your journey through the Web. When you come across a description of an image that sounds particularly appealing, you can enable the image-display feature.

Let's Hear It: How to Enable Sound

The simplest way to listen to sounds (audio files) on the WWW is to purchase a computer that meets the standards for multimedia PCs. The Multimedia PC Marketing Council (which consisted of Microsoft and other leading hardware and software companies) published a standard—the Multimedia PC (MPC) Standard—for future developments in PC-based multimedia. The standard was founded on the Windows graphical user interface enhanced with multimedia software components and programming tools. Basic PCs typically have a single, small mono speaker that emits sound levels ranging from barely audible to adequate. The more recent 80486 and Pentium-based IBM-compatible computers go beyond these initial standards. Table 5.3 tells you what your system should have to be able to take full advantage of using sound in multimedia applications.

Sound cards play, record, or generate sounds of any kind, including speech, music, and sound effects. With an MPC-compatible PC and appropriate driver software, you can travel through the Web and listen to a jazz session, a volcanic eruption, or a debate on taxes. MPC computers require sound cards with specific requirements. Table 5.4 lists the common audio file formats that you are likely to come across. Table 5.5 shows two NCSA-recommended audio players.

Table 5.3   MPC Sound-Card Requirements

External Connections	Input and Output
Microphone	Built-in amplifier
Speakers/headphones	Synthesizer
Stereo system	Stereo channels
MIDI devices	8-bit DAC/ADC (16-bit recommended)
CD-ROM drive	22.05 KHz sampling rate (44.1 KHz recommended)

Table 5.4   Common Audio Formats

File Type	Description
UNIX AU	UNIX audio-file format
WAV	Waveform audio

Table 5.5   NCSA-Recommended Audio Players

Medium Type	PC
WAV sounds	Media Player
AU sounds	WHAM

Note

PCs that meet the MPC standard can play sound. Here is what you do to set up a PC that has a speaker but doesn't have a sound board. The PC speaker driver for basic PC speakers was developed by Microsoft and is available at no charge to licensed users of Windows 3.1. Download the file speak.exe from the URL address **http:// www.ncsa.uiuc.edu/SDG/Software/WinMosaic/speak.html** or FTP to **ftp.ncsa.uiuc.edu** directory **Mosaic/Windows/viewers/** file speak.exe (21,236 bytes).

You can use WWW browsers or search software to search other file archives. The file speak.exe is a self-extracting file. From within DOS, place speak.exe in a new directory, and type **speak** at the DOS prompt. Extraction will produce a speaker.drv file. Do not place that file in a separate directory from oemsetup.inf.

Lights, Camera, Action: How to Enable Movies

In the 1930s and '40s, audiences could watch the latest news events in movie theaters that played newsreels. In the 1950s, '60s, and '70s, television crews traveled all over the world to capture current events and bring them back home. In the 1980s, with the invention and wide distribution of video camcorders, individuals who captured interesting and newsworthy events could get their footage broadcast. Now, at the turn of the century, the Internet opens a vast avenue for video (news, entertainment, commercials, and so on) that individual people and companies record and place on the WWW.

By bypassing the traditional outlets for video—broadcast and cable companies—the Web promises to deliver a tremendous amount of specialized video information that we otherwise would not be able to access. In addition, because Web video is "on-demand" video, we can watch when our own schedule permits. One example of WWW video, for a very small target audience, is a QuickTime movie (on a server at Stanford University) that shows people hang-gliding from ridges and mountains in California. Table 5.6 shows some of the video file formats that you may come across.

You can get digital movies through WWW browsers, using MPEG (Motion Picture Experts Group) and QuickTime file formats. Download time, however, may be excessive if you are using SLIP/PPP dial-up connections. Regardless, expect a comparatively short playback time (for example, a 5-minute download at 14.4 Kbps for a 10-second video clip). These frustrating time factors will become less of a problem as larger bandwidths and faster modems become available.

Special movie-viewer software plays the movies. PC Mosaic uses MPEGPLAY to play MPEG movie files. You can retrieve QuickTime viewers for Microsoft Windows from the URL address **http://cougar.stanford.edu:7878/ MoviePage.html**. You can also get a set of files that will modify Windows Media Player to play QuickTime videos from the URL **ftp:// ftp.ncsa.uiuc.edu/Web/Mosaic/Windows/viewers/qtw11.zip.** NCSA recommends a set of viewers for image, audio, and video display. Table 5.7 lists some of the video viewers that are available.

Table 5.6 Video Formats	
Format	**Description**
AVI	Video for Windows
MPEG (Motion Picture Experts Group)	Standard for compressed video
QuickTime	Apple Computer's cross-platform movie format

Table 5.7 NCSA-Recommended Video Viewers	
Medium Type	**PC**
AVI	Media Player
QuickTime movies	QuickTime or Media Player (with modifications)
MPEG movies	MPEGPLAY

How to Find Multimedia Viewers

▶ See "Internet and World Wide Web Resources," p. 568

This section provides a list of viewers that you can use to view graphics, photographs, and movies and to listen to sounds that are available on the Web. Most of these viewers are shareware or freeware products. The list includes viewers that NCSA recommends for use with NCSA Mosaic; they also may work well with other Web browsers. (You may have to experiment a bit.)

The NSCA FTP site is very popular and is frequently busy. If you can't get through, you may want to check out some of the other Web sites that contain viewer shareware. These sites are listed in Chapter 22, "Computers." Some viewers also are included on the CD-ROM that accompanies this book (refer to Chapter 34, "What's on WebCD").

▶ See "Personal Computers and PC Software," p. 578

▶ See "Viewers," p. 989

To use the viewers on the Windows platform, you may have to configure the software from the program menu or add a statement to the INI file of the browser (Mosaic, Cello, and so on) to let the browser know what directory the viewer resides in. (The remainder of the sections in this chapter provide information on installing viewers and configuring browsers to use them.) Specific configuration instructions come with many of the viewers in a readme text file. The NSCA Web site **http://www.ncsa.uiuc.edu** also has information about viewer installation.

- LView

    Description: freeware GIF/JPEG viewer

    FTP site: **ftp.ncsa.uiuc.edu**

    Directory: /Mosaic/Windows/viewers

    File: lviewp1a.zip

    File size: 304,843 bytes

- MPEGPLAY

    Description: shareware MPEG movie viewer

    FTP site: **ftp.ncsa.uiuc.edu**

    Directory: /Mosaic/Windows/viewers

    File: mpegw32h.zip

    File size: 641,702 bytes

- PC speaker driver

    Description: for basic PC speakers; available at no charge to licensed users of Windows 3.1

    FTP site: **ftp.ncsa.uiuc.edu**

    Directory: Mosaic/Windows/viewers

    File: speak.exe

    File size: 21,236 bytes

- QuickTime

    Description: video player from Chinese University in Hong Kong

    FTP site: **ftp.ncsa.uiuc.edu**

    Directory: /Web/Mosaic/Windows/viewers

    File: qtw11.zip

    File size: 325,867 bytes

II

Browsing with Mosaic

■ WHAM

> Description: Waveform Hold and Modify Version 1.31; freeware plays AU and AIFF sound files for systems with Windows-supported sound cards
>
> FTP site: **ftp.ncsa.uiuc.edu**
>
> Directory: /Mosaic/Windows/viewers
>
> File: wham131.zip
>
> File size: 138,130 bytes

Many viewer programs can handle the different types of media files that you find on the Web. Some of these programs are commercial software packages; others are shareware that you can find on the Internet. If you have more questions about viewers or can't find the viewers that you need, here are some additional sources of information:

■ Read the FAQ (frequently asked questions) file by opening the **H**elp menu and choosing **F**AQ Page. If you scroll to the bottom of the document, you find a hyperlink titled Viewer Software Information. Click this hyperlink to load a document that gives you general information on how to customize Mosaic to use different viewers. This document also has links that enable you to load some of the more popular shareware viewers.

■ Use Gopher or FTP to go to some of the big software repositories on the Internet, and look around for viewer programs. Chapter 33, "Hot FTP and Gopher Sites," lists some of these servers.

■ Chapter 34, "What's on WebCD," has a section that talks about the viewers that are included on WebCD.

■ If you have UseNet access, read the newsgroup **comp.infosystems.www.users**. A discussion of viewers that work with Mosaic is an appropriate topic with this group.

■ Using Mosaic, you can get more information about different viewers and where to find them from the URL **http://www.ncsa.uiuc.edu/SDG/Software/WinMosaic/viewers.html**.

> **Note**
>
> If you already have software for viewing a particular type of file (such as Media Player for WAV, AVI, and MID files), you can set up Mosaic to use this software, rather than the programs listed earlier. For instructions on setting up Mosaic to use the software, see "Configuring Mosaic to Use Viewers" later in this chapter.

Retrieving Multimedia Viewers

A number of the viewers discussed in "How to Find Multimedia Viewers" earlier in the chapter can be found on WebCD. If the viewer you want is not on the CD, you may be able to pick it up directly from the NCSA viewers page.

Open the URL **http://www.ncsa.uiuc.edu/SDG/Software/ WinMosaic/viewers.html** and look at the list of viewers that are on the page. Most of the links on the page are to the viewer files themselves. To load one of these viewers, simply Shift+click the hyperlink, fill in the information on where you want to put the file in the Save As dialog box that appears, and then choose OK. The viewer will be loaded to your disk, and you are ready to install it.

If the viewer that you want is not on the NCSA viewers page but is on an FTP server, use the FTP application that came with your Internet communications software to connect to that FTP server and retrieve the file. (An example of using WS_FTP to retrieve a file can be found in Chapter 4, "Getting Mosaic Running in Windows.") Or use Mosaic to connect to the FTP server and load the file.

◀ See "Where to Get the Basic Mosaic Software," p. 65

▶ See "Connecting to an Anonymous FTP Server," p. 154

Setting Up Mosaic for Multimedia

You can run Mosaic without installing any additional viewers or configuring Mosaic to use them. But you may want to install these viewers so that you can view images, watch movies, and listen to sounds that you download through Mosaic. In general, to install a viewer for Mosaic, you load the viewer program on to your local disk and then tell Mosaic where the program is located and what type of files you can view with it.

MIME—A Multimedia Standard

All the multimedia viewers that you come across will handle MIME (Multi-purpose Internet Mail Extensions) standard multimedia files. MIME was developed to extend the Internet e-mail standard (originally developed for text-only messages) to allow any type of data to be sent via e-mail. The WWW browsers use this same standard for identifying the type of multi-media files.

The basic MIME types identified by WWW browsers are text, audio, image, video, and application. (Application is a catch-all category that lets you associate almost any type of file with an application that will be able to display that file.) Browsers can be configured to use different viewers for different subtypes (video/avi and video/mpeg, for example).

Mosaic has a list of standard MIME types/subtypes on the Preferences Viewers configuration sheet. You can also add your own MIME types to this sheet. If you want to see what the MIME type definitions look like, edit your mosaic.ini file and look at the Viewers section. To configure the MIME types, see the section "Configuring Mosaic to Use Viewers" later in this chapter.

Installing Multimedia Viewers

After you've found a viewer that you want to use and have downloaded the viewer file to your PC, you will most likely need to install the viewer. This may be as simple as unzipping the file you've retrieved, or it may involve going through a Windows setup procedure. In general, to install a multime-dia viewer, follow these steps:

▶ See "Installing Software from WebCD," p. 974

1. If you haven't already downloaded the files for the viewer that you need, consult "How to Find Multimedia Viewers" earlier in this chapter and then use FTP to transfer the files. Alternatively, find a viewer that interests you on WebCD, and follow the installation instructions in Chapter 34, "What's on WebCD." (Remember that the software in-cluded with the CD is shareware and must be registered and paid for if you use it.)

> **Note**
>
> If you are using a program that you already have installed as a viewer, skip to the next section, "Configuring Mosaic to Use Viewers."

2. If the viewer comes as a ZIP file, create a directory for the viewer and move the ZIP file there. If the viewer comes as a self-extracting archive (EXE file), create a temporary directory and place the viewer file there.

3. If the viewer files are compressed with PKZIP, unzip them in the new directory. Look for a readme file and follow any instructions that are in that file. This will probably be all you need to do for viewers that come as ZIP files.

4. If the viewer file is a self-extracting archive, start Windows (if it isn't already running) and double-click the file to unpack it.

5. If the viewer has an install or setup program, run it from Program Manager or File Manager by opening the **F**ile menu and choosing **R**un. Enter the path to the install or setup file in the command line text box of the Run dialog box as follows:

Tip
Double-click the install or setup file to execute it.

```
c:\viewer\install.exe
```

To install the viewer, follow the directions on-screen.

Configuring Mosaic to Use Viewers

Once you have installed viewers on your PC, you need to configure Mosaic to use these viewers. Older versions of Mosaic required you to edit the mosiac.ini file, which you can still do if you'd rather. However, there is now a sheet in the Preferences dialog box to let you easily specify which viewers you have and what file types they can handle.

1. Open the **O**ptions menu and choose **P**references. In the Preferences dialog box that appears, select the Viewers tab for a sheet that allows you to customize Mosaic to use viewers (see fig. 5.2).

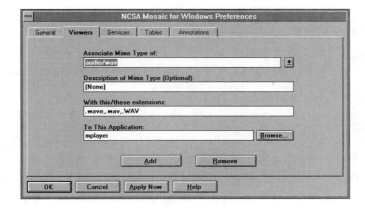

Fig. 5.2
The Viewers sheet in the Preferences dialog box lets you tell Mosaic to start a viewer automatically when it finds a file of a particular type.

2. Click the arrow to the right of the Associate MIME Type of: box and scroll through the list until you find the MIME type for the viewer you are installing.

3. If you want, enter a description of the MIME type in the indicated text box (this is optional).

4. Enter the file extension(s) that are associated with this MIME type. If you have multiple file extensions, separate them with a comma. Be sure to include the dot at the beginning of the file extension.

5. In the To This Application: text box, enter the path to the viewer. You can click Browse to bring up a Browse dialog box to let you look through your directories to find the viewer. If you click the viewer in the Browse dialog box, its path will be automatically entered in the text box.

6. Once all the information on this sheet is entered correctly, click OK to close the Preferences dialog and save the viewer information to your mosaic.ini file.

You can make additional changes to installed viewers at any time.

Configuring Application Viewers

One of the nice features of Mosaic is that you can define viewers for file types such as Word or ZIP, so that if Mosaic loads one of these file types, it automatically starts the correct application to display the file. You can add viewers like these by adding a new MIME type of application/<*name*>. For example, you can add a MIME type of application/word or application/zip. To add a new MIME type and its associated viewer, follow these steps:

1. Open the **O**ptions menu and choose **P**references. In the Preferences dialog box that appears, select the Viewers tab for a sheet that allows you to customize Mosaic to use viewers.

2. To add a completely new viewer, click **A**dd to get a blank viewer sheet (see fig. 5.3).

3. Enter the new MIME type in the Associate MIME Type of: text box (remember, it should be of the form application/<*name*>).

4. Fill in the remainder of the text boxes as described in steps 3, 4, and 5 of the previous section, "Configuring Mosaic to Use Viewers."

MIME type ——————

File extensions ——————

Viewer path ——————

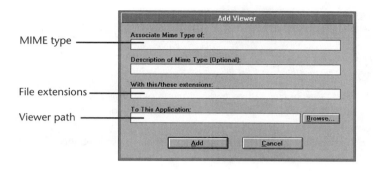

Fig. 5.3
This Add Viewer
dialog box has been
filled in to direct
Mosaic to start Word
when it loads files
with the DOC
extension.

5. Click **A**dd to add that MIME type to the list (or **C**ancel to skip adding it).

6. Once all the information on this sheet is entered correctly, click OK to close the Preferences dialog box and save the viewer information to your mosaic.ini file.

Using Viewers

When you have viewers installed and have configured your browser to use the viewers, you're ready to go. If you're viewing a document that contains links to multimedia files, or if you're browsing an FTP or Gopher site, all you need to do is click the link to the multimedia document. Your browser will load the document, automatically starting the viewer that you defined for displaying that type of multimedia file.

At least, that's the way it should work. It is likely that there may be a few glitches to iron out before your viewers work flawlessly with Mosaic. The following sections discuss some of the problems you may run into with the popular viewers.

> **Caution**
>
> Mosaic seems to develop serious problems after using video viewers. Once Mpegplayer and the QuickTime MediaPlayer modifications are installed, they can be used to view a video *once*. If you try to load a second video, Mosaic stops transferring the file (or never starts transferring it). You might or might not be able to abort the transfer, but even if you can, eventually your PC will lock up, requiring a reset.

II

Browsing with Mosaic

Troubleshooting

I downloaded a picture, and it opened fine in Lview (or any other multimedia viewer). But I went back to view the picture later, and the file wasn't there. What happened?

The problem isn't with Lview or any of the viewers. When Mosaic downloads multimedia files for viewing, it creates a temporary file, and that is what you view. If you close the viewer without saving the file, the file will be gone when you exit Mosaic. So if you want to save multimedia files that you download for later use, save them before you exit the viewer application.

I have Mosaic configured to use a viewer for the file type I loaded but nothing happened after the file transfer was completed. What happened?

If there is not enough memory available to start your viewer, Mosaic will download the file but nothing will happen. You do not even get a message telling you that there was not enough memory. If you are going to download large image or video files, you might want to try it with Mosaic as the sole application running on your PC.

I installed my viewer and told Mosaic where to find it, but when I tried to load a file type that uses the viewer, Mosaic told me it couldn't find the viewer. What happened?

Although the Apply Now button on the Viewers sheet of the Preferences dialog box does appear to save the information immediately to the mosaic.ini file, Mosaic does not seem to refer to this configuration information when it tries to load a file. You may have to exit and restart Mosaic for it to properly locate viewers that you've just configured.

Media Player (Modified for QuickTime)

After downloading and unzipping the qtw11.zip file, be sure to follow the terse instructions in the readme.txt file carefully. You must modify the two files indicated, and copy all the unzipped files (except for the readme.txt) to the Windows system directory, or Media Player will not be able to play QuickTime movies.

When you load a QuickTime movie, the Media Player control panel will open, and the file that you loaded will open in a Media Player window. You must use the Media Player control panel to start the movie before you see anything in the window.

LViewPro

After you unzip the LView files into a working directory, you need to move (or copy) the file ctl3dv2.dll to the c:\Windows\system directory. If you do not, you will get an error when Mosaic tries to start LView after loading the file you want to view.

The readme.1st file that comes with LView discusses the limitations of the unregistered version of this application. The registered version (which costs $30) is designed to work in the Win32 environment (the unregistered version is a 16-bit application), and you can get a registered version specific to your machine architecture (386, 486, or Pentium).

MPEGPLAY

If you are using an unregistered version of MPEGPLAY, you will get the About box everytime you view a video with MPEGPLAY. In addition, the unregistered version of MPEGPLAY is limited to viewing MPEG files that are smaller than 1M (which is not very big for an MPEG file). So, if you are going to be using MPEGPLAY a lot, you probably want to register it and get the better version (a $25 cost for individual users).

From Here...

To learn more about using Mosaic and to find interesting WWW documents, refer to these chapters:

- Chapter 6, "Navigating with Mosaic," tells you how to use Mosaic to find and view documents on the WWW.

- Chapter 7, "Mosaic Shortcuts and Tips," tells you how to become an expert WWW navigator.

- Chapter 34, "What's on WebCD," tells you about the browsers that are included on WebCD.

II

Browsing with Mosaic

Chapter 6

Navigating with Mosaic

by Mary Ann Pike

The World Wide Web (WWW) is one of the best examples of *cyberspace*, the electronic world of interconnected computers. The Web is a system that links documents together so that you can move between them with little effort. You can literally travel to many different places around the world, learning about any topic imaginable. Like any traveler in a new place, however, you can easily get lost.

Mosaic is an easy-to-use interface that lets you traverse the Web. Mosaic has many convenient features that help you keep track of the places you've been and get back to those places quickly. The concepts discussed in Chapter 1, "Introduction to the World Wide Web," are used throughout this chapter.

In this chapter, you learn to do the following:

- Start up Mosaic and use its basic features

- Move between WWW documents

- Configure Mosaic to your preferences

- Handle errors you may encounter

What Is a Home Page?

The designers of Mosaic define a *home page* (or *home document*) as the document that you tell Mosaic to display when it starts. This document should contain links to the documents and WWW sites that you use most frequently. Many people mistakenly use the term "home page" for the welcome page that you get when you connect to a WWW site. A home page provides you with access to the WWW sites or documents that you use most. Your

◀ See "Hypertext and Hypermedia Concepts," p. 24

◀ See "What Happens When You Connect to the Web?" p. 27

project or company may have its own home page to give members easy access to needed information. You can load someone else's home page or design your own.

When you start the Mosaic software, it comes with the home page predefined as the NCSA Mosaic welcome page. You probably want to change this because, for one thing, the NCSA Mosaic page is probably not very useful to you unless you are involved in the installation and maintenance of Mosaic at your site and you want to keep up with the latest information from NCSA. In addition, retrieving a document causes a load on the machine where the document is located. If everyone used the NCSA Mosaic welcome page as their home page, the NCSA WWW server would become considerably slower.

Telling Mosaic What Home Page to Load

Mosaic finds the URL for your home page in the Main section of your mosaic.ini file.

You can use Mosaic's Preferences dialog box to set your default home page. To use the Preferences dialog box, follow these steps:

1. Open the **O**ptions menu and choose **P**references. The Preferences dialog box, shown in figure 6.1, appears. Choose the General tab if it's not already selected.

> **Note**
>
> If you're selecting **P**references from the **O**ptions menu using the keyboard, you must press "p" twice to select it. The first time you press "p," Presentation Mode is highlighted. The second time you press "p," Preferences is highlighted. Press Enter to bring up the Preferences dialog box.

2. Click the text field in the box labeled Home Page.

3. Enter the URL of the document you want to use as your home page.

4. Choose OK to save your preferences to your mosaic.ini file and exit the Preferences dialog box.

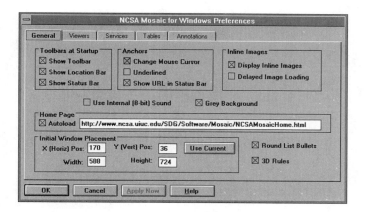

Note

If you want to apply the changes you've made in the Preferences dialog box without exiting the dialog box, choose **A**pply Now.

Your home page can be a document on your computer or any document that you can access at a WWW site. (See Chapter 14, "Creating Home Pages with HTML," for details on how to make your own home page or how to turn a file saved on your computer into a home page.)

By default, when Mosaic starts up, it displays the home page that was specified in your mosaic.ini file. After the home page loads, the URL for that page appears in the URL bar (if you have it enabled). After your home page is loaded, you can click any of its links to load the documents you use frequently.

If you want to return to your home page at any time, open the **N**avigate menu and choose **H**ome. This reloads your home page document.

You also can tell Mosaic not to load any page when it starts. You can use Mosaic's Windows Preferences dialog box to turn off the loading of a home page. To use the Preferences dialog box, follow these steps:

1. Open the **O**ptions menu and choose **P**references. The Preferences dialog box, shown in figure 6.2, appears. Choose the General tab if it's not already selected.

Tip
You can use the Home button (the one that looks like a house) on the toolbar to quickly reload your home page.

Fig. 6.2
Tell Mosaic whether to load a home page from the Preferences dialog box.

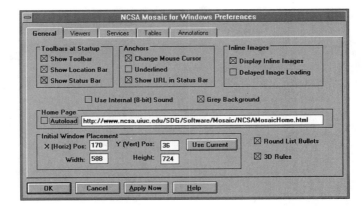

2. Deselect the Autoload check box in the Home Page box.

3. Choose OK to save your preferences to your mosaic.ini file and exit the Preferences dialog box.

When you start Mosaic, your document viewing area is blank, and you can begin your navigation of the WWW from there.

Moving between Documents

After you start Mosaic, you can move between WWW documents in several ways—you can click links in the document you are viewing, or you can use Mosaic's Open URL dialog box to enter a URL. If you load a home page, it probably includes links to other documents. After all, the purpose of the WWW is to let you move quickly between related documents without having to enter long path names. If there are no links in a document, it's not a very useful WWW document. But, even if your current document has no links, you can still move between documents by directly entering the URLs for the documents you want to view.

▶ See "Create Lists of Your Favorite URLs," p. 128

▶ See "Quick Access to Your Favorite URLs," p. 135

> **Note**
>
> A third way to move between documents is to use hotlists that contain items with predefined URLs. Creating and using hotlists is covered in Chapter 7, "Mosaic Short-cuts and Tips."

Moving between Documents Using Links

Links are simply references to other documents (or to pictures, movies, or sounds). But they aren't just stated references like "see page 2 for more information." They are actual live links, where you can activate the link and cause the thing it references to appear on your screen. When someone writes a hypertext document, he or she can insert links to other documents that have information relevant to the text in the document.

There are two parts to a link. One part is the *anchor*. The author of a document can define the anchor to be a word, a group of words, a picture, or any area of the reader's display. The reader activates the anchor by pointing to it and clicking with a mouse (for a graphical-based browser) or by selecting it with arrow keys and pressing Enter (for a text-based browser).

The second part of a hypertext link is the item referenced by the anchor. That item can be a document, picture, movie, or sound. In the case of the WWW, the item being referenced could be within the current document, or it could be anywhere on the Internet.

Mosaic can indicate the hypertext links in a document in a number of different ways. If your monitor is color, the links can be displayed in a different color than other text (or outlined in color if they are graphics). If you have a black-and-white monitor, the links can be underlined.

By default, Mosaic is set so that when you move your cursor over an area of the screen that has an active link, your cursor changes from an arrow to a pointing hand. The URL associated with each link that you pass over appears in the status bar (if it is enabled). When you activate a link by placing your cursor over the link and clicking, Mosaic loads the document and displays the URL for that document in the URL bar (if it is enabled). All of these settings are configurable. See the "Customizing Your Mosaic Window" section for more information about configuring Mosaic's link-related attributes.

◀ See "Hypertext and Hypermedia Concepts," p. 24

▶ See "Understanding HTTP and HTML: the Languages of the WWW," p. 321

II

Browsing with Mosaic

Note

If you click the right mouse button while your cursor is over a hyperlink (the anchor), you will get a pop-up menu that gives you a number of options (these are explained in the "What You See When a Document Is Loaded" section, later in this chapter). If you select Spawn Mosaic from Anchor, this opens a new Mosaic window containing the document referenced by the hyperlink. You can use this window to view WWW documents just as you can your original Mosaic window, and you can open any number of Mosaic windows this way. To close any of your open Mosaic windows, open the **F**ile menu in that window and choose E**x**it.

Look at the Mosaic home page in figure 6.3. The words "World Wide Web," "National Center for Supercomputing Applications," "University of Illinois, Urbana-Champaign," "highlighted phrase," "NCSA Mosaic for the X Window System," "NCSA Mosaic for the Apple Macintosh," and "NCSA Mosaic for Microsoft Windows" are all links. When you run Mosaic on a color display, you see the links in blue (they are underlined in the figure), the default hyperlink color. The URL of the active link (with the pointing hand over it) is shown in the status bar.

Fig. 6.3
The Mosaic welcome page has a number of hyperlinks that can be displayed in color or underlined, as shown here.

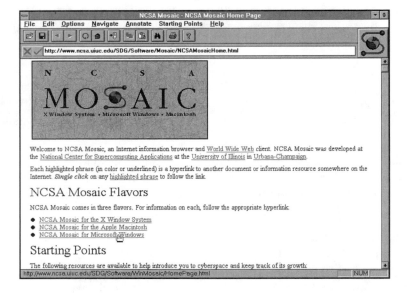

Moving Backward and Forward

Typing long URLs and scrolling through documents to look for the links you want can get rather tedious. If you're jumping between a number of documents, take advantage of three helpful navigating commands: **B**ack, **F**orward, and **R**eload.

▶ See "How to Get Where You Were," p. 126

Mosaic keeps information about what documents you have loaded (see a discussion of the history list in Chapter 7, "Mosaic Shortcuts and Tips"), and lets you move quickly between these documents using the **B**ack and **F**orward commands. The **B**ack command takes you to the previous document that you had opened. To go back, open the **N**avigate menu and choose **B**ack.

The next command is **F**orward. What you have to remember about **F**orward is that you can move forward only after moving back. (This concept is rather confusing, but makes more sense when you read about history lists in Chapter 7, "Mosaic Shortcuts tand Tips.") To move forward, open the **N**avigate menu and choose **F**orward.

▶ See "How to Get Where You Were," p. 126

The last command is **R**eload. This command tells Mosaic to read the document from its URL, and display it again. To reload the current document, open the **N**avigate menu and choose **R**eload.

When you are reading documents, you often move back and forth between one document and others which are linked to that document. To keep from having to load the main document from its URL every time you view it, Mosaic keeps copies of the last few documents you viewed on your local computer. This is called *caching*.

Caching is good because it keeps Mosaic from making unnecessary demands on Internet resources. It does take up resources on your own computer, though, so you can only cache a limited number of documents. In Windows Mosaic, you can edit your mosaic.ini file and set the number of documents you want to cache by setting the Number line in the Document Caching section of the file (the default is 2).

Follow these steps:

1. Open the **O**ptions menu and choose **P**references. Choose the Services tab in the Preferences dialog box (see fig. 6.4).

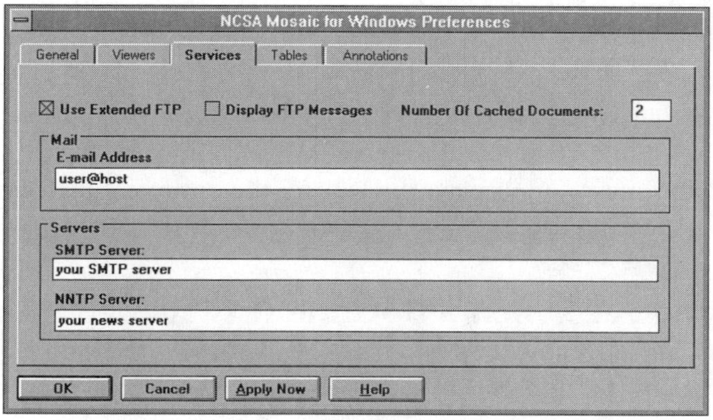

Fig. 6.4

The Services tab in the Preferences dialog box lets you give Mosaic information about using other Internet services, as well as allowing you to set the number of documents cached.

2. Enter the number of documents you want to cache in the Number of Cached Documents text box.

3. Choose OK to save your preferences to your mosaic.ini file and exit the Preferences dialog box.

Moving between Documents Using URLs

▶ See "Links and URLs Transport You from Place to Place," p. 27

If you don't want to go to any of the documents whose links are displayed in the current document, or if you did not load a home page, or if you do not currently have a document displayed, you can load a new document by specifying its URL to Mosaic. Refer to Chapter 1, "Introduction to the World Wide Web," for information about how to correctly format a URL. To enter a URL directly, follow these steps:

1. Open the File menu and choose Open URL.

2. The Open URL dialog box appears (see fig. 6.5). The contents of the URL box (set to the first item in your current hotlist) are highlighted. Click the URL box.

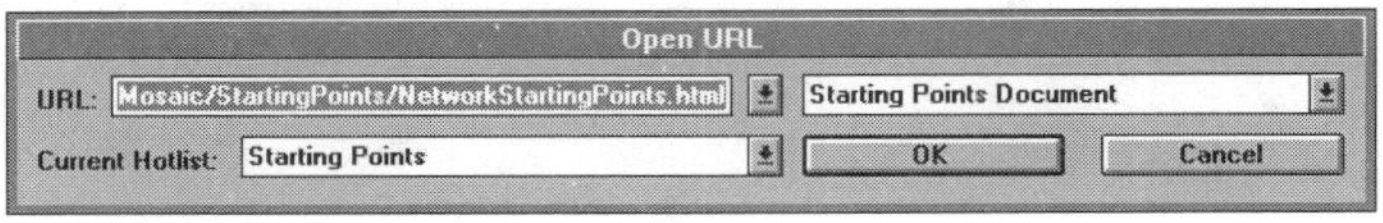

Fig. 6.5
The Open URL dialog box lets you directly enter the URL for the next document that you want to view.

3. If you want to enter a completely new URL, just begin typing the URL in the box, and the old contents are deleted. If you want to modify the URL that is shown, click the box again and your cursor is inserted in the text, where you can edit the current URL.

Tip
You can type the URL directly in the URL bar to load a new document. After typing the URL, press Enter or click the check mark (✓).

4. Choose OK to load the URL that you entered, or choose Cancel if you do not want to load that document. If you choose OK, Mosaic loads that document and displays the URL for the document in the URL bar (if you have it enabled).

What You See When a Document Is Loaded

When you load a document, Mosaic gives you a lot of information about what is happening. The globe in the upper-right corner of the window rotates, with its beacon flashing. A number of different messages appear in the status bar. These messages can include the following:

■ `Doing nameserver lookup on:<hostname>`

■ `Connecting to HTTP server` (If it is another type of server, such as Gopher or FTP, that protocol is indicated rather than HTTP.)

- Reading response

- Transferring:*<counter>*/*<total>* bytes

- Transferring inline image *<filename.gif>*:*<counter>*/*<total>* bytes

It's nice to be able to follow the status of the document load because you can see at the first (or sometimes the only) indication that there is a problem. For example, if you try to load a document that's a type Mosaic doesn't recognize, Mosaic makes the connection to the server, but simply aborts the load because it does not recognize the document type. If Mosaic aborts a load in this way, it shows an initial connecting message, but then doesn't show a transferring message in the status bar. Mosaic gives no other indication that it aborted the document load.

It's also nice to be able to watch the counter increase as the document is loaded. If you know the file size of the document you are loading, you have an idea of how far along you are and how much longer you can expect it to be before the document is loaded. Mosaic shows the total number of bytes that will be loaded for a document if it can get the information from the server where the document is kept.

Tip

Another indication of a transfer error is that the globe in the upper-right corner of the window stops spinning.

II

Browsing with Mosaic

Caution

If you attempt to click a hyperlink while images are still loading, Mosaic may lock up your machine.

Loading documents can take a few minutes, especially if the document contains large graphics and your computer has a relatively slow (less than 9600 bps) connection to the Internet. There are a couple of things you can do to speed up the loading of the document: tell Mosaic not to load the inline graphics from the document; or tell Mosaic to delay the loading of inline graphics (load and display the text for the page with placeholder icons for the graphics, and then load the graphics).

To stop the loading of inline images in Windows Mosaic, complete the following steps:

1. Open the **O**ptions menu and choose **P**references. Choose the General tab in the Preferences dialog box (see fig. 6.6).

Fig. 6.6

The Display Inline Images check box lets you speed up Mosaic by turning off image loading.

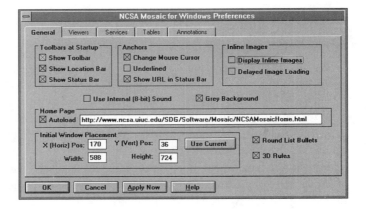

2. If you don't want Mosaic to load the inline graphics in a document, click the check box next to Display Inline Images. (The x in the box disappears when the option is turned off.)

3. If you want Mosaic to load the inline graphics after loading the text, first make sure that Display Inline Images is enabled (there should be an x in the check box next to it), and then click the check box next to Delayed Image Loading so that there is an x in it.

4. Choose OK to save your preferences to your mosaic.ini file and exit the Preferences dialog box.

If you turn off the loading of inline graphics, Mosaic displays placeholder icons in the document instead of the images. If you want to see one of the images that was not loaded, click the placeholder icon for that image with the right mouse button. You will get a pop-up menu that gives you a number of options, including Load **I**mage. Select Load **I**mage, and Mosaic loads and displays that image.

Troubleshooting

Why don't I get the Load Image option on the pop-up menu when I click a placeholder icon?

If you have Display Inline Images turned on and you get an error while transferring an image from the WWW server, you will have an error placeholder icon in your document where that image should have been (you have to look closely to differentiate it from an image icon). If you try to click this icon with the right mouse button, you do not get the Load **I**mage option in the pop-up menu. You will need to reload this page if you want to see that image.

The right mouse button gives you several other options for images. Save **Im**age lets you save the image under your cursor in a file on your local disk. When you select Save **I**mage, you get a submenu asking if you want to save it in Windows **B**MP Format or the **R**emote Site Format (the original format of the image). You can then select the name and location of the file in the Save As dialog box that appears, as you would when saving any WWW document (see "Saving and Printing Documents" later in this chapter).

You can also get information about the source of an image by selecting **Im**age Information from the pop-up menu, which brings up the Anchor Information window (see fig. 6.7). If the image associated with this window is represented with a placeholder icon, the window lets you load the image into the document.

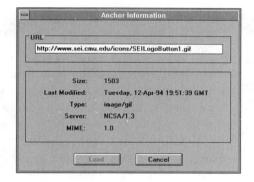

Looking for Information in a Document

If the WWW document you are reading is short, it's easy to scroll through the document (or use Page Up and Page Down) to find information of interest to you. If you have loaded a very long document, though, Mosaic does provide a quick way to look for information. Follow these steps:

1. Open the **E**dit menu and choose **F**ind to open the Find dialog box.

2. Click the Fi**n**d What text box and enter the word for which you want to search.

3. Click Match **C**ase if you want Mosaic to match exactly the capitalization of the word you entered.

4. Choose **F**ind Next to begin the search. If a match is found, Mosaic scrolls the window to the section where the match is. An alert box informs you if no match is found.

Caution

The Find feature does not work properly in the current version of Mosaic. It does not always find matching words when they do exist and does not always notify you when no matches are found. Sometimes, the Find feature causes your PC to lock up, requiring you to reboot your computer. This is a known bug.

Saving and Printing Documents

In general, the purpose of the World Wide Web is for you to be able to have one copy of a document that many people can view, although there are times when you might want to save a copy of a document to your local computer. Mosaic gives you several options for saving documents.

The first way to save a document is to open the **F**ile menu and choose **S**ave. This brings up the Save As dialog box which lets you browse through your directories and store the current document wherever you like.

Tip

To save a document instead of viewing it, place the cursor on the hyperlink, click the right mouse button, and select **L**oad Anchor to Disk.

There is another way to save files. Open the **O**ptions menu and choose **L**oad to Disk. A check mark appears next to the item, and the feature is enabled. The next time you click a hyperlink, rather than have Mosaic load the document for viewing, it brings up the Save As dialog box. You then specify a file on your local disk where the document can be saved. You can save any format document in this manner—HTML file, image file, sound file, or unformatted text.

Remember to turn off the option if you want to go back to viewing files with Mosaic (open the **O**ptions menu and choose **L**oad to Disk again to turn it off).

Tip

If you want to save the file you are currently viewing to disk, choose **L**oad to Disk from the **O**ptions menu, and then choose **R**eload from the **N**avigate menu. This brings up the Save As dialog box.

Note

If you want to load a single file to disk, in Windows Mosaic you can Shift-click the hyperlink rather than choosing **L**oad to Disk from the **O**ptions menu. This loads only that one file to disk, and you won't have to worry about forgetting to turn off Load to Disk.

You can also get information about the source of a hyperlink by selecting **A**nchor Information from the pop-up menu, which brings up the Anchor Information window (see fig. 6.8). Choose Load to view the document associated with this hyperlink.

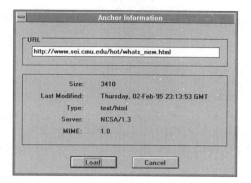

Fig. 6.8
The Anchor Information window gives you the URL for the hyperlink under your cursor, along with the size and type of the document file, the last time the file was modified, and the type of server the file lives on.

When you save an HTML document to your local disk, remember that the document probably contains hyperlinks in it. These links can be *relative* or *absolute*. An absolute reference contains the complete address of the document that is being referenced, including the host name, directory path, and file name. A relative reference assumes that the previous machine and directory path are being used, and just the file name (or possibly a subdirectory and file name) is specified.

If the document references other documents with relative addresses, you cannot view those documents unless you copy them to your local disk and set them up with the same directory structure they had at the original site. You might want to set up a document and its linked documents on your local disk if you want to be able to view the document without connecting to the Internet. One problem is that if the original document changes, your local copy will be outdated, and you may not be aware that this has happened.

Absolute references always work unless your Internet connection fails or the referenced documents are moved.

In addition to being able to save documents, you can print documents directly from Mosaic. Open the **F**ile menu and choose **P**rint to send a copy of the current document to your printer. You can select your printer in the same manner you do for any other Windows application. If you select Print Preview from the **F**ile menu, you get an on-screen preview of what the file will look like when it is printed.

▶ See "Adding Hyperlinks to Other Web Documents," p. 334

II

Browsing with Mosaic

Customizing Your Mosaic Window

This chapter has covered some of the features of Mosaic that let you move between documents. It is possible to customize a number of these features; you can set up Mosaic to behave in a way that is most convenient for you. This section discusses how to set up Mosaic to your preferences.

Customizing the Hyperlink Indicators

You can change the default appearance and color of the hyperlinks in the documents Mosaic loads. The 2.0a9 version of Mosaic has eliminated the need to edit your mosaic.ini file to customize many of Mosaic's features. To customize Mosaic's link attributes, follow these steps:

1. Open the **O**ptions menu and choose **P**references. The Preferences dialog box, shown in figure 6.9, appears. Select the General tab for a page that allows you to customize the Mosaic window.

Fig. 6.9
Customize the link appearance from the Preferences dialog box.

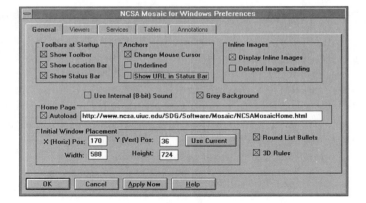

2. To have anchors underlined in a document, select the Underlined check box in the Anchors area of the dialog box (an x indicates the option is selected).

3. If you don't want your cursor to change shape over hyperlinks, deselect the Change Mouse Cursor check box in the Anchors area of the dialog box.

4. If you don't want to see the URL of a link in the status bar when you place the cursor over the link, deselect the Show URL in Status Bar check box.

5. When you have the options set to your satisfaction, choose OK. The information is written to your mosaic.ini file. Mosaic puts these options into effect immediately.

> **Note**
>
> If you want to apply the changes you've made in the Preferences dialog without exiting the dialog box, choose **A**pply Now.

If you want to edit your mosaic.ini file instead of using the Preferences dialog box to customize your links, you can edit the following variables in the [Main] section of the file:

```
[Main]
Anchor Underline=no
Anchor Cursor=yes
Show URLs=yes
```

Setting Anchor Underline to yes causes the anchors to be underlined. Setting Anchor Cursor to no causes Mosaic to not change the cursor to a pointing hand over anchors. Setting Show URLs to no causes Mosaic to not display the URL of the anchor under the cursor in the status bar.

To configure the color Mosaic uses to indicate links, you must edit your mosaic.ini file and set the Anchor Color variable as you wish:

```
[Settings]
Anchor Color=0,0,255
```

The Anchor Color variable takes values from 0 to 255 for red, green, and blue components to create the hyperlink identifying color. You need to play around with the values of each color component to find something that you like.

Customizing the Displayed Fonts in Windows

You can customize the fonts that Mosaic uses when displaying documents. HTML documents use standard paragraph tags to describe each paragraph in the document. Mosaic lets you specify the font family, size, and style for each of the standard HTML paragraph tags.

1. Open the **O**ptions menu, and select **C**hoose Font. A submenu appears that lists the different HTML paragraph tags (see fig. 6.10).

Fig. 6.10
You can customize the fonts for any of Mosaic's paragraph formats.

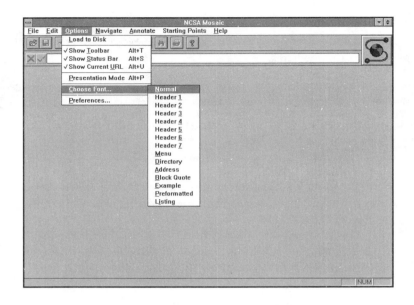

▶ See "HTML Basics: Title, Heading, and Text," p. 327

2. From this submenu, select the paragraph tag of the font you want to change. Even if you aren't familiar with HTML, you can guess what the different paragraph types are. For example, Normal is the regular text font, Header 1 is usually the large heading at the top of a document, and so on.

3. When you select a paragraph tag, the Font dialog box appears, as shown in figure 6.11.

Fig. 6.11
The Font dialog box lets you define the font for the paragraph type you selected.

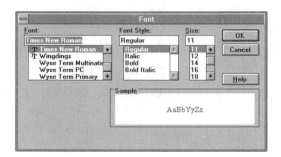

4. Scroll down through the **F**ont list until you find the font you want and select it. You also can set the Font St**y**le (bold, italic, and so on) and the **S**ize.

5. Choose OK to make the selections take effect, or Cancel if you decide not to change the fonts.

The changes that you make take effect immediately and are used by Mosaic in future sessions.

Customizing Graphical Elements

There are a few different graphical elements that Mosaic gives you the option of simplifying to make your display time faster. Open the **O**ptions menu and choose **P**references to bring up the Preferences dialog box. Set the following options on the General page to your satisfaction, and choose OK to make them take effect:

- To set Mosaic's document viewing area to white instead of grey, deselect the Grey Background check box. (Note that some WWW documents are written to expect a grey background for Mosaic.)

- By default, Mosaic uses round graphical elements for bullets. To change the bullet indicator to a hyphen, deselect the Round List Bullets check box.

- By default, Mosaic draws heavier lines for certain types of rules in WWW documents. If you want only a thin line drawn for all rules, deselect the 3D Rules check box. (The 3-D rules feature seems to be broken in the 2.0a9 version of Mosaic. All rules are thin.)

Customizing the Display of Tables

The 2.0a9 version of Mosaic has added support for graphical display of tables. Tables can be viewed as simple flat tables with thin black rules between the cells, or you can view tables as three-dimensional. Three-dimensional tables have colored, shaded rules between the cells of the table. You can customize the color and the dimension of the viewed tables by following these steps:

1. Open the **O**ptions menu and choose **P**references.

2. Click the Tables tab (see fig. 6.12).

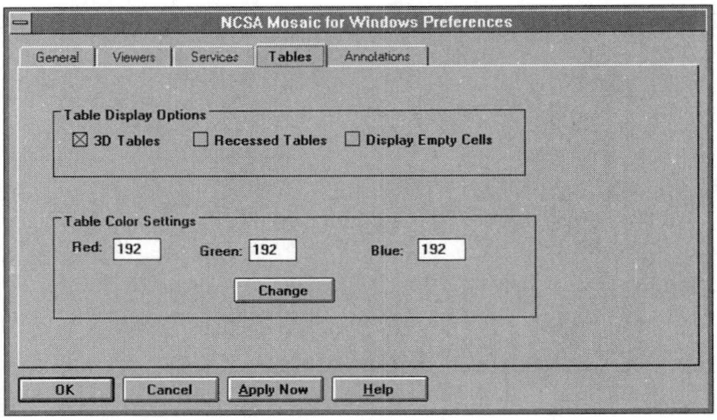

Fig. 6.12
Customize the appearance of tables in Mosaic from the Preferences dialog box Tables tab.

Tip
Load the table at **http://www.ncsa.uiuc.edu/SDG/Software/Mosaic/Tables/Elements.html** and turn Recessed Tables on and off to see what it does.

3. If you want tables to appear three-dimensional, select the 3D Tables check box.

4. If you want to hide borders where no cells exist in irregular tables, select the Recessed Tables check box. (This affects only 3-D tables.)

5. If you want empty cells in a table to be filled with the rule color, deselect the Display Empty Cells check box. If this check box is selected (has an X in it), empty cells are outlined in color with the cell interior set to the normal Mosaic background color. (This feature only works with 3-D tables.)

6. When you have all of the parameters on the Tables page set to your liking, choose **A**pply Now to make them take effect (you can choose Cancel to keep the settings the way they were), and then choose OK to exit the Preferences dialog box. You should be able to choose OK to make your settings take effect when you exit (without choosing Apply Now), but this seems to be broken in the 2.0a9 version of Mosaic.

To set the color of the table rules, either fill in the red, green, and blue components of the color in the boxes under Table Color and choose OK, or click the Change button, which brings up the Color dialog box (see fig. 6.13).

1. You can set the color of the rules by selecting one of the color squares in the **B**asic Colors section of the dialog box. The selected color and its offset color are shown in the Color|**So**lid box under the color palette.

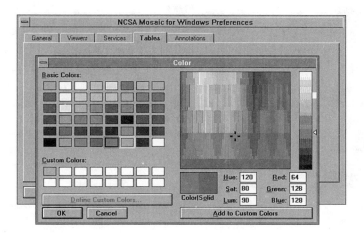

Fig. 6.13
Table rule colors
can be set from the
Color dialog box.

2. You can also set the color of the rules by clicking anywhere in the palette. This gives you a two-tone value in the Color|Solid box. There doesn't seem to be any way of setting the two colors in the box independently.

3. Click the vertical color bar to the right of the palette to set the intensity of the colors. Click towards the top for less intense colors; click towards the bottom for more intense colors. (The solid part of the two-tone is black when the arrow is close to the bottom.) An arrow appears to the right of the bar to indicate the current setting.

Tip
Try clicking the palette and dragging the mouse straight up and down to get variations on a single color.

> ### Note
>
> You can also set the colors by directly entering values in the **H**ue, **S**at, **L**um, **R**ed, **G**reen, and Bl**u**e boxes. (The corresponding two-tone value is shown in the Color|S**o**lid box as you do this.) However, this is a difficult way to find a color combination you like unless you have some idea what the different number combinations will produce.

4. When you've set the colors to your liking, click OK. You return to the Tables tab of the Preferences dialog box. Click **A**pply Now on this page to make the table settings take effect immediately.

Browsing with Mosaic

Caution

If you do not choose **A**pply Now on the Tables tab of the Preferences dialog box, your changes will not take effect, even if you click OK to exit the Preferences dialog box. This is a bug.

---

5. Click OK to exit the Preferences dialog box.

Troubleshooting

Why does my custom color palette get wiped out when I leave the Preferences dialog box?

The **C**ustom Colors feature of the Color dialog box does not appear to be working in the 2.0a9 release of Mosaic. You can set one custom color for the current color of your table rules. If you build a palette, it gets wiped out when you leave the Preferences dialog box.

The colors of the rules in my table don't look like the ones I set in the Color dialog box.

Because of the relative thinness of the rules, some colors do not show up well. For example, very light colors usually don't show up well; but very dark colors, like maroon and olive, don't show up well either. Bright colors are your best bet.

Customizing the Displayed Window Areas

Many of the different window areas in Mosaic are optional (except the document viewing area—Mosaic wouldn't be very useful without that!). The title bar and menu bar cannot be removed, but the toolbar, URL bar, and status bar all can be turned off. Turning off these window areas gives you a bigger viewing area but removes some timesaving and informational features. The following list describes how to turn these features off (or back on):

■ To turn off the toolbar, open the **O**ptions menu and select Show **T**oolbar. The check mark next to the menu item disappears, and the toolbar is removed from the window.

■ To turn off the URL bar, open the **O**ptions menu and select Show Current **U**RL. The check mark next to the menu item disappears, and the URL bar is removed from the window.

■ To turn off the status bar, open the **O**ptions menu and select Show **S**tatus Bar. The check mark next to the menu item disappears, and the status bar is removed from the window.

You can set the startup values of these options from the Preferences dialog box. Whenever you start Mosaic, it then uses the values in the Preferences dialog box to decide what areas of the window to display. Open the **O**ptions menu, choose **P**references, and select the General tab. In the Toolbars at Startup box on the General tab, deselect the check boxes of the window areas that you want to get rid of (so that the x is no longer present): Show Toolbar, Show Location Bar, Show Status Bar. These options only take effect when you start Mosaic, and you can change them from the Options menu anytime during your session. But they are reset to the values in the Preferences dialog box each time you start Mosaic.

Setting the Default Window Size and Position

The startup size and position of the main Mosaic window can be set from the Windows Preferences dialog box. To do so, follow these steps:

1. Open the **O**ptions menu and choose **P**references. Choose the General tab. The Initial Window Placement area of the General tab allows you to set the startup size and position of the main Mosaic window.

2. To set the size of the window, click in the Width and Height text boxes and enter the desired values in pixels.

3. To set the position of the window, select the X (Horiz) Pos: and Y (Vert) Pos: text boxes and enter the desired placement of the upper-left corner of the window in pixels.

4. To set the size and position of the Mosaic window quickly, use the resize borders on the window to set it to a size you like, and drag the window to a position you like. Then select Use Current to fill in the size and position boxes with the current values.

5. When you set the options to your satisfaction, choose OK. The information is written to your mosaic.ini file. Mosaic uses these new settings the next time your start Mosaic.

Viewing Multimedia Files

One of Mosaic's best features is that it enables you to view documents of many different types. If you remember from the introductory chapters, Mosaic is a *multimedia application,* which means that you can view files containing a number of different types of media—pictures, sound, and animation.

◀ See "Multi-media—Using Viewers," p. 81

II

Browsing with Mosaic

Mosaic can display text and inline graphics directly, but to display other types of files, you must have viewers for these files installed on your machine.

After you have your viewers installed and Mosaic knows where to find them and what type of files they display, Mosaic automatically starts the correct viewer when you click the hyperlink for a file of a recognized type. Mosaic can recognize any of a number of standard image, sound, and animation formats. Some of the more common ones are shown in table 6.1.

Table 6.1	Multimedia File Types Recognized by Mosaic
Media	**File Type**
Audio	WAV, MIDI
Image	JPEG, GIF, TIFF
Video	MPEG, AVI, MOV
Formatted text	PS, RTF, DOC

Once you have your viewers set up, you only need to select the hyperlink for the file, and Mosaic launches the viewer application with the file loaded. You now can use any of the features of the viewer application to examine, modify, or save the file you loaded. Figure 6.14 shows an example of a GIF file loaded in the LView image viewer.

Fig. 6.14
When Mosaic loads a file type that it recognizes, the viewer you specify for that file type displays the image, sound, animation, and so on.

Notice that because the image is loaded in an external application, you can use Mosaic at the same time you view the image.

Working with Local Files

When you think of using Mosaic, you think of retrieving documents from WWW servers on the Internet to view. Mosaic can read documents from your local file system as well as from halfway around the world. If you share documents among members of your organization, many of the documents you view may be on a local file server, or possibly on your local computer.

Mosaic provides an option to make it easy to load a local file. If you want to load a local file, open the **F**ile menu and click Open **L**ocal File. This brings up the Open dialog box shown in figure 6.15; this dialog box lets you browse through all your local disks to find a file.

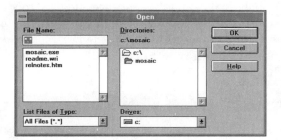

Fig. 6.15
The Open dialog box lets you enter a local file name or browse your local file system to find the next document that you want to view.

You also can load a local file in the same manner that you load any URL. Open the **F**ile menu and choose **O**pen URL. To specify a local file in the URL box, precede the directory path of the file with **file:///c|** (you can substitute any of your local disks for c). The three slashes tell Mosaic that you are looking for a local file, and the bar is used instead of a colon, because the colon has a specific purpose in a URL. Use slashes in the directory path you enter, even if you are describing a directory on a PC where the backslash is usually used. Mosaic properly translates the slashes when it retrieves the file.

Local URLs can be used anywhere URLs are used—as items in hotlists, links in documents, and so on.

◄ See "Links and URLs Transport You from Place to Place," p. 27

Problems that Occur while Navigating the WWW

The World Wide Web is really a concept still under development, and Mosaic is definitely an application still under development. For an alpha release, it works pretty well. But, with a complex application like Mosaic and a conceptually young Internet service like the WWW, there are bound to be occasional problems.

Some problems that occur are related to limited resources on any particular Internet host (for example, the number of people who can connect to the host at one time may be limited). Traffic over the Internet is steadily growing and communications may be slow. Other problems may be actual bugs in Mosaic. Throughout the Mosaic chapters, problems related to a certain topic are discussed when that topic is discussed. This section deals with problems that are common to many different Mosaic functions and not mentioned elsewhere.

Mosaic Bugs

Mosaic admittedly has its flaws. After all, it is an alpha release, not yet to the point of a beta (which is usually pretty close to the final release). The designers realize this is somewhat of an inconvenience and have tried to provide some help by publishing a list of known bugs. To see a list of bugs for Windows Mosaic, open the **H**elp menu and click **B**ug List. Mosaic loads a document that describes all known Windows Mosaic bugs and tells you how to get in touch with the developers if you find a bug that they don't know about.

> **Note**
>
> The developers of Mosaic did a great thing by putting the help files for Mosaic online. When you open the **H**elp menu and choose **O**nline documentation or **B**ug List, you are loading a WWW page with this information from the NCSA Web site. This way, the developers can constantly update the list so you always have access to the most current information. The bad news is, if you can't get Mosaic to work or if the NCSA Web server is overloaded and you can't get connected, these online files aren't much help!

Most Mosaic bugs are discussed in the sections of this book that are related to the functions that cause the bugs. Currently in the Windows version, the only Mosaic bug that is common enough to mention is Help buttons that fail in some windows. Sometimes a window that Mosaic brings up has a Help button that brings up a blank Windows Help window. One such window is the Save As window that you see when you are loading files to disk. Also, sometimes you see the message For Help, Press F1 in the status bar while you are using Mosaic. Pressing F1 has the same effect of bringing up a blank Windows Help window.

User Errors

Sometimes you can inadvertently ask Mosaic to do something it can't do. You can make a mistake when typing in the URL, or try to fetch the right document from the wrong machine. Here are a few of the more common user errors and Mosaic's reaction to them.

■ *Enter an invalid protocol.* Windows Mosaic gives you an `Access not available` error alert like the one shown in figure 6.16. Choose OK to make the alert disappear, and then try to load a valid URL.

Fig. 6.16
When Mosaic encounters an error, it usually brings up an alert box like this one to let you know what happened.

■ *Try to load a document that doesn't exist.* You get a `File/directory does not exist` error alert. Choose OK to make the alert disappear, and then try to load a valid URL.

■ *Try to load from a site that doesn't exist.* You get a `Failed DNS Lookup` error alert. Choose OK to make the alert disappear, and then try to load a valid URL.

Network Errors

A number of network-related errors can be caused by many problems—a machine down, too much traffic on the network, too many people using a host's resources, or any number of other problems. These types of problems are associated with having a large number of different types of machines and services on a large network.

The following list of error alerts is by no means all-inclusive, but it does show some of the most common errors. If you load the Bug List document from the Windows Mosaic Help menu and scroll down to the bottom, you see the link `Common Error Messages` in a section entitled Bug Like Features. This link loads a document (**http://www.ncsa.uiuc.edu/SDG/Software/ WinMosaic/errors.html**) that lists most of the errors that you can see—it doesn't tell you what caused them or how to avoid them.

■ `SOCKET:Connection has been refused`. This error usually occurs when the maximum number of people allowed to use the host's resources are currently online. Try again later.

■ `SOCKET:Connection timed out`. This message comes up if Mosaic tries to communicate with a host and receives no answer in a specific time period. The host is too busy to answer, or the machine is hung up.

■ `SOCKET:Host is down`. The host that you tried to reach is down. Try to reach another host that provides the same service, or try this one again later.

■ `Failed DNS Lookup`. The host that you tried to reach does not exist. This may or may not be a real error. If you typed the name of the host incorrectly, it is an error. This error also seems to occur if Mosaic tries to look up the host and doesn't get a response from the name server in a specific period of time.

■ `Transfer canceled`. This error is uncommon, but seems to occur when there are communication problems. For example, if you connect to your Internet provider using the SLIP protocol, and the phone line that you use to dial in becomes noisy for some reason, it causes a transfer to abort.

From Here...

Mosaic was one of the first graphical interfaces to the WWW and is still one of the most popular because it's free. With Mosaic, you can view nicely formatted WWW documents and associated files of other media types (sound, animations, and so on) if you have the appropriate players. Mosaic allows you to quickly load documents that are linked to the current document, and to make quick-access lists of the documents you use most frequently. These features make accessing the Internet friendlier than it has ever been.

To learn more about using Mosaic and to find interesting WWW documents, refer to these chapters:

■ Chapter 4, "Getting Mosaic Running in Windows," shows you how to get Mosaic and set it up on your PC.

■ Chapter 5, "Multimedia—Using Viewers," tells you how to get viewers for different types of multimedia files set up to work with Mosaic.

■ Chapter 7, "Mosaic Shortcuts and Tips," describes how you can become an expert WWW navigator.

■ Chapter 19, "Web Searching," discusses how to use automated software to find some of the most interesting collections of WWW documents.

Mosaic Shortcuts and Tips

by Mary Ann Pike

The WWW lets you move easily between documents. Although this is convenient, it also can be a curse. While moving back and forth, you easily can get lost...and URLs can be long, complicated, and difficult to remember.

Mosaic has many features that allow you to keep track of where you were and allow you to get to places quickly. This chapter assumes you have read Chapter 6, "Navigating with Mosaic."

In this chapter, you learn to do the following:

- Navigate the WWW efficiently

- Keep track of sites that interest you

- Quickly access the sites you use the most

- Annotate documents to remind you why they interest you

Effective Browsing Techniques

Navigating between WWW documents can be confusing. Documents often connect back to documents you've already read. You don't know you're going to a document you've already seen because different words or pictures are used for the hyperlink than the ones you used originally.

Sometimes you can't tell from the hyperlink whether the document is of interest to you, and loading documents uses valuable time. Often, you waste time loading documents that you dismiss immediately. This section helps you learn to reduce unnecessary document loading and circular navigating.

How to Keep Track of Where You've Been

Keeping track of where you are and where you were is one of the biggest challenges of using Mosaic. For example, say you're reading a document that deals with agriculture and you click a hyperlink to take you to Hay Field Seeding Suggestions. The document turns out to be one you loaded earlier, when you found a hyperlink for Pasture Management Techniques. How can you avoid this frustrating repetition?

One suggestion is to have a home page that provides links to your most-visited WWW pages. This home page is useful, for example, if you work on a group project and frequently use documents with known locations. You can create your own home page, or someone can create a project home page for your group. In this scenario, you probably are already familiar with the servers, if not the exact documents.

But what if you're navigating in uncharted waters on the WWW? Although it sounds difficult, you probably can learn to recognize the URLs of the sites that keep information of interest to you. If the URL bar is displayed, the URL for the current document is shown there. If you have the status bar displayed, open the **O**ptions menu and choose **P**references. On the General tab sheet, make sure the Show URL in Status Bar check box in the Anchors box is selected, and choose OK. The status bar shows the URL of a hyperlink when you move the cursor over it (see fig. 7.1). As you move between documents, you begin to remember some of the URLs you see frequently; when you put your cursor over a hyperlink, you recognize documents you know.

How to Get Where You Were

Trying to navigate back to a document you viewed in the current Mosaic session also can be challenging. In general, to go to the document you viewed prior to the current document, open the **N**avigate menu and choose **B**ack (or the left arrow in the toolbar). Choosing **F**orward (or the right arrow) takes you to the last document you viewed after this document. This sounds rather confusing, but is understandable if you look at how Mosaic determines these links.

The **N**avigate menu has an item called **H**istory that brings up a window, similar to the one shown in figure 7.2. Notice there is a list of URLs in this window and the URL for the current document is highlighted.

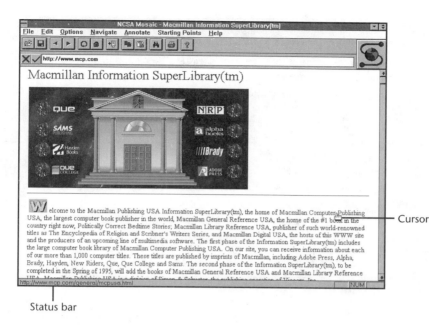

Fig. 7.1
The status bar displays the URLs of hyperlinks when the cursor is on top of them.

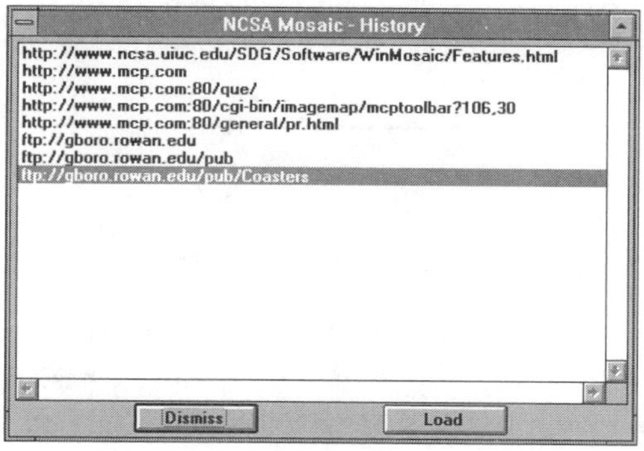

Status bar

Fig. 7.2
The NCSA Mosaic History window shows a linear list of URLs you visit.

Tip
If the History window is open when you use the **F**orward and **B**ack commands, you can see the highlighted item move in the list of URLs.

The history list shows you the URLs of the document chain that led you to this point and any documents that you visited after the current document. If you use the **B**ack navigation command, you move up in the list. If you use the **F**orward navigation command, you move down the list. Click any URL in the list and choose Load to jump to that document (and that point in the list).

> **Caution**
>
> If you move up to one of the higher level links and then jump to a new URL from that document, it wipes out all the URLs past the current document. So, while you can use the **B**ack and **F**orward navigation commands to move between documents you already visited, if you jump to a new document while in the middle of the list, you erase the links at the end of the list.

To move quickly between documents that you load, use the history list. If you want to add a new document to the list of ones you're viewing, make sure that you're at the end of the list before you jump to that document. You don't have to use hyperlinks to add the document you load to the history list. Load the document, by opening the **F**ile menu and choosing **O**pen URL or by using the URL toolbar button, and it is added to the list.

> **Troubleshooting**
>
> *I can't see the right-most part of the URLs in the History window.*
>
> The horizontal scrolling feature of the History window is not working in the 2.0.a8 release of Mosaic. The only thing you can do is resize the History window to be wider so that you can see the end of long URLs.

Create Lists of Your Favorite URLs

If you don't want to learn how to use HTML commands to create a home page with all your favorite WWW documents, Mosaic has an alternative. To quickly access your favorite URLs, Mosaic lets you create up to 20 personal menus and submenus. In addition, you can have a QUICKLIST that lets you access your favorite documents.

Creating Your Own Menus

You can create up to 20 menus in Mosaic. These 20 menus can either be top-level menus that appear in your menu bar, or submenus that you access from the top-level menu. By default, Mosaic has one preconfigured top-level menu and several submenus. The Starting Points menu lets you access a number of documents on the WWW that help you learn about the World Wide Web and the Internet, and gives you quick access to Internet services and information repositories. You may want to create your own menus, though, to gain access to documents and services that you use most. For example, you might want to have a menu for each project you work on, with each menu giving you access to the documents and services you need for that project.

The Personal Menus dialog box allows you to add, delete, and edit Mosaic menus. To open the Personal Menus dialog box, open the **N**avigate menu and choose **M**enu Editor (see fig. 7.3).

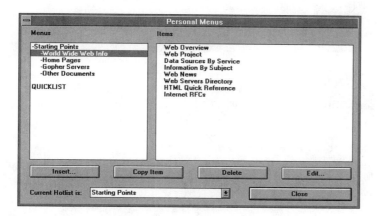

Fig. 7.3
The Mosaic Personal Menus dialog box shows current menus and items on those menus, and lets you create, delete, and edit those menus.

The existing user-configurable menus are shown in the Menus section of the dialog box. If you click a menu in this list, the items from that menu are displayed in the Items section. After you finish modifying your personal menus, click Close to close the dialog box.

Creating a New Menu

Personal menus let you group WWW documents that you use frequently. For example, you may want to have a menu for each project on which you work. The top-level menus you add are displayed in the menu bar, between the Starting Points menu and the Help menu (see fig. 7.4 for an example of a user-configured menu). You can click the menu and select items from it, just as you can with the other menus built into Mosaic. Mosaic has a limit of 20 total user-configurable menus and submenus.

To create a new menu, follow these steps:

1. Open the **N**avigate menu and choose **M**enu Editor to open the Personal Menus dialog box.

2. Click the blank line above the word QUICKLIST in the Menus section of the dialog box. The Add Item dialog box appears (see fig. 7.5).

Fig. 7.4
The menus
Internet Resources
and Cool Sites
have been added
to the menu bar.

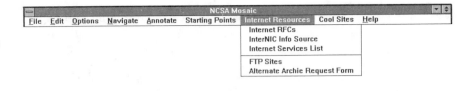

Fig. 7.5
Enter the title of
the menu you're
adding in the Add
Item dialog box.

3. Click the box next to Title and enter the name of the menu you want to add. Notice that the Menu radio button is selected automatically; you can't deselect it or select another radio button.

4. Click OK. The new menu appears highlighted in the Menus section of the Personal Menus dialog box. You are now ready to add items to the menu.

Tip
If you have a
SuperVGA moni-
tor, use Windows
setup to choose a
driver for a higher
screen resolution
(such as 800 ×
600) to get more
menu items on-
screen.

> **Note**
>
> Choose descriptive, short names for your menus. Mosaic displays these names in the menu bar; there isn't much room! If the menu list becomes longer than one line, Mosaic expands the size of the menu bar as many lines as it needs to display all of the menu names.

Adding Items to a Menu

After you create a new menu, you can add the items you want to appear in the menu—you can also add items to any existing menu. Mosaic currently has a limit of 40 items per menu.

To add items to a menu, follow these steps:

1. To open the Personal Menus dialog box, open the **N**avigate menu and choose **M**enu Editor.

2. In the Menus section of the dialog box, click the name of the menu to which you want to add items.

3. If there are existing items in that menu, you can place the new item anywhere in the list. If you click the name of an item in the Items section, the new item is added before the selected one. If you don't select one of the current items, the new item is added to the end of the list.

4. After you have selected the menu and item position, choose Insert. The Add Item dialog box appears (see fig. 7.6).

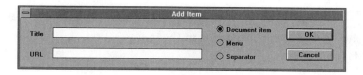

Fig. 7.6

In the Add Item dialog box, enter the name of the menu item you are adding and the URL associated with it, if there is one. You also can identify the type of the item.

You now can add items to the menu. The items can be of three types: a Document (with its associated URL), a Menu (submenu), or a Separator (to let you visually group items in a menu). The following three sections explain how to add the three different types of items at the current menu position.

Adding a Document. You probably add documents most often to your menus. In this case, *document* indicates any valid Web URL; you can actually access more than just documents. Your URL can use any Internet protocol that Mosaic recognizes, including Gopher, FTP, and Telnet.

Tip

A quick way to add a document to the end of the menu you selected as your current hotlist is to open the **N**avigate menu and choose **A**dd Current To Hotlist.

To add a document item to a menu, follow these steps:

1. Select the Document Item radio button in the Add Item dialog box. The fields pertaining to this item type become active (see fig. 7.7).

Fig. 7.7

When you select the Document Item radio button, the URL and Title fields become active.

2. Click the box next to Title and enter the name you want to appear in the menu. By default, the title and URL of the current document appear in the fields.

II

Browsing with Mosaic

3. Click the box next to URL and enter the complete URL used to access this document, if it isn't already in the field.

Caution

If you enter an incomplete URL (for example, if you leave off the http:// at the beginning) and then try to access the menu item, it may cause your PC to lock up.

---

4. Choose OK. The item appears in the Items section of the Personal Menus window.

Note

If you want to have a menu item that is the same or similar to an existing menu item, you can copy that menu item to the Add Items buffer. Select the menu that contains the desired item in the Personal Menus dialog box. Select the desired item in the Items section, and then choose Copy Item. The title and URL of the selected item appear in the Add Item dialog box the next time it is opened.

Adding a Submenu. Another way to group related items in your menus is to create a submenu that contains the related items. Remember, Mosaic has a limit of 20 total user-configurable menus and submenus.

To create a submenu, follow these steps:

1. In the Add Item dialog box, select the Menu radio button. The field that pertains to this item type becomes active, as shown in figure 7.8.

Fig. 7.8
When you select the Menu radio button, only the Title field is active.

2. Click the box next to Title and enter the name you want to appear in the menu.

3. Choose OK. The item appears in the Items section of the Personal Menu dialog box. Notice that it has a right angle bracket next to it to indicate that it's a menu.

Adding a Separator. If you don't want to add any submenus, but you still want to group some of your menu entries, you can visually group items in a menu by putting a thin line called a *separator* between groups of related items.

To add a separator, follow these steps:

1. In the Add Item dialog box, select the Separator radio button. There are no active entry fields in the Add Item dialog box (see fig. 7.9).

Fig. 7.9
When you click the Separator radio button, all entry fields become inactive; you don't need to enter any information for this type of item.

2. Choose OK. A line appears in the Items section of the Personal Menu dialog box.

Editing a Menu Item

After you create a menu, you may want to change the names or URLs of some of the items in the menu. You can do this using the Edit button in the Personal Menus dialog box.

To edit menu items, follow these steps:

1. Open the **N**avigate menu and choose **M**enu Editor. The Personal Menus dialog box appears.

2. Click the name of the menu that has the item you want to change.

3. Select the item in the Items list you want to change and choose Edit. The Edit Item dialog box appears (see fig. 7.10).

Tip
Double-clicking either a menu or an item in the Personal Menus dialog box brings up the Edit Item dialog box for that item.

Fig. 7.10
The Edit Item dialog box lets you change the title or URL of an existing menu item.

4. Edit the title and/or URL for that item, and then choose OK.

Your menu item is now changed as you specified. You also can edit any of the menus in the Menu section to change its title (the URL field is automatically omitted when you edit a menu).

Deleting a Menu Item

Mosaic also lets you delete a menu item or an entire menu. To delete menus or menu items, follow these steps:

1. Open the **N**avigate menu and choose **M**enu Editor. The Personal Menus dialog box appears.

2. Click the name of the menu or menu item that you want to delete, and choose Delete. You see a Menu Editor alert box asking you to confirm the deletion (see fig. 7.11).

Fig. 7.11
The Menu Editor alert box makes sure you want to delete the item or menu.

3. Choose OK to delete the menu or item.

If you are deleting an item, it is removed. If you are deleting a menu, you're asked if you want to recursively delete the menu—meaning it deletes everything under the menu. Choose OK; it is confusing to delete a menu, but not items on that menu.

Caution

Menu deleting does not work properly. Although Mosaic asks if you want to recursively delete a menu, it does not do this. Although it looks like the menu is deleted from the window, it deletes only the menu title from the mosaic.ini file. The items that were under that menu are left in your mosaic.ini file and will probably appear the next time you add a menu. If you press Cancel when it asks about the recursive deletion, it does the same thing—deleting the menu title and leaving the items under the menu in the mosaic.ini file.

Creating Your Own QUICKLIST

The QUICKLIST is a permanent hotlist that you can't delete or change the title of. The QUICKLIST doesn't show up as a menu in the menu bar; the only way to access it is to make it the current hotlist and select an item from it in the Open URL dialog box (this procedure is explained in more detail in the section, "Setting and Using the Current Hotlist," later in this chapter).

You can insert, edit, and delete items in the QUICKLIST the same way you do for any of the other user-configurable menus by using the Personal Menus dialog box. Unlike the other user-configurable menus, which have a limit of 40 items, there's no limit to the number of items in the QUICKLIST.

Quick Access to Your Favorite URLs

Now that you have all these hotlists set up, how do you use them? You can select items directly from the user-configurable menus, or you can select them in the Open URL dialog box. This saves you the trouble of having to remember and type in long URLs.

Accessing Items in a Hotlist

The user-configurable menus and QUICKLIST comprise the hotlists. You can access items from the user-configurable menus either directly or from the Open URL dialog box. The QUICKLIST items can only be accessed from the Open URL dialog box.

Setting and Using the Current Hotlist

One way to use a hotlist is to make it the current hotlist in the Open URL dialog box. There are two ways to do this. The first way is as follows:

1. Open the **F**ile menu and choose **O**pen URL (or click the Open URL button on the toolbar). The Open URL dialog box appears. The Current Hotlist field shows the current hotlist (see fig. 7.12).

2. Click the Current Hotlist field to display a drop-down list of available hotlists (see fig. 7.13).

Tip

To add the current document to the current hotlist, open the **N**avigate menu and choose **A**dd Current to Hotlist. The document is added to the end of the current hotlist.

Fig. 7.12

You can change the current hotlist in the Open URL dialog box.

II

Browsing with Mosaic

Fig. 7.13

You can select any of the user-configurable menus to be the current hotlist.

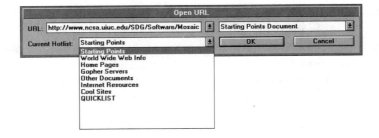

3. Click the hotlist you want to be designated the current hotlist.

4. Now click Cancel to keep the hotlist you selected, or select a URL to open from this dialog box.

The other way to set the current hotlist is from the Personal Menus dialog box. To do this, follow these steps:

1. Open the **N**avigate menu and choose **M**enu Editor. The Personal Menus dialog box appears (see fig. 7.14).

Fig. 7.14

You can set the current hotlist from the Personal Menus dialog box.

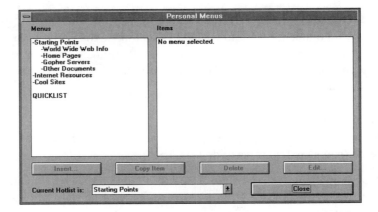

2. To display a drop-down list of available hotlists, click in the Current Hotlist field (see fig. 7.15).

3. Select the hotlist you want to designate as the current hotlist.

4. Choose Close to dismiss this dialog box.

Now that you have the current hotlist set, how do you use it? The Open URL dialog box gives you quick access to the items in the current hotlist. The URL field and the field to its right contain information from the current hotlist. If you click the URL field, you can select any of the URLs from the items in the current hotlist. If you click the field to its right, you can select any of the items in the current hotlist by title. To load the item you select, choose OK.

Remember, the only way to access an item in the QUICKLIST is to make it the current hotlist and load the items it contains from the Open URL dialog box.

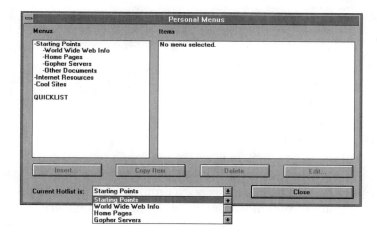

Fig. 7.15
You can scroll through the list of the user-configurable menus and select any one of them to be the current hotlist.

Loading a Document from a Menu

All documents in your hotlists (except for those in the QUICKLIST) are accessible from the menus you create. These menus appear between the Annotate and Help menu items in the menu bar. To access a document in one of these menus, simply follow these steps:

1. Click the menu.

2. Choose an item from the menu. If the item you choose is also a menu, a submenu pops up, and from it you choose an item (see fig. 7.16).

When you release the mouse button after selecting an item, Mosaic loads the URL for that item.

Fig. 7.16

The personal menus you create let you quickly load URLs from the menu bar.

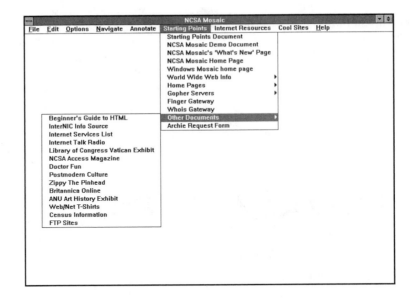

Sharing Hotlists

Sharing hotlists is a good way to make coworkers and colleagues aware of information resources they would otherwise not know of. At this time, Mosaic doesn't have an automated way of exporting and importing hotlists. However, if you edit your mosaic.ini file, you find the hotlists defined at the end of the file, after the Annotations section (see fig. 7.17 for an example of a hotlist entry). Entries have headings, such as User Menu1, followed by the name and URL for each item in the menu. You can copy these menu definitions from your mosaic.ini file into an e-mail message or file, and distribute them to people you think might be interested in them. They can then edit their mosaic.ini file and insert these menus into the file.

Using Built-In Hotlists

Mosaic, as distributed from NCSA, comes with two built-in hotlists: the Starting Points hotlist and the QUICKLIST. You can edit both lists to suit your particular needs, and you can delete the Starting Points hotlist just as you can delete any other user-configurable menu.

The Starting Points Hotlist

If you're new to the Internet and the World Wide Web, you might want to use the Starting Points hotlist to do some exploring and familiarize yourself with some of the most common Internet and WWW resources available. Some items in the Starting Points hotlist are:

- *The Starting Points document.* This contains links to many documents that provide introductory information to the Internet and the World Wide Web.

- *The NCSA Mosaic What's New page.* This gives an overview of new WWW resources. There are links to previous months' announcements at the beginning of this document.

- *World Wide Web Info menu.* This is a menu containing links to documents that give background information about the WWW and have links to interesting WWW sites.

- *Home pages.* This is a menu that links you to some of the more interesting home pages on the WWW.

- *Gopher servers.* There are connections to a number of different Gopher servers that also give you access to Veronica searches.

- *Other documents.* This menu contains links to some interesting WWW and Internet services, such as a Beginners Guide to HTML and a summary report from the 1990 Census.

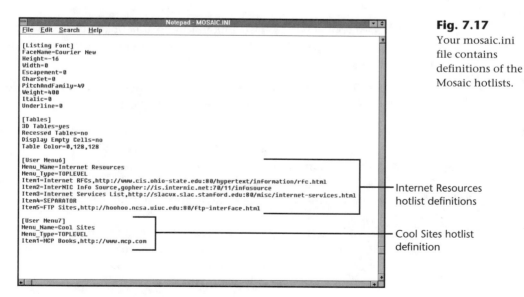

Fig. 7.17
Your mosaic.ini file contains definitions of the Mosaic hotlists.

Internet Resources hotlist definitions

Cool Sites hotlist definition

The QUICKLIST Hotlist

The built-in QUICKLIST hotlist gives you access to some of the same places as the Starting Points hotlist. In addition, the QUICKLIST gives you access to the following:

- Your local hard disk

- Several large FTP software archives

- Online weather forecast information

You may want to explore the items included with this list when you first start using Mosaic. If they're not of any use to you, replace the items with ones you use frequently.

Using Internet Shortcuts

The 2.0a9 version of Mosaic has added a new way of saving URLs, one that is more easily shared with others. You can save the address of a document in a file that can be quickly opened. When you find a document that you'd like to keep track of, follow these steps to create a quick way of accessing the document:

1. Place your cursor over the link to this document and click the right mouse button. Choose Create Internet Shortcut from the pop-up menu that appears.

2. This brings up a Save As dialog box that lets you store this URL into a file (with the extension URL) on your hard disk.

Tip
Drop the shortcut file onto the Open button on the toolbar to open the document associated with it.

3. When you want to view the document associated with that file, drag the file from the Windows File Manager and drop it onto the URL bar. Mosaic will open the document associated with this file. You can also view the document associated with this file by opening the **F**ile menu, choosing Open **L**ocal File, and opening the URL file.

If you use this method of keeping track of documents, you will have a collection of files that contain the URLs you are interested in. If you want to share these URLs with anyone, all you need to do is copy the files. Anyone can then open the documents by opening the files.

Annotations

Sometimes when you explore the WWW, you might find a document that has lots of information, but only a small amount of it is important to you. It would be nice if you could somehow mark the information of importance so that you could find it quickly. Mosaic has a feature that lets you make notes in a document to remind you of why this document is important to you and where the important information is.

Setting Up Mosaic to Use Annotations

Mosaic stores any annotations that you make as files. The first thing that you need to do is set up Mosaic so that it knows where to store these files. You can also specify a default title for your annotations.

To set up the annotation information in your Mosaic, follow these steps:

1. Open the **O**ptions menu and choose **P**references. This opens the Windows Preferences dialog box.

2. Click the Annotations tab to bring up the Annotations page (see fig. 7.18).

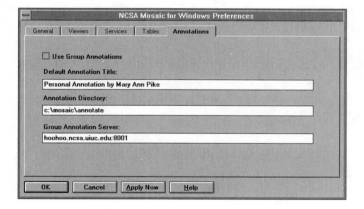

Fig. 7.18
Set up your annotation information from the Annotations page of the Windows Preferences dialog box.

3. Change the text in the box under Default Annotation Title to the default title you want for your annotations.

4. Change the text in the box under Annotation Directory to the path of the directory in which you want the annotation files to be stored.

II

Browsing with Mosaic

5. If you're going to be using group annotations, select the Use Group Annotations check box. If you're only using personal annotations, make sure this box is not selected. (See the discussion of group annotations in the section "Group and Personal Annotations" later in this chapter.)

6. If you're going to be using group annotations, enter the address of your annotations server.

7. When you have all of the parameters on the Annotations page set to your liking, choose OK (you can choose Cancel to keep the settings the way they were). Your settings will take effect immediately.

Although Mosaic doesn't support an e-mail protocol at this time, it lets you define a default e-mail address, and uses this address as the default value for the Author field in the Annotations window (as well as using it when you send bug reports to the Mosaic developers). To set your e-mail address:

1. Open the **O**ptions menu and choose **P**references. Click the Services tab to bring up the Services page (see fig. 7.19).

Fig. 7.19
The e-mail address you specify on the Windows Preferences Services page is used for the annotation author information.

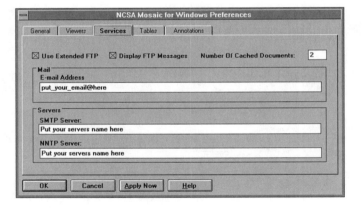

2. Change the text in the box under E-mail Address to your e-mail address.

3. Choose OK to set your e-mail address, or choose Cancel if you decide not to make the changes. (Since the Apply Now function is not yet working in the Windows Preferences dialog box, you will have to exit and restart Mosaic in order for this change to take effect.)

You can also set all of the annotation options discussed here by directly editing your mosaic.ini file, if you prefer to do that. To set your annotation options this way, follow these steps:

1. Edit the mosaic.ini with a text editor like Notepad.

2. Find the Annotations section of the file.

3. Change the Directory entry to point to the directory in which you want the annotation files to be stored.

4. Change the Default Title entry to the default title for your annotations.

5. Set Group Annotations to yes or no, depending on whether you're using personal or group annotations.

6. Set Group Annotations Server to the address of the server that you'll be using for group annotations.

7. To set your e-mail address, scroll to the top of your mosaic.ini file and under the [Main] section, change the E-mail entry to your e-mail address.

Group and Personal Annotations

There are two different types of annotations you can put in WWW documents. *Personal annotations* are stored in the directory on the hard disk that you have configured Mosaic to use. Only you (or someone who is using your computer) can read personal annotations.

You can also place *group annotations* in WWW documents. Mosaic is supposed to allow you to specify a server that will manage the group annotations. However, the author could find no documentation describing how you set up the group server to recognize group members or keep track of the annotations, so until the Mosaic developers provide more information on how to do this, it will be left as an exercise to the readers.

Using Mosaic's Annotation Feature

To add an annotation to a document, follow these steps:

1. Open the **A**nnotate menu and choose **A**nnotate. The Annotate Window dialog box, shown in figure 7.20, appears.

Fig. 7.20

The Annotate
Window dialog
box lets you create
annotations for
Mosaic docu-
ments.

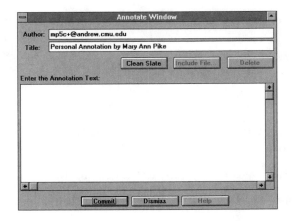

2. Enter the Author information. It defaults to the e-mail address you
   defined on the Services page of the Windows Preferences dialog box.

3. Enter the Title of this annotation, if you want it to be something other
   than the default.

4. Enter the text of the annotation text where indicated (refer to fig. 7.20).
   You can make notes here about anything: interesting links in this document, why this document is useful to you, and so on. If you want to
   erase all of the annotation text you entered, choose Clean Slate and
   re-enter the annotation text.

5. If you are satisfied with this annotation, choose Commit. This saves the
   annotation in a file in the annotation directory that you specified on
   the Annotations page of the Windows Preferences dialog box. If you
   decide that you don't want to add this annotation, choose Dismiss.

The next time you load this document, the title of your annotation and the
date it was entered show up as a link at the end of the document (see fig.
7.21). Click the link to read your annotation. To return to the document after
you have read the annotation, open the **N**avigate menu and choose **B**ack.

You can have more than one annotation in a document. Click the title of the
one that you want to read.

> **Caution**
>
> Note that in Windows Mosaic, the Delete, Include File, and Help buttons in the Annotations window are not yet working. Also, the Edit This Annotation and Delete This Annotation items on the Annotate menu do not seem to work. This means that once you create an annotation, you can't edit it or get rid of it. In addition, the author had problems with annotations being displayed on some WWW pages.

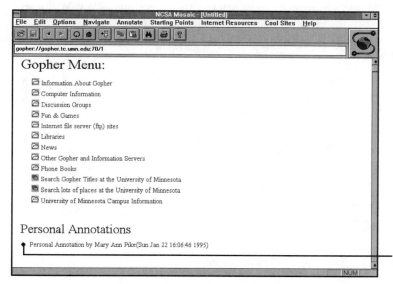

Fig. 7.21
Your annotations show up as hyperlinks at the end of a document.

Hyperlink to annotation

From Here...

Mosaic was one of the first graphical interfaces to the WWW, and is still one of the most popular because it's free. Mosaic allows you to quickly load documents that are linked to the current document, and to make quick-access lists of the documents you use most frequently. These features make accessing the Internet friendlier than it has ever been.

To learn more about using the WWW and Mosaic, refer to these chapters:

- Chapter 1, "Introduction to the World Wide Web," gives you some background information about the WWW and tells you how you can learn more about it.

- Chapter 4, "Getting Mosaic Running in Windows," tells you how to get Mosaic and set it up on your PC.

- Chapter 5, "Multimedia—Using Viewers," tells you how to get viewers for different types of multimedia files set up to work with Mosaic.

- Chapter 6, "Navigating with Mosaic," tells you how to quickly get started browsing the WWW with Mosaic.

- Chapter 19, "Web Searching," discusses how to use automated software to find some of the most interesting collections of WWW documents.

Chapter 8

FTP and Mosaic

by Mary Ann Pike

Although the initial intent of the WWW was to have a system that allowed easy retrieval of hypermedia documents for viewing, the designers of Mosaic saw the potential of having an interface that accessed not only WWW documents, but other Internet services as well. One of the oldest Internet services in existence is FTP, the File Transfer Protocol, which allows a person to transfer files from one Internet site to another. Mosaic's GUI (Graphical User Interface) allows easy FTP browsing and file retrieval without the need to learn the cryptic FTP commands.

Although the Internet FTP service can be used to transfer files from any account on the Internet, Mosaic supports only anonymous FTP service. Anonymous FTP sites are set up so that anyone on the Internet can access that site, browse the files there, and download any files of interest.

In this chapter, you learn to do the following:

- Find information on anonymous FTP servers

- Connect to anonymous FTP servers

- Retrieve files

Locating the FTP Information You Want

One of the big problems with the Internet is that there is no central source where you can go to find out where the information you want is located. One Internet service that is specifically designed to locate information on anonymous FTP servers is *Archie*.

◀ See "File Transfer Protocol,"
p. 14

Using Archie to Find Information on FTP Servers

Archie is an Internet service that allows you to search a database of FTP information for a particular program or file. Sites that provide anonymous FTP servers can register with the maintainers of the Archie database so that the information about their server is in the database. The Archie servers periodically check the computers that are registered with them and update the Archie databases to reflect the current directory structure of the registered FTP sites. Archie is a good way to look for the source of a program or particular document that you are interested in, but is not too useful for finding out information about particular topics.

> **Note**
>
> An Archie search only matches file names at the FTP sites that are registered, so if the file you are looking for is at an unregistered site, Archie cannot locate it.

◀ See "Locate Files at FTP Sites," p. 15

▶ See "Using Mosaic to Access Telnet," p. 179

Mosaic does not support Archie protocol in URLs, but there are a few different ways to do an Archie search from Mosaic. One way is to connect to an Archie server using Telnet. The other way is to use the Archie search form that is available from the Starting Points menu. The steps that follow show you how to do an Archie search using this form:

> **Note**
>
> Another Archie WWW page can be found at **http://www.lerc.nasa.gov/Doc/archieplex.html**.

Tip
Windows users whose Starting Points menu is missing or altered can access this form by opening the URL **http://hoohoo.ncsa.uiuc.edu/archie.html**.

1. Open the **S**tarting Points menu and choose **A**rchie Request Form. The Archie Request Form, shown in figure 8.1, appears.

2. Enter the file name (or part of the file name) you want to search for in the What Would You Like To Search For box.

3. Choose from the There Are Several Types Of Search list box to change the default value. Archie can do any of the searches shown in table 8.1.

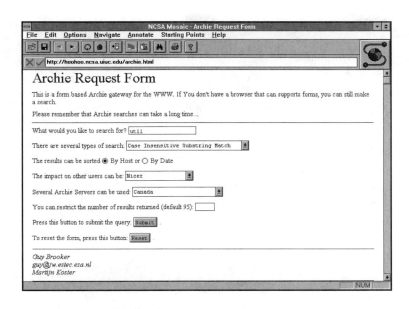

Fig. 8.1
The Archie Request
Form is available
from Mosaic's
Starting Points
menu.

Table 8.1	Archie Search Types
Type	**Description**
exact	File name must match the search string you enter exactly, including the case of all letters.
case-insensitive substring	File names that contain the search string will match, regardless of the capitalization.
case-sensitive substring	File names that contain the search string with the same capitalization will match.
regular expressions	File names that contain the complicated character patterns that you specify will match.

4. In The Results Can Be Sorted radio buttons, click the radio button (By Host or By Date) for the sorting method you prefer. Archie can return the results of the search sorted by hostname (sorted alphabetically by domain, then by organization), or by date of update of the file's information in the database (with more recent files shown first).

II

Browsing with Mosaic

> **Note**
>
> A *regular expression* is a way of specifying the possible values for a search string without specifying the exact letters. For each letter position, you can specify ranges of letters to find (in square brackets), ranges of letters to exclude (precede the letters with ^), any number of occurrences of a specific character (follow the character by a *), or any number of characters to ignore (use .*). For example, [0-9] would match any number; [^a-zA-Z] would match any non-letter; [0-9]* would match any number of numbers; win.*[0-9] would match any file name that started with "win" and ended in a digit, with any number of other characters in between. If you want to search for a special character (like a period), you can precede it with a backslash (\).

5. Choose the priority at which your search is done in The Impact On Other Users Can Be list box. You have six options, from Not Nice At All to Extremely Nice. The middle choice (Nicer) is probably a good compromise between making unnecessary demands on network resources and waiting a long time to get your search results.

6. The Several Archie Servers Can Be Used list box allows you to select the Archie server you want to use to do the search. You might want to select an Archie server that is geographically close to you because it's likely to be physically close to you on the network, giving you a faster response time. Of course, your response time also depends on how busy the host running the server is and the number of people making requests to the server.

The servers in the U.S. are listed by the organization that provides them, and other servers are listed by country. Some of the servers that are available to use are:

- InterNIC (New Jersey)

- University of Nebraska (Nebraska)

- ANS Archie server (New York)

- Rutgers University (New Jersey)

- SURAnet (Maryland)

- Australia

- Canada

- Germany

- Japan

- Sweden

- United Kingdom

7. If you want to limit the number of matching files that are returned to you, you can enter a number in the You Can Restrict The Number Of Results Returned (Default 95) box.

8. When you have all of the fields filled, choose Submit. Your search is sent to the Archie server that you requested. When the search is finished, the results are returned to you, as shown in figure 8.2.

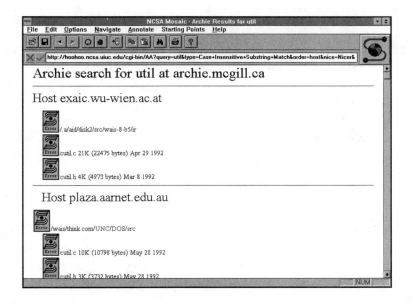

Fig. 8.2
The results of an Archie case-insensitive search on the substring "util" are shown from the Archie Request Form.

II

Browsing with Mosaic

Troubleshooting

Why does my Archie search show error icons in the results?

This seems to be the way that this Archie form works. Any results that are returned have error icons in front of each item. The links that are created for these items work with no problem, though.

Why does my Archie search take so long?

Archie servers work by queuing the requests they get, and processing the requests in the order they were received. If you connect to an Archie server using Telnet, the Archie server notifies you of what number you are in the queue and the estimated amount of time until your request is processed. When you use the Archie Request Form, you don't receive any of this queue information. So, if the Archie server you've selected is busy, you may find yourself sitting for a number of minutes waiting for the results of your search. (And, if the Archie server you've chosen is not responding, you aren't notified of this error; the form continues to indicate that it is attempting to do the search.)

If the search is taking a long time and you want to cancel it, click the Mosaic icon (spinning globe). You can now select a new server and choose Submit, or you can set all of the fields in the window back to their default values by choosing Reset, and set up another search.

---

9. After you have the results of your search, you can connect to an FTP server that has the file in which you are interested. Click one of the links in the list of results to connect to a directory that contains the file in which you are interested. You can now load the file for viewing or save it to your local disk. (This is discussed in more detail in the "Retrieving a File from an Anonymous FTP Server" section later in this chapter.)

Browsing FTP Servers

One way of finding information available at anonymous FTP servers is to browse through the directories on the server. At a server that is set up correctly, there should be a lot of informational files that tell you exactly what is on the server. The section "Exploring an Anonymous FTP Server," later in this chapter, discusses how to approach browsing on a server.

Other Ways to Find Information on FTP Servers

Although Archie is the primary means of locating files on FTP servers, there are a few other ways that you can find servers that may be of interest to you.

A summary of anonymous FTP servers can be found at the URL **http:// hoohoo.ncsa.uiuc.edu:80/ftp-interface.html**. A quick way to access this list is to open the Starting Points menu and choose Other Documents. From the drop-down menu that appears, choose FTP Sites. This brings up the document shown in figure 8.3.

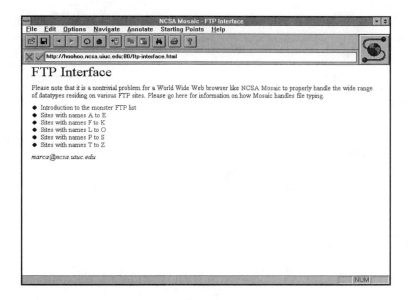

Fig. 8.3
The Monster FTP List document has pointers to the alphabetically organized files that make up the list.

This WWW page allows you to view a series of documents containing an alphabetical listing of a large number of anonymous FTP servers. A description of each document in the series is found in the first item on the page, "Introduction to the monster FTP list." Each document in the series contains a synopsis of anonymous FTP servers whose names fall in a particular range of the alphabet, including the server's address (which is a hypertext link to that site), the e-mail address of its administrator, the organization that manages the server, and a brief summary of what can be found on the server.

▶ See "Using
Mosaic to
Access UseNet
Newsgroups,"
p. 185

> **Note**
>
> The Monster FTP List that you can access from the Starting Points menu is somewhat
> out of date. There is a more recent list of FTP servers posted regularly to the UseNet
> newsgroup **news.answers**. Go to that newsgroup and look for the posts with head-
> ings like "Anonymous FTP: Sitelist Part 1 of 18" (the list is currently divided into 18
> pieces).

▶ See "Using
Mosaic to
Access WAIS,"
p. 188

Another way of finding documents that may be of interest to you is to use
WAIS. Using WAIS to find information is discussed in Chapter 10, "Using
Mosaic to Access Other Internet Services."

Connecting to an Anonymous FTP Server

When you want to connect to an anonymous FTP server on the Internet, you
do it the same way that you do anything in Mosaic—by using a URL. However, because you are not retrieving a WWW document, you do not use the
HTTP protocol in the URL. Instead, you specify the FTP protocol. An example
of a URL that you might use to connect to an anonymous FTP server is
ftp://ds.internic.net.

When you use **ftp:** in a URL, you tell Mosaic to communicate with the
Internet host that you specify using FTP. If you have ever used FTP, you know
that the normal sequence of events is to open a connection to an Internet
host, do a directory of the host after you are connected, change directories if
necessary, get any files that you are interested in, and disconnect from the
host.

Mosaic gives you a graphical interface that hides these FTP commands. A
graphical representation of the file structure appears on the Internet host,
and you can point and click to open files just like you do in File Manager. In
reality, Mosaic is interpreting your pointing and clicking and is sending the
corresponding FTP commands to the Internet host. It then takes the information that the host sends back and changes it to a picture instead of printing
the information as text.

After you are connected to an anonymous FTP server, you can easily navigate
around the server using Mosaic's navigation commands. Navigating at an FTP
server is not that different from navigating between WWW hypertext documents—but, with an FTP server you are viewing directories and their

contents. The contents may be text, image, sound, or even HTML files. Mosaic shows you the directories, but to see the contents of the files, you have to have the correct viewers installed and set up for Mosaic to use (text and HTML files can be displayed by Mosaic itself).

> **Note**
>
> Mosaic users should note that using FTP from Mosaic is not quite the same as using FTP from an application like WS_FTP. Most dedicated FTP applications open a connection to the FTP server and leave that connection open until the user closes it. Mosaic opens and closes a connection for each FTP command it needs to do.
>
> For example, when you change directories, Mosaic connects to the FTP server, executes the "cd" command, and then disconnects from the server. This can make FTP operations in Mosaic time-consuming, since you must try to connect to the server for every operation. It also means that at any time while trying to browse an FTP server, you may get a Connection refused error when Mosaic tries to execute the next FTP command.
>
> If you want to see what Mosaic is doing while browsing an FTP server, you can tell Mosaic to open a window that shows the FTP commands it is sending. On the Services page of the **P**references dialog box (open the **O**ptions menu and choose Preferences), the Display FTP Messages check box bring ups the FTP Messages window the first time you connect to an FTP server. You see all the commands that Mosaic sends to the FTP server in the FTP Messages window as you browse the server.
>
> You must choose Close to get rid of this window. However, if you are still browsing the FTP server (or if you start browsing another FTP server), the window will reappear unless you turn off the Display FTP Messages option.

Retrieving Information Using FTP

After you have found an anonymous FTP server that has information of interest to you, you can use Mosaic to connect to the server, explore its holdings, and retrieve any files you may want. This section explains how to do this.

Exploring an Anonymous FTP Server

When you connect to an anonymous FTP server, Mosaic shows you the directory structure of the server. You start at the top directory level, and can move down into any subdirectories in the server.

1. Open the **F**ile menu and choose **O**pen URL. In the Open URL window, enter the URL of the FTP server you want to connect to and choose OK. Figure 8.4 shows an example of what you see when you connect to an anonymous FTP server.

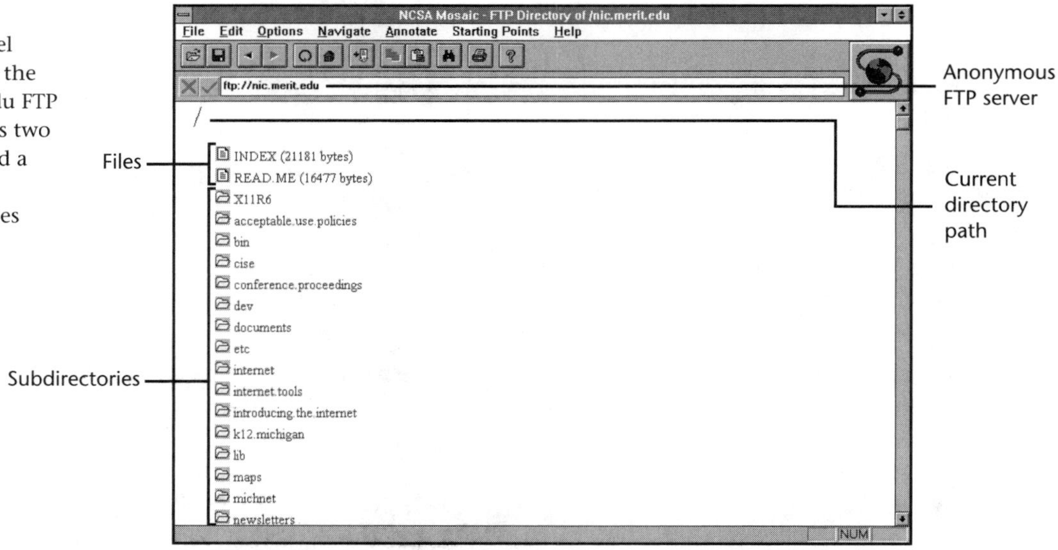

Fig. 8.4

The top-level directory of the nic.merit.edu FTP server shows two text files and a number of subdirectories (folders).

Files ——

Subdirectories ——

Anonymous FTP server

Current directory path

In figure 8.4, notice that the title bar tells you that you are in the FTP directory of the Internet host /nic.merit.edu. In the document viewing area, you see a / (slash) that tells you that you are in the root directory for that host.

You also see a list with icons next to the entries. The first two items in the list are INDEX and READ.ME. Notice that the icons look like a sheet of paper, and that they have a size (in bytes) to the right of them. The sheet-of-paper icons indicate that these two files are text files that Mosaic knows how to display. The items that follow these two files all have folder icons next to them. These files are subdirectories that you can browse by clicking the subdirectory names.

Note

On the Services page of the Preferences dialog box (open the **O**ptions menu and choose **P**references), you find a check box labeled Use Extended FTP. If this option is selected, FTP directories are shown as described in this section (icons next to the file and directory names, sizes next to files, and so on). If this option is turned off, all directories and files are shown only with a dot to the left of the name, and no sizes are given for files (although not all sites are set up to show file sizes, even if extended directory parsing is enabled).

2. If you can find a document called README, READ.ME, or readme.txt, click it and Mosaic displays it. It is common to place a file with a name like this on FTP servers. The file is used to describe what is on the server, list any restrictions on the use of the server, or other administrative-type messages. You should always look for one of these files when you connect to an unfamiliar FTP server. Figure 8.5 shows the contents of a typical READ.ME document.

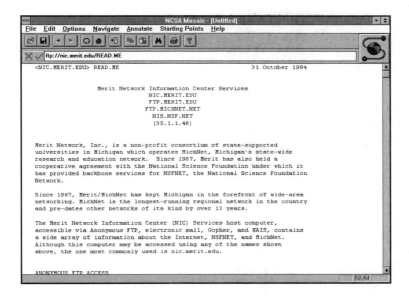

Fig. 8.5
The READ.ME document from the nic.merit.edu FTP server describes the server and what you can find there.

II

Browsing with Mosaic

3. After you have finished reading about the FTP server to which you are connected, open the **N**avigate menu and choose **B**ack to return to the top-level directory of the server. From there, you can click some of the subdirectories that look interesting to you. When you click a subdirectory, the contents of that directory are displayed, with the directory path shown at the top of Mosaic's document viewing area (see fig. 8.6).

Tip
FTP servers often show you the size of the files in each directory. You can have some idea of how long the file transfer will take when you load the file for viewing in Mosaic or when you save it to your local disk.

Fig. 8.6
The
/nic.merit.edu/
documents
directory is an
example of one
directory you can
view.

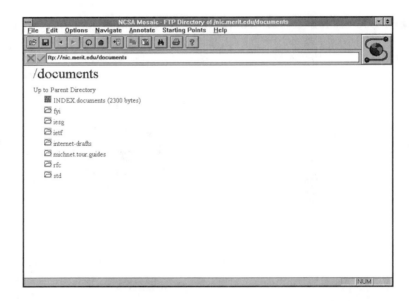

4. The first item underneath the directory path in figure 8.6 is labeled Up to Parent Directory. Click this item to return to the directory level above the current one. This is a quick way to get to the directory above you when you have been browsing through directories at a server. You might think that the Navigate/Back command in Mosaic takes you to the directory above you, but this command just takes you to the previous link, which may be in the directory under you!

> **Note**
>
> Near the top of the directory list in figure 8.6 is the INDEX.documents file. Notice that the icon next to this file is not recognizable as anything. That's because Mosaic does not recognize the file-type of this file. If Mosaic retrieved this file, it would not know how to display it. If you click this file, Mosaic attempts to retrieve it, but when it realizes that it doesn't know what to do with the file, Mosaic simply aborts the transfer.
>
> Mosaic is an application under development. The developers may eventually offer you an option for displaying a file of unknown type. When Mosaic aborts a transfer, it usually does not inform you. You just notice that there is no activity in the status bar and your document viewing area has not changed (and the globe in the Mosaic icon button is no longer spinning).

Retrieving a File from an Anonymous FTP Server

After you have found a file that you're interested in (either through an Archie search or by browsing through an FTP server), you can retrieve the file and view it from Mosaic, or you can save it to your local disk.

Viewing a File

To view a file on an anonymous FTP server, follow these steps:

1. Place the cursor on the document name and click it. After Mosaic has finished loading a document, you should see something similar to figure 8.7.

> **Note**
>
> Many of the files you find on an anonymous FTP server are text files without any HTML commands in them. These files are displayed like the one in figure 8.7, without any nice formatting. If you click a file that needs an external viewer and you have set up Mosaic to work with that viewer, Mosaic launches the viewer with the selected file loaded into it. You can then use any of the viewer's features (including saving the file to your local disk).

◀ See "Multi-media—Using Viewers," p. 81

II

Browsing with Mosaic

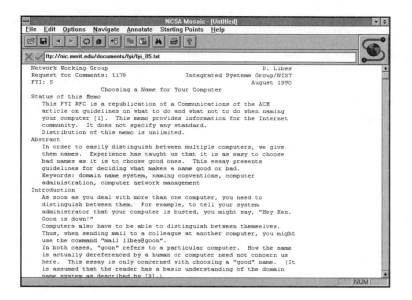

Fig. 8.7
The fyi_05 document from the /nic.merit.edu/ documents/fyi directory tells you about naming conventions for computers.

Troubleshooting

Why can't I view some documents on FTP servers?

If Mosaic can't display a file directly (HTML or text), and if you don't have a viewer configured for that file type, Mosaic cannot display the file. Mosaic may try to load the file but never finish (in which case you have to click the spinning globe to abort the load). Or it may just refuse to load the file (do nothing when you click the link).

---

2. When you are finished viewing a document at an FTP server, open the **N**avigate menu and choose **B**ack to return to the directory the file came from. The files viewed at FTP servers are likely to be plain text files (if they were hypertext files, they would be on a WWW server), image files, or sound files. Because these documents have no hyperlinks in them, they don't link you to other documents or other WWW servers. To navigate around an FTP server, you simply move through the directory structure (folders).

Saving a File to Your Local Computer

If you want to save the document you are reading, there is a **S**ave option under the **F**ile menu. The steps for saving a file using the Save command are as follows:

1. While you are viewing a document you want to save, open the **F**ile menu and choose **S**ave. You see a Save As dialog box, similar to the one shown in figure 8.8, that asks you where you want to save the file.

Fig. 8.8
When you save a file to disk, you can put it anywhere on your local directory system.

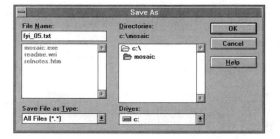

2. Enter the information in the dialog box and choose OK. Mosaic attempts to save the file to your local disk.

There is another way that you can save files from Mosaic. The following procedure saves the file associated with a URL to a file on your local disk:

1. Open **O**ptions and choose **L**oad to Disk.

2. Click the hyperlink for the document you want to save. You see a Save As dialog box, such as the one shown in figure 8.8, that asks you where you want to save the file.

3. Enter the information in the dialog box and choose OK. Mosaic attempts to load that URL to disk instead of displaying it in the document viewing area.

4. Open the **O**ptions menu and choose **L**oad to Disk again to turn off the feature.

If you forget to turn off Load to Disk, Mosaic tries to load the URL of the next hyperlink you click to disk instead of loading it to view. If this happens, you have to select Cancel in the Save As dialog box, and then turn off Load to Disk before you can view another document.

Retrieving an Embedded FTP File

While looking through a WWW document, you may find links to files on anonymous FTP servers. You can find this out by looking at the URL of the document in the status bar (the URL begins with **ftp:**). If the file is of a type that Mosaic can handle (either directly or with an external viewer), you can click this file and load it. Even if Mosaic doesn't know what to do with it, you can use Mosaic to transfer this file and save it directly to disk instead of trying to display it. (See "Saving a File to Your Local Computer" earlier in this chapter for instructions.) Figure 8.9 shows an example of a WWW document with embedded FTP files.

Tip

To load a single file to disk quickly, click the right mouse button while your cursor is over the URL for the file and select **L**oad Anchor to Disk.

Tip

If you want to load a single file to disk, you can Shift+click the hyperlink rather than choosing **O**ptions, **L**oad to Disk. This loads only that one file to disk; you won't have to worry about forgetting to turn off Load to Disk.

Tip

If you want to save the file you are currently viewing to disk, choose **O**ptions, **L**oad to Disk, and click Reload from the **N**avigate menu. This brings up the Save As dialog box.

II

Browsing with Mosaic

Fig. 8.9

The Multimedia section of the Macmillan Software Library page contains links to FTP files that you can retrieve.

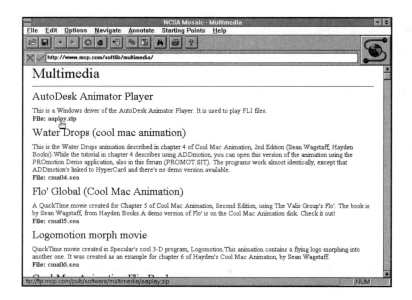

From Here...

Mosaic can be used in place of FTP to transfer files from one Internet host to another. Mosaic also allows you to access other Internet services in addition to the WWW.

To learn more about using the WWW and Mosaic, refer to these chapters:

- Chapter 1, "Introduction to the World Wide Web," gives you background information about the Internet and the WWW.

- Chapter 6, "Navigating with Mosaic," familiarizes you with the Mosaic features that help you find and view documents on the WWW.

- Chapter 10, "Using Mosaic to Access Other Internet Services," gives you information on using WAIS to find information on the WWW, and tells you how to use Telnet and access UseNet newsgroups with Mosaic.

- Chapter 33, "Hot FTP and Gopher Sites," gives you some pointers on where to find interesting files you can view and retrieve.

Chapter 9

Gopher and Mosaic

by Mary Ann Pike

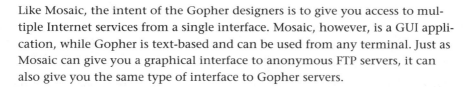

Like Mosaic, the intent of the Gopher designers is to give you access to multiple Internet services from a single interface. Mosaic, however, is a GUI application, while Gopher is text-based and can be used from any terminal. Just as Mosaic can give you a graphical interface to anonymous FTP servers, it can also give you the same type of interface to Gopher servers.

Gopher servers are similar to anonymous FTP servers in that anyone on the Internet can access the server, browse around it, and download any files of interest. However, unlike anonymous FTP servers, which are viewed simply as directory structures with the actual file and directory name displayed, Gopher servers are menu-oriented. Also, Gopher servers let you connect to other Internet services—such as Telnet, WAIS, and other Gopher servers—and view and retrieve files.

In this chapter, you learn how to:

- Find Gopher servers that have the information you want

- Navigate through Gopherspace

- Retrieve files from a Gopher site

- Use other Internet services from a Gopher site

Connecting to a Gopher Server

If you want to connect to a Gopher server on the Internet, you do it the same way you do anything in Mosaic—you use a URL. Because you aren't retrieving a WWW document, you don't use the HTTP protocol in the URL. You specify the Gopher protocol instead. An example of a URL that you might use to connect to a Gopher server is **gopher://gopher.nsf.gov**.

◀ See "Retrieve Information with Gopher," p. 16

Understanding the Gopher Protocol

Tip
Many Internet sites precede their server names with the type of service they provide. For example, the fictitious company "Bigcorp" might have the servers ftp.bigcorp.com, gopher.bigcorp.com, and www.bigcorp.com.

When you begin a URL with gopher:, you tell Mosaic that you want to use the Gopher protocol to communicate with the Internet host. Gopher was originally developed to be used from an ASCII terminal, not from a GUI interface. When you use a Gopher program from a terminal, the normal sequence of events is to connect to a Gopher server on an Internet host, select one of the menu items that is presented to you, change directories or connect to other Internet services if necessary, get any files that you're interested in, and exit from the Gopher program.

Mosaic gives you a graphical interface that hides these Gopher commands; you see a graphical representation of each item in the Gopher menu. You can point and click to change directories, open files, and connect to other Internet services. In reality, Mosaic is interpreting your pointing and clicking and sending the corresponding Gopher commands to the Gopher server. Mosaic then takes the information that the server sends back and changes it to a picture instead of printing the information as text.

After you're connected to a Gopher server, you can easily navigate around the server by using Mosaic's navigation commands. Navigating at a Gopher server is not that different than navigating between WWW hypertext documents, except at a Gopher server you're viewing menus, which are displayed by Mosaic in a format similar to the FTP servers. The menus are shown as lists of items with icons next to them, marked either as files, directories, or other Internet services.

One of the main differences between the Gopher and FTP servers is that with FTP, you're limited to accessing files and directories on the host where the server resides. With Gopher, a menu item might be on the same host, or it might take you to another host at a very distant site. Menu items can be text, image, sound, HTML files, or connections to other Internet services. To see the contents of the files, you must have the correct viewers installed for Mosaic (text and HTML files can be displayed by Mosaic itself).

Locating Gopher Information

A big problem with the Internet is that there is no central information source where you can find the location of items that interest you. You can always connect to servers that you know exist and just browse around the servers looking for things that might interest you. However, there's an Internet service called Veronica that is specifically designed to locate information on Gopher servers.

Browsing Gopher Servers

One way of finding information available at a Gopher server is simply to browse through the menus on the server. At a server that is set up correctly, there should be lots of informational files that tell you exactly what's on the server. The section later in this chapter, "Exploring Gopher Servers," discusses how to approach browsing on a Gopher server.

Finding Information on Gopher Servers

Although Gopher itself was designed as an information-finding aid, there are some other sources of information about interesting Gopher servers. WAIS is an Internet service that allows you to look through databases of documents to find information. Also, you can use Archie to search for a file on an anonymous FTP server and see if the Internet site where the file resides has a Gopher server. Internet sites often have a Gopher server that lets you access the information found on the site's anonymous FTP server, as well as additional resources.

▶ See "Using Mosaic to Access WAIS," p. 188

◀ See "Using Archie to Find Information on FTP Servers," p. 148

Using Veronica to Search Gopherspace

Just as Archie is a service that allows you to search file names and directories on anonymous FTP servers, Veronica allows you to search menu items on Gopher servers. You can limit your Veronica search to directories that contain the word(s) that you're interested in, or you can search through all of Gopherspace to find files and directories that might interest you.

The first thing that you need to do is figure out what words you want to search for. Your search string should contain enough words to make the search as specific as possible (otherwise, thousands of matches might be found). After you have built your search string, you can use Veronica to do the search.

Building Your Search String

Veronica allows you to search for just one word, or use multiple word search strings. There are also two options that you can use in your search: one to specify the number of items that are returned, and one to specify the type of items that are returned.

Using Boolean Operators and Wild Cards. If you want to do a simple multiple word search, you can just enter the words you want to search for with spaces between them. This type of search finds items that contain all the search words, although the words will not necessarily be adjacent or in the same order.

You can also use Boolean operators (and, or, not) and wild cards (*) in your searches, and group words with parentheses. Table 9.1 shows you how to use these different operators in your search string.

Table 9.1 Operators for Veronica Search Strings	
Operator	**Description**
and	Directs the search to return items that contain the words (or grouped words) before and after "and"
or	Directs the search to return items that contain either the word (or grouped words) before "or" or following "or"
not	Directs the search to return items that do not contain the word specified after "not" (usually grouped with other operators)
*	Used at the end of a word (or part of a word); matches words that begin with the characters that precede "*"
( )	Used to group words so that operators work on groups of words rather than individual words

Some examples of search strings that you might use when doing Veronica searches are "women and politics," "chicken and (casseroles or rice)," "financ*," and "education not primary."

Options. You have two options in your Veronica search string (you can place the options either before or after the search words). The first option is -m<*number*>, which allows you to limit the items returned by the search to the number you specify. If you search with no limits specified, most Veronica servers will return the first 200 items and will put a note at the end of the list telling you how many additional items were found (some servers have a different default number than 200). By using the -m option without an argument, you tell Veronica to return all of the matches it finds.

The second option, -t*<type>*, allows you to limit the types of files that Veronica returns from its search. For example, you can limit the files to text, sound, HTML, and so on. Table 9.2 shows the types of files that can be specified.

Table 9.2 Veronica Search File Types	
Type	**Description**
0	Text file
1	Directory
2	CSO name server
4	Mac HQX file
5	PC binary
7	Full text index (Gopher menu)
8	Telnet session
9	Binary file
s	Sound
I	Image (other than GIF)
M	MIME multipart/mixed message
T	TN3270 session
g	GIF image
h	HTML, hypertext markup language

Performing a Search

To use Veronica, you have to be connected to a Gopher server that gives you access to a Veronica server. The following steps show you how to connect to a Gopher that provides Veronica search service and how to do a search.

1. Open the Starting Points menu and choose Gopher Servers, Veronica Search. Mosaic displays a menu that looks like the one in figure 9.1.

Note

In addition to giving you easy access to a Veronica Search menu, the Gopher Servers option on the Starting Points menu lets you quickly connect to some of the more popular Gopher servers (including the one at the University of Minnesota where Gopher was developed).

Notice that the title bar tells you that you're running NCSA Mosaic, but you're in an Untitled document. Remember, Mosaic is an application still under development, so some things might not look as you expect them to.

Fig. 9.1
The Gopher menu appears when you open the Starting Points menu and choose Gopher Servers, Veronica Search.

Files

Subdirectory

Gopher positions Mosaic cannot interpret

Searchable indexes

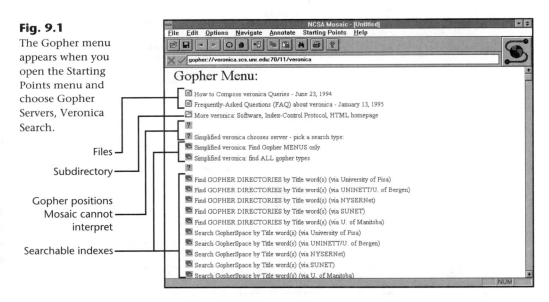

At the top of the document viewing area, it says Gopher Menu:. This lets you know that what you're viewing is a Gopher server. What you see below that heading looks the same as what you see when you use the

FTP protocol—folders, which represent directories, and files. (The icon that looks like a stack of cards represents a searchable index.) Notice, however, that directory or file names are not next to these folders. Instead, there are descriptive phrases.

> **Note**
>
> If you don't have the default Starting Points menu and can't access the Gopher Servers and Veronica Search options from this menu, you can directly connect to a Gopher that gives you access to Veronica. To do so, open the **F**ile menu and choose **O**pen URL. Enter the URL **gopher:// veronica.scs.unr.edu** and choose OK. After you're connected to this Gopher server, choose the menu item Search ALL of Gopherspace (4800 Servers) Using Veronica. You can continue with step 2 from here to do a Veronica search.

2. You can select a specific Veronica server, or let the Veronica search select the server for you. To select a specific server, click one of the entries in the list that has a server name following it in parentheses. Entries that begin with `Search GopherSpace by Title Word(s)` will find files or directories that contain your search word(s). Entries that begin with `Find GOPHER DIRECTORIES by Title Word(s)` will find just directories that contain the search word(s).

   The line `? Simplified veronica chooses server—pick a search type:` is a description of the two items that follow it. (Notice that these two items have the stack of cards icon that indicates a search function.) Click the Simplified Veronica: Find Gopher MENUS Only item to let Veronica choose the server to use for a directory-only search. Click the Simplified Veronica: Find ALL Gopher Types item to let Veronica choose the server to use for a comprehensive Gopher search. A search form, like the one shown in figure 9.2, is loaded in the document viewing area.

3. Click in the Search Index box at the bottom of the screen and enter the words you want to search for. Then press the Enter key.

Fig. 9.2
The Gopher
Search Index form.

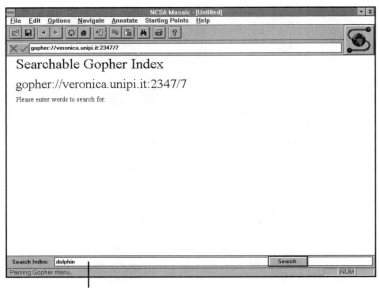

Enter search words

Troubleshooting

Why does my Veronica search take so long?

The Veronica is searching a list of the menu items of all known Gopher servers. That takes a long time. Also, if there are a lot of people connected to that server doing searches, the server will be slow.

If the search is taking too long and you want to cancel it, click the Mosaic icon (spinning globe). You can go back to the list of Veronica servers and try your search from a different server.

4. The Veronica search builds the Gopher menu shown in figure 9.3 (the viewing area has been scrolled so that it shows the middle of the list). Notice that the search found both image and text files. Veronica can build a menu that has any type of Gopher item in it—Telnet connections, animations, and so on. You can now click these items to view them.

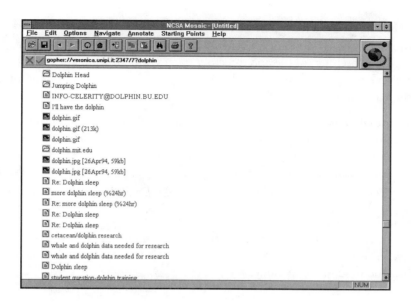

Troubleshooting

Why can't I get Veronica to repeat my search after I get a Too many connections error?

If you get an error returned to you as the result of your search (for example, `0***Too many connections  Try again soon.***`), you'll need to do your search over. However, doing a search on the same string is not straightforward. If you just return to the search window and press Enter again, it will return you to the error screen since that was the result of the search for that string (Mosaic can't tell the difference between a good result and an error). To get Veronica to try another search, you must change the search string—for example, reverse the order of some of the words because order does not matter.

When you're done looking through the menu built by the Veronica search, open the **N**avigate menu and choose **B**ack to take you back to the search window. From there, you can navigate back to other menus on this Gopher server or go to a completely new URL.

Exploring Gopher Servers

Tip

If you find a Go-
pher server that
you use often, add
it to one of your
hot lists so that
you can access it
quickly.

Veronica can help find items of interest to you at Gopher servers, but it's limited to searching for file and directory names only. It would be nice if you could search the contents of the files, but it would take an enormous amount of time to search every file on every Gopher server that exists.

Some individual Gopher servers have a full-text search service as one of their menu items. These search services search the text of the items (or a subset of the items) found on that particular Gopher. So if you can find a Gopher server that has information that you're interested in, you can use the full-text search to find the particular files that would interest you.

Browsing with a Gopher Server

Just looking around is often an effective way to find things at a Gopher server, especially if it's a well-run server that has a lot of informational documents and descriptive menu item names.

The following steps show you how to browse a Gopher server:

◀ See "Create
Lists of Your
Favorite URLs,"
p. 128

1. Open the **F**ile menu and choose **O**pen URL. In the Open URL dialog box, enter the URL of the Gopher server you want to explore and choose OK. After Mosaic loads the main menu for this Gopher server, you should see something similar to figure 9.4.

Fig. 9.4
The top-level menu of the gopher.nsf.gov Gopher server, showing some text files, a number of subdirectories (folders), and some search indexes.

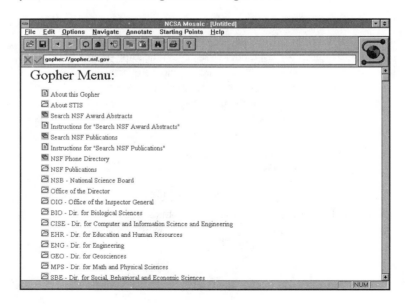

> **Note**
>
> Notice that a number of messages flash by in the status bar at the bottom of the window when you connect to a Gopher server. Sometimes they go by too quickly to see, but if the network is slow or there is a problem, the message might remain there. Some of these messages include: `Doing Name Service Lookup`, `Parsing Gopher Menu`, and `Transferring`. These messages let you know the progress Mosaic has made and can help you diagnose any problems that occur when connecting to the server.

The first item in the menu in figure 9.4 is About this Gopher, which is shown as a text file (indicated by the sheet of paper icon). If you place your cursor over the hyperlink for this item, you will see the URL for the item in the status bar. What is actually being retrieved when you click this hyperlink is a file called About.

The next item in the menu has a folder icon next to it. This item takes you to another Gopher menu. Several of the menu items following the folder have icons that look like stacked index cards. These items give you access to a search index that lets you do a full-text search on files at this Gopher.

> **Troubleshooting**
>
> *Why can't I view some documents on Gopher servers?*
>
> If you have the correct viewers installed, you can load any files you find at a Gopher server and view them. The problem, though, is that you don't know the format of the files in a Gopher menu. Even if you place your cursor over the hyperlinks for the animations and images, the file names that are shown in the status bar have no extensions, so you don't know what type of viewer you need for them.
>
> If Mosaic can't display a file directly (HTML or text) and you don't have a viewer configured for that file type, Mosaic will not be able to display the file. Mosaic may try to load the file, but it will never finish (in which case you will have to click the spinning globe to abort the load). Or, it may just refuse to load the file (do nothing when you click the link).

2. To find out information about the Gopher server, look for a file like the About this Gopher document shown in figure 9.4. Most Gopher servers have a document like this in their top-level menu to give you some idea

II

Browsing with Mosaic

of what you can do from that server. To read the document, just place your cursor on the name and click. When Mosaic finishes loading the document, you should see something that looks similar to figure 9.5.

Fig. 9.5

The About this Gopher document from the gopher.nsf.gov Gopher server briefly describes the server and what you can find there.

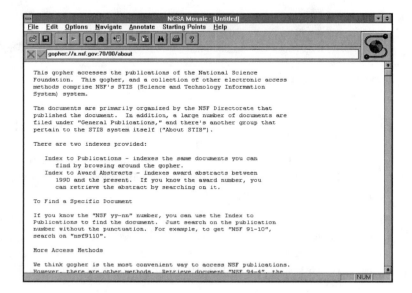

This is a short document that tells you what's on this Gopher server and how to locate the items in which you are interested. You probably want to go back to the main menu now and look for a file that interests you. Although you can browse through a Gopher site like you do an anonymous FTP site, Gopher servers are really structured to help you find information on a particular topic that is of interest to you.

3. Open the **N**avigate menu and choose **B**ack to return to the main menu for this Gopher server. Now that you're back at the main menu, there are a number of options. You could keep clicking menu items that sound interesting, looking at files and jumping to different menus (possibly on different Gopher servers) as you go along. Or, if there are any index items that tell you what is available from this Gopher server, try looking up something.

> **Note**
>
> Unlike Mosaic's anonymous FTP screens, which give you an Up to Parent Directory link, the Back command in the Navigate menu is the only hypertext command available to move you along your link path. There isn't an item in the document viewing area that takes you to the previous menu, because, in most cases, the Gopher server doesn't know what menu you came from. Unlike a directory structure where every piece of the directory is fixed and can be accessed with complete certainty, a Gopher menu can have a number of different menus that link to it.
>
> Use the navigating tips discussed in Chapter 7, "Mosaic Shortcuts and Tips," to help you figure out how to keep track of where you've been.

Doing a Full-Text Search of a Gopher Server

A search index is one of the easiest ways to find something that interests you on the Gopher server. If the Gopher server has a full-text search index available, click that item in the Gopher menu. You will get a search form in which you can do a search, as described in the "Using Veronica to Search Gopherspace" section earlier in this chapter.

Saving Files from a Gopher Server

If you want to save the document you're reading, there is a Save option in the File menu. The steps for saving a file using the Save command are as follows:

1. While you're viewing a document that you want to save, open the **F**ile menu and choose **S**ave. You'll get a Save As dialog box, like the one shown in figure 9.6, that asks you where you want to save the file.

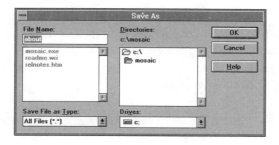

Fig. 9.6
When you save a file to disk, you can put it anywhere on your local directory system.

2. Fill in the information in the dialog box and choose OK. Mosaic attempts to save the file to your local disk.

There is another way you can save files from Mosaic. The following procedure saves the file associated with a URL to a file on your computer.

Tip
To load a single file to disk quickly, click the right mouse button while your cursor is over the URL for the file and select **L**oad Anchor to Disk.

1. Open the **O**ptions menu and choose **L**oad to Disk.

2. Click the hyperlink for the document you want to save. You get a Save As dialog box that asks you where you want to save the file (refer to fig. 9.6).

3. Fill in the information in the dialog box and choose OK. Mosaic attempts to load that URL to disk instead of displaying it in the document viewing area.

4. Open the **O**ptions menu and choose **L**oad to Disk again to turn off the feature.

> **Note**
>
> If you want to load a single file to disk, you can Shift-click on the hyperlink rather than choosing **L**oad to Disk from the **O**ptions menu. This loads only that one file to disk; you won't have to worry about forgetting to turn off Load to Disk.

> **Note**
>
> If you want to save the file you're currently viewing to disk, choose **L**oad to Disk from the **O**ptions menu, and then choose Reload from the **N**avigate menu. This brings up the Save As dialog box.

If you forget to turn off Load to Disk after saving a document, Mosaic continues trying to load the URL of the next hyperlink you click to disk instead of loading it to view. If this happens, you have to choose Cancel in the Save As dialog box, and then turn off Load to Disk before you can view another document.

Retrieving an Imbedded Gopher File

While looking through a WWW document, you may find links to files on Gopher servers. You can find this out by looking at the URL of the document in the status bar (the URL will begin with gopher:). If the file is a type that Mosaic can handle (either directly or with an external viewer), you can click this file and load it. But even if Mosaic doesn't know what to do with it, you can use Mosaic to transfer this file and save it directly to disk instead of trying to display it. (See the earlier section, "Saving Files from a Gopher Server," for instructions.)

Connecting to Other Internet Services from a Gopher Server

In addition to items we've already discussed, there are a few other types of items that you might find in a Gopher menu that let you access other Internet services. Some Gopher menu items connect to other Gopher servers (you can do this without realizing it if the menu item label doesn't indicate that it connects to another server).

One other item that you might find in a Gopher menu is a Telnet connection to a service on another Internet host. To do a Gopher Telnet command, Mosaic must use the Telnet program that came with your TCP/IP communications program (you must configure Mosaic so that it knows where the Telnet program can be found). It starts up the Telnet program, giving it the host information that is contained in the Gopher menu item. A Telnet window then appears that connects you to the Internet host that was specified in the Gopher menu item.

▶ See "Using Mosaic to Access Telnet," p. 179

From Here...

Mosaic provides a nice interface to older Internet services as well as the World Wide Web. To learn more about using the WWW and Mosaic, refer to these chapters:

- Chapter 1, "Introduction to the World Wide Web," gives you background information about the WWW.

- Chapter 6, "Navigating with Mosaic," familiarizes you with the Mosaic features that help you find and view documents on the WWW.

- Chapter 10, "Using Mosaic to Access Other Internet Services," gives you information on how to use WAIS to find information on the WWW, in addition to telling you how to use Telnet and access UseNet newsgroups with Mosaic.

- Chapter 33, "Hot FTP and Gopher Sites," gives you some pointers on where to find interesting files that you can view and retrieve.

II

Browsing with Mosaic

Using Mosaic to Access Other Internet Services

by Mary Ann Pike

Besides Gopher and FTP, which were discussed in previous chapters, Mosaic can also directly access a number of other Internet services.

In this chapter, you learn to do the following:

- Use Mosaic to access Telnet

- Use Mosaic to access UseNet newsgroups

- Use Mosaic to access WAIS

- Use Mosaic to access E-mail

Using Mosaic to Access Telnet

This section discusses using Telnet directly from Mosaic. Telnet can be used to connect to some informational BBS systems on the Internet, or to log in to an account on a remote machine (of course, you have to have an account and know the password, just as you would to log in to a machine directly).

Getting Telnet to Work with Mosaic

Mosaic can communicate using the Telnet protocol, but it needs the Telnet program that comes with the TCP/IP software that's installed on your PC. To use the Telnet protocol in a URL, your mosaic.ini file must contain a statement at the end of the Viewers section that shows the complete directory path to your Telnet software (see fig. 10.1).

Fig. 10.1

The mosaic.ini file, with the Telnet path specified at the end of the Viewers section of the file.

```
                                   Notepad - MOSAIC.INI
 File  Edit  Search   Help

[Viewers]
rem     Links to the viewer applications can be found from the viewers link on the Mosaic home pa
rem     http://www.ncsa.uiuc.edu/SDG/Software/WinMosaic/viewers.html
TYPE0="audio/wav"
TYPE1="application/postscript"
TYPE2="image/gif"
TYPE3="image/jpeg"
TYPE4="video/mpeg"
TYPE5="video/quicktime"
TYPE6="video/msvideo"
TYPE7="application/x-rtf"
TYPE8="audio/x-midi"
TYPE9="application/sgml"
TYPE10="application/pdf"
rem     You can define other MIME types in a simular manner.  Check out this URL for
rem     more info on MIME types:  ftp://isi.edu/in-notes/media-types/media-types
rem     YOU MUST DEFINE THE PATHS TO YOUR VIEWERS.
application/postscript="ghostview %ls"
application/x-rtf="write %ls"
image/gif="c:\winapps\lview\lview31 %ls"
image/jpeg="c:\winapps\lview\lview31 %ls"
video/mpeg="c:\win32app\mpegplay\mpegplay %ls"
video/quicktime="mplayer %ls"█
video/msvideo="mplayer %ls"
audio/wav="mplayer %ls"
audio/x-midi="mplayer %ls"
application/sgml="c:\winapps\hotmetal\hotmetal.exe %ls"
application/pdf="c:\winapps\acroread\acroread.exe %ls"
telnet="c:\trumpet\telw.exe"

[Suffixes]
application/postscript=.ps,.eps,.ai,.ps
application/x-rtf=.rtf,.wri
audio/wav=.wave,.wav,.WAV
audio/x-midi=.mid
```

Telnet program location

If your PC is directly connected to the Internet, your mosaic.ini file is probably preconfigured with the appropriate address (you can ask your system administrator for help if you have problems making Telnet connections from Mosaic). If you're running over a SLIP or PPP connection, the TCP/IP communications software that you installed should include a Telnet program.

Troubleshooting

Why does the Telnet URL I've entered fail even though I have the correct host and port number?

When you specify a Telnet address in a URL, it sometimes contains a port number in addition to the host name (see the example in the next section, "Using the Telnet Protocol from Mosaic"). Mosaic separates the host name and port with a colon (:), but some Telnet programs do not handle this properly and the connection fails. (This often happens when you're trying to start a Telnet connection from a Gopher menu, where the host name and port number are defined with a colon separating them.)

If the connection fails, it will probably fail with the Telnet window open. If this happens, open the Connect menu item and select it. This dialog box should have the host name and port of the failed connection in it. You can correctly enter the host name and port number here and complete the connection.

Using the Telnet Protocol from Mosaic

To use the Telnet protocol from Mosaic, open a URL just as you do to use any of the Internet services. The URL for a Telnet session should specify the Internet host you want to connect to and any special port number that may be needed. The following steps show you how to use the Telnet protocol:

1. Open the **F**ile menu and choose **O**pen URL.

2. Enter the URL for the Internet host you want to connect to (for example, **telnet://downwind.sprl.umich.edu:3000**) in the URL field of the Open URL dialog box.

   If you're connecting normally to a host, you'll get its login prompt. If you're connecting to an Internet BBS (like the one shown in figure 10.2), you'll get the welcome screen for the BBS.

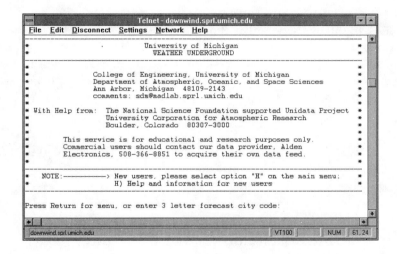

Fig. 10.2
When using Telnet to connect to the Weather Underground System at the University of Michigan, this is the BBS welcome screen you get.

3. When you're finished with your remote connection, be sure to log off or exit from the BBS. The Telnet window remains open when you close the remote connection. Close the Telnet window if you won't be using it any more.

Troubleshooting

Why does my Telnet command fail when I have the right host name and port entered?

If the Telnet command reports an error, the remote computer may be unavailable, or the network between the two machines may be broken. If this happens, you should wait a while and try again.

Note

Because your Telnet connection is running in a separate window, you can do other things with Mosaic while you're connected to the Telnet service.

Using Archie from Telnet

◄ See "Using Archie to Find Information on FTP Servers," p. 148

Archie is an Internet service that allows you to search a database containing the contents of anonymous FTP servers for a particular program or file. Chapter 8, "FTP and Mosaic," showed you how to do an Archie search using forms. The following steps show you how to connect to an Archie server and perform a search using the Telnet protocol:

1. Open the **F**ile menu and choose **O**pen URL.

2. Enter the URL for the Archie server you want to connect to in the URL field of the Open URL dialog box.

Note

There are a number of Internet Archie servers that you can connect to using Telnet. Some of the ones you might want to try are the following:

Server	Location
archie.internic.net	New Jersey
archie.unl.edu	Nebraska
archie.ans.net	New York
archie.rutgers.edu	New Jersey
archie.sura.net	Maryland
archie.au	Australia

Server	Location
archie.cs.mcgill.ca	Canada
archie.th-darmstadt.de	Germany
archie.wide.ad.jp	Japan
archie.switch.ch	Switzerland
archie.doc.ic.ac.uk	United Kingdom

Tip

For faster response time, you might want to pick an Archie server that's in a time zone where most people are sleeping.

3. A welcoming message appears, and the remote computer asks you to log in an account name. Type **archie** as the account name (see fig. 10.3).

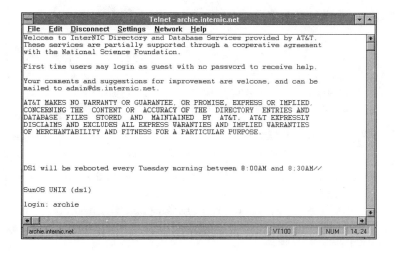

Fig. 10.3
The Telnet window that appears when you connect to **archie.internic.net** through Mosaic shows the Archie server welcoming message.

4. Enter the command **set pager** to allow you to read what appears on-screen more easily.

5. Enter the command **set search subcase** to tell the Archie program to search for substrings and to let you match upper- and lowercase letters in the search.

6. To search for the file you're interested in, enter **find** followed by the name (or part of the name) of the file you're interested in (see fig. 10.4). The server will tell you what position you are in the search queue and the estimated time of completion of your search, usually in minutes and seconds.

II

Browsing with Mosaic

Fig. 10.4

The Telnet window shows a search being performed on an Archie server.

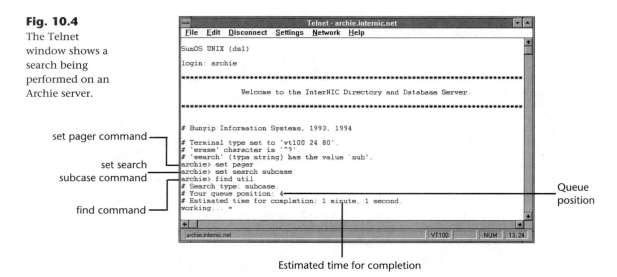

set pager command ⎯

set search subcase command

find command ⎯

Queue position

Estimated time for completion

7. After Archie finishes searching its database for files that match what you're looking for, it displays the results a page at a time (see fig. 10.5). For each matching file, Archie displays several pieces of information that can help you download the file:

   ■ The computer on which the file is located (giving the host name and Internet address numbers for the host).

   ■ The last time that the Archie server connected to this host system to update its database. This date can be important, because the file may have been deleted from the displayed computer system after the Archie server updated its database. If the date displayed for the last update is more than a few weeks old, you may want to choose a different matching file.

   ■ The location of the matching file (generally a directory on the host machine) and information about the matching file, such as the full name, the size of the file, and when the file was created.

8. Press the space bar to move to the next page of output. You should note the names of the servers that have a recent copy of the file you're look-ing for so that you can connect to one of these servers using anony-mous FTP and retrieve the file.

9. Type **q** to get back to the main Archie prompt. You can do this at any time while viewing the search results.

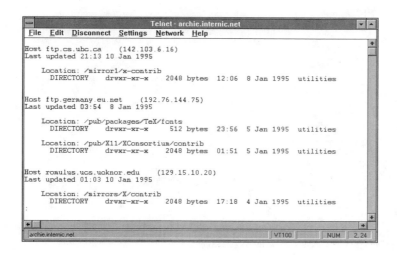

Fig. 10.5
The Telnet
window shows the
result of the Archie
search for fyi.

10. After you finish searching the Archie database, type **quit** at the archie>
prompt. This disconnects you from the Archie server, but leaves your
Telnet window open. If you're not going to be making any other Telnet
connections, you can close the Telnet window.

Using Mosaic to Access UseNet Newsgroups

One of the Internet protocols that Mosaic can use directly is the UseNet news
protocol (properly called the NNTP protocol). This protocol allows Mosaic to
browse and load UseNet newsgroups. These newsgroups are discussion groups
that cover thousands of different topics.

◀ See "Get the
News with
Newsgroups,"
p. 17

Setting Up Mosaic to Read UseNet Newsgroups

To read newsgroups, you must be able to specify a news server to which
Mosaic can connect. If you're directly connected to the Internet and have
a local news server at your site, your system administrator probably has
preconfigured your mosaic.ini file to use this server. If you have dialed in to
a SLIP or PPP connection, ask your Internet provider whether it has a news
server, or knows of one, to which you can connect. You must then enter the
name of the news server on the Services sheet of the Preferences dialog box.
Open the **O**ptions menu and choose **P**references. Choose the Services tab to
open the Services sheet; then enter the name of your news server in the
NNTP Server text box as shown in figure 10.6.

Fig. 10.6

You need to specify your UseNet news server in the Servers box on the Services sheet of the Preferences dialog box.

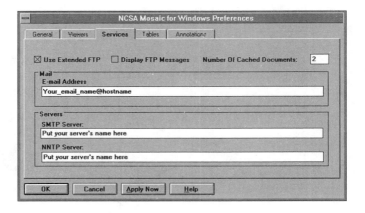

Reading UseNet Newsgroups

Mosaic is actually not an elegant interface to UseNet. To understand why, you must understand something about the structure of UseNet. UseNet is a collection of thousands of different discussion groups. Each group has a main topic that, hopefully, the participants stick to; but, under that main topic, there may be dozens of sub-topics, with hundreds or even thousands of messages in a single group.

There are many different newsreaders, but there are a number of features that are common to most newsreaders. One basic feature shared by most newsreaders is some method of telling you the names of the newsgroups that exist on your news server so that you can choose which groups you want to read from that list. Some newsreaders group all of the articles related to a particular topic so that you can glance over the headers and skip to the next topic in which you're interested. Many newsreaders allow you to post follow-up messages (reply to a post with a post of your own), and messages on a new sub-topic. And, a useful feature found in a number of newsreaders allows you to automatically exclude posts on topics in which you're not interested, or from people you dislike. Unfortunately, the Mosaic UseNet interface lacks all of these features.

From the Mosaic UseNet interface, there's no way of finding the names of any of the newsgroups that exist. Messages are shown in the order that the news server received them, with the newest messages displayed first. No topic grouping of any kind is possible. You can't post messages from Mosaic; you can only read them. And there's no way of excluding messages in advance (by topic or author). Mosaic's only advantages are that news articles read with Mosaic are nicely formatted, and Mosaic provides direct links from follow-up articles to related articles.

An Example of Reading News with Mosaic

The following is an example of reading the newsgroup **news.announce.newusers**. You should read this newsgroup to familiarize yourself with UseNet before you dive in.

Tip
UseNet URLs consist of the protocol **news:** followed by the name of the newsgroup.

1. Open the **F**ile menu and choose **O**pen URL.

2. Enter the URL for the newsgroup you want to read in the URL field of the Open URL dialog box (for example, **news:news.announce. newusers**). A list of article titles preceded by bullets appears, as shown in figure 10.7.

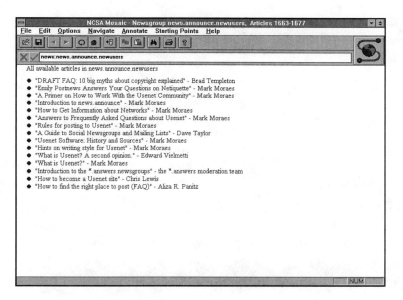

Fig. 10.7
The list of current articles in the newsgroup **news.announce. newusers**.

Browsing with Mosaic

II

3. Click a title that interests you. The body of that article appears in the document viewing area. For example, figure 10.8 shows the body of the article *Introduction to news.announce*.

   The top of the window contains the date of the posting, followed by the author's name on the next line. The title of the article appears next. After that is a list of other newsgroups where the article is posted (posting to multiple groups is called *crossposting*). Next is some historical information about the article, followed by the actual text of the article.

4. You now can click one of the newsgroup names to read that newsgroup, or open the **N**avigate menu and choose **B**ack to return to the list of articles.

Fig. 10.8
The date of posting, author, and title appear at the top of the display, with the crossposted newsgroups and text of the article following the header information.

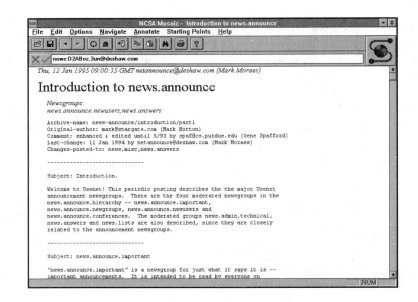

If the article shown in figure 10.8 were a follow-up article (which it is not), there would be references to the original articles before the article text. These references are hyperlinks to the original articles. If you click these hyperlinks, the original articles are loaded (if they're still on your news server).

If you read a newsgroup that has more than one page of articles, there are hyperlinks at the top (Earlier Articles) and bottom (Later Articles) of each page that move you backward and forward in the list of articles.

> **Note**
>
> If you want a WWW browser that gives you the capability to post new and follow-up messages (and has other convenient features) you should probably try Netscape.

▶ See "Using Other Internet Services," p. 250

Using Mosaic to Access WAIS

One of the big problems with the Internet is that there's no central information source where you can find the location of items that interest you. You can always connect to servers that you know exist and just browse around them looking for things that might be of interest to you. However, there is an Internet service, called WAIS, that is specifically designed to locate information sources on the Internet. WAIS allows you to search a set of databases that have been indexed with keywords, and returns addresses where you can locate documents that would be of interest to you.

If you want to do a WAIS search, you first have to connect to a WAIS server. Although Mosaic directly supports WAIS protocol, it does so only on UNIX at this time. However, if you want to use WAIS from Windows Mosaic, you have a number of options. You can use Telnet to connect to a WAIS server, find a Gopher server that has a WAIS form, or use one of the WAIS to WWW gateway forms.

Using WAIS to Search for Information

One way to do a WAIS search is to Telnet to a public WAIS server. This type of search requires you to use a text-based interface, which is not as convenient as a GUI. Another way to do a WAIS search is to connect to a Gopher server that offers WAIS as one of its menu items. Examples of both types of searches are given here.

Using WAIS from Telnet

There are a number of public sites that allow you to log in to WAIS servers—including **sunsite.unc.edu** (log in as **swais**) and **quake.think.com** (log in as **wais**). The following steps show you how to use the server at **quake.think.com**:

1. Open the **F**ile menu and choose **O**pen URL.

2. Enter the URL **telnet://quake.think.com** in the URL field of the Open URL dialog box.

   Assuming that you have Telnet set up properly on your PC, a Telnet window opens with the login prompt shown in figure 10.9. (For more information about setting up Telnet to work with Mosaic, see the section "Using Mosaic to Access Telnet" earlier in this chapter.)

3. You're asked to provide an account to log in to. Type **wais** to log in and use a simple WAIS text-based client program.

4. You're asked to enter your Internet address. Then the system prompts for the kind of terminal you're using. Type **vt100** (see fig. 10.10).

   Now the remote computer system starts up the WAIS program. After a minute or so, you see the main screen shown in figure 10.11.

   Rather than look through all the databases available (there are hundreds of them), you can use a directory of databases, called the directory-of-servers, to find ones containing the information you want.

Fig. 10.9
Connecting
to the public WAIS
server at
quake.think.com.

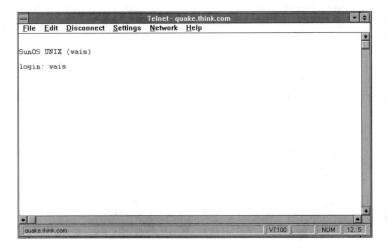

Fig. 10.10
Most computer
systems and
communications
programs let you
use the terminal
type vt100. If you
use a different
terminal type, you
can enter that type
here instead.

5. The WAIS program on the **quake.think.com** machine lets you look for a particular database by typing a slash (/) and the name of the database, and then pressing Enter. Because you want to find the directory-of-servers database, type **/directory-of-servers** (your screen should look like figure 10.12), and then press Enter. Other WAIS programs may use a different command.

6. Press the space bar to tell the program that you want to use this database. An asterisk appears next to the line containing the database name.

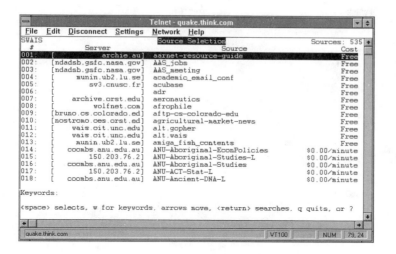

Fig. 10.11
The WAIS main screen shows the different databases of information that are available for you to search.

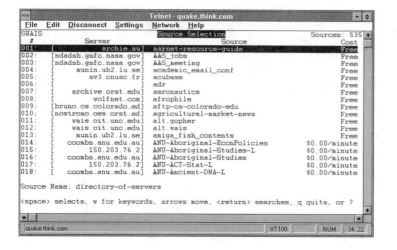

Fig. 10.12
Note that the slash you typed doesn't show up, but causes the program to prompt for the Source Name (the database you want to search).

II

Browsing with Mosaic

7. To look for the information you want within the selected database, do a keyword search (by using the w command), Enter **w** (which prompts you for keywords) followed by your keyword(s). Figure 10.13 shows a search for the word "clinton."

When you press Enter to start the search, the system goes through the directory-of-servers database looking for all the databases that have information about the keyword(s) you entered. You see a list of any matches it finds on a new screen, as shown in figure 10.14.

Fig. 10.13

The WAIS search screen has the directory-of-servers starred and the word "clinton" entered in the command line.

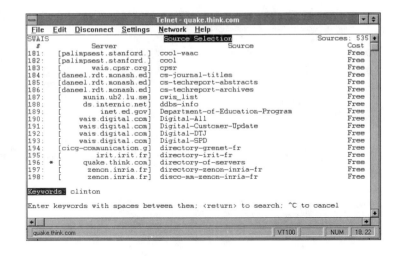

Fig. 10.14

In this example, the search finds two databases: clinton-speechess and White-House-Papers.

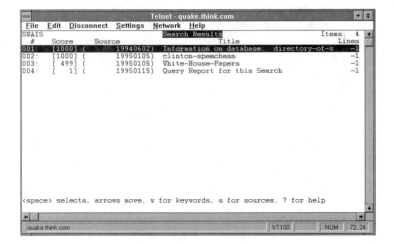

Note

If you press the space bar while on the directory search results screen, information about the selected directory displays.

---

8. Go back to the list of databases by typing **s**.

9. Press the space bar to tell WAIS that you won't be searching through the directory-of-servers database any more (the asterisk next to the entry disappears).

10. You should now use one of the databases returned from your search of the directory-of-servers to try to find the information that you're interested in. Type / followed by the name of the database.

> **Note**
>
> You can use just a part of the database name when searching, if the part is unique.

11. Press the space bar to tell WAIS to use this database for searching. An asterisk appears next to the database listing.

12. Now search the database for keywords related to the information you're looking for using the **w** command again. You can enter multiple words to make the search more specific to your topic.

The WAIS program looks through the database for documents with these words in them, and assigns a score to each one. The better the match with the search words, the higher the score is. So, if documents with all of your search words in them are available, they will have a high score and appear near the top of the results list. See figure 10.15 for an example of a search result.

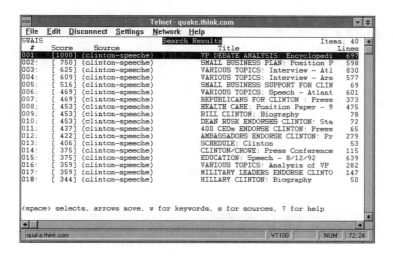

Fig. 10.15
After searching the database clinton-speechess for the keywords "clinton," "atlanta," and "georgia," the system finds a number of documents that matched at least some of the keywords.

13. To display a document, move to the document and press the space bar (see fig. 10.16). Press the down-arrow key to move down one document in the list. Press the up-arrow key to move up one document in the list.

Fig. 10.16
The WAIS program displays the document, a copy of a speech given by President Clinton in Atlanta, Georgia.

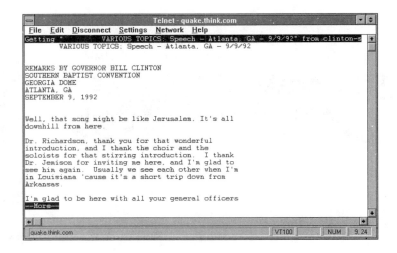

Tip
You can get more information about the WAIS commands by typing **h** or **?** in the WAIS program.

You can quit the WAIS program by typing **q**. This terminates the connection to **quake.think.com**, but leaves the Telnet window open. If you're not going to make any other Telnet connections, close the Telnet window.

Using WAIS from a Gopher Server

There are a number of public Gopher servers that give you access to WAIS servers—including **launchpad.unc.edu** and **gopher-gw.micro.umn. edu**. The following steps show you how to use the Gopher server at **launchpad.unc.edu** to do a WAIS search:

1. Open the File menu and choose **O**pen URL.

2. Enter the URL **gopher://launchpad.unc.edu** in the URL field of the Open URL dialog box. You get a short Gopher menu.

3. Select the menu item Surfing the Net! This loads a menu that contains, among other things, the item Search WAIS Based Information.

4. Select Search WAIS Based Information. This brings up a list of WAIS search directories.

5. Scroll down through the list of servers until you find the entry directory-of-servers.src—it should be a little over halfway through the list (see fig. 10.17).

6. Selecting this menu item loads a search form in the document viewing area that interfaces to a WAIS server to allow you to do a keyword search on the master list of databases. You should see something similar to what is shown in figure 10.18.

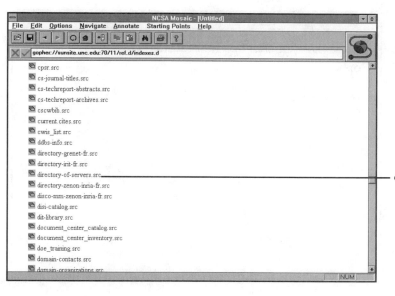

Fig. 10.17
Search the directory-of-servers to get a list of directories that contains the information you're looking for.

— directory-of-servers entry

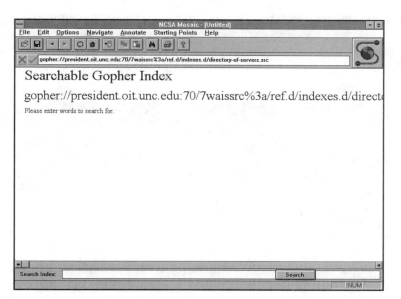

Fig. 10.18
The WAIS search form allows you to search for keywords in the selected database.

7. Click in the area next to the Search Index at the bottom of the screen, type in a keyword describing the information you want to search for, and then press Enter. A list of databases containing items that match your search displays (see fig. 10.19).

Fig. 10.19

The result of the WAIS search for the word "clinton" shows the clinton-speechess and White-House-Papers databases.

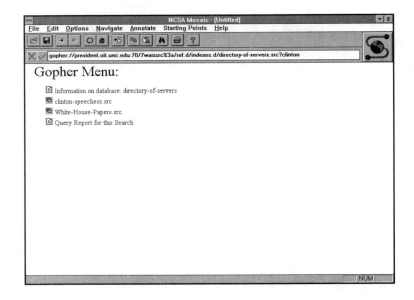

8. You now can search the databases that were found by your initial search for documents that contain the information you're interested in. Use the **B**ack command from the **N**avigate menu twice to return to the list of WAIS databases. Scroll through the list until you find one of the databases that matches your initial keyword search.

> **Note**
>
> When the list of matching databases is returned from your initial search, you would think that you should be able to click these databases and continue the search from that point, but the Gopher server returns an error when you try to do this. Instead, return to the master list of databases and search from there. (If you use a WAIS server from a Telnet connection, you also have to return to the main list of servers to continue the search.)

9. Click the database that you want to search through and another search form appears. Enter the keywords that you would like to search for in the Search Index box, and press Enter (you can enter multiple words separated by a space to narrow the search). A list of documents appears in the document viewing area (see fig. 10.20).

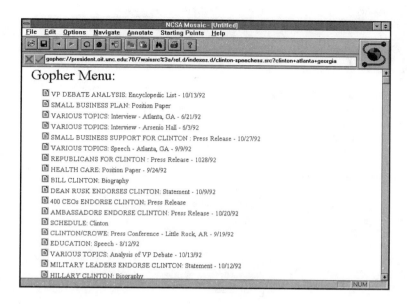

Fig. 10.20
The list of documents is the result of doing a search on the words "clinton atlanta georgia."

You now can click the documents to view them. After you finish, open the **N**avigate menu and choose **B**ack to return to the search window. From here, you can navigate back to other menus on this Gopher or go to a completely new URL.

Using a WAIS to WWW Gateway Form

WAIS Inc., provides a WWW form to let you do WAIS searches more easily. Using this form is comparable to using one of the Gopher-based WAIS search forms, but is a little easier to use. Although the form is designed to let you search databases quickly, it does not appear to work exactly as advertised at this time. However, you still can use it to do your WAIS searches.

1. Open the **F**ile menu and choose **O**pen URL.

2. Enter the URL **http://server.wais.com/waisgate-announce.html** in the URL field of the Open URL dialog box. This puts you at the WAIS search information page (see fig. 10.21).

3. To search for databases that contain the information you are looking for, click the directory of servers link. The search page in figure 10.22 appears.

Fig. 10.21

The WAIS Inc. WAISGATE page gives you access to a WAIS search form and other information about WAIS searches.

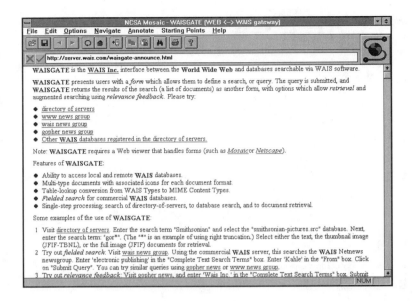

Fig. 10.22

The WAIS search form gives you a description of the database you are searching, tells you whether there is any cost involved in doing the search, and allows you to enter the search string.

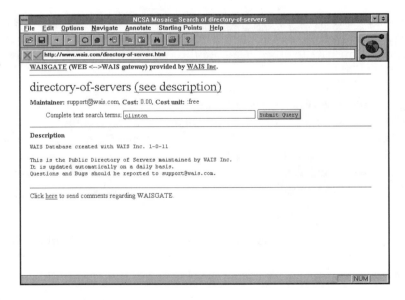

4. Enter the keywords you want to search for and choose Submit Query. When the search is finished, a list of databases that contain documents matching the keywords is shown at the end of the form (see fig. 10.23).

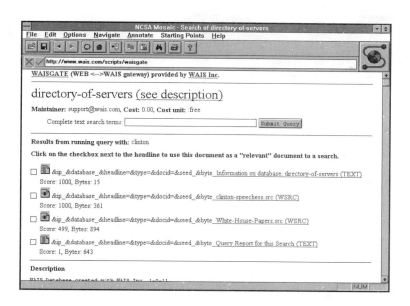

Fig. 10.23
When you search the directory-of-servers, the list of databases that match your keyword search is displayed at the end of the search form.

5. The instructions seem to indicate that you should be able to click the check box next to the database you want to search and then enter keywords in the text box and choose Submit Query to search that database. This does not work in Mosaic, however (see the Caution that follows for more information about this problem). In order to search one of the databases in the list, you must go back to the WAISGATE information page shown in figure 10.21 and choose the Other WAIS databases registered in the directory of servers link to bring up the entire list of databases.

6. Scroll through this list of databases until you find the one that you want to search. Click it and you get another form like the one in figure 10.22. Enter the keywords you want to search for and choose Submit Query. A list of items in that database that match the keywords is shown at the end of the form (see figure 10.24). You can click one of these items to load it (if it is text or HTML), or start a viewer for it if you have a viewer defined for that file type.

II

Browsing with Mosaic

Fig. 10.24
When you search a database, the items that match your keywords are shown at the end of the search form.

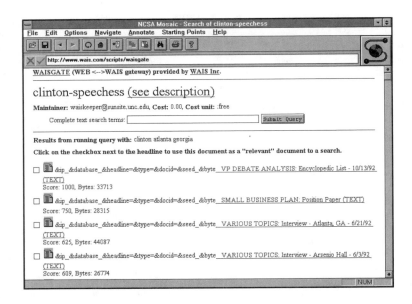

Caution

This form seems to have been designed using HTML statements that cannot be understood by Mosaic, but are understood by Netscape. When the search results are returned in Mosaic, you see HTML statements preceding the names of the databases or documents in the list. When you try to load the documents, you get an error from Mosaic.

If you use this form from Netscape, you don't see the HTML code in the results lists, and it loads the documents with no problems when you click them. In addition, when you search the directory of servers and get the list of databases that contain documents that match your keywords, you don't need to go back to the complete list of databases to search through one of the matching ones. All you need to do is click the database you want to search in the results list, and a new form allowing you to search that database appears. If you want to use this form as it is currently, you should really do it from Netscape.

Retrieving a WAIS Document

WAIS servers were designed for viewing documents, not for retrieving them. So, if you use WAIS via Telnet, there's really no way of retrieving the document that you're viewing (unless the WAIS server shows you the actual address of the file you're viewing—then you can use anonymous FTP to retrieve the file). When you use WAIS from a Gopher server, however, you can use Mosaic's file-saving features to store the file on your local disk.

If you want to save the document you're reading, there is a **S**ave option under the **F**ile menu. The steps for saving a file using the Save command are as follows:

1. While you're viewing a document that you want to save, open the **F**ile menu and choose **S**ave. A Save As dialog box appears, like the one shown in figure 10.25, asking you where you want to save the file.

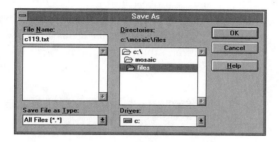

2. Fill in the information in the dialog box and choose OK. Mosaic attempts to save the file to your local disk.

There's another way you can save files from Mosaic. The following procedure saves the file associated with a URL to a file on your PC:

1. Open the **O**ptions menu and choose **L**oad to Disk.

2. Click the hyperlink for the document that you want to save. A Save As dialog box appears, like the one shown in figure 10.25, asking you where you want to save the file.

3. Fill in the information in the dialog box and choose OK. Mosaic attempts to load that URL to disk instead of displaying it in the document viewing area.

If you forget to turn off Load to Disk after saving a document, Mosaic tries to load the URL of the next hyperlink you click to disk instead of loading it to view. If this happens, you have to choose Cancel in the Save As window, and then turn off Load to Disk before you can view another document.

Tip
To save a document instead of viewing it, place the cursor on the hyperlink, click the right mouse button, and select **L**oad Anchor to Disk.

Fig. 10.25
You can save a file to anywhere on your local directory system.

Tip
To save the file you are viewing to disk, choose **O**ptions **L**oad to Disk; then choose Reload from the **N**avigate menu. The Save As dialog box appears.

Tip
To load a single file to disk, you can Shift-click the hyperlink rather than choose **L**oad to Disk. This loads only that one file to disk, and you don't have to worry about forgetting to turn off **L**oad to Disk.

II

Browsing with Mosaic

Using Mosaic to Access E-Mail

Windows Mosaic gives you a limited capability to use e-mail from WWW documents. If a document contains a URL that uses the `mailto:` protocol, you can send mail to the address specified in that URL. You cannot read e-mail at all from Mosaic, nor can you use the Open URL dialog to send mail to any address.

In order to send mail at all, you must have access to a mail server that Mosaic can use. If you're directly connected to the Internet and have a local mail server at your site, your system administrator probably has preconfigured your mosaic.ini file to use this server. If you have dialed in to a SLIP or PPP connection, ask your Internet provider whether it has a mail server, or knows of one, that you can use. You must then enter the name of the mail server on the Services sheet of the Preferences dialog box. Open the **O**ptions menu and choose **P**references. Choose the Services tab to open the Services sheet, then enter the name of your mail server in the SMTP Server text box as shown in figure 10.26.

Fig. 10.26

You need to specify your mail server in the Servers box on the Services sheet of the Preferences dialog box.

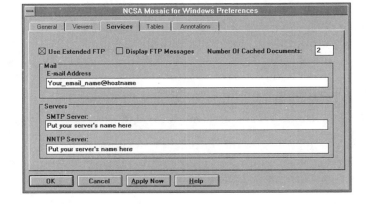

Once you have your mail server configured, you can send mail from any URL that uses the `mailto:` protocol. When you click a link containing one of these URLs, you get a Mail dialog box like the one shown in figure 10.27. Enter the Subject and text of your message. (Mosaic does not let you send the message if you leave either of these fields blank.) Then choose **S**end to send the mail, or **A**bort to cancel it. If you send the mail, a confirmation dialog asks if you really want to send the mail to that address. If you choose **Y**es (and your mail server is correctly specified), the mail is sent. Choose **N**o to abort the mail at this point.

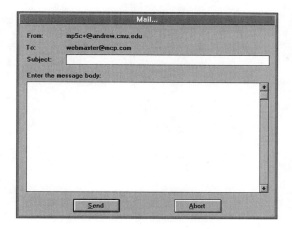

Fig. 10.27
Mosaic fills in the
From field with
your e-mail address
as you've config-
ured it, and the To
field with the
address in the URL.

From Here...

Mosaic and many of the other WWW browsers allow you to do much more
than just view WWW documents. You can access many other Internet services directly through URLs, and those that can't be accessed through URLs
are often accessible from easy-to-use forms.

To learn more about using the WWW and Mosaic, refer to the following
chapters:

- Chapter 1, "Introduction to the World Wide Web," gives you background information about the WWW and the Internet.

- Chapter 6, "Navigating with Mosaic," familiarizes you with the Mosaic
  features that help you find and view documents on the WWW.

- Chapter 9, "Gopher and Mosaic," gives you general information on
  using Gopher servers.

II

Browsing with Mosaic

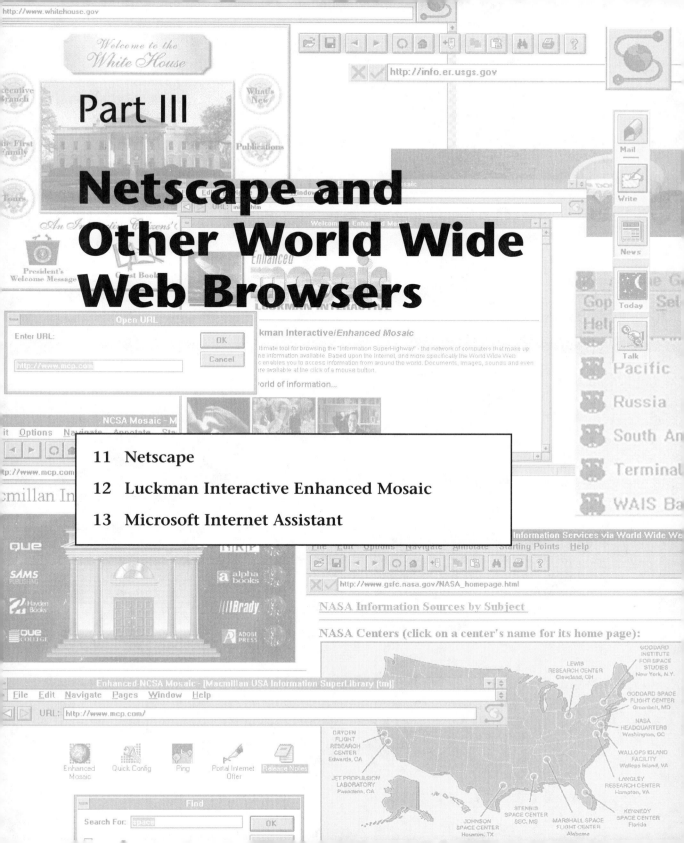

Part III

Netscape and Other World Wide Web Browsers

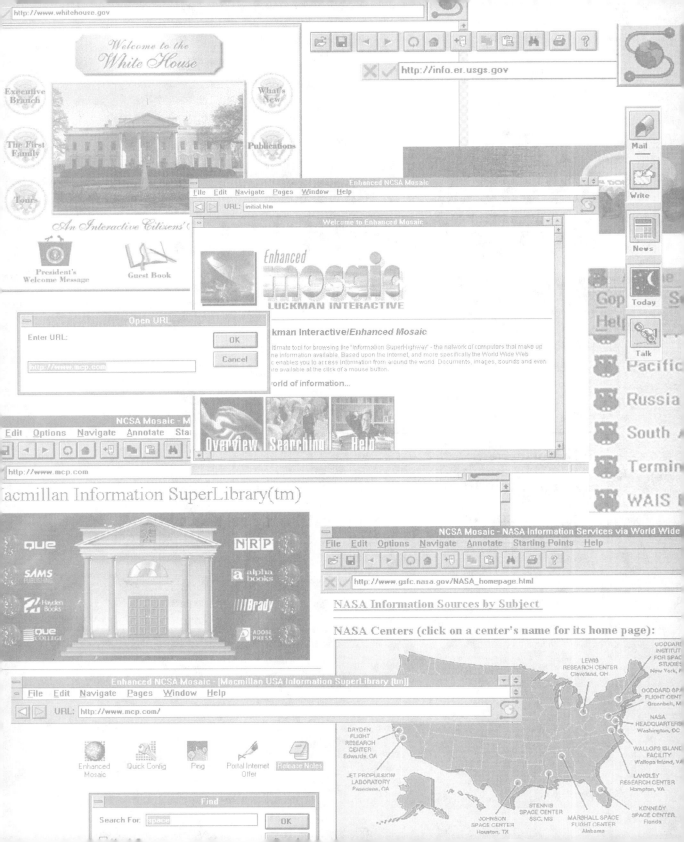

Chapter 11

Netscape

by Mary Ann Pike

Netscape is another popular Web browser that you can pick up on the Net. Although not free, Netscape is no more expensive than many of the commercial games that you might purchase—and it's a great deal more useful. Netscape has many nice features, including background image loading, secure data transmission, and multiple document windows.

In this chapter, you learn how to do the following:

- How to find and install Netscape 1.0

- How to use the Netscape interface

- How to navigate the Web with Netscape

- How to customize Netscape to your taste

Getting Netscape Up and Running

Trying the Netscape browser is easy. If you have an FTP program, you can retrieve the browser and evaluate it for 30 days for free (after that, you have to register and pay for it). Before you get the software, however, you should make sure that your system is properly set up to run Netscape. When you do get the Netscape software, you probably will want to get some external applications that allow you to automatically view movies, hear sounds, and experience all the multimedia documents that are available on the Web.

Will Your Computer Run Netscape?

Before you can run Netscape for Windows on your personal computer, you must make sure that your computer system is capable of running the software. Although this requirement may seem to be fairly basic, it is disappointing (not to mention annoying) to spend several hours getting software and setting it up, only to discover that Netscape does not run under your operating system or that your modem is too slow to use Netscape effectively.

First, your computer system must be capable of running Microsoft Windows version 3.1 or later (for example, Windows NT or Windows for Workgroups). If you do not already have Windows 3.1 or later, you must purchase and install this software before you can run Netscape.

The basic Netscape for Windows configuration requires about 2M of disk space for the Netscape software and documentation. You also need some temporary disk space (about 1M) to hold the compressed Netscape files while you are unpacking them. In addition to this basic disk space requirement, Netscape requires some disk space to hold temporary files while it is running; disk space for documents that you want to store locally; and disk space for any viewers that you need to display movies, image files, sound files, and so on.

Needless to say, if you want to take full advantage of Netscape and use it to browse the WWW, you need an Internet account. If your PC is not directly connected to the Internet via Ethernet and you are using a SLIP or PPP connection, you need a relatively fast modem (14,400 bps is the minimum recommended speed, although the Netscape documentation says that 9600 will work).

In addition to the system requirements, Netscape for Windows requires a direct connection to the Internet, through an Ethernet card in your system or through some kind of modem connection. If you need help getting a connection to the Internet, see Chapter 2, "Connecting to the World Wide Web."

Where to Get Netscape and Associated Software

Although the Netscape software is not free, it is available through anonymous FTP. Netscape Communications is allowing people to pick up the software from its FTP site, use the software for a 30-day trial period, and then pay for the software (a moderate $39 at the time this book went to press) if they decide to keep it. This section discusses how to get this software and any additional software that you will need to run Netscape.

The basic Netscape software is available through anonymous FTP at the machine **ftp.mcom.com** under the Netscape directory. This site has versions of Netscape for several different machine types, but you are interested in the Netscape software for PC machines running Windows, located in the file ns16-100.exe.

If you have a Windows-based FTP program, such as WS_FTP (included on the WinCD that comes with this book), and you want to retrieve the Netscape software from the Internet, use the following procedure:

1. Connect to your Internet provider.

2. Start the FTP program.

3. Click **C**onnect, and enter the address of the site that you are using. Enter **anonymous** as the user ID and your e-mail address as the password.

4. Navigate to the directory that you need by double-clicking the directory name in the Remote System window.

> **Note**
>
> When you retrieve the Netscape software, transfer it directly to a temporary directory where you can unpack it.

5. When you reach the correct directory, select the files to be transferred from the Remote System window, and then click the left-arrow button to make the transfer.

> **Note**
>
> Transferred files are saved in the directory in the Local System window. To change this directory, click the desired directory.

6. After transferring all the files you need, click **C**lose to close your FTP connection; then click E**x**it to exit FTP.

You may encounter one problem in obtaining the Netscape software; because this software is so popular, the mcom site often is very busy. A limited number of users can connect to the site at the same time; at busy times, you may not be able to connect. If this happens, be patient and try again.

III

Other Browsers

Another thing to keep in mind when you are looking for this software is that just as you move files around on your computer, the system administrators of the FTP sites occasionally move files or rename directories. If you can't find the files that you are looking for, look in another directory; they may be somewhere else.

Obtaining Auxiliary Software for Netscape

◀ See "How to Find Multime-dia Viewers," p. 88

Although Netscape directly displays the text and inline graphics from HTML documents, you may want to obtain additional software to enable Netscape to handle pictures, sounds, and animations (movies). Chapter 5, "Multime-dia—Using Viewers," discusses how to get and install viewers.

Installing Netscape on Your System

◀ See "Installing Multimedia Viewers," p. 92

After you obtain all the files you need to run Netscape on your PC, you can go through the process of getting the software ready to run. This section covers the steps necessary to set up the basic Netscape software. (For a discus-sion of installing auxiliary viewer applications, see Chapter 5, "Multimedia—Using Viewers.")

To set up the software, follow these steps:

1. If you did not transfer the ns16-100.exe file directly into a temporary directory where it can be unpacked, move this file into a temporary directory.

2. Execute the file to unpack the Netscape software. Simply enter the file name as a DOS command, or double-click the file name in the Win-dows File Manager.

3. Open the **F**ile menu and choose **R**un.

Tip
You also can double-click setup.exe in File Manager to execute it.

4. If the temporary directory that you used is called c:\temp, type the command **c:\temp\setup** in the Run dialog box. Then choose OK to run the setup program.

5. Click **C**ontinue in the first installation dialog box (see fig. 11.1).

6. The next dialog box asks where you want to install your Netscape soft-ware (see fig. 11.2). Change the path, if necessary, and then click **C**ontinue.

7. The next dialog box asks in which program group you want to place the Netscape icon (see fig. 11.3). The default is a new Netscape group; you can specify your own new group name, or you can select one of your

existing groups. Click **C**ontinue to install Netscape and create a program group for it.

Fig. 11.1
The initial Netscape setup dialog box.

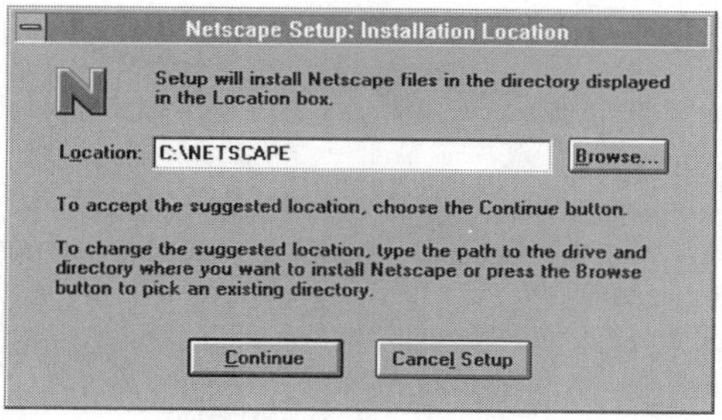

Fig. 11.2
You are prompted for your Netscape directory.

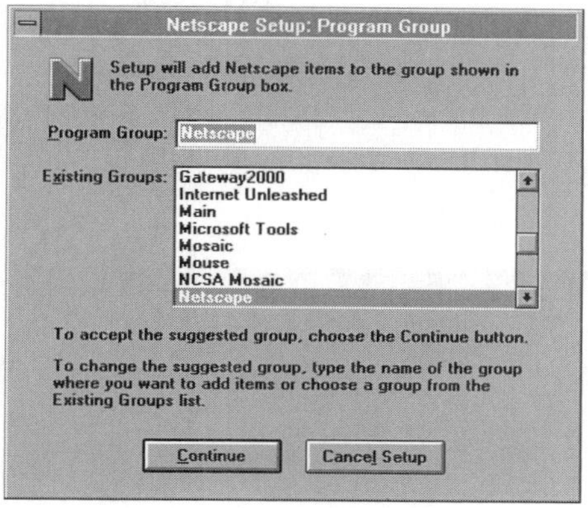

Fig. 11.3
You are prompted for your Netscape program-group information.

8. The progress of the installation is shown in a linear graph. When the installation is complete, you see the dialog box shown in figure 11.4 that asks if you want to read Netscape's README file now. Click **Y**es to read the file or **N**o to exit the installation.

III

Other Browsers

Fig. 11.4
A dialog box asks
if you want to read
the README file
now.

Note

The readme.txt file tells you how to find information about the new features
and known problems of Netscape. This information can be found at the URL
**http://home.mcom.com/home/released/netscape/windows/
relnotes-1.0N.html**).

The readme file also tells you how to get in touch with the developers to
provide them with feedback. If you need to contact the developers, open
the **H**elp menu and select How To Give **F**eedback, or send e-mail to
win_cbug@mcom.com. If you are reporting a problem, let the developers
know what version of Netscape Navigator you are using, what your hardware
configuration is, and what operating system you are running under. Also, be
as specific as possible in describing the problem, and provide a URL that ex-
emplifies the problem if possible.

9. When you exit the installation, the Netscape program group, shown in
   figure 11.5, appears in your Program Manager. (You can shrink the
   program group to a more appropriate size.) Alternatively, the Netscape
   icon appears in the new or existing program group that you specified
   during setup.

Fig. 11.5
The installed
Netscape program
group.

10. The setup of the Netscape software is complete. You can remove the temporary directory in which you unpacked the software, if you want; it is no longer needed.

Although you can customize the Netscape software to meet your needs, you can run the software without any further work. You will, of course, need to set up your Internet-connection software before using Netscape to access WWW documents.

Using the Netscape Interface

After you installed all the software that you need to run Netscape, you can connect to your Internet provider and start Netscape. Netscape is a very powerful application, but it is graphically oriented and not difficult to use after you are familiar with all of its features.

Starting Netscape

Before starting Netscape, you should be connected to the Internet. If your Internet connection is via your LAN, be sure that you are logged on to your network. If you are connected to the Internet through a modem, start your TCP/IP software, and log in to your account.

After you establish your Internet connection, open the Netscape program group (or whatever program group you put Netscape in), and double-click the Netscape icon. You are ready to explore the Internet with Netscape.

The Netscape License

The first time you start Netscape, you see the Netscape License Agreement dialog box shown in figure 11.6. If you choose Accept, you agree to the terms specified in this document. (You can use the scroll bar to read the entire document.) If you choose Do Not Accept, Netscape will not start.

Netscape is free for educational or not-for-profit use. For all other purposes, it can be used free of charge for a 30-day trial period, after which the user must send the specified registration fee ($39, as of the printing of this book) to Netscape Communications Corporation. Send e-mail to **info@mcom.com** or call 1-800-NETSITE for ordering and registration information.

III

Other Browsers

Fig. 11.6

The Netscape License Agreement dialog box appears the first time you start Netscape.

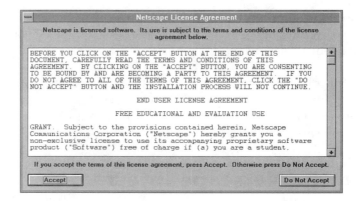

The Netscape Window

When Netscape starts, it loads the document that is specified as the home page in the Preferences dialog box (choose Options, Preferences). Unless you have specified a personal home page, your window should look like the one shown in figure 11.7 (which shows the default Netscape welcome page).

Fig. 11.7

The different parts of the Netscape window appear on the default Netscape Communications welcome page.

Toolbar   Title bar   Menu bar

Location bar ‌—

Directory buttons ‌—

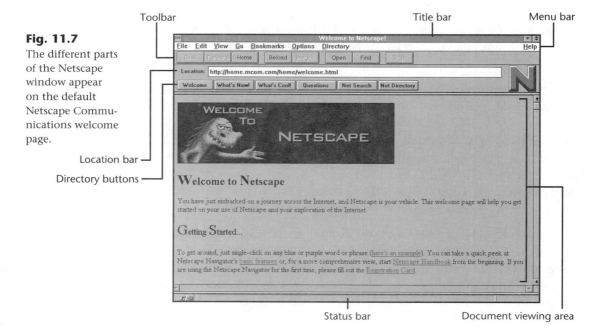

Status bar   Document viewing area

The full URL for the default home page is the following:

http://home.mcom.com/home/welcome.html

The following list briefly describes each window part. The remainder of this chapter contains detailed discussion of Netscape's features.

Tip
Don't load the Netscape welcome page as your home page. See "Telling Netscape What Home Page to Load," later in this chapter, for more information.

- The *title bar* contains the usual window-function buttons (Control-menu box, and Maximize and Minimize buttons), as well as the name of the application (Netscape) and the name of the WWW document that you are viewing.

- The *menu bar* gives you access to all the functions that you need to use Netscape. You can retrieve documents to view, print documents, customize your Netscape window, navigate between documents, annotate documents, save files, and access Netscape's online help system.

- The *location bar* shows the URL of the current document. When you open a document, its URL is displayed, and the Netscape logo (at the right end of the bar) blinks while the document is being retrieved.

- The *directory buttons* give you quick access to the items in the **D**irectory menu.

- The *document viewing area* is the area of the window in which you see the text of a document and any inline images that it may contain.

- The *status bar* serves two functions. While Netscape is loading your document, it shows the progress of the different document elements (text and individual graphics) that are being loaded. At the left end of the status bar, a counter shows the number of bytes loaded compared with the size of the document or image that is being loaded. At the right end of the status bar, a bar graph shows what percentage of the entire document has been loaded.

  When you are viewing a document, the status bar shows the URL of the hyperlink on which your cursor rests.

- The *toolbar* gives you quick access to some of the most-used features in Netscape (see fig. 11.8). By default, the toolbar contains buttons labeled to describe the actions that they perform. You can configure the toolbar to show pictures that represent the actions or pictures with the descriptions printed below them.

III

Other Browsers

Fig. 11.8
The buttons in the
toolbar are found
at the top of the
screen.

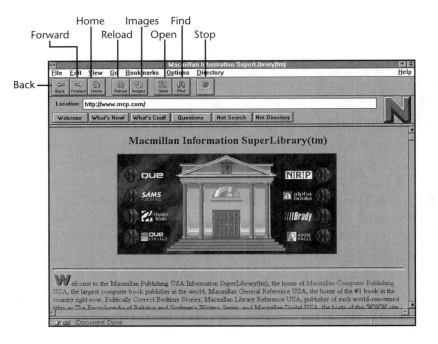

The following list provides basic descriptions of the toolbar buttons:

- *Back* displays the preceding document in the history list.

- *Forward* displays the following document in the history list.

- *Home* goes to the default home page.

- *Reload* reloads the current document.

- *Images* loads the images in a document, if you had image loading turned off.

- *Open* enables you to open a URL.

- *Find* locates a text string in the current document.

- *Stop* stops the loading process for the current document.

What Is a Home Page?

Your *home page* (or home document) is the document that you tell Netscape to display when it starts. This document should contain links to the documents and WWW sites that you use most frequently. Many people mistakenly use the term home page for the welcome page that you see when you connect to a WWW site. A home page gives you access to the WWW sites or documents that you use most. Your project or company may have its own home page to give members easy access to needed information. You can load someone else's home page or design your own.

When you start the Netscape software, it comes with the home page pre-defined as the Netscape Communications Corporation welcome page. You probably will want to change this page, because the Netscape page may not be very useful to you. In addition, retrieving a document causes a load on the machine on which the document is located. If everyone used the Netscape welcome page as his or her home page, the Netscape WWW server would become considerably slower.

Telling Netscape What Home Page to Load

Netscape allows you to set your home page in its Preferences dialog box. To use the Preferences dialog box, follow these steps:

1. Open the **O**ptions menu and choose **P**references. The Preferences dialog box appears.

2. Select Styles in the drop-down list at the top of the dialog box (see fig. 11.9).

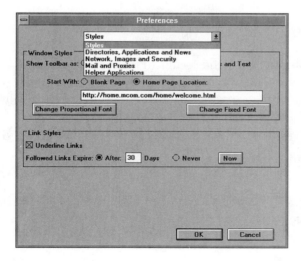

Fig. 11.9
Choose the Preferences page that you want to modify from the drop-down list at the top of the Preferences dialog box.

III

Other Browsers

3. Click the text box below the Home Page Location radio button (see fig. 11.10).

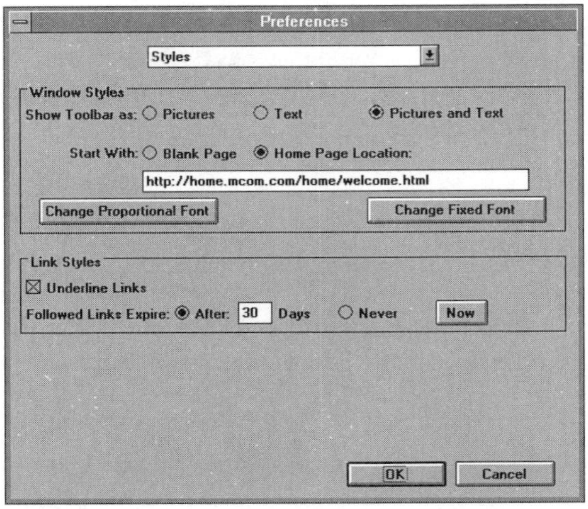

Fig. 11.10
Select Styles from
the drop-down list
in the Preferences
dialog box to set
the Netscape
home page.

4. Enter the URL of the document that you want to use as your home
   page.

5. Choose OK to save your home page setting and exit the Preferences
   dialog box.

Your home page can be a document on your computer or any document that
you can access at a WWW site. (See Chapter 14, "Creating Home Pages with
HTML," for details on creating your own home page or turning a file that's
saved on your computer into a home page.)

When you start Netscape, the document that you defined as your home page
will be displayed in the document viewing area. After the home page loads,
the URL for your home page appears in the location bar (if you have the location bar enabled). When your home page is loaded, you can click any of the
links on your home page to load the documents that you use frequently.

Tip
You can click the
Home button (the
one that looks like
a house, if you
have pictures
turned on) in the
toolbar to reload
your home page
quickly.

If you want to return to your home page at any time, open the **G**o menu and
choose **H**ome. This command reloads your home-page document.

You also can tell Netscape not to load any page when it starts. You can use
Netscape's Preferences dialog box to turn off the loading of a home page.
Follow these steps:

1. Open the **O**ptions menu and choose **P**references. The Preferences dialog
   box appears.

2. In the drop-down list at the top of the dialog box, select Styles.

3. Click the Blank Page radio button (see fig 11.11).

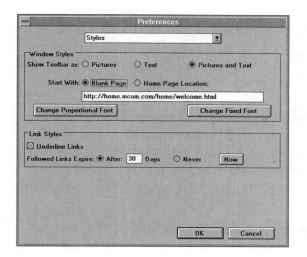

4. Choose OK to save your preferences and exit the Preferences dialog box.

When you start Netscape, your document viewing area will be blank, and you can begin your navigation of the WWW from there.

Moving between Documents

After you start Netscape, you can move between WWW documents in several ways; you can click links in the document that you are viewing, or you can use Netscape's Open Location dialog box to enter a URL. You can also type a URL directly into the text box in the location bar (press Enter at the end of the URL to load that document).

If you loaded a home page, that page probably includes links to other documents. After all, the purpose of the WWW is to enable you to move between related documents quickly, without having to enter long path names. If a document contains no links, it's not a very useful WWW document. But even if your current document has no links, you can still move between documents by entering the URLs for the documents that you want to view.

III

Other Browsers

> **Note**
>
> Netscape gives you a few other ways to move between documents. You can use bookmarks that contain items with predefined URLs. Creating and using bookmarks is covered in the section "Create Lists of Your Favorite URLs," later in this chapter.
>
> In addition, the Directory menu gives you access to some interesting, important Internet documents, and directory buttons enable you to load these documents.

Using Links to Move between Documents

◄ See "Hypertext and Hypermedia Concepts," p. 24

A link can be a word, a group of words, or an image. Netscape can indicate the hypertext links in a document in several different ways. If you have a color monitor, the links can be displayed in blue and other text in black. (Graphics that contain links can be outlined in blue.) If you have a black-and-white monitor, the links can be underlined (the default).

If you have a color display, Netscape enables you to keep track of the links that you've visited recently. After you load a document, the next time you come across a link to that document, the link is displayed in magenta rather than blue. You can set up Netscape so that the memory of your visit to a link expires after a certain period of time (or you can set it so that it never expires). You also can reset the expiration state of all links so that all links start out blue again.

When you move your cursor over an area of the screen that contains an active link, your cursor changes from an arrow to a pointing hand. The URL associated with each link that you pass over appears in the status bar (if the status bar is enabled). To activate a link, click it. Netscape loads that document and displays the URL for the document in the location bar (if the location bar is enabled).

Look at the Netscape home page in figure 11.12. The phrases, *here's an example, basic features*, *Netscape Handbook*, and *Registration Card* are links. When you run Netscape on a color display, you see the links in blue (they are underlined in the figure), which is the default hyperlink color. The URL of the active link (with the pointing-hand pointer over it) appears in the status bar.

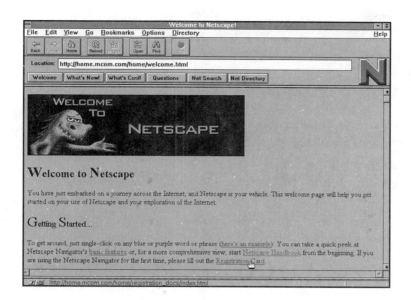

Fig. 11.12
The Netscape
home page shows
the hyperlinks
underlined.

Customizing the Hyperlink Indicators

You can change the default appearance and color of the hyperlinks in the
documents that Netscape loads. To customize Netscape's link attributes, follow these steps:

1. Open the **O**ptions menu and choose **P**references. The Preferences dialog
   box appears.

2. Select Styles from the drop-down list that appears at the top of the
   Preferences dialog box.

3. To have links underlined in a document or to get rid of the underlining, select the Underline Links check box in the Link Styles area of the
   dialog box (see fig. 11.13).

4. You can set the number of days after which followed links (URLs that
   you've previously loaded) expire. Click the box next to the After radio
   button, and enter the number of days. When the amount of time since
   you have accessed a link is longer than this time, the link becomes
   blue again.

   If you click the Never radio button, any link that you follow will be
   shown in magenta until you clear all links.

Fig. 11.13
Customize the link
appearance in the
Preferences dialog
box.

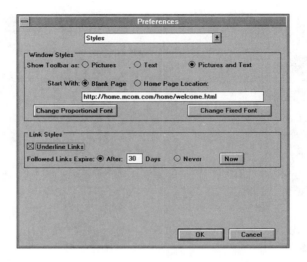

5. Click Now to clear the expiration information from all of your links immediately. A confirmation box appears, asking whether you definitely want to mark all of your links as not visited. If you choose **Y**es, all links will be displayed in blue, whether or not you have accessed them recently (until you access them again). Choose **N**o to leave the expiration information on your links as is.

6. When you have the options set to your satisfaction, choose OK.

Moving Backward and Forward

Typing long URLs and scrolling through documents to look for the links you want can get rather tedious. If you're jumping between several documents, take advantage of three helpful navigating commands: **B**ack, **F**orward, and **R**eload.

Netscape keeps information about what documents you have loaded (see the discussion of the history list in "How to Get Where You Were," later in this chapter) and allows you to move between these documents quickly by using the **B**ack and **F**orward commands. The **B**ack command takes you to the preceding document that you had open. To go back, open the **G**o menu and choose **B**ack.

The next command is **F**orward. What you have to remember about **F**orward is that you can move forward only after moving back. (This concept is rather confusing, but it will make more sense after you read about history lists in

"How to Get Where You Were," later in this chapter.) To move forward, open the **G**o menu and choose **F**orward.

The last command is **R**eload. This command redisplays the document that you are currently viewing. To reload the current document, open the **V**iew menu and choose **R**eload.

When you are reading documents, you often move back and forth between one document and others that are linked to that document. To keep from having to load a document every time you view it, Netscape keeps copies of the last few documents that you viewed on your local computer. Keeping copies of previously viewed documents is called *caching*.

Caching keeps Netscape from making unnecessary demands on Internet resources. Caching does take up resources on your own computer, though, so you can cache only a limited number of documents. Netscape enables you to specify the amount of memory and disk that it can use for caching. Follow these steps:

1. Open the **O**ptions menu and choose **P**references. The Preferences dialog box appears.

2. In the drop-down list at the top of the dialog box, select Network, Images, and Security.

3. The Network area enables you to set up the amount of memory and disk space that Netscape can use for caching (see fig. 11.14). The default settings are 600K of memory and 5M (5000K) of disk space.

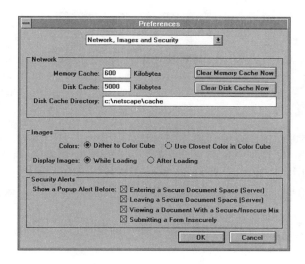

Fig. 11.14
Set the amount of memory and disk space to as much as you can spare to keep from reloading documents frequently.

III

Other Browsers

4. You can set the directory that Netscape uses for disk caching. To do so, enter the path in the Disk Cache Directory text box.

5. If you want to clear the current contents of your memory or disk caches, click Clear Memory Cache Now or Clear Disk Cache Now. When you click either of these buttons, a confirmation box asks whether you definitely want to clear that cache. If you click Yes, the cache is cleared immediately. Click No if you decide not to clear the cache.

6. When you have the options set to your satisfaction, choose OK.

Using URLs to Move between Documents

◀ See "Links and URLs Transport You From Place To Place," p. 27

If you don't want to go to any of the documents for which links are displayed in the current document, or if you did not load a home page (you do not currently have a document displayed), you can load a new document by specifying its URL to Netscape. Refer to Chapter 1, "Introduction to the World Wide Web," for information on how to correctly format a URL. To enter a URL directly, follow these steps:

1. Open the File menu and choose Open Location. The Open Location dialog box appears (see fig. 11.15). The URL for the last document that you loaded appears highlighted in the text box.

Fig. 11.15
The Open Location dialog box allows you to directly enter the URL for the next document that you want to view.

2. If you want to enter a new URL, begin typing the URL in the box; the old contents are deleted. If you want to modify the URL that is displayed, click the box; your cursor is inserted into the text, where you can edit the current URL.

Tip
Type a URL into the text box in the location bar and press Enter to open a document.

3. Choose Open to load the URL that you entered, or click Close if you do not want to load that document. If you choose OK, Netscape loads that document and displays the URL for the document in the location bar (if you have it enabled).

Opening Multiple Documents

A very useful feature of Netscape is its capability to display multiple documents at the same time. To open another document window, open the **F**ile menu and choose **N**ew Window. This window has the same history list as the window from which it was opened, with the displayed document being the oldest document in the history list. You now can view any document you want in any of the open Netscape document windows.

What You See When a Document Is Loaded

When you load a document, Netscape gives you a great deal of information about what is happening. The big N in the location bar blinks, the Stop button in the toolbar turns red, and messages appear in the status bar. All these signals help you follow the progress of a document load.

Status Bar Messages

Viewing a WWW document involves many different activities. Netscape needs to contact the server where the document lives, ask the server whether it has the document, and then ask the server to transfer that document to your computer. Through messages in the status bar, Netscape tries to tell you what steps have been accomplished and what still needs to be done as it is loading the document. These messages can include the following:

- `Connect: Looking up Host:<hostname>`

- `Connect: Contacting Host:<hostname>`

- `Connect: Host Contacted: Waiting for reply...`

- `Document: Received <nnn> of <nnnn> bytes`

- `Transferring data`

- `Document: Done`

The blinking N is a useful indicator of the status of the document load. A blinking N with no other action can be the first (and sometimes, the only) indication that a problem exists—if, for example, your counter stops increasing, even though it hasn't reached the full load size.

It is nice to be able to watch the counter increase (and the bar graph) as the elements of the document are loaded. These features give you an idea of how far along you are and how much longer you can expect to wait before the document is loaded.

III

Other Browsers

Stopping a Document Load

Occasionally, you may want to abort the loading of the current document. Perhaps you clicked a link inadvertently, or perhaps you discovered the document that you wanted to view contains huge graphics that you don't have time to download.

You can stop a document load in two ways. If your toolbar is displayed, click the Stop button to cancel the load. (The Stop button should be red while a document is loading.) You also can open the **G**o menu and choose **S**top Loading to abort the load.

You will find that if you stop a load, you are likely to get a partial copy of the document that was loading. (A Transfer interrupted! message probably will appear at the end of the partial document.) Open the **G**o menu and choose **B**ack to return to the preceding document, and continue your navigation from there.

Controlling the Loading of Graphics

Tip

The Images button in your toolbar becomes active when Auto Load Images is turned off.

Loading documents can take a few minutes, especially if the document contains many large graphics and your computer has a relatively slow (less than 9600 bps) connection to the Internet. You can do one thing to speed the loading of the document; tell Netscape not to load the inline graphics from the document. To do this, open the **O**ptions menu and choose **A**uto Load Images, as shown in figure 11.16.

Fig. 11.16

You can turn off image loading from the **O**ptions menu.

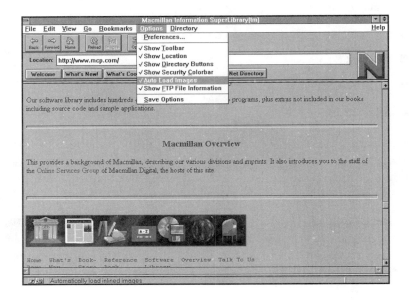

The next new document that you load will not have any graphics displayed; instead, placeholder icons will be displayed where the graphics should be (see fig. 11.17). To load the images in the current document, click the Images button in the toolbar, or open the **V**iew menu and choose Load **I**mages.

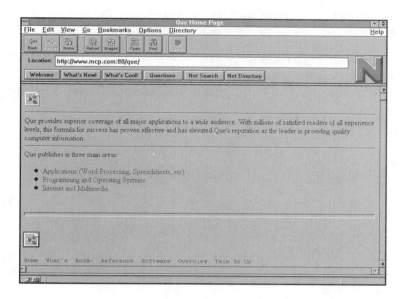

Fig. 11.17
When you tell Netscape not to load inline graphics, it places icons where the graphics would be.

You can configure several other image-related features of Netscape:

■ By default, Netscape begins to display an image while it loads it. You can set Netscape so that it loads an entire image first and then displays it. This procedure may be faster if you have a good Internet connection.

■ You also can set Netscape to dither colors so you can create the closest match to the color that is specified. It takes longer to do this, but it produces more accurate images.

■ You can set Netscape so that it displays the palette color closest to the one specified in the graphic. This method loads images faster, but the

III

Other Browsers

colors may be slightly off; however, it should be adequate for most graphics that you would be viewing online.

To set Netscape's image options, follow these steps:

1. Open the **O**ptions menu and choose **P**references. The Preferences dialog box appears.

2. In the drop-down list at the top of the dialog box, select Network, Images, and Security. The Images area of the dialog box enables you to specify how you want Netscape to load images and display colors (see fig. 11.18).

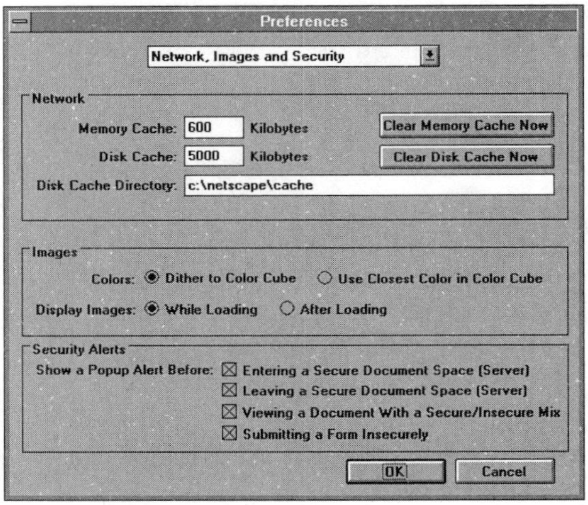

Fig. 11.18
The default image settings are Dither to Color Cube and Display Images While Loading.

3. Select the Colors and Display Images options you want.

4. Choose OK.

Looking for Information in a Document

If the WWW document that you are reading is short, you can scroll through the document (or press the PgUp and PgDn keys) to find information that interests you. If you have loaded a very long document, though, Netscape provides a quick way to look for information. Follow these steps:

1. Open the **E**dit menu and choose **F**ind to bring up the Find dialog box (see fig. 11.19).

Fig. 11.19
The Find dialog box enables you to specify the search words and the direction of the search.

2. In the Fi**n**d What text box, enter the word for which you want to search.

3. To specify the direction of the search, click **U**p (toward the beginning of the document) or **D**own (toward the end).

4. Click Match **C**ase if you want Netscape to match the exact capitalization of the word that you entered.

5. Choose **F**ind Next to begin the search. If a match is found, Netscape scrolls the window to the section where the match appears and highlights the matching text. An alert box informs you if no match is found.

Saving Documents

In general, the purpose of the World Wide Web is to provide one copy of a document that many people can view. At times, however, you may want to save a copy of a document to your local computer. Netscape gives you several options for saving documents.

The first way to save a document is to open the **F**ile menu and choose **S**ave As. The Save As dialog box appears, enabling you to browse through your directories and store the file wherever you want.

When you save an HTML document to your local disk, remember that the document probably contains hyperlinks. These links can be relative or absolute. An *absolute reference* contains the complete address of the document that is being referenced, including the host name, directory path, and file name. A *relative reference* assumes that the preceding machine and directory path are being used; only the file name (or possibly a subdirectory and file name) is specified.

If the document references other documents that have relative addresses, you cannot view those documents unless you copy them to your local disk and set them up with the same directory structure that they had at the original site. You may want to set up a document and its linked documents on your local disk, if you want to be able to view the document without connecting

Tip
Shift-click a link to save the document associated with that link to disk instead of displaying it.

III

Other Browsers

to the Internet. One problem is that if the original document changes, you are not aware that you are viewing an outdated version of the document.

Absolute references always work unless your Internet connection fails or the referenced documents are moved.

Printing Documents

In addition to being able to save documents, you can print documents directly from Netscape. Open the **F**ile menu and choose **P**rint to send a copy of the current document to your printer.

One of the nice features of Netscape is that you can preview the current document before printing it. Open the **F**ile menu and choose Print Pre**v**iew. Netscape creates a preview of the document in a separate window (see fig. 11.20). This preview window enables you to look at each page of the document, zooming in and out wherever you want. When you are satisfied with the print preview, you can print the document directly from this window.

Fig. 11.20
The print preview window enables you to see what your document will look like before it is printed.

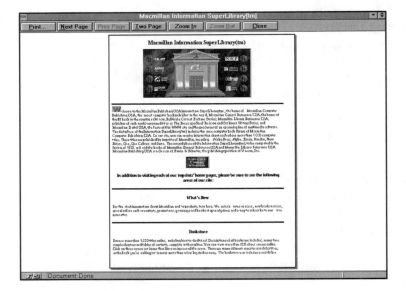

Customizing the Displayed Fonts

Unlike Mosaic, Netscape allows you to define only two basic fonts for your document window. One of these fonts is the *proportional font*, which is used for most of the text that you see in your window (the font size and style are varied to create distinctive headers and emphasize text). The other font is the *fixed font*, which is used for editable fields and some preformatted paragraphs.

Netscape allows you to specify the font family and size for the basic variety of each of these two fonts. Follow these steps:

1. Open the **O**ptions menu and choose **P**references. The Preferences dialog box appears.

2. In the drop-down list at the top of the dialog box, select Styles.

3. Click the button for the basic font that you want to change: either Change Proportional Font or Change Fixed Font. The Choose Base Font dialog box appears (see fig. 11.21).

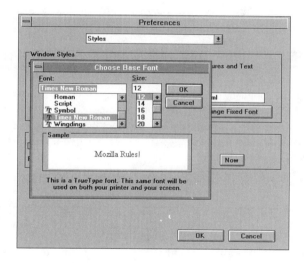

Fig. 11.21
The Choose Base Font dialog box allows you to define the font for each of the basic font types.

4. Scroll through the **F**ont list, and select the font family that you want to use.

5. If you want, set the font **S**ize that will be used for normal paragraph text (headings will be a variation on the size and style of this font).

6. Choose OK to make the selections take effect, or click Cancel if you decide not to change the fonts.

The changes that you make take effect immediately and are used by Netscape in future sessions.

III

Other Browsers

Customizing the Displayed Window Areas

Some of the window elements in Netscape are optional (not, however, the document viewing area; Netscape wouldn't be very useful without that!). The title bar and menu bar cannot be removed, but the toolbar, location bar, and directory buttons can be turned off. Turning off these window elements gives you a bigger viewing area, but it also removes some time-saving and informational features. The following list describes how to turn these features off (or back on):

■ To turn off the toolbar, open the **O**ptions menu and choose Show **T**oolbar.

■ To turn off the location bar, open the **O**ptions menu and choose Show **L**ocation.

■ To turn off the directory buttons, open the **O**ptions menu and choose Show **D**irectory Buttons.

Caution

If you remove two of the three bars at the top of the viewing area, the large blue N shrinks to a size that is more difficult to see. If you remove all three of the bars, the N disappears, causing you to lose one of the visual clues that gives you information about document loading. In addition, you lose the ability to cancel document transfers quickly, because the Stop button in the toolbar has been removed from the window. (You can still cancel transfers by opening the **G**o menu and choosing **S**top Loading.)

Although these changes take effect immediately after you select the menu item, Netscape does not automatically save them as your default settings. To save the current settings as the default, open the **O**ptions menu and choose **S**ave Options.

Viewing Multimedia Files

◀ See "Using Viewers," p. 95

One of Netscape's best features enables you to view documents of many types. If you remember from the introductory chapters, most WWW browsers are multimedia applications, which means that you can view files that contain different types of media—pictures, sound, and animation. Netscape can display text and inline graphics directly; to display other types of files, you must have viewers for these files installed on your machine.

After you have your viewers installed, and when Netscape knows where to find those viewers and what type of files they display, Netscape automatically starts the correct viewer when you click the hyperlink for a file of a recognized type. Netscape can recognize several standard image, sound, and animation formats. Table 11.1 shows some of the most common formats.

Table 11.1 Multimedia File Types Recognized by Netscape	
Medium	**File Type**
Audio	WAV, MIDI
Image	JPEG, GIF, TIFF
Video	MPEG, AVI, MOV
Formatted text	PS, RTF, DOC

All of the WWW multimedia viewers that you come across will let you configure viewers for MIME (Multipurpose Internet Mail Extensions) standard multimedia files. MIME was developed to extend the Internet e-mail standard (originally developed for text-only messages) to allow any type of data to be sent via e-mail. The WWW browsers use this same standard for identifying the type of multimedia files.

Configuring Netscape for Viewers

Once you have installed viewers on your PC, you need to configure Netscape to use these viewers. The Preferences dialog box lets you easily specify which viewers you have and what file types they can handle.

1. Open the **O**ptions menu and choose **P**references. The Preferences dialog box appears. In the drop-down list at the top of the dialog box, select Helper Applications (see fig. 11.22).

2. Scroll through the list of MIME types and associated files until you find the MIME type for the type of viewer you are installing.

3. If you need to add a new file extension to the list of extensions associated with that MIME type, enter them in the Extensions text box, separated by commas. Do not include the dot at the beginning of the file extension.

III

Other Browsers

Fig. 11.22
The Helper
Applications
option lets you tell
Netscape to start a
viewer automati-
cally when it finds
a file of a particu-
lar type.

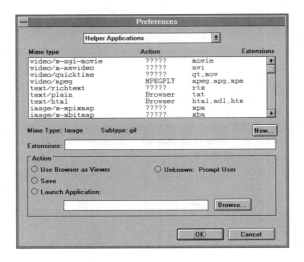

4. In the Action area, choose the radio button that describes what you
   want Netscape to do when it loads files associated with this MIME type.

   ■ Choose Save if you want to save the files directly to disk.

   ■ Choose Use Browser as Viewer if you want Netscape to try to load
     and display the file itself. Netscape can only handle files that
     contain information formatted as text, HTML, JPEG, or GIF
     information.

   ■ Choose Launch Application if you want to launch a viewer with
     the file loaded into it. Enter the path to the application in the
     text box below the radio button. You can click Browse to bring
     up a Browse dialog box in which you can look through your
     directories to find the viewer. If you click the viewer in the
     Browse dialog box, its path will be automatically entered in the
     text box.

   ■ You can also click the Unknown: Prompt User radio button if you
     want Netscape to bring up a dialog box that asks what you want
     to do with the file when it finds a file of that MIME type.

5. When all the information is entered correctly, click OK to close the Preferences dialog box and save the viewer information.

You can make additional changes to installed viewers at any time.

> **Note**
>
> Even though they are not specifically mentioned in the Helper Applications area of the Preferences dialog box, Netscape will automatically launch many of the standard applications (like Word and Paintbrush) when it finds files whose extensions are associated with those applications.

Adding a New Mime Type

One of the nice features of the MIME standard is the *MIME type application*. The application MIME type lets you specify any subtype, so you can have a MIME type for any application that you run frequently. If you would like Netscape to be able to start an application when it tries to load a file of a particular type, just add a new MIME type for that application. To do so:

1. Open the **O**ptions menu and choose **P**references. The Preferences dialog box appears. In the drop-down list at the top of the dialog box, select Helper Applications.

2. Select New to bring up the Configure New Mime Type dialog box (see fig. 11.23).

Fig. 11.23
Use the Configure New Mime Type dialog box to specify a MIME type and subtype.

3. Enter **application** in the Mime Type text box. Then enter a word that describes the subtype in the Mime SubType text box.

4. Click OK to add this new MIME type to the Helper Applications scroll list. The entry for this new type will be highlighted in the scroll list. You can continue with step 3 from the previous section, "Configuring Netscape for Viewers," to finish configuring the file extension and viewer information for this new MIME type.

III

Other Browsers

> ### Caution
>
> When you add a new MIME type, the type and subtype information should be entered correctly. Once you choose OK in this area of the Preferences dialog box and add that type, there does not appear to be a way of editing or removing the MIME type and subtype information from the scroll list.

Loading a File with an Unknown Viewer

If you selected the Unknown radio button as the action for a particular MIME type, Netscape will bring up the dialog box shown in figure 11.24 when you try to load a file associated with that MIME type. Choose Save to Disk to bring up a Save As dialog box that lets you store the file anywhere on your local disk.

Fig. 11.24

The Unknown File Type dialog box lets you tell Netscape to save a file it doesn't know how to display, or lets you configure a viewer to display that file type.

If you choose Configure a Viewer, you get the Configure External Viewer dialog box (see fig. 11.25). Enter the path of the viewer you want to use for this MIME type in the text box, or choose Browse to browse your local disk for the viewer application that you want (click the application and the path of the viewer will be entered in the text box). When the viewer information is correct, click OK. Netscape will load the file into the viewer. Netscape will now automatically start this viewer anytime it loads a file of this MIME type.

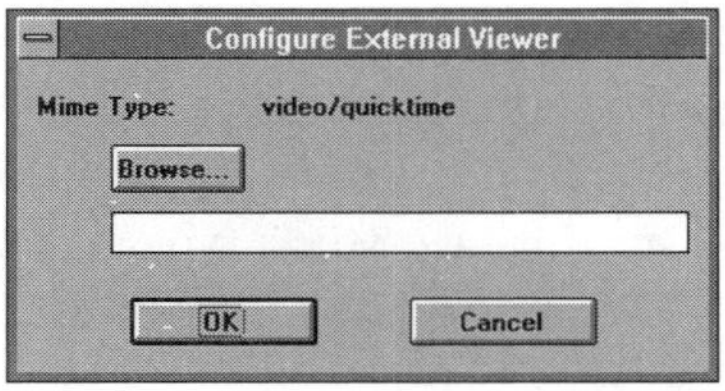

Fig. 11.25

This is the dialog box in which you specify the path for a viewer when you encounter an unassociated file type.

Loading a File with a Known Viewer

When you have your viewers set up, you need only click the hyperlink for a file of a known type (or open its URL), and Netscape launches the viewer application with the file loaded. You now can use any of the features of the viewer application to examine the file.

Notice that because the image is loaded in an external application, you can use Netscape while the helper application loads and displays the image.

Specifying Netscape's Temp Directory

When Netscape loads files into viewers, it first loads a copy of the file to a temporary directory, and then starts the viewer with a pointer to that temporary file. You can tell Netscape where to put these temporary files in the Preferences dialog box:

1. Open the **O**ptions menu and choose **P**references. The Preferences dialog box appears. In the drop-down list at the top of the dialog box, select Directories, Applications, and News (see fig. 11.26).

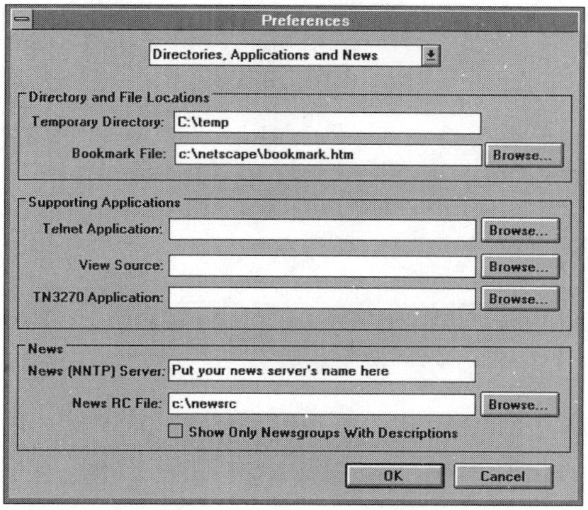

Fig. 11.26
The Directories, Applications, and News area of the Preferences dialog box lets you tell Netscape where to store files temporarily when displaying them with external viewers.

2. In the Temporary Directory text box, enter the path to the directory where you want temporary files stored.

3. Click OK to close the Preferences dialog and save the temporary directory information.

III

Other Browsers

Troubleshooting

I downloaded a picture, and it opened fine in Lview (or any other multimedia viewer). But I went back to view the picture later, and the file wasn't there. What happened?

The problem isn't with Lview or any of the viewers. When Netscape downloads a multimedia file for viewing, it creates a temporary file, and that is what you view. If you close the viewer without saving the file, the file will be gone when you exit Netscape. If you want to save a multimedia file that you downloaded for later use, save it before you exit the viewer application. Or, if the viewer doesn't give you the option of saving the file, move the file from Netscape's temporary directory to another directory on your disk.

Working with Local Files

When you think of using Netscape, you think of retrieving documents from WWW servers on the Internet. Netscape can read documents from your local file system, as well as from halfway around the world. If you share documents among members of your organization, many of the documents that you view may be on a local file server or your local computer.

Netscape provides an option that makes loading a local file easy. If you want to load a local file, open the **F**ile menu and choose Open **F**ile. The File Open dialog box appears (see fig. 11.27). This dialog box enables you to browse through all your local disks to find a file.

Fig. 11.27
The File Open dialog box enables you to enter a local file name or browse your local file system to find the next document that you want to view.

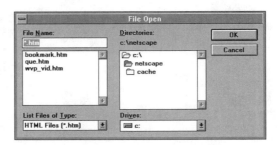

You also can load a local file in the same manner that you load any URL. Open the **F**ile menu and choose Open **L**ocation box. To specify a local file in the text box in the Open Location dialog box, precede the directory path of the file with **file:///c|** (you can substitute any of your local disks for c). The three slashes tell Netscape that you are looking for a local file; the bar is used instead of a colon because the colon has a specific purpose in a URL. Use slashes in the directory path that you enter, even if you are describing a directory on a PC that usually uses the backslash. Netscape translates the slashes properly when it retrieves the file.

Local URLs can be used anywhere that URLs are used—as bookmarks, links in documents, and so on.

◀ See "Links and URLs Transport You from Place to Place," p. 27

Effective Browsing Techniques

Navigating between WWW documents can be confusing. Documents often connect to documents that you have already read. You can't always remember which of several related documents contains the information that you really need.

Sometimes, you can't tell from the hyperlink whether the document is of interest to you, and loading documents uses valuable time. Often, you waste time loading documents that you dismiss immediately. This section helps you learn to reduce unnecessary document loading and circular navigating.

How to Keep Track of Where You've Been

Keeping track of where you are and where you were is one of the biggest challenges of using the WWW. Suppose that you're reading a document that deals with agriculture, and you click a hyperlink that takes you to Hay Field Seeding Suggestions. The document turns out to be one that you loaded earlier—when you found a hyperlink for Pasture Management Techniques. How can you avoid this frustrating repetition?

One suggestion is to have a home page that provides links to your most-visited WWW pages. This home page is useful, for example, if you work on a group project and frequently use documents with known locations. You can create your own home page, or someone can create a project home page for your group. In this scenario, you probably are already familiar with the servers, if not with the exact documents.

But what if you're navigating in uncharted waters on the WWW? Although it sounds difficult, you probably can learn to recognize the URLs of the sites that keep information that interests you. If the location bar is displayed, the URL for the current document appears there. The status bar shows the URL of a hyperlink when you move the cursor over it (see fig. 11.28). As you move

III

Other Browsers

between documents, you begin to remember some of the URLs that you see frequently; when you put your cursor on a hyperlink, you recognize documents that you know.

Fig. 11.28
The status bar displays the URLs of hyperlinks when the cursor is on top of them.

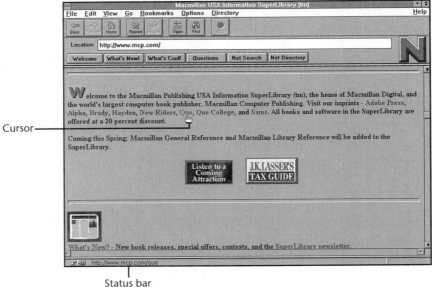

How to Get Where You Were

How to Get Where You Were

Trying to navigate back to a document that you viewed in the current Netscape session also can be challenging. In general, to go to the document that you viewed before the current document, open the **G**o menu and choose the **B**ack command (or click the Back button in the toolbar). Opening the **G**o menu and choosing the **F**orward command (or clicking the Forward button) takes you to the last document that you viewed after the current document. This arrangement sounds rather confusing, but it is understandable if you examine how Netscape determines these links.

Tip
If the History dialog box is open when you use the **F**orward and **B**ack commands, you can see the highlighted item move in the list of URLs.

The **G**o menu contains an option called **H**istory, which displays a dialog box similar to the one shown in figure 11.29. Notice that a list of URLs appears in this dialog box; the URL for the current document is highlighted.

The history list shows you the URLs of the document chain that led you to this point, as well as any documents that you visited after the current document. If you use the **B**ack command, you move up in the list; if you use the **F**orward command, you move down the list. Click any URL in the list and click Go To to jump to that document (and that point in the list).

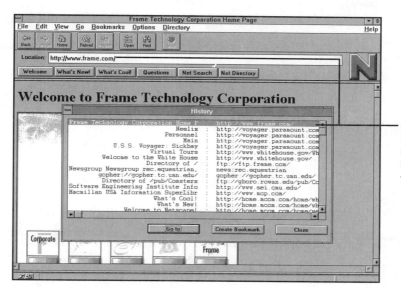

Fig. 11.29
The Netscape History dialog box shows a linear list of URLs that you visit.

Current URL is high-lighted in history window

Caution

You can use the **B**ack and **F**orward commands to move between documents that you already visited (which are shown in the history list). If, however, you jump to a new document while you are in the middle of the list, you erase the links at the end of the list and cannot use the Forward command to return to those documents. The link for the document you just jumped to replaces all of the links past your current point in the list.

To move quickly between documents that you load, use the history list. If you want to add a new document to the list of documents that you're viewing, make sure that you're at the end of the list before you jump to that document. You don't have to use hyperlinks to add the document you load to the history list. Load the document (open the **F**ile menu and choose **O**pen Location, or click the Open toolbar button), and it is added to the list.

You will notice when you open the **G**o menu that the last few documents that you visited (a maximum of 15) are displayed at the bottom of the menu (see fig. 11.30). The documents are shown in the order in which you opened them, with the most recent document appearing at the top of the list. The 10 newest documents are numbered so that you can access them quickly without using the mouse. A zero appears to the left of the most recently visited document; the nine documents following it are numbered sequentially.

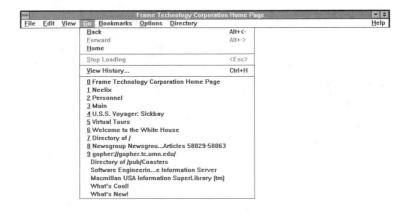

Fig. 11.30
The Go menu enables you to quickly access the last few documents that you visited.

Create Lists of Your Favorite URLs

If you don't want to learn to use HTML commands to create a home page that contains all of your favorite WWW documents, Netscape offers an alternative. To quickly access your favorite URLs, you can create *bookmark files*. You can have any number of bookmark files and can save any number of URLs to each file.

Setting Your Current Bookmark File

The default bookmark file is bookmark.htm. You can have any number of bookmark files, although only one can be set as the current bookmark file. To set your current bookmark file, follow these steps:

1. Open the **O**ptions menu and choose **P**references. The Preferences dialog box appears.

2. In the drop-down list at the top of the dialog box, select Directories, Applications, and News.

3. Click the Bookmark File text box (see fig. 11.31), and modify the existing path, or delete it and enter the path for the file that you want to use.

4. You can click the Browse button to browse through your local files. Click the file that you want to use as the current bookmark file (the path is entered in the text box automatically when you click the file).

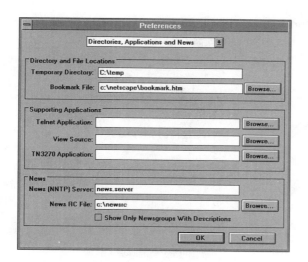

Fig. 11.31
You can select
your current
bookmark file in
the Preferences
dialog box.

5. Choose OK to make the selections take effect, or click Cancel if you decide not to change the current bookmark file.

Creating and Editing Bookmarks

After you define your current bookmark file, you can create bookmarks in several ways. The simplest way is to open the **B**ookmarks menu and choose **A**dd Bookmark. This command writes the title and URL of the current document as the last item in your bookmark file. You do not need to visit a document, however, to add it to your bookmark file. The Bookmark List dialog box allows you to add and edit bookmarks in the current bookmark file.

To use the Bookmark List dialog box, follow these steps:

1. Open the **B**ookmarks menu and choose View **B**ookmarks. The Bookmark List dialog box appears (see fig. 11.32).

2. To add the address of the current document as a bookmark, select the item in the list that you want the bookmark to follow, and then click Add Bookmark. The title of the current document will be added after the selected item. The address of the current item will appear in the text field below the bookmark list.

3. To search for an item in your bookmark list, enter the string of characters that you want to search for in the Find text box, and then click Find. Netscape finds all occurrences of the character string (regardless of capitalization), whether the string occurs as part of a word or as an entire word.

The Find command searches from the current bookmark down, and will find strings in the URLs associated with entries.

Fig. 11.32

The Bookmark List dialog box enables you to add and go to documents in your bookmark file.

In addition to adding the current document, you can add any document to the list, edit the documents that currently appear in the list, and add headings and separators in the lists. To access these functions, click the Edit button in the lower-right corner of the Bookmark List dialog box; this action expands the dialog box, as shown in figure 11.33.

Fig. 11.33

When you click the Edit button, the Bookmark List dialog box expands so that you can edit the bookmark list.

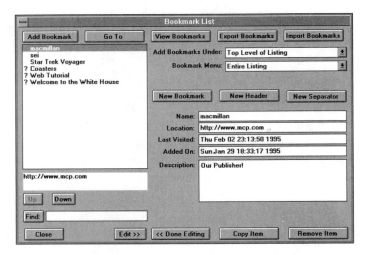

If you want to edit one of the bookmarks in the list, select it. Information about that bookmark appears in the text boxes labeled Name, Location, Last Visited, Added On, and Description. You can edit the Name, Location, and Description entries. The *name* is the entry that appears in the bookmark list. The *location* is the URL of the document. The *description* appears below the name when you view the bookmark file as a document.

To add a new item to the list, select the item that you want the new item to follow. Then click New Bookmark, New Header, or New Separator. These three buttons do the following:

- New Separator causes a line to be added below the selected item. This line appears when the bookmarks are displayed in the Bookmarks menu.

- New Header causes the words *New Item* to appear in the bookmark list and the Name text box. Change the Name entry to whatever you want the header to be. The new name appears in the bookmarks list as you type it in the Name box.

- New Bookmark causes the words *New Item* to appear in the bookmarks list and the Name text box, and enters the current time and date in the Added On box. Change the Name entry to whatever you want it to be. Then enter the URL of the document you are adding in the Location box. If you want to, you also can add a description of the document in the Description box.

To remove an item from the bookmarks list, select the item, and then click Remove Item. To copy an item, select it, and then click Copy Item. This action creates a copy of the item below the item. You can edit the copy or move it by pressing the up- and down-arrow keys. (Select the item and then press the up-arrow key to move the item higher in the list, or select the item and then press the down-arrow key to move the item lower in the list.) Notice that the arrow keys can have the effect of indenting items, as explained in the following section.

Structuring Your Bookmarks Menu

You can set up your bookmarks list so that all or part of it appears at the end of the Bookmarks menu. In addition, you can structure the bookmarks list so that it is hierarchical, allowing you to have submenus for the items in the Bookmarks menu. You can do all of this from the expanded Bookmark List dialog box.

III

Other Browsers

Open the **B**ookmarks menu and choose View **B**ookmarks. Click the Edit button in the lower-right corner of the Bookmark List dialog box to expand it. The box next to Bookmark menu is a drop-down list that enables you to specify what items from the bookmarks list are shown in the Bookmarks menu. The drop-down list contains the option Entire Listing, as well as any headers that you have added to the bookmarks list. You can select Entire Listing if you want to see all the entries from the bookmarks list in the Bookmarks menu. You also can limit the bookmarks shown in the Bookmarks menu to the items below one of the headings in your bookmarks list.

Also in the expanded Bookmark List dialog box, you can tell Netscape where to place the items that you add by choosing **B**ookmarks, **A**dd Bookmark. The box next to Add Bookmarks Under is a drop-down list that enables you to specify where items added this way are placed in the bookmark list. You can select Top Level of Listing if you want all new items to be added at the end of the bookmarks list. If you want all the entries to be added at the end of a particular section of your bookmarks list, choose the header for that section from the drop-down list.

One final thing that you can do with the Bookmarks menu is structure the way the entries in the bookmarks list are displayed in the menu. Normally, all entries in the bookmarks list are displayed sequentially as they appear in the list. You can click the Up and Down buttons at the bottom of the bookmarks list to structure items to appear in submenus of the Bookmarks menu.

If you select an item immediately below a heading and then press the up-arrow key, the item is indented to the right. This indentation indicates that the item will appear in a submenu of that heading in the Bookmarks menu. Whenever you select an item that is below an indented item and then press the up-arrow key, the selected item also is indented. In this way, you can build submenus like the one shown in figure 11.34.

If you want to get rid of your submenus and have everything at the top level, you can press the down-arrow key to remove the indents from items in the bookmarks list. Select the item at the end of an indented section, and then press the down-arrow key to move the item to the left. Repeat this procedure for each item in that section, moving up from the last one, until you move all the items to the left. A submenu no longer appears below the pertinent heading; all the items are in the top-level menu.

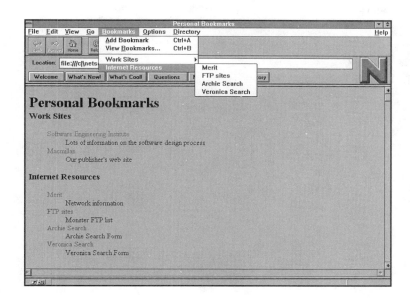

Fig. 11.34
You can structure
your bookmarks
list to group items
in submenus of
the Bookmarks
menu.

Using Bookmarks

Bookmarks enable you to access documents quickly. You simply open the
Bookmarks menu and select any of the bookmarks that appear at the end of
the menu. Netscape loads the document associated with that bookmark. If
the Bookmark List dialog box is open, you can select any item in the bookmarks list and then click Go To to load that document in Netscape.

Another way to use your bookmarks is to click View Bookmarks in the Bookmark List dialog box. This action loads your current bookmarks file in
Netscape for you to view (see fig. 11.35). This file is formatted exactly the way
that your bookmarks list is. Any headings in the list appear as headings in the
document, and items in the document fall below the same headings as in the
list.

Below each item is the description that you entered when you added the item
to the bookmarks list (if you entered one). Each item in the document is a
normal hypertext link. Click any of the items to load its documents.

Sharing Bookmarks

Netscape makes it very easy for you to share your bookmarks with other
users. If you want to share entire bookmark files, simply give the users a copy
of your bookmark files. Those people then can specify any of those files as
their current bookmark file, and they will be able to access the same documents that you can.

III

Other Browsers

Fig. 11.35

You can view your bookmarks file as a document in Netscape.

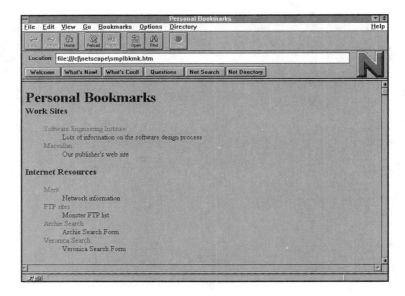

You also can save the current version of your bookmarks list to a file from the Bookmark List dialog box. Simply click Export Bookmarks, and use the Browser dialog box that appears to select the directory and file to which you want to write the bookmarks. You then can give that file to other people.

If you get someone else's bookmark files, and you don't want to bother changing files all the time to use them, you can add the bookmarks from those files to your main bookmarks file. Set the current bookmarks file to be the one that you use most often. In the Bookmark List dialog box, click Import Bookmarks. You get a Browser dialog box that allows you to select the file that you want to import from your file system. When you select the file that you want to import, all the bookmarks from that file are added to the end of the current bookmarks list, preserving any menu structure that was in the imported list.

Security

Many people seem to feel that because computers are machines, communications between computers is secure (no people are involved). Nothing could be farther from the truth.

Communication on the Internet involves data being forwarded from the sending computer to the receiving computer through several intermediate computers. A possibility exists that someone could be looking at the information passing through the intermediate computers. He or she could even set up another computer to pretend to be the receiving computer, so that everything you send goes to someone who was not intended to see the information.

For this reason, sending sensitive information (such as your credit card number) over the Internet is not a good idea. Any information sent over the Internet is at risk—e-mail messages, file transfers, and particularly information from electronic forms that you may fill out with your WWW browser.

There is, however, a solution to this problem. Netscape Communications Corporation has built security features into its Web browser and server. A very secure encryption standard can be used for transmitting information between the Netscape browser and a Netscape server. This encryption prevents anyone who is observing the information at an intermediate point from making any sense of it. The Netscape browser shows the security status of the document that you are viewing in several ways:

- If the key symbol to the left of the status bar is broken, the current document is not secure. If the key is unbroken on a blue background, the document is secure.

- A gray bar above the viewing area in your document indicates an insecure document; a blue bar indicates a secure document.

- Dialog boxes can warn you when you are entering or leaving a secure WWW server, and also warn you when you are going to submit information with an insecure form.

The Security Alerts area that appears in the Preferences dialog box when Network, Images, and Security is selected enables you to specify whether you want to see the alert dialog boxes for different security conditions (see fig. 11.36).

You also can get security information about the document that you are currently viewing from the Document Information dialog box (see fig. 11.37). Open the **F**ile menu and choose **D**ocument Info to display this dialog box.

III

Other Browsers

Fig. 11.36
Netscape can alert you about the security status of the WWW servers and documents that you visit.

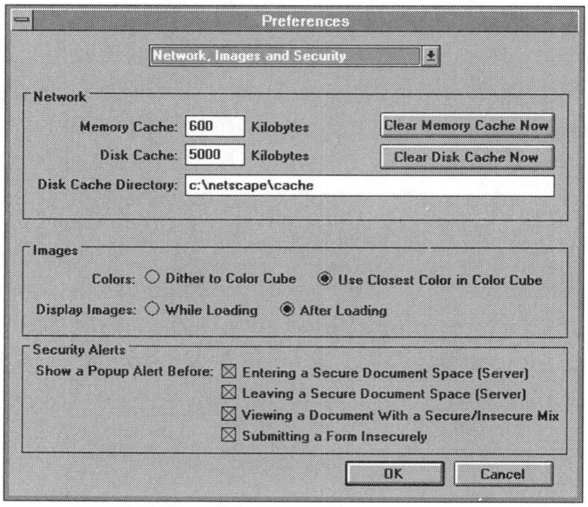

Fig. 11.37
The Document Information dialog box tells you the document title and location, and when it was last modified, in addition to information about the security of the document.

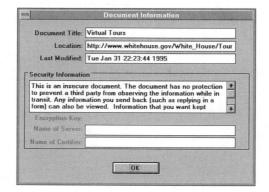

Using Other Internet Services

Like Mosaic, Netscape provides a friendly interface to some of the older Internet services. Conceptually, using Netscape to access these services is the same as using Mosaic to access the services, so the following sections simply show you how Netscape displays the services. (You may want to read the corresponding Mosaic chapters for in-depth information about the services.)

◀ See "Connecting to an Anonymous FTP Server," p. 154

FTP

Like Mosaic, Netscape provides a nice way to browse FTP sites. Instead of having to use cryptic FTP commands from a terminal interface, you can use the FTP protocol in a URL to connect to and graphically view an FTP site.

FTP sites are viewed as file systems; when you connect to a site, you see the top-level directory for that site. From there, you can click subdirectories to examine their contents, and you can click files to load them into Netscape.

> **Note**
>
> Remember that if you try to load a file that Netscape cannot view directly, and if you don't have a viewer set up (or available) for that file, you will have wasted your time loading that file. You can, however, Shift+click the link for that file and save the file to your local disk, if you want.

Netscape allows you to display FTP directories as simple lists of file and directory names, or as annotated lists similar to the way Mosaic shows them. The annotated lists have icons representing the type of file or directory, and show information about file and directory attributes. By default, Netscape gives you the elaborate FTP information. If you want to turn this feature off, open the **O**ptions menu and choose Show FTP **F**ile Information. Figure 11.38 shows the elaborate FTP listing format.

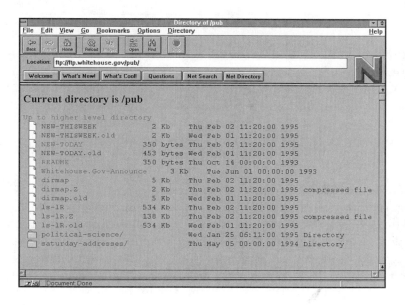

Fig. 11.38
Netscape gives you a wealth of information about files at FTP sites.

Gopher

Netscape provides an easy way to navigate through Gopherspace, presenting the Gopher menus in an annotated fashion similar to the way Mosaic does. Icons are used to represent the different types of items that you find in

◀ See "Locating Gopher Information," p. 164

III

Other Browsers

Gopher menus. To view a menu item, click its icon. Figure 11.39 shows a Gopher menu displayed by Netscape.

Fig. 11.39
Netscape gives you a graphical interface to Gopher servers.

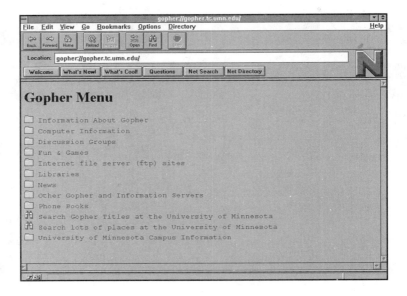

UseNet

◄ See "Get the News with Newsgroups," p. 17

◄ See "Using Mosaic to Access UseNet Newsgroups," p. 185

Netscape provides a full-featured interface to the thousands of UseNet newsgroups. If you can provide the name of an NNTP server for Netscape to use, you can have full access to newsgroups from Netscape; you can read existing articles, post new articles, and post follow-up articles. This is a great improvement over NCSA Mosaic, which only allowed you to read newsgroups.

Configuring Netscape to Read Newsgroups

Netscape keeps the information about the newsgroups that you read in a file on your local disk. To set up your NNTP server information and the information about where to find this file, open the **O**ptions menu and choose **P**references to display the Preferences dialog box. Then select Directories, Applications and News to display those options (see fig. 11.40). Enter the name of your news (NNTP) server and the path to your News RC file in the indicated text boxes (or click the Browse button to browse your file system). If you do not have a News RC file the first time that you try to read a newsgroup, Netscape will create one for you.

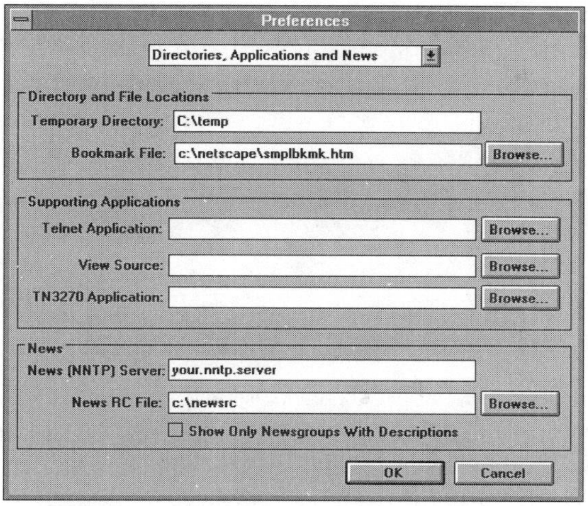

Fig. 11.40
If you can provide
the name of an
NNTP server, you
can use Netscape
to read UseNet
newsgroups.

Subscribing to Newsgroups

If you are going to be reading a newsgroup on a regular basis, you should
subscribe to it so that it appears on a list of newsgroups that you read most
often. To view your list of subscribed newsgroups, open the **D**irectory menu
and choose **G**o to Newsgroups. A document appears that contains a list of the
newsgroups to which you subscribe (see fig. 11.41). From this page, you can
click the name of one of the subscribed newsgroups and read the articles in
that group.

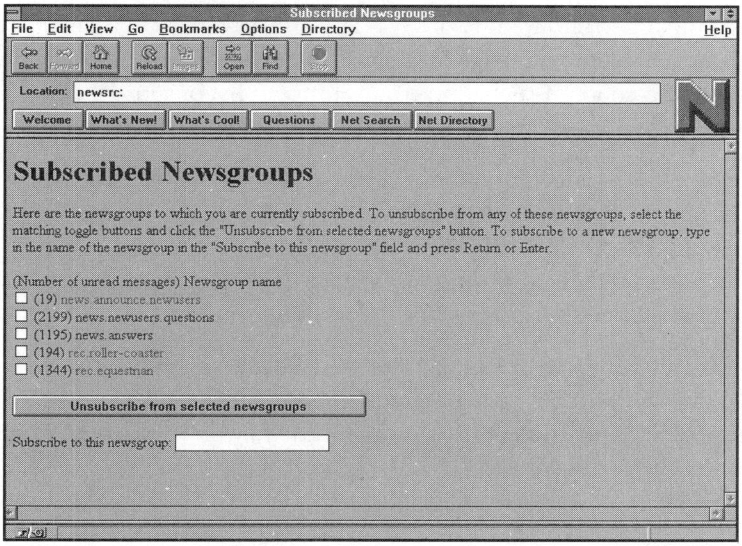

Fig. 11.41
Netscape's
Subscribed
Newsgroups page
gives you a list of
links to the
newsgroups you
subscribe to. The
number of unread
articles in each
group is shown
in parentheses to
the left of the
newsgroup name.

III

Other Browsers

You can subscribe to newsgroups by entering the name of the newsgroup in the Subscribe to this Newsgroup text box. To unsubscribe from a newsgroup, click the check box to the left of the newsgroup name and choose Unsubscribe from Selected Newsgroups. The page will redisplay with that newsgroup removed from your list.

Note

It can be tough to find a particular newsgroup among the thousands available. If you know the general newsgroup hierarchy where you want to look for some interesting groups, Netscape can make it a little easier to search for ones of interest to you.

To find a list of all newsgroups under a particular hierarchy, enter the first part of the newsgroup name, followed by an asterisk. For example, enter as a URL news:comp.* to get a document that contains a list of all the newsgroups in the comp hierarchy. When you have a list of newsgroups that you might be interested in, open the **E**dit menu and choose the **F**ind command to look for newsgroup names that are related to a specific topic. You may want to search through the comp hierarchy for any newsgroups that discuss networks, for example.

Another way to subscribe to a newsgroup is to first read a newsgroup that you don't subscribe to by opening its URL. While you are viewing that newsgroup, press the Subscribe button at the top of the page. This will add the current newsgroup to your list of subscribed groups.

Reading Newsgroups

You can read a newsgroup in two ways. The first way is to click the link to that newsgroup from your page of subscribed newsgroups. Open the **D**irectory menu and choose **G**o to Newsgroups for your list of subscribed newsgroups.

You can also open a newsgroup just as you would any WWW document. You must specify a URL that uses the news protocol. For example, open the **F**ile menu and choose Open **L**ocation, and then enter a URL in the format news:<newsgroup name>. A window appears, displaying a list of articles that have been posted to this group since the last time you read it (see fig. 11.42).

If you have a recently updated NNTP server, the articles will be shown grouped by topic within the newsgroup. These topics are also known as *threads*. Articles that are responses to other articles will be indented to the right under the original article.

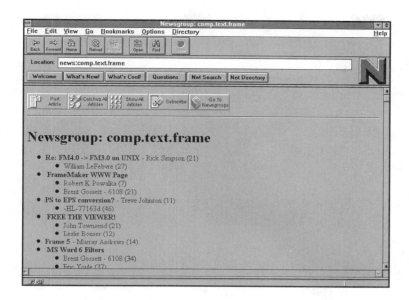

Fig. 11.42
Entering the URL
**news:comp.text.
frame** will take
you to a
newsgroup that
discusses the
FrameMaker
desktop publishing
application.

Note

If you get your news from an older NNTP server, Netscape may not show your related articles grouped together. Instead, what you get is a list of articles in the order that they were received by your news server.

There are a number of buttons at the top of your newsgroup window (they are repeated at the bottom of the list of articles, also). Their functions are as follows:

■ Post Article allows you to submit a new article to this newsgroup.

■ Catchup All Articles marks all of the articles in this newsgroup as being read and removes them from the page.

■ Show All Articles shows all of the articles in the newsgroup that currently exist on the NNTP server, even the ones you've read previously.

■ Subscribe/Unsubscribe lets you add the current newsgroup to your list of subscribed newsgroups, or remove it from the list if you are currently subscribed to this group.

■ Go To Newsgroups returns you to your list of subscribed newsgroups.

III

Other Browsers

To read any of the articles, simply click the link to that article and Netscape will load it (see fig 11.43).

Fig. 11.43

When you read an article, Netscape lets you post a follow-up message and send e-mail to the person who posted the article, among other things.

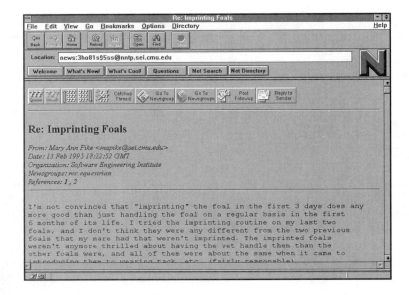

There are a number of buttons at the top of your article window (they are repeated at the bottom of the article, also). Their functions are as follows:

- Left Arrow moves you to the previous article about this topic.

- Right Arrow moves you to the next article about this topic.

- Up Arrow moves you to the first article in the previous topic.

- Down Arrow moves you to the first article in the next topic.

- Catchup Thread lets you mark all of the articles in this current topic as read.

- Go To Newsgroup returns you to the list of articles in the current newsgroup.

- Go To Newsgroups returns you to your list of subscribed newsgroups.

- Post Followup lets you post an article with the same topic as the current message.

- Reply to Sender lets you send e-mail to the author of the current article.

If the article that you are reading is in response to another article, there are links listed in the References line of the article header. You can click these links to go to those referenced articles (this is particularly useful if you have an old NNTP server that doesn't show you the articles grouped by topic).

Also, if the current article is crossposted to other newsgroups, those groups will be listed in the Newsgroups line of the article header. You can click the newsgroup name to read that newsgroup.

Posting to Newsgroups

If you would like to start a new topic of discussion in a newsgroup, you can post a new article to the newsgroup. You can also make a follow-up post that continues the discussion on a particular topic. To post a new article, press the Post Article button while you are viewing the article list of a newsgroup. To post a follow-up article, press the Post Followup button while you are reading the article you want to respond to.

When you post an article, you get the form shown in figure 11.44. If you are posting a new article, fill in the Subject line (if you are posting a follow-up, it will contain the subject of the article you are responding to).

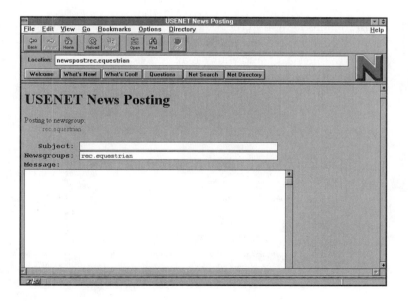

Fig. 11.44
The USENET News Posting form lets you submit a new article or respond to an existing article in a newsgroup.

Tip
Press Enter when
your line reaches
the edge of the
message box, or
your posted mes-
sage will be too
wide for most
people to display.

Enter the text of your message in the Message box. If you are posting a
follow-up message, the text of the original message is quoted at the beginning of the box. Leave the quoted material only if you need to refer to it
specifically in your reply.

When you have finished entering your message text, scroll to the bottom of
the form and click the Post Message button. Netscape will display an Article
Posted Successfully page that contains a link to take you back to the
newsgroup. If you decide to cancel the post, simply open the **G**o menu and
choose **B**ack.

E-mail

Netscape also allows you to use e-mail in a limited way. You can e-mail the
current document you are reading to yourself or someone else. In order to
send e-mail, you must be able to access an e-mail server. To set up your e-mail
server information, follow these steps:

1. Open the **O**ptions menu and choose **P**references to display the Preferences dialog box.

2. Select Mail and Proxies from the drop-down list.

3. Fill in the information in the Mail area (see fig. 11.45). Enter the name
   of your e-mail server, your name as you want it to appear in the From
   line of your messages, and your e-mail address so that people who receive your messages can respond to you.

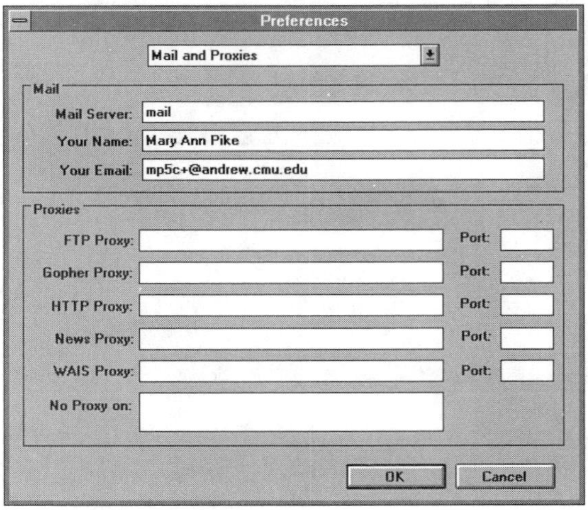

Fig. 11.45
Fill in the
information in the
Mail area of the
Mail and Proxies
section of the
Preference dialog
box.

To mail the current document, open the **F**ile menu and choose **M**ail Document. The form shown in figure 11.46 will appear. Enter the address of the recipient in the To text box, and add any explanatory text that you would like to precede the document in the large box in the middle of the form. Choose Send Mail when you are ready to send the document.

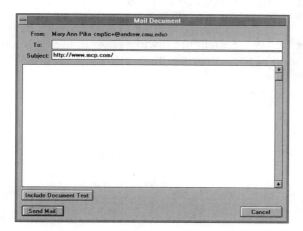

Fig. 11.46
The Mail Document form lets you mail a document to someone with comments.

Telnet

Netscape gives you the option of using Telnet (a terminal interface program) to connect to hosts that require connecting to a special port or to hosts that actually require you to log in to use a service. Like Mosaic, Netscape must use the Telnet program that comes with your Internet communications software. You must tell Netscape where to find your Telnet program. Open the **O**ptions menu and choose **P**references to display the Preferences dialog box. Select Directories, Applications, and News. Enter the path of your Telnet application in the indicated text box (or click the Browse button to browse your file system). Choose OK to exit the dialog box. Netscape now can properly handle URLs that use the Telnet protocol by starting the Telnet application.

◀ See "Using Mosaic to Access Telnet," p. 179

From Here...

Netscape is a full-featured WWW browser that has a number of improvements over NCSA Mosaic. This chapter was a brief introduction to this powerful WWW interface. For a more in-depth look at this application, you may want to check out *Using Netscape*, a Que publication.

III

Other Browsers

To learn more about using Mosaic and to find interesting WWW documents, refer to these chapters:

- Chapter 6, "Navigating with Mosaic," tells you how to use Mosaic to find and view documents on the WWW.

- Chapter 7, "Mosaic Shortcuts and Tips," tells you how to become an expert WWW navigator.

- Chapter 19, "Web Searching," discusses how to use automated software to find some of the most interesting collections of WWW documents.

Chapter 12

Luckman Interactive Enhanced Mosaic

by Mary Ann Pike

A number of companies have licensed the original Mosaic from NCSA in order to develop their own customized WWW browser. *Luckman Interactive Enhanced Mosaic* is one of these browsers and is included on WebCD. Luckman is a light version of Mosaic, giving you all the features you need to access the WWW, but less confusing for the new Internet user.

> **Note**
>
> NCSA has licensed Mosaic to several companies, including Spyglass. Spyglass has in turn licensed Mosaic to Luckman and several other companies under the name Enhanced Mosaic. Many other companies are likely to begin marketing versions of Mosaic similar to this one. The features in all these versions will be similar so that if you purchase or receive one of these, you will find that many of the procedures explained in this chapter will apply to your version.

In this chapter, you learn the following:

- How to install Luckman Mosaic
- How to use the Luckman interface
- How to navigate the Web with Luckman
- How to customize Luckman Mosaic to your preferences

Getting Luckman Up and Running

Trying out the Luckman browser is easy since the software is included on WebCD. You should make sure that your system is properly set up to run Luckman before loading the software, however. And once you do get the Luckman software installed, you probably will want to get some external applications that enable you to view movies, hear sounds, and experience all the multimedia documents that are available on the Web. Many of these applications are on the included WebCD in the \viewers directory.

Will Your Computer Run Luckman Mosaic?

◀ See "Can Your Computer System Run Mosaic for Windows?" p. 61

The system requirements of Luckman are similar to those of the other Web browsers. Check out Chapter 4, "Getting Mosaic Running in Windows," to get an idea of what your system requirements are. In addition, depending on the type of Internet connection you plan to have, you may need additional programs (like Winsock, which is on the included WebCD) to get connected to the Internet. Chapter 4 discusses the types of software you may need and how and where to get them.

Luckman directly displays the text and inline graphics from HTML documents, and automatically starts viewers for a limited number of other file types. Unlike with Mosaic and Netscape, you cannot configure Luckman Mosaic to directly use external viewers for use with other file types. You will have to save these files to your local disk and load them into the viewer yourself.

> **Note**
>
> Que licensed this software for purchasers of this book. Luckman Interactive Enhanced Mosaic is *not* shareware, public-domain software, or freeware; it may not be copied or redistributed by any means.

Installing Luckman on Your System

Setting up the basic Luckman software consists of running an installation program in Windows for the Luckman software itself. To set up the software, follow these steps:

1. Open the WebCD in the Windows File Manager, and go to the \luckman\disk1 directory.

2. Execute the setup.exe file by double-clicking the file name from the Windows File Manager.

3. Click **C**ontinue on the first installation screen shown in figure 12.1. (To stop the installation, click **E**xit).

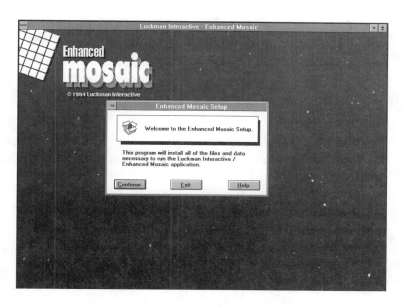

Fig. 12.1
The Initial Luckman Enhanced Mosaic setup screen tells you what you are installing.

4. The next screen, shown in figure 12.2, asks where you want to install your Luckman software and informs you that it will be adding a new program group to the Program Manager. Note that the default installation directory is c:\mosaic. If you already have another version of Mosaic (NCSA Mosaic, for example) installed in that directory and you don't want to overwrite it, enter a different directory name.

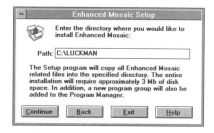

Fig. 12.2
Enter the name of the directory where you want to install the Luckman Interactive Enhanced Mosaic software. In this example, the user is installing the software to C:\LUCKMAN instead of the default setting of C:\MOSAIC.

5. Click **C**ontinue to continue the installation.

The progress of the installation is shown on a linear graph. Once the installation is complete, you will get the dialog box shown in figure 12.3.

Other Browsers

Fig. 12.3
Enhanced Mosaic
informs you that
you need to install
the Win32s
software.

◄ See "Installing
the Windows
32-bit Librar-
ies," p. 69

Since Luckman Mosaic is on WebCD instead of the Luckman distribution disks, do not follow the directions in the dialog box to install the
Win32s software. If you haven't install Win32s, you can install it from
the \win32s directory on WebCD. See Chapter 4, "Getting Mosaic Running in Windows," for more information on installing the Win32s
software.

6. When you exit the installation, the Enhanced Mosaic program group
   shown in figure 12.4 will appear in your Program Manager.

Fig. 12.4
After the installa-
tion is complete,
the Enhanced
Mosaic program
group window
displays. (You can
adjust its size.)

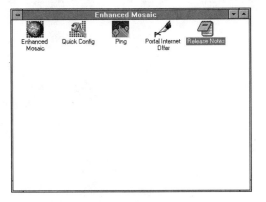

Configuring Your Internet Connection

You need to set up your software to connect to the Internet before using
Luckman Enhanced Mosaic to access WWW documents. When you run
Luckman Mosaic for the first time, you see the dialog box in figure 12.5.

Fig. 12.5
Luckman En-
hanced Mosaic
asks if you want
to do a Quick
Configuration the
first time you run
the software.

Choose **Y**es to start the Quick Configure program. The dialog box shown in figure 12.6 appears.

Fig. 12.6
When you start the
Quick Configure
program, it informs
you that you can
manually configure
your connection
software if you are
not going to use
the Portal Internet
service.

After you choose OK in this dialog box, you get the dialog box shown in figure 12.7.

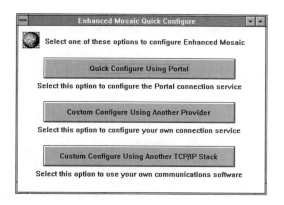

Fig. 12.7
The Enhanced
Mosaic Quick
Configure dialog
box enables you
to set up your
Internet connec-
tion information
for Luckman
Mosaic.

III

Other Browsers

Quick Configure Using Portal

If you do not have an Internet provider, Luckman Mosaic comes with an offer for a 30-day free trial with the Portal Information Network, a national provider of Internet services. To sign up for this provider, go to the Enhanced Mosaic program group and double-click the Portal Internet Offer icon.

Clicking this icon opens a form in Windows Write that you need to complete to get an account. Fill in this form and fax or mail it to Portal at the given address or fax number.

At this point, you have to wait, usually just a day or so if working by fax, for Portal to set up your account and send you the information you need to finish the quick configure.

Once you get the information back from Portal, follow these steps:

1. Double-click the Quick Config icon to start the configuration.

2. Click OK in the dialog box shown in figure 12.6.

3. Click Quick Configure Using Portal when you get the dialog box shown in figure 12.7.

4. In the Portal Quick Configure dialog box, click the arrow next to the Portal Phone number box and choose a local phone number in your area. If you don't see a number in your area, call Portal at 1-800-848-8980 to see if the company has recently added a local number for you. Portal has local numbers in most areas now.

5. Enter your Portal account name and password in the boxes provided.

6. Select the port where your modem is connected in the Modem Port box.

7. Set the speed for your modem in the Modem Speed box. (If you have a 14.4 Kbps modem, you should use 19200 for the speed.)

8. Click Configure. When the configuration is complete, click OK in the dialog box and you're finished.

Custom Configure Using Another Provider

> **Caution**
>
> This option is not recommended unless you are an experienced Internet user and understand TCP/IP addresses and how to script an automatic login procedure.
>
> If you already have an Internet connection and you can connect using the software you have, you are better off choosing the Custom Configure Using Another TCP/IP Stack option described in the next section.

Luckman also comes with the Distinct communications software that you can use to connect to another Internet provider. To make this connection, follow these steps:

1. Choose Custom Configure Using Another Provider in the dialog box shown in figure 12.7.

2. In the SLIP/PPP configuration dialog box, open the SLIP/PPP menu and choose **P**hone book, and the Phone Book dialog box displays.

3. Enter the name and phone number of the provider. Provide the name of your dialing script, and provide either your address information or the type of addressing used.

4. Either select SLIP or PPP depending on which type of account you use.

5. When you are finished, click **E**xit.

Note

If you accidentally click on the wrong configuration button, Luckman Mosaic will automatically configure itself for that option even if you don't save any changes. If this happens to you, just restart Quick Configure and click on Yes when Quick Configure warns you that you are about to make changes. You can then select a different configuration button and re-configure Luckman Mosaic.

Notice that when you rerun Quick Configure, it will warn you that Enhanced Mosaic has already been configured and you will replace the current settings if you continue.

You will probably need to help to configure this option properly, so if you have problems configuring this, contact your service provider and tell them you are using Distinct TCP/IP and need to configure it to work with their service.

Custom Configure Using Another TCP/IP Stack

You also have the option of using your current Internet connection software. To do this, choose Custom Configure Using Another TCP/IP stack. You will get the dialog box shown in figure 12.8.

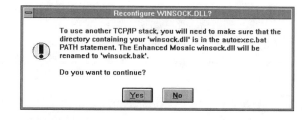

Fig. 12.8
If you decide to use your current communications software, Luckman informs you that the winsock.dll must reside in a directory that is in your path variable.

When you click Yes, the configuration will be complete. You should verify that the directory containing your Winsock program files, including winsock.dll, is in your path.

III

Other Browsers

While there are some customizations that you can do to the Luckman Mosaic interface to make it meet your needs, you can run the Luckman software without any further work.

Using the Luckman Enhanced Mosaic Interface

After you have installed the Luckman software, you can connect to your Internet provider and start Luckman Interactive Enhanced Mosaic. Luckman Mosaic is an easy-to-use, graphically oriented WWW browser.

Starting Enhanced Mosaic

Before starting Luckman, you should first be connected to the Internet. If your Internet connection is through your LAN, be sure that you are logged onto your network. If you are connected to the Internet by a modem, start your SLIP or PPP software and log in to your account.

> **Note**
>
> If the Winsock program you use to connect to the Internet, such as Trumpet Winsock or the Portal software, is in a directory in your path statement, you can double-click the Enhanced Mosaic icon and it will start your Winsock, too.

After you have established your Internet connection, open the Enhanced Mosaic program group, and double-click the Enhanced Mosaic icon. You are now ready to explore the Internet with Luckman Mosaic.

The Luckman Mosaic Window

When Luckman Mosaic starts, it loads the document specified as the home page in the Preferences dialog box. (See "Telling Luckman Mosaic What Home Page to Load" later in this chapter to see how to change this.) Unless you have specified a personal home page, your window should look like the one shown in figure 12.9 (which shows the default Luckman Mosaic home page).

A brief description of each window part is given in this section. The remainder of this chapter contains detailed discussion of Luckman Mosaic's features.

■ The *title bar* contains the usual window function buttons (Control Menu box, and Maximize and Minimize buttons). In addition, it has the name of the application (Enhanced NCSA Mosaic).

■ The *menu bar* gives access to all the functions you need to use Luckman Mosaic. You can retrieve documents to view, print documents, customize the look of your Luckman Mosaic window, navigate between documents, save files, and access Luckman's online help.

Menu bar —
URL bar —
Document title —
Document window —
Status bar —

Title bar

Fig. 12.9
The default Luckman home page is found in the directory where you installed the software in the file initial.htm.

■ The *URL bar* shows the URL of the current document. When you open a document, its URL is displayed here, and the globe icon on the right side of the URL bar spins while the document is being retrieved. The left arrow takes you to the page from which you came to the current page. The right arrow takes you to the last document you visited from this page.

◄ See "Links and URLs Transport You from Place to Place," p. 27

■ The *document window* is a separate window within the Enhanced NCSA Mosaic window in which you see the text of a document and any in-line images it may contain. This document window has a separate Maximize/Restore button just beneath the one for the application. You can have multiple document windows open at one time. The title bar of each document window contains the title of the document displayed in that window.

■ The *status bar* serves two functions. While Luckman Mosaic is loading your document, it shows the progress of the different document elements (text and individual graphics) that are being loaded. On the right of the status bar will be a bar graph that shows what percentage of the current document element has been loaded.

III

Other Browsers

When you are viewing a document, the status bar shows the URL of the hyperlink that is under your cursor.

What Is a Home Page?

▶ See "Program-
ming Your
Home Page,"
p. 326

Your *home page* (or home document) is the document that you tell Luckman Mosaic to display when it starts. This document should contain links to the documents and WWW sites that you use most frequently. Many people mistakenly use the term *home page* for the welcome page that you get when you connect to a WWW site. A home page provides you with access to the WWW sites or documents that you use most. Your project or company may have its own home page to give members easy access to needed information. You can load someone else's home page or design your own.

◀ See "Moving
between Docu-
ments," p. 102

When you start the Luckman software, it comes with the home page predefined as a local Luckman welcome page. The use of a default local document as Luckman Mosaic's home page was a good idea on the part of the developers. The document loads quickly, and it doesn't waste Net resources by attempting to connect to a remote machine that you aren't interested in anyway. This default home page has some interesting pointers to WWW and Internet resources for someone who is new to the Net. You might want to keep this home page for a while, and, when you are more familiar with the WWW and know the addresses of documents you use frequently, you may want to make up your own home page.

Telling Luckman Mosaic What Home Page to Load

Luckman lets you set your home page in its Preferences dialog box. To use the Preferences dialog box, follow these steps:

1. Open the **E**dit menu and choose **P**references. The Preferences dialog box appears (see fig. 12.10).

Fig. 12.10
You can set your default home page in the Preferences dialog box.

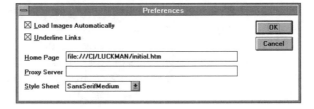

2. Click in the text box next to **H**ome Page, delete the text in the box, and enter the URL of the document you want to use as your home page.

3. Choose OK to save your home page setting and exit the Preferences dialog box.

Your home page can be a document on your computer or any document that you can access at a WWW site. (See Chapter 14, "Creating Home Pages with HTML," for details on how to make your own home page or how to turn a file saved on your computer into a home page.)

When you start Luckman Mosaic, the document that you defined as your home page displays in a separate window inside the main Enhanced NCSA Mosaic window. After the home page loads, the URL for your home page appears in the URL bar. Once your home page is loaded, you can click any of the links to load the documents you use frequently.

If you want to return to your home page at any time, open the **N**avigate menu and choose Ho**m**e. This reloads your home page document.

Tip
Another way to reload your home page is to open the **P**ages menu and choose **H**ome.

> **Note**
>
> Unlike with many other Web browsers, you cannot set Luckman Mosaic to start with a blank display. If you try to wipe out the home page information in the Preferences dialog box, Luckman Mosaic will still default to the initial.htm document in its working directory.

Moving between Documents

After you start Luckman Mosaic, you can move between WWW documents in several ways—you can click links in the document you are viewing, or you can use Luckman Mosaic's Open URL dialog box to enter a URL. If you loaded a home page, it probably includes links to other documents. After all, the purpose of the WWW is to let you move quickly between related documents without having to enter long path names. If there are no links in a document, it's not a very useful WWW document. But, even if your current document has no links, you can still move between documents by directly entering the URLs for the documents you want to view.

> **Note**
>
> Luckman Mosaic gives you a few other ways to move between documents. You can use a hotlist that contains items with predefined URLs. Creating and using hotlists is covered in the "Create Lists of Your Favorite URLs" section later in this chapter.
>
> Also, the **P**ages menu gives you access to the interesting Internet and Web documents found in the default home page.

Moving between Documents Using Links

◄ See "Hypertext and Hypermedia Concepts," p. 24

A link can be a word, a group of words, or an image. Luckman Mosaic can indicate the hypertext links in a document in a number of different ways. If you have a color monitor, the links can be displayed in blue while other text is black (graphics containing links can be outlined in blue). If you have a black-and-white monitor, the links can be underlined (this is the default).

► See "Understanding HTTP and HTML: the Languages of the WWW," p. 321

Luckman Mosaic enables you to keep track of what links you've visited recently if you have a color display. After you've loaded a document, the next time you come across a link to that document, the link displays in green rather than blue.

When you move your cursor over an area of the screen that has an active link, the URL associated with each link that you pass over appears in the status bar. To activate a link, place your cursor over the link and click. Luckman Mosaic loads that document and displays the URL for the document in the URL bar.

Look at the Macmillan Publishing welcome page in figure 12.11. The words *Adobe Press*, *Alpha*, *Brady*, *Hayden*, *New Riders*, *Que*, *Que College*, and *Sams* are all links. When you run Luckman Mosaic on a color display, you see the links in blue (they are underlined in the figure), the default hyperlink color. The URL of the active link (with the pointer over it) is shown in the status bar.

Fig. 12.11
The Macmillan home page has links to home pages for each of the publishing groups. Each publishing group name is an underlined hyperlink.

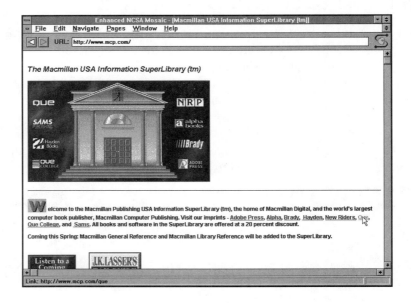

Customizing the Hyperlink Indicators

Luckman Mosaic is not as customizable as some other WWW browsers (notably, NCSA Mosaic and Netscape). The only link parameter that you can customize is whether links are underlined. To set this feature, follow these steps:

1. Open the **E**dit menu and choose **P**references.

2. To have anchors underlined in a document or to get rid of the underlining, click the **U**nderline Links check box (an x indicates the option is selected).

3. When you have the option set, choose OK.

Moving Backward and Forward

Typing long URLs and scrolling through documents to look for the links you want can get rather tedious. If you're jumping between a number of documents, take advantage of three helpful navigating commands: **B**ack, **F**orward, and **R**eload.

Luckman Mosaic keeps information about what documents you have loaded (see a discussion of the history list in the "How to Get Where You Were" section later in this chapter) and lets you move quickly between these documents using the **B**ack and **F**orward commands. The **B**ack command takes you to the previous document that you had open. To go back, open the **G**o menu and choose **B**ack.

The next command is **F**orward. What you have to remember about **F**orward is that you can only move forward after moving back. (This concept is rather confusing, but makes more sense when you have read about history lists in the "How to Get Where You Were" section later in this chapter.) To move forward, open the **N**avigate menu and choose **F**orward.

The last command is **R**eload. This command tells Enhanced Mosaic to reread and display the current document from its URL. To reload the current document, open the **N**avigate menu and choose **R**eload.

Moving between Documents Using URLs

If you don't want to go to any of the documents whose links are displayed in the current document, you can load a new document by specifying its URL to Luckman Mosaic. Refer to Chapter 1, "Introduction to the World Wide Web," for information about how to format a URL correctly. To enter a URL directly, follow these steps:

◀ See "Links and URLs Transport You from Place to Place," p. 27

III

Other Browsers

1. Open the File menu and choose Open URL.

   The Open URL dialog box appears (see fig. 12.12). The URL for the last document that you loaded appears highlighted in the text box.

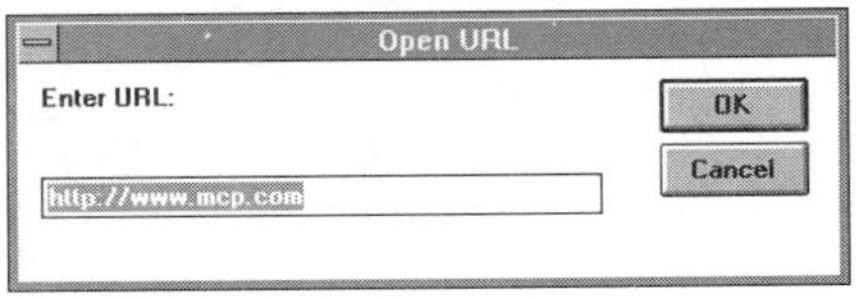

Fig. 12.12
Using the Open URL dialog box, you can directly enter the URL for the next document that you want to view.

2. To enter a completely new URL, begin typing the URL in the box and the old contents are deleted. To modify the URL that is shown, click in the box and your cursor is inserted in the text. You can then edit the current URL.

Tip
A quicker way of entering a URL is to type it directly into the URL bar and then press Enter.

3. Choose OK to load the URL that you entered, or choose Cancel if you do not want to load that document. If you choose OK, Luckman Mosaic loads that document and displays the URL for the document in the URL bar (if you have it enabled).

Opening Multiple Documents

A very useful feature of Luckman Mosaic is that you can view multiple documents at one time. Open the File menu and choose New Window to get another document window. This window will have the same history list as the window it was opened from, with the displayed document being the oldest document in the history list. You can now view any document you want in any of the open Luckman document windows.

Tip
Press Alt and click a link to open the document associated with that link in a new window.

Any new document windows that you open are contained within the main Enhanced NCSA Mosaic window. They can be minimized and maximized, just like regular windows. The titles of the documents in all the document windows appear at the end of the Windows menu (the active document window is checked).

To make a document window active, choose it from the list. There is a number next to the first nine windows in the list to let you select them from the keyboard. If there are more than nine windows, More Windows appears at the bottom of the list. If you select this, the Select Window dialog box appears with a list of all the document windows. Scroll through the list and select the window that you want to be active.

The Window menu gives you some control over the placement of the individual document windows. If you open the Window menu and choose Tile, the document windows are resized so that they all can be displayed in the main window simultaneously. If you open the **W**indow menu and choose **C**ascade, all the windows are stacked neatly on top of one another, slightly offset. If you have your document windows minimized, open the **W**indow menu and choose **A**rrange Icons to neatly arrange the icons in the main window.

Troubleshooting

Why can't I see all my open document windows in the Enhanced NCSA Mosaic main window?

You must make sure that you don't have one of the open document windows maximized. Once you restore this window to its regular size, you should be able to see all the open document windows.

What You See When a Document Is Loaded

When you load a document, Luckman Mosaic gives you a lot of information about what is happening. The globe in the URL bar spins, and a number of different messages appear in the status bar. All these signals help you to follow the progress of a document load.

Status Bar Messages

Viewing a WWW document involves many different activities. Luckman Mosaic needs to contact the server where the document resides, ask the server if it has the document, and then ask it to transfer the document to your computer. Luckman Mosaic tries to let you know what steps have been accomplished and what still needs to be done as it is loading the document. It does this through messages in the status bar. These messages can include the following:

- ■ `Finding the address for the system '<hostname>'`

- ■ `Connecting to HTTP server`

- ■ `Accessing URL:<URL>`

- ■ `Fetching image: <filename>`

- ■ `Loading images`

- ■ `Reformatting text`

III

Other Browsers

The spinning globe is a useful indicator of the status of the document load. A spinning globe with no other action can be the first (or sometimes the only) indication that there is a problem (if your bar graph stops increasing even though the document is not yet loaded, for example).

It is nice to be able to watch the bar graph increase as the elements of the document are loaded. This gives you an idea of how quickly the document is loading.

Stopping a Document Load

You may find that occasionally you need to abort the loading of the current document. Perhaps you clicked a link inadvertently, or you've discovered the document you wanted to view contains huge graphics that you don't have time to download. To stop a document from loading, press Esc.

If you stop a load, you are likely to get a partial copy of the document that was loading. Use the **B**ack command from the **N**avigate menu to return to the previous document and continue your navigation from there.

Controlling the Loading of Graphics

Tip

You can load individual images from a document by right-clicking the box containing the image name.

Loading documents can take a few minutes, especially if the document has many large graphics and your computer has a relatively slow (less than 9600 bps) connection to the Internet. There is one thing you can do to speed up the loading of the document: tell Luckman Mosaic not to load the inline graphics from the document. To do this, open the **E**dit menu and choose **P**references. The Preferences dialog box shown in figure 12.13 appears. Click the **L**oad Images Automatically check box to turn off image loading.

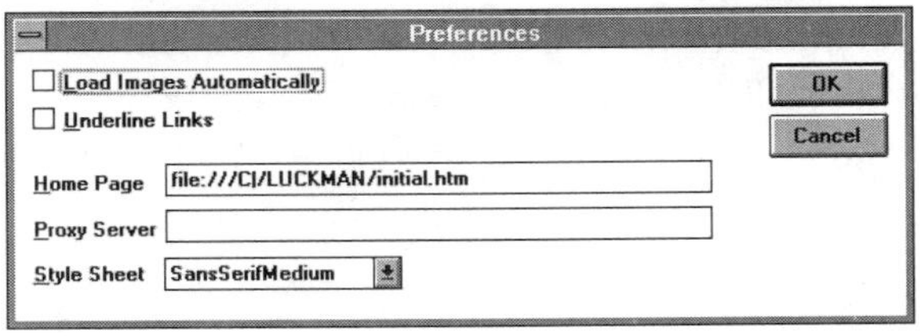

Fig. 12.13

The Load Images Automatically check box should be blank if you don't want to load inline images in your documents.

The next new document you load will not have any images displayed but will instead have boxes containing the names of the missing images (see fig. 12.14) or a Not Loaded icon. To load the images in current document, open the **N**avigate menu and choose **L**oad Missing Images.

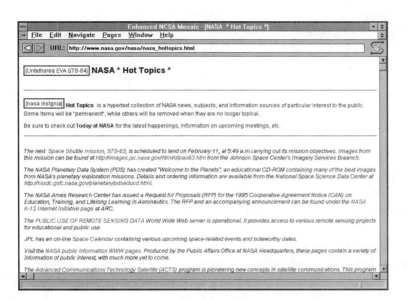

Fig. 12.14
When you tell Luckman Mosaic not to load inline images, it places the names of the images in boxes where the images would be.

> **Note**
>
> The **L**oad Missing Images item in your **N**avigate menu will become active only when Load Images Automatically is turned off.

Looking for Information in a Document

If the WWW document you are reading is short, it is easy to scroll through the document (or use Page Up and Page Down) to find information of interest to you. If you have loaded a very long document though, Luckman Mosaic does provide a quick way to look for information. Follow these steps:

1. Open the **E**dit menu and choose **F**ind to bring up the Find dialog box (see fig. 12.15).

Fig. 12.15
In the Find dialog box, you can specify the search words and starting point of the search.

2. Click the box next to Search For and enter the word or words for which you want to search.

Other Browsers

3. If you want to search the entire document, click the Start From Top check box (if there is not already an X in it). If this box is not checked, the search will go from the current point in the document to the end.

4. Click Match Case if you want Luckman Mosaic to match exactly the capitalization of the word you entered.

5. Choose OK to begin the search. If a match is found, Luckman Mosaic scrolls the window to the section where the match is and highlights the matched text. An alert box informs you if no match is found.

To search for exactly the same string again, open the **E**dit menu and choose Find Again.

Saving Documents

In general, the purpose of the World Wide Web is to be able to have one copy of a document that many people can view, although there are times when you might want to save a copy of a document to your local computer. Luckman Mosaic gives you several options for saving documents.

To save a document, open the **F**ile menu and choose Save **A**s. A Save As dialog box appears in which you can browse through your directories and store the file wherever you like. You have the option of storing the file as plain text or as the HTML source code. Choose the option you want from the list box under Save File as **T**ype.

You can also save any file associated with a hyperlink directly to disk instead of loading it into Luckman Mosaic. Press Ctrl and click a link to load the document associated with that link to disk rather than display it. The document will be stored in whatever format it exists on the remote server—HTML, GIF, WAV, and so on.

When you save an HTML document to your local disk, remember that the document probably contains hyperlinks in it. These links can be *relative* or *absolute*. An absolute reference contains the complete address of the document that is being referenced, including the host name, directory path, and file name. A relative reference assumes that the previous machine and directory path are being used, and just the file name (or possibly a subdirectory and file name) is specified.

If the document references other documents with relative addresses, you cannot view those documents unless you copy them to your local disk and set them up with the same directory structure they had at the original site. You might want to set up a document and its linked documents on your local disk if you want to be able to view the document without connecting to the

Tip

Press Ctrl+G to repeat a search quickly.

Tip

Press Ctrl and click to load to disk documents that Luckman Mosaic can't display; then use your own viewers to display the file. (See "Viewing Multimedia Files" later in this chapter.)

▶ See "Adding Hyperlinks to Other Web Documents," p. 334

Internet. One problem is that if the original document changes, you don't know it and view an outdated version of the document.

Absolute references always work unless your Internet connection fails or the referenced documents are moved.

Printing Documents

In addition to being able to save documents, you can print documents directly from Luckman Mosaic. Open the **F**ile menu and choose **P**rint to send a copy of the current document to your printer.

You can set up the margins, headers, and footers of your document by opening the **F**ile menu and choosing Pa**g**e Setup. You can also set up your printer options by choosing **S**etup from the Print dialog box.

> **Note**
>
> The **F**ile has a P**r**inter Setup option, but it brings up the Print dialog box instead of the Print Setup dialog box.

Customizing the Displayed Fonts

Unlike NCSA Mosaic, Luckman Mosaic offers a limited choice of font style combinations for your window. You can choose to have a serif font used for all text, a sans-serif font used for all text, or mixed fonts, which gives you sans-serif fonts for headings and serif fonts for body text. For each of these combinations, you can choose to have a small, medium, or large font size.

1. Open the **E**dit menu and choose **P**references. Click the **S**tyle Sheet list box to get a list of font options (see fig 12.16).

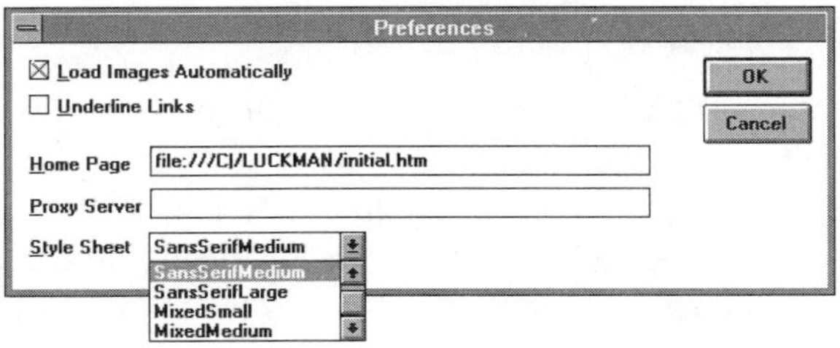

Fig. 12.16
In the Style Sheet list box, you can select from a list of font combinations and sizes.

2. Scroll down through the list until you find the type style and size combination that you want.

3. Choose OK to make the selections take effect, or choose Cancel if you decide not to change the fonts.

The changes that you make take effect immediately and are used by Luckman Mosaic in future sessions.

Viewing Multimedia Files

Luckman Mosaic is much more limited in its capability to display multimedia files than most of the other WWW browsers. It has a built-in capability to display GIF, JPEG, and BMP files using its own image viewer application, and will use Windows Media Player to play WAV files. If you have Microsoft Video for Windows installed, it uses that to display AVI files. Table 12.1 lists the multimedia files that Luckman Mosaic can display.

Table 12.1 Multimedia File Types Recognized by Luckman Mosaic	
Media	**File Type**
Audio	WAV, AU
Image	JPEG, GIF, BMP
Video	AVI

▶ See "Viewers," p. 989

When you click the hyperlink for a file of a recognized type, Luckman Mosaic starts its built-in viewer and either displays the image or plays the sound file or animation. If Luckman Mosaic does not recognize the file type, it will bring up a Transfer To Disk dialog box that lets you load the file directly to disk. You can then use another application to view that file if you have one that will do it.

The included WebCD has viewers for all of the file types you're likely to encounter on the Internet. For graphics files (GIF, JPEG, PCX, BMP, etc.) check out the Lview, WinJPEG, or WinECJ programs. To play animation files (AVI or MPEG) use Mpegplay, Video for Windows, or Video Audio Viewer. For sound files, use Video Audio Viewer, WPlany, or Play Wave. All of these programs are on the enclosed WebCD in the \viewers directory.

Working with Local Files

When you think of using a WWW browser, you think of retrieving documents from WWW servers on the Internet to view. Luckman Mosaic can read documents from your local file system as well as from halfway around the world. If you share documents among members of your organization, many of the documents you view may be on a local file server or possibly on your local computer.

Luckman Mosaic makes it easy to load a local file. To load a local file, open the **F**ile menu and click **O**pen Local. The Open Local dialog box, shown in figure 12.17, appears. By default, only files of type HTM are shown, but you can see all files in your directories by selecting All Files (*.*) in the List Files of **T**ype list box.

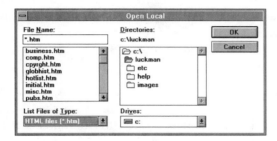

Fig. 12.17
In the Open Local dialog box, you can enter a local file name or browse your local file system to find the next document that you want to view.

◀ See "Links and URLs Transport You from Place to Place," p. 27

You also can load a local file in the same manner that you load any URL. Open the **F**ile menu and choose Open **L**ocation. To specify a local file in the URL box, precede the directory path of the file with **file:///c|/path/ filename** (you can substitute any of your local disks for *c*). The three slashes tell Luckman Mosaic that you are looking for a local file, and the bar is used instead of a colon because the colon has a specific purpose in a URL. Use slashes in the directory path you enter, even if you are describing a directory on a PC where the backslash is usually used. Luckman properly translates the slashes when it retrieves the file.

Local URLs can be used anywhere URLs are used—as entries in your hotlist, as links in documents, and so on.

Effective Browsing Techniques

Navigating between WWW documents can be confusing. Documents often connect back to documents you already read. You can't always remember which of several related documents has the information you really need.

Sometimes you can't tell from the hyperlink whether the document is of interest to you, and loading documents uses valuable time. Often, you waste time loading documents that you dismiss immediately. This section helps you learn to reduce unnecessary document-loading and circular navigating.

How to Keep Track of Where You've Been

Keeping track of where you are and where you were is one of the biggest challenges of using the WWW. Documents are often cross linked to many sites and tagged to different hyptertext links. Keeping track of how you arrived at an interesting destination can be difficult. Finding your way back can be impossible—especially if you were just surfing from site to site when you found something that interested you. Luckily, most WWW browsers include features that let you minimize these navigation problems.

One suggestion is to have a home page that provides links to your most-visited WWW pages. This home page is useful, for example, if you work on a group project and frequently use documents with known locations. You can create your own home page, or someone can create a project home page for your group. In this scenario, you probably are already familiar with the servers, if not the exact documents.

But what if you're navigating in uncharted waters on the WWW? Although it sounds difficult, you probably can learn to recognize the URLs of the sites that keep information of interest to you. If the location bar is displayed, the URL for the current document is shown there. The status bar shows the URL of a hyperlink when you move the cursor over it (see fig. 12.18). As you move between documents, you begin to remember some of the URLs you see frequently—when you put your cursor over a hyperlink, you recognize documents you know.

Fig. 12.18
The status bar displays the URLs of hyperlinks when the cursor is on top of them.

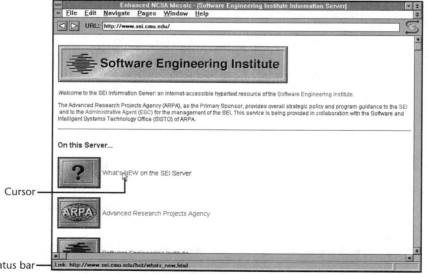

How to Get Where You Were

Trying to navigate back to a document you viewed in the current Luckman Mosaic session also can be challenging. In general, to go to the document you viewed prior to the current document, open the **N**avigate menu and choose the **B**ack command (or the left arrow in the toolbar). Choosing the **F**orward command (or the right arrow) takes you to the last document you viewed from this document. This sounds rather confusing, but the more you use the buttons, the more you get the hang of what they do.

The **N**avigate menu has an item called **H**istory that brings up a window, similar to the one shown in figure 12.19. Notice that a list of URLs is in this window. This list shows all the URLs you have visited; the highlighted URL at the top of the list is the last new document that was visited.

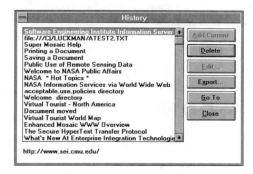

Fig. 12.19
The Luckman Mosaic History window shows a linear list of URLs you've visited.

Unlike many of the other WWW browsers, Luckman Mosaic does not show you a list of documents you've visited in the order in which you visited them. Rather, it organizes them according to their relationship with other documents. If you jump from a parent document to a linked document, move back to the parent document, and then jump to a different document, both documents to which you jumped will be shown under the parent document's entry in the list.

> **Note**
>
> Luckman Mosaic's way of implementing the history list makes it very confusing to figure out how you got to a document. Using the Back and Forward navigation commands do not move you linearly in the history list. These commands actually keep track of what document you came from and what document you last visited from the current document (which is how the history list is implemented in most other Web browsers). So there are some documents in the history list that you cannot get to by using the Forward and Back navigation commands.

III

Other Browsers

You can go directly to any document in the History dialog box. Click any URL in the list and choose **G**o To to jump to that document. This loads the document and moves the position of that document up to near the top of the history list.

The best strategy for getting back to where you were changes, depending on how you have been viewing documents. If you have been moving progressively from one document to another and not jumping back and forth to the parent document, the Back and Forward navigation commands will easily move you among the documents you've visited.

On the other hand, if you've been using a central document to visit many other documents or if you have been jumping in circular paths or otherwise leaving a confusing trail of where you've been, you probably want to use the history list to just select a document you've previously visited and jump directly back to it.

Luckman Mosaic saves the history of your Internet travels from session to session in a cumulative list. This feature makes it easy to go back to places you've visited previously, even if you didn't remember to add the site to your hotlist or a bookmark file.

Create Lists of Your Favorite URLs

If you don't want to learn to use HTML commands to create a home page with all your favorite WWW documents, Luckman Mosaic has an alternative. To quickly access your favorite URLs, Luckman Mosaic lets you export your history list to create what is commonly called a *bookmark* file. You can have any number of bookmark files with any number of links in them. You can also use Luckman's Hotlist feature to make a list of documents that you can quickly load.

Creating and Using Bookmark Files

You can use the history list to create a bookmark file containing a list of documents that you've visited in this current session. Each item in the list is a link to that document. You can load any bookmark file that you create in this way and jump to any of the documents it points to. To create a bookmark file from the current history list, follow these steps:

1. Open the **N**avigate menu and choose Hi**s**tory (see fig. 12.20).

2. Delete any documents you don't want to save by selecting the document and choosing **D**elete. The document will be removed from the History list.

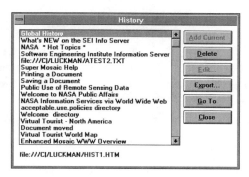

Fig. 12.20
Using the History dialog box, you can export a list of the documents you've visited in this session.

> **Note**
>
> According to the Luckman Mosaic documentation, you should be able to use the **E**dit button in the History dialog box to change the title and copy the URL of any item in the list, but this does not seem to work in the current version of the software.

3. Choose E**x**port to write the list of documents to an HTM file. This brings up the Export History dialog box, which lets you name the file and save it anywhere in your directory structure.

When you save the file and choose Close, Luckman Mosaic loads that file as your current document (see fig. 12.21).

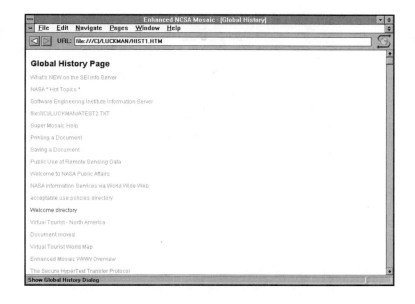

Fig. 12.21
Saving your history list creates the Global History Page document that contains a list of links to the documents that were in your history.

III

Other Browsers

4. Choose **C**lose to dismiss the History dialog box.

Tip
Create a book-
marks directory to
store your ex-
ported history lists
so that you can
find them quickly.

You can load any of the bookmark files that you've created by opening the **F**ile menu, choosing **O**pen Local, and browsing your file system until you find one of the files that you've saved. Once the file is loaded, you can click any of the document titles to load that document. You can also share these files with your friends.

Creating and Using Hotlists

Besides saving your history lists, Luckman Mosaic provides another way for you to create a list of URLs that you can access quickly. Luckman lets you add any documents that you visit to your hotlist, open the hotlist, and quickly jump to those documents. To use the hotlist, follow these steps:

1. Open the **N**avigate menu and choose **H**otlist (see fig. 12.22). The first time you do this, the list will be blank, and you will only be able to add the current document to the list.

Fig. 12.22
In the Hotlist dialog box, you can add documents to your hotlist, edit and delete them, and save the hotlist to a file.

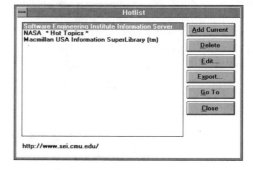

2. To add the current document to the hotlist, choose **A**dd Current. The item will be placed at the end of the hotlist.

3. Delete any documents you don't want to save by selecting the docu-ment and choosing **D**elete. The document will be removed from the hotlist.

4. You can choose **E**dit to change the title or URL of the selected item in the hotlist (see fig. 12.23).

Fig. 12.23
In the Edit Title-URL dialog box, you can change the title or URL of any item in your hotlist.

5. Choose E**x**port to write the list of documents to an HTM file. This brings up the Export Hotlist dialog box, which lets you name the file and save it anywhere in your directory structure. You must manually enter the .htm extension when saving this file.

When you save the file, Luckman Mosaic then loads that file as your current document (see fig. 12.24).

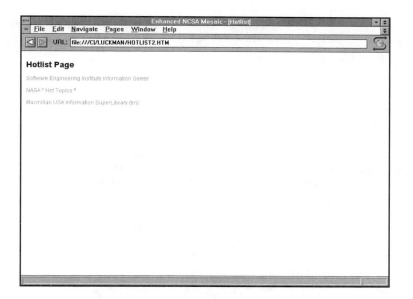

Fig. 12.24
Saving your hotlist creates the Hotlist Page document that contains a list of links to the documents that are in your hotlist.

6. Choose **C**lose to dismiss the Hotlist dialog box.

You can change the hotlist that Luckman Mosaic loads when it starts by re-naming any of your hotlist files to hotlist.htm. Remember to first rename the existing hotlist.htm file. The next time Luckman Mosaic starts up, it will load the file hotlist.htm from its working directory as its current hotlist. By saving and renaming various hotlist files, you can easily change the default hotlist presented by Luckman Mosaic.

Tip
Create a hotlists directory to store your exported history lists so that you can find them quickly.

III

Other Browsers

You can also load any of the hotlist files that you've created directly into Luckman Mosaic. Open the **F**ile menu, choose **O**pen Local, and browse your file system until you find one of the files that you've saved. Once the file is loaded, you can click any of the document titles to load that document. You can also share these files with your friends.

Security

Many people seem to feel that because computers are machines, communications between computers is secure (no people involved). Nothing could be further from the truth.

Communication on the Internet involves data being forwarded from the sending computer to the receiving computer through a number of intermediate computers. A possibility exists that someone could be looking at the information passing through the intermediate computers. They could possibly even set up another computer to pretend to be the receiving computer so that everything you sent went to someone who was not intended to see the information.

◀ See "Security," p. 248

For this reason, sending sensitive information (like your credit card number) over the Internet is not a good idea. Any information sent over the Internet is at risk—e-mail messages, file transfers, and particularly information from electronic forms that you may fill out using your WWW browser.

Luckman Mosaic has no provisions for guaranteeing the security of information you enter to a form. If you need to send sensitive information using a WWW browser, see the information on security in Chapter 11, "Netscape."

Using Other Internet Services

Like NCSA Mosaic, Luckman Mosaic provides a more friendly interface to some of the older Internet services. Conceptually, using Luckman Mosaic to access these services is the same as using NCSA Mosaic to access the services, so these next sections just show you how Luckman Mosaic displays the services. (You may want to read the corresponding NCSA Mosaic chapters for more in-depth information about the services.)

FTP

Like NCSA Mosaic, Luckman Mosaic provides a nicer way of browsing FTP sites. Instead of having to use cryptic FTP commands from a terminal interface, you can use the `ftp:` protocol in a URL to connect to and graphically view an FTP site. FTP sites are viewed as file systems; when you connect to a site, you see the top-level directory for that site. From there, you can click subdirectories to examine their contents, and you can click files to load them into Luckman Mosaic.

◀ See "Locating the FTP Information You Want," p. 147

Caution

Luckman Mosaic does not always seem to correctly display URLs that use the ftp: protocol. It sometimes gives an error telling you that the attempt to load that URL failed. In addition, if you connect to an FTP server and then try to connect to different FTP server, Luckman Mosaic seems to connect you to the new server, but in reality takes you back to the top-level directory for the first FTP server. The current version of the software seems unreliable to use for viewing FTP servers.

Unlike NCSA Mosaic, Luckman Mosaic enables you to display FTP directories only as simple lists of file and directory names. Figure 12.25 shows you the format Luckman Mosaic uses to display the directory information from FTP servers. Note that you have no way of knowing what any particular entry in a directory is unless the files in that directory use standard file extensions.

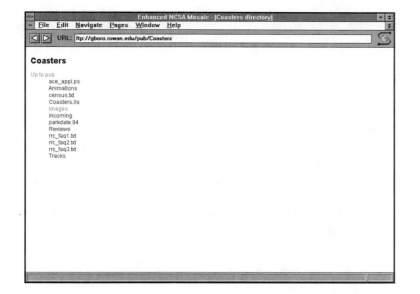

Fig. 12.25
Luckman Mosaic gives little information about the content of the directories on FTP servers.

III

Other Browsers

If you try to load a file that Luckman Mosaic does not know how to display, it will bring up the Transfer File To dialog box, enabling you to save the file directly to your local disk. If you cancel the load to disk, Luckman Mosaic attempts to load the file for viewing instead of aborting the loading. Press Esc to abort the loading.

Gopher

◀ See "Locating Gopher Information," p. 164

Luckman Mosaic provides a simple interface to Gopher servers, similar to its FTP server interface. You see a textual representation of the Gopher menu with no indication of what the items in the menu are. You can point to a menu item and click to view that item. If the item is another menu, that menu displays. If the item is a file type that Luckman Mosaic can display, it loads the file and displays it. Figure 12.26 shows a Gopher menu displayed by Luckman Mosaic.

Fig. 12.26
Luckman Mosaic gives you a graphical interface to Gopher servers.

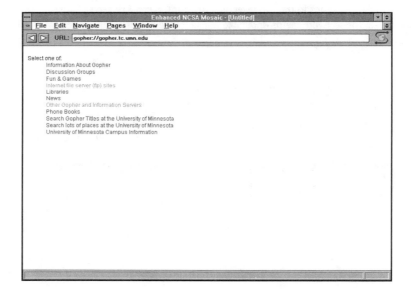

◀ See "Saving Files from a Gopher Server," p. 175

If you try to load a file that Luckman Mosaic does not know how to display, it will bring up the Transfer File To dialog box, enabling you to save the file directly to your local disk. If you cancel the load to disk, Luckman Mosaic attempts to load the file for viewing instead of aborting the loading. Press Esc to abort the loading.

UseNet

Like NCSA Mosaic, Luckman Mosaic provides an interface to the thousands of UseNet newsgroups. If you can provide the name of an NNTP server for Luckman Mosaic to use, you can read any UseNet newsgroup. To tell Luckman Mosaic what NNTP server to use, edit the line beginning NNTP_Server= in your lmosaic.ini file in Luckman Mosaic's working directory and put the name of your NNTP server after the equal sign.

◀ See "Using Mosaic to Access UseNet Newsgroups," p. 185

The Luckman Mosaic interface to newsgroups is almost identical to NCSA Mosaic's interface to newsgroups. You can only read articles—you cannot post new or follow-up articles—and the articles are shown in the order they were received on the server (they cannot be grouped by topic). See the discussion on newsgroups in Chapter 10, "Using Mosaic to Access Other Internet Services," for more information on how to use this interface to read newsgroups.

Telnet

Unlike Mosaic, Luckman Mosaic does not give you the option of using Telnet (a terminal interface program) to connect to hosts that require connecting to a special port, or hosts that actually require you to log in to use a service. If you enter a URL with the Telnet protocol, or click a link that uses the Telnet protocol, Luckman Mosaic brings up a dialog box telling you to run your communication software's Telnet program and use it to connect to the hostname in the URL.

Luckman Interactive InfoWeb

Luckman Interactive has another useful product you may find interesting for browsing the Web. Through a partnership with Que, Luckman has created the InfoWeb, an electronic version of the site listings in *Using the World Wide Web*. With this product, you can access any of the sites listed in the reference chapters of *Using the World Wide Web* by clicking a hyperlink instead of entering the URL by hand. The text relating to the sites is included, too.

InfoWeb works as a collection of HTML files saved on your hard drive. After InfoWeb is installed, the default home page in Luckman Mosaic is changed so that it looks like figure 12.27.

III

Other Browsers

Fig. 12.27
Luckman Enhanced Mosaic with the InfoWeb added to the default home page.

To use the InfoWeb, click the InfoWeb link. This will open the main InfoWeb page, shown in figure 12.28.

Fig. 12.28
This is the main InfoWeb page showing the various categories of listed Web pages.

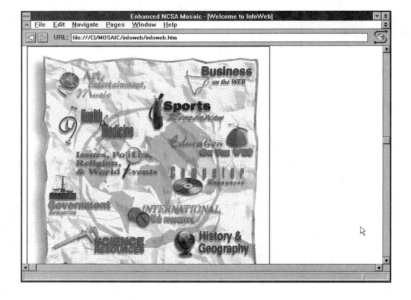

On this page, there is a large clickable image map (again, this is stored locally to save time loading) with areas to click for each of the subject areas in the *Using the World Wide Web* listings. For example, clicking Computers brings up the page shown in figure 12.29 and from there you can jump to any of the pages in the listings.

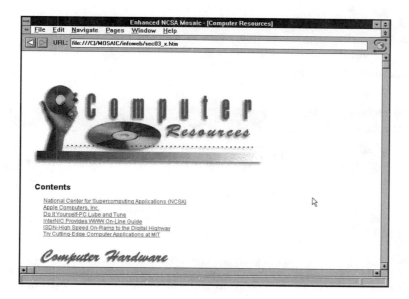

Fig. 12.29
The InfoWeb Computer Resources page lists all the computer listings from *Using the World Wide Web*.

> **Note**
>
> You may notice that some of the listings in InfoWeb are not exactly the same as those in *Special Edition Using the World Wide Web and Mosaic*. That's because in writing this special edition, we have added new listings, updated listings, and made other changes to keep this new version of the book completely up to date.

Although InfoWeb is designed to work with Luckman's Enhanced Mosaic, you can use it with any Web browser since the pages are in standard HTML Web format. To use it from another browser, open the c:\mosaic\infoweb\infoweb.htm file.

If you are interested in purchasing InfoWeb, see the Luckman Interactive advertisement near the back of this book.

The Future of Enhanced Mosaic

As explained in the chapter introduction, Spyglass licensed Mosaic from NCSA and commercialized it to license to other companies. The version of Enhanced Mosaic from Luckman with this book is based on the version 1 of Enhanced Mosaic from Spyglass.

III

Other Browsers

Spyglass has announced a new version of Enhanced Mosaic that will add security features, improve speed, and improve graphics viewing. This version is expected to be available to the companies having Spyglass licenses by the time you read this. However, it was several months after the licensees received the first version before any of the companies had them ready to resell to the public. (Luckman Interactive is the first.) You can expect it to be several months after Spyglass finishes version 2 before any of the licensees have their version 2 products ready to sell.

> **Note**
>
> For more information on Spyglass, the companies licensing Mosaic, and Enhanced Mosaic version 2, see **http://www.spyglass.com/mos_home.htm**.

From Here...

This chapter covered the Luckman Interactive version of Enhanced Mosaic.

To learn more about using Mosaic and to find interesting WWW documents, refer to these chapters:

- Chapter 6, "Navigating with Mosaic," tells you how to use Mosaic to find and view documents on the WWW.

- Chapter 7, "Mosaic Shortcuts and Tips," tells you how to become an expert WWW navigator.

- Chapter 19, "Web Searching," discusses how to use automated software to find some of the most interesting collections of WWW documents.

Chapter 13

Microsoft Internet Assistant

by Mary Ann Pike

In preparation for its Windows 95 environment and the Microsoft Network (which will give people access to Internet services from Windows 95), Microsoft has released their Internet Assistant, a WWW browsing and authoring extension to Microsoft Word. While it was still being beta tested as of this writing, expect it to be released by the time you read this.

In this chapter, you learn the following:

- How to install Internet Assistant

- How to access Internet Assistant

- How to view Web documents with Internet Assistant

> ### Caution
>
> The version of Internet Assistant used while writing this chapter was a beta release. It had little in the way of error messages, and would occasionally hang without warning or generate a general protection fault while downloading a document (often because it ran out of temporary disk space). Take necessary precautions to avoid permanent loss of data on your system if you are running a beta version of this application. If you tried the beta version, you should upgrade to the release version as soon as it is available. Be sure to read any documentation with the release regarding switching versions.

III

Other Browsers

Getting Internet Assistant Up and Running

If you already have an Internet connection, you can get the files for Internet Assistant from Microsoft's FTP or WWW sites. You should make sure that your system is properly set up to run Internet Assistant before loading the software, however.

If you don't have Internet access (or don't want to download this for some reason), Microsoft will send a copy on disk to registered users of Word 6. If you don't have an Internet connection, you will need to get one in order to take full advantage of this software.

Will Your Computer Run Internet Assistant?

You must be running Windows 3.1 or better (including Windows for Workgroups 3.1 or better, Windows NT, or Windows for Pen Computing). You must also be running MS-DOS 3.0 or later, and should have a minimum of 6M of RAM (8M recommended) and 2M of hard disk space (plus another 1M or so to unpack the software).

You need to be running Word 6.0a or later to integrate Internet Assistant with Word. If you do not have Word 6.0a or better, there is a program called Word Viewer (available from Microsoft) that will allow you to view documents created in Word. The current version of Internet Assistant is a 16-bit application, so you must be running 16-bit Word for Windows in order to use Internet Assistant with Windows NT.

The Internet Assistant does not currently run in any of the international language versions of Word 6. Support for international versions is planned for later.

> **Note**
>
> If you are not sure which version of Word 6 you have, choose **H**elp, **A**bout to see the version. If you have version 6.0 instead of 6.0a, contact Microsoft for information about getting the patch to upgrade to version 6.0a.

◀ See "Obtaining Auxiliary Software for Mosaic," p. 68

You might want to check out Chapter 4, "Getting Mosaic Running in Windows," to get an idea of what auxiliary software you might need while running Internet Assistant.

Installing Internet Assistant on Your System

You first need to get a copy of the Internet Assistant file from the Microsoft WWW site or the Microsoft FTP site. If you have access to another WWW browser, open the URL **http://www.microsoft.com/pages/deskapps/ word/ia/default.com**. Scroll to the middle of the document to a section called "How to download Internet Assistant," where you will find the hyperlink `download Internet Assistant` near the bottom of the page. To load this file, simply click on the hyperlink, fill in the information on where you want to put the file in the Save As dialog box that appears, and then choose OK. Internet Assistant will be loaded to your disk, ready to install.

> **Note**
>
> The Internet Assistant self-extracting archive file is about 1.17M, and will take a while to load if you are working over a SLIP or PPP connection.

If you do not already have a WWW browser, but do have an Internet connection, you can use the FTP application that came with your Internet communications software to connect to the Microsoft FTP server (**ftp.microsoft.com**) and retrieve the file /deskapps/word/winword-public/ ia/wordia.exe. (An example of using WS_FTP to retrieve a file can be found in Chapter 4, "Getting Mosaic Running in Windows.")

After you have a copy of the Internet Assistant, follow these steps to install it:

1. Make sure that the Internet Assistant self-extracting archive is in a temporary directory.

2. Execute the self-extracting archive by double-clicking on the archive file from the Windows File Manager. When the file has finished extracting, you may have to press Enter to return to Windows.

3. To execute the setup.exe file, simply double-click the file name from the Windows File Manager. (You may need to choose **W**indow, **R**efresh to see the files that you extracted).

4. Choose OK at the first installation screen (shown in fig. 13.1) to proceed with the Internet Assistant installation. (If you want to stop the installation, choose E**x**it Setup.)

Tip

You can also pick up Internet Assistant from the Macmillan Information SuperLibrary software page at **http:// www.mcp.com/ softlib/ Internet/**.

◄ See "Where to Get the Basic Mosaic Software," p. 65

◄ See "Connecting to an Anonymous FTP Server," p. 154

Tip

You can also retrieve this from the Macmillan FTP site at **ftp.mcp.com** in /pub/que/net-cd/wordia.exe.

III

Other Browsers

Fig. 13.1
The initial
Internet Assistant
setup screen tells
you to exit all
other applications
before starting the
installation.

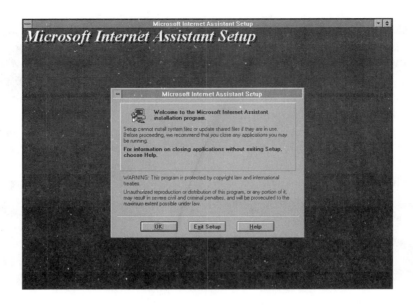

5. The next three screens show you the Internet Assistant license agreement. Click **C**ontinue on the first two screens and **A**gree on the final
   screen (shown in fig. 13.2) to begin the installation.

Fig. 13.2
On the final
Internet Assistant
license screen,
click **A**gree to
accept the license
terms or E**x**it
to exit the
installation.

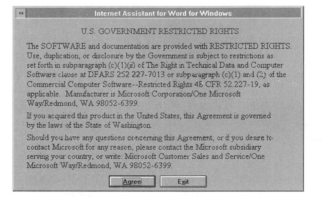

6. The next screen lets you specify the directory where Internet Assistant is
   to be installed (see fig. 13.3). The default is a directory called internet
   under your Word 6 directory. You can browse your local disk to specify
   a different directory.

Fig. 13.3
Click the **C**ontinue button with the terminal on it when you are satisfied with the location of the Internet Assistant directory.

7. Before Internet Assistant installs the Web browsing component, it brings up the screen shown in figure 13.4. Click **Y**es to install the Internet browsing software if you have Internet access.

Fig. 13.4
Internet Assistant tells you that the browsing component will not be useful if you don't have an Internet connection, and tells how to find out about connecting to the Internet.

8. The progress of the installation is shown on a linear graph. When the installation is complete, you will get the dialog box shown in figure 13.5.

Fig. 13.5
After the Internet Assistant installation is complete, you can Launch Word or Exit the setup program.

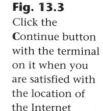

III

Other Browsers

9. To exit the setup program, click OK in the dialog box shown in figure 13.6.

Fig. 13.6
After setup is complete, Internet Assistant informs you that the installation was successful.

The installation of the Internet Assistant software is now complete. You can remove the temporary directory where you unpacked the software if you want—it is no longer needed.

Using the Internet Assistant

Before starting Internet Assistant, you must be connected to the Internet. If your Internet connection is via your LAN, be sure you are logged onto your network. If you are connected to the Internet by a modem, start your TCP/IP software and log in to your account.

After you have established your Internet connection, start Word 6. You now can use Word 6 and Internet Assistant to author WWW documents and explore the Internet.

The Internet Assistant Interface

Tip
Click the eyeglasses button at the left of the formatting toolbar to enter Web browser mode without loading the default home page.

When you run Word 6 with Internet Assistant loaded, you can use Word 6 to edit Word documents. When you get the urge to surf the Internet, however, instead of leaving Word and starting a Web browser, all you need to do is open the File menu and choose Browse Web. The Internet Assistant screen shown in figure 13.7 appears.

A brief description of each window part is given in this section. The remainder of this chapter contains detailed discussion of the Internet Assistant's browser features.

- The *title bar* contains the usual window function buttons (Control Menu box and Maximize and Minimize buttons). The title of the loaded Web document is not currently shown in the title bar.

- The *menu bar* gives access to all the functions you need to use Internet Assistant, in addition to the normal Word functions.

■ The *toolbar* gives you access to some of the most used browsing commands. The following list gives basic descriptions of these buttons:

- *Go Back* displays the document from which you jumped to this document.

- *Go Forward* displays the last document you visited from this one.

- *URL* opens a dialog box to enter a URL to jump to.

- *Title* opens a dialog box where you can insert information about the current document in the head of the documents.

- *Open Favorite* opens your list of favorite places.

- *Add Favorite* adds the URL of the current document to your list of favorite places.

- *History* brings up a list of the last 50 URLs that you've visited.

- *Home* loads your home page.

- *Stop* aborts a document load.

■ The *document window* is a separate window within the Word window where you see the text of a document and any inline images it may contain. You can have multiple document windows open at one time.

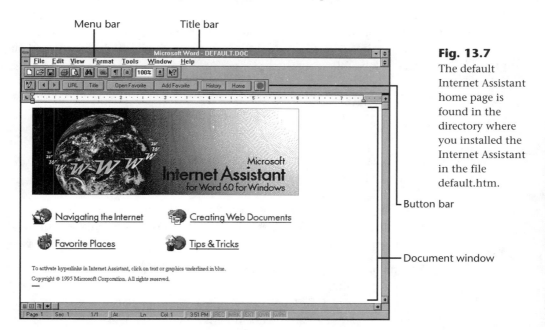

Fig. 13.7
The default Internet Assistant home page is found in the directory where you installed the Internet Assistant in the file default.htm.

III

Other Browsers

What Is a Home Page?

Your *home page* (or home document) is the document that you tell the Internet Assistant to display when it starts. This document should contain links to the documents and WWW sites that you use most frequently. Many people mistakenly use the term home page for the welcome page that you get when you connect to a WWW site. A home page provides you with access to the WWW sites or documents that you use most. Your project or company may have its own home page to give members easy access to needed information. You can load someone else's home page or design your own.

When you start the Internet Assistant browser, it comes with the home page predefined as a local page for the Internet Assistant. The use of a default local document as the Internet Assistant home page was a good idea on the part of the developers. The document loads quickly, and it doesn't waste Net resources by attempting to connect to a remote machine that you aren't interested in anyway. This default home page has some interesting pointers to WWW and Internet resources for someone who is new to the Net. You might want to keep this home page for a while, and when you are more familiar with the WWW and know the addresses of documents you use frequently, you may want to make up your own home page.

Telling Internet Assistant What Home Page to Load

Tip
Rename the original default.doc if you replace it, just in case you want to refer to it later.

Internet Assistant lets you use any document as your home page. One way to do this is to rename a local document to be default.htm and put it in the Internet directory under your Word 6 working directory. You can also edit your wordhtml.ini file and set the home page to be any document on your local disk by following these steps:

1. Edit the wordhtml.ini file found in your c:\windows directory.

2. Edit the line StartDoc= and place the path to the file containing your home page after the equal sign.

3. When you have the option set to your satisfaction, exit your editor, making sure to save the file.

Your home page can be a document on your computer. (See Chapter 14, "Creating Home Pages with HTML," for details on how to make your own home page or how to turn a file saved on your computer into a home page.)

When you start Internet Assistant, the document that you defined as your home page will be displayed in a separate window inside the main Word window. Once your home page is loaded, you can click any of the links on your home page to load the documents you use frequently.

If you want to return to your home page at any time, open the **W**indow menu and choose H**o**me. This reloads your home page document.

Tip

Click the Home button on the toolbar to quickly reload your home page.

> **Note**
>
> Unlike many other Web browsers, you cannot set Internet Assistant to start with a blank display. However, you can click the eyeglasses button at the left of the formatting toolbar to enter Web browser mode without loading the default home page.

Moving between Documents

After you start Internet Assistant, you can move between WWW documents in several ways—you can click links in the document you are viewing or you can use Internet Assistant's Open URL dialog box to enter a URL. If you loaded a home page, it probably includes links to other documents. After all, the purpose of the WWW is to let you move quickly between related documents without having to enter long path names. If there are no links in a document, it's not a very useful WWW document. But, even if your current document has no links, you can still move between documents by directly entering the URLs for the documents you want to view.

> **Note**
>
> Internet Assistant gives you a few other ways to move between documents. Use your Favorite Places document to create a list of URLs that point to your favorite documents. Creating and using hotlists is covered in the section "Create Lists of Your Favorite URLs" later in this chapter.

Moving between Documents Using Links

A link can be a word, a group of words, or an image. The Internet Assistant browser can indicate the hypertext links in a document in a number of different ways. If your monitor is color, the links are displayed in color while other text is black (graphics containing links are outlined in the link color; blue is the default). Also, text containing links is underlined.

Look at the Macmillan Publishing welcome page in figure 13.8. The words Adobe Press, Alpha, Brady, Hayden, New Riders, Que, Que College, and Sams are all links. When you run Internet Assistant on a color display, you see the links in blue (they are underlined in the figure), the default hyperlink color.

◀ See "Hypertext and Hypermedia Concepts," p. 24

▶ See "Understanding HTTP and HTML: The Languages of the WWW," p. 321

III

Other Browsers

Fig. 13.8
The Macmillan
Publishing home
page, with
hyperlinks
underlined.

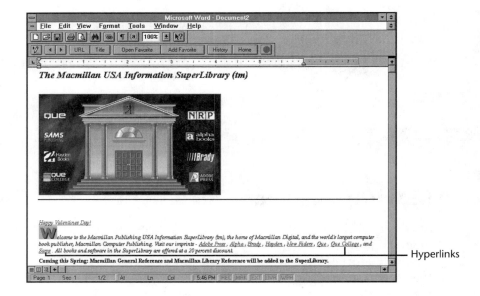

Hyperlinks

Customizing the Hyperlink Indicators

Internet Assistant is not as customizable as some other WWW browsers (notably, NCSA Mosaic and Netscape). The only link parameter that you can customize is what color the links are. To set this feature, follow these steps:

1. Edit the wordhtml.ini file found in your c:\windows directory.

2. Add the line AnchorColor= to the [Misc] section and place a color from the following list after the equal sign.

Black	DarkCyan	DarkGray
Magenta	DarkYellow	Green
DarkBlue	Cyan	White
DarkRed	Yellow	DarkMagenta
Blue (default)	DarkGreen	LightGray
Red		

3. When you have the option set to your satisfaction, exit your editor, making sure to save the file.

This change will take effect the next time you close and restart Word.

> **Note**
>
> This change does not affect documents in Word .doc format. It only affects true HTML. So you will not see the links change color in the default.doc document or the other .doc files that come with Internet Assistant.

Moving Backward and Forward

Typing long URLs and scrolling through documents to look for the links you want can get rather tedious. If you're jumping between a number of documents, take advantage of three navigating commands: Go **B**ack, Go **F**orward, and **R**eload.

Because you can have multiple document windows open at one time in Internet Assistant, the Go Back and Go Forward commands are not as important as they are in browsers where only one document at a time can be open. And the commands don't work in quite the same way.

To access either the Go **B**ack or Go **F**orward command, open the **W**indow menu and choose the command. These commands will take you to the document window that you came from (back) and that you last jumped to (forward) from the current document window. They are most useful for moving quickly between a few of the document windows you've visited recently. They are not as useful for trying to get back to a document that you visited a while ago (see "How to Get Where You Were" later in this chapter).

One command that may be of use to you occasionally is Reload (particularly if there has been an error while loading your document). This command tells Internet Assistant to read the current document in from its URL and display it again. To reload the current document, open the **F**ile menu and choose **R**eload.

Moving between Documents Using URLs

If you don't want to go to any of the documents whose links are displayed in the current document, you can load a new document by specifying its URL to Internet Assistant. Refer to Chapter 1, "Introduction to the World Wide Web," for information about how to correctly format a URL. To enter a URL directly, follow these steps:

1. Open the **F**ile menu and choose Op**e**n URL.

2. The Open URL dialog box appears (see fig. 13.9). The URL for the last document that you loaded appears highlighted in the text box.

Tip
The left and right arrows in the toolbar are (respectively) the Go Back and Go Forward commands.

◄ See "Links and URLs Transport You from Place to Place," p. 27

Tip
Click the URL button in the toolbar to bring up the Open URL dialog box.

III

Other Browsers

Fig. 13.9
The Open URL dialog box lets you directly enter the URL for the next document that you want to view.

3. If you want to enter a completely new URL, just begin typing the URL in the box and the old contents are deleted. If you want to modify the URL that is shown, click in the box and your cursor is inserted in the text, where you can edit the current URL.

4. Choose OK to load the URL that you entered, or choose Cancel if you do not want to load that document. If you choose OK, Internet Assistant loads that document and displays the URL for the document in the URL bar (if you have it enabled).

Opening Multiple Documents

A very useful feature of Internet Assistant is its ability to view multiple documents at one time. Any time you open a document, it opens in a new document window. You can move between any of the open Internet Assistant document windows.

Any new document windows that you open are all contained within the main Word window. They can be minimized and maximized, just like regular windows. The titles of the documents in all the document windows appear at the end of the Windows menu (the active document window is checked).

> **Note**
>
> Although having a new window for each document you visit can be a nice feature, it can quickly get out of hand if you are jumping to a lot (dozens) of different documents on the Web in a short period of time. You end up with a huge number of open windows, and it's difficult to find the window you want because the title bars do not contain the name of the documents—just a document number.
>
> You'll need to learn to close the windows of documents you won't be needing again so that you can quickly find the documents you do need.

To make a document window active, simply choose it from the list. There is a number next to the first nine windows in the list to let you select them from the keyboard. If there are more than nine windows, More Windows... appears at the bottom of the list. If you select this, the Select Window dialog box appears with a list of all the document windows. Scroll through the list and select the window that you want to be active.

The Window menu gives you some control over the placement of the individual document windows. If you open the **W**indow menu and choose **A**rrange All, the document windows are resized so that all of them can be displayed in the main window simultaneously.

To close all your open document windows and exit the Web browser mode, open the **F**ile menu and choose Close All **W**eb Documents.

Troubleshooting

Why can't I see all my open document windows in the Word main window?

You must make sure that you don't have one of the open document windows maximized. When you restore this window to its regular size, you should be able to see all the open document windows.

What You See When a Document Is Loaded

Internet Assistant loads documents by first loading and formatting the text of a document, and then loading each of the image files that belongs in the document. As you are opening a document, Internet Assistant displays a bar that shows you the percentage loaded for each piece of the document (see fig. 13.10). It's nice to be able to watch the bar graph as the elements of the document are loaded. This gives you an idea of how quickly the document is loading.

Fig. 13.10
The Downloading bar graph shows you the progress of each piece of the document you are loading.

Stopping a Document Load

You may find that, occasionally, you would like to abort the loading of the current document. Perhaps you clicked on a link inadvertently. Or perhaps you've discovered the document you wanted to view contains huge graphics that you don't have time to download. To stop a document from loading, click the button that looks like a red stop sign in the toolbar. You can also click the Cancel button in the Downloading bar graph to cancel the remaining images in the document.

Controlling the Loading of Images

Loading documents can take a few minutes, especially if the document has a lot of large graphics and your computer has a relatively slow (less than 9600 bps) connection to the Internet. There is one thing you can do to speed up the loading of the document: tell Internet Assistant not to load the inline images from the document. To do this, open the **V**iew menu and choose Load **I**mages. If you want to turn image loading on again, open the **V**iew menu and choose Load **I**mages again.

The next new document you load will not have any images displayed, but will instead show the name of the missing images in brackets (see fig. 13.11). The only way to load the missing images in your current document is to open the **V**iew menu and choose Load **I**mages to turn image loading on again, and then open the **F**ile menu and choose Re**l**oad.

Fig. 13.11
When you tell Internet Assistant not to load inline images, it places the names of the images in brackets where the images would be.

Placeholder brackets for missing images

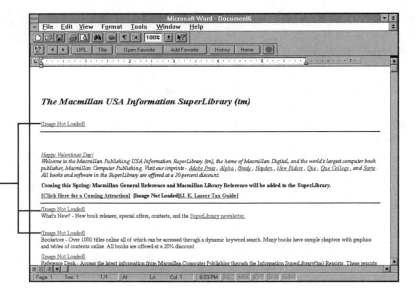

Looking for Information in a Document

▶ See "Microsoft Internet Assistant for Microsoft Word," p. 380

If the WWW document you are reading is short, it is easy to scroll through the document (or use Page Up and Page Down) to find information that interests you. If you have loaded a very long document, though, you can use Word's find command to search for information. Word will change to view the HTML source of the current document as it searches through it. When you close the Find box, the document view returns to normal, and you are positioned back at the beginning of the document.

Saving Documents

In general, the purpose of the World Wide Web is to be able to have one copy of a document that many people can view, although there are times when you might want to save a copy of a document to your local computer. Internet Assitant gives you several options for saving documents.

To save a document, open the **F**ile menu and choose Save **A**s. This brings up a Save As dialog box that lets you browse through your directories and store the file wherever you like. You have the option of storing the file as a number of standard Word output formats, or as the HTML source code. Choose the option you want from the list box under Save File as **T**ype:.

When you save an HTML document to your local disk, remember that the document probably contains hyperlinks in it. These links can be *relative* or *absolute*. An absolute reference contains the complete address of the document that is being referenced, including the host name, directory path, and file name. A relative reference assumes that the previous machine and directory path are being used, and just the file name (or possibly a subdirectory and file name) is specified.

If the document references other documents with relative addresses, you cannot view those documents unless you copy them to your local disk and set them up with the same directory structure they had at the original site. You might want to set up a document and its linked documents on your local disk if you want to be able to view the document without connecting to the Internet. One problem, though, is that if the original document changes, you will not be aware of it and will view an outdated version of the document.

Absolute references always work unless your Internet connection fails or the referenced documents are moved.

Because Internet Assistant is not just a Web browser, like Mosaic or Netscape, but can also edit Web documents, the Save feature can be much more valuable. See Chapter 16, "HTML Editors and Filters," for details on using Internet Assistant to edit HTML documents.

Printing Documents

In addition to being able to save documents, you can print documents directly from Internet Assistant. Open the **F**ile menu and choose **P**rint to send a copy of the current document to your printer.

You can set up the margins, headers, and footers of your document by opening the **F**ile menu and choosing Pa**g**e Setup. You can also set up your printer options by choosing **S**etup from the Print dialog box.

III

Other Browsers

Viewing Multimedia Files

◀ See "Multi-
media—Using
Viewers," p. 81

At this time, Internet Assistant is much more limited in its ability to display multimedia files than most of the other WWW browsers. It has a built-in capability to display GIF and JPEG, PCX, and a few other image file types.

When you click on the hyperlink for a file of a recognized type, Internet Assistant opens a new window containing the downloaded image (see fig. 13.12).

Fig. 13.12
If Internet
Assistant under-
stands how to
display the image
you download, it
brings it up in a
new window.
(Here you see the
holographic
doctor from the
Star Trek: Voyager
series.)

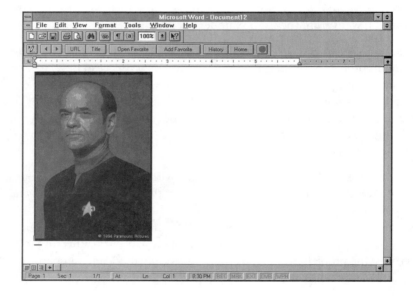

Caution

If Internet Assistant does not recognize the type of the file associated with the link you click, it will try to load the file anyway (which is very time-consuming). When it completes the loading process, it will give you an error. You will not be given the option of saving the file to disk.

Working with Local Files

When you think of using a WWW browser, you think of retrieving documents from WWW servers on the Internet. Internet Assistant can read documents from your local file system, as well as from halfway around the world.

If you share documents among members of your organization, many of the documents you view may be on a local file server, or possibly on your local computer.

You can load a local HTML file to view just like you load any file in Word. To load a local file, open the **F**ile menu and choose **O**pen. This brings up the standard Word Open dialog box. By default, only files of type HTM are shown, but you can see all files in your directories by selecting All Files (*.*) in the List Files of Type list box.

Effective Browsing Techniques

Navigating between WWW documents can be confusing. Documents often connect back to documents you already read. You can't always remember which of several related documents has the information you really need.

Sometimes you can't tell from the hyperlink whether the document is of interest to you, and loading documents uses valuable time. Often, you waste time loading documents that you dismiss immediately. This section helps you learn to reduce unnecessary document loading and circular navigating.

How to Keep Track of Where You've Been

Keeping track of where you are and where you were is one of the biggest challenges of using the WWW. For example, say you're reading a document that deals with agriculture and you click a hyperlink to take you to Hay Field Seeding Suggestions. The document turns out to be one you loaded earlier—when you found a hyperlink for Pasture Management Techniques. How can you avoid this frustrating repetition?

One suggestion is to have a home page that provides links to your most-visited WWW pages. This home page is useful, for example, if you work on a group project and frequently use documents with known locations. You either can create your own home page or someone can create a project home page for your group. In this scenario, you probably are already familiar with the servers, if not the exact documents.

Browsing with Internet Assistant is particularly difficult because you can't see the URL of a link before you load it. You need to rely more on your history list and on the list of favorite URLs that you can create.

How to Get Where You Were

Trying to navigate back to a document you viewed in the current Internet Assistant session also can be challenging. The Go Back and Go Forward

III

Other Browsers

commands from the Window menu take you through the open document windows in the order that you opened them. If you delete one of the document windows, though, you can't get back to that URL with these commands.

Tip
Click the History button in the toolbar to open the History List dialog box.

If you open the **W**indow menu and choose **H**istory, you get a dialog box, similar to the one shown in figure 13.13, that shows you the last 50 URLs you visited. The URL of the current document is highlighted. This list is maintained between Internet Assistant sessions. When you exit Word, the history list is saved; it's reloaded the next time you start Internet Assistant.

Fig. 13.13
The Internet Assistant's History List dialog box shows a list of URLs you've visited.

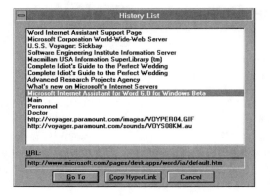

You can go directly to any document in the History List dialog box. Select any URL in the list and choose **G**o To to jump to that document. This loads the document.

The best strategy for quickly accessing documents is probably to leave the windows of documents that are of greatest interest to you open and close all other documents. This way, you can quickly move between documents by switching document windows. And, if you need to return to a document whose window you've closed, open the history list and reopen that document.

Tip
Click the Add Favorite button in the toolbar to add the current URL to the Favorite Places document.

Create Lists of Your Favorite URLs

If you don't want to learn to use HTML commands to create a home page with all your favorite WWW documents, Internet Assistant has an alternative. Internet Assistant maintains a file of *Favorite Places,* where you can store URLs you visit often and quickly access them.

To save the URL of the current document to your Favorite Places document, open the **T**ools menu and choose Add to **F**avorite Places. This stores the current URL in the Favorite Places document, briefly displaying the Favorite Places document as it stores the URL.

To view the Favorite Places document, open the **T**ools menu and choose Open Favorite **P**laces. Your Favorite Places document will appear in a new window (see fig. 13.14). Just click on any of the links to go to your favorite documents.

Tip
Click the Open Favorite button in the toolbar to view the Favorite Places document.

Fig. 13.14
Store URLs you access frequently in the Favorite Places document.

Security

Many people seem to feel that because computers are machines, communications between computers is secure (no people involved). Nothing could be further from the truth.

Communication on the Internet involves data being forwarded from the sending computer to the receiving computer through a number of intermediate computers. A possibility exists that someone could be looking at the information passing through the intermediate computers. They could even set up another computer to pretend to be the receiving computer so that everything you sent went to someone who was not intended to see the information.

III

Other Browsers

For this reason, sending sensitive information (like your credit card number) over the Internet is not a good idea. Any information sent over the Internet is at risk—e-mail messages, file transfers, and particularly information from electronic forms that you may fill out using your WWW browser.

◄ See "Security," p. 248

Internet Assistant has no provisions for guaranteeing the security of information you enter in a form. If you need to send sensitive information using a WWW browser, see the information on security in Chapter 11, "Netscape."

> **Note**
>
> Forms look a little different in Internet Assistant than they do in other browsers you may have seen, such as Mosaic or Netscape. Instead of a box with a line around it, input areas on forms will be gray shaded areas in Internet Assistant, as shown in figure 13.15. Initially, the shaded area may appear smaller than the size of the box you would see in another browser. As you enter text in an input box, it will expand to the full size of the box if needed.

Fig. 13.15
Forms in Internet Assistant have gray shaded areas for input.

Input box for text ———

Check box ———

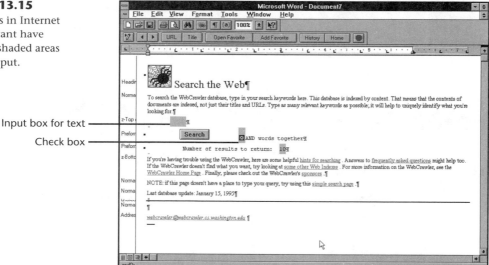

Using Other Internet Services

The beta release of Internet Assistant that was used while writing this chapter was not able to use the URL protocols for other Internet servers, such as FTP or Gopher servers. If you want to access these servers with a Web browser, you will need to use one of the Web browsers that supports these protocols, such as Netscape or Mosaic.

From Here...

Internet Assistant is an innovative step toward integrating document authoring and viewing applications. In its current form, it does not provide a full feature interface to the WWW and the Internet, but the missing features may be added to the released version.

To learn more about using Mosaic and to find interesting WWW documents, refer to these chapters:

- Chapter 6, "Navigating with Mosaic," tells you how to use Mosaic to find and view documents on the WWW.

- Chapter 7, "Mosaic Shortcuts and Tips," tells you how to become an expert WWW navigator.

- Chapter 11, "Netscape," tells you how to use Netscape, one of the best of the existing Web browsers.

- Chapter 19, "Web Searching," discusses how to use automated software to find some of the most interesting collections of WWW documents.

III

Other Browsers

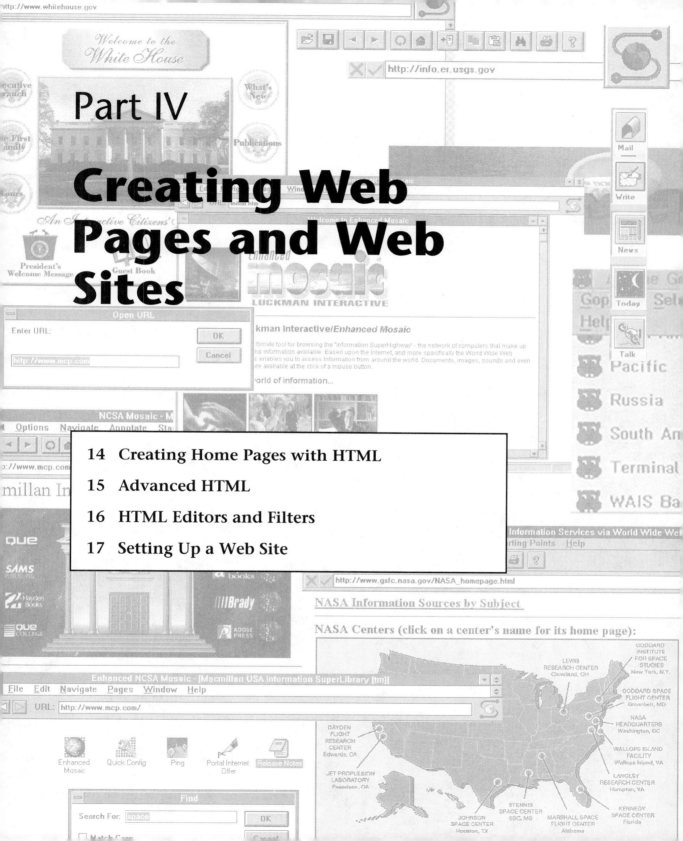

Part IV

Creating Web Pages and Web Sites

Chapter 14

Creating Home Pages with HTML

by Bill Eager

A *home page* is a place where you begin to explore the resources on the WWW. Two types of home pages exist. The first type consists of the home pages that reside on Web servers around the world. When you enter in your multimedia browser (Mosaic, Internetworks, Cello, and so on) an URL (Uniform Resource Locator) address that points to a home page, you connect with the home page on the remote Web server. When you type the URL address **http://www.doc.gov/**, for example, you establish a connection to the U.S. Department of Commerce (USDOC) Information server; within seconds, the home page for this service appears.

The home page usually is a starting point for information about a specific subject or company. The USDOC home page offers hypermedia links to various information about business and commerce, as well as links to other government agencies, such as the National Institute for Standards and Technology (NIST). When you jump to NIST, the home page for this agency appears. Some USDOC resources that you jump to from this home page are hypertext documents that exist in subdirectories on the server.

The WWW electronic malls illustrate the difference between a home page and other documents. Suppose that you jump to the home page for the Electronic SuperMall (a fictitious mall), which resides on a computer in Wyoming. The SuperMall home page has links to the Rodeo Clothing Store, the Western Music Shop, Rugged Trucks Automotive, and Big Sky Video. Just as you would enter a main door in a real shopping mall, you first enter the

▶ See "Electronic Malls," p. 883

home page and then jump to individual stores. The individual "stores" can be subdocuments on the SuperMall computer, or they can reside on separate computers. Therefore, the owner of Big Sky Video can operate a separate WWW computer that simply has a link on the SuperMall home page.

In this chapter you will learn:

- About the HTML Web page programming language

- How different browsers display Web pages

- Step-by-step directions for creating a home page

- How to custom tailor your web documents with graphics and pictures

> **Note**
>
> If you want to have a presence on the Web without the headaches of running a Web server, many service providers now operate and rent space on their Web sites. Also, check out some of the companies that have Web pages listed in Chapter 22, "Computers." Many of these firms place your page on their server—usually for a fee.

A Home Page on Your PC

There is a second type of home page—a *local* home page—which is a personalized document that you create and maintain on your PC. You develop this document with the same computer language that is used to create home pages on Web servers. A high-school music teacher could create a home page that contains links to all the Web's music resources; a travel agent may develop a home page that's full of interesting travel destinations; a stockbroker might produce a home page with links to global financial information—and you can develop a home page with links to your favorite Web resources.

You can configure your WWW browser (such as Mosaic) to display your home page each time the program loads. If you own a high-speed, dedicated (full-time) Internet connection, you can let the rest of the world jump into your computer and visit your home page. Your computer and Internet connection, however, must be on 24 hours a day; otherwise, people who try to jump to your "server" will get a blank screen or error message.

The rest of this chapter provides step-by-step directions that help you create a home page. The directions refer specifically to creating a home page with

Microsoft Windows and displaying the home page with Mosaic. The programming language, however, is common across all computer platforms, and most WWW browsers will load the home page in a similar fashion.

Understanding HTTP and HTML: The Languages of the WWW

You are about to learn how to be a computer programmer. Don't worry—creating a home page is almost as simple as writing a letter.

The WWW uses several protocols to transport and display the hypertext and multimedia resources that reside on computers around the world. One of these protocols is *HTTP* (Hypertext Transport Protocol). HTTP works with Web servers to provide a client-server environment for the Internet. Normally, your PC is the client and the remote Web computer is the server. CERN, the European Laboratory for Particle Physics in Switzerland, proposed the HTTP protocol, along with several other software applications and network standards, for the WWW client-server environment. HTTP supports the capability of the Internet to provide access to an enormous quantity of interlinked resources.

HTTP is a fairly simple communications protocol that takes advantage of the fact that the documents it retrieves contain information about future links that the user may reference. By contrast, with FTP or Gopher, information about the next possible links must be transmitted via the protocol.

Although you don't need to know anything about the HTTP protocol to view documents on the WWW, if you are interested, you can find a copy of the IETF HTTP specification at the URL address **http://info.cern.ch /hypertext/WWW/Protocols/HTTP/HTTP2.html**. This specification is the standard specification of the HTML protocol that has been developed and accepted by the Internet community.

The individual multimedia documents (pages) on the Web use a computer programming language called *Hypertext Markup Language*—HTML for short. HTML commands are inserted around blocks of text in a document to describe the text. Within a document, for example, text is marked as headings of various levels, simple paragraphs, page headings, footers, bulleted items, and so on. Some commands enable you to import other media (images, sounds, animation, and so on); other commands enable you to create links to Web documents or other Web computers (or to text within the same document). Your browser gets the document and interprets the HTML commands, formatting each structure in the document (headings, bullets, plain paragraphs, and so on) in a way that looks best on your display.

You can write the HTML code that becomes a document or home page in several ways. You can write the code from scratch (by using a simple word processor), copy it from another document, or generate it with a HTML authoring program. HTML uses a simple, common text format that allows people who use a variety of computer systems (PC, Macintosh, and UNIX) to create Web documents.

Hypertext Glossary

Several terms describe the hypermedia programming language, protocols, and information components. These terms are basic to the development and use of WWW hypermedia documents.

Term	Definition
Home page	The first page of information in a hypermedia document
HTTP	Hypertext Transfer Protocol—the protocol used by WWW servers to provide rules for moving information across the Internet
HTML	Hypertext Markup Language—the language that defines the style and information in a WWW hypermedia document
Hyperlink	A reference point in a document for linking information. The link usually stands out, with words being highlighted or underlined
Hypermedia	A multimedia document that contains and links text, audio, and video
SGML	Standard Generalized Markup Language—a standard that describes markup languages
URL	Uniform Resource Locator—an address that identifies and locates multimedia information on the WWW

Comparing Web Pages in Different Forms

Before you get into the programming details that make HTML work, look for a few examples of Web pages in different forms. Comparing an HTML source document with what you see on-screen in Mosaic or Cello should give you a better idea of how HTML translates into the hypertext Web documents that you browse on-screen.

First, look at the Web page (the Tori Amos home page, URL address **http://www.mit.edu:8001/people/nocturne/tori.html**) shown in Mosaic in figure 14.1 and in Cello in figure 14.2. Notice the similarities between the two views of this same page. The views have the same title and address, have the same graphic image, and show the same text and hyperlinks.

> **Note**
>
> Cello is a Web browser created by the Legal Information Institute (LII) at Cornell Law School. Cello software is available from LII without charge, but limits of warranty and license restrictions apply. You can download Cello from the Cornell FTP site, which is **ftp.law.cornell.edu**. The program (cello.zip) is in the subdirectory /pub/LII/Cello. You need to uncompress the program to use it.

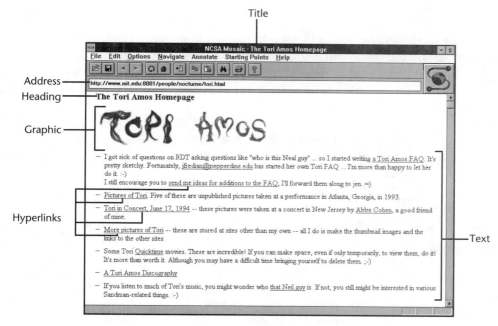

Fig. 14.1
The Tori Amos home page in Mosaic.

Fig. 14.2
The Tori Amos
home page in
Cello.

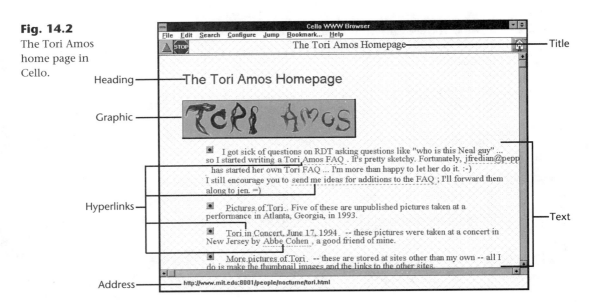

How can two programs display the same information? Both programs are
reading from the same HTML document. To see what the HTML document
for this page looks like, you can view it in Mosaic. To do this, open the **F**ile
menu and choose **D**ocument Source. The window shown in figure 14.3
opens. If you look carefully at the areas called out on the figure, you can see
which parts of this document translate to the hypertext document that you
see in the normal Mosaic screen shown in figure 14.1.

Fig. 14.3
The source
document for the
Tori Amos home
page in Mosaic.

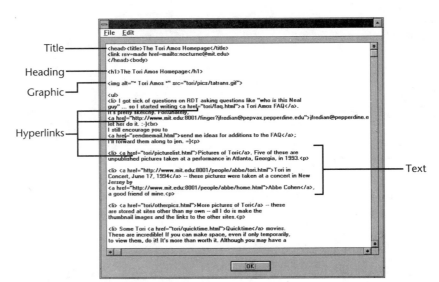

The main difference that you see is the use of the markup codes in the angle brackets (< >). HTML uses these codes to define the parts of the home page. Mosaic reads the codes and applies them to what you see on-screen.

Cello works essentially the same way. Open the **E**dit menu and choose View **S**ource; a window like the one shown in figure 14.4 opens.

> **Note**
>
> By default, Cello uses Notepad to view the HTML source. This display of the HTML code is a little more difficult to follow than Mosaic's built-in editor. Also, if the HTML document runs too wide, be sure to turn on word wrap in Notepad by opening the **E**dit menu and choosing **W**ord Wrap.

Title   Heading   Graphic

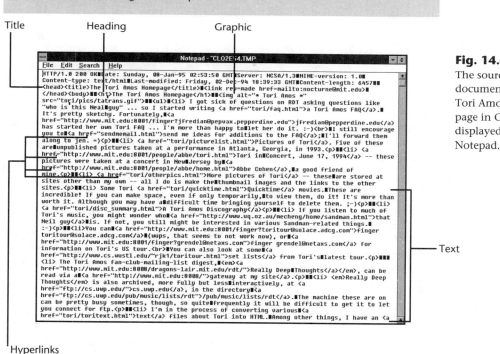

Hyperlinks

Fig. 14.4
The source document for the Tori Amos home page in Cello is displayed in Notepad.

Text

This view in Cello is not as easy to follow, but Cello has one advantage. If you just want to see the text without any of the markup codes, open the **E**dit menu and choose View as **C**lean Text. Notepad opens again and displays the document in the form shown in figure 14.5.

Fig. 14.5

The clean-text version of the Tori Amos home page in Cello, opened in Notepad.

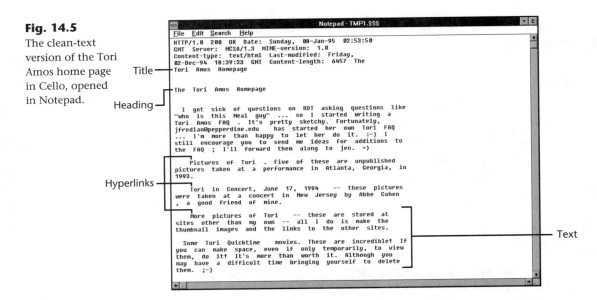

Title

Heading

Hyperlinks

Text

Although a few HTML codes identify the size of letters, style of type (such as italic), and graphic features (such as underlining), much of the appearance of text is determined by the configuration choices in your browser. So even though you create the basic text and layout of your Web documents, the browser itself determines how the text appears in terms of things like the color and font.

In Mosaic, you access these font choices by opening the **O**ptions menu and choosing **C**hoose Font. In Cello, open the **C**onfigure menu and choose **F**onts. In either program, a submenu appears, enabling you to set the font for titles, headings, and all the other text parts of documents.

Programming Your Home Page

This section describes the commands that you need to create a single document (home page) from scratch, using simple keyboard commands to write the HTML language in a plain text editor. A simple word of advice: have patience. Computers occasionally can be frustrating, but computer programming can be worse—especially when it doesn't work. Computers and software

are extremely picky; one misspelled or misplaced keystroke can prevent a program (here, the program for your home page) from working properly. If something doesn't work, go back and make sure that your "code" is written exactly as it is presented here. To begin creating your home page with HTML, open your text editor (or word processing program) and then open or start a new document. Now that you have a "clean slate" ready, it's time to learn how to fill it with HTML code.

> **Note**
>
> The examples in this chapter occasionally show screens from Notepad, a Windows-based text editor. However, you can follow the same basic procedure on a Macintosh or even on a computer running UNIX. To enter HTML commands, just use a text editor such as Teach Text on the Macintosh or vi (Visual Editor) or emacs (Editor Macros) for UNIX systems. One terrific aspect of HTML is the fact that it works on all types of computer systems.

HTML Basics: Title, Heading, and Text

The most common HTML codes are for the title, heading, and paragraph text. The following example shows title, heading, and paragraph tags. *Tags* consist of a left angle bracket (<) followed by the function or directive of the tag (usually, a single letter) and a right angle bracket (>). Beginning and ending tags usually surround the text that you write; a slash (/) appears just before the directive in the ending tag. Directives are enclosed in brackets (<TITLE>). The following table describes the directives that help you format most basic documents:

Directive	Purpose
TITLE	Gives the window title
H#	Formats a header in larger typeface
P	Designates the end of a paragraph
IMG	Points at a picture to be placed on the page
A	Creates a hypertext link to another page or resource

Browsers interpret these tags and directives to determine how to format information and when to start and stop formatting. Within the text on the text file, characters such as the carriage return have no effect. The HTML formatting tags determine when a paragraph occurs. The tags in HTML are case-insensitive—that is, it doesn't matter whether you write the information in uppercase or lowercase letters. Therefore, the tag <Title> is the same as <TITLE>.

> **Note**
>
> If a browser doesn't understand an HTML tag, it ignores the tag.

Here is the HTML code that creates a home page with a title, a heading, and two separate paragraphs. Enter this code in your editor for your home page. Figure 14.6 shows this code written in the Microsoft Notepad editor.

```
<Title>My Home Page</Title>
<H1>This Is A Level One Heading</H1>
Here is an example of a home page paragraph.<P>
Here is a second paragraph.<P>
```

Fig. 14.6
Notepad editor with simple HTML code for a home page.

How to Save the Document

The next step is saving this home-page code in a file that your browser can read. Use your editor's Save command to save the file. You must save the file with the extension htm or html, which tells Mosaic and other browsers that the file is an HTML file.

> **Note**
>
> DOS allows only three-letter extensions, so the file name must end with .htm, as in homepage.htm.

Name the file when you save it; then close the document and exit your text editor.

Load and Test the Document

You should occasionally load and test your home-page creations. Follow these steps:

1. Start Mosaic.

> **Note**
>
> You may have to start the SLIP or PPP connection software first. In a typical PC installation, Mosaic needs to have the network software started, but not necessarily connected to the network, to run.

2. Open the **F**ile menu and choose Open **L**ocal File. A dialog box like the one shown in figure 14.7 appears, allowing you to open your home-page file.

◄ See "Working with Local Files," p. 121

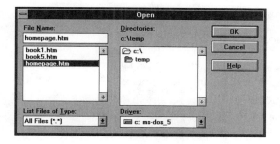

Fig. 14.7
The Open dialog box in Mosaic.

3. Select the drive, directory (or folder), and file name for your home page.

4. Choose OK to finish the entry and load the new home page (see fig. 14.8).

Fig. 14.8

This is your home page in Mosaic. Notice the file:///c| designation at the beginning of the URL; this is how Mosaic identifies local files and drives. Keep in mind that the size of the headings is dependent on your font choices in Mosaic.

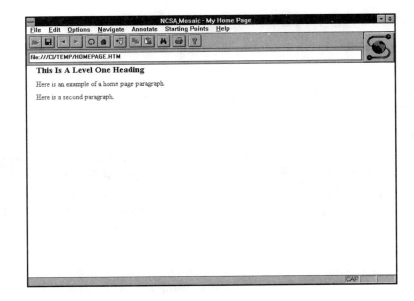

You can do the same thing with another browser. In Cello, for example, the procedure is almost the same. Follow these steps:

1. Start Cello.

2. Open the **J**ump menu and choose Launch via **U**RL. A dialog box like the one shown in figure 14.9 appears; you use this dialog box to open your home-page file.

Fig. 14.9

This is where you indicate the local file to be opened in Cello.

3. Type **file://localhost/c:/temp/homepage.htm**, in which c is the drive letter, temp is the directory, and homepage.htm is the file name. file://localhost/ designates this file as a local file for Cello.

4. Choose OK to finish the entry and load the new home page (see fig. 14.10).

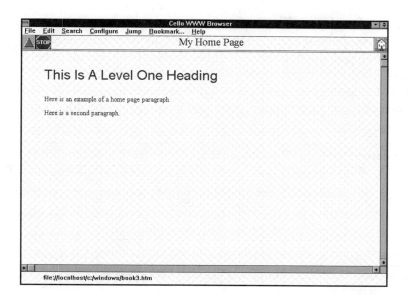

Fig. 14.10
This is your home
page in Cello.
Notice that it is
the same as this
page in Mosaic,
except for font
differences.

You can repeat the process of editing the home-page text, saving the file in a
text editor, and opening the local file as you add to and develop your home
page. In the Windows environment, be sure to close the text editor after every change so that Mosaic can access the file. You can configure Mosaic, as
described in the browser-configuration section, so that it automatically displays your home page when you start the browser.

Troubleshooting

I can't find my homepage document.

In all likelihood, you will have saved your homepage.htm file in the C: subdirectory
for your text editor or word-processing program. Check there first, and if you're
using Mosaic when you get to the Open local file dialog box, type ***.HTM** in the File
Name field—this will show you only the html files.

My homepage won't load; why?

There are a couple of things to check. First, make sure that the file has been saved as
an ASCII text file (not as a word-processing file format). Second, make sure the extension on your file is HTM—other extensions may not work.

Customize Your Text

You may want to add a bit of flair to your copy by changing the appearance of the headers or the text. Notice that the header for the sample page is tagged <H1>. You can use six levels of headers, ranging from H1 (the largest) to H6 (the smallest). You also can style the text by making it boldface, italic, or underlined, or by adding a rule across the page. The following table describes a few more directives that you can use to create these effects:

Directive	Purpose
B	Applies boldface formatting
I	Applies italic formatting
U	Applies underline formatting
strong	Makes letters more intense; similar to boldface
blockquote	Makes text look like a "quote"
HR	Places a rule (horizontal line) across the page

Figure 14.11 shows what these formatting directives look like in NCSA Mosaic.

Fig. 14.11
By using simple tags, you can spice up the appearance of your Web home page or documents.

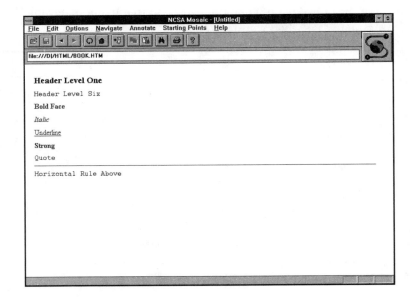

Following is the code for this page:

```
<h1>Header Level One</h1><p>
<h6>Header Level Six</h6><p>
<b>Bold Face</b><p>
<i>Italic</i><p>
<u>Underline</u><p>
<strong>Strong</strong><p>
<blockquote>Quote<p><p>
<hr><p>
Horizontal Rule Above
```

How to Create a List

You can use HTML codes to present text lists as numbered or unnumbered lists. The list itself is surrounded by an opening and a closing tag. You don't need to use paragraph separators to separate the list items, because each item starts with a tag that separates it from the other items.

Following is the code that you use to create an unnumbered list in which the list items are preceded with a small on-screen dash:

```
<b>Here's an unnumbered list.</b><p>

    <UL>
    <LI> First
    <LI> Second
    <LI> Third
    <LI> Fourth
    </UL>
```

To create a numbered list, you change the opening and closing tags from <UL> and </UL> to <OL> and </OL>. The list-item tag remains <LI>. Following is an example of how you write a numbered list with HTML—this creates list items that are preceded with numbers:

```
<b>Here's a numbered list.</b><p>

    <OL>
    <LI> First
    <LI> Second
    <LI> Third
    <LI> Fourth
    </OL>
```

Figure 14.12 shows a screen that contains an unnumbered list and a numbered list that were created with the preceding code.

Fig. 14.12

The top part of this Web page displays an unnumbered list; the bottom portion shows what a numbered list looks like.

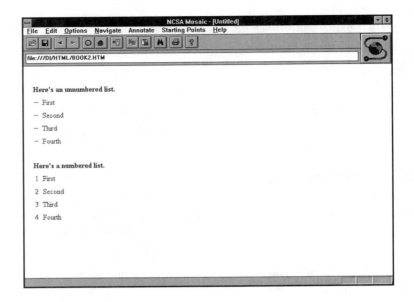

Adding Hyperlinks to Other Web Documents

If you are going to use a document that you create as a home page, you need to add some hyperlinks so that you can jump to other pages. You can jump to other pages that you create locally (this capability may be useful if you develop a page that will be accessed by other people who use the pages that you create), or you can link to pages on other WWW servers. These links, also created in your HTML document, enable you to click a word, a phrase, or even an image to connect with other Web resources. URLs are the mechanism used by the WWW to find a particular page, image, or sound. Basically, you can think of a URL as the address by which you find a page. (URL, often pronounced *Earl*, is short for Universal Resource Locator.)

There are two types of URLs. The first is an *absolute URL*. This URL is a complete address, and nothing more is needed to find the information. The second type of URL is a *relative URL*. A relative URL is one that only contains the necessary address to find what you want from where you currently are.

For example, your street address might be:

1700 S. Stadium Dr.

Bontia, CT 47052

This would be an absolute address, as it is all that is necessary to find you. However, once I'm standing in your front lawn, the relative address of:

1800

would be all that is necessary for me to find a house on the next block. I no longer need the street, city, or state because I am already there.

HTML uses a similar mechanism when specifying addresses of where to find documents.

A typical absolute URL consists of the following items:

service://host:port/path/file.ext

service:// indicates how the document is being accessed. Some of the more frequently used services include:

file://	Use FTP to retrieve the file
ftp://	Use FTP to retrieve the file
http://	Use a WWW server to retrieve the file
gopher://	Use a Gopher mechanism
telnet://	Access a remote machine
news:	Read remote news

Notice that news: differs from the rest of the services in that it does not include the // characters. The // characters are not required on all the services, only on the ones shown with it.

host indicates in what machine the information you wish to get resides (for example, your host might be www.somewhere.com).

:port is optional, and needs only be included if the information is not available using the default port specified by the service: (for example, Gopher uses a default port of 70, HTTP uses 80).

path indicates the route from the URL home directory to the desired information (for example, the path to your home directory on machine www.somewhere.com might be usr/people/me).

file.ext indicates the actual name of the file you wish to retrieve.

In many situations, a URL need not have the path and file.ext. In these cases, a default document will be provided from the requested system.

An example of an absolute URL would be:

http://www.iquest.net/cw/cookware.html

This accesses the file cookware.html, which exists in the directory cw on the host www.iquest.net. The file will be accessed using the host's WWW server, as indicated by http://.

Relative URLs include only a piece of the full address. Relative URLs are only used inside an HTML document to find other information relative to that document and also stored on the same machine. For example, if the cookware.html file requires a p1.gif picture, the URL can be done one of two ways:

| Absolute: | <img src="http://www.iquest.net/cw/p1.gif"> |
| Relative: | <img src="p1.gif"> |

The first syntax we understand, as it is absolute. The second relative syntax is a little more confusing. Because we had already retrieved the cookware.html file from the cw directory, the system will look in the cw directory to satisfy any relative requests.

Troubleshooting

My URL command isn't working. It refuses to connect to the proper document.

Check the URL to see if any / separator characters were accidentally entered as \ characters. Users who are familiar with DOS frequently enter the incorrect slash out of habit.

Why do some of my URLs not work correctly with anchors?

Depending on your browser, you may find that relative URLs may not work correctly when using them with anchors (<A>). This may especially be true when using HTML files local to your computer. In cases where a relative URL fails, replace it with an absolute URL to fix the problem.

Defining a Hyperlink in the Text Editor

Again, open your text editor, and open the HTML document that you created. Now insert a new line of code where you want the hyperlink to appear, as follows:

```
<A HREF= "http://www.doc.gov/">U.S. Dept. of Commerce</A>
```

Examine the parts of this code. The left angle bracket (<), followed by the *anchor* code A, indicates the start of the hypertext link. HREF indicates that the anchor for this link is *sensitive* text; when a reader clicks the text, he or she jumps to the link. The URL address for the link is contained in quotation marks.

> **Note**
>
> The quotation marks (" ") that surround the resource are very important; you should use them for links to other Web documents, images, FTP files, and so on.

Following the first ending angle bracket is the name or the text that you want to give the link. This name can be the actual name of the document, as it is defined in the document, or any other name that you give it. Whatever name or text you put here, it is linked to the address in the A HREF statement.

The code for this link ends with the /A code in angle brackets. All that the reader will see on the page is the text—in this case, *U.S. Dept. of Commerce*. Figure 14.13 shows this statement in place in the text editor.

Fig. 14.13
This Notepad document has the HTML code for a hyperlink to the U.S. Dept. of Commerce added.

IV

Creating Web Pages & Sites

You can save the document now to test it, or you can add more hyperlinks or other elements. Depending upon which Web browser you are using, you may need to close the document and exit your editor before trying to test with the browser.

If you want to add a hyperlink to a document on your local computer, the code looks like this:

```
<A HREF="file://localhost/c:/temp/funpage.htm">A Local Home Page
with Some Fun Links</A>
```

In this code, the `file://localhost/c:` part of the hyperlink definition states that the file is a local file and defines the drive on which the file is located. The rest of the statement essentially is the same text used to define a link to a page on another Web site.

> **Note**
>
> Putting hyperlinks on separate lines in your text editor does not place the links on separate lines when you load the HTML document. To force a new line for your links, use the <P> (paragraph) code.

Checking to See Whether Your Hyperlinks Work

The next time you start Mosaic and load this page, any new hypertext links that you added to the page should be active (see fig. 14.14).

Fig. 14.14
Here Mosaic shows the new hyperlinks you've added to the home page.

Hyperlinks —

Address for hyperlink below mouse pointer —

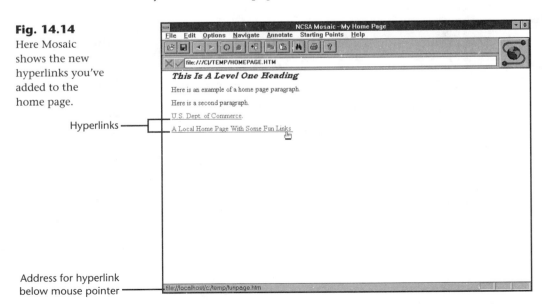

Putting in a Link that Goes to Text on the Same Page

You can create an anchor that links the reader to text that is in the same page or document that is currently loaded. Suppose that you turn your address book into one big HTML document. At the top of the page, you list the letters of the alphabet: A, B, C, D, and so on. When the reader clicks M, he or she jumps not to a new document, but simply down the page to the people whose last names begin with M.

The capability to jump to another location in one document is a good way to help people get to the destination of a link rapidly. Of course, you could chop the address book into 26 documents—one for each letter of the alphabet—but getting to the M listings would take longer, because a new document would have to load. On the flip side, if your address book contains 2,000 names, loading this single document would take a very long time.

Tip

As a rule, an HTML document should contain no more than about five screens' worth of text.

To create a link that goes to another location within the same document, you actually put two codes in the text: one is the link, and the other is the location to which the link jumps. Following is an example:

```
<A HREF="#far"> Click here to visit the Far East.</a>
```

The sentence *Click here to visit the Far East* now is a link that jumps the reader to the anchor *far*. The pound sign (#) means that the link jumps to an anchor in the same document. You need to add the end point of this link, as follows:

```
<A NAME=far>China</a> is a good country with which to begin our
travel of the Far East.
```

The word *China* now is associated with the anchor *far* and becomes the destination of the link. You could have four pages or screens of text between the link and the anchor.

Adding a Graphic to Your Home Page

As you probably noticed in the Web pages that you have seen, you can add images to your documents. These images are called *inline* images. The pictures that you see in home pages do not reside in the code for the home page. Instead, the code that you write simply tells the browser where to find the picture, which is located on your hard drive (or on the Web server, if you are creating an external Web document).

You can use inline images for several purposes, including the following:

■ Enhancing the appearance of the document (for example, a logo)

■ Offering useful information (such as a map)

■ Providing a link to a full-screen version of the image

■ Providing a link to another Web resource

The Mosaic browser can view GIF and XBM graphics. To create your own graphic or picture for a home page, you need software that can save or translate images into one of these file formats. If you can't do this, you may be able to download a public-domain image from an Internet/Web site to include in your home page.

Caution

As with anything on the Web, don't use someone else's copyrighted material (text, images, audio, and so on) in violation of their copyright. Many copyrighted images are available for purchase. Although this warning seems to be common sense, graphic images often are copied on the Web without the rightful owner's permission.

Defining an Inline Image in the Text Editor

Again, start the text-editor application, and load your home-page file. Now insert a new line of code where you want the image to appear, as follows:

```
<IMG SRC="file:///c¦/temp/money1.gif">
```

Note that the graphic file (money1.gif) is on the C drive in a directory named temp.

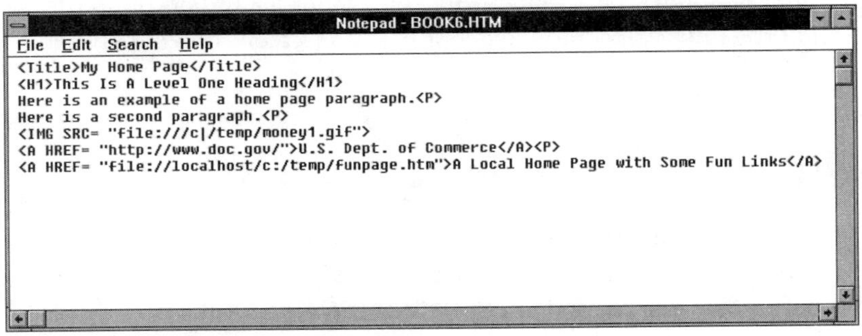

Fig. 14.15
The image is in the same line as the hyperlink to the Department of Commerce.

This places the image money1.gif in the same line as the Department of Commerce hyperlink (because no <P> code is used to start a new line after the graphic).

You also can move the text next to the graphic by using the *align* attribute. Suppose that you want to have a caption at the top instead of near the bottom of the image. You would write the code as follows:

```
<IMG ALIGN=top SRC= "file:///c¦/temp/money1.gif"> U.S. Dept of
Commerce
```

The command ALIGN=top moves the caption up. (Another option is ALIGN=middle.) Again, you can add links to other graphics, or you can save the file and close the text editor when you finish.

> **Note**
>
> Keep your inline images small and simple. You don't want too much visual clutter on the page and you don't want to waste time waiting for the image to load.

Testing the Document with the Graphic in Mosaic

The next time you start Mosaic and load this page, any new inline images that you added should be visible (see fig. 14.16).

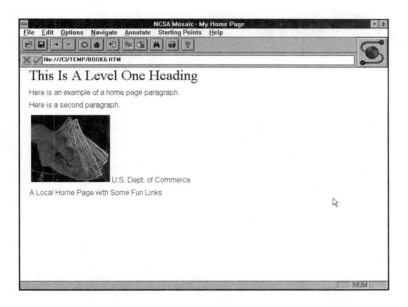

Fig. 14.16
The page shows the inline image, viewed in Mosaic.

> **Note**
>
> Some browsers don't display graphic images. Home-page design should consider the fact that the page will look different when it is viewed by a line browser, as well as when the Inline Images option is off.

Linking an Inline Image to Another Image or Web Resource

Inline images themselves can be links to larger versions of the same picture. When you click the inline image, a larger picture downloads and then is displayed with a graphics viewer. Following is an example of the necessary code:

```
<A HREF= "big_money.jpeg"><IMG SRC= "money1.gif"></A>
```

Now the file money1.gif appears as an inline image and is itself a link to the image big_money.jpeg.

The inline image also could be a link that enables you to do other things, such as jumping to a Gopher site, playing an audio message, or retrieving a file from an FTP site, as in the following example:

```
<A HREF= "ftp://solomon.technet.sg/pub/misc/money-rates.txt"><IMG
SRC= "money1.gif"></A>
```

If we replace the image command from the previous example with this, and include

```
Money Rates<P>
```

after it as text, the image becomes the link and the text is not a link, as shown in figure 14.17.

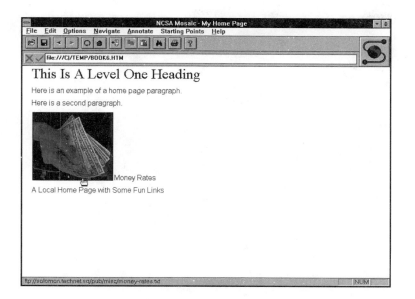

IV

Creating Web Pages & Sites

Fig. 14.17
The image is now a link. Note that with the mouse pointer over the image, the URL that it is linked to is visible in the status bar.

The blue border around the image in Mosaic signifies that it is a link to another resource.

From Here...

In this chapter you've learned how to use the HTML programming language to create a home page. Web pages can even have more elaborate features. To find out more, see the following chapters:

- Chapter 15, "Advanced HTML," explains the process of creating and using forms.

- Chapter 16, "HTML Editors and Filters," describes software programs that help you create HTML.

- Chapter 17, "Setting Up a Web Site," which explains how to get, install, and use a software program that can transform your PC into a Web site.

Chapter 15

Advanced HTML

by David Cook with Bill Eager

In the last chapter you learned how to use the HTML programming language to create simple home pages. You could use these pages on your PC and load them when you want to jump to links that you have saved. You also can place these pages on the Web for the world to see—either by having someone who runs a Web server maintain the pages or by turning your PC into a Web server. Chapter 17, "Setting Up a Web Site," provides greater detail on the hardware requirements, techniques, and software that enable you to maintain a Web site.

This chapter provides instructions on how you can use HTML to create (actually, program) some advanced features on your Web pages. These features include special on-screen characters, pages that provide forms for readers to fill in, and advanced inline images that are mapped and have several areas that the reader can click. Obviously, you will use these features if you are creating Web documents that other people will access; these documents will reside on a Web server. To use this chapter, you should first be familiar with the concepts presented in Chapter 14, "Creating Home Pages with HTML."

The sudden popularity of the World Wide Web caused WWW developers to see the need for advanced capabilities. HTML+ and other new standards add elements to HTML that provide many components for successful commercialization of the Web.

In this chapter, you learn to do the following:

- Create special characters on your page(s)

- Understand the function of forms

- Use basic form elements

- Create a form

- Understand how forms are processed

- Create imagemaps

Special Characters

Because many keyboard characters have special meanings in HTML, you must use special character sequences for those characters to show up. You can use the same mechanism to produce foreign-language characters.

Because the < and > characters are used to delimit an element, you may begin to suspect that using these characters in a document may be a problem. In fact, the < and & characters are reserved within HTML. As you already know, < is used to signify the start of an element. The & character is used to access characters that are not available on the keyboard (for example, characters that have accent marks). To correctly represent the <, >, and & symbols in a document, you must replace them with alternative characters when you do not intend for them to be interpreted as HTML commands. Following is a partial list of the most frequently used special characters:

&lt	Replaces < (less-than sign)
&gt	Replaces > (greater-than sign)
&amp	Replaces & (ampersand by itself)
&quot	Replaces " (double quotes)
	Nonbreaking space

Suppose that you need to place the following text in HTML form:

The "A & B" new price is <$10.99>

The HTML version of this text is:

The &quot A &amp B &quot new price is &lt $10.99 &gt

Although this procedure seems to be awkward, it solves the problem of using the special characters without confusion and is not too difficult to remember or implement.

> **Note**
>
> Not all browsers support the entire set of special characters. Additionally, some browsers ignore the first space after a special character. If you experience trouble using a special character, revert to the original character and check the results. To fix spacing problems, try adding spaces around your special characters.

Comments

You can include comment lines in HTML that do not show up in browsers. The format for a comment is as follows:

<!— Everything in here is part of the comment. —>

> **Note**
>
> Server-side include commands (see Chapter 10, "Using Mosaic to Access Other Internet Services") embedded in HTML use the same character sequence as comments so that the server-side include commands do not show up, even when a server does not support server-side includes. Documents that use server-side includes, however, must have the extension .shtml.

Foreign-Language Characters

HTML uses the ISO-Latin1 character set, which includes characters for all Latin-based languages, as the name implies. Like the other special character sequences in HTML, foreign-language character sequences begin with an ampersand (&), followed by a written-out description of the character. Table 15.1 lists the available foreign-language sequences.

Tip

This table is included on WebCD in HTML format, in the file \html\examples \foreign.htm. You can use this file to copy and paste the characters into your own HTML files without risk of typing errors.

Table 15.1   Foreign-Language Characters in HTML

Character	Sequence
Æ,æ	Æ,æ
Á,á	Á,á
Â,â	Â,â
À,à	À,à
Å,å	Å,å
Ã,ã	Ã,ã

Table 15.1 **Continued**	
Ä,ä	&Auml,&auml
Ç,ç	&Ccedil,&ccedil
Ð,ð	&ETH,&eth
É,é	&Eacute,&eacute
Ê,ê	&Ecirc,&ecirc
È,è	&Egrave,&egrave
Ë,ë	&Euml,&euml
Í,í	&Iacute,&iacute
Î,î	&Icirc,&icirc
Ì,ì	&Igrave,&igrave
Ï,ï	&Iuml,&iuml
Ñ,ñ	&Ntilde,&ntilde
Ó,ó	&Oacute,&oacute
Ô,ô	&Ocirc,&ocirc
Ò,ò	&Ograve,&ograve
Ø,ø	&Oslash,&oslash
Õ,õ	&Otilde,&otilde
Ö,ö	&Ouml,&ouml
ß	&szlig
Þ,þ	&THORN,&thorn
Ú,ú	&Uacute,&uacute
Û,û	&Ucirc,&ucirc
Ù,ù	&Ugrave,&ugrave
Ü,ü	&Uuml,&uuml
Ý,ý	&Yacute,&yacute
Ÿ	&yuml

> **Note**
>
> Different Web browsers may display the foreign-language characters with slight variations.

Interactive Forms

One of the most powerful and exciting capabilities of the World Wide Web is the capability to send data from Web clients back to the Web server. This capability enables Web users to enter search words and phrases; comments; suggestions; and, in the growing world of electronic commerce, even credit-card numbers and addresses for purchases made over the Internet. Future Web servers and clients are likely to support the capability to post entire files and remote servers, simulating an environment similar to dial-up bulletin-board systems or many online services.

► See "Finding the Elusive Resource: Web Searchers," p. 450

HTML's capability to handle interactive forms allows interaction with users in ways that simple links cannot manage. The following list offers just a few of the ways that people on the Web use forms:

- User surveys and polls

- Search criteria for database retrieval

- Button mechanisms for option selection

- Order entry

- Interactive message and newsgroup handling

- Game mechanisms

At the heart of the Web's interactive capabilities is support for forms and scripts. On the client side, data is entered through fill-in forms. Form data then is sent to the server for processing.

Setting up a form system involves two basic steps: creating your form in your HTML document, and determining the mechanism to be used to retrieve the information. For the second step, you can write the mechanism yourself, find an existing method, or have someone write it for you. This section explores all these issues.

> **Note**
>
> A good understanding of form elements is necessary even when you use HTML editors such as HoTMetaL. Most of the editors and filters that offer form capability do so without WYSIWYG previewing.

How Forms Are Processed

Before you explore the elements used in the construction of forms, you need to have a basic understanding of how forms are processed.

Forms require the use of a World Wide Web server known as an *HTTP daemon*. HTTP (Hypertext Transfer Protocol) is often referred to as HTTPD because it is a daemon (a background-running process). The purpose of the HTTP server is to handle your form when it is submitted. After a user fills in a form, he or she submits it. To whom is the form submitted? What happens to the information? And what type of HTML response is returned to the user?

These questions indicate that some computer intelligence must handle the form information. This intelligence must be able to determine the type of form, handle the incoming data, and produce some type of response to the user. This is handled by a program or script running on an HTTP server. After a form is filled out, it is submitted to the server indicated in the form's URL. By analyzing the URL, the server hands the form to the appropriate program or script that deals with that form.

All these facts mean that although forms are extremely useful, they cannot be used unless they are accompanied by software running on the Internet to process that form.

As you learn how to create forms, you will discover the mechanisms by which the server knows how to deal with a form and what options are available. You also will see what options exist for form builders who lack the expertise or time to create their own form-handling systems.

The Basic Form Element

As previously discussed, a form is the mechanism for getting information back from a user. A document may contain more than one form, but forms never appear inside other forms. A form contains many elements that describe different aspects of the form. HTML form elements are:

- Radio buttons
- Check boxes

- Lists

- Text-entry areas

A form contains one or more of these elements. There are no limits on the number of elements that can be used.

The <FORM> element defines the beginning of a form. Because a form encompasses a block of other elements, the <FORM> element is, obviously, a nonempty element. Use </FORM> to define the end of the form.

The <FORM> element contains two parameters: ACTION and METHOD. Following is an example of a <FORM> element:

```
<FORM ACTION="url" METHOD="technique">
```

The ACTION parameter specifies a valid RELATIVE or ABSOLUTE URL. The form will be transmitted to the URL specified by ACTION when the form is submitted.

The METHOD specifies the technique that the server uses to send the form data to the program specified by the ACTION. Two basic types of METHOD parameters exist: GET and POST.

The GET method is the older method, as well as the default. If you do not specify a method, GET is used automatically. When an HTTP server receives a form that uses the GET method, the form elements are converted to a command-line statement and are passed to the program or script specified by the ACTION.

The POST method is newer and more powerful than GET. Because of the limitations of GET, using POST is recommended. In fact, most HTML documentation recommends that you change existing GETs to POSTs to remain compatible with future versions of the HTML language and HTTP servers. Instead of passing the form information to the ACTION via the command line, POST submits the form information via standard input (STDIN). Although this procedure may appear to be confusing, it does not need to be a crucial decision made by you, the form designer; the software to which you are interfacing will dictate whether the POST method or the GET method should be used.

Following is an example FORM element:

```
<FORM ACTION="http://www.com/cgi-bin/top" METHOD="POST">
```

In this FORM element, you can see that the form data will be sent to the ACTION specified as a server (http://) named www.com. The server will access the program or script named top, which appears in the server's cgi-bin directory. The METHOD indicates that the form will be submitted to the top program using the POST method.

Knowing what to use for an ACTION or METHOD consists of talking to the staff at your server site or reading the documentation that accompanies your server's form-handling software.

The INPUT Element

The <INPUT> element is the most common form command because it enables you to create many types of controls that allow the user to make choices. Controls include two types of buttons that the user can turn on and off, as well as windows in which text can be typed. The INPUT element is an empty element, requiring no termination.

The INPUT element has many parameters; the most important one is TYPE. The TYPE parameter specifies what kind of INPUT to expect from the Web site user and can be assigned any of the following values:

Value	Description
Check box	Implements a button that can be toggled on or off
Radio button	Allows you to implement a group of buttons in which only one of the group can be turned on at any time
Text	Allows the user to enter a line of text
Password	Same as Text, but the characters entered by the user are displayed as asterisks (or similar concealing characters)
Reset	Causes a button to appear that, when selected, resets all the other form elements to their default values
Submit	Displays a button that will transmit the form to the URL (Action) when selected

If no TYPE is specified in the INPUT element, TYPE=TEXT is assumed by default.

Following is an example of a simple <INPUT> command that implements a CHECKBOX style button. (The NAME parameter is shown for completeness and is discussed in the following section.) Remember that this command can appear only between a <FORM> and </FORM> element.

```
<INPUT TYPE="CHECKBOX" NAME="test">
```

Each TYPE element has its own parameters to further define the element.

The following sections show examples of the TYPE elements and explain their parameters. Almost all the elements use the NAME parameter; therefore, the NAME parameter is discussed first.

> **Note**
>
> SUBMIT and RESET are the only two FORM elements that do not use the NAME parameter.

Using the NAME Parameter

NAME is a required parameter for all INPUT elements except the SUBMIT and RESET elements. The NAME parameter creates a label that will be associated with the user response, and allows the server that interprets the form to determine which response from the user goes to which form element.

The word that you equate with NAME can be any word; it never appears to the user in any form. Examples of the NAME parameter include the following:

```
NAME="user_text"
NAME="variable1"
NAME="variable2"
NAME="their_email_address"
NAME="a"
```

NAME is used in the examples of most of the other INPUT parameters. Please refer to these examples as working examples of the NAME parameter.

Creating CHECKBOX TYPE Input Elements

```
<INPUT TYPE="checkbox" NAME="name" VALUE="value" CHECKED>
```

The CHECKBOX TYPE, which allows you to create a button that the user can turn on or off, is like a toggle switch. The checkbox function allows you to ask a simple question, for which you get one of two possible responses.

You can have any number of check boxes in your document. Each check box is independent of all the others. When a form is submitted, only the boxes that are checked by the user are actually submitted. The server always assumes that all the other boxes are unchecked. If you want to have a check box checked by default (so that when the user initially sees it, the box is already checked), place the parameter CHECKED in the element. The CHECKED parameter functions like a switch and requires no data or argument following the parameter.

Tip

You should use names that are short but descriptive, because this practice reduces the amount of data that is transmitted. Descriptive names also help you locate names when you need to modify the form.

IV

Creating Web Pages & Sites

Check-box elements also can contain a VALUE parameter, which allows you to set a string that is sent for the on state. If no VALUE parameter appears, the default—on—is selected. VALUE is used in conjunction with NAME, which is set to a symbolic label equated with the VALUE. If you set parameters for NAME="setting" and VALUE="on", when the user selects that check box, the server will be sent setting=on.

If more than one check box uses the same NAME, each box that the user selects will be sent to the server. For example, if one check box has NAME="pet" and VALUE="dog", and another check box has NAME="pet" and VALUE="cat", and if both check boxes have been selected, both pet=dog and pet=cat will be sent to the server.

▶ See "Creating a Complete Form," p. 366

Following are some examples of check boxes (this code must appear within a <FORM> and </FORM> element).

```
<INPUT TYPE="CHECKBOX" NAME="brochure" VALUE="yes" CHECKED> Would
you like a brochure?
```

This example places a check box next to the string `Would you like a brochure?`

By default, the check box will be checked (CHECKED). When the information is sent to the server, it will be sent brochure=yes (because of NAME and VALUE).

> **Note**
>
> WebCD includes HTML documents with all the code for the examples shown in the figures in this chapter in \html\examples. The file names match the figure names. The code for figure 15.1, for example, is in the file 15-1.htm.

Following is a more complex example:

```
<FORM>
<INPUT TYPE="checkbox" NAME="pet" VALUE="dog" > Dog<P>
<INPUT TYPE="checkbox" NAME="pet" VALUE="cat" > Cat<P>
<INPUT TYPE="checkbox" NAME="pet" VALUE="fish" > Fish<P>
<INPUT TYPE="checkbox" NAME="pet" VALUE="horse" > Horse<P>
<INPUT TYPE="checkbox" NAME="pet" VALUE="bird" > Bird<P>
<INPUT TYPE="checkbox" NAME="pet" VALUE="snake" > Snake<P>
</FORM>
```

This HTML script produces the output shown in figure 15.1.

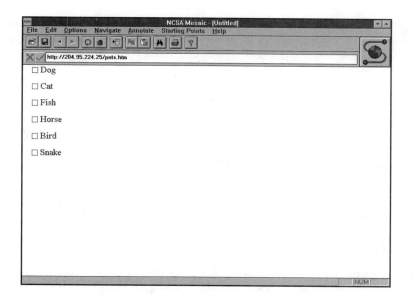

Fig. 15.1
The user can select any or all of these check boxes.

Six check boxes are displayed. Each box is labeled by a type of pet, allowing users to indicate whether or not they have that type of pet. A user can mark any of the boxes. For each box that is marked, a string consisting of the NAME and the VALUE will be sent to the server. If the user selects Dog and Horse, for example, pet=dog and pet=horse will be sent to the server.

Because each check box is unique, you never should have two check boxes with the same NAME and VALUE parameter. You can, however, have check boxes with the same NAME and different VALUEs or with the same VALUE and different NAMEs.

Creating RADIO TYPE Input Elements

```
<INPUT TYPE="radio" NAME="name" VALUE="value" CHECKED>
```

The RADIO TYPE allows you to create a button that acts just like CHECKBOX in that you can turn it on and off. Radio buttons differ, however, in that within a group of buttons, only one can be selected at a given time. Selecting a button in a group deselects the button that is currently selected and turns on the newly selected button. This element is useful when you want the user to select only one choice from a series of choices.

Note

To allow the user to make more than one selection from a group of choices, use the CHECKBOX parameter. To force the user to select only one option, use the RADIO parameter.

Like CHECKBOXes, RADIO buttons have a NAME field that allows you to label the box for the server. Each RADIO button that has the same NAME is in the same group. In that group, only one button can be activated at any time.

The VALUE field acts just as it does for CHECKBOX and specifies a unique word that is sent with the form when that particular button is activated.

If one of the buttons in a group has the CHECKED parameter, that button is automatically selected when the form is first displayed to the user. This feature allows you to select a default button in a group.

Following are examples of radio buttons:

```
<FORM>
What type of credit card are you using?<P>
<INPUT TYPE="radio" NAME="credit" VALUE="visa" CHECKED> Visa<P>
<INPUT TYPE="radio" NAME="credit" VALUE="mc" > MasterCard<P>
<INPUT TYPE="radio" NAME="credit" VALUE="discover" > Discover<P>
<INPUT TYPE="radio" NAME="credit" VALUE="diners" > Diners Club<P>
<INPUT TYPE="radio" NAME="credit" VALUE="ae" > American Express<P>
</FORM>
```

This HTML script produces the output shown in figure 15.2.

Fig. 15.2
Only one radio button can be selected at any time.

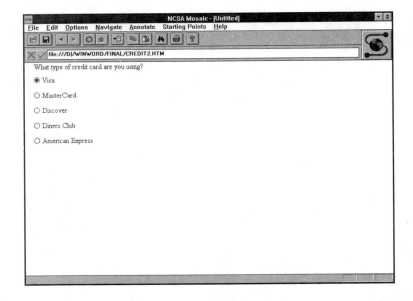

Tip
Radio buttons that are in the same group do not necessarily need to be grouped together on-screen.

This example displays five radio buttons below the string What type of credit card are you using? Each radio button belongs to the group called credit.

The first button, Visa, is selected by default (CHECKED). If the user were to select Discover, for example, when the form is submitted, the server will receive credit=discover (NAME=VALUE) for this group of buttons.

Creating TEXT TYPE Input Elements

```
<INPUT TYPE="type" NAME="name" VALUE="value" SIZE=40 MAXLENGTH=100>
```

It frequently is useful to accept single lines of free-form input from a user. This approach can be used to take e-mail addresses, phone numbers, credit-card numbers, comments, and any other simple typed information.

Like most of the other INPUT elements, TEXT regions have a NAME field that allows you to label the box for the server. Place a symbolic name for this text box in the NAME parameter. Setting NAME="email", for example, will send the server email=, followed by whatever text the user enters in that field.

The VALUE parameter sets a default string to appear in the box when it is first displayed. If no VALUE parameter is encountered, the box will be empty when first displayed.

A SIZE parameter allows you to set the size of the displayed text box. Setting SIZE="40", for example, will set a text window 40 characters wide. If text is typed that is longer than 40 characters, the text will scroll correctly. Many browsers support multiple lines of text and allow you to set SIZE=width,height to specify more than one line. Setting SIZE="40,10", for example, sets a text window 40 characters wide by 10 lines high. Because HTML also supports a multiple-line TEXTAREA command, you should not use this feature within TEXT itself.

If you do not include the SIZE parameter, the TEXT window is automatically set to 20 characters.

Tip

Only the physical size of the window on-screen is affected by SIZE, not the amount of text that the user can type in the window.

Troubleshooting

I created a text area of a specific SIZE, but my characters don't fit.

Different browsers handle SIZE differently. Some equate SIZE with the number of characters; others equate it with different width rules. As a good practice, do not make SIZE too large, as it may not fit on all users' screens. A normal size of between 10 and 40 characters works fine in most cases.

A MAXLENGTH parameter is included to set a maximum number of characters that can be entered for text fields. If no MAXLENGTH parameter appears, the text field is an unlimited length. If you set MAXLENGTH="100", for example, only 100 characters can be typed per line.

Following is an example of a text window. (As mentioned in "Creating a Complete Form" later in this chapter, this script must appear within a <FORM> and </FORM> element.)

```
Please enter your E-MAIL address: <INPUT TYPE="text" NAME="email">
```

This line will place a text-entry window next to the string `Please enter your E-MAIL address:`. Whatever the user enters will be transmitted to the server as email=, followed by his or her typed text. If the user types debi@high.tech.com, for example, the server receives email=debi@high.tech.com.

Following is another example:

WebCD

```
<FORM>
Enter your first name: <INPUT TYPE="text" NAME="first"
MAXLENGTH=20> <P>
Enter your last name: <INPUT TYPE="text" NAME="last"
MAXLENGTH=20><P>
Enter your address: <INPUT TYPE="text" NAME="address" SIZE=80><P>
Comments: <INPUT TYPE="text" NAME="comments" VALUE="Please send
info" SIZE=80><P>
</FORM>
```

This HTML script produces the output shown in figure 15.3.

Fig. 15.3
You can create a Web form where the user can enter information into a specific text area.

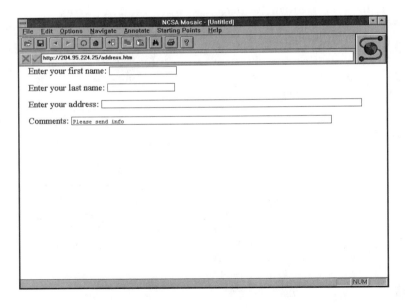

Tip
MAXLENGTH is useful when you are using forms with databases; it ensures that the information that the user types is not longer than the maximum size allowed by your particular database.

This example displays four lines. The first line allows the user to enter his or her first name. The first name is limited to 20 characters of typed text (MAXLENGTH). When the user submits the form, first= will be sent to the server, followed by the information that the user typed.

The second line repeats the actions of the first line for the user's last name. Again, the name is limited to a maximum 20 characters.

The third line allows the user to enter an address. The address window is 80 characters wide (SIZE=80), but the user can type unlimited amounts of information in that window (because no MAXLENGTH statement is used).

The final line allows the user to enter a comment. The size of the window again is set to 80 (SIZE=80). The window initially displays to the user with the string `Please send info` already in it as a default string (VALUE=). The user can change the string by typing in the window.

Creating PASSWORD TYPE Input Elements

```
<INPUT TYPE="password" NAME="name" VALUE="value" SIZE=40
MAXLENGTH=100>
```

You may want to accept information from a user but not have that information appear on the user's screen. This approach allows you to collect passwords, credit-card numbers, and other personal data while assuring the user that prying eyes will not see what is entered. The PASSWORD TYPE allows this action. Although this approach does not encrypt the data in any way, it keeps the data from appearing on the user's screen as he or she types it (just in case someone's looking over their shoulder).

The NAME, VALUE, SIZE, and MAXLENGTH parameters work exactly as they do for TEXT.

Following is an example of a password window (it must appear within a <FORM> and </FORM> element):

```
Please enter your account password: <INPUT TYPE="password"
NAME="pass" SIZE=10>
```

This line will display a text window after the string `Please enter your account password`.

The window will be sized to display only 10 characters (SIZE=10) but will accept a string of any length (because no MAXLENGTH statement is used). When the typed information is sent to the server, pass= is transmitted, followed by the user's typed text (NAME=). The user sees only asterisks or similar characters (depending on the browser), regardless of what he or she types.

Creating a Button to RESET a Form

```
<INPUT TYPE="reset" VALUE="value">
```

HTML has the capability to define a single button that can reset a form. The form is reset to all its default values, as specified by the various parameters of each of the form's elements.

Tip

PASSWORD is not a secure mechanism for transmitting data. The typed information is inhibited only from being displayed on the user's screen. No encryption of the data is performed while the data is transmitted by the server.

IV

Creating Web Pages & Sites

The RESET TYPE button does not have a corresponding NAME= parameter, because it is never transmitted to the server. RESET is handled in the user's browser automatically as the user clicks the button.

The only parameter that RESET uses is the VALUE= parameter. Whatever you set VALUE= to will be used as the label for that button.

Following is an example of the RESET button (this code must appear within a <FORM> and </FORM> element):

```
<INPUT TYPE="reset" VALUE=" Push here to reset this form ">
```

This line will result in the creation of a button that contains the string `Push here to reset this form`. When the user clicks the button, all text fields will be set to their default values. Text fields for which no default value is specified will be cleared. Check boxes and radio buttons with CHECKED set in their definitions are turned on automatically, and the non-CHECKED definitions are turned off automatically. TEXT and PASSWORD areas with VALUE= statements will be set to the string specified by VALUE= or will be blanked if no VALUE= statement appears.

Creating a Button to SEND a Form

```
<INPUT TYPE="submit" VALUE="value">
```

The INPUT element TYPE="submit" is used to create the button that submits the form to the server. When this button is selected, the form and its current contents will be sent to the server specified by the ACTION of the <FORM> line, using the <FORM> line's METHOD.

The SUBMIT TYPE button does not have a corresponding NAME= parameter, because the button itself is never transmitted to the server. Instead, SUBMIT causes the entire form to be transmitted when the user clicks the button.

The only parameter that SUBMIT uses is the VALUE= parameter. Whatever you set VALUE= to will be used as the label for that button.

Following is an example of the SUBMIT button (it must appear within a <FORM> and </FORM> element, as mentioned in "Creating a Complete Form" later in this chapter):

```
<INPUT TYPE="submit" VALUE=" Push here to send this form ">
```

This line will result in the creation of a button that contains the string `Push here to send this form`. When the user clicks the button, all filled-in fields will be sent to the server specified in the <FORM> statement. Fields and buttons that are not set to anything will not be transmitted. The example from figure 15.3 is shown in figure 15.4 with the RESET and SEND buttons added.

Fig. 15.4
Here the form
includes both a
RESET and a SEND
button for the user
to either start over
or submit his/her
message.

Following is the code for this example:

```
<FORM>
Enter your first name: <INPUT TYPE="text" NAME="first"
MAXLENGTH=20> <P>
Enter your last name: <INPUT TYPE="text" NAME="last"
MAXLENGTH=20><P>
Enter your address: <INPUT TYPE="text" NAME="address" SIZE=80><P>
Comments: <INPUT TYPE="text" NAME="comments" VALUE="Please send
info" SIZE=80><P>
<INPUT TYPE="reset" VALUE=" Push here to reset this form ">
<INPUT TYPE="submit" VALUE=" Push here to send this form ">
</FORM>
```

Using the TEXTAREA Element

```
<TEXTAREA NAME="NAME" ROWS=10 COLS=40> </TEXTAREA>
```

Often, the capability to accept a block of text from the user is useful. Having
this capability allows users to cut and paste entire documents into HTML
pages. This capability in turn allows large quantities of information to be
passed back and forth. This feature can save both HTML-page room and database room by combining what would be many TEXT elements in a single
TEXTAREA.

The TEXTAREA element is not a TYPE of the INPUT command; it is a specific
element, just as INPUT is.

Like most of the other INPUT elements, TEXT regions have a NAME field that allows you to label the area for the server. Place a symbolic name for this text box in the NAME parameter. Setting NAME="body", for example, will send the server body=, followed by whatever the user types for that TEXTAREA.

The TEXTAREA element also has ROWS and COLS parameters. These parameters specify the size of the TEXTAREA window that is displayed to the user. This does not limit the user in how much he or she can type, but merely limits the size of the window displayed to the user. As the user types and overfills the window, the window should automatically create a vertical scroll bar to aid in moving the view for the user.

To use ROWS and COLS, simply set them equal to the number of rows and columns that you want in your TEXTAREA. Setting ROWS=10 and COLUMNS=80, for example, sets a field 10 characters high and 80 lines wide.

The TEXTAREA element is a NON-EMPTY element, which means that it must have a </TEXTAREA> terminator. Anything between the <TEXTAREA> and </TEXTAREA> elements will appear as default information inside the text area. If nothing appears between the two elements, no default information will be placed in the text area when it appears to the user.

Following is an example of the TEXTAREA element (this must appear within a <FORM> and </FORM> element; see "Creating a Complete Form" later in this chapter):

```
<TEXTAREA NAME="resume" ROWS=8 COLS=80></TEXTAREA>
```

In this example, a text area is created that is 8 lines high by 80 characters wide. The user can type any amount of information into this area. The area contains no default information.

Following is another example:

```
Please enter any special instructions:<P>
<TEXTAREA NAME="instructions" ROWS=5 COLS=40>No special instruc-
tions</TEXTAREA>
```

Troubleshooting

My Web browser displays input text outside of the text area. Why does this happen and what can I do to fix it?

Some browsers will not deal with the default text specified between the <TEXTAREA> and </TEXTAREA> elements. When displayed by these browsers, the text will appear outside the text area.

> One solution is to try the VALUE= parameter within the <TEXTAREA> element. Some browsers recognize this code as an alternative mechanism for specification of default text. Your browser may not accept either mechanism, in which case you cannot have default text.

Incorporating this code into the example shown in figure 15.4 (in place of the comment box) would yield the result shown in figure 15.5.

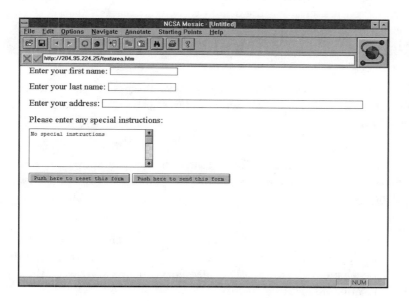

Fig. 15.5
TEXTAREA accepts more than one line of typed text.

Following is the code for this example:

```
<FORM>
Enter your first name: <INPUT TYPE="text" NAME="first"
MAXLENGTH=20> <P>
Enter your last name: <INPUT TYPE="text" NAME="last"
MAXLENGTH=20><P>
Enter your address: <INPUT TYPE="text" NAME="address" SIZE=80><P>
Please enter any special instructions:<P>
<TEXTAREA NAME="instructions" ROWS=5 COLS=40>No special instruc-
tions</TEXTAREA><P>
<INPUT TYPE="reset" VALUE=" Push here to reset this form ">
<INPUT TYPE="submit" VALUE=" Push here to send this form ">
</FORM>
```

IV

Creating Web Pages & Sites

> **Note**
>
> A <P> was added after the text-area definition so that the two buttons will appear on the next line.

This example creates a text window 5 lines high by 40 characters wide. The window is named instructions and will be passed to the server as instructions=, followed by whatever text the user enters. The first time the field is presented to the user, it has the default content No special instructions.

Using the SELECT Element to Create a List

```
<SELECT NAME="LIST"> </SELECT>
```

HTML form handling allows you to create several types of lists. Each list presents one or more items to the user, who can select a single item or several items from the list.

When lists are displayed, they appear in an inset window or in a pop-up window. Inset windows that contain a list larger than the window itself have a scroll bar on the side that allows you to access other items in the list. When check boxes are useful for small lists, the <SELECT> element allows lists of any size to be created.

Lists are bounded by the <SELECT> and </SELECT> elements. Only two things can appear between these two elements: any free-form text, and the <OPTION> element. No other HTML elements can appear between the <SELECT> and </SELECT> elements.

The <SELECT> element starts a list. The NAME parameter, which must be associated with the <SELECT> element, allows you to label the list for the server. Place a symbolic name for this text box in the NAME parameter. Setting <SELECT NAME="list1">, for example, will send the server list1=, followed by the name, for each item selected in the list. If the list contains Dog, Cat, and Mouse, for example, and if Dog and Cat are selected, both list=Dog and list=Cat will be sent to the server. Dog, Cat, and Mouse are specified with the <OPTION> element (discussed later in this section).

The <SELECT> element has an optional SIZE parameter. If the SIZE parameter is missing, the parameter is assumed to be equated to the value 1 (one). When size is set to 1, the list is a pop-up window, in which you can select only one of the items in the list. This use is similar to the use of radio buttons, in which only one of a group may be selected.

When the SIZE parameter is larger than 1, it is presented as an inset window that contains a list of selectable items. The number that is assigned to SIZE sets the maximum number of items that are in the inset window at any time. If the list is set to SIZE=5, for example, five items from the list are visible at one time. Items that are not visible in the list can be accessed by the scroll bar that appears to the right of the list.

Another optional parameter of the <SELECT> element is the MULTIPLE parameter. MULTIPLE has no value associated with it. Using MULTIPLE forces the list to be displayed in a scrollable inset window. Additionally, when MULTIPLE is present, the user can select more than one item from the list by holding down the Ctrl key while selecting additional items in the list.

The <OPTION> element appears between the <SELECT> and </SELECT> elements. One <OPTION> is used for every item that may be picked in the list.

<OPTION> has one parameter associated with it: SELECTED. If SELECTED is set, the item associated with that <OPTION> is selected by default. If MULTIPLE is specified in the <SELECT> element, more than one SELECTED parameter may appear.

Following is an example of the SELECT element:

```
<FORM>
Please select your favorite ice cream toppings:<P>
<SELECT NAME="list1" SIZE=3 MULTIPLE>
<OPTION SELECTED> Chocolate
<OPTION> Fruit Preserves
<OPTION> Nuts
<OPTION> Butterscotch
<OPTION> Candy sprinkles
</SELECT>
</FORM>
```

This HTML script produces the output shown in figure 15.6.

In this example, a select box is created that is large enough for three items. The rest of the items are accessible by scrolling (SIZE=3). The select area allows the user to select more than one item (MULTIPLE), and each item selected will be transmitted to the server as list1=, followed by the item that was selected. The select box in this example contains five items that the user can choose.

Chocolate is selected by default (because almost everybody loves chocolate) but can be deselected by the user.

Fig. 15.6
The inset list
window shows
three items; the
scroll bar allows
the user to select
the options that
are hidden.

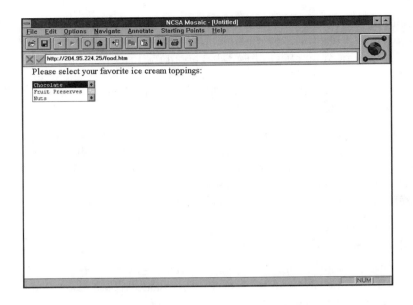

Creating a Complete Form

Now that you have examined the fundamental elements necessary to complete a form, try putting them all together to see how a form actually looks.

For this example, you will create an order form that allows the user to purchase a new car (see fig. 15.7).

The order form begins by accepting free-format text from the user for a name,
phone number, and address. The form displays a series of radio buttons that
allow the user to pick the color of the car. Below the radio buttons is a list of
options for the car. The user can pick one option from the list or hold down
the Ctrl key to select multiple options. After the inset box, a series of check
boxes allows the user to select a method of response. Finally, the SUBMIT
button is displayed, which enables the user to send the form to the HTTP
server. The HTML code to create this form is as follows:

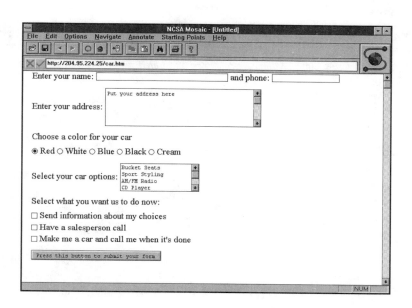

Fig. 15.7
The new car order
form combines
most of the FORM
elements.

```
<FORM ACTION="http://www.car.com/cgi-bin/sellcar" METHOD=POST>
Enter your name: <INPUT TYPE="text" NAME="name" SIZE=40> and phone:
<INPUT TYPE="text" NAME="phone" SIZE=20><P>
Enter your address: <TEXTAREA NAME="address" ROWS=5 COLS=50>Put
your address here</TEXTAREA><P>
Choose a color for your car<P>
<INPUT TYPE="radio" NAME="color" VALUE="red" CHECKED> Red
<INPUT TYPE="radio" NAME="color" VALUE="white" > White
<INPUT TYPE="radio" NAME="color" VALUE="blue" > Blue
<INPUT TYPE="radio" NAME="color" VALUE="black" > Black
<INPUT TYPE="radio" NAME="color" VALUE="cream" > Cream<P>
Select your car options:
<SELECT NAME="options" MULTIPLE SIZE=4>
<OPTION> Bucket Seats
<OPTION> Sport Styling
<OPTION> AM/FM Radio
<OPTION> CD Player
<OPTION> Turbo charged engine
<OPTION> Tinted Windows
</SELECT> <P>
Select what you want us to do now:<P>
<INPUT TYPE="checkbox" NAME="dispose" VALUE="mail"> Send informa-
tion about my choices<BR>
<INPUT TYPE="checkbox" NAME="dispose" VALUE="sale"> Have a sales-
person call<BR>
<INPUT TYPE="checkbox" NAME="dispose" VALUE="make"> Make me a car
and call me when it's done<P>
<INPUT TYPE="submit" VALUE=" Press this button to submit your form
">
</FORM>
```

Troubleshooting

I created my forms, but everything appears to be a text area, even my radio buttons and check boxes.

Some browsers are not case-independent in the button type, so make sure that you use radio, checkbox, and text when defining these buttons. Using uppercase for these words may not work in many browsers.

This example begins by opening the form with a <FORM> statement. In this statement, you specify that the form is to use the POST method of transferring data and that it is to send any filled-out form to the URL http://www.car.com/cgi-bin/sell car, as specified by the ACTION statement.

Next, you accept the user's name, address, and phone number by using TEXT windows. The address is entered in a multiple-line TEXTAREA; the phone numbers and user's name are single-line text windows.

Next, the user is allowed to select the color of his or her car as one of five possible choices. Notice that the default color is Red and that only one color can be selected from the list because it is a RADIO type group of buttons.

Below the car color choices is a select box that contains various options for the car. The user can select any number of these options because the <SELECT> element contains the MULTIPLE parameter.

Toward the end of the form, the user can select up to three METHODs of follow-up. The user can check any or all of the three CHECKBOX elements.

Finally, the last button allows the user to send the form to the server specified (car.com) by the ACTION parameter of the <FORM> element.

Understanding How Forms Are Submitted

Anybody can design a form. The resulting form will be usable, in that it can be filled out and submitted. At this point, however, you must ask, "Submitted where?" For a form to be useful, it must be submitted to some place that will know what to do with the data in the form. Because every form is different, the submission process often requires custom solutions.

Two problems are associated with determining how a form is handled. The first problem is where to send the form data—in other words, what to set the ACTION parameter of the <FORM> element to.

Second, you must determine what you want to do with the data. You may want the data to be e-mailed to you, or you may want the data to be integrated into a database. The database can be designed to provide instant feedback to the user, so that immediately after the user submits the form, the entire HTML system is modified to incorporate the user's information. You can do an infinite number of things with form data, depending on your needs.

Interestingly enough, both problems have the same solutions. If you can write a shell script or a fairly simple program in C or a similar language, you probably have enough skill to write your own form-handling software. For people who do not have the programming or script skills, or who simply lack the time, off-the-shelf solutions already exist for many form needs.

Before you see how a solution can be implemented, you need a better understanding of exactly how a server deals with a form. Examine a simple example in which you play the role of the user. You have just filled out a form, and you clicked the SUBMIT button. At that moment, the user's browser software accumulated the information contained in the form and transmitted it to the URL pointed to by the ACTION parameter of the <FORM> element.

So far, so good. Your information is somewhere between you and the server that is going to handle it. When the information reaches the server, it is examined by the server. The URL must direct the server where to find a program that will handle your form data. For example, the following may have been your ACTION URL:

```
<FORM ACTION="http://www.com/cgi-bin/remailer?bob@www.com"
METHOD="POST">
```

In this FORM element, you see a valid URL for the ACTION that points to a server (http://) named www.com. The server finds a program named remailer in the cgi-bin directory (more information on cgi-bin appears later in this chapter). The METHOD is POST, so the server will communicate with the remailer program by using that method. If there is information to be passed to the remailer program in the command line, that information is separated by the question-mark character (?) from the program name itself.

Back to your data—as your data enters the server (www.com), the server examines the URL information and (in this example) invokes the remailer program. The server hands the string bob@www.com in the command line to the remailer program and also transmits the contents of your filled-out form to the remailer program. The transmission occurs in the command line for GET methods and through standard input for POST methods.

The server's software (remailer, in this case) examines and handles the form information, and formats a response for you, the user. The response is sent back to you via the server and arrives on your screen.

Again, you can see the two basic problems: where do you send your data, and what do you do with it?

The simplest way to handle a form is to have all the submitted forms e-mailed to a single destination, where they can be examined at will. This process is known as FORM REMAILING, and many server sites already provide some type of form-remailing service. Commercial form remailers typically impose a small monthly charge for forwarding your e-mailed forms. Form remailers require you to provide a single e-mail address to send the contents of all forms. Remailers then take all incoming forms, format them in readable responses, and send the forms to you. This method is easiest because you can use it even if you don't have access to a server site. This method means that you can run pages out of a directory, using file://, and still take advantage of form-handling capabilities.

If you have access to a server site and can design your own software or scripts, you can implement your own form-handling program easily. It is beyond the scope of this chapter to provide details on constructing server form-handling software, as this subject would be a book in itself. The methods, however, are simple enough that anyone who has a moderate level of experience in writing scripts should be able to implement simple form-handling programs.

Another solution involves finding archives of existing software. Many form-handling systems have been placed in the public domain on the Internet. These systems often can be used outright or modified slightly to accommodate any special needs. Use of existing software requires that you have access to a server on which to implement it.

Finally, many consultants and service bureaus are more than happy to implement custom-designed form solutions. These groups will write your software as well as help you find a cost-effective server site on which to place it.

A Brief Look at cgi-bin

At the end of the preceding section, you saw an example of the use of cgi-bin in what appeared to be a path. Here is the line again, for your reference:

```
<FORM ACTION="http://www.com/cgi-bin/remailer?bob@www.com"
METHOD="POST">
```

Although cgi-bin looks like a path, in effect it is a special word recognized by the server (in this example, www.com). CGI (Common Gateway Interface) is a special mechanism for interfacing Web servers with programs, allowing them to handle form and other input. Cgi-bin programs can be pointed to from any link or form. Links pass all information to the form in the command line, as though a GET were issued. Forms pass information by GET or POST METHOD.

When a server sees an URL coming across that contains the cgi-bin directory, it knows to call the program referenced by the URL and to hand that program the data in the URL and form (if a form is present). The server also knows to expect a response from the cgi-bin program that it sends back to the user.

Any time that a browser submits a form to a server, it expects a valid HTML response from the server. If no response is received in a reasonable period of time (two to three minutes in most browsers), the browser returns an error. All cgi-bin programs must return some form of HTML response to the user via the server. This return is accomplished by the cgi-bin program's writing the desired response, as valid HTML, to standard out (STDOUT). The server receives the output and sends it back to the user's browser.

Using cgi-bin programs allows you to create new Web capabilities, offering new features and data-handling capabilities to users. One of the primary attractions of the Web is its capability to change and modify itself to fit its users' needs.

Forms: Diverse Applications

As you can see, HTML forms provide a quick, easy method for the document user to transmit data back to the document's originator. HTML documents and their forms undoubtedly will prove to be popular mechanisms for individual users, groups, and companies to provide information to the Internet community in an exciting, attractive manner. In the future, companies will consider HTML documents for advertising and HTML forms for product ordering to be common marketing tools.

Imagemaps

You already know (from Chapter 14) that you can make inline images act like graphical buttons by making them hypergraphic anchors. In addition, you can subdivide images into regions by using imagemaps. Imagemaps are a capability of the National Center for Supercomputing Applications (NCSA's)

◀ See "Link an Inline Image to Another Image or Web Resource," p. 342

server (and other servers) that allows a single GIF image to contain several hot regions. Different links will be followed depending on where in the image the reader clicks. This technique can be used to create graphical buttons or even interactive maps.

Understanding How Imagemaps Work

An imagemap actually is a single hypergraphic that links to a specific server script named imagemap. When a reader clicks the image, the mouse coordinates relative to the image are sent back to the imagemap script. The script then looks in the corresponding map file to decide which hyperlink to follow, based on the mouse coordinates.

Creating Imagemaps

For imagemaps to work, several configuration steps are necessary. First, your browser must support imagemaps. (All the popular graphical browsers support imagemaps, and no special browser configuration is required, so this step is easy.) Second, certain imagemap-support files must be present on your server. Third, you must create the graphic and define the coordinates of the various regions.

Configuring the Server for Imagemaps

▶ See "Overview of Web Servers," p. 409

The server requires two files for imagemap support. The first file is a script called imagemap, which must be compiled for your machine and placed in the cgi-bin directory. If you installed the server as a precompiled binary for UNIX, this script should already be compiled and in place; if not, you will have to compile it first.

> **Note**
>
> The imagemap script usually goes in the cgi-bin directory, but it could be placed in any CGI script directory as created by the ScriptAlias directive.

You also need write permission to the file imagemap.conf in the server's conf directory. This file maps image names, which you create, to their associated map files. If you do not have write access to this file, your administrator will have to add a line to this file for each new imagemap created. The format of the imagemap.conf file is simple, as the following example shows:

```
image_name : real_path
```

The path to the .map file is not a URL; it's the actual path on your system. A sample imagemap.conf is included in the following example:

```
homepage : /top/homepage.map
buttonbar : /top/buttons.map
usmap : /top/countries/us.map
```

Creating an Imagemap

You can use any image-editing program or GIF conversion tool to make the GIF file itself. The difficult part of making an imagemap is mapping image coordinates to corresponding actions.

The current version of the imagemap script handles only rectangular coordinate regions. These regions are defined in a map file. The map-file format looks like this:

```
rect url upper_left(x,y) lower_right(x,y)
```

Each line defines one rectangular region and its associated URL. Coordinates are in the order (x,y), with (0,0) being the upper-left corner. The first line of a map file is the default, which specifies what action to take if the coordinates fall outside any defined region. The following sample map file divides a 400-by-200 box into four equal "buttons":

```
default /top/homepage.html
rect /box/upper_left.html 0,0 199,99
rect /box/upper_right.html 200,0 399,99
rect /box/lower_left.html 0,100 199,199
rect /box/lower_right.html 200,100 399,199
```

> **Note**
>
> Virtual buttons in a map file also can point to full URLs on other servers. For example, a map file could contain rect ftp://ftp.internic.net/ 0,0 199,99.

To simplify the process of defining the image coordinates, you should use an image editor that displays the coordinates of selected areas. Lview is useful for this purpose. Follow these steps:

1. Open the file that you plan to use as the image map.

2. Select an area that you want to make clickable, and don't release the mouse button.

> **Note**
>
> If you are creating regions in a picture that has odd shapes, such as the faces in figure 15.8, make the regions a little bigger than shapes (the faces, in this case) to make it easier for the user to click what he or she wants. That way, if the mouse is just a little off where it should be, the user still jumps to the right place.

3. Notice the numbers in the status bar, as shown in figure 15.8. The first pair of numbers is what you should use for the upper-left coordinates.

Fig. 15.8

The status bar display makes defining image coordinates much easier.

Image area selected

Click this tool to select it

Use this pair of numbers for the upper-left coordinates

Use this pair of numbers for the lower-right coordinates

4. To get the lower-right coordinate, add the two pairs of numbers. (Add the first numbers in each pair, and then add the second number in each pair.)

5. Repeat steps 2 through 4 for each area that you want to map.

> **Caution**
>
> The regions should not overlap. It's OK if not all of the image is used, but the same part of the image should not be part of two different regions.

Linking to the Imagemap

After you create a map file for an image, you must include it in an HTML file by making it an anchor, as follows:

```
<A HREF="/cgi-bin/imagemap/box"><IMG SRC="box.gif"></A>
```

The hypertext reference must contain the URL to the imagemap script, followed by a slash (/) and the name of the map defined in imagemap.conf. The actual picture then is included with the <IMG SRC> tag.

In summary, creating clickable images involves three steps:

1. Create the map file.

2. Create an alias to the map file in imagemap.conf.

3. Make the image a hypergraphic anchor in an HTML document.

From Here...

This chapter covered how to create special characters, construct simple FORM documents, and create imagemaps using HTML elements. As this chapter pointed out, it is important to work with your WWW provider to correctly handle the processing of the information in a form when the user submits it. To learn more about HTML, refer to these chapters:

■ Chapter 14, "Creating Home Pages with HTML," gives a basic overview of the HTML language.

■ Chapter 16, "HTML Editors and Filters," gives you details on some of the software programs that make authoring easier.

■ Chapter 17, "Setting Up a Web Site," shows you how to get Web server software and use it to run a Web site.

Chapter 16

HTML Editors and Filters

by Bill Kirkner

It's easy to write an HTML document. After all, the main document is nothing but ASCII text, and much of that is often the plain-language text that you're trying to communicate on the page. The tricky part is getting the proper tags in the right place to make your text and images come out looking like you want them to. Browser programs are very literal in the way that they interpret HTML, so errors in your HTML syntax make your page look very unusual. You need to take extra care to ensure that your page comes out looking like you planned.

Because HTML documents are all ASCII code, originally Web documents were written with simple text editors, such as the Windows Notepad. As people began writing longer and more complex documents, many turned to their favorite word processing programs (which can save documents in plain ASCII text) and wrote macros and tools to help them.

As the Web has expanded, dedicated HTML editing programs (similar to word processing programs, but designed to produce results for the screen and not the printed page) began to appear. These programs allow Web page creators to more quickly format their text into proper HTML format by allowing authors to have codes placed automatically around text at the click of a toolbar button. The popularity of these editors has driven developers to produce dozens of new editors, filters, and utilities, all aimed at making a Web author's life easier (as well as ensuring that the Hypertext Markup Language is properly used.)

As you can see, there are many ways you can write your HTML documents; you can use your favorite line editor, a word processor, or a dedicated HTML tool. The choice of which system to use depends on personal preference and your confidence in your use of HTML.

Because many HTML-specific tools have checking routines or filters to verify that your documents are correctly laid out and formatted, they appeal to new writers of Web documents. They also tend to be friendlier and more graphically based than non-HTML editors.

On the other hand, if you're a veteran programmer or writer, you may want to stick with your favorite editor and use a filter or syntax checker afterwards. Luckily, there are ample tools available for whichever approach you take.

This chapter looks at four types of applications that are useful in developing HTML documents:

- Plain-text editors

- Tools and macros for word processing programs

- Stand-alone HTML authoring tools

- Tools, converters, and filters for importing other types of documents into HTML

> ### Note
>
> One of the best sites to look for new editors and filters is CERN. Through the WEB, connect to **http://info.cern.ch/WWW/Overview.html**. Also useful is the NCSA site, accessible through the Web at **http://www.ncsa.uiuc.edu/SDG/Software/Mosaic/Docs** where the document *faq-software.html* contains an up-to-date list of offerings. You can also find a good index of HTML editors from Yahoo at **http://akebono.stanford.edu/yahoo/Computers/World_Wide_Web/HTML_Editors/**.
>
> Many of the editors discussed in this chapter are included on WebCD.

WebCD

Plain-Text Editors

You can use any ASCII editor to write HTML pages. The tags necessary to indicate special effects that a Web browser should show are only combinations of ASCII characters (such as <BLINK> at the beginning of text that's supposed to blink and </BLINK> at the end). In contrast, most word processing programs embed special binary codes in the text to indicate changes in font styles or the location and format of graphics. Because hypertext authors know the HTML codes, they can write in various formatting effects as easily as they can enter sections of text.

This simplicity can be extremely useful. Many veteran HTML authors rely on a simple plain-text editor as they tweak specific points on any given page. Plain-text editors have the advantage of taking up less memory, which allows experienced authors to open up multiple Web browser programs simultaneously to see how their page looks in each format. (Although a code for something to be bold is read by Cello, Mosaic, and Netscape as bold, the way bolded text appears may vary slightly with each browser.)

A major annoyance with plain-text editors is that HTML codes are not treated as complete units. You have to edit each and every keystroke in the HTML code, whereas many editor programs treat the code as an entire entity. In a plain-text editor, getting rid of the code combination <B> and </B> around text requires deleting each keystroke. Some of the dedicated editors recognize the combination and eliminate the code <B> (and even delete its companion code on the other side of the text, </B>).

Nevertheless, you will probably need to use a simple editor some time. Become familiar with at least one, even if it's not what you usually use to compose your HTML files.

You can use Notepad to edit HTML documents, as long as the documents are not too long. Notepad has a file size limit; any particularly complex HTML document probably exceeds its capacity.

One advantage that Notepad has is that it creates files in ASCII format. This capability saves you the step of translating the file from a word processor format into ASCII, which is necessary if you use some of the add-on templates for word processors.

Notepad can also prove useful if you just need to make a quick tweak on a document that's already mostly edited. You may be able to open the HTML document in Notepad and make the minor adjustment without having to go through the hassle of opening your word processor and activating the proper template.

HTML Editing Tools for Use with Word Processors

Because many people are already familiar with the editing features of their favorite word processor, many HTML authors have turned to creating specialized macros and tools that take advantage of the properties of the word processing programs to make editing HTML even easier. Now, even developers are getting into the act, and produce programs designed explicitly as add-ons for commercial word processors.

Tip

If you use a plain-text editor for most of your HTML authoring, it's a good idea to check the syntax in your documents before putting them on the Web. To check the syntax, use a program with HTML filtering, such as Quarterdeck's HTML Authoring Tools for MS Windows.

For whatever reason, be it the strong use of styles or an easy, powerful macro language, Microsoft's Word seems to be the word processor of choice for people writing HTML editing tools; the vast majority of these types of tools are written expressly for Word for Windows. It is, perhaps, this obvious demand in the Word market that has compelled Microsoft to release its own package of utilities for using Word on the World Wide Web.

Microsoft Internet Assistant for Microsoft Word

Internet Assistant is a no-cost add-on offered by Microsoft for Word for Windows that turns Word into a Web browser and includes styles, toolbars, and tools for authoring HTML.

> **Note**
>
> The following information is based on the beta test version of this software. It is expected that by the time this book reaches publication, Microsoft will have formally released the official version of this product. References to some menu items or toolbars may be different as a result.

> **Note**
>
> You can find a copy of Internet Assistant under the "What's New" heading of Microsoft's home page on the World Wide Web. The URL is **http://www.microsoft.com/**. Microsoft will also ship a copy on floppy disk to registered owners of Word 6 for a shipping and handling charge of $5. Call (800) 426-9400.

Besides turning Word into a functional Web browser, Microsoft's Internet Assistant for Word provides two ways to create documents for use on the Internet. First, this add-on offers a set of tools for editing HTML documents. These tools are an extensive set of styles that you can apply to text. They enable you to drag and drop links to other documents.

▶ See "Using the Internet Assistant," p. 300

Second, Microsoft has created a viewer for Word documents that allows you to place Word-formatted documents directly on the Web. When the user opens a link to one of these documents, he can activate the Word viewer and look at the document. Users who have Microsoft Word theoretically can treat the document as a Word document, including copying text and graphics to use in other documents.

Using Internet Assistant to Edit HTML

After you install Internet Assistant (see "Installing Internet Assistant on Your System," in chapter 13 for details), you will find that you have access to two new templates, called HTML.DOT and WEBVIEW.DOT. Opening a new file using the WEBVIEW template causes Word to act like a Web Browser, whereas activating HTML.DOT provides a set of styles and tools for editing HTML.

To open a new document using the HTML template:

1. Open the **F**ile menu and choose **N**ew. This opens a dialog box with a list of templates.

2. Select HTML and click the OK button. When the new document opens, you will see a new toolbar, with several regular Word functions removed.

In the example presented in figure 16.1, both the Standard and Formatting toolbars are open. Keep in mind that these toolbars, like all of the toolbars in Word, can be customized by adding buttons and rearranging their order—so your tools may look different.

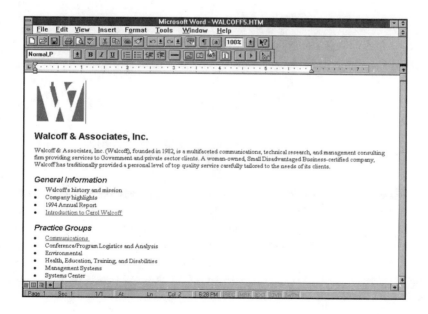

Fig. 16.1
Internet Assistant lets you edit HTML using standard Word tools.

If you want to edit an already existing HTML document, Word will automatically open the HTML template when you select a document with an HTM extension. (In the beta version used for this section, Word didn't present an option to select HTML documents in its Open Document dialog box.)

As you type in the text of your Web page, you can mark it for specific text effects such as bold or italic using the standard Word tools. Word automatically translates those effects into HTML tags. You also can format text in HTML modes such as Strong or Preformatted by using the styles available under the HTML template. You can select a style using the Styles tool in the Formatting toolbar, or you can open the Format menu and choose either **S**tyle or Style **G**allery.

Entering Special Characters Using Internet Assistant. Internet Assistant also provides a way to place special codes such as diacritical marks, copyright and trademark symbols, or other special punctuation. To access these special characters, open the **I**nsert menu and choose **S**ymbol. This opens a dialog box with listings of special characters, as shown in figure 16.2. Double-click on the name of any specific character to place it in the text where the I-beam cursor is located.

Fig. 16.2
Special characters
and symbols can
be inserted
through this
dialog box.

Handling HTML Codes That Are Not Supported by Internet Assistant.
There are also several HTML tags and effects that Internet Assistant does not accommodate through styles or tools. It is possible to enter these additional tags (or any extra HTML code) by opening the **I**nsert Menu and choosing **H**TML Markup. This opens a dialog box with a large window for entering direct HTML code, as shown in figure 16.3. The entered text is handled and displayed as HTML code without ever being translated into Word format.

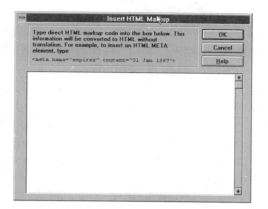

Fig. 16.3
HTML tags that aren't supported by the tools in Internet Assistant are entered through this dialog box.

Creating Forms Using Internet Assistant. Internet Assistant has some fairly extensive features for creating interactive forms. You can begin a form by opening the **I**nsert menu and choosing the For**m** Field option. This causes Internet Assistant to enter the HTML tags that surround a form, and a Forms Toolbar and dialog box to help you create the form field pop-up, as shown in figure 16.4.

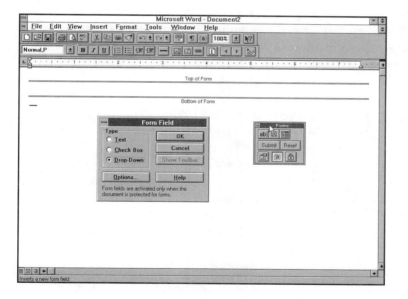

Fig. 16.4
Internet Assistant has several tools for editing forms.

If you've created forms in Microsoft Access, you may recognize the look of some of these form tools. The Forms toolbox gives you point-and-click access to creating click-boxes, pull-down menus, and text boxes, as well as providing a standard Reset button. When you place a field in the form area, additional dialog boxes open to help you create the necessary choices for a pull-down menu or other controls to help make the form work. You even can add help text that may appear in the browsers status bar. Form fields also can be linked to macros to help automate the exchange of data.

Linking a Web Page to a Database. If you open the Insert menu, you will see an option called Database, which, if used by itself, will let you enter a database table (or a table of query results) into the text of an HTML document. While this could be useful if you needed to put tabular data online in its tabular format, this is probably not a good way to create an effective and exciting Web document. The Insert, Database option has much more potential to be used as an element in macros that could then be linked to your interactive forms.

By combining the forms that you create with macros using the Insert Database option, you can create HTML documents that would provide dynamic responses to searches whose terms are specified by the user viewing your Web page. This allows you to make the information contained in your databases available to a much wider audience, and increases the utility of your documents.

Saving Documents in HTML Format. Internet Assistant saves documents in HTML format by default. The resulting document is then ready to be used on your Web server. This is a contrast to many of the third-party templates discussed in this chapter, which require you to translate the document from Word DOC format into ASCII/HTML text.

Using Word Documents on the World Wide Web

Along with the HTML editing tools, Microsoft has released a viewer that allows users who do not own Word to view Word documents from the World Wide Web. This means that authors can use the various formatting tools and special design capabilities of Word to design documents that exceed the capability of HTML. Users who own Word are able to treat the online document as any other Word document, and consequently can take advantage of features such as Word's ability to interact with other Microsoft products, such as Access or Excel.

Unfortunately, people who don't have Word probably won't be able to take advantage of all of these capabilities. This means that if you design a Web page in Word—even though everyone may be able to get a viewer to look at the document—some percentage of the audience will be unable to fully interact with the document unless they invest in additional Microsoft products.

There are potentially two negative side effects to this: first, if the majority (or even a large percentage of Web pages) were designed in Word format, more people would eventually be compelled to use one company's products to interact with the Web. This could eventually have the effect of giving a large percentage of control of the future of the Web to a single company. The opposite could also be true; people who don't want to deal with the Microsoft family of software products could stay away from your site in droves, knowing that they wouldn't have full accessibility.

Nevertheless, this ability presents new options for the Web page designer, who can now incorporate functional links to databases and spreadsheets into their documents. The ability to drag and drop components will undoubtedly help to spur the creativity of at least some Web authors, which may force the rest of the Internet community to come up with other ways of accomplishing the same kinds of tasks through a revised and expanded HTML.

Note

You can find a link to a copy of the Word Viewer on the same Web page as Internet Assistant under the What's New heading of Microsoft's home page. The URL is **http://www.microsoft.com/**.

Quarterdeck's WebAuthor

Quarterdeck recently released a commercial package of HTML authoring tools for use with Microsoft Word 6 for Windows called WebAuthor.

Note

The information in this section was based on our evaluation of a beta version of Quarterdeck's WebAuthor for Word for Windows; the final version may look slightly different as Quarterdeck changes or adds features.

Setting up Quarterdeck's WebAuthor for Windows is relatively simple; it comes with a fairly standard install program. This installation creates a program group that contains a Windows-standard help file and a Write document with release information. The main body of the tools are not apparent, however, until you open Microsoft Word.

To activate WebAuthor, open the **T**ools menu. An option called **H**TML Authoring should appear at or near the bottom of this menu (see fig. 16.5). Choosing this option opens the HTML Authoring Tools dialog box.

Fig. 16.5

You can access Quarterdeck's WebAuthor through this menu selection.

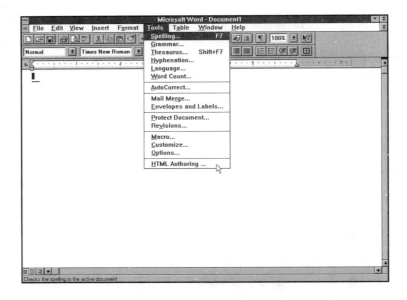

If you ran a complete installation of Word (or Microsoft Office), you've probably already installed the proper filter. If you haven't, the first time that you try to open WebAuthor, a dialog box informs you that the filter isn't installed (see fig. 16.6).

Fig. 16.6

If you haven't configured a GIF filter for Word, this dialog box will appear.

Quarterdeck's WebAuthor requires you to have the CompuServe GIF filter installed to be able to take advantage of the WYSIWYG interface for your HTML documents. But you don't need to belong to CompuServe to get it; it actually comes with Word, and is available as one of the options that you can install.

It's easy to install the filter; follow these steps:

1. Run your Word Setup program (or your Office Setup program, if your copy of Word is part of the Microsoft Office suite).

2. When you're in the setup program, choose Add/Remove.

3. Next, select Converters, Filters, and Data Access and click Change Option.

4. This brings up a list of different types of filters for text and video. The CompuServe GIF option is the only one you need to worry about; make sure that it's selected, and then click OK. Insert the required disks, as prompted.

After you activate WebAuthor, you should see a box that provides several options (see fig. 16.7). You can Create a New HTML Document (Blank), in which case Word opens a new document. You can Import and Convert an Existing HTML Text File, in which case the tools take an HTML file and convert it to Word format so that you can edit it. Or you can Open a Word Document (HTML Original) for Editing and change the document to an HTML file. One of the things that you can't do is take a document that's already open and turn it into HTML. You'll need to save and close the document and re-open it in WebAuthor if you want to modify it as an HTML document.

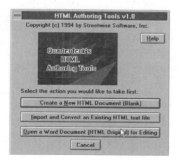

Fig. 16.7
You're given several options after you choose HTML Authoring from the Tool menu in Word.

Opening and Editing a New File

If you open a new file, when you get the blank screen, notice that there are some notable differences to the toolbars. According to Quarterdeck, the different toolbars remove some of the Word functions that are almost exclusively designed for print features. Likewise, some additional tools (more relevant to processing HTML) appear. WebAuthor provides tooltips to help you identify the new tools. *Tooltips* are the little labels that appear when you let your pointer rest on a tool for more than a second. Table 16.1 is a quick synopsis of the new tools presented by WebAuthor.

Table 16.1   WebAuthor Tools

Tool	Name	Description
	New	Opens a new Word document based on your default template, similar to its Word counterpart.
	New HTML	Opens a new HTML document.
	Open	Opens a directory containing both Word and HTML documents.
	Open from HTML	Opens a document in hypertext format as a Word document.
	Save	Saves a file; you can choose from a number of formats. HTML is *not* an available format, but you can save the file as a DOS file.
	Save to HTML	Saves a Word document as an HTML document. As you work, your document is in Word format; you need to save it to HTML format before you can place it on the Web.
	Document View Toggle	Changes the view of the document, gives you several options as to the type of editing screen on which you can work.
	Style	Specifies the appearance of text on your page.
	Format Character	Specifies one of the standard HTML character formatting types (such as Strong, Citation, or Emphasis).
	Anchor Manager	Specifies anchors on your page.
	Image Manager	Specifies graphics in your page design.

Tool	Name	Description
▦	Form Manager	Inserts the basic codes necessary for having a form in your document.
▦	List	Creates lists on your page; specifies the type of list you want to create.
®	Insert Symbol	Enters special codes, such as the copyright or trademark symbol, on your page.

For the beginning user, this collection of tools speeds up the editing of many types of HTML documents.

Opening an Existing HTML File

If you choose to open an existing HTML file, Authoring Tools asks if you want the program to filter the existing document (see fig. 16.8). This helpful step checks the syntax of your existing file for errors and displays the errors, along with some good fixes. Using this option provides you with the HTML Editing toolbar.

Fig. 16.8
When you open an HTML document created by another editor, WebAuthor asks if you want to check the existing tags.

Note

The filtering feature is particularly useful if you've been editing your HTML documents in some other fashion, such as with a plain-text editor. The filter catches mistakes in syntax that you might not otherwise notice (including some cases where types of markers are incompatible with each other). This feature is particularly nice because some of these errors may be transparent to the author and the user (they don't necessarily show up on the page), but may confuse the browser programs and eventually lead to errors.

It may take a minute or two for Authoring Tools to revise your document so that it's in the proper format, but the wait may be worth it. What you end up seeing isn't exactly WYSIWYG, but it's closer than you'd get using a plain-text editor (see fig. 16.9).

Fig. 16.9
The almost-WYSIWYG view of a page in WebAuthor.

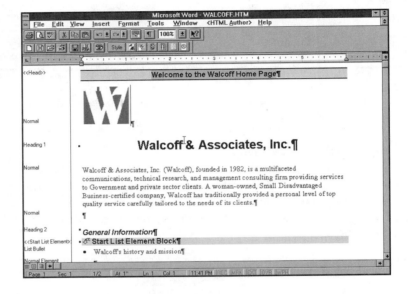

WebAuthor also enters some markers that help show what the effects of certain codes will be. Hypertext links show up in green; click them to open up a dialog box that shows their destination (see fig. 16.10).

Fig. 16.10
Clicking high-lighted links displays the URL to which the text is linked.

Unfortunately, WebAuthor doesn't let you directly edit the text labels for anchors; that is, if you try to click-position your I-beam bar on the label, it selects the whole label. If you need to edit the label for a link, click the Anchor Manager tool. The Anchor Definition dialog box appears (see fig. 16.11). Clicking the Next button provides you with an opportunity to change the visible text. It also seems to be impossible to give a label a special effect (such as italic or bold) and still have WebAuthor treat it as an anchor.

Fig. 16.11
Specify the URL to be connected to an anchor in the Anchor Definition dialog box. Clicking the Next button lets you edit the anchor text.

Opening a Word Document (HTML Original) for Editing

If you've been editing an HTML document in Word, but haven't yet saved it in HTML format, this option opens the document and brings up the appropriate HTML editing toolbar. By contrast, if you've written a Word document that you want to convert to HTML format, this option doesn't make that automatic conversion (nor does it bring up the HTML toolbars).

Your best bet for doing this sort of conversion is to follow this process:

1. Save the Word document in MS-DOS Text format. To do this, open the File menu and choose Save As.

2. Select MS-DOS Text as your file type, and use HTM as your file extension when you name the file. This allows you to open up the file as an HTML file when you start Authoring Tools.

When you create a document with Authoring Tools, it saves the file as a Word document until you explicitly save it in HTML format. The Word format includes embedded binary codes, which are unreadable to Web browsers. Therefore, when using Authoring Tools, you have to save the file as an HTML document, otherwise it's worthless on the Web.

Files saved in the appropriate format have the HTM extension. If Word saves the document with a DOC extension, it's still in Word format. Go back into the document and resave it in the appropriate format before trying to use it on the Web.

> **Note**
>
> Suggested retail price for Quarterdeck's WebAuthor is $149.95. You can get more information about WebAuthor by calling (310) 392-9851. You can also check Quarterdeck's Internet Web site at **http://www.qdeck.com/**; or you can send an e-mail request to **info@qdeck.com**. You can also write to Quarterdeck at Quarterdeck Office Systems, Inc., Pico Boulevard, Santa Monica, CA, 90405.

The ANT Template for Word

The ANT template is a low-cost shareware program designed to help edit HTML documents that also works with Word for Windows for the Macintosh. With ANT's toolbar you can edit a document and insert the appropriate HTML codes. ANT also reads your document's formatting and converts styles (where possible) to equivalent HTML tags. Another big plus of the ANT_HTML template is that it works with all of the international language versions of Word, giving an added degree of flexibility to authors who create multilanguage versions of their pages.

Unfortunately, ANT_HTML can't incorporate the tags created in another program the way that Quarterdeck's Authoring Tools can. It's also somewhat fussy during installation, at least under Windows.

Installing ANT

To install ANT, copy all of the ANT files into a subdirectory, then open a document called ANT_INST.DOC in Word. This opens a document with an install button (see fig. 16.12).

Fig. 16.12
Opening the file ANT_INST.DOC reveals this document. Double-click the button to install the ANT template.

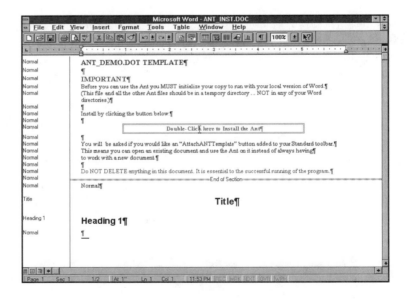

When you click the install button, ANT installs itself in Word. A dialog box asks you if you want to add ANT to your standard Word toolbar. If you choose Yes, a tool with an A appears on your regular toolbar. If you have an open document, clicking the A tool reveals the ANT toolbar (see fig. 16.13) with the buttons as shown in table 16.2.

Table 16.2	The ANT Toolbar	
Tool	**Name**	**Description**
	Convert and Save	Changes the document from Word into HTML.
	The Ant	Gives information about the ANT_HTML template.
	Check styles for HTML codes	Reads Word styles and converts to HTML equivalents.
	Hidden Text	Hides or reveals HTML tags.
	Address	Places HTML Address tags.
	Normal	Marks text as plain text.
	Title	Places HTML Title tags.
	Pre	Places HTML tags to maintain text exactly as created by the author.
	Styles	Activates dialog box of styles to be applied to text.
through	Heads 1-6	Places HTML tags for first six levels of headings.
	Horizontal Rule	Places a tag for a horizontal line to appear on the page.
	P	Marks the end of a paragraph.
	BR	Makes a break.
	GIF	Activates a dialog box for inserting a GIF image in the document.
	Placeholder	Enters a placehoder image where a graphic image will later be placed.
	URL	Links selected text to a specific URL.
	Local Anchor Ref	Creates a link to another section of the Web document.

(continues)

IV

Creating Web Pages & Sites

Table 16.2 Continued		
Tool	**Name**	**Description**
	Local Anchor Destination	Marks an area that can be linked to within the Web document
	Description List Entry	Marks selected text as a description list.
	Numbered List	Marks selected text as a numbered list.
	Unnumbered list	Places tags to mark text as an unnumbered list.
	Form Entry	Creates several types of tags for HTML forms.
	ANT to HTML demo	Transforms demonstration Word document into WYSIWYG format.

Fig. 16.13
Clicking the tool marked A reveals the ANT toolbar beneath your standard Word toolbar.

Using ANT to Place HTML Tags

When you open a new document, Word prompts you to select a template for the document's format. At this point, you should select the ANT_HTML template if you want to use ANT.

Clicking the A tool reveals the ANT toolbar. The ANT toolbar features fairly extensive tooltips that tell you what each tool does. Most of the tools are designed to insert tags around a particular piece of text. To get ANT to place the appropriate tags, follow these steps:

1. Highlight the text you want to tag.

2. Click the appropriate tool.

3. The appropriate tags are entered on either side of the text.

Unfortunately, ANT doesn't recognize the tags as entire entities. To remove a tag, you must delete each character in the tag one at a time. Furthermore, you must be careful to remove the companion tag (if one exists).

Using the ANT_HTML Template in Style Gallery

ANT also installs a style template that contains many of the standard HTML formats. Using these styles, you can quickly link sections of text to the appropriate format. When you apply a specific style, the text, as it appears on-screen, appears with the attributes of that particular HTML style, but the HTML codes don't appear.

If you save a document created using the ANT_HTML styles in ASCII (MS-DOS) format, the resulting document contains the proper HTML codes.

Changing a Word Document into an HTML Document with ANT

If you've created a Word document that you'd like to translate into HTML format, ANT can help make the conversion simpler.

The Check Styles for HTML Codes tool causes ANT to check the open document's styles to see if there are formatting codes that have an HTML equivalent. ANT tags words that are bold, italicized, or underlined with the appropriate HTML codes.

Because the original document was formatted for the printed page, you will probably still have to go back and reformat some of the document.

Note

If you've created a document using the ANT_HTML template styles, clicking the Check Styles for HTML Codes tool reveals all of the HTML codes (see fig. 16.14 and 16.15). To hide these codes again, click the Hidden Text tool.

Fig. 16.14
A Web page
created using ANT
styles.

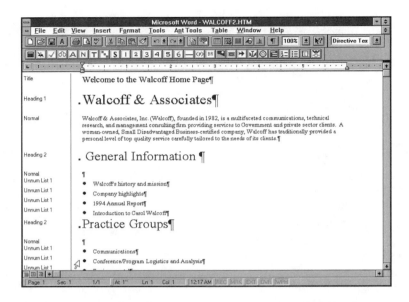

Fig. 16.15
The same page
with HTML tags
revealed.

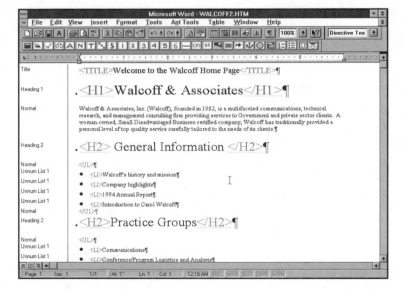

Saving Your Word Document in HTML Format

The documents that you create using the ANT templates are in Word format
as you create them (regardless of whether you're using the styles or the
toolbars to enter the appropriate tags). To use these documents on the Web,
you need to save them in ASCII format. To do this, you can either click the
Convert and Save tool, or you can use the standard Word commands.

To save the file as you would in Word, open the File menu and choose Save As. When the Save As dialog box opens, select ASCII (or MS-DOS) as your File Type, and then enter a file name and click OK.

Clicking the Convert and Save tool brings up a dialog box with two options (see fig. 16.16). The first option allows you to run a basic filter over the document that adds appropriate formatting tags where necessary. The second option allows you to skip the filtering process, and save the file directly as an ASCII file.

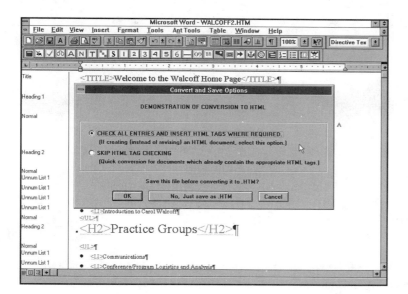

Fig. 16.16
When ANT converts your document to HTML, it can check your tags and formatting.

Note

You can obtain ANT_HTML by anonymous FTP from **ftp.inet.net** in the directory `EINet/pc`. The latest version is usually available as **ANT_DEMO.ZIP**.

CU_HTML

CU_HTML, named after the Chinese University of Hong Kong where it was created by Kenneth Wong and Anton Lam, is a template-based add-on for Word 2 and Word 6.

CU_HTML comes with installation instructions in an HTML format. Use your browser to open the file CU_HTML.HTM (see fig. 16.17). If your browser isn't working, just open the Word document CU_HTML.DOC.

Fig. 16.17
CU_HTML comes with installation instructions in HTML format that can be read using a Web browser.

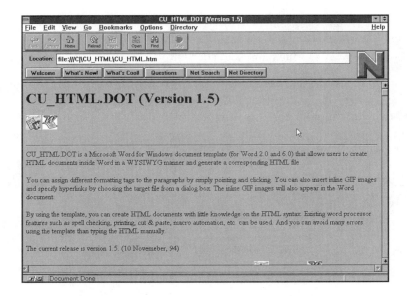

After you install CU_HTML's files, you can select the CU_HTML template when you open a new document in Word.

If you choose this template, some styles equivalent to HTML tags are loaded. There's also an extra menu item, called **H**TML (see fig. 16.18). This menu item provides you with some options for tagging text, mostly for linking text in the document to other files (such as graphics or other hypertext links). For tags to format text, open the Format menu and select Styles (or Style Gallery). CU_HTML provides tags for most of the basic HTML text formatting functions.

CU_HTML requires that you save a copy of the file before it lets you put tags on anything. So after you open a new document, save it. This allows you to insert GIF files.

After you've entered text, you can use the options under the HTML menu to format links to other files. You can link to a graphics file with the Insert Gif option, or another locally stored HTML file with Insert Link. You can create a link to another section of your Web document with Insert Local link, or link to another document on the Web with Insert URL.

Like most of the templates for Word, CU_HTML creates files in Word format. Save the completed document in HTML format before you try to use it on the Web. To do this using CU_HTML, open the **H**TML menu and choose **W**rite HTML.

Fig. 16.18
CU_HTML creates a new menu item, called HTML, that gives the user access to several useful HTML editing tools.

> **Note**
>
> You can obtain CU_HTML from the Chinese University of Hong Kong by anonymous FTP from **ftp.cuhk.hk**. It's stored in the directory /pub/www/windows/util. The file name is usually CU_HTML.ZIP.

GT_HTML Template for Word

GT_HTML is a simple template designed to provide some access to HTML tags to Word for Windows users.

Installation of the template is simple; just copy the template into your templates subdirectory for Word. If you activate the template when you open a new document in Word, you have the ability to add two new toolbars. These toolbars give you the ability to apply HTML tags to highlighted text (see fig. 16.19).

This template doesn't provide a WYSIWYG view of the HTML document. However, the Browser tool will activate a browser to view the document as it's being created.

Another button allows you to hide all of the HTML codes so that you can see the plain text as it should appear on the completed page. The HTML Save tool allows you to automatically save the Word document in HTML format, eliminating the need to use the Save As feature in Word.

What this template doesn't do is provide a lot of preset styles for formatting text. In fact, the only styles supported are three levels of Headers. Nevertheless, this template will meet your needs if you need to create some basic, information-only pages for your Web site.

Fig. 16.19
When you install GT_HTML, you have the option of turning on two toolbars to help you edit HTML.

Stand-Alone Editors for HTML

Beyond the templates for word processors, some stand-alone editors are designed completely for the purpose of editing HTML documents. This section covers some of the most common stand-alone editors for HTML.

HTML Assistant

HTML Assistant is a pretty thorough HTML editor for Microsoft Windows. Like most of the stand-alone editors, it inserts HTML tags around highlighted text and links to images and other URLs through a dialog box in which you insert the appropriate code into the HTML document.

Unlike several of the other editors, it incorporates a full set of tools aimed at supporting the creation of forms, and provides a menu option that translates MOSAIC.INI files and Cello bookmark files into HTML files that can be used as personal home pages.

Furthermore, HTML Assistant allows you to build files of URLs, so that you can pull up URLs that you use repeatedly at the click of a button.

Tags at the Click of a Button

HTML Assistant has a toolbar that sports most of the common HTML tags. The organization of the toolbar separates tags into particular types; tags which adjust the appearance of text are grouped together, as are the tags that link the document to other files (see fig. 16.20).

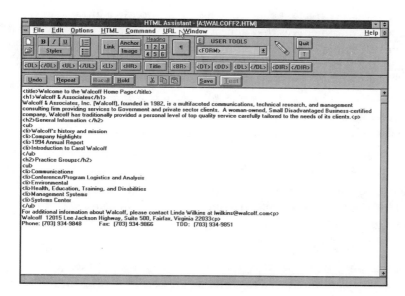

Fig. 16.20
HTML Assistant has a toolbar that puts access to tags at the author's fingertips.

The toolbar also has drop-down lists in which the user can create tags for other functions that aren't otherwise supported on the toolbar. This is where HTML Assistant stores most of the forms-related tags.

If the toolbar is taking up too much of your desktop, it can be hidden by opening the **O**ptions menu and then toggling the option Hide Lower toolbar. (The toolbar can be restored in the same fashion.)

HTML Assistant has a button for repeating a tag, a function that can be particularly useful when you prepare HTML documents with lists, or for inserting standard icons next to links to other files (such as a standard audio icon next to the links for each of a series of WAV or AU files).

Some Additional Helpful HTML Assistant Features

One of the useful features of HTML Assistant is the ability to create files of URLs that you can call up while creating an HTML text document. This is particularly helpful if you're creating a Web site that requires references to certain key index pages.

Like some other editors, HTML Assistant has the ability to save Mosaic.INI files and Cello bookmark lists as HTML files. The MOSAIC.INI translator even retains the menu structure of your original Hotlists from Mosaic. (Mosaic refers to its bookmark files, or its lists of frequently used sites as *hotlists,* which are stored as part of the MOSAIC.INI file.)

HTML Assistant can also be linked to a Web browser to allow you to view your HTML documents as they appear when translated by the browser. After you link the browser to HTML Assistant, you can activate the browser by clicking the Test button on the toolbar.

HTML Assistant Pro and Some Liabilities in the Shareware Version

You can find a shareware version of HTML Assistant on the net that contains the features most HTML editors need to create some fairly sophisticated Web pages.

Unfortunately, the shareware version has a file size limit of 32K. You can create larger files by editing the file in pieces in HTML Assistant, and then stitching the pieces together in a word processor or an editor with an ability to handle larger files.

HTML Assistant Pro is the commercial version of the software. It doesn't have a file size limit and has more complete support for the Expanded Character set, as well as a feature called the Automatic Page Creator, which works like a Microsoft-style wizard to create an HTML page.

> **Note**
>
> As of January 1, 1995, the price for HTML Assistant Pro was $99.95, plus postage and handling ($10 in North America, $15 elsewhere). To order a copy of HTML Assistant Pro, contact Brooklyn North Software Works at 25 Doyle Street, Bedford, Nova Scotia, Canada, B41 1K4, or fax (902) 835-2600.
>
> You can get a copy of the freeware version of HTML Assistant from many of the Windows Utilities and WWW Utilities archives. Set your Archie client to look for a file called htmlasst.zip. One site that carries HTML Assistant is the Chinese University of Hong Kong (anonymous FTP at **ftp.cuhk.hk**). HTML Assistant is stored with several other HTML editors in the directory /pub/www/windows/util.

HTMLed

HTMLed is a great little shareware HTML editor for Microsoft Windows. Running the HTMLed program opens up a simple editing screen with a menu bar and toolbar (see fig. 16.21). Even though it looks pretty basic, this program has a lot of useful features.

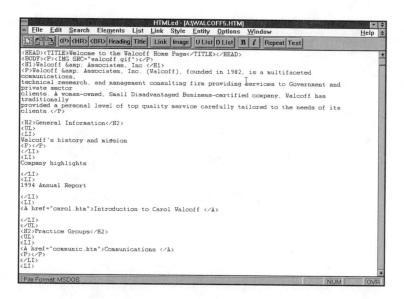

Fig. 16.21
HTMLed contains a wealth of useful features, particularly if you're working in several languages.

HTMLed Toolbars

Toolbars are probably one of the best features of this program. Instead of depending on icons, developer Peter Crawshaw has chosen to either put the tag itself or the plain-English name for the tag (or type of tag) on the buttons. This requires novices to know a little more about HTML code, but it's probably for the best.

Clicking the Link or Image tool brings up a dialog box into which you enter the appropriate file name or URL. Once a URL is entered in the dialog box, it is saved in a list that can be used to pull up the same URL if you need to create a link to it in other locations throughout the document.

If you're tagging a set of text items that need the same tag (such as items in a list), you might find useful the ability to repeat a tag. HTMLed provides both a toolbar button and a menu item (Elements, Repeat Last Markup) for repeating tags.

Furthermore, HTMLed provides a few extra toolbars that are particularly useful for heavy-duty HTML authors. The first is a Headings toolbar, which allows you to click a tool and automatically format text with the appropriate Header tag. A second toolbar, called the Common Tags toolbar, provides a tool for inserting 15 common tags. The Extended Character toolbar provides access to 62 characters beyond the standard ASCII set, such as accented vowels, which are particularly useful when creating the other-than-English language versions of your Web pages. Figure 16.22 shows these toolbars.

Fig. 16.22
HTMLed features three "floating" toolbars that you can activate.

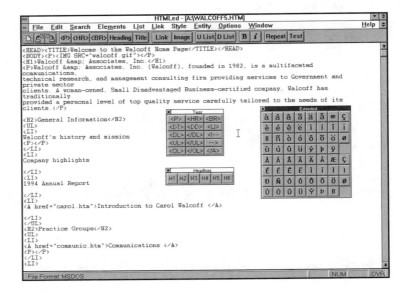

You can also create your own custom button by entering a brief description of the tag and the keystrokes that comprise the tag that it should enter.

Some Interesting HTMLed Menu Items

The HTML menu bar breaks down standard tags into fairly easy-to-understand groupings. You can find the standard divisions of an HTML document under the Elements menu. One option, Standard Document Outline, drops in the opening and closing codes, as well as the tags for the head and body sections of your HTML document.

The List menu provides access to tagging styles for each of the major types of lists. The Style menu allows you to tag text with most of the HTML text styles.

There are some punctuation marks, letter formats, and other common text items for which HTML must use special codes. These include greater than and less than (><), and the ampersand (&), which HTML uses as part of tags or other extended codes. The Entity menu provides access to these text extended text elements and codes by providing the proper code in HTML format.

There's also a set of menu items for providing diacritical marks. This is a particularly slick set of tag controls because it reads the letter that you're trying to place the diacritical mark on and then assigns the appropriate HTML code. Furthermore, it won't let you place an accent or other diacritical mark on a letter that's not supposed to have one.

Configuring HTMLed

Under the **O**ptions menu, there's a Setup option. The Setup dialog box allows you to specify whether you want HTMLed to display Extended characters as they will appear or as they are coded in HTML. You can also choose to have several of the special toolbars appear every time you start the program.

HTMLed also provides an option for linking the editor to Mosaic so that you can test your HTML files with the browser before putting them on the Web. In the Setup dialog box, there's an option for specifying the path of your Web browser. This links your browser to the Test button on the Standard toolbar and to the **T**est HTML Document option under the **F**ile menu.

Other Features

HTMLed also has a few other fairly useful features. One feature under the Options menu (Convert MOSAIC.INI to HTML file) does just that—it enables you to turn your MOSAIC.INI file into an HTML file (thus turning all of your favorite links into a personal home page). HTMLed also allows you to save files in a variety of formats: as a DOS, UNIX, or plain text file (without the HTML tags included).

All in all, this is a pretty sharp editor that should prove particularly useful for new HTML authors and users with some experience. HTMLed doesn't cover some of the tags for forms and other advanced HTML features that some of the other editors do, but it's useful for the vast majority of your HTML editing needs.

> **Note**
>
> You can get a copy of HTMLed via anonymous FTP from **ftp.cuhk.hk**. In the directory /pub/www/windows/util, you'll find HTMLed saved as htmed10.zip (later versions may increase the number), along with several other programs and templates for editing HTML.

HoTMetaL

HoTMetaL is an HTML editor created by NCSA and distributed by SoftQuad for Microsoft Windows (and for X-Windows running under UNIX). The first thing you need to know about HoTMetaL is that it's very big. The files take up about 5M of disk space, and require about 3M of memory to run.

The second thing that you need to know is that HoTMetaL is probably the strictest editor with respect to requiring absolute adherence to HTML syntax rules. In some respects, it's like riding a bike with training wheels—you're guaranteed not to make any mistakes, but you're not likely to be able to use it to do the cool stuff that more experienced authors are doing.

As an example, HoTMetaL doesn't recognize any of the so-called HTML2 tags (such as Center and Blink) that are supported by Netscape. Documents containing these codes can't be opened by HoTMetaL. Likewise, older HTML documents or HTML documents with *nested* tags (an italic tag inside of an anchor, for example) are often rejected. Many files created in editors other than HoTMetaL can't be imported to this editor.

But HoTMetaL does provide an exceptionally good interface for people who are first learning how to write HTML documents. There's a certain amount of enforced precision that comes from working in HoTMetaL that encourages good authoring practices down the road. All of HoTMetaL's templates are in perfect HTML form, complete with all HEAD and BODY tags intact and properly placed (see fig. 16.23).

Tip

It is possible to turn Rules Checking off if you're trying to create a document that uses newer standards than those contained in your Rules file. Check under the **M**arkup menu for the option Turn Rules Checking Off, or try Ctrl+K.

Fig. 16.23
HoTMetaL provides an easy-to-understand interface with HTML tags indicated as labels.

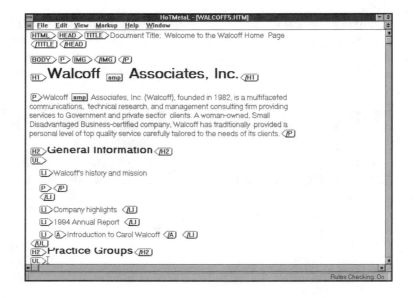

HoTMetaL provides quite a few templates of standard formats for WWW pages. All the new author needs to do is delete the placeholder text and replace it with his own, and a proper WWW page is instantly created.

Moreover, the HTML tags are handled entirely as complete entities by HoTMetaL. They're displayed on-screen as large markers, and it's impossible to delete one half of a tag pair without deleting the other half.

HoTMetaL's import filter is incredibly demanding. You can be sure that if your HTML document passes through this filter that it's without HTML syntax errors. Likewise, the filter doesn't allow you to save a document that has HTML syntax errors in it. If strict adherence to HTML syntax is your goal, HoTMetaL will help you achieve it.

> **Note**
>
> A reduced-function version of HoTMetaL is available as freeware at most utility sites. Look for it at NCSA or CERN. Try the WWW page **http://info.cern.ch/ hypertext/WWW/Tools**, and look for the file HoTMetaL.html.

Converting Documents to HTML

HTML filters are a useful tools that let you convert a document produced with any kind of editor (including ASCII text editors) to HTML. Filters are useful when you work in an editor that has its own proprietary format, such as Word, WordPerfect, and Rich Text Format (RTF).

HTML filters are attractive if you want a utility to convert your document with tags to HTML as you continue to work in your favorite editor. Filters tend to be fast and easy to work with, because they take a file name as input and generate an HTML output file.

Converting Word

Word for Windows and Word for DOS documents can be converted to HTML using the CU_HTML and ANT_HTML extensions mentioned earlier. A few stand-alone conversion utilities have also began to appear. Because Word can read other word processor formats (including WordPerfect and RTF), you can use these filters when error checking is required or when a dedicated filter for your word processor is not available.

Converting WordPerfect

The utility WPTOHTML converts WordPerfect documents to HTML. WPTOHTML is a set of macros for WordPerfect versions 5.1, 5.2, and 6.0. You can also use the WordPerfect filter with other word processor formats that WordPerfect can import.

> **Note**
>
> WPTOHTML is available through anonymous FTP from **oak.oakland.edu** in the directory SimTel/msdos/wordperf as the file wptXXd10.zip, where XX is the version number of WordPerfect.

From Here...

This chapter covered various types of programs for developing HTML documents. It discussed plain-text editors, add-ons for word processing programs, and stand-alone authoring tools. Additionally, there was coverage of filters, tools, and converters for importing other document types into HTML.

For more information related to the topics in this chapter, see the following:

- Chapter 14, "Creating Home Pages with HTML," provides a basic overview of the HTML language.

- Chapter 15, "Advanced HTML," covers creating and using forms.

- Chapter 17, "Setting Up a Web Site," explains how to get, set up, and use a software program that transforms your computer into a Web site.

Chapter 17

Setting Up a Web Site

by David Chandler

This chapter takes you through the process of getting a Web server up and running for the first time under Microsoft Windows. The server comes with default configuration files that gets your server up and running quickly.

The information presented in this chapter shows you how to install and run the server for the first time. It does not cover many details of server configuration. If your Web site is more than just a hobby and you need to make changes to the defaults, you should take a look at Que's book *Running A Perfect Web Site,* which covers many of the details of configuring and managing a server.

Specifically, you learn the following in this chapter:

- How to install the server software

- How to start and stop the server

- How to use the server's command line options

- How to tune your system and troubleshoot common problems

- Where key files and directories are located

- Where to put your home page

Overview of Web Servers

NCSA (National Center for Supercomputing Applications) developed a UNIX server originally. This is one of the most popular Web servers in use on the Internet. Since the original NCSA server for UNIX, various authors have ported the server to other platforms or based their work on NCSA's server.

◀ See "Key WWW Developments: A Recipe for Success," p. 29

These servers are listed in table 17.1. This chapter focuses on Windows httpd. Most of the principles and terminology covered here are the same for NCSA-based servers running on any platform.

Table 17.1 Servers Closely Related to NCSA's	
Platform	**Internet Address**
UNIX	**http://hoohoo.ncsa.uiuc.edu/docs/Overview.html**
Windows	**http://www.alisa.com/win-httpd/**
OS/2	**ftp://ftp.netcom.com/pub/kfan/overview.html**
Mac	**http://www2.uth.tmc.edu/machttp_info.html**

Many other Web servers exist; the principles covered are applicable to more than just the NCSA servers.

Windows httpd

Windows httpd is included with this book and is one of the easiest Web servers to install. *HTTPD* stands for *HyperText Transfer Protocol Daemon,* which is simply a type of information server that uses the HTTP protocol. It features simple installation and a wide variety of useful features, including:

■ Low memory consumption and fast operation

■ True multithreaded operation for supporting multiple simultaneous requests

■ Ready to run "right out of the box"

■ Compatible with nearly all Web browsers and Windows TCP/IP packages

■ Automatic directory indexing for file serving

■ Script support using DOS BAT files and Visual Basic

■ Support for graphical usage statistics using VBStats

■ Support for fill-in forms and imagemaps

■ Built-in diagnostics

The only feature lacking in the Windows httpd that is found in the UNIX version of NCSA httpd (and the OS/2 port) is support for *server-side includes,* which allows HTML pages to include certain elements, such as date and time, that are generated on the fly. However, anything that can be done with server-side includes can also be done with *CGI scripts,* which are supported by the Windows httpd. CGI scripts allow the Web server to interact with other applications, such as databases.

Getting Started with Windows httpd

This section is a tutorial on running Windows httpd, from copying the necessary files to starting the server. The next section contains detailed information on configuration.

Requirements

In order to use Windows httpd, your computer must meet certain system and network requirements. In addition, you should already be familiar with using Windows.

System Requirements

The recommended configuration for a busy Web server is at least a 486/66 with 8M RAM running Windows 3.1 or Windows for Workgroups. If you plan to use the Visual Basic script support built in to Windows httpd, you must also have the Visual Basic run-time library VBRUN300.DLL.

Network Requirements

In order to run any Web server and most client software, your computer must be configured to speak TCP/IP over a network or SLIP/PPP connection. If you can already run Mosaic, Netscape, or another browser that uses TCP/IP, no additional configuration is needed to run your Web server. If not, you will have to get one of these browsers running first. For more information on this, see Chapters 4 and 11.

◀ See "Account Types," p. 40

> **Note**
>
> Web servers require a true SLIP or PPP connection because your server must have its own IP address. You can't run a server using a SLIP emulator, such as the Internet Adapter or TwinSock. Programs which work with true SLIP/PPP connections include the shareware Trumpet Winsock (included on the WebCD) and NetManage Chameleon.

Tip

You can provide Internet connectivity to several machines, via a single dial-up connection by using a *dial-up router* like the Rockwell NetHopper (**http://www.rns.com/**). This makes a SLIP/PPP modem connection appear as a regular leased line to the Internet.

WebCD

If you're setting up a full-time Web server, you need a full-time connection to your Internet service provider. This can be a dial-up line, as long as the server is always connected (obviously, you only want to do this with a local provider). Dedicated access costs from $150–$400/month for a connection using 28.8 Kbps modems.

If you're setting up a part-time Web server for limited use, you don't need a full-time connection, but you do need a *static IP address* so that your server always has the same address. Some providers assign IP addresses dynamically, which means that your address changes every time you log in to the service provider. This kind of connection is useful only for very limited experimental purposes because users must frequently be told the server's address.

Installation

Windows httpd is included on WebCD in the back of this book.

> **Note**
>
> Windows httpd is free for personal and education use. It is included with this book for your convenience; however, by buying the book, you have not purchased the software in any way. No rights have been rented, leased, or assigned to you. For more information on the WebCD, see the license agreement and disclaimer opposite the CD at the back of the book and Chapter 34. The Windows httpd license agreement is distributed with the software as LEGAL.HTM. Commercial users must pay a small fee after 30 days, which is described in the license agreement.

To install Windows httpd, follow these steps:

1. Create a new directory HTTPD on your hard drive (for example, C:\HTTPD). You must use this name for the installation.

2. Unzip the Windows httpd using your favorite file extraction utility and be sure to preserve the directory structure. If you don't preserve the directories, Windows httpd will not run correctly.

   If you use PKUNZIP, the command to use is

   ```
   pkunzip d:\www\whttpd\whttpd14.zip c:\httpd -d
   ```

   assuming WebCD is in your D drive and you are installing to C.

   If you use a Windows based utility to unzip the files, be sure to select to preserve the directories. For example, in WinZip 5.5, the **U**se Directory Names option must be selected in the Extract dialog box.

3. Edit your C:\AUTOEXEC.BAT file and add a line to set the TZ variable to your time zone. This line should include your time zone abbreviation, the number of hours from Greenwich Mean Time (GMT), and the abbreviation for daylight time in your zone if your state is on daylight time. Table 17.3 lists time zone abbreviations in the United States. For example:

```
SET TZ=CST5CDT (Central Standard Time Zone)
```

Table 17.3 Settings for the Timezone Variable in the United States

Time Zone	Setting
Eastern Standard Time	EST4EDT
Central Standard Time	CST5CDT
Mountain Standard Time	MST6MDT
Pacific Standard Time	PST7PDT

You need to reboot for the AUTOEXEC.BAT change to take effect.

That's all there is to it. Your Web server is now ready to run.

Starting the Server

Assuming you have a SLIP or network connection to the Internet, simply follow these steps to start your server:

1. If you're using SLIP or PPP over a dial-up account, dial and log in to your account as you normally would to run Mosaic or another browser. Make a note of your IP (internet address, like **167.142.100.115**).

2. From the Windows Program Manager, create an icon pointing to C:\HTTPD\HTTPD.EXE.

3. To start the server, double-click the server icon. The server icon appears on your desktop showing the server initializing and then idle (waiting for connections).

Figure 17.1 shows Windows httpd after it's been opened.

Tip

You can quickly create an icon by dragging the file from File Manager into a Program Manager group.

Tip

If you plan to run your server whenever Windows is running, copy the Winsock and server icons into the Program Manager Startup group. The Winsock icon should come first so Windows starts it first.

Fig. 17.1
Windows httpd.

4. To test your server, start your Web browser and open a connection to
http://<your IP>/ or **http://localhost/**. For example, if your IP is
167.142.100.115, you would select **F**ile, **O**pen URL in Mosaic (or another browser) and type **http://167.142.100.115/**. If your machine
also has a name, you can use this as well, like **s115.infonet.net**. If
your server is running properly, the label on the server icon will say
httpd_active (1), where 1 is the number of active connections.

If the transfer was successful, you will see the server's home page in your
browser. Figure 17.2 shows the default server home page in Mosaic for
Windows. By default, the server's home page is in C:\HTTPD\HTDOCS\
INDEX.HTM. To learn how to write your own home page, see Chapter 14,
"Creating Pages with HTML."

Tip
You should always
close all Winsock
applications, like
the Web server,
before closing the
Winsock program
itself in order to
prevent Windows
from locking up.

Stopping the Server

To quit running Windows httpd, double-click the server icon and choose **E**xit
from the **C**ontrol menu. Alternatively, you can choose **C**lose from the pop-up
menu that appears when you click the server icon.

Troubleshooting and System Tuning

This section contains descriptions of many common problems and the appropriate solutions. If you are having performance problems with your server,
make sure the following items have been addressed.

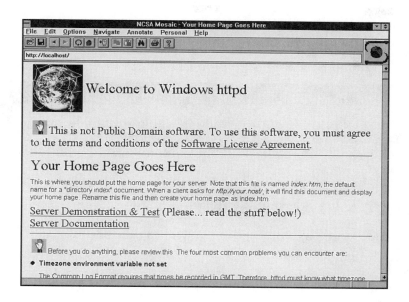

IV

Creating Web Pages & Sites

Fig. 17.2
Default home page
for Windows
httpd.

Broken Winsock

A common problem with running Windows httpd is that some Winsock software, which is at the heart of your TCP/IP connection, is not fully compliant with the Windows Sockets 1.1 standard used by Windows httpd. Fortunately, Windows httpd provides a workaround. Stop the server and restart it by using the -n option on the command line C:\HTTPD\HTTPD.EXE -n. This disables multithreaded operation, which means the server will answer only one request at a time, but allows it to work with incompatible Winsock programs.

To start the server with the -n option using the server icon, click the icon and choose **F**ile, **P**roperties in Program Manager to edit the command line.

Time Zone Not Set

This is required for proper access logging. Make sure your time zone variable is set correctly in your AUTOEXEC.BAT file, as described in the previous section.

CommandEnvSize

Certain pages in the documentation and applications you may write require DOS scripts. These will fail if you don't have enough DOS environment space for DOS sessions running under Windows. If you're having problems running

▶ See "Software for Connecting to the Internet (TCP/IP)," p. 980

WebCD

Tip
If you're using the shareware Trumpet Winsock version 2.0a, you probably need to use the -n option with HTTPD.EXE. In Trumpet version 2.0b, this is no longer necessary. If you're using version 2.0a, you should upgrade to 2.0b, which is on WebCD.

DOS scripts, add this line to the [NonWindowsApp] section of your SYSTEM.INI file:

```
CommandEnvSize=8192
```

> **Note**
>
> For changes to your Windows SYSTEM.INI and WIN.INI to take effect, you must restart Windows.

What's in the Server

This section gives you an overview of the files and directories that come with the server. This section explains the command line options and directory structures.

Files and Directories

◄ See "A Brief Look at cgi-bin," p. 370

This section contains information on the files and directories included as part of the Web server. After you install the server, you will find several directories underneath the server root directory (C:\HTTPD). These include:

- cgi-bin
- cgi-src
- conf
- icons
- logs
- support

The cgi-bin directory is where all scripts will be placed.

> **Note**
>
> There are no sample scripts included with Windows httpd so the cgi-bin has only one file, which is just junk used to create the directory with PKZIP. For information about scripting, see Que's *Running a Perfect Web Site*.

The cgi-src directory contains source code used to implement script capabilities. You should not need to modify anything in this directory, but it may be a useful reference.

The conf directory contains all the server configuration files. These include:

- httpd.con

- srm.con

- access.con

- mime.typ

httpd.con is the top-level server configuration file. It defines the server's name and port and points to other configuration files. *srm.con* is the server resource map. This provides information on the location and type of documents on the server. *access.con* defines who can access which directories on the server. Finally, *mime.typ* associates file names with document types.

The *icons directory* contains images that may be useful to include in documents residing on your server. The icons directory also contains small GIF images that are used as file icons in server-generated directory indexes.

The *logs directory* is the default location for both the error log and access log files, which record all accesses to the server.

The *support directory* contains several utility programs. Htpasswd converts document usernames and passwords into a format readable by the server. Htpasswd is part of server access control. The support directory also contains WinCron, which runs scheduled programs at specified times.

In Windows httpd, four additional directories are created by default. These are listed below.

- CGI-DOS

- CGI-WIN

- HTDOCS

- VBSTATS

The CGI-DOS and CGI-WIN directories contain already written scripts that run under DOS and Windows, respectively. These can help you get started writing your own scripts. For more information on forms see Chapter 15, "Advanced HTML."

HTDOCS is the top-level document directory by default. Normally, all HTML documents are placed under this directory. The documentation on the server itself is located in the HTTPDDOC subdirectory. By default, the server's home page is C:\HTTPD\HTDOCS\INDEX.HTM.

VBSTATS contains a utility to record and graph Web server usage statistics.

Command Line Options

Windows httpd can be started with command line options for various configuration and troubleshooting purposes. These options are:

- -d server_root_directory

- -f server_configuration_file

- -I DLL_name

- -n

- -r

- -x 0xnnn

Tip
The -d option is a convenient way to run multiple Web servers with different sets of configuration files and different documents. For example, you can run an internal and external Web server on the same machine by using the -d option to point to different sets of configuration files.

Specifying -d followed by a directory name changes the location of the server root directory, which is where the server looks for the server configuration file by default. Under Windows httpd, this value defaults to C:\HTTPD.

The -f option is similar to the -d option, but changes only the location of the server configuration file, not the entire server root directory. You can use this to test changes in one or more of the server configuration files without having to create an entirely new test directory.

This chapter's troubleshooting section discusses the -n option. The -n option disables multithreading to allow the server to run with network or SLIP software that does not meet the Windows Sockets 1.1 standard.

The -r option enables reverse DNS lookups, which causes the server to look up the name of each client that connects to the server using its IP address. By default, the server doesn't do this automatically. Reverse DNS lookups must be turned on if you're using name-based access control or if you want client names to appear in the log files.

> **Note**
>
> VBStats, the usage statistics program that comes with Windows httpd, looks up address names when it's processing the usage log files, so you can still see address names even when the server -r option isn't turned on.

The -I option is used to load a DLL file (dynamic link library) when the server is started and keep it loaded until the server is stopped. This option was designed for use with VBRUN300.DLL, which is used by servers using Visual Basic scripts. Without this option, the DLL is loaded and unloaded each time it is used, resulting in substantial overhead if it's used a lot.

The -x option is used for debugging, and is useful mainly for those very familiar with the HTTP and TCP/IP protocols.

From Here...

This chapter provides the basics for setting up a World Wide Web server. When you think about it, it's pretty incredible that you can transform a PC which costs less than $2,000 into a communications center which can reach millions of people all over the world. From here you will find additional information that will help you manage your Web site and become proficient at authoring Web documents in the following chapters:

- Chapter 2, "Connecting to the World Wide Web," details the various Internet accounts—both dedicated and dial-up—that you can get for your Web server.

- Chapter 15, "Advanced HTML," is where you will find step-by-step instructions for authoring advanced HTML scripts to create interactive Web page forms and graphic imagemaps.

- Chapter 16, "HTML Editors and Filters," offers an overview of the software programs which make the process of HTML scripting a little easier.

- Chapter 22, "Computers," provides a comprehensive list of Web sites devoted to computers, software, and the Internet.

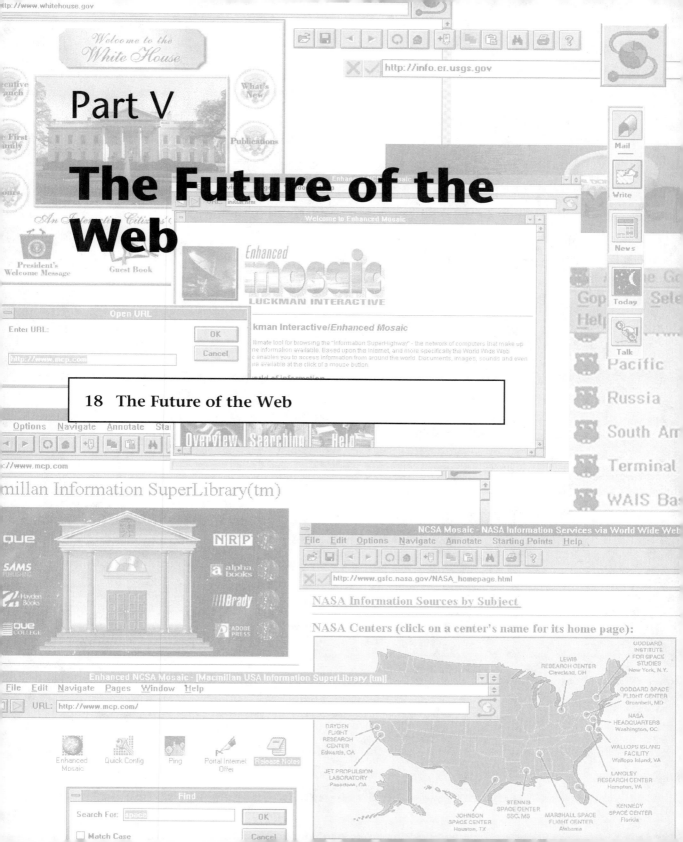

Part V

The Future of the Web

18 The Future of the Web

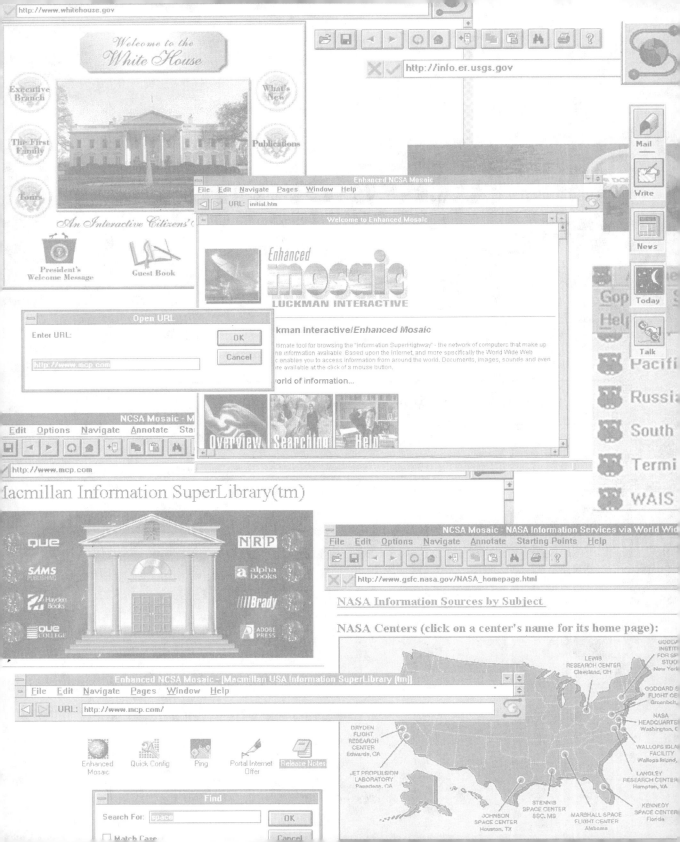

Chapter 18

The Future of the Web

by Bill Eager

When a communications medium is successful, changes are inevitable. Two significant areas of change exist; one involves the technology that lies behind the medium, and the other involves the applications for which the medium is used.

For example, television has evolved technically from a state in which stations broadcast black-and-white transmissions to the point at which signals are relayed via satellite and cable systems. Color, stereo, and closed captioning also are available, and high-definition images (HDTV) are on the horizon. As television became widespread, the applications also evolved, moving from general-interest entertainment to specialized education, news, first-run movies, and shopping at home.

The phenomenal growth of the Web means that changes are in store; in fact, they're happening today. This chapter looks at the major trends in technology, applications, and management that affect the future of the Web. In this chapter, you learn about the following:

- ■ Technical changes that make the Web easier to use

- ■ The dramatic increase in the number of commercial firms that have a presence on the Web

- ■ Financial applications and browsers that ensure security of commerce via the Web

- ■ Cutting-edge Web sites that provide remote sensing (where you can see and interact with devices that are in other parts of the world) and virtual reality

Web Connectivity Gets Faster and Faster

On the technology side, the most significant change—from the point of view of Web users—is the rapid increase in the speed of Internet connections. The popularity of the Web comes from its delivery of graphics, audio, and video. As all Web surfers know, the files are big, and they take forever to get into our PCs. With some home pages, you have time to get a cup of coffee and a sandwich before the page loads. These big files also eat up space on Internet lines.

To solve this problem, the communication lines of the Internet are rapidly being upgraded. The NSFNET backbone now runs T3 lines (lines that provide transmission speeds of 45 Mbps), and commercial networks are quickly surpassing NSFNET in terms of the volume of Internet transmissions and speed. By mid-1995, MCI's backbone will have more than 35,000 miles of fiber-optic and digital radio links, connect 400 locations, and deliver data at 155 mbps. To put this situation in perspective, the system could deliver a 90-minute video in three minutes or about 10,000 pages of text in a second. The MCI system is significant because it serves many regional Internet service providers, such as BARRnet, JVNCnet, Merit, NEARnet, SURAnet, and other networks (including Canada's CA*net and Japan's WIDEnet) that manage as much as 40 percent of Internet traffic.

One other area needs to increase in speed, of course: the connection between your PC and the Internet. This change is occurring as well. You can purchase a 28.8 Kbps modem that works with standard telephone lines. If that modem isn't fast enough, you can use Motorola's BitSURFER TA210 digital modem. The BitSURFER uses a special telephone service—Integrated Services Digital Network, or ISDN—that is available from all regional Bell companies and most other telephone companies. ISDN service offers two 64 Kbps channels. You can use one for voice, and the other for data—or, for maximum speed, use both for a data rate of 128 Kbps. This modem connects to the serial port of a PC or Macintosh computer and is compatible with Windows, DOS, and Apple operating systems. The BitSURFER has a built-in feature that allows users to plug directly into ISDN lines. You still need to have an Internet account that will serve you at these high speeds. Many service providers offer the speed, but the price usually goes up.

Another option in the not-too-distant future will be to tie your PC into the Internet and Web via service from cable-television companies. The same cable that delivers HBO and Showtime can transmit data to and from the

Internet by means of a special black box that you place in your house. This setup represents the ultimate in high-speed connectivity, at 500,000 bps.

One example of this trend is a joint effort of Boston-based Continental Cablevision and Performance Systems International, the nation's largest Internet service provider. Together, these companies potentially can offer this high-speed link to the Internet to as many as 3 million subscribers. Jones Intercable is offering similar service as a test in the Washington, D.C. area.

Advertising and Commerce on the Web

The explosive growth of the Web has not gone unnoticed by companies that sell products and services. After all, the Web is a marketing manager's dream come true. With its inherent capability to display pictures and movies, play audio, and enable users to interactively request information and order products instantly, the Web is an all-in-one market research, advertising, and sales mechanism.

The number of commercial sites that have Internet registrations (.com addresses) has risen dramatically. In 1990, 93 such sites existed; by August 1994, the number exceeded 18,000. And the growth is not stopping. The publication *Internet Info* reported that the November 1994 snapshot of commercial domains registered with InterNIC shows 24,762 unique domains, compared with 21,777 as of October 15, 1994. This increase of 2,985 registered domain names represents a 13.7-percent month-to-month gain. According to telecommunications giant MCI, 38 percent of all publicly traded companies with sales that exceed $400 million annually have some type of presence on the Internet. Often, however, this presence is only e-mail access.

Fortunately, the interactive nature of the Internet helps the Web remain immune to the type of obnoxious promotion (advertising) that we so often find on television and radio. Indeed, several companies that placed blatant ads on UseNet newsgroups and mailing lists were severely *flamed*—that is, instead of receiving orders for their services, they received hundreds of thousands of nasty e-mail messages, basically forcing them off the Net.

The trend for commercial Web sites, therefore, is for companies to have Web documents that offer useful product information, news, articles, interactive brochures, free software utilities, and even games—the sort of information and tools that provide value and that intrigue Web travelers.

Consider the inviting copy that begins a journey into the Web site for Time, shown in figure 18.1 (**http://www.timeinc.com**). The copy reads, "On this page, you'll find a compass to some of the world's greatest writing and photography and a whole lot of other Internet goodies. Click on any of the blue underlined words to explore the stories featured here, on any logo to visit a home page, or to TIMELINE to see today's news from TIME, Money, and Entertainment Weekly."

Fig. 18.1
Time is one of thousands of commercial firms that run Web sites, offering useful and fun information.

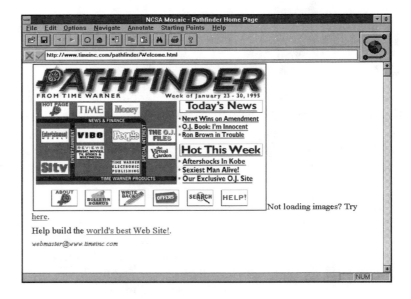

Who could resist a whole lot of Internet goodies? The offerings include reviews of books, movies, and TV shows; samples of articles; copy from cover stories; and a series of special-interest bulletin boards that cover subjects ranging from health and medicine, to the sexes, to Washington, D.C. You may not have time to read the magazine if you get on this site.

Another good example of a commercial site is the Macmillan Computer Publishing site (**http://www.mcp.com**). The home page has a link to a bookstore that contains information on more than 1,000 different computer-related books. There are also sample chapters and pictures of the covers of many of the book; both give you a nice preview of the titles—kind of a "try it before you buy it" approach. You can also order online at a discount. Another section of this site offers hundreds of shareware, freeware, and demo software programs. If you find that you have an unanswered computer question, try the Reference Desk link. This link opens a digital room full of the latest computing information (see fig. 18.2). In addition to reference articles, you can subscribe to receive reports from an Information SuperLibrary that has more than 35 categories, such as Children's Computing, Databases, and Games.

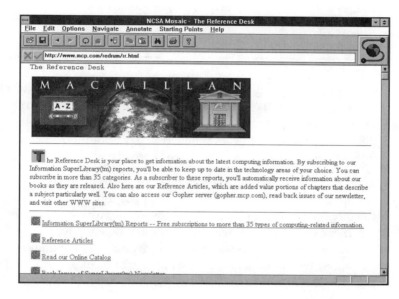

Fig. 18.2
Macmillan Computer Publishing maintains a Web site that offers useful reference information and sample chapters of computer books.

Steve Bennett wrote a MIT working paper titled "Recent Developments in Business Use of the Internet: Emerging Uses of the World Wide Web by Lead Users." According to this report, the 10 commercial Web sites that have received the most visits are those in the following table.

Site	URL Address
1. CommerceNet	**http://www.commerce.net**
2. Canadian Airlines International	**http://www.cdnair.ca**
3. Ericsson Netherlands Server	**http://www.ericsson.nl**
4. Securities & Exchange Commission (Edgar Server at NYU)	**http://town.hall.org/cgi-bin/srch-edgar**
5. Internet Shopping Network	**http://www.internet.net**
6. Quote.Com	**http://www.quote.com**
7. Global Network Navigator	**http://nearnet.gnn.com/gnn/gnn.html**

(continues)

The Future of the Web

V

Site	URL Address
8. AT&T Bell Laboratories	**http://www.research.att.com**
9. Digital Equipment Corporation	**http://www.digital.com**
10. World Real Estate Listing Service	**http://interchange.idc. uvic.ca/wrels/index.html**

You also can order products directly from Web pages. Many of the electronic malls and stores on the Web enable you to see and purchase merchandise by using a *forms interface*: a page that contains boxes in which you can enter information (such as your credit-card number) to have clothing, flowers, wine, or other items shipped to your home the very next day.

The Web not only can help companies get new customers and make money, but it also can help them save money. Companies pay more than $2 to print and mail a color brochure or catalog to one prospective customer. On the Web, companies can create electronic brochures that potentially reach millions of people for pennies per viewer. Another advantage is that unlike printed brochures, Web information can be updated immediately if a product or price changes. The consumer wins as well. Online retail firms can dramatically reduce their overhead expenses for personnel, paperwork, and inventory, and pass these savings on to Web customers.

Security of Web Transactions

The first thought that may come to your mind when you see a Web page that asks you to input your credit-card number is "No way!" There has been a great deal of discussion about the security of financial transactions and electronic commerce on the Web. These activities include purchasing products with credit cards, processing purchase orders, and sending confidential reports over the Internet/Web. The concept of *digital cash* is now moving from transactions once conducted solely by banks into the homes of Internet users. It won't be long before you can pay a large number of your bills directly through the Internet by transferring funds from your bank account directly into the accounts of firms you do business with, such as the electric company.

With estimates of electronic financial transactions reaching as high as $5 billion a year by the turn of the century, many companies and Internet organizations are pursuing methods of ensuring that this information cannot be stolen as it moves across the Net.

A low-tech security approach involves instructing Web mall operators to ask customers to use their telephones to call in credit-card information. Users then get a password that admits them to mall stores. This approach is used by the Internet Shopping Network (**http://www.internet.net**), which now is owned by the Home Shopping Network.

In a more technical approach, Enterprise Integration Technologies (**http://www.eit.com**), the National Center for Supercomputing Applications (NCSA), and RSA Data Security have developed Secure Mosaic. Ordinarily, merchants would have difficulty proving that their online customers are who they say they are. When you use Secure HTTP to purchase a product, however, the program generates a session key, which, in conjunction with the merchant's special public key, encrypts the contents of the order form—mainly your credit-card and address information—and then delivers the form to the Web server, where the information is decoded.

Most of the companies that are developing new Web browsers are supporting the Secure HTTP standards. Spry, the company that offers Internet-In-A-Box, is releasing a system called Mosaic Express, which uses these standards. In addition, the Netscape browser currently provides encryption based on the RSA system.

◀ See "Security," p. 248

All this security is spawning new Web services. For example, MCI is using Netscape to secure transactions on its interMCI Web shopping mall, and BankAmerica has joined forces with Netscape to help its customers perform secure financial transactions via the Internet. To top off the list, a company called Portfolio Accounting World Wide now operates a Web site that enables users to purchase and sell stocks online. The site shown in figure 18.3 (**http://pawws.secapl.com**) connects users to The Net Investor, a discount brokerage arm for New York Stock Exchange member Howe Barnes Investments. Again, Netscape is used for security; investors establish several passwords to protect their accounts. Future services will include mutual funds, bonds, and options.

V

The Future of the Web

Fig. 18.3
Buy and sell stocks
at the PAWWS
Web site, shown
here via the
Netscape browser,
which helps
secure financial
transactions with
encryption.

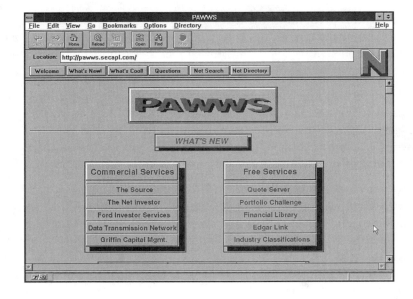

Shopping, banking, and stock-market transactions represent a significant portion of consumer applications for financial transactions. After these services prove to be successful on the Web, other applications (such as corporate payroll, and tax payments to the Internal Revenue Service) will begin to appear.

Remote Sensing and Control

Two aspects of the Web that have tremendous potential, and are now being explored, are *remote sensing* and *remote control*. This means that you can connect many devices other than computers to a computer network—for example, video cameras, thermostats, robots, and even vending machines. People like you, who may be hundreds of thousands of miles away from these devices, can access and control these devices directly through Web pages.

Remote sensing specifically refers to the monitoring of information at a remote site. This information can be statistical, such as the outdoor temperature or the number of cans of soda in a pop machine. Or, it can be visual, such as the image of Fifth Avenue in Manhattan relayed from a video camera. Remote control enables you to control a device that is in a distant location. You can, for example, adjust another building's thermostat.

Although this concept may sound more like science fiction than fact, you can try it today. Some of these applications really are just fun experiments, but all of them provide great demonstrations of the potential of this medium.

Mark Cox, a Ph.D. candidate at the University of Bradford in England, has established a Web site with links to several remote sensing devices. (His site is **http://www.eia.brad.ac.uk/mark/fave-inter.html.**) In the realm of video sensing, you can try links to cameras that take a picture of an iguana in his cage every 10 minutes, of the San Diego Bay every 30 minutes, or of a coffeepot in an office every 10 seconds.

At New York University (**http://found.cs.nyu.edu/cgi-bin/rsw/ labcam**), try Labcam, a video camera that you can control, panning or tilting to suit your desired image of this computer lab. The Labcam experiment had an interesting and relevant outcome. Before the camera went online, several pieces of equipment were stolen from the lab; after Labcam began operating, the thievery stopped. Think about it. This type of application turns millions of Web cruisers into the security force for any video-connected Web site. At any point someone out in cyberspace could capture a still image of a thief in action!

Other machines and devices can be connected to Web servers. With security-controlled Web access, you can control the thermostat and lights in your home if you are away on vacation. One Web site, for example, has a hot tub (**http://www.msen.com/~paulh**) with a Web-connected thermometer. You can check out the temperature of the hot tub by visiting the site, but you can't change the temperature. Thirsty? Tie into the Coke machine at Rochester Institute of Technology (there are several such sites; this one is **http:// www.csh.rit.edu/proj/drink.html**) to find out what sodas are in the machine and how cold they are.

You can control more than video cameras from Web sites. At the University of Southern California, a robot arm sits in a sandbox with a camera mounted near it. You can control the robot arm through the Web page (**http:// www.usc.edu/dept/raiders**) and dig for artifacts buried in the sandbox.

The California State Department of Transportation (CDOT) offers a somewhat more practical application. The department's Web site (**http:// www.scubed.com:8001/caltrans/transnet.html**) monitors and displays current traffic conditions in various cities in California. You can view a map that shows current traffic speeds and the locations of possible accidents. If you live in these areas, you can reduce drive-time problems by checking the site before you leave the house. CDOT also may place kiosks at public places, such as airports and bus stations. Figure 18.4 shows one of the maps for the Los Angeles area.

Fig. 18.4
Remote sensing devices enable you to monitor the current status of highway speeds in California at the California State Department of Transportation Web site.

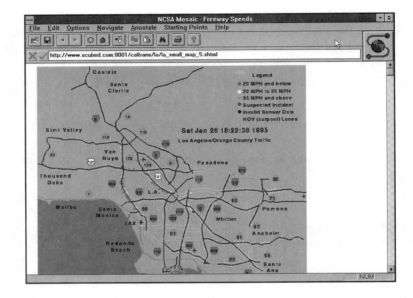

Other interesting examples of remote control include an LED sign outside a building (you enter the message via the Web form) and a Christmas tree (you turn the lights on and off).

The Web Brings People Together

With applications such as *distance learning* and information sharing, the Web holds the potential to enrich the lives of millions of people and to bring the world closer together. The concept of distance learning is simple: you study a subject at your home or office and tap into a network of top-notch educators who may work in distant cities.

One Web example of distance learning is the Virtual Online University (**http://core.symnet.net/~VOU**). This site helps you take courses with professors from around the world. In the area of natural sciences, for example, the university offers high-end courses such as "Principles of Protein Structure," from Birkbeck College, England; "Biocomputing," from the University of Bielefeld, Germany; and "Quantum Mechanics in Simple Matrix Form," from the University of Hamburg, Germany. Best of all, transferrable college credit is available.

The world itself will benefit as people begin to learn more about foreign cultures and customs through Web-based information. You can, for example, explore the languages, religion, and music of India through the India page (see fig. 18.5). Try the URL address **http://www.cs.clemson.edu/~nandu/india.html**.

▶ See "Public Policy and World Events," p. 795

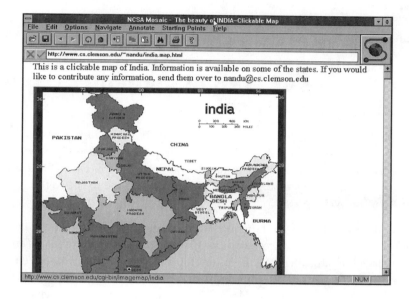

Fig. 18.5
The world may become a better place through the sharing of cultural information on the Web.

Virtual Reality Lives on the Web

Virtual reality refers to a computer-generated world that you can enter and explore. In the most advanced form of virtual reality, you put on a computer helmet or glasses (perhaps even special computer gloves) and then wander through artificial worlds, viewing scenes as you walk along and touch or pick up objects.

The Web isn't quite that elaborate, but a simple version of virtual reality is quite alive on the Web, which offers a variety of electronic places to visit. These sites include virtual cities; you get an interactive map of the town, and you click different parts of the map to visit those places. The Web also offers virtual museums, in which you walk through exhibits and click doors to go to special displays. These museums even include tour guides that tell you what you're looking at (click a button and listen to the guide's voice).

The U.S. Library of Congress gets credit for being at the cutting edge of interactive Web museums. The library offers a series of electronic exhibits in

V

The Future of the Web

which you can browse through information just as you do in a real museum. A recent exhibit is the American Memories project, which focuses on American culture and history. When you visit, you can view photographs of artists such as Billie Holliday and Martha Graham; use keywords to search for Civil War photographs (more than 1,000 are available); and listen to audio recordings of Franklin D. Roosevelt and Calvin Coolidge. If you're in the mood for a little Web virtual reality, try the URL address **http://lcweb.loc.gov/ homepage/lchp.html** (you don't have to whisper!).

The Future of Web Management and Technical Protocols

If no single entity controls the Internet or the Web, how will the system develop to address the concerns and requirements of new users? Who will ensure the realization of the one inherent goal of the Web: to provide a system that any person, using any type of computer, can use to access the resources of the Web?

The good news is that several organizations are devoted to these goals. The Internet Society (**http://www.isoc.org**), based in Reston, Virginia, is an international organization that helps establish standards and coordinate the ongoing development of the Internet. Members include Internet providers, not-for-profit organizations, government agencies, and private citizens. Executive Director Tony Rutkowski believes that the Web plays an important role in expanding the use and applications of the Internet because it's easy to use and makes Internet navigation much simpler. In an online interview, Rutkowski conveyed his enthusiasm for the future of the Web when he wrote: "The WWW allows people to be really clever and innovative in multiple ways on a global scale. There is no comparable human communications medium."

The W3 Organization (W3O) is another organization that focuses on issues surrounding the ongoing development of the Web. CERN (the European Laboratory for Particle Physics in Switzerland) and the Laboratory for Computer Science at the Massachusetts Institute of Technology (MIT) are the founding W3O member organizations. MIT operates several research groups that tie into the Web, including the Media Lab and the Artificial Intelligence Lab. Before W3O, CERN was the only organization that played a significant role in the ongoing definition of the Web. The W3O intends to join with other institutes and sites to provide centers of excellence and local contact points. In Europe, W3O aims to establish a contact point in each country.

W3O's initial focus is the development of new international data-entry and data-retrieval standards for the Web; the standards are expected to make finding information much easier. Because the Web is becoming a huge electronic library, standard ways to catalog will improve the accessibility of information. Evolving from existing Web standards, these standards will supply a common architecture for use by commercial developers of browser software. The standards also will ensure that software created by different companies will be compatible.

For global commercial application of the Web, W3O will address issues related to security, privacy, and electronic transfers of funds. Funding for this project will come from the U.S. government, the European Economic Community (EEC), and various international companies. Although it is not a standards organization, W3O works with developers and researchers to create awareness of the implications of converging and emerging technologies. Specific areas of technical and operational development include the following:

- Name and address syntax and semantics (universal identifiers)

- Network transfer protocols (Hypertext Transfer Protocol, or HTTP)

- Data formats for hypertext and hypermedia (Hypertext Markup Language, or HTML)

- Encoding methods for compression and security

- Protocols for billing and for transferring legally binding documents

- Protocols that enhance the functions of the Web (such as caching, replication, and optimal request routing)

- The use of alternative high-speed-network technology, such as Asynchronous Transfer Mode (ATM)

WWW Reference Information

A variety of governmental, educational, and private institutions participate in the development of the World Wide Web and provide information about it. Information is readily available through mailing lists and news groups. Following are a few sources of information to get you started.

Government Entities, Organizations, and Companies

CERN
URL address: **http://info.cern.ch**

> **Note**
>
> Also try CERN's W3 project page at **http://info.cern.ch/hypertext/WWW/ TheProject.html**, where you'll find information about Web software, servers, conferences, protocols, and source code.

Swiss site:
European Laboratory for High Energy Physics
H - 1211 Geneva 23 (Switzerland)

French site:
Organisation Europeenne pour la Recherche Nucleaire
F - 01631 CERN Cedex (France)
Central telephone exchange: +41 22 767 6111

Enterprise Integration Technologies
URL address: **http://www.eit.com/**

459 Hamilton Avenue
Palo Alto, CA 94301
Phone: (415) 617-8000
Fax: (415) 617-8019

The Internet Network Information Center (InterNIC)
URL address: **http://is.internic.net/**

P.O. Box 85608
San Diego, CA 92186-9784
Phone: (800) 444-4345 or (619) 455-4600
Fax: (619) 455-4640
Electronic mail: **refdesk@is.internic.net**

InterNIC makes current documentation on the NSFNET available via a mail server and by anonymous FTP, Gopher, WAIS, and the World Wide Web.

Internet Society
URL address: **http://info.isoc.org/home.html**

12020 Sunrise Valley Drive, Suite 270
Reston, VA 22091
Phone: (703) 648-9888

The Internet Society is an international organization that helps establish standards and coordinate the ongoing development of the Internet.

National Center for Supercomputing Applications (NCSA)
URL address: **http://www.ncsa.uiuc.edu**

152 Computing Applications Building
605 East Springfield Avenue
Champaign, IL 61820
Phone: (217) 244-0072

National Science Foundation (NSF)
URL address: **http://www.nsf.gov/**

4201 Wilson Boulevard
Arlington, VA 22230
Phone: (703) 306-1234

World Wide Web Consortium
URL address: **http://www.lcs.mit.edu/**

545 Technology Square
Cambridge, MA 02139
Phone: (617) 253-5851

The MIT World Wide Web Consortium is managed by the Laboratory for Computer Science at the Massachusetts Institute of Technology. The consortium was established in support of the CERN-MIT W3O initiative.

Web-Specific Newsgroups

alt.hypertext
This newsgroup focuses on hypertext.

comp.infosystems.www.misc
This newsgroup is a forum for general discussion of WWW-related topics that are not covered by the other newsgroups, including the Web's future, the politics of changes in the structure, and protocols of the Web that affect both clients and servers.

V

The Future of the Web

comp.infosystems.www.providers

This newsgroup is a forum for discussion of WWW server software. Topics include server design, setup questions, server bug reports, security issues, and HTML page design.

comp.infosystems.www.users

This newsgroup is a forum for discussion of WWW client software and for use in contacting various Internet information sources. Acceptable topics for this group include new-user and client setup questions, client bug reports, information on how to locate information on the Web that can't be found by the means detailed in the FAQ, and comparisons of client packages.

comp.text.sgml

This newsgroup features technical discussions of Standard Generalized Markup Language (SGML). HTML (the Hypertext Markup Language used by the World Wide Web) is a subset of SGML, so this newsgroup may be of interest to you.

Web Mailing Lists

A robot-like computer program called a *list server* maintains W3 mailing lists and enables users to retrieve documents on request. You subscribe to the W3 mailing lists by sending e-mail to the robot. Address your mail to **listserv@info.cern.ch**, and leave the subject line blank. In the first line of the e-mail message, type the following:

· **subscribe www-announce [*your name*]**

If your name is Angela Douglas, the first line of your subscription request is

subscribe www-announce Angela Douglas

You don't need to include your e-mail address in the subscription request; the robot picks up your address. If you have problems or questions that you want a person to answer, include them in an e-mail message to **www-request@info.cern.ch**.

www-announce

This list is for people who are interested in the Web and its progress, new data sources, and software releases.

www-html

This list provides technical discussions of the Hypertext Markup Language (HTML) and HTML+ designs.

www-proxy

This list provides technical discussions about Web proxies, caching, and future directions.

www-rdb

This list provides discussions about using gateways to integrate relational databases into the Web.

www-talk

This list provides technical discussions for people or institutions that are developing Web software.

WWW Interactive Talk

WWW Interactive Talk (WIT, for short) is a new type of discussion group that has been formed for the WWW. In some ways, WIT is similar to UseNet newsgroups. The creators of this forum, however, tried to overcome some of the limitations of UseNet groups by structuring the discussion of a particular topic. Each topic is presented in a form that shows the topic and proposals for discussion of the topic. Under each proposal are arguments for and against the proposal.

> **Note**
>
> The designers of WIT hope that this format allows readers to see whether a topic has been adequately discussed before they submit their own comments. By comparison, a point often is made over and over again in UseNet newsgroups, because readers respond before they see whether someone else has already brought up the point.

This discussion format is new and somewhat experimental. Currently, a WIT discussion area is set up at **http://info.cern.ch/wit/hypertext/WWW**.

This area is not limited to WWW discussions (any topic can be introduced), but it is a place where you are likely to find some people to talk to you about the WWW.

From Here...

In this chapter you've read about some of the things to come in the months and years ahead on the Web. If you're ready to learn more, try these chapters:

- Chapter 19, "Web Searching," has tips about how to use the Web searching mechanisms. You can use these tools to find out about the latest developments on the Internet and the Web.

- Chapter 22, "Computers," provides a comprehensive review of Web sites that focuses on computer applications, including developments in the World Wide Web.

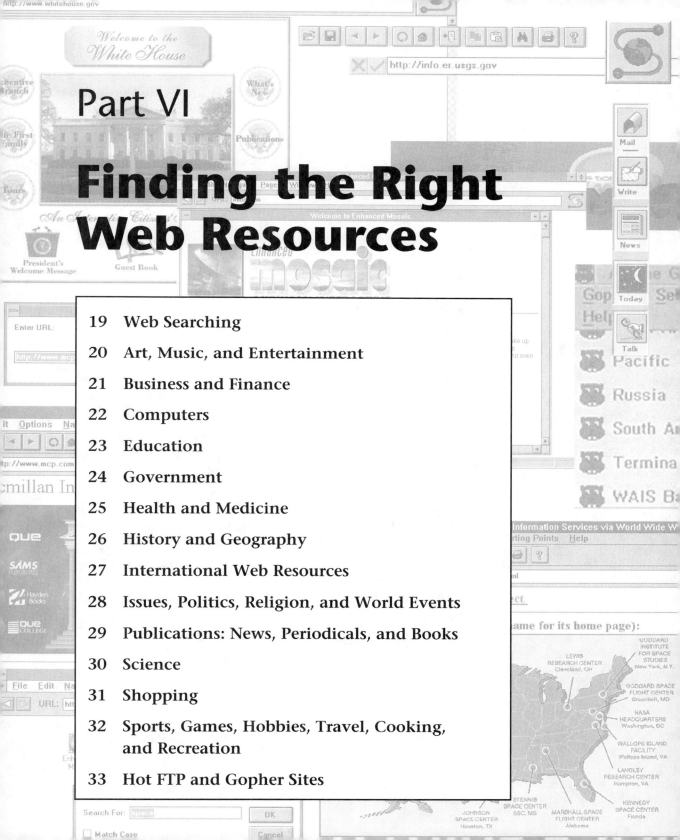

Part VI

Finding the Right Web Resources

Chapter 19

Web Searching

by Bill Eager

You don't need to create a home page or author hypermedia documents to enjoy the World Wide Web. You can get a thrill and a sense of satisfaction when you connect to a WWW site that has exactly the information you need—perhaps a lesson on how to rewire the electrical outlet that's on the fritz in your basement, a database of bird images that identifies the new feathered friend sitting on your bird feeder, or a lesson plan for a sixth-grade science class that explains how solar energy works. There is a real sense of adventure as you jump from link to link, looking for resources that will make your life a little richer.

For practical purposes, there are two main reasons for using the Web. Either you want to accomplish a specific task—locate information or order a bouquet of flowers—or you simply want to explore the global cyberspace, take a journey, even a mini-vacation. In either case, it helps to have a starting point, a place where you can literally jump in and get started. *Special Edition Using the World Wide Web and Mosaic* provides listings of the resources on the Web—in all, more than 1,500 Web pages you can visit to begin your global exploration!

This chapter introduces techniques that will help you search for and locate Web information that is of interest to you. The first technique involves using the resource listings in Chapters 20–32 of this book. Using these along with the index, you should be able to find pages on any topic you want. But what if the specific information you need isn't on a page that is listed in this book? You can then search the Web using one of several Web searchers described in this chapter. You'll learn the following in this chapter:

- Tips for loading and saving URL addresses

- Techniques which can make Web "surfing" faster

- What Web searchers are and how to use them

- Reviews (and URL addresses) of the most popular Web searchers

> **Note**
>
> You may be wondering why you needed to buy a book that lists Web sites if you can simply search the Web itself to find information and resources. The answer is that you'll want to use both of these methods. This book doesn't list every home page— and new ones appear on a regular basis. We have, however, tried to list the best pages that have been around for more than a day or two (things do change fast on the Web). The information on these pages will be a good source of reference, like a phone book, or "Yellow Pages," that will point you either directly to the resource you want or to a very good starting point. Depending on your service provider's fee structure, you may pay as much as $10 per hour for Web connect time. Weaving your way through thousands of Web home pages can be a very expensive proposition. By helping you quickly get where you want to go, this book will save both time and money.
>
> While valuable, use of the Web searchers does not guarantee that you will find all the pages related to a given topic, and these searchers are prone to turning up a lot of unrelated topics.

The Resource Listings

The WWW resources are divided into 13 separate chapters, which represent broad categories, including:

Chapter	Topic
20	Arts, music, and entertainment
21	Business and finance
22	Computers
23	Education
24	Government
25	Health and medicine
26	History and geography
27	International Web resources

Chapter	Topic
28	Issues, politics, religion, and world events
29	Publications: news, periodicals, and books
30	Science
31	Shopping
32	Sports, games, hobbies, travel, cooking, and recreation

The table of contents and index further break down these categories to help you rapidly locate a specific subject, such as interactive art museums or scuba diving.

> **Note**
>
> We have worked to make the index as comprehensive as possible. We've listed every possible occurrence we could find of company names, topics, and subtopics with the hope that it would make finding information in this book and on the Web easier.

Each chapter begins with an in-depth review of several of the sites that meet the criteria of the chapter. The review discusses the merits of the resources at the site, the multimedia aspects of the site (whether there are images or audio samples), and where the major hyperlinks on the home page take you. For example, Chapter 27, "International Web Resources," reviews the following home pages:

Gateway to Antarctica

New Zealand

Singapore Online Guide

Japan—Nippon Telephone and Telegraph Corporation

Window-to-Russia

After these reviews, the remainder of the chapter provides shorter summaries of other WWW sites. Here, for example, is one of the listings in Chapter 30, "Science," under the subcategory Meteorology:

Current Weather Maps and Movies

URL address: **http://rs560.cl.msu.edu/weather**

VI

Finding Web Resources

This weather database receives weather information from around and above the globe, including the Department of Meteorology at the University of Edinburgh, Scotland, and NASA readings. Maps in this database are updated every hour so that you can view weather patterns as they happen—almost as good as TV weather. In addition to still images, you can view (with the right software) weather movies.

The first line in each listing is either the actual name of the WWW home page or a description that tells you what you will find there. The second line is the URL (Uniform Resource Locator) address that you need to enter in your browser to get to the site. The following section provides a short overview of the resource.

URL Address Tips

Tip

If pages are loading too slowly, disable inline images. (You can always reload the page if you need or want to see an image.)

Hopefully, if you're ready to use a resource, you already have your WWW browser installed and know how to load it. For both Macintosh and Windows, this is a point-and-click procedure. After you find a resource that suits your needs or interest, you must load the URL address. (This procedure is described in detail in Chapter 6, "Navigating with Mosaic," for NCSA Mosaic for Windows.) Nine times out of ten, you will enter an address and be at your site within seconds. However, there are times when you can't connect. There are a few rules about URL addresses that will help prevent you from becoming frustrated:

Note

Some WWW sites are slower than others as a result of the telecommunications lines that get you to them. Always try a site that is in your region/country first to see if it has the information you need. This also helps reduce unnecessary burden on the entire Internet/WWW system.

■ Always make sure you enter the address exactly as it appears. Let's look at a few examples that show where problems can occur.

URL address: **http://www.latrobe.edu.au/Glenn/KiteSite/ Kites.html**

This is an address for a server that has information about the hobby of kite flying. The address begins with the http://. Notice that there are a few capital letters in the address. You must type uppercase letters if they are uppercase in the address. If you don't, you won't connect.

URL address: **http://herald.usask.ca/~maton/bahai.html**

This is the address of a WWW server that focuses on the Baha'i religion. The character ~ appears frequently in URL addresses. Again, you must have it. This character is the uppercase of the backwards apostrophe, usually found to the left of the number 1 on your keyboard.

URL address: **http://ananse.irv.uit.no/trade_law/nav/ trade.html**

This address connects you to a server in Norway that contains information about trade law. Notice that there is an underscore between the words trade and law. Make sure you put this in your address.

The number one reason for not connecting to a Web site is incorrectly entering the proper address. If you get an error message such as `Error Accessing` or `Failed DNS lookup`, enter the address a second time. You may have accidentally made a typographical error. Even an extra space in an address can prevent a connection.

■ Enter the URL address at the very beginning of the entry box. Some browsers will not connect if you have a space before the beginning of the address.

■ If a URL address doesn't work, try a root address. Many home pages actually reside in complex subdirectories on a computer. It's possible that the information has moved to another location on the computer. If you use a long, complex address and it doesn't work, try entering a shorter version of the address. This may connect to a higher directory where you'll be able to locate the information you need. For example, the following is the address for an electronic art gallery in New York City.

Tip

WWW documents and servers *do* change their addresses. Good ones will leave a forwarding address; bad ones just seem to disappear.

URL address: **http://www.egallery.com/egallery/ homepage.html**

The address tells you that this home page resides on a commercial server (**www.egallery.com**) that has a special area for the gallery. It's possible that the company also lets other vendors operate Web pages on the computer. If the full address doesn't work, try again but eliminate the ending:

URL address: **http://www.egallery.com/egallery**

And if that doesn't work, go one more step:

VI

Finding Web Resources

URL address: **http://www.egallery.com**

It's very likely that you will connect with the commercial company's home page and then be able to find links to the art gallery.

Troubleshooting Troublesome Addresses

You're certain that you entered the correct address and you still can't connect. All the WWW site addresses in this book have been carefully checked for accuracy. There are a few other things that can prevent a connection:

Tip
Don't give up on an address, because you may not connect for several reasons besides a bad address. For example, the server could be down or could only allow a certain number of users at a time.

- ■ *The host is busy.* Wait a few minutes (longer if necessary) and try again. By using the reload feature, you don't have to retype the URL address. With some 30 million plus people using the Internet, it's possible that the WWW server you are trying is busy with other people who are connecting. Or, the lines to the host may be overcrowded—like when you try to call home on Christmas day.

- ■ *The server is down.* The WWW server may be literally unplugged. Sometimes computers are pulled offline to be repaired or upgraded. Good WWW server owners will either use another computer during downtime, or do repair work during off hours. If the server is down, it can take between five minutes to five days before it is back online.

- ■ *The server/home page has moved.* It's possible for a server to get a new IP address. If this happens, your old address will no longer work. It's also possible for someone who maintains a home page to move his or her home page and data to another WWW computer. Responsible WWW home page owners will post a message that you receive when you try the URL. The message tells you the new address, and may have a hyperlink to the new server, which is similar to when you have the phone company place a forwarding message that plays when you move to a new home and get a new phone number. But, like the phone company, the WWW message may not last forever—be sure to write down the new address before it disappears!

- ■ *The server or home page has died.* Yes, it is possible for a server to completely vanish. You can be pretty confident that NASA will not permanently pull the plug on its WWW computer. However, with the increasing age of commercialism on the Net, it's possible that commercial companies or information providers who host WWW home pages may go out of business. If they do, the server is gone. More likely, however, some of the home pages for small businesses will come and go. After all, if Bill's Barber Shop doesn't get any new business after six months, Bill may decide not to sponsor the interactive haircut database. Likewise, if Joyce is a graduate student at a university and she operates a home page about rocket science, it may disappear when she graduates and no longer maintains the information. These are all worst-case scenarios. Ninety percent of the time you will be able to connect to a WWW site, but occasionally it's nice to know why you can't.

> **Note**
>
> If you're mysteriously not connecting to any of the resources, it is possible that your TCP/IP connection has been dropped. Depending upon your system and software, you may not realize it (unless you can hear the phone connection disconnect) and your system may, or may not, automatically try to reestablish the connection.

Tips for Web Navigation

Here are a few more tips that should make your journey through the Web more enjoyable. Many WWW home pages incorporate a lot of graphic images, often too many. Because the graphics are large files, it takes a long time to load them. The larger the graphic, or the more graphics on a home page, the longer it will be before you can actually use the information or links on the page. Some home pages take in excess of five minutes to load at 14.4 Kbps.

◀ See "What You See When a Document Is Loaded," p. 106

If you start to get bothered by the amount of time it takes to load and then use home pages, turn off the browser feature that lets these images load. In NCSA Mosaic (alpha 9), you can turn the graphics feature on or off by opening the **O**ptions menu and choosing Preferences. Then, a Preferences screen appears where you can select or deselect (check on or off) Display Inline Images which appears as an option on the Preferences General Tab screen. You save a tremendous amount of time when fully retrieving a home page. Then, if you find information that is exciting, you can always reload the home page after you turn on the graphics feature.

◀ See "Moving Backward and Forward," p. 104

VI

Finding Web Resources

◀ See "Moving Backward and Forward," p. 104

Another feature on browsers that is worth noting when it comes to Web navigation is the *cache*. Cache (pronounced "cash") is the amount of computer RAM memory that the program sets aside to store information about the home pages or documents you visit during a session. A larger cache means that you can store more of the home page HTML documents in your computer's memory. As a result, you can navigate or jump back to a site you have recently visited because it's still in your computer's memory—you don't actually reload the home page. There are some pros and cons here. A large cache means you can quickly jump back through two, three, or four home pages. The bad news is that an extremely large cache may hinder your computer's functionality—things may simply slow down. Start with the program's default, and then adjust as necessary.

◀ See "Quick Access to Your Favorite URLs," p. 135

As you journey through WWW sites, you'll find new home pages that you'll want to return to. It's easy to think, "Well, I'll be back there in a minute and then I'll write down that address." If you really like a home page, write down the address immediately, or, better yet, add it to the hotlist, quicklist, or bookmark in your browser. It's very easy to get lost in cyberspace and never find that home page again.

Finding the Elusive Resource: Web Searchers

With more than a 3,000 percent annual increase in the number of WWW sites, the resources available on the Web expand faster than you can possibly visit the sites. There are more than 10,000 WWW servers, and more than 1.5 million hypermedia documents, images, sound, and video files with URL addresses. The resources in this book will get you either to the information you need or to a Web page that has links to that information. However, the time will come when you're looking for something unique or esoteric, such as a tour guide company that will help you climb Mount Everest.

That's when you want to connect with one of the WWW *searchers*. Generally, searchers are computer programs that search the Web on a periodic basis collecting information about new Web documents and servers. Depending upon the searcher, the information collected may contain only the names and addresses of home pages, or it may also include information about the contents of a page, the words in a text-based document, or information about multimedia files. Other searchers don't go out to look for information, but rather ask people who create home pages to send in details of their page. In either case, the information is stored in a database that resides on the searcher's World Wide Web server.

You connect to a searcher just as you do any other WWW resource, by entering the URL address into your browser. When the searcher home page appears, you have an opportunity to enter keywords or phrases to search for resources that meet your needs. It's important to recognize that some browsers (or clients), like recent versions of NCSA Mosaic or Spry's Air Mosaic, support a *forms* feature. Developed by NCSA programmers, forms is a software program/code that allows users to interact by supplying information (or requests for information) to the HTTP-based Web server.

◀ See "Moving Backward and Forward," p. 104

◀ See "Interactive Forms," p. 349

The forms function enables your browser to present fill-in boxes that resemble forms on-screen. The form entry box can be used for several applications. You can enter keywords for a Web searcher search, supply order entry information (such as your credit card number and address) to purchase products online via the WWW, or supply comments that you send back to an editor of an electronic publication. Most Web browsers support the forms function (see fig. 19.1), but a few do not (see fig. 19.2). You can still perform keyword searches using these searchers, as they provide a link to an alternative interface. This interface opens a dialog box in your browser in which you can enter information.

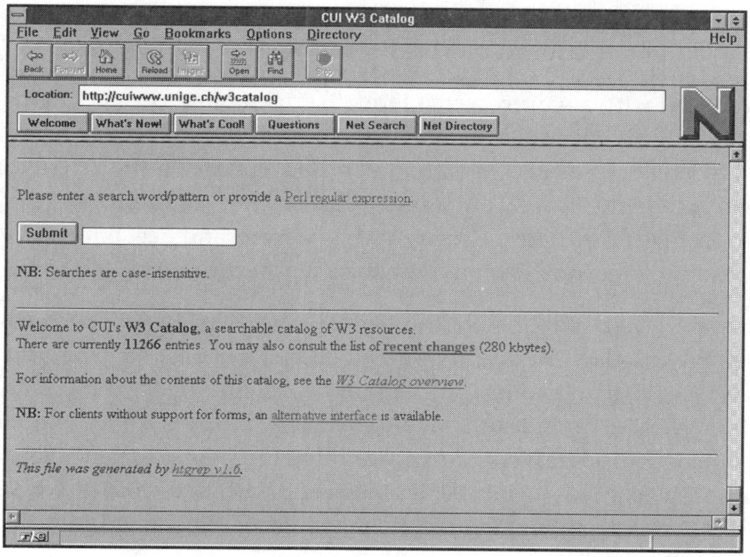

Fig. 19.1
The Netscape browser uses the forms interface in a search using the W3 Catalog. Enter your search words in the form box.

VI

Finding Web Resources

Fig. 19.2
The Cello browser
does not use the
forms interface.

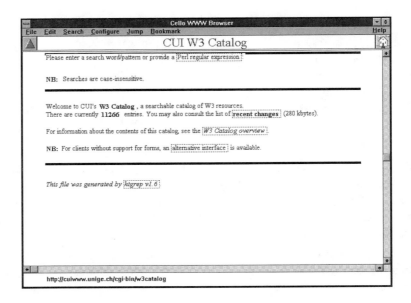

The result of a search is a list of Web locations that may contain the information you request, along with hyperlinks that take you directly to those sites. Sometimes, the list simply has the name of the home page. At other times, it includes a short description of what the site offers.

You can start with a narrow search term, like "climbing" or "Everest." However, it's unlikely this will find much. So, to continue your quest, broaden the search to single words like "mountains" or "adventure." If this doesn't work, go even broader to "travel" or "sports." One of these will probably get you to the peak of Everest. There are many Web searchers, and new ones appear all the time. The following sections describe a few of the best Web searchers.

The current generation of Web searchers do have a few flaws, which you'll notice fairly quickly. For one, they aren't all updated on a daily or even weekly basis, so you do miss some resources. Perhaps the biggest problem is that they're based on indexes that are created by humans. Unless a home page title or URL address contains a word that fits your search profile, or the creator of the page or document has indexed it with that word, it is possible to miss resources that meet your search criteria *and* get search results that *don't* meet your criteria.

For example, there may be a home page that contains links to "Stocks and Bonds" information. If you search for "money," the search could miss this page unless it has been identified with the word "money." Likewise, you will often get erroneous information from a search. For example, a keyword search for "money" produces a home page titled "Web T-Shirts" via one of the searchers. It is possible, although unlikely, that the T-shirts page offers apparel with images of money.

ALIWEB

URL address: **http://web.nexor.co.uk/public/aliweb/aliweb.html**

People who maintain a Web home page write descriptions of their services in the HTML file format. This file has a link to their home page. They then tell ALIWEB about the file, which ALIWEB retrieves and combines into a searchable database. The search input page for ALIWEB is shown in figure 19.3, and the results of an ALIWEB search is shown in figure 19.4.

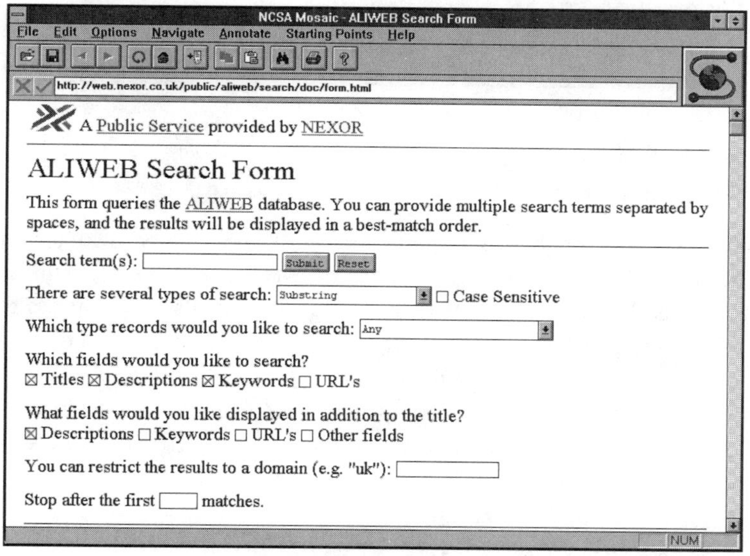

Fig. 19.3
There are several different front ends for ALIWEB; this is only one of them.

> **Note**
>
> The ALIWEB searcher is mirrored on several other Web servers. This means that the database and the search forms have been copied and are available for access via these other Web sites. For Web users who live in the U.S., the mirror site at Indiana University often has faster response time than the site in the United Kingdom. The URL address for the Indiana mirror site is: **http://www.cs.indiana.edu/aliweb/search**.

Fig. 19.4
The search looks
for matching
keywords in the
description of
what the site
offers.

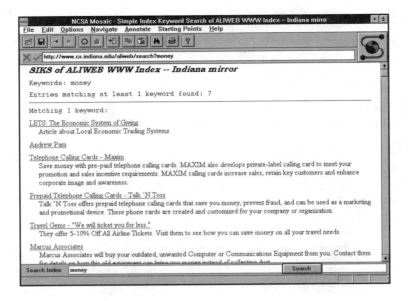

CUI Search Catalog

URL address: **http://cuiwww.unige.ch/w3catalog**

W3 Catalog is a searchable catalog of resources that's created from a number
of manually maintained lists available on the Web (see fig. 19.5). The result
of a search, as shown in figure 19.6, is a chronological list of resources that
meet your search criteria. Thus, if you do a search in January, the first entries
on the list represent sites that came online in January; later entries date back
to December, November, and so on. Listings also usually include short paragraph descriptions of the sites. The names of the sites (which are underlined)
are hyperlinks that take you to that site if you click it.

EINet Galaxy—Search the World Wide Web

URL address: **http://galaxy.einet.net/www/www.html**

This searcher maintains an index that points to Web home pages around the
world. Figure 19.7 shows an example of a search input page for EINet's
search; the results of the search are shown in figure 19.8. When you connect,
the home page automatically opens a search dialog box. The result of a search
is a name-only hyperlink list of possible resources. The list is prioritized in a
fashion similar to a WAIS (Wide Area Information Server) search, with the
first entry receiving 1,000 points and the remaining entries getting fewer

points. Each entry also indicates the size of the document or home page that you will jump to. This is useful because it tells you how long it will take to load that page.

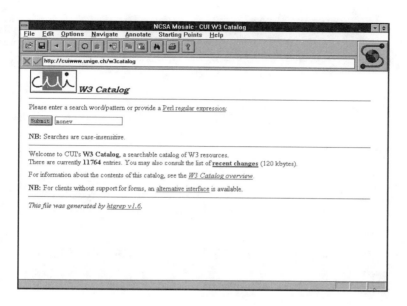

Fig. 19.5
The CUI W3 Catalog search form is very simple. It doesn't matter if you type in your search word(s) in upper- or lower-case.

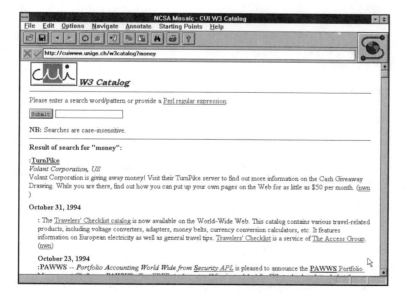

Fig. 19.6
Here is the result of a search for the keyword "money" with the CUI W3 Catalog.

Fig. 19.7
The search input page for EINet's search asks you to enter your keywords.

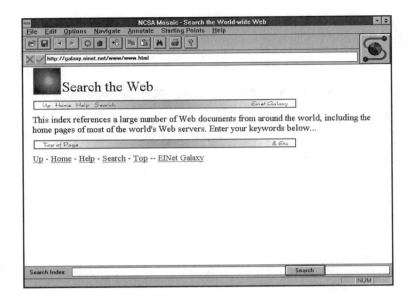

Fig. 19.8
The search results for EINet's search results in a succinct list, including a priority rating system and size of the documents and files.

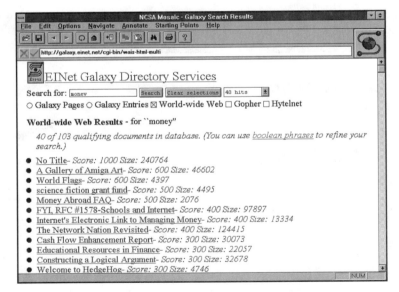

Global Network Academy Meta-Library

URL address: **http://uu-gna.mit.edu:8001/uu-gna/
meta-library/index.html**

GNA is a non-profit corporation based in Texas. Affiliated with the UseNet
University project, GNA has a long-term goal of creating a fully accredited

online university. This searcher is one of the information management tools that GNA offers. The search input page for GNA is shown in figure 19.9, and the results of the search are shown in figure 19.10.

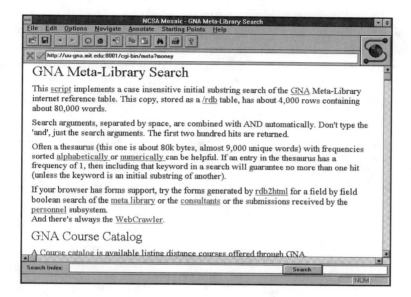

Fig. 19.9
You can use the search input page to find out more information about the Global Network Academy Meta-Library.

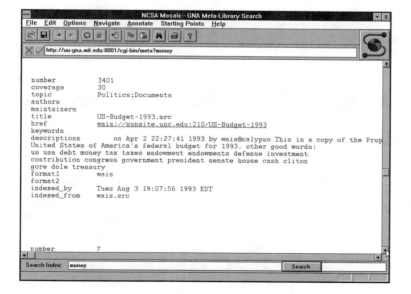

Fig. 19.10
You can see the results of the search with GNA.

VI

Finding Web Resources

Lycos

URL address: **http://lycos.cs.cmu.edu/**

Lycos is a research program that focuses on information retrieval and discovery in the WWW. You can see the search input page for Lycos in figure 19.11. Lycos currently does its retrieval based on abstracts of Web documents, and it claims to have a database of more than 1.5 million URLs. There are several computers connected to this searcher, and you can pick and choose the one that is currently the least busy, which means you'll get your results faster. You can see the search results page for Lycos in figure 19.12, which includes descriptive text with the search term highlighted.

Fig. 19.11
The search input page for Lycos is ready to receive your keyword to begin the search.

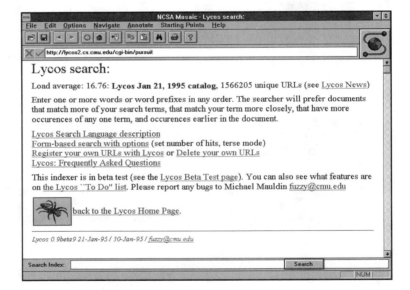

Nomad Gateway

URL address: **http://www.rns.com/cgi-bin/nomad**

This Web resource searching site represents a joint effort between Rockwell Network Systems and Cal Poly, San Luis Obispo, to develop a pool of replicated Web resource locators (see fig. 19.13). The result of your search is a list of single line entries, each of which is a hyperlink to another Web resource (see fig. 19.14).

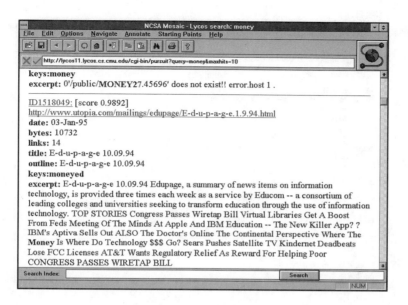

Fig. 19.12
The search results page for Lycos. The search for the keyword "money" retrieved 2,000 documents.

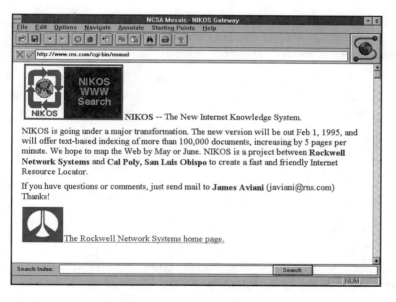

Fig. 19.13
The search input page for Nomad.

Fig. 19.14
The search results for Nomad.

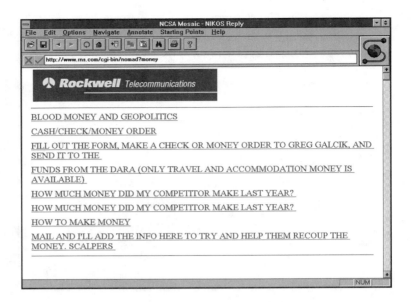

WebCrawler Searcher

URL address: **http://webcrawler.cs.washington.edu/WebCrawler/ Home.html**

Developed by Brian Pinkerton at the University of Washington, the WebCrawler program focuses on accumulating information about the specific documents that reside on Web servers; the search input page is shown in figure 19.15. It creates indexes of the documents it locates on the Web and lets you search these indexes. The result of a search is a list of sites, home pages, and documents that match your criteria. As shown in figure 19.16, the list is prioritized—the first resource receives a rating of 1,000 and should most closely match your criteria, while a resource farther down on the list is less likely to match.

WWWW—The World Wide Web Worm

URL address: **http://www.cs.colorado.edu/home/mcbryan/ WWWW.html**

This searcher gets used more than 300,000 times every month. You can see the search input page in figure 19.17; the search results are shown in figure 19.18. The home page tells us, "The Worm scours the Web for resources and provides search capabilities on its database of 300,000 multimedia objects."

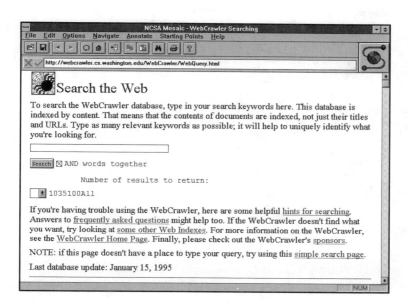

Fig. 19.15
The search input page for the WebCrawler.

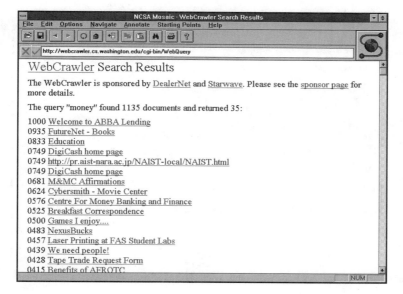

Fig. 19.16
The results of a WebCrawler search provide a priority-based list of hyperlinks to resources.

Fig. 19.17
The search input page for the World Wide Web Worm offers several types of searches, including a search by home page title and names of URLs.

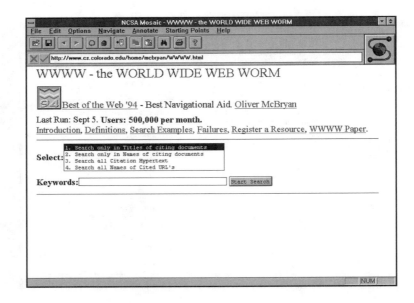

Fig. 19.18
The search results from World Wide Web Worm contain one match—Myers Equity Express.

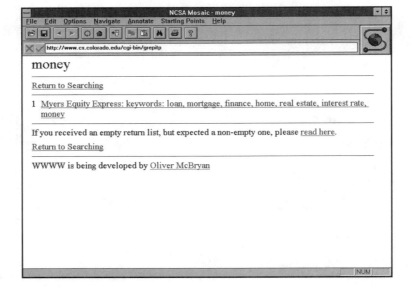

Yahoo

URL address: **http://akebono.stanford.edu/yahoo**

Yahoo is a comprehensive database of Web sites and pages. There are more than 27,000 entries that reference different Web resources (see fig. 19.19).

The site adds about 100 to 200 new links each day. Web pages are organized into subject categories such as art, entertainment, and social sciences. The results of a Yahoo search put links into these subject categories, as shown in figure 19.20. You can search the entire database for specific keyword matches. According to the statistics (which are available via a link on the home page), the site has had more than 2.5 million visits.

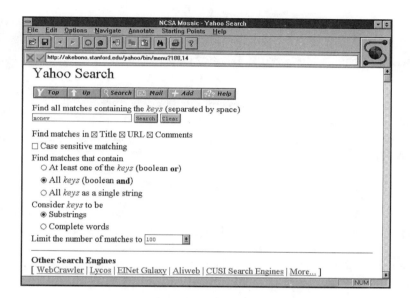

Fig. 19.19
With links to more than 27,000 entries, Yahoo has become a very popular Web searcher.

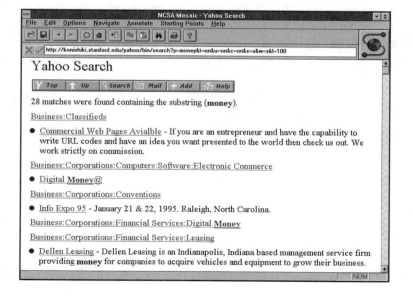

Fig. 19.20
The results of a Yahoo search put links into subject categories.

WWW Directories and Index Home Pages

Unlike the searchers, the following WWW home pages are directories and indexes of searchers. The directories represent a list of resources that you may find useful. You can cross-reference the subjects and resources in these directories. The indexes are pages that have pointers to, or search boxes for, several different Web searchers.

Global News Network Directory

URL address: **http://nearnet.gnn.com/gnn/GNNhome.html**

GNN is a directory of the resources compiled by this commercial service. Many links in this directory are to businesses and companies.

Harvest

URL address: **http://harvest.cs.colorado.edu/brokers/www-home-pages/query.html**

This site indexer has links to some 21,500 WWW home pages. One of the Harvest pages states, "Harvest is an integrated set of tools to gather, extract, organize, search, cache, and replicate relevant information across the Internet. With modest effort, users can tailor Harvest to digest information in many different formats, and offer custom search services on the Internet. Moreover, Harvest makes very efficient use of network traffic, remote servers, and disk space."

NCSA What's New

URL address: **http://www.ncsa.uiuc.edu/SDG/Software/Mosaic/Docs/archive-whats-new.html**

This home page provides a month-by-month, year-by-year list of new WWW resources (see fig. 19.21).

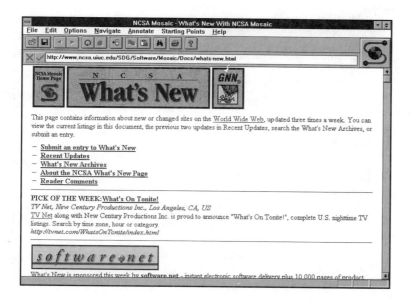

Fig. 19.21
The What's New
catalog home page.

W3 Search Engines

URL address: **http://cuiwww.unige.ch/meta-index.html**

This is the same computer system that brings you the CUI Catalog. Here the home page presents a list of several different Web searchers. Next to the name of each searcher is a box where you can enter your search phrase and then submit it directly to the searcher. As an alternative, you can click the name of the searcher and go to its home page.

Web of Wonder

URL Address: **http://www.digimark.net/wow**

This is a hierarchical list of more than 6,000 links from all over the world.

World Wide Web Virtual Library

URL address: **http://info.cern.ch/hypertext/DataSources/bySubject/ Overview.html**

This is a subject catalog that begins with the subject of Aboriginal Studies (see fig. 19.22) and ends with Unidentified Flying Objects, providing access to a wide range of categories.

VI

Finding Web Resources

Fig. 19.22
The main subject
listing appears in
the Virtual
Library.

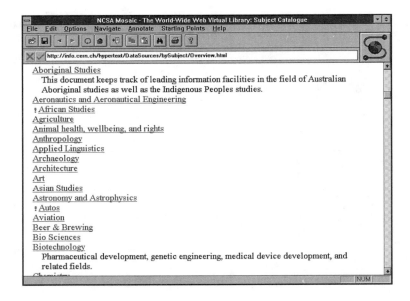

Now get going and enjoy the resources in this book as you explore the information, services, and multimedia that the World Wide Web offers.

From Here...

This chapter provided an overview of the tools and techniques which make it easier for you to locate information and Web sites to match your requirements, interests, or hobbies. From here you'll find other useful navigational techniques in the following chapters:

- Chapter 6, "Navigating with Mosaic," describes how you use NCSA Mosaic to navigate through the Web.

- Chapter 7, "Mosaic Shortcuts and Tips," provides some techniques for getting from here to there in the fastest way possible using the NCSA Mosaic browser.

- Chapters 20–32 provide listings of Web pages on many topics.

Chapter 20

Art, Music, and Entertainment

by Bill Eager

One of the most powerful applications of the World Wide Web is the storage and distribution of multimedia. Artists, musicians, gallery owners, museum curators, and library directors take advantage of this aspect of the Web. You can view a painting by Georgia O'Keefe, listen to audio samples of ZZ Top music, or review the schedule for next week's satellite television broadcasts.

Electronic museums represent a new avenue for the public display of art. Now, rather than waiting for museum hours or pushing through crowds to view a masterpiece, you can connect to an electronic museum, such as the Frederick R. Weisman Art Museum, and leisurely browse through works of art. If your taste runs more toward current endeavors, visit an exhibition in an online New York art gallery (where you can even buy a painting if you see one you like), glance through scripts of *Star Trek* episodes, or download a collection of songs by the music group Quagmire.

Art is universal. You can appreciate a painting created by a Japanese painter of the 13th century as easily as a print created in the 1950s by an American artist. Art on the Web makes it simple to transcend some of the cultural and linguistic barriers that occur when we try to communicate with people in foreign countries. The diversity of art, music, and entertainment on the Web is tremendous; you can find a resource that will help you develop a research paper on Greek architecture as easily as you can pull up a review of the latest Tom Hanks movie.

Collections can be quite large and WWW home pages frequently incorporate search mechanisms that help you locate a specific work of art or information

▶ See "Authors," p. 811

about a specific artist or musician. If your keyword search doesn't produce the results you want, try to broaden the search, perhaps from "New Orleans Jazz" to simply "Jazz." Many of the home pages listed here have links to other art-based WWW resources—so, jump in and have fun.

The broad categories for these resources include:

- Art
- Dance
- Movies
- Museums
- Music
- Publications
- Television
- Radio

Cardiff's Movie Database

URL address: **http://www.msstate.edu/Movies**

Fig. 20.1
You can search Cardiff's WWW Movie Database to find out about films and the many people that played a role (acting, writing, and directing) in each movie.

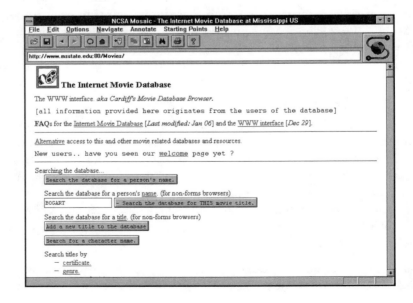

Have you ever watched a movie, trying to recall the name of the actress or actor? Or placed a bet with a friend that you can name the entire cast of *The Maltese Falcon*? Or wondered how many movies Henry Fonda and Paul Newman starred in together? If you've ever had any question about a movie regarding plot, characters, actors, actresses, directors, writers, or anything else, this is the home page for you!

A hypertext front-end to the **rec.arts.movies** newsgroup database, this is a wonderful example of interactive information. The home page provides a variety of search options that let you enter names of characters, actors, or movie titles to begin a search. The information is vast. The database contains more than 85,000 listings of actors and actresses, some 34,835 titles (including TV series), and 1,500 plot summaries.

As an example of how this works, click the home page button that is labeled "Search the database for a person's name." A new page appears where you can enter the last name **HOLDEN** for a name search. This query delivers a list of approximately 35 Holdens (Amy Holden Jones, the writer; David Holden, the writer; Gloria Holden, the actress, and William Holden, the actor). Now click William Holden to get a list of some 72 films he acted in. You didn't know he was a character in the 1967 film *Casino Royale*? Click this film name and you get a description of the film that tells you it was a James Bond spoof originally written by Ian Fleming and that many other actors and actresses, including Woody Allen, were in the film.

EXPO Ticket Office

URL address: **http://sunsite.unc.edu/expo/ticket_office.html**

This is a WWW must-visit! The home page refers to the EXPO Ticket Office as "the world's most exciting electronic exposition." This isn't far off. From the home page, you can jump onto one of six guided tour buses that take you to one of the six EXPO pavilions (buses leave every few microseconds). Selections include:

The *Vatican Exhibit* includes precious maps, books, and manuscripts.

The *Soviet Archive* boasts of being the first public display of secret Russian records.

1492: An On-Going Voyage examines the events that settled the "new world."

Dead Sea Scrolls describes the history and discovery of these artifacts.

The *Paleontology Exhibit* includes fossil life from the University of California, Berkeley.

The *Spalato Exhibit* describes the history and architecture of this Roman village.

Fig. 20.2
You can jump on board an interactive bus tour and visit six interesting pavilions at the EXPO Ticket Office.

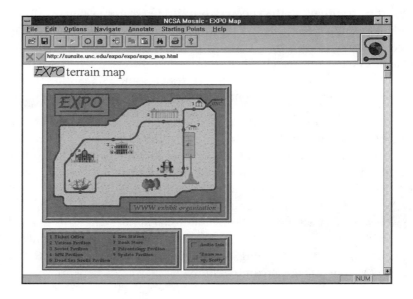

Most of the information and multimedia exhibits were donated by the Library of Congress. What makes this Web resource unique is the interactive manner in which you move through information. As you move through one of the pavilions, a little icon of footsteps appears to help guide your journey. From the home page, you can jump to an almost 3-D map that shows the location of the pavilions and includes an audio clip.

There is even an EXPO restaurant, Le Cordon Bleu, for the weary traveler. Every day of the week there is a different menu; Wednesday's special is split pea soup with bacon, sorrel, and lettuce. Inline GIF images display your electronic lunch. Have fun!

Traditional Folk Song Database

URL address: **http://web2.xerox.com/digitrad**

This server provides a searchable index of the Digital Traditional Folk Song database. The database contains the lyrics and music for thousands of folk songs, many esoteric, with some including audio sample files that you can play. Dick Greenhaus and his friends are credited with developing this collection.

To find a song, you perform a keyword search. Search results bring up a list of songs that either contain or relate to your search word. You click a song name to retrieve the lyrics. A search using the word "Russian" delivers "It's Sister Jenny's Turn To Throw the Bomb," whereas a search for the keyword "Spring" produces four songs: "Birds In the Spring," "So Early In the Spring," "Flower Carol," and "Spring Glee." This is a fun and extensive resource—try it out!

The Online Museum of Singapore Art & History

URL address: **http://king.ncb.gov.sg/nhb/museum.html**

Fig. 20.3
Travel around the world and back in time when you download images from this online collection of historical artwork from the Museum of Singapore.

Art history offers a unique opportunity to appreciate artistic endeavors from another era and a chance to learn about society and life at a particular point in time. The Online Museum of Singapore Art & History lets you explore paintings and documents by early Singapore artists. One of the exhibitions is a collection of 19th-century prints of Singapore.

When you click the title for a print, a picture of the artwork appears along with a description of the piece and an overview of the artist. This particular exhibition is interesting because many of the prints show you images of Singapore in the early 1800s—not only do you get to travel halfway around the world to view the artwork, you also travel back in time.

For example, when you select "Plate 5: View from the Mouth of the Singapore River, 1830," you get a wonderful image that shows a view of Singapore from the mouth of the river. You can "look" upstream and see where European merchants used warehouses for their products.

You can view and save the pictures as JPEG files—even start your own personal museum of images in your PC. You can also learn about the artists, engravers, and specific details about each print, such as their size (this one was 31.5 × 23 cm) and where they currently are stored or displayed. Other choices from the main menu include:

Pioneer Artists	Early Singapore artists
Raffles Revisited	A history of the founder of Singapore
Ponts des Art	Explores the influence on area artists who studied in France
From Ritual to Romance	An exhibition of paintings inspired by Bali

Star Trek: The Next Generation

URL address: **http://www.ee.surrey.ac.uk/Personal/STTNG/ index.html**

Fig. 20.4
Connect with this Star Trek Web site to find out whether Klingons really like humans.

It is the year 2364 and the phrase "Beam Me Up" transmits across the galaxy. This WWW server is located in the UK, where, despite its non prime-time slot, ST:TNG (the abbreviation for Star Trek: The Next Generation) often came in as one of the top 10 rated shows for BBC2, sometimes the highest rated show on the channel.

The home page has so many links that you don't have time to visit the Holosuite. There is information about the cast, guest roles, descriptions of all major alien species (even the nasty Borg), episode summaries, and movie rumors. A trivia section keeps you busy with facts like Professor Steven Hawking (the famous physicist) is the only person to ever appear as himself in the show. Here is one example of an episode summary:

Peak Performance

A simulated war game turns deadly when the crew is ambushed by a Ferengi battleship. With the Enterprise crippled in the attack, Picard must try to get Riker, Geordi, and the others back on board.

> **Note**
>
> For trekkies who are devoted to every Star Trek series there's also a Star Trek Voyager page at **http://voyager.paramount.com**.

CBC Radio Trial

URL address: **http://debra.dgbt.doc.ca/cbc/cbc.html**

The Canadian Broadcasting Corporation and the New Broadcast Services Laboratory of the Communications Research Centre (CRC), in association with the Communications Development and Planning Branch of Industry Canada, sponsor this WWW radio service.

From the home page, you can jump to a list of CBC radio products, an overview of the available program transcripts, program listings, and samples of digital radio programs. The digital radio program files are in the AU audio file format. A 10-minute story takes approximately 5M. Program samples include:

- *Quirks and Quarks*. CBC Radio's science program.

- *The Idea of Canada*. A program in which Canadians talk about what Canada means to them.

- *Sunday Morning*. A current affairs program.

- *Basic Black*. A program featuring people who have unusual jobs and hobbies.

- *Brand X*. A pop culture entertainment magazine.

> **Note**
>
> Another WWW site, **http://www.cs.cmu.edu:8001/Web/Unofficial/
> Canadiana/CBC-News.html**, maintains audio files of the daily Canadian Broadcast
> News programs.

Art

Art on the Web includes all the forms that exist in the real world. There are paintings, sculpture, and photography. This section is broken first into "Art Study, Research, and Resources," which includes databases of historical art, mailing lists, and so on. The section "Artists" displays the works of individual artists; "Sculpture" shows the 3-D world of art; "Exhibits and Galleries" shows both temporary and permanent collections; and "Photography" includes both color and black-and-white images.

Art Study, Research, and Resources

African Art: Aesthetics and Meaning
URL address: **http://www.lib.virginia.edu/dic/exhib/93.ray.aa/
African.html**

This site is an electronic exhibition catalog sponsored by the Bayly Art Museum and the University of Virginia, Charlottesville, Virginia. This Web server is a nice introduction and exhibition of African art, with links to elements of the African aesthetic, the exhibition, and a detailed bibliography.

Architecture—ANU Art History
URL address: **http://rubens.anu.edu.au**

This Web server offers a variety of art-history images. There are two image databases you can access from the main page. One includes 2,800 images and associated descriptions about the history of printmaking from the 15th century to the end of the 19th century.

A second collection includes images that focus on the classical architecture of the Mediterranean. For the prints collection, users can choose between menus that provide inline images and ones that don't. The server is adding an additional 2,500 images of classical architecture and architectural sculpture in this collection.

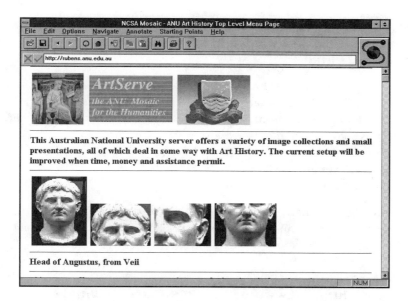

Some main menu selections include database access to prints, print history, the architecture of Islam, a few images of contemporary Hong Kong architecture, a brief illustrated tour of a few of the classical sites in Turkey, and work at the Canberra School of Art.

ArtSource

URL address: **http://www.uky.edu/Artsource/artsourcehome.html**

This is a gathering point for networked resources on art and architecture. The content is diverse and includes pointers to resources around the Net, as well as original materials submitted by librarians, artists, and art historians. You can select discipline-specific resources, general resources, and bibliographies from the home page. There are also links to art journals, image collections, and electronic exhibitions.

Art Topics Mailing Lists

URL address: **http://www.willamette.edu/~jpatters/art-lists.html**

Perhaps you prefer to talk about art rather than simply look at it. This Web page has a list of more than 100 art-related mailing lists. From the "Ceramic Arts" discussion list to the "Medieval Performing Arts" list, you are sure to find a group of other people who share your specific interest in the arts.

Fine Art Forum
URL address: **http://www.msstate.edu/Fineart_Online/art-resources.html**

This home page provides a directory of links to different art resources on the Web. The broad categories that you start with include Events, General and Academic Resources, Electronic Art, Galleries, and E-journals and Individual Artists. It is a great place to start exploring art on the WWW.

University of Art and Design
URL address: **http://www.uiah.fi/**

The University of Art and Design in Helsinki provides information on the International Symposium on Electronic Art (ISEA) and the International Conference on Color Education.

World Art Treasures
URL address: **http://sgwww.epfl.ch/BERGER/index.html**

This Web project is a collaboration between the J. E. Berger Foundation and the Swiss Federal Institute of Technology. As the home page states: "Its principal purpose is to promulgate the discovery and love of art." You can start your journey into these treasures by selecting a link to one of two programs. Program one offers 100 images from different civilizations (Egypt, China, India, Japan). The second program is a visual and historic pilgrimage to Abydos, a site in ancient Egypt. Text is available in both English and French.

Artists

Berryhill, Tom—Pictures and Poetry
URL address: **http://wimsey.com/anima/NEXUS/TomStuff/Travelling.html**

The online hyperbook, "Travelling with Light," by Tom Berryhill is a collection of the artist's poetry and pictures connected through hypertext links. Features include options to browse just the pictures or the poetry, or to just follow the links that bring you through this interesting collection. Also featured are clickable pictures that download into a JPEG viewer for modification by the reader.

Dali, Salvador
URL address: **http://www.eunet.es/spain/images-dali/**

Do you remember the famous melting clocks in Salvador Dali's painting "La Persistenciade la Memoria" (translated "The Persistence of Memory")? This is one of the color images that loads on the home page of this Web server, which is in Spain, homeland to Salvador Dali. If you have your inline images turned on, be prepared for a *long* load time as the home page has numerous GIF images of Dali's work. Even though the small amount of text is in Spanish, you can easily find the images you want.

Di Leo, Belinda
URL address: **http://gort.ucsd.edu/mw/bdl.html**

The paintings in "Ancestry: Religion, Death, and Culture" document the native culture of Central Appalachia. The work portrays the character and spirit of this region of the country. Originally shown as a University of California, San Diego MFA Project, Appalachian artist Belinda Di Leo explores relationships between religion and death.

Jacobsen, John E.
URL address: **http://amanda.physics.wisc.edu/show.html**

"Strange Interactions" is a WWW art show of paintings, drawings, and prints by this artist.

Kandinsky, Wassily (1866–1944)
URL address: **gopher://libra.arch.umich.edu/11/Kandinsky**

This Gopher site contains some text files about modern artist Kandinsky, as well as several GIF files that you can view online or download.

Menczer, Erico
URL address: **http://www-cse.ucsd.edu/users/fil/erico.html**

Here you find the home page for a painter, photographer, and cinematographer from Rome, Italy. This is a gallery containing his biography and some of his paintings (acrylic on wood) and photographs.

Sculpture

Research into Artifacts
URL address: **http://brains.race.u-tokyo.ac.jp/RACE.html**

From the University of Tokyo, Japan, this WWW site and its links explore the relationship between art, technology, and the environment. There are links to an artist-in-residence program, images, and descriptions of the professors involved in these efforts.

Sculpture Tour
URL address: **http://loki.ur.utk.edu/sculpture/sculpt.html**

This Web site contains photographs of the pieces included in the 1992–93 Sculpture Tour of the Knoxville campus. In all there are 26 separate pieces of sculpture located on campus. You can jump to GIF images of each piece (the files are 100K+ but resolution is quite good), and learn a little about the artist who created the work.

Galleries and Exhibits

911 Gallery
URL address: **http://www.iquest.net/911/iq_911.html**

The "real" 911 is in Indiana and it specializes in art based on electronic media—so the Web is a good place to showcase their work. From the home page you can jump to either the current exhibit or to previous shows. Some examples of what you'll find include small images of computer-generated art displayed on screens or printed on canvas, and video art. Some of the art carries a price tag just in case you want to buy.

Access Art
URL address: **http://www.mgainc.com/Art/HomePage.html**

This is the home page for a commercial service run by Medium for Global Access, which helps artists and collectors connect electronically. You can access links to artists like William Buffet, Edson Campos, Olivia Deerardinis, Ted Kimer, Jean-Giraud Moebius, and Alberto Vargas. See their work and use an on-screen order form to add art to your collection. One home page link lets you look at art by subject category, such as fantasy or landscape.

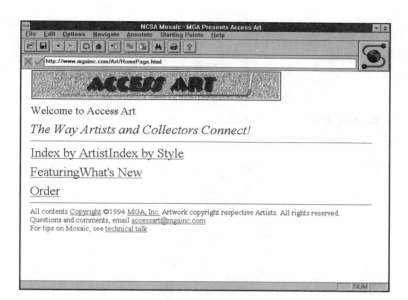

Fig. 20.6
This WWW gallery lets you look at artwork in several different media and categories (such as landscapes).

Asian Art

URL address: **http://www.nets.com/asianart**

Trek through exhibitions in private galleries, new and rare color publications, and discoveries in Asian Art. One typical link is to the Himalayan Art image bank, which provides a sample of antique Himalayan sculpture and paintings.

Electric Gallery

URL address: **http://www.egallery.com/egallery/homepage.html**

You can forget the expenses involved in flying to the Big Apple, renting a limousine and tuxedo, and fighting traffic to visit an exclusive art gallery. Now you can appreciate quality art electronically via the WWW; the Electric Gallery contains an ever-changing collection of paintings.

FineArt Forum Gallery

URL address: **http://www.msstate.edu/Fineart_Online/gallery.html**

To browse through several areas in this electronic gallery, you need a JPEG viewer. The Gallery is constantly being expanded and developed. Some installations include:

Joseph DeLappe—Recent Work

Helaman Ferguson—Mathematics in Stone and Bronze

Celeste Brignac—Photographs

Kaleidospace—Artists and Multimedia
URL address: **http://kspace.com**

Fig. 20.7
The graphic display on the Kaleidospace home page is "mapped"—when you click different sections you jump to various art-related areas, including painting and music.

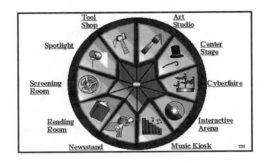

Kaleidospace provides a WWW site for the promotion of independent artists, musicians, performers, CD-ROM authors, writers, animators, and filmmakers. Artists provide samples of their work, which Kaleidospace integrates into a multimedia display available via the Internet.

Media West Editions
URL address: **http://www.wimsey.com/Pixel_Pushers**

Media West Editions showcases digital artists for the Pixel Pushers Exhibition of Original Digital Art. Included in the line-up are Oscar-winning composer and musician, Buffy Sainte-Marie; some of Canada's graphic artists, including Yuri Dojc and Louis Fishauf; Vancouver-based typographer, Stephen Herron; and digital art innovators from the U.S., including Diane Fenster, Jeff Brice, Helen Golden, and Kai Krause.

Ohio State University at Newark
URL address: **http://www.cgrg.ohio-state.edu:80/mkruse/osu.html**

The Ohio State University at Newark Art Gallery made its exhibition "Roy Lichtenstein Pre-Pop, 1948–1960" available for view via the WWW. The Art Gallery includes over 30 works of the famous American artist, most of which have never been shown to the public. This exhibition provides insight into how the Lichtenstein arrived at his famous Pop Style. The Art Gallery also exhibits local, national, and international artists.

REIFF II Electronic Museum
URL address: **http://www.informatik.rwth-aachen.de/Reiff2**

If you enjoy German art (and can read German), you may enjoy this Web site. The art association "Mehrwert e.V." is online. Its staff has established an electronic museum, REIFF II, which is open for all Internet users. The Museum was developed in cooperation with the Department of History of Art, the Center of Computing, and the Department of Computer Science.

Photography

Ansel Adams
URL address: **http://bookweb.cwis.uci.edu:8042/AdamsHome.html**

This site houses an exhibition of photographs by Ansel Adams called "Fiat Lux." You can browse through the digital photographs, which comprise his portrait of the University of California created for the 1968 Centennial celebration.

California Museum of Photography
URL address: **gopher://galaxy.ucr.edu/11/Campus%20Events**

This provides an overview of photo exhibits and schedules for exhibits held at the California Museum of Photography, located at the University of California, Riverside.

Jazz Photography of Ray Avery
URL address: **http://bookweb.cwis.uci.edu:8042/Jazz/jazz.html**

Here is an interesting combination of two art forms. Learn about Ray Avery—a photographer who took pictures of jazz greats and has more than 100 album covers to his credit. There are links to special exhibits of his work and also links with music by the musicians and an extensive discography.

Peoria Art Guild—Online Juried Art
URL address: **http://www.bradley.edu/exhibit/index.html**

Fig. 20.8
Tour through the galleries in this electronic photo exhibition.

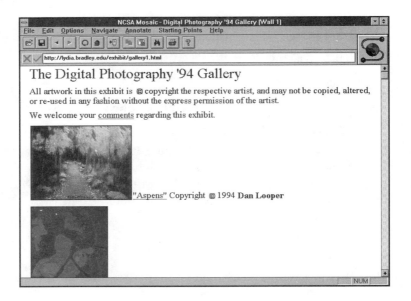

The Peoria Art Guild of Peoria, Illinois, provides this electronic version of their juried exhibition "Digital Photography '94." This exhibit has entries nationwide from photographers whose work involves digital photography. You move from the home page into electronic galleries where inline images of the photographs appear. Click the inline image to download or display a complete JPEG image of the photograph.

Dance

American Dance Festival

URL address: **http://www.nando.net/adf/adfmain.html**

Fig. 20.9
Visit this Web site and learn about the American Dance Festival, which orchestrates and sponsors dance perfor- mances across the country.

Established in 1934 in Bennington, Vermont, the American Dance Festival (ADF) encompasses a school with 350 professional and pre-professional dancers. Currently at Duke University in Durham, North Carolina, the ADF has sponsored more than 350 premieres and hosted major American modern dance companies. This resource has a complete schedule of ADF events and activities.

Dance & Technology

URL address: **http://www.dance.ohio-state.edu/files/ Dance_and_Technology/tech-menu.html**

This is an Ohio State WWW server that promotes the combination of technology and dance. It provides information that encourages people in dance to investigate the cutting edge applications of dance and technology, including the use of computers with dance performances. There is research, a bibliography, and a listing of "Who Is Doing What & Where."

Global Dance Directory

URL address: **ftp://ftp.std.com/pub/dance**

This is a Gopher site that has extensive information on global dance resources, including the countries of Brazil, Ireland, Spain, Venezuela, and Yugoslavia. There is also dance clipart, dance steps documents, and access to the **rec.arts.dance** newsgroup.

International Association of Gay Square Dance Clubs

URL address: **http://hawg.stanford.edu/~sgreen/IAGSDC/**

The IAGSDC is an organization of 40 modern western square dancing clubs throughout the U.S. and Canada. Information provided at this site includes details of programs and a convention that attracts more than 1,000 dancers.

Ohio State University, Department of Dance Home Page

URL address: **http://www.dance.ohio-state.edu**

This is a WWW server that focuses on original material related to dance. Topics include dance history, musicians in dance, and dance resources.

UK-Dance

URL address: **http://www.tecc.co.uk/public/tqm/uk-dance/**

This resource includes information and stories on clubs, parties, events, record shops, and radio, with a focus on the underground dance and the music scene in the United Kingdom. It also provides details on an Internet mailing list for people to discuss dance music culture in the U.K.

Movies

Buena Vista Pictures

URL address: **http://bvp.wdp.com/BVPM**

This site belongs to a division of the Walt Disney Company. It's a great source for information and previews of movies from Walt Disney Pictures, Touchstone Pictures, and Hollywood Pictures. Visit the Movie Plex, where you find movie trailers in QuickTime format, a trivia game, and movie gossip. There are also JPEG stills from films and press kits. If you don't have QuickTime, there are links to players for UNIX, Macintosh, and Windows.

Computer Animation—ReZn8 Productions

URL address: **http://www.rezn8.com**

ReZn8 is a Hollywood animation and video graphics production company that serves clients ranging from ABC to Disney. You can see some sample graphics and even view a short movie trailer from the action film *Clear and Present Danger*.

Computer Animation

URL address: **http://mambo.ucsc.edu/psl/thant/thant.html**

This great site has more than 100 links — in alphabetical order — to sites on the Web that serve computer animations and videos. Try an animation of the Big Bang, or a QuickTime movie of the music group Pearl Jam.

MCA Universal Cyberwalk

URL address: **http://www.mca.com**

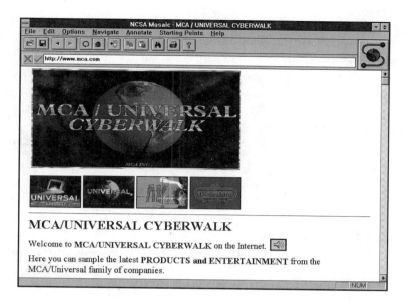

Fig. 20.10
The MCA/
Universal Web site
provides multime-
dia previews of
current files. Lots
of graphics here!

Do you like entertainment? This Web site is devoted to exploring, reading about, and being entertained by movies and music from MCA/Universal. There are interactive previews of movies. You can, for example, jump into a multimedia presentation about the action-adventure film *Street Fighter,* where you receive reports on the crisis in the imaginary country where the action occurs. Or, join movie stars for gala premieres of new films. It's fun and it's funky—but be warned—the home page loads slowly with a lot of graphics!

Movies

URL address: **http://www.vortex.com**

This site links to several interesting topics. You can read film reviews and news about film and television releases, publicity photos, and audio/video clips in "Professor Neon's TV & Movie Mania." You also can learn about the history of computing when you connect with the Computer History Association of California. Last, but not least, you can check out the Los Angeles weather conditions.

Movies Database

URL address: **http://www.cm.cf.ac.uk/Movies**
URL address: **http://ballet.cit.gu.edu.au/Movies/**

VI

Finding Web Resources

The Web interface to the **rec.arts.movies** database is mirrored in the U.S. and in Australia. There is information on over 30,000 titles, 75,000 actors and actresses, 6,500 directors, and 7,900 writers. All the information can be searched. Whether you are a movie fan or just need answers to movie trivia questions, this is for you.

Movie Reviews

URL address: **http://b62528.student.cwru.edu/reviews/reviews.html**

This WWW home page offers movie reviews. Some movies reviewed here include *Evil Dead, Army of Darkness, Crimewave,* and *Darkman.* It doesn't look like *Mary Poppins* will be reviewed any time soon.

UseNet Postings on Movies

URL address: **http://www.lysator.liu.se/sf_archive/sub/movies.html**

These postings to UseNet focus on science fiction movies. Many reviews are indexed by title.

Wisdom and Lore

URL address: **http://cad.ucla.edu/repository/useful/useful.html**

From UCLA, this is a WWW home page that offers an enormous hodge-podge of information. Much of it is about entertainment, movies, and literature, including things to do in L.A. There's a kosher restaurant city guide, hypertext movie information, movie info lists (actors and actresses), movie rating information, and ratings such as the Billboard charts and Nielson TV ratings.

Museums

Frederick R. Weisman Art Museum

URL address: **http://www.micro.umn.edu/weisman/museum.html**

Although it says the museum hours are 10:00 a.m. to 6:00 p.m., you can use the WWW to view many of the museum's collections any time, day or night. Small icons of individual paintings are displayed, and when you click them you can view full-frame images of artwork by the likes of Georgia O'Keefe and Robert Motherwell. GIF and JPEG images are the choices offered.

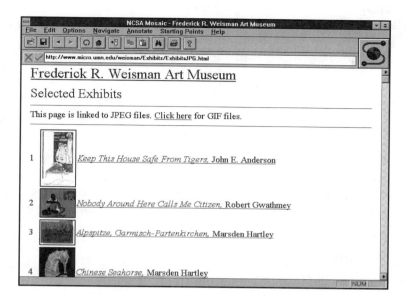

Fig. 20.11
This WWW site shows paintings by some of America's most famous 20th-century artists.

Le WebLouvre

URL address: **http://mistral.enst.fr/~pioch/louvre**

Take a trip to Paris. Start with an inline image of the Pyramid in front of the Louvre. This collection of electronic paintings is maintained by Nicolas Pioch. The server won a "Best of the Web 1994" award in the category of "Best Use of Multiple Media." You should know that this server/resource is not officially connected with the Louvre in Paris.

La Trobe University Art Museum

URL address: **http://www.latrobe.edu.au/Glenn/Museum/ ArtMuseumHome.html**

Located in Australia, this museum hosts a variety of exhibitions, including painting and sculpture. Jump from the home page to an overview of the current exhibition, where a series of color thumbnails of the artwork is displayed. Then, if you want, you can retrieve a more detailed JPEG image of any work of art. Be prepared for slow load times.

VI

Finding Web Resources

Music Hall
URL address: **http://www.ncsa.uiuc.edu/SDG/Experimental/ vatican.exhibit/exhibit/e-music/Music.html**

This Web page is a subset of the Vatican Exhibit, which can be found via the WWW EXPO (described earlier in this chapter). It deserves special mention here because of its unique music resources and because it might be easy to miss otherwise.

The focus of this exhibition is on the music of the Renaissance, which was closely tied to the religions and artistic ideals of the 16th century. There are three music rooms that you can access via this page. Each room offers a slightly different collection of musical information and artifacts. There are pictures of musical instruments, music scores, and images of singers.

Russian Virtual Exhibits
URL address: **http://www.kiae.su/www/wtr/exhibits.html**

This page features virtual exhibitions from Russia (by Relcom). You can jump between the Kremlin, the Contemporary Fine Arts Center, the Paleontology Institute, and the Soviet Archives. The Russian WWW servers are all under development, but are worth a visit.

San Francisco Exploratorium
URL address: **http://www.exploratorium.edu**

The San Francisco Exploratorium has a large collection of both art and science exhibits. The focus here is on interactive exhibits that incorporate technology to give the viewer a learning experience.

University of Illinois at Urbana-Champaign
URL address: **http://www.ncsa.uiuc.edu/General/UIUC/ KrannertArtMuseum/KrannertArtHome.html**

Don't miss this one. Created by the NCSA publications group, the Krannert Art Museum and Kinkead Pavilion have very extensive collections of works, including sculpture, European and American painting, Asian, African, Pre-Columbian, and Medieval art, and Old World antiques. In addition to viewing works of art, you can jump from the home page to the Education Resource Center, which offers instructional materials and educational workshops.

Fig. 20.12
The Krannert Art Museum Web page maintains a diverse collection of Asian, African, and Medieval art, as well as educational resources.

Music

Music Study, Research, and Resources

American Music Network
URL address: **gopher://tmn.tmn.com:70/00/Artswire/amn/infoamn**

Created to further the appreciation, performance, creation, and study of American music, this home page has links to all historical and contemporary styles. You will also find other information about events, speakers, and important dates in the history of American music.

Batish Institute
URL address: **http://hypatia.ucsc.edu:70/1/RELATED/Batish**

The Batish Institute of Indian Music and Fine Arts maintains this WWW server. The Institute, formed in 1973 by the Batish family, holds classes in vocal and instrumental music and publishes *RagaNet*, an electronic journal about Indian music and art. Pandit Shiv Dayal Batish and his son, Ashwin Batish, create and offer via this Web site material that teaches the theory and practice of Indian music. This is a comprehensive examination of Indian music.

BMI
URL address: **http://metaverse.com/bmi/index.html**

This is the home page for BMI, a music-performing rights organization that represents more than 150,000 songwriters and composers. You can search through a database of songs with title, artist, and publisher. There are also links and information about the music industry.

Digital Music
URL address: **http://metaverse.com/knet/**

Take your pick—there are digital music selections labeled as "the hottest tracks from the New Jersey Warehouse" hosted by Adam Curry or "Cool Jazz from the Big Apple." Audio files range from seven minutes to one hour (a whopping 53M in the MPEG Layer 2 format).

Hyperreal—the Techno/Ambient/Rave Archive
URL address: **http://hyperreal.com**

As the home page states, "There's a lot of stuff here." The stuff includes links to various music archives, mailing lists, publications, and even art-based shareware.

Indiana University Music Library
URL address: **http://www.music.indiana.edu/misc/music_resources.html**

This is a great collection of music links carefully organized into areas such as academic, geographic, individual artists, and so on.

Mammoth Music Meta-List
URL address: **http://www.timeinc.com/vibe/mmm/music.html**

This Web site has lists of lists, giving you access to links about every subject you can think of that pertains to music.

Music References
URL address: **http://freeabel.geom.umn.edu:8000/music.html**

This is a terrific home page for music information; there's everything from links to music lyrics to digital sound clips of The Doors and Pink Floyd.

Rare Groove Charts
URL address: **http://rg.media.mit.edu/RG/charts/top.html**

This Web site shows you ratings charts based on access of song samples, and it lets you make a graph of your top 20 tracks. You fill in the genre, your name, assigned password if you are a DJ, and the artist, title, and label for each hit.

Usenet Music FAQs

URL address: **http://www.cis.ohio-state.edu/hypertext/faq/usenet/
music/top.html**

Boy, there are many questions (and answers) here! Try Q&A on a cappella,
Billy Joel, music composition, Deep Purple, percussion drum equipment suppliers, listings of open musical jam sessions, MIDI, and reggae, to name a few.

Web Wide World of Music

URL address: **http://american.recordings.com/wwwofmusic/
index.html**

You may never get out of this site! The link to the Ultimate Band List serves
up 1782 links for 565 bands with 477 Web pages. Major Music Links offers a
comprehensive list of other music sites on the Web. The hotlist is described
as a place to post your favorite links and where you can remove everybody
else's dull, boring links.

Blues

Delta Snake Blues News

URL address: **http://www.portal.com/~mojohand/delta_snake.html**

If you like to sing or even learn about the blues, stop at this home page.
There are fun and heartfelt reviews of new albums such as John Brim's "The
Ice Cream Man" on TONE-COOL RECORDS or Roomfull of Blues' "Dance All
Night" on BULLSEYE BLUES. Also, there's the Delta Snake kitchen, which
provides recipes like blackened catfish.

Classical

Leeds University

URL address: **http://www.leeds.ac.uk/music.html**

The home page for the Leeds University Department of Music has a lot of
links. First, find out about the department and programs in music. Next,
search for music information by type, genre, period, artist, or area. Then,
learn about Organ Recitals from St. Bartholomews, Armley, jump to the Op-
era Schedule Server from the Process Control Department of the Technical
University of Budapest, find out about the Oregon Bach Festival, or... well,
you get the idea.

Oregon Bach Festival
URL address: **http://jrusby.uoregon.edu/obf/obfhome.html**

This Web site tells you about the annual festival, provides a schedule of events (which run through the summer months), and offers bios of the musicians, conductors, and composers.

Ethnic

Songs of Abayudaya Jews
URL address: **http://www.intac.com/PubService/uganda/music.html**

The Abayudaya music you can listen to was recorded by Kohavim Tikvah, a youth singing group of the Abayudaya congregation. Every week Kohavim Tikvah comes together to sing for the community. Much of the music played by the Abayudaya are versions of American-Jewish songs. The Lecha Dodi and Sh'ma are sung in original Abayudaya tunes, written by Gershom Douglas King, a Jewish man from Britain who visited the community. The audio files are between 1M and 2M.

Jazz

Jazz Server
URL address: **http://www.acns.nwu.edu/jazz**

Jump through a collection of album charts and a fun "mediamap" timeline of jazz, which lets you link to different jazz eras from 1900 to today. There are also links to other jazz sites and newsgroups.

Rock, Pop, and Alternative

Bad Taste
URL address: **http://www.centrum.is/badtaste**

No, this site doesn't offer reviews of frozen dinners, but rather information about the Icelandic record label Bad Taste. So, if you're into unusual music and recording artists that you may not find at the local record store, visit this site.

Burnett
URL address: **http://www.cecer.army.mil/~burnett/MDB/musicResources.html**

Are you a fan of a musical group? Well, this home page offers links to other Web servers and documents for numerous artists, from the Beatles to Alice In Chains.

Communications Research Group
URL address: **http://www.crg.cs.nott.ac.uk/~mjr/Music/index.html**

This server focuses on the music scene in the United Kingdom. It is sponsored by the Department of Computer Science at the University of Nottingham.

Jazz Butcher Conspiracy
URL address: **http://purgatory.ecn.purdue.edu:20002/JBC/jbc.html**

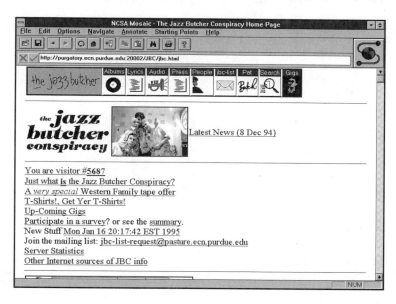

Fig. 20.13
With everything from reviews of releases to info on mailing lists and bootleg recordings, this is a fun WWW music group home page—you'll enjoy the little smoking penguins.

This is a hypermedia presentation of information about the Jazz Butcher, an English pop group. Included at this site are albums, lyrics, photos, audio clips, and T-shirt information.

Online Digitized Music
URL address: **http://ftp.luth.se/pub/sounds/songs**

This is the Web site for the San Diego State University sound archives. From Abba to ZZ Top, this server offers a comprehensive index of songs, many with audio sound clips.

Quality In Sound Consortium
URL address: **http://purgatory.ecn.purdue.edu:20002/JBC/quality.html**

The Quality In Sound Consortium maintains this site for the British pop group The Jazz Butcher Conspiracy, the Czechoslovakian experimental techno group The Black Eg, and the American group, Vergiftung. There are links to photographs, discographies, discussion, and audio.

Rolling Stones
URL address: **http://www.stones.com**

Fig. 20.14
Visit the Stones' home page to review samples of their music, see Mick in action, or find out about upcoming concerts.

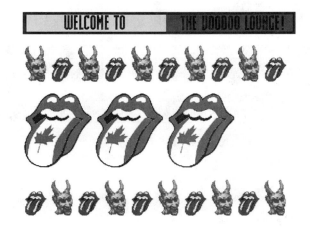

Often billed as the greatest rock-n-roll band, the Rolling Stones may also have made cyberspace history as they broadcast 20 minutes of their Cotton Bowl concert live on the Web. This is a graphics intensive site where you will get all kinds of satisfaction as you jump to links.

Tom Waits
URL address: **http://www.nwu.edu:80/music/waits/**

Everything you need to know about Tom, starting with an FAQ document. You can check out concert appearances, pictures, and his musical influences.

Underground Music Archive
URL address: **http://sunsite.unc.edu/ianc/index.html**

Information about new, underground bands such as Bedazzled—gothic, epic music from Rob Wyatt and Steve Willet's recording label—and TeenBeat. One group, Quagmire, presents, in its entirety, a full length music CD available on the World Wide Web—*for free*. Don't ask about download time.

Web Wide World of Music
URL address: **http://american.recordings.com/wwwofmusic/index.html**

This site may be a tongue twister to pronounce, but it is definitely worth a visit for fans of modern music and rock-and-roll. You may want to start with a jump to the Ultimate Band List, a page that contains 746 links to more than 170 bands (wow). There is also band trivia and a forum for interactive discussion of music.

Record Labels

PolyEster Records & Books
URL address: **http://www.aus.xanadu.com/PolyEster/polyester.html**

How hip are you? Find out about underground and above ground media from Australia. Local bands, books, and electronic zines (magazines) are available through this online catalog. You can keyword search the record collection and place your order online (with a forms-capable browser).

Warner Brothers
URL address: **http://WWW.iuma.com/Warner**

Fig. 20.15
If you want to hear a digital sample of a song by Tom Petty or any other Warner Brother artist, check out this home page.

Warner Bros. Records, one of the big players in the music industry, has a Web site where you can find out all sorts of details about the record label's artists. You can download sound clips from some of the chart-rising singles.

Resources for Musicians

Banjo Tablature Archive

URL address: **http://www.vuw.ac.nz/who/Nathan.Torkington/ banjo/tab/home.html**

This home page provides you with both original and transcribed tablature for a five-string banjo. The styles range from bluegrass to classical. You may also want to try the Guitar and Bass Tablature at **ftp://ftp.nevada.edu/pub.**

Bottom Line Archive

URL address: **http://syy.oulu.fi/tbl.html**

In this magazine for acoustic and electric bass players, you can jump to compact disc reviews, descriptions of equipment, comments from bass players, and even some GIF pictures.

Drums and Percussion Page

URL address: **http://www.cse.ogi.edu/Drum**

Did you know that a "quinta" is the smallest of the conga drums? If you like any form of percussion, this is a great WWW resource. The home page offers a link to an encyclopedia of percussion, a list of FAQs, a list of percussionists, a Drum mailing list, and a Drum Equipment Suppliers list—and if you get bored, a link to drummer jokes.

Guitarland

URL address: **ftp://ftp.netcom.com/pub/jcarson/guitar/gl.html**

When the home page opens with a color photograph of Jimi Hendrix, you know that you've found a resource for guitar lovers. Connections here take to you to newsletters, newsgroups, acoustic and classical guitar archives, and even a section on guitar lessons, which ranges from the Basic Blues to the Major Triads.

Hammered Dulcimer

URL address: **http://tfnet.ils.unc.edu/~gotwals/hd/dulcimer.html**

Make beautiful music. This site has information for hammered dulcimer players—documents on the history, playing, building, workshops, music from around the world, instructional books, festivals, and a catalog of instruments.

MIDI Home Page

URL address: **http://www.eeb.ele.tue.nl/midi/index.html**

MIDI is the digital standard for connecting musical instruments to computers and to each other via computers. This site offers information about the specifications. You also can access some MIDI sequences, MIDI-related newsgroups, or jump to info on specific MIDI instruments such as Yamaha synthesizers.

Clubs

Alberto's Nightclub

URL address: **http://and.com/albertos/**

This server offers a taste of Alberto's nightclub in downtown Mountain View, California. You can find out about the live music and shows. Musical styles represented include: Tango, Latin Rock, Reggae, Cajun, Samba, World Beat, Brazilian, African, and Soca.

Anecdote

URL address: **http://anecdote.com**

A club in downtown Ann Arbor, Michigan, the Anecdote serves as an open forum for artists. You can view artwork and listen to music.

Georgia Tech's Student Radio Station

URL address: **http://www.gatech.edu/wrek/wrek.html**

WREK Atlanta, 91.1 FM, has a WWW home page. WREK offers diverse programming, from rock to blues to jazz. *WREKology* is WREK's quarterly program guide.

Miller Tap Room

URL address: **http://www.mgdtaproom.com**

Fig. 20.16
Enjoy the nightclub scene without the hassles of crowds at Millers' Tap Room.

Wet your whistle by dropping in at the Miller Genuine Draft home page, the Tap Room—a virtual pub where you can share what Miller describes as progressive lifestyle information.

This includes information on trends in music, fashion, nightlife, art, sports, food, and social issues from around the country. In a press release, James Taylor, brand director Miller Genuine Draft/Miller Genuine Draft Light, notes that "MGD is perfect for providing a forum for anyone interested in tapping into the latest happenings in popular culture." So grab a beer, get a designated driver, and tap into the Tap Room.

Publications

The following electronic publications offer the same variety of articles and images that you find in hard copy publications; however, because they are electronic, you move through the publication by pointing and clicking.

Cambridge University Science Fiction Society
URL address: **http://myrddin.chu.cam.ac.uk/cusfs/ttba**

The magazine of the Cambridge University Science Fiction Society contains fiction, reviews, poetry, and artwork.

Computer Music Journal
URL address: **file://mitpress.mit.edu:/pub/Computer-Music-Journal/ CMJ.html**

The Computer Music Journal Archive is provided for *Computer Music Journal* readers and the computer music community. It includes a table of contents, abstracts, and editor's notes for several volumes of *CMJ*, including the recent bibliography, discography, and taxonomy of the field, and the list of network resources for music. There are also related documents such as the complete MIDI and AIFF specifications, a reference list, and the text of recent articles.

Cyberkind
URL address: **http://sunsite.unc.edu/shannon/ckind/title.html**

This is a WWW magazine of Net-related fiction, nonfiction, poetry, and art. *Cyberkind* features prose and art submitted by the Internet population. All genres and subjects are included, with the condition that there is some connection to the Internet, cyberspace, computers, or the networked world. Features range from articles on writers and the Internet to computer-related mysteries to hyperlinked poems. There is also a variety of graphic art. Send submissions or queries to **shannon@sunsite.unc.edu**.

Depth Probe E-Zine
URL address: **http://www.neo.com/Depthprobe/zine/index/home.html**

Depth Probe E-Zine is an esoteric collection of movie, book, and modern culture reviews—some interesting, some amusing, and some ridiculous. Check it out.

Quanta
URL address: **http://nearnet.gnn.com/wic/scifi.03.html**

The electronic magazine *Quanta* contains a variety of amateur fiction.

Webster's Weekly
URL address: **http://www.awa.com/w2**

Fig. 20.17
Webster's Weekly is an online magazine with articles and images about the arts.

Webster's Weekly—a weekly WWW features magazine on the Web—offers columns on music and movies, politics, psychology, mad rantings, and dangerous toys. The magazine also distributes photographs, poems, cartoons, and a response column.

Mother Jones Magazine
URL address: **http://www.mojones.com/motherjones.html**

This contains online current and back issues of *Mother Jones Magazine*, and includes an assortment of links to shareware, interactive kiosks, music reviews, and the kitchen sink.

Secular Web
URL address: **http://freethought.tamu.edu**

This site includes secular issues including atheism, agnosticism, humanism, and skepticism. The site also offers an archive of free-thought literature called The Freethought Web.

Television

It's very interesting that televison and radio networks are using the Internet and Web as a means to promote themselves and to offer detailed program listings. For users, it's a convenient way to find out what's happening in the local and national television and radio scene. And, even if you don't happen to live in the town where a network or station has a Web site, you often find useful and interesting information, such as program schedules for radio current playlists, or sample video and audio files.

BBC
URL address: **http://www.bbcnc.org.uk/bbctv/sched.html**

This nine-day schedule for BBC TV and radio programs is categorized into areas such as childrens' shows, sports, and so on. You also can get a daily listing of all TV shows in chronological order.

C-SPAN
URL address: **gopher://c-span.org/**

Find out about the current week's program schedule for the 24-hour-a-day cable channel devoted to government issues. This site also includes transcripts and information for educators.

Corporation for Public Broadcasting
URL address: **http://www.cpb.org**

You know this is a great organization that funds many of the programs we watch on our local PBS stations. Links here tell you about CPB and their various educational outreach programs.

Doctor Who
URL address: **http://www.phlab.missouri.edu/c621052_www/ Dr.Who/**

An archive of Dr. Who programs is maintained at this university in Missouri.

Mystery Science Theatre 3000

URL address: **http://alfred1.u.washington.edu:8080/~roland/mst3k/mst3k.html**

If you like *Mystery Science Theater*, you will love this home page! It contains very complete information on all episodes.

The Prisoner

URL address: **http://itdsrv1.ul.ie/Entertainment/Prisoner/the-prisoner.html**

This is a site for a classic television program from the BBC.

Satellite TV Page

URL address: **http://itre.uncecs.edu/misc/sat.html**

This Web server is a database for information relating to the hobby of satellite television and radio, also known as TVRO. Lists and charts are compiled by Robert Smathers. You can find out about the programs and schedules for satellites that carry radio and TV programs, including specific transponders.

Science and Engineering Television Network

URL address: **http://www.service.com/stv/setncall.html**

SETN is a consortium of scientific organizations formed to offer a television network for scientists and engineers. Find out about the network, programming, societies, and government agencies that participate in this network. SETN begins broadcasting in 1995.

Star Trek—British Starfleet Confederacy and Others

URL address: **http://deeptht.armory.com/~bsc**

The British Starfleet Confederacy is a non-profit organization run by the fans of *Star Trek* for the fans of *Star Trek*. There's information about the British Starfleet Confederacy, the Tardis FTP archive, *Star Trek* information, Science Fiction Resource Guide, and UK Science Fiction Fandom Archives. Another Star Trek home pages includes Brigitte Jellinek's Star Trek resource guide (**http://www.cosy.sbg.ac.at/rec/startrek/index.html**).

Ultimate TV List

URL address: **http://tvnet.com/UTVL/utvl.html**

The home page sets the stage for this one. It states: "Ok Everyone, this is the Ultimate Modifyable List of TV pointers, Link away.... Containing 355 Links for 111 Shows, including 108 WWW Pages." You can find out about your favorite TV shows by clicking links to genre, resources (such as newsgroups), or follow an alphabetical list of the shows.

Vanderbilt Television News Archive

URL address: **http://tvnews.vanderbilt.edu**

Are you a news junkie? This site offers an indexed listing of national news-casts dating back to 1983. You can keyword search or search by date; then get an abstract of the news for *any* day.

Radio Networks

Canadian Broadcast News

URL address: **http://www.cs.cmu.edu:8001/Web/Unofficial/ Canadiana/CBC-News.html**

This WWW site maintains daily audio files of the CBC radio news broadcasts. There are two daily newscasts—an International broadcast at 8:00 EST and Canadian Domestic News at 17:00 EST. The audio files are 10–15 minutes long. (You can also see the detailed overview of the CBC Radio Trial.)

MIT Radio Station List

URL address: **http://www.mit.edu:8001/activities/wmbr/ otherstations.html**

The home page touts this site as having "to the best of our knowledge, the most comprehensive list of radio stations on the Internet." There are easily over 100 links to Web and Gopher sites for radio stations. You can even save the page to disk to have a quick link to the world of radio.

National Public Radio

URL address: **http://www.npr.org**

NPR reaches millions of homes across the U.S. via member stations. This site has links to news and cultural program information, job opportunities, and links to many public radio station Web and Internet sites. And no request for pledges!

Radio Japan

URL address: **http://www.ntt.jp/japan/NHK/**

Radio Japan provides international shortwave radio transmissions by NHK (the Japan Broadcasting Corporation). This page also includes links to broadcasting information and timetables.

International Radio

CFUV 102 FM Victoria, British Columbia

URL address: **http://www.uvic.ca:70/1/general/cfuv**

Here you'll find links to detailed programming info.

CHMA 107FM New Brunswick, Canada

URL address: **http://aci.mta.ca/TheUmbrella/CHMA/ chmastart.html**

This is a campus and community radio station. The site includes links to sound files, job opportunities, programming, and music projects.

98 FM Dublin, Ireland

URL address: **http://www.ieunet.ie/ois/98fm/98fmrequest.html**

This site takes the concept of asking for music requests to an all-time high. You actually fill in a form and send it back to the station. Odds are you'll never hear it.

Stads Radio Rotterdam, the Netherlands

URL address: **http://morra.et.tudelft.nl/~remcob/srr.html**

There are not a lot of links here, but you can find out what folks listen to in the Netherlands.

Fréquence Banane, Switzerland
URL address: **http://fbwww.epfl.ch**

This server is direct from Switzerland. Are you surprised to learn that one of the top songs for this student radio station is the Pixies hit "Where Is My Mind?" Links offer details about the programming.

Rock Radio

KDKB 93.3 Phoeniz, AZ
URL address: **http://www.getnet.com/kdkb/**

The site for this classic rock station links to a current list of top hits and concerts in the area.

WAOA 107.1 FM Melbourne, FL
URL address: **http://www.wa1a.com/wa1a.html**

In addition to the standard song lists, concerts, and promotions, there is *real time radio*—10 and 20 second downloadable files of music playing on this station right now!

WNNX 99 FM Atlanta, GA
URL address: **http://www.com/99x/**

Need to know who's hot and who's not? There are links to the most current radio playlists, bands, station promotions, and images of musicians.

WFBQ 95 FM Indianapolis, IN
URL address: **http://www.iquest.net/Q95/**

Labeled as "Indy's Best Music," this home page has some fun links such as "Canned Laughter." It also offers many links to other Web music sites.

WZLX 100.7 FM Boston, MA
URL address: **http://www.wzlx.com/wzlx/**

Here's a fun stop that you don't have to live in Boston to enjoy. It has links to the history of rock, new CD releases, rock trivia, and station promotions.

College Radio

KFJC 89.7FM Los Altos Hills, CA
URL address: **http://www.cygnus.com/misc/kfjc.html**

A campus station, this Web site has links to top artist and detailed program notes, giving you a nice overview of music you may not have heard yet.

KCRW 89.9 FM Santa Monica, CA

URL address: **http://www.webcom.com/~gumbo/kcrw-info.html**

Here you'll find album recommendations and links to the top pop, classical, and jazz recordings.

WXYC, North Carolina

URL address: **http://sunsite.unc.edu/wxyc**

The home page boasts that this is the "first real-time 24 hour Internet radio station."

WSRN 91.5 FM Swarthmore, PA (Swarthmore College)

URL address: **http://sccs.swarthmore.edu/~justin/Docs/WSRN.html**

Download an audio clip of the station ID, or find out about the mixture of classical, jazz, and rock music that this station plays. There are also links to other radio stations on the Web.

KVRX 91.7 FM Austin, TX

URL address: **http://wwwhost.cc.utexas.edu/finearts/kvrx.html**

This site includes one great link to an A–Z list of women-based bands.

Country Radio

New Country 94.1 FM Seattle, WA

URL address: **http://www.solutionsrc.com/KMPS**

This country music radio station offers news and reviews of country CD releases. You have to register online as a "loyal listener."

Jazz Radio

Ohio University Public Radio

URL address: **http://www.tcom.ohiou.edu/radio.html**

This site provides information about the station, program listings, a jazz playlist, and *Family Health*—a series of audio files about health subjects.

Talk

Internet Talk Radio

URL address: **http://juggler.lanl.gov/itr.html**

This is a daily information service that focuses on news and technology about the Internet. Internet Talk Radio is similar in format to National Public Radio and provides in-depth technical information to the Internet community. There are also some general interest program features such as "Taking Care of Planet Earth" and "Technology and Health Care." You download the program to your PC, and then play it back with a sound program. Each half-hour program consists of 64,000 bits per second or 15M total. ITR produces between 30 and 90 minutes of programming each day. This digital, cyberspace radio show is produced by the Internet Multicasting Service—a non-profit corporation that resides in the National Press Building. Initial support for the project comes from Sun Microsystems and O'Reilly & Associates.

RadioNet—KSCO AM 1080
URL address: **http://www.radionet.com/radionet**

This site is a combination real and cyberspace station. It includes interesting talk shows that focus on "the magical fusion of computers, video and telecommunications." Don't miss the still images that are captured and sent from the studio every couple of minutes!

From Here...

It's fun to have fun. The Web sites in this chapter focus on information and activities that are enjoyable. Going to a museum, listening to music, and looking at paintings are all things that we enjoy doing with our leisure time. If you still have time on your hands after you've tried these sites, then try:

- Chapter 29, "Publications: News, Periodicals, and Books," lists enough electronic textbooks to satisfy the most voracious bookworm.

- Chapter 32, "Sports, Games, Hobbies, Travel, Cooking, and Recreation," has many sites devoted to the exploration of amateur and professional recreation, hobbies, games, and vacation opportunities.

Chapter 21

Business and Finance

by Bill Eager

Business is booming on the Internet and the WWW. One clear sign that the world of business considers this global network to be a useful mechanism for commerce is that business people now include an Internet address on their business cards. And, if that isn't good enough, DHM Information Management of Redondo Beach, California, will imprint your Internet address on a license plate frame to enable other drivers to find your electronic mailbox.

Thousands of companies now race to get information about their products and services transformed into hypermedia documents so that potential customers around the world can access this information via the WWW. Some companies operate their own Web servers, whereas others contract with a service provider to maintain the information. Generally, companies that put information onto the WWW focus on informational documents more than strict advertising documents.

Computer and telecommunications companies have a large presence on the Web. This is not too surprising when you consider that these companies play a significant role in the development of software, hardware, and infrastructure components that make the Web a reality. Increasingly, however, information, products, and services reach a broad business audience. Web servers at Harvard University, The Kellogg School, and Wharton School of Business provide resources on business education.

Other Web resources include home pages in foreign countries that have links to detailed tips and information about doing business with companies in those countries. Some Web servers have up-to-the-minute stock price information, and other servers provide information for entrepreneurs and people who work at home. In other words, whether you own a small, one-person firm or a multinational company, resources exist on the Web that can help you expand and improve your business. Here's a summary of what you'll find in this chapter:

- Business development and business resources

- Companies: computers and telecommunications

- Companies: general

- Consulting

- Financial

- International

- Internet services

- Science and business

- Small business and individual resources

AT&T Toll Free Numbers

URL address: **http://att.net/dir800**

Fig. 21.1
The AT&T toll-free Web site helps you quickly find toll-free phone numbers for products and companies.

Who can resist a toll-free telephone number? Well, if you're looking for toll-free numbers for travel reservations, catalogs, or anything else, you can now turn to the Web instead of a switchboard operator. Now, the AT&T 800 directory is on the Web. This online directory has more than 150,000 listings from AT&T's business and consumer yellow-page 800 directories.

The home page tells us: "It's designed to help you shop for the things you need and want without leaving the comfort of your home or office. You can use this directory to buy almost anything from anywhere in the United States—from gifts and flowers to things for the home and unique and hard-to-find items."

You can search through the listing in two ways. First, choose an A to Z category. For example, the letter E hyperlinks to eggs, engines, exports, and so on. Or, you can choose by company name. Again, select the letter E and you get a list of companies that include Ebony, Eaton, and Exxon.

CommerceNet

URL address: **http://www.commerce.net**

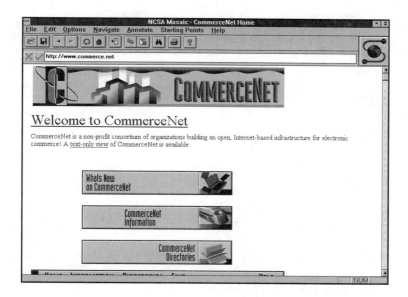

Fig. 21.2
The CommerceNet
home page. You
can access
additional
information by
clicking inside one
of the boxes.

From marketing and selling products to transmitting electronic orders and
payments, Silicon Valley-based CommerceNet focuses on the business applications of the WWW. Many of the world's largest companies, including Intel,
Apple, Lockheed, Bank of America, and Dun & Bradstreet, belong to the initial phase of CommerceNet in order to create a virtual storefront. Any size
business, from one person to a multinational business, can join
CommerceNet to promote its products and services.

◀ See "Security of
Web Transac-
tions," p. 428

From the CommerceNet home page, you can jump to a directory of all companies involved with CommerceNet. If these companies operate Web servers,
you can jump directly to them. When CommerceNet is complete, you can get
detailed product information, do online price comparisons, and conduct
financial transactions electronically.

Half of the initial funding for CommerceNet comes from a Federal grant from
the government's "Technology Reinvestment Program" (TRP), sponsored by
the Defense Department's Advanced Research Projects Agency (ARPA), the
National Institute of Standards and Technology (NIST), the National Science
Foundation (NSF), and other government agencies. Matching funds come
from the State of California and participating companies.

VI

Finding Web Resources

CommerceNet's goal is to make public computer networks such as the Internet "industrial strength" for business use. CommerceNet addresses issues including low-cost, high-speed Internet access using newly deployed technology such as Integrated Services Digital Network (ISDN) services and multimedia software. CommerceNet supports a range of commercial network applications such as online catalogs, product data exchange, and engineering collaboration.

It also offers outreach services such as technical assistance to small- and medium-size businesses that want to access public networks. CommerceNet is currently testing a system that uses public key cryptography and a version of Mosaic known as Secure Mosaic to ensure the security of financial transactions over the vast Internet. Initially, CommerceNet serves the needs of businesses and customers in California, but service is expected to extend around the world in less than two years.

The CommerceNet consortium is sponsored by Smart Valley, Inc., a non-profit organization chartered to create a regional electronic community, and the State of California's Trade and Commerce Agency. Enterprise Integration Technologies, a company that specializes in electronic commerce, is leading the effort. If you want to become an online vendor on CommerceNet, you can either place informational pages online at the CommerceNet server, or set up a private WWW server and connect it to the CommerceNet. Subscribers who pay an annual fee receive training and are listed in CommerceNet's vendor directory—a logo or listing connects to your server. Sponsors who pay a larger annual fee receive advanced training classes and the opportunity to participate in the governance of the network.

(For more information on CommerceNet, send e-mail to **info@commerce.net**.)

Hong Kong WWW Server

URL address: **http://www.hk.super.net/~rlowe/bizhk/bhhome.html**

This server offers a wealth of information about doing business in Hong Kong, which, as many business people know, is a leading manufacturing and financial center and a gateway to doing business with China. A link to BizHK provides a trade contacts service. This home page matches Hong Kong businesses with potential trading partners worldwide. More information is available by sending e-mail to **rlowe@hk.super.net**.

Through this server, you can access a database of more than 1,000 companies in Hong Kong. You can click alphabetically through the database and find company contacts, financial data, product information, addresses, and phone numbers. Special sections focus on two major areas for business opportunities: the Hotel, Tourism, and Travel industry, and Textiles, Fabrics, and Clothing. The home page also has links to economic statistics that relate to Hong Kong and press releases about business trade, such as an overview of the imports and exports between Hong Kong and the United Kingdom.

Fig. 21.3
On the BizHK home page, use the scroll bar to view additional information about doing business in Hong Kong.

IRS

URL address: **http://www.ustreas.gov/treasury/bureaus/irs/ irs.html**

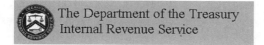
The Department of the Treasury Internal Revenue Service

Now, instead of worrying about getting a call from the IRS, you can knock on its door. The home page explains: "Our presence on the Internet and the World Wide Web is part of our continuing efforts to provide broad and immediate electronic access to IRS tax information and services." There are four main links:

Fig. 21.4
Whether you've already finished your taxes or are beginning to plan for next year, the IRS Web site offers lots of information.

- Tax forms and instructions

- Frequently asked questions

- Where to file

- Where to get help

Choose the first link to see a list of all forms or search through the forms. Link 2 presents FAQs, such as how to check the status of your return. Link 3 is a state-by-state list of where to file; Link 4 provides a series of help phone numbers for individuals, small businesses, and the handicapped.

VI

Finding Web Resources

MCI

URL address: **http://www.mci.com**

This is Gramercy Press.

MCI is hot on the Internet. In addition to offering Internet access to its customers, MCI has a strong presence on the Web. This site has information about the company's Internet services and a link to its online mall. Using encryption from RSA Data Security, online transactions are protected, so you can use your credit card to purchase products. MCI anticipates Internet commerce to exceed $2 billion by the turn of the century.

There is also a home page link to MCI's cyberspace-based publishing firm called "Gramercy Press" (URL address: **http://www.mci.com/gramercy/ intro.html**). This is a company that exists only on the Web—but it has the look and feel of a real company. Start your visit by clicking on windows of an office building to learn more about the people who "work" here. The site explains: "Gramercy's archives contain all kinds of literature: everything from critical essays and short stories to poetry, even an entire novel. You'll be able to browse through our art books covering everything from oil paintings and etchings to wonderful photography and funny cartoons. You'll find movies and sounds everywhere when you come to visit, all of it ready to be downloaded for your personal enjoyment."

One other link on the home page brings you to information (and more links) about networkMCI (URL address: **http://www.mci.com/net_mci/ net_mci.html**). networkMCI represents a full range of connectivity and Web-based services for businesses and individuals.

The World Bank

URL address: **http://www.worldbank.org**

Fig. 21.6
The World Bank
home page.

▶ See "Public
Policy and
World Events,"
p. 795

If you need to find out what is going on in international finance or trends in the economies of specific countries, this is the Web server for you! The World Bank Group consists of:

- The International Bank for Reconstruction and Development (IBRD), which is the primary lending arm of the World Bank.

- The International Development Association (IDA), the World Bank affiliate that lends funds on concessional terms to poor countries.

- The International Finance Corporation (IFC), which finances private sector projects and advises businesses and governments on investment issues.

- The Multilateral Investment Guarantee Agency (MIGA), which promotes foreign direct investment through guarantees, policy advice, and promotional services.

You can jump from the home page to two areas that contain a wealth of information on the financial status, economic development projects, and social and environmental conditions in countries around the world. Some of the available information is found in books, articles, and documents (many of which are for sale) in the World Bank Publications section.

A second area, the World Bank Public Information Center (PIC), maintains a variety of economic reports and environmental data sheets. You can view these reports online or download and print one copy. The World Bank maintains copyright on all information. Here are a few examples:

- Privatization and adjustment—Bangladesh

- Public finance reforms in the transition—Bulgaria

- Policies for private sector development—Caribbean countries

VI

Finding Web Resources

- Environment and development: challenges for the future—Indonesia

- Nutrition and national development: issues and options—Morocco

- Social protection during transition and beyond—Russia

EINet Galaxy

URL address: **http://galaxy.einet.net/galaxy.html**

Fig. 21.7
A peek at some of the many sites you can access via EINet Galaxy's home page.

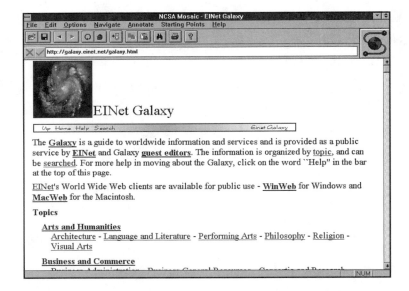

This is a guide to worldwide information and services. It includes public as well as commercial information and services provided by EINet customers and affiliates.

The site provides an overview of the latest release of WinWeb, a World Wide Web browser for Microsoft Windows, along with downloading instructions. Similar information is provided for MacWeb, a Web browser for Macintosh computers.

EINet Galaxy's most exciting feature from an information-access point of view is its generous collection of links to home pages on a variety of topics. Figure 21.7 shows only a partial listing.

The Business General Resources link takes you to a range of business-related sites, including the Koblas Currency Converter, a comparative chart of currency values updated weekly.

Apple Computer Home Page

URL address: **http://www.apple.com/**

This server provides links to information about Apple computers, Apple customer support services, the Apple Library of Tomorrow, code snippets, Apple-oriented resources, Internet resources for the Macintosh, a variety of media resources, and much more.

Besides being a comprehensive resource for information about using Apple computers, the site presents the latest business statistics about Apple Inc. You can weave your way through several links to a server at MIT (URL address **http://www.ai.mit.edu/stocks/graph?AAPL**), where you can check out stock market performances on a variety of companies, including Apple. Figure 21.8 shows a sample graph of Apple's ups and downs, as accessed through this link.

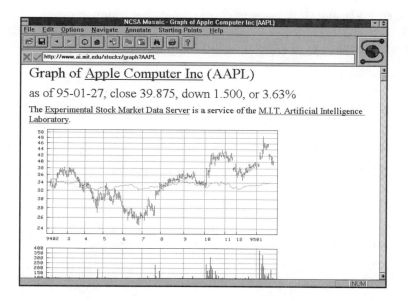

Fig. 21.8
The savvy business person needs up-to-date information about a company's earning potential. Now it's available on the Web.

Novell Inc. World Wide Web Home Page

URL address: **http://www.novell.com**

Fig. 21.9
Novell's novel home page, which uses a bookshelf metaphor to point to different categories of information.

Novell's home page makes good use of the WWW's graphic capabilities. It is just a system designed to help answer questions you have about Novell or its products. But the categories, which include technical support databases, searchable FTP and Gopher archives, an online product buyer's guide, and links to the Novell European Support Center, are represented by a row of books resting on a bookshelf.

The book metaphor doesn't carry through smoothly to all the links at the site. In fact, most of the links are to plain text files or Gopher servers. But the page demonstrates how navigation of Internet hypertext files is easier when familiar metaphors and motifs are used.

Canadian Airlines International Ltd.

URL address: **http://www.CdnAir.CA**

This home page provides service and information about "Canada's premier customer-driven airline." Buttons point to the services presently offered via the home page. These services include the capability to query flight arrival and departure databases and to obtain pricing information. News updates as well as weather and leisure information for the traveler are also provided.

As shown in figure 21.10, the site also includes clickable route maps of the airline's service areas. Although this site is as yet incomplete, it has the potential to be a very useful and user-friendly repository.

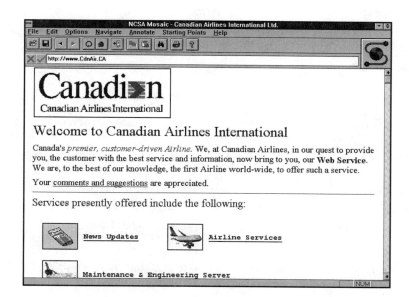

Fig. 21.10
Query flight times,
pricing databases,
and more at this
home page.

Business Development and Business Resources

American Business Women's Association

URL address: **http://freenet3.scri.fsu.edu:81/ht-free/abwa.html**

This site provides a menu about the association. Items include the mission of the ABWA; officers and contact people; meeting information; and minutes of meetings and club events.

Translation Service

URL address: **http://www.trib.com/service/braille.html**

This site provides contact information for this Casper, Wyoming, company that translates text into English Grade II Braille. This is a helpful service for companies wishing to meet the requirements of the Americans with Disabilities Act.

Business Schools

URL address: **http://riskweb.bus.utexas.edu/bschool.html**

This home page provides links to Harvard University, The Kellogg School, Wharton School, and other prestigious business school WWW servers. You find detailed information about business programs and get access to campus-wide online phone books and library databases.

Currency Converter
URL address: **http://www.ora.com/cgi-bin/ora/currency**

Need to know how many pesos or rubles to the dollar? The Web currency converter shows you current exchange rates between most of the world's money systems.

Distributed Electronic Telecommunications Archive (DELTA)
URL address: **http://gozer.idbsu.edu/business/nethome.html**

This project is intended to demonstrate how telecommunications and data communications education can be facilitated by sharing teaching and learning materials over the Internet.

Federal Express
URL address: **http://www.fedex.com**

Fig. 21.11
When you want to see where your FedEx package is, check out this Web site.

At this site, you find information about the company, the services, the service areas and, most impressively, a link to a form that you can use to track the status of a FedEx package!

GE Corporate Research and Development CE-Toolkit Home Page
URL address: **http://ce-toolkit.crd.ge.com/**

The Concurrent Engineering Toolkit (CE-Toolkit) provides a broad and well-organized collection of resources for implementing manufacturing networks. This site has links to information about services, software, papers, and some related items available to you on the WWW.

IBC: Internet Business Center

URL address: **http://tig.com/IBC/index.html**

Fig. 21.12
Learn about
business use of
the Internet at
this page.

The Internet Business Center is a WWW server for information specifically related to business use of the Internet.

Internet Multicasting Service

URL address: **http://www.town.hall.org/**

The Internet Multicasting Service is an NSF- and corporate-funded program that compiles unusual, interesting, and important data. Although the data at this site is ostensibly intended for business use, individuals might find it interesting and useful, too.

Master-McNeil, Inc.

URL address: **http://www.naming.com/naming.html**

This site provides product and corporate naming services to companies worldwide. One section is devoted to information on trademarks, including the full list of international trademark classes and digitized copies of the USPTO trademark application forms.

SURAnet NIC Home Page

URL address: **http://www.sura.net/index.html**

SURAnet is the networking arm of the Southeastern Universities Research Association, Inc., a non-profit research consortium that serves organizations throughout the Southeast US, the Caribbean Basin, and South America. It provides Internet access and promotes sharing of networked information and computing resources. This Web page briefly describes SURAnet's Network Information Center services.

Telephone Customer's Corner

URL address: **http://www.teleport.com/~mw/cc.html**

Explore links that take you to 800-line shopping numbers. Other links exist to telephone company-related Web sites.

VI

Finding Web Resources

The College of Business Administration (Univ. of Nebraska)

URL address: **http://unicron.unomaha.edu/home.htm**

Located at University of Nebraska, Omaha, this server provides text-oriented information on the College of Business Administration, which is rated in the top 20 percent of the business schools in the nation.

U.S. Department of Commerce Information Services via World Wide Web

URL address: **http://www.doc.gov/**

Fig. 21.13
From the Department of Commerce page, you can access more government information than you imagined.

▶ See "U.S. Government," p. 667

Welcome to the U.S. Department of Commerce

This server provides general information on the activities and missions of the Department, contacts and resources within this department, and links to various department-wide and federal government-wide information services. It also provides links to the Bureau of the Census, National Telecommunications Information Administration (NTIA), National Institute for Standards and Technology (NIST), National Oceanic and Atmospheric Administration (NOAA), and the Patent and Trademark Office (PTO).

UniForum WWW Server Home Page

URL address: **http://www.uniforum.org/**

UniForum is a professional consortium, the goal of which is to help individuals and organizations use open systems effectively. The Web site provides a membership roster, conference and seminar schedules, publications and product catalogs, and other information.

United States Patent and Trademark Office (USPTO)

URL address: **http://www.uspto.gov/**

This site includes information about the USPTO's Working Group on Intellectual Property Rights, and provides access to its draft report on the intellectual property implications of the national information infrastructure, or the *information superhighway*. The server also provides a link to the complete transcripts, prepared remarks, and e-mail comments from the Patent Office's public hearings on software patent protection and lists job openings.

Utah Wired

URL address: **http://www.comnet.com/**

This server provides information about living and doing business in Utah. A new feature, CONNECTions, is an online version of the newspaper in Utah that provides information about the computer and information industry within the state. The server also features an "Interesting Link of the Week," which is someone's favorite WWW find.

▶ See "Travel—Places to Go, United States," p. 935

Companies—Computers and Telecommunications

AT&T Bell Laboratories Research

URL address: **http://www.research.att.com**

Learn how to obtain videotapes of "Live from AT&T Bell Labs" broadcasts and how to access AT&T FTP sites. The site also lists conferences and calls for papers, as well as information or papers on topics such as anonymous credit cards, document marking, multimedia, and the Clipper chip.

Bellcore Home Page

URL address: **http://www.bellcore.com/**

Bellcore is the communication research arm of Bell. The Web page, which is experimental, provides information about Bellcore products, telecommunications, and the following:

- Bellcore's catalog of information products. To access the catalog, log in with the user ID `cat10`

- Bellcore TEC Training Catalog

- National ISDN Information

- Bellcore Digest of Technical Information

- MIME (Multipurpose Internet Mail Extensions)—an FTP repository of MIME information

- Telecommunications Industry Forum Information Products Interchange Committee (TCIF/IPI) and S/key authentication system.

Berkeley Software Design: Home Page
URL address: **http://www.bsdi.com/**

This server provides information about new features, questions and answers, technical features, and a support summary. The company designs, develops, markets, and supports the BSD/386 operating system.

Bristol Technology
URL address: **http://bristol.com**

Bristol is a developer of graphical user interface development tools. On its Web page, you find copies of the company newsletter, pointers to downloadable product demos, a bibliography of published articles about the company, and more. The "What's New" link shares new product information and even personal news about company employees—such as a birth announcement complete with a photograph of the new baby.

California Software Incorporated
URL address: **http://www.calsoft.com:80/**

In addition to CalSoft corporate and product information, this server provides links to InterAp product information. In describing the company, the page announces, "InterAp is a Microsoft Windows-based suite of Internet applications that clarify for businesses how to approach using the Internet."

Carnation Software
URL address: **file://ftp.netcom.com/pub/carnation/
HT.Carn.Home.html**

Carnation Software specializes in connecting Macs to host computers running relational databases. The server provides company, product, and ordering information.

Cellular One Home Page
URL address: **http://www.elpress.com:80/cellone/cellone.html**

This server provides links to information about Cellular One's line of cellular telephones, as well as about services, coverage areas, rate plans, and billing.

Commodore Amiga Information Resources

URL address: **http://www.cs.cmu.edu:8001/Web/People/mjw/ Computer/Amiga/MainPage.html**

Amiga users will appreciate this comprehensive server, which provides information topics such as "What's New on This Site," magazines, newsletters, rumors, hardware, software, projects, and user support. There is a link to "A Gallery of Amiga Art," where you find Shoemaker-Levy Comet animation, and you also appreciate reviews of the Amiga Software/Hardware Archives.

CYGNUS TECHNOLOGY Ltd.

URL address: **http://www.cygnus.nb.ca/cygnus/cygnus.html**

Cygnus Technology Ltd. provides a control system used for applications requiring remote intelligence and control. This server supplies information about its products and services, and links to a general telecommunication technology information site sponsored by the same company.

Digital

URL address: **http://www.digital.com/**

This is a suite of servers providing corporate and product information on Digital Equipment Corporation, as well as information on several professional organizations, the Grace Hopper Women In Computing Conference, a gallery of 32 cloud photographs, and more.

EDI and Electronic Commerce

URL address: **http://www.premenos.com**

This Web server provides information about EDI (Electronic Data Interchange) standards, industry implementation guidelines, organizations, EDI mailing lists on the Internet, network information, a calendar of events, and other documents for those interested in Electronic Commerce.

Farallon WWW Server

URL address: **http://www.farallon.com/**

Farallon makes networking products that attach personal computers to AppleTalk, TCP/IP, and 10BASE-T networks. This Web site provides information about Farallon's products and services, including Replica, an application for creating and viewing multiplatform online documents.

Hitachi, Ltd.

URL address: **http://www.hitachi.co.jp**

Fig. 21.14

The Hitachi home page.

Lots of visuals and graphics here. Topics include labs, products, divisions, what's new, headquarters, and special information. They are also very polite, with an introductory statement that says, "We appreciate you sparing your time to visit our booth."

HP Business World

URL address: **http://www.wsg.hp.com/wsg/Business/business.html**

The home page says, "This part of the Web provides information and contacts for doing business with HP." Links are to HP dealers and HP sales offices locally and nationally.

IBM

URL address: **http://www.ibm.com/**

Links are provided to the following IBM departments: Industry Solutions, Products and Services, and Technology. You can also find out how IBM plans to support the Internet and Web—both with access via OS/2 Warp and with the WebExplorer browser.

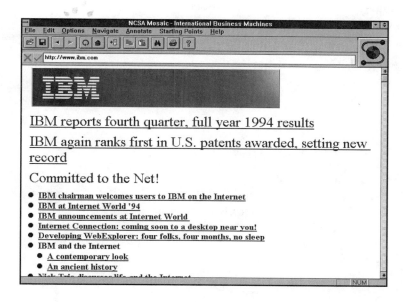

Fig. 21.15
IBM's home page offers links to IBM information, as well as Internet information.

InfoSeek

URL address: **http://www.infoseek.com**

According to its home page, the company's mission is "to deliver products that make it possible for computer users to quickly find information anywhere in the world." You can learn how to get an InfoSeek account so that you can take advantage of this timely service.

Intel Corporation

URL address: **http://www.intel.com**

This is the Web server for the company that manufactures microprocessors for the vast majority of IBM-compatible PCs. In addition to Intel corporate and product information, you find pointers to companies that use Intel chips in their products, to an assortment of other commercial enterprises, and to Web documentation.

Logic-Users Mosaic Page

URL address: **http://www.mcc.ac.uk/~emagic/emagic_page.html**

The server, located in the United Kingdom, provides information for users and future users of Emagic software, with an emphasis on Logic (formerly called Notator Logic), but also including Notator SL, SoundSurfer/ SoundDiver, and Logic Audio.

VI

Finding Web Resources

Microsoft

URL address: **http://www.microsoft.com**

The WWW server for the world's largest computer software company includes the usual corporate and product information, public information about research, and job openings.

NCD Home Page

URL address: **http://www.ncd.com/**

Network Computing Devices, Inc.'s home page offers information about all NCD products, including the three major product lines: NCD X terminals, NCD PC-Xware, and Z-Mail Enterprise-wide electronic mail. NCD's sales office locations, whitepapers, technical support bulletins, new product announcements, press releases, and corporate information are also available on the server.

Pacific Bell Home Page

URL address: **http://www.pacbell.com**

This server explains CalREN, "a $25 million program to stimulate the development of new applications for high-speed data communications services" which "will establish a foundation for broad band services including telemedicine research, diagnosis, and treatment and online schools and business partnerships." Other information, including a link to the Pacific Bell Gopher system, is also available.

Quadralay Home Page

URL address: **http://www.quadralay.com/home.html**

Fig. 21.16
The Quadralay
home page.

The Quadralay Corporation is a designer of a commercialized version of Mosaic. This server provides product and company information and a link to the Quadralay FTP Server. In addition, a link called Austin City Limits makes available "everything you ever wanted to know (and more) about Austin,

Texas," and, just for fun, a lighthearted but factual collection of coffee-related information is stored under the heading "Caffeine Archive." There's also more, both serious (C++ Forum) and fun (Dilbert). Pay this site a visit.

Racal-Datacom Corporate Headquarters

URL address: **http://www.racal.com/racal.html**

This home page offers Racal-Datacom product information and announcements, some WWW data communications and networking links and files, and Internet navigation links.

Robelle WWW Home Page

URL address: **http://www.robelle.com:80/**

Robelle Consulting develops and supports software tools for Hewlett-Packard minicomputers and workstations. You find corporate and product information here, as well as Robell and Union Software FTP archives.

RSA Data Security, Inc.'s Home Page

URL address: **http://www.rsa.com/**

RSA is a recognized world leader in cryptography, with millions of copies of its software encryption and authentication installed and in use worldwide. The company's server, characterized at press time as "under development," lists product information, news bulletins, and technical documents, among other topics.

Silicon Graphics' SILICON SURF Home Page

URL address: **http://www.sgi.com/**

This server makes good use of graphics. You select one of the following:

- Headlines (press release and amp product announcements)

- Products and Services (catalog of products)

- The Classroom (education)

- Techno Corner (technical information)

- Free Lunch (free software and graphics)

- SGI Investor (info on SGI stock)

- What's New! (what's new in Silicon Surf)

Sony Computer Science Laboratory

URL address: **http://www.csl.sony.co.jp**

The Sony Computer Science Laboratory conducts research relating to computer science and aims toward achieving breakthroughs in computer development. The Web page describes the lab's research environment, its members and their interests, and some of the lab's projects. It also has links to other, more general WWW sites and links to information and updates on the status of activities regarding the large earthquake that rocked Japan in early 1995.

Sprint

URL address: **http://www.sprintlink.net**

Find out about the products and services of this major telephone carrier. The home page relies on graphics for links, so have your graphics on!

Sun Microsystems Home Page

URL address: **http://www.sun.com/**

This server makes good use of graphics to provide information about products and services from Sun Microsystems, including current and in-press books, research reports, and other public information.

Sunergy Home Page

URL address: **http://www.sun.com/sunergy/**

The Sunergy program offers satellite television broadcasts, newsletters, and whitepapers designed to educate members of the computer industry worldwide. The site includes broadcast summaries, the text of printed documents, and transcripts of educational materials originally presented in a variety of electronic media.

T3plus Networking Inc.

URL address: **http://www.t3plus.com**

T3plus Networking supplies T3 and SONET broad band wide-area networking solutions. The server provides corporate and product information, as well as examples of network applications.

Technology Board of Trade

URL address: **http://www.tech-board.com/tbot/**

The Technology Board of Trade, recently acquired by Corporate Software, Incorporated, assists businesses in defining, valuing, and exchanging intellectual property and provides for the transfer of commercial technology. The server lists corporate and product information and links to a database of software technology available for licensing as well as for technology being sought.

The Numerical Algorithms Group Ltd.

URL address: **http://www.nag.co.uk:70/**

The server, located in the United Kingdom, provides non-commercial information about NAG's mathematical and scientific software products and services. Information includes technical reports, availability, user notes, installation notes, demos, and downloadable software. The server is also the home of the FORTRAN 90 Software Repository.

UniPress Software, Inc.

URL address: **http://www.unipress.com**

UniPress, a developer and distributor of UNIX software, has designed its server for users to browse its product listings, which range from PC-UNIX connectivity solutions to development tools and applications. Users can also request more information through a form provided on the server. UniPress hosts an online T-shirt contest, includes a "rogues' gallery" of company employee photographs, and allows you to link to individual employees' hotlists of favorite Web sites. Spend a little time poking around here. It's fun.

Xerox

URL address: **http://www.xerox.com**

Xerox is one of the companies involved in the development of CommerceNet. This home page links with information about Xerox products and services as well as a listing of Xerox activities on a month-by-month basis.

VI

Finding Web Resources

Companies—General

Automobiles

URL address: **http://akebono.stanford.edu/yahoo/Economy/Business/Corporations/Automobiles/Parts/**

▶ See "Products and Gifts," p. 895

Westex Automotive Inc. is a company that distributes high quality automotive parts and supplies. The site, although a little confusing to navigate, links you to classified ads and other sources for automotive parts and supplies.

Blacksburg

URL address: **http://www.bev.net/welcome/welcome.html**

Fig. 21.17
The Blacksburg home page offers access to an experimental networked community.

All types of information about this community in southwest Virginia. Learn about the business opportunities, the educational offerings, and jump to links about local companies or access area maps.

General Electric

URL address: **http://www.ge.com**

General Electric is a big company—it owns NBC among other holdings. It is so big, in fact, that this site offers a hypertext-based alphabetical listing. Check out its annual report or jump to the Web pages for specific divisions such as Capital Services, Information Services, Plastics, Power Systems, and Corporate Research.

Homebuyer's Fair

URL address: **http://www.homefair.com/**

Buying or selling a home? Trying to get a mortgage? This Web site has links to all sorts of real estate information. With one link, you can obtain a free subscription to a housing guide from any one of 23 metro areas in the U.S.

and Canada. And, if you're moving but not quite ready to buy, try the Apartment Relocation listings in cities across the U.S. You fill in your requirements in a forms-based questionnaire and the company gets back to you with listings that meet your needs.

Lockheed Missiles Company

URL address: **http://www.lmsc.lockheed.com**

Provides information on many of Lockheed's operations, including an artist's rendering of the Hubble Telescope, press releases describing Lockheed's technological successes, and links to other online services.

What Is Wavefront Technologies?

URL address: **http://wavefront.wti.com/whatis.html**

Wavefront supplies 2D and 3D animation software for creating high-end animation and simulations. Product and corporate information, employees' home pages, newsgroup links, and animation are featured here.

Consulting

Hundred Acre Consulting

URL address: **http://www.pooh.com/**

Hundred Acre Consulting, located in Nevada, does software engineering and development. Through this server, you can link to GNU online documentation and an FTP archive, among other services.

Dainamic Consulting

URL address: **http://www.netpart.com/dai/home.html**

Dainamic Consulting offers overall marketing strategy and management services for high technology companies. The server provides company information and service descriptions.

Financial

Chicago Mercantile Exchange

URL address: **http://www.interaccess.com:80/cme/**

This is the home page for the World's Largest Marketplace, trading approximately $200 trillion annually in financial and agricultural futures and options. Here you will find links and information about CME background, volume, membership price and charts. There is also a link to a model for federal financial regulation, a proposal for streamlining government oversight of financial institutions, and a glossary of futures-related terms—just in case you don't already know them.

Credit Card Application
URL address: **http://www.its.com**

This site is billed as the location of "the first online credit card application." Check out how you can get a Rolling Stones MasterCard, provided in conjunction with Chevy Chase Bank and the Rolling Stones.

DowVision
URL address: **http://dowvision.wais.net/**

The Wall St. Journal, New York Times, and Dow Jones News Service are all online as part of DowVision. There is a limited time testing of this service. At some time, it will be a commercial service with fees.

Dun & Bradstreet Information Services
URL address: **http://www.dbisna.com/**

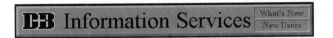

Fig. 21.18
The Dun & Bradstreet information services page.

A great Web server for locating financial information about companies and industries and lots of good jumping-off links to other Web financial resources. Learn how to market your business globally or manage your vendors.

Experimental Stock Market Data
URL address: **http://www.ai.mit.edu:80/stocks.html**

This page provides a link to the latest stock market information. It is updated daily to reflect the current day's closing information. It consists of general market news and quotes for selected stocks.

FINWeb Home Page
URL address: **http://riskweb.bus.utexas.edu/finweb.htm**

FINWeb bills itself as a financial economics WWW server. It offers links to economics and finance-related WWW servers. You can locate drafts of working papers from the National Bureau of Economic Research, jump to stock market reports, and access thousands of federal, state, and local government WWW sites.

Interactive NestEgg
URL address: **http://nestegg.iddis.com/nestegg/nestegg/
backnest.html**

NestEgg is a personal finance publication distributed to more than 2 million
homes. Interactive NestEgg has indexed links to all articles published in
NestEgg plus additional features including regularly updated mutual fund
and securities performance charts and a financial bookstore provided by the
New York Institute of Finance.

J.P. Morgan & Company
URL address: **http://www.jpmorgan.com**

Fig. 21.19
J.P. Morgan brings
investment tools
to the Web.

The banking and financial giant J.P. Morgan has jumped "head first" into the
Internet and Web. To position themselves as a leader in the world of finance,
the company began a risk-measurement service called RiskMetrics. This service uses complex mathematical formulas to help investors (primarily institu-
tional) evaluate risks of investments. These risk data sets are posted daily to
the Web.

In addition, there is information about the government bond index, mortgage refinance index, and mortgage purchase index on the Web. The firm
also has digital recruiting brochures to attract new talent.

Myers Equity Express
URL address: **http://www.internet-is.com:80/myers/mortform.html**

This service allows you to request a loan interest rate quote via the Internet.
You may request a quote for a home loan by filling in as much of the provided form as you care to, using a point-and-click procedure as shown in
figure 21.20. The company responds with a current quote.

Fig. 21.20

Use the Myers Equity Express page to check on home loan rates.

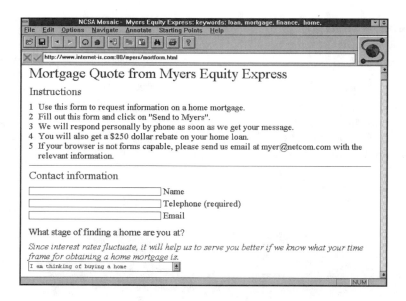

NASDAQ Financial Executive Journal

URL address: **http://www.law.cornell.edu/nasdaq/nasdtoc.html**

Financial Executive Journal is a shared project of the Legal Information Institute at Cornell Law School and The Nasdaq (SM) Stock Market. The server provides back issues of the journal for your review.

QuoteCom

URL address: **http://www.quote.com**

QuoteCom provides financial market data to Internet users, both for free and on a subscription basis, if you require more detailed data. This server provides information on the company and its services.

International

E-EUROPE

URL address: **http://freenet3.scri.fsu.edu:81/doc/eebn.doc**

Designed to help persons wanting to do business in Eastern Europe, this server is a text-only collection of files, e-mail addresses, lists of business possibilities, and agencies that can be of assistance.

Interfinance Limited
URL address: **http://intergroup.com/interfinance**

Located in the Netherlands, this company provides advisory and intermediary services in areas of investment banking, real estate, commercial and industrial project loans, and venture capital. The WWW site contains newsletters, statement of policies, and application forms.

Internet Guide to Japan Information Resources (Experimental)
URL address: **http://fuji.stanford.edu**

Internet X-Guide to Japan Information, Stanford University's experimental guide to Japanese information, represents a first cut at organizing the widely diverse information sources about Japan currently available over the Internet.

Major categories of Japanese information currently maintained in the X-Guide include the following: Japanese science and technology information; Japanese business, economic, and financial information; U.S.-Japan relations and policy; working, studying, traveling and living in Japan; Japanese language computing; teaching Japanese and about Japan; internship opportunities in Japan; Japan industry and technology management training program (JITMT) universities; and a program guide.

You have access to text and graphics that previously were available only in print—in Japan.

Japan (via Nippon Telephone & Telegraph server)
URL address: **http://www.ntt.jp**

This server opens doors to a tremendous amount of information on Japanese businesses and documents that help you learn how to do business in Japan. One of the great multimedia aspects is a color map of Japan that has pointers to various companies and institutions. Just click an icon and jump to that resource—the URL for the map is **http://www.ntt.jp/japan/map/**.

Russian and East European Studies Business and Economics Resources
URL address: **http://www.pitt.edu:80/~cjp/rsecon.html**

The Central Library of the Budapest University of Economics has produced ECONINFORM, an information system that allows you to display information in German, Hungarian, or English. The system contains a bibliographic database of special economic literature and business information, developed on the basis of UNESCO CDS Micro ISIS 2.3 with the cooperation of MTA SZTAKI KFIIR-labor. It is sponsored by the Information Infrastructure Development Programme.

Fig. 21.21
This page sports a clickable map to find information about various companies in Japan.

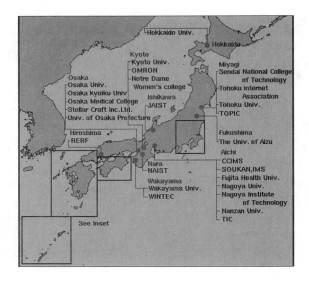

Internet Services

Atlantic's Home Page
URL address: **http://www.atlantic.com/index.html**

This is a server for the Atlantic Computing Technology Corporation, which provides networking/Internet access consulting to Connecticut businesses. Corporate and service information are provided, as well as links to Internet Starting Points, information about living and doing business in Connecticut, and advertisements of Web space for rent.

Canadian Domain Information Server
URL address: **http://www.csi.nb.ca/domain/**

Cybersmith Inc.'s Canadian Domain Information Server lets you use an interactive form to keyword search on "the organizations registered in the Canadian portion of the Internet," as the home page states.

DataFlux Systems

URL address: **http://www.dataflux.bc.ca/home.html**

DataFlux is an Internet provider in Victoria, British Columbia, Canada. The server provides information about the company and its services.

Electric Press, Inc.

URL address: **http://www.elpress.com/homepage.html**

Electric Press displays your information—catalogs, brochures, newsletters—in full-color multimedia format on the WWW. The server provides sample online catalogs, newsletters, and brochures, so you can preview the quality of the work.

Enterprise Integration Technologies

URL address: **http://www.eit.com**

Enterprise Integration Technologies is a Palo Alto-based R&D and consulting company that develops software and services to promote commercial use of the Internet. Its home page includes an overview of the company and its services, as well as descriptions of some of its projects.

Fnet

URL address: **http://www.fnet.fr**

This site is an association that provides Internet access in France and in Europe. The Web page is in French, but you have the option to select pages in English. There is company and technology information, plus pointers to research services.

InteleNet Home Page

URL address: **http://www.intelenet.com/**

This server describes the services offered by InteleNet Consulting Services. The company's areas of expertise include Internet connectivity, support and maintenance; Network design, installation, support and maintenance; UNIX systems administration and software development; ISDN design, installation and support, and the maintenance of ISDN-based telecommuting applications.

Internet Business Directory

URL address: **http://ibd.ar.com**

The Internet Business Directory (IBD) home page will take you to an "electronic" catalog/index of many companies that have Web sites. The other service of the IBD is helping Web surfers locate new jobs and post resumes.

Internet Distribution Services

URL address: **http://www.service.com/**

Internet Distribution Services, Inc. provides electronic marketing, publishing, and distribution services on the Internet. You can learn about the company's products, services, and clients, and can link to some of those clients' home pages, through this server.

MCSNet Home Page

URL address: **http://www.mcs.net/**

Contains information about Macro Computer Solutions, Inc., owners and operators of the MCSNet Internet Provider in the Chicago area. It has a provision of an automated scanner that runs nightly for subscriber home pages, which appear in the server's domain every night shortly after midnight central time. An "Interesting Places" link points readers to useful Internet resources. You also can access an online bookstore.

Online System Services (OSS)

URL address: **http://www.ossinc.net**

This site proves that business can be fun. The home page opens with a click-on graphic that shows the interior of a rocket ship headed towards a variety of interesting planets. Click on planets and visit "worlds" of amusement, Internet resources, and Web search tools. There are also links (on the control panel inside the spaceship) to information about OSS. The company provides several levels of Internet connectivity, offers training classes for beginner and advanced users, and designs, develops and maintains Web pages for clients.

Real/Time Communications

URL address: **http://kaleidoscope.bga.com/**

They provide international marketing and sales opportunities through the World Wide Web/Internet, as well as news and information concerning the growth and advances in telecommunications, networking, and events of interest to the Internet community.

StrategyWeb Pre-Home Page

URL address: **http://fender.onramp.net/~atw_dhw/precom.htm**

You can browse StrategyWeb for information on developing strategic plans, regardless of your business or service area. The Web page is very much under construction, but contains interesting links to information on education, management, and cognitive psychology, among others.

Welcome to XOR Network Engineering, Inc.

URL address: **http://xor.com:80/xor/**

XOR Network Engineering provides Internet services for companies who can't afford to maintain their own Internet connection and services or who choose not to. They also coordinate training and trade show services for clients. The home page describes these services in detail.

Science and Business

Alberta Research Council

URL address: **http://www.arc.ab.ca:80/**

The Alberta Research Council carries out applied science, engineering, and technology development for the benefit of the province of Alberta. Its home page describes the services it provides, including video and audio clips. The home page also presents company news and links the reader to related Web sites, including the Best of the Web (**http://wings.buffalo.edu/ contest/**).

BEST North America

URL address: **http://medoc.gdb.org/best.html**

Identify and locate researchers with interests and expertise which match yours—assuming you are a researcher. This site has an online inventory of researchers, inventions, and facilities at U.S. and Canadian universities, and other organizations. In all, there are 40,000 records of individuals, 5,000 inventions, and 2,000 facilities.

NREL's WWW Server

URL address: **http://www.nrel.gov/**

Fig. 21.22
The NREL home
page logo.

▶ See "Environ-
mental Sci-
ences," p. 858

The National Renewable Energy Laboratory is a national laboratory of the
U.S. Department of Energy. Located in Colorado, NREL's server provides information about the laboratory and its research, and about renewable energy research, development, and applications. Other information includes
technology transfer of renewable energy research to the private sector; accumulated energy data and resource maps; publications; and business and job
opportunities.

Small Business and Individual Resources

About Home-Based Businesses

URL address: **http://freenet3.scri.fsu.edu:81/ht-free/hbb1.html**

This site provides the history of working from home and information about
doing it. Through the Tallahassee, Florida, Freenet, links are provided to topics such as Information About the HBB; Membership in HBB; Meeting Information; Questions/Comments; Featured Business of the Month; The HBB
Newsletter, and HBB References.

Company Corporation

URL address: **http://www.service.com/tcc/home.html**

This server gives you information on how you can incorporate your business.
It provides links to the company introduction, advises on why it is a good
idea to incorporate, explains the four types of corporations and which one is
right for you, suggests 16 reasons to incorporate in Delaware, provides basic
incorporation costs for all 50 states, and explains additional services the
Company Corporation provides.

Corporate Agents, Inc.

URL address: **http://www.corporate.com**

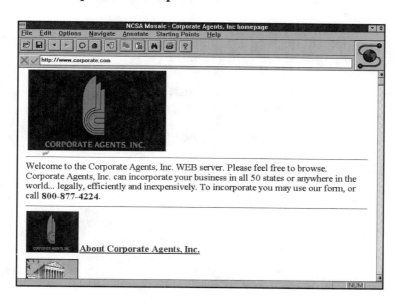

Fig. 21.23
You can incorporate your business by using a form at this server.

A service to help people form their own corporations or limited liability companies (LLC) over the Internet. You can form a corporation in almost any U.S. state, country, or jurisdiction worldwide and the process takes about 10 minutes. The server also has information on the advantages of incorporation.

Entrepreneurs on the Web

URL address: **http://sashimi.wwa.com/~notime/eotw/EOTW.html**

Provided by No Time Enterprises, this is a server for entrepreneurs. It offers a variety of business information, products, and services of interest to entrepreneurs, including a FAQ document about advertising on the Internet.

Even/Anna, Ltd

URL address: **http://www.ais.net/evenanna**

This company (and site) offers a variety of promotional products to advertise a business. Find out about clothing, pens, mugs, and other products. Perhaps a key chain that looks like a floppy disk or a mouse pad imprinted with your company name and logo.

Execusoft

URL address: **http://www.utw.com/execusoft/homepge.html**

Execusoft is a high-technology consulting firm that uses its Web page both to advertise its services and to recruit new consultants. The page describes job opportunities in various computer-related projects.

MelaNet Information and Communications Network

URL address: **http://www.melanet.com/melanet/**

MelaNet is a Web site that helps African-American business people market their goods and services to an Internet-based audience. MelaNet highlights businesses looking for a sub-contractor match in performing U.S. government contracts. Other links offer demographic and economic data relevant to the African-American community, educational opportunities, and non-profit organizations.

Westcoast Interchange

URL address: **http://interchange.idc.uvic.ca/**

Fig. 21.24
Communicopia Environmental Research is one of the pages that links from the Westcoast Interchange.

Located in Victoria, British Columbia, Canada, Westcoast Interchange is a startup Internet service business initiating a few small ventures. The company is receptive to proposals from others interested in partnering in business via the WWW. It currently offers a free listing service for real estate and links to Communicopia Environmental Research and Communication, an environmental communication firm.

What Is the American Risk and Insurance Association (ARIA)?

URL address: **http://riskweb.bus.utexas.edu/whataria.htm**

ARIA is an association of insurance scholars and other insurance and risk-management professionals. The server describes the risk-management profession and answers questions about risk theory, as well as about meetings, conferences, publications, and educational opportunities available to risk-management and insurance professionals.

From Here...

If the saying "knowledge is power" is even vaguely true, then the resources in this chapter can help any individual or business become more competitive. Other business tools can be found in:

- Chapter 22, "Computers," where you'll find numerous sites which offer information about computer technology.

- Chapter 27, "International Web Resources," which opens the doors to international commerce.

- Chapter 31, "Shopping," where you'll find numerous electronic malls and stores where you can purchase many different products via the Web.

VI

Finding Web Resources

Chapter 22

Computers

by Bill Eager

With approximately 80 million computers sitting in homes and offices across the United States, it's safe to declare that computers are an integral part of our lives and our society. There are almost as many applications for computers as there are vocations and hobbies. Computers help architects design houses, enable musicians to electronically compose and record songs, and allow scientists to create 3-D models of DNA—the building blocks of life. It is the application of this technology to specific tasks and industries that makes computers useful to people. The listings in this section portray the diverse applications for computers, and highlight the fact that a tremendous amount of information about these applications exists on the World Wide Web.

The "Educational Resources" and "Personal Computer" sections of this chapter help you locate information and answer questions about the operation of your computer. The use of multimedia, the foundation of the World Wide Web, now stretches into many different fields; the "Multimedia" listings provide resources that range from software tools to WWW servers that demonstrate multimedia. If you're in the mood for some high-tech reading, visit electronic computer publications for copy that ranges from articles about the industry to science fiction stories. There are listings of organizations, companies, and educational institutions that contribute to the ongoing development of computer hardware, software, and networks—resources valuable to anyone who has an interest in advanced computer technology. The Internet and World Wide Web resource listings provide addresses of home pages that can help you learn more about the Internet and the Web—everything from technical specifications of servers to articles and frequently asked question (FAQ) files about resources and navigational techniques. Here is a breakdown of the categories of computer resources in this chapter:

- Computer hardware and software

- Educational resources

- Graphics, 3-D imaging, and virtual reality

- Infrastructure and networks

- International

- Internet and World Wide Web resources

- Multimedia

- Music

- Organizations and associations

- Personal computers and PC software (IBM-compatible, Macintosh)

- Publications, magazines, and articles

- Research—government agencies

- Research—universities

- Security

- Supercomputing

National Center for Supercomputing Applications (NCSA)

URL address: **http://www.ncsa.uiuc.edu/demoweb/demo.html**

If you want to learn more about the Mosaic WWW browser, update your version of the software, or simply explore interesting Web links, travel to the server at the National Center for Supercomputing Applications (NCSA)—the same organization that gave birth to Mosaic. This home page provides a fantastic demonstration of the multimedia capabilities of Mosaic and the Web. The page begins with an overview of the history of Mosaic, complete with audio messages. There's a brief explanation of hypermedia, complete with a picture of Vice President Al Gore. The home page also has more than 100 links (with short descriptions) to Web sites around the world.

You can also jump to the NCSA Mosaic home page (**http://www.ncsa.uiuc.edu/SDG/Software/Mosaic/ NCSAMosaicHome.html**), which has links that focus on information resources specific to Mosaic. You can find out about the latest developments and features of this browser, such as a version that will ensure security of financial transactions via the Internet.

Another useful link from the home page is to the NCSA "What's New" page (**http://www.ncsa.utuc.edu/SDG/Software/Mosaic/Docs/ whats-new.html**). This page offers a chronological listing of new WWW resources. The listings start with the week you connect and date back about three weeks. Each listing includes a brief description, and the name of the resource is a hyperlink to that Web server. Here are two examples:

> "The office of USA Vice President, Al Gore, announces *FinanceNet*, providing access to financial management documents and information pertaining to all levels of government: foreign, Federal, state, and local."

> "The World's Greatest Rock 'n' Roll Band is proud to announce their very own Web Server. They are the *Rolling Stones* and they are now giving you the best place in netland for the real Stones fan to hang out."

In both instances, the highlighted text (shown here in italics) represents a link. If these descriptions have piqued your interest, the FinanceNet address is **http://www.financenet.gov**, and you can find the Rolling Stones at **http://www.stones.com/**.

Apple Computers, Inc.

URL address: **http://www.apple.com**

Apple Computers continues to develop unique, computer-based products and services. The Apple Newton is a hand-held personal digital assistant (PDA) that manages information and can be used to send electronic mail messages to and from remote locations; the Power PC is a high-speed computer that uses both Macintosh and IBM-compatible files and programs; and E-World is a commercial online service similar to CompuServe or America Online.

Perhaps you need to learn how to expand your 4M PowerBook 150 to 8M RAM, or you'd like to participate in a local Apple user group. You can learn about these products and services when you connect to the Apple WWW home page. The main menu offers the following selections:

- What's New

- Information about Apple

- Apple Products and Support

- Apple Developer Services and Products

- Apple Research & Technology

- Apple Programs and Products for Special User Communities

- Outside Resources

About 50 percent of these links open hypertext documents that contain other links and informational documents. The other half connect to Gopher menus where you navigate through easy-to-understand subdirectories to get the information you need. The freeware/shareware sites link offers a list of non-Apple places where you can get free advice and software applications for many different Apple products. Examples include the University of Michigan (**ftp://mac.archive.umich.edu/mac/**), Washington University (**http://www.uwtc.washington.edu/JonWiederspan/ MacSupportOnInternet.html**), and University of Iowa (**ftp:// newton.uiowa.edu/pub/NewtonSoftware**).

Fig. 22.1

Visit this home page if you own or use an Apple Computer product or service.

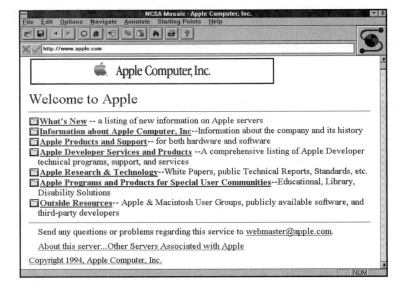

Digital Equipment's Reading Rooms

URL address: **http://www.digital.com:80/.i/info/edu/**

This is a great page for teachers, librarians, and researchers. There are three different links which offer hypertext links to selections of the best sites for books, information, and periodicals fitting into the categories of education, research, libraries, and museums.

The links just never seem to stop. For example, if you try the education link, you get new options for primary, secondary, and higher education. There are "hot site" links that bring you to major educational resources that focus on the Internet. Choose Primary Education and you get a slew of new links— K–12 Internet projects, Internet curriculum, and Internet indexes. This page might fit under the category of education, except that there are entirely different series of connections for researchers and librarians. Also, a lot of the links provide extremely useful information about the Internet and the Web. It's only a guess, but it seems like there are at least 500 links to explore from this one page.

Fig. 22.2
Digital Equipment has a home page that offers an endless series of links to information about the Internet and Web.

Do It Yourself—PC Lube and Tune

URL address: **http://pclt.cis.yale.edu/pclt/default.htm**

The PC Lube and Tune (PCLT) home page represents the ultimate in electronic "self-service"—first you learn about a subject, and then you apply that knowledge to suit your needs. PCLT supplies introductions, tutorials, directions, and education on technical subjects for ordinary computer users through hypertext articles. Examples of a few of the articles include:

- Introduction to PC Hardware

- Introduction to SNA

- Introduction to TCP/IP

- PC Serial Communications

- "Windows on the World" (a project to add Internet software to Windows and OS/2)

InterNIC Provides WWW Online Guide

URL address: **http://www.internic.net**

Fig. 22.3
Established by the National Science Foundation, InterNIC offers many resources for people and companies that use the Internet.

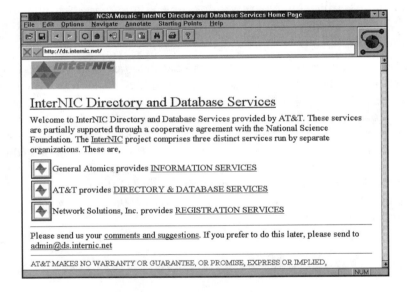

If you could only visit one WWW server for information about the Internet, this would be the place to go. The Internet Network Information Center, known as simply InterNIC, was established in January of 1993 by the National Science Foundation and went into operation on April 1, 1993. The InterNIC is a collaborative effort of three organizations that work together to offer a variety of services, which include information about how to access and use the Internet, assistance in locating resources, and registration of network components for Internet connectivity. The goal of InterNIC is to make network-based information accessible to researchers, educators, and the general public. The term "InterNIC" comes from the cooperative effort between the Network Information Centers, or NICs.

From the InterNIC home page, you can access Information Services, provided by General Atomics; Directory and Database Services, provided by AT&T; and Registration Services, provided by Network Solutions, Inc. The Information Services InfoGuide (**http://internic.net/infoguide.html**) is an online source of information about the Internet, offering pointers to online resources, Internet organizations, access providers, usage statistics, basic and advanced user guides, and a hypertext version of the National Science Foundation Network News. There's a simple electronic index, similar to a library card catalog system, where you select an index based on subject, title, and author, and then follow hyptertext links to specific documents, images, sounds, or video. Another source of online information are Scout Reports, weekly reports that keep users aware of current network activities and offer reviews of new WWW and Internet resources. The reports contain hyperlinks to the resources mentioned.

ISDN—High Speed On-Ramp to the Digital Highway

URL address: **http://www.pacbell.com/isdn/isdn_home.html**

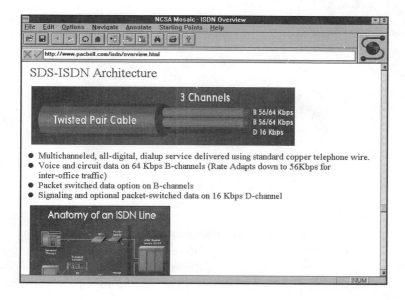

Fig. 22.4
The Pacific Bell home page provides an overview of Integrated Services Digital Network for both beginners and advanced computer users.

Pacific Bell and AT&T Network Systems present information on ISDN, Integrated Services Digital Network. ISDN is a high-speed, digital telephone service delivered to businesses and homes over standard copper telephone wires. ISDN offers usage-based pricing, is easy to use, and provides high speed data service with voice capability. You can access inline graphics that illustrate how you can use ISDN for Internet access, telecommuting, and video conferencing. Links included in this home page include:

- ISDN overview

- ISDN User's Guide

- Pacific Bell ISDN Service Options and Rates

- How to order ISDN or learn more

- ISDN for Internet access

- ISDN for videoconferencing

Try Cutting-Edge Computer Applications at MIT

URL address: **http://tns-www.lcs.mit.edu/tns-www-home.html**

Fig. 22.5
MIT's Telemedia, Networks, and Systems Group WWW server lets you try some of the cutting-edge applications of computer-network multimedia.

The MIT Laboratory for Computer Science is an interdepartment laboratory that focuses on research in computer science and engineering. The Telemedia, Networks, and Systems Group (TNS) is a research group at the MIT Laboratory for Computer Science. The group studies topics in distributed multimedia systems—the hardware, software, and networks that enable multimedia information to travel to computers.

The TNS home page offers hyperlinks that help you navigate the world of computers and computing. For example, you can jump from the WWW Index to Multimedia Information Sources. Another interesting link is to The National Information Infrastructure: Agenda for Action, where you can hear a speech by Secretary Brown on the topic of The National Information Infrastructure, and view clips of the video "Toward a National Information Infrastructure."

Computer Hardware

Compaq Computer Corporation

URL address: **http://WWW.Compaq.Com/homepage.text.html**

From this page, you can follow links to online support and information on Compaq products, programs, and service.

Network Hardware Suppliers List

URL address: **http://www.ai.mit.edu/datawave/hardware.html**

This site has a list of dealers in new and used telecommunications and computer hardware that have been favorably discussed on the Internet. Many of the hardware systems and drivers are for systems running BSDI's UNIX OS.

PicturePhone Direct

URL address: **http://ppd.gems.com/ppd**

This is an online catalog of desktop video-conferencing products and accessories. Links take you to individual descriptions of products, such as still and full-motion video cameras, Photo CD players, digital to analog converters, and more.

Telecommunications Products

URL address: **http://www.hello-direct.com/hd/**

This site has descriptions of various telecommunications products, including headsets, teleconferencing units, call controllers, and cellular accessories.

VI

Finding Web Resources

Computer Software

AppleScript at Notre Dame

URL address: **http://www.nd.edu**

The University of Notre Dame WWW server is online for general information and includes images, sounds, and AppleScript-based services.

Consensus Development—Collaboration Software

URL address: **ftp://ftp.netcom.com/pub/consensus/www/ConsensusFrontDoor.html**

Consensus Development provides this service, which covers software support for collaboration. This includes *groupware* (defined as software to support collaboration and intentional group processes), decision support, facilitation, electronic democracy, hypertext authoring, online documentation, document architecture, shared spaces, virtual organizations, and online knowledge management.

Genome Software

URL address: **http://www-hgc.lbl.gov/GenomeHome.html**

The Human Genome Center at the Lawrence Berkeley Lab (LBL), in Berkeley, California, provides samples of computer software developed at LBL for use in various Genome studies. For more information about Genome studies, see Chapter 30, "Science," later in this book.

Lumina Decisions Systems, Inc.

URL address: **http://www.lumina.com/lumina/**

Lumina Decision Systems, Inc. of Palo Alto, California, maintains a WWW server that provides information about software for modeling and decision support. Lumina's DEMOS software (Decision Modeling System) is a Macintosh-based, visual environment for creating, analyzing, and communicating probabilistic models for business, risk, and decision analysis.

Numerical Algorithms Group Ltd.

URL address: **http://www.nag.co.uk:70/**

The Numerical Algorithms Group Ltd. (NAG) WWW server provides (non-commercial) information about NAG's mathematical and scientific software products and services. Information includes technical reports, availability, user notes, installation notes, demos, and downloadable software. The server is also the home of the Fortran 90 Software Repository.

Project GeoSim

URL address: **http://geosim.cs.vt.edu/index.html**

Project GeoSim has a WWW server to distribute Geography Education software, developed by the Departments of Geography and Computer Science at Virginia Tech. The software runs on MS-DOS, Macintosh, and DECstations running X-Windows. The Gopher address **gopher://geosim.cs.vt.edu/1** is also available.

Software Development

URL address: **http://www.center.org/csd/home.html**

Do you develop software? Do you need to develop or test on every type of UNIX, PC, Apple Macintosh, pen-based or wireless system, printer, or network available? The Center for Software Development can help you. The Center is a non-profit organization that promotes the growth of software companies. It acts as a catalyst between areas of the software industry—software developers, hardware and software vendors, and service providers. This Web site has information about the Center and resources to help software developers.

Software Forum

URL address: **http://software.net/index.htm**

The software forum offers links to descriptions (and sales) of more than 7,500 software programs for all platforms. There are also links to other publications and a help desk that may solve some of your software-related problems.

Fig. 22.6
Software.Net helps you find out about thousands of software products for all computer platforms.

UNIX Index

URL address: **gopher://ici.proper.com/77c/unix/.cache**

This is a searchable database of information on the Internet that relates to UNIX. There are many UNIX-related Gopher and WWW servers on the Internet that have interesting information. If you are primarily an e-mail user, there are UNIX mailing lists. Much of the current information is found in UseNet newsgroups. The UNIX frequently asked questions (FAQ) files, produced in the UseNet newsgroups, have become repositories for UNIX-related information on the Internet.

Educational Resources

▶ See "Department of Education," p. 676

The following resources list general educational resources, such as online computer dictionaries and bibliographies of texts devoted to computers. If you have an interest in college and university programs devoted to computer science, check out the resources in Chapter 23, "Education," which focus on educational programs around the world.

CERN—High Energy Physics and the World Wide Web
URL address: **http://info.cern.ch/hypertext**

Visit the home page for the European High Energy Physics Laboratory—the organization that began the World Wide Web and continues to contribute to its development. There are some terrific WWW resources and links here—everything from online Web tutorials to searchable indexes of WWW servers.

Computational Science Education Project
URL address: **http://csep1.phy.ornl.gov/csep.html**

This home page provides links to a variety of educational teaching materials for undergraduate and graduate students in computational science and engineering.

Computer Dictionary
URL address: **http://wombat.doc.ic.ac.uk**

This WWW site provides a free online dictionary of computing terms. If you want to keep up with all the latest buzzwords, try finding them here. This is a great source of information for browsers who aren't computer experts, but who need to know the "language."

Computer-Mediated Communication
URL address: **http://www.rpi.edu/~decemj/cmc/center.html**

The Computer-Mediated Communication Studies Center serves the needs of researchers, students, teachers, and practitioners interested in computer-mediated communication (CMC)—in plain English, communication that is created and distributed via computer. This center and Web site help people share information, make contacts, collaborate, and learn about developments and events related to CMC. The home page has links to the *CMC Magazine*, which has a directory of people interested in the topic (you can add your name and e-mail address) and a list of activities, such as conferences and other resources.

Computer Science Bibliography

URL address: **http://www.ira.uka.de/ftp/ira/bibliography/index.html**

This Web site offers a computer science bibliography collection that contains more than 400 bibliographies and 240,000 references to journal articles, conference papers, and technical reports. Subjects include artificial intelligence, databases, neural networks, and parallel processing.

DELTA

URL address: **http://gozer.idbsu.edu/business/nethome.html**

Distributed ELectronic Telecommunications Archive (DELTA) is an archive of information related to teaching and learning about business telecommunications and data communications. This is a good site for higher level educators.

Great Computer Minds

URL address: **http://www.sun.com/sunergy/**

Sun Microsystem's Sunergy program offers satellite television broadcasts, newsletters, and white papers. Sunergy presents the views of people who work in the computer industry.

Help for UNIX Novices

URL address: **http://www.ucs.ed.ac.uk/Unixhelp/TOP_.html**

Unixhelp is an experimental WWW server with helpful information for new users of the UNIX operating system. For anyone wanting to learn the ins and outs of UNIX, this is worth browsing.

IBM Kiosk for Education

URL address: **http://ike.engr.washington.edu/ike.html">**

IKE, the IBM Kiosk for Education, is a free information service for IBM users in the higher education community. IKE offers IBM product information and news, as well as software to download and a bulletin board for exchanging ideas with colleagues.

Jargon File

URL address: **http://web.cnam.fr/Jargon/**

This is an electronic dictionary of computer jargon—the foundation of the book *The New Hacker's Dictionary*.

National Center for Supercomputing Applications (NCSA)

URL address: **http://www.ncsa.uiuc.edu**

◄ See "Key WWW Developments: A Recipe for Success," p.29

This is the address for the NCSA home page. NSCA has been instrumental in the development of the World Wide Web, notably for the creation of the Mosaic browser. There is a tremendous amount of information on Mosaic and the WWW at this site, and numerous links to WWW demos and other servers.

Online Educational Technology

URL address: **http://ccat.sas.upenn.edu**

Educational Technology Services (ETS) and SAS Computing in the School of Arts & Sciences at the University of Pennsylvania maintain this server. ETS supports the instructional and research computing and technological needs of the School of Arts & Sciences. Incorporated in the server is the CCAT (Center for Computer Analysis of Texts, a sub-unit of ETS) Gopher server, which contains one of the largest online text archives in the world. Other areas under development are the digital language lab, an attempt to distribute audio/video materials traditionally delivered in a cassette language lab digitally over the Internet; and the digital slide library, an initiative to make slides for Art History and other courses using images available on the Internet.

Online World

URL address: **http://login.eunet.no/~presno**

This is an electronic handbook about how to use online information resources. The hypertext document explores selected computer applications including online services, databases, entertainment, special services for professionals, and organizations.

Technical Glossary

URL address: **http://www.careermosaic.com/cm/seagate/ seagate8.html**

Fig. 22.7
The Seagate-sponsored technical glossary is a hypertext reference guide to hundreds of computer terms and abbreviations.

If you think the "landing zone" is where your plane screeches to a halt, you need this Web page. Sponsored by Seagate, this page is a large technical glossary of computer terms—in all, there are some 300 industry terms and 200 abbreviations. At the top of the page, there is an A–Z selection of links that quickly get you to the word or term you want. By the way, the *landing zone* is where the read/write heads on your hard drive sit when they're not active.

Web66

URL address: **http://web66.coled.umn.edu**

The University of Minnesota College of Education offers this site to help K–12 educators learn how to set up their own Web servers, link K–12 servers, and find and use K–12 appropriate resources on the Web. The Web66 server features a Server Cookbook that has "recipes" with step-by-step instructions for establishing a Web site using a Macintosh computer.

Graphics, 3-D Imaging, and Virtual Reality

Computer Graphics

URL address: **http://info.mcc.ac.uk/CGU/CGU-intro.html**

The Computer Graphics Unit (CGU) at Manchester College maintains this interesting server. Included here are CGU services, software, research, images, computer graphics, and scientific visualization information. This server is officially mandated and representative of the CGU.

Computer Graphics

URL address: **http://info.mcc.ac.uk/CGU/ITTI/gravigs.html**

The ITTI Gravigs project produced complete teaching packs on the use of computer graphics and scientific visualization for scientists, engineers, and medics. Some packs have been released; you can read about the pack contents, scope, and prices for the following:

Standards for Computer Graphics

Color in Computer Graphics

Visualization 1: Graphical Communication

Visualization 2: Graphical Exploration

Computer Graphics at the University of Manchester
URL address: **http://info.mcc.ac.uk/CGU/CGU-intro.html**

The Computer Graphics Unit at the University of Manchester provides computer graphics and scientific visualization services. They are now serving information on the Web, including descriptions of graphical software they have developed (much of which is freely available) and graphics research they are doing (which means lots of pretty pictures and several MPEG movies).

Online Searchable Map
URL address: **http://www.cica.indiana.edu/**

The Center for Innovative Computer Application (CICA) Web server provides information about CICA, articles and projects by CICA staff, computer graphics, visualization, sonification, high-performance computing, special computing needs, and other areas of interest to CICA. It also contains the Indiana University Bloomington Searchable Campus Map and the Graphical Bloomington Weather Report.

Virology Images and Animation
URL address: **http://www.bocklabs.wisc.edu**

The Institute for Molecular Virology at the University of Wisconsin offers their WWW server, which provides computer-generated images and animations of viruses, topographical maps, digitized electron micrographs of viruses, and tutorial information on selected topics in virology.

Virtual Reality and 3-D Computing
URL address: **http://www.dataspace.com/**

Lateiner Dataspace supports this server of information on high-performance 3-D computation, including the ARPA proposal done in partnership with Kendall Square Research for a real-time volume rendered virtual reality with real-time physical simulation. This is a rather technical, but worthwhile Web resource.

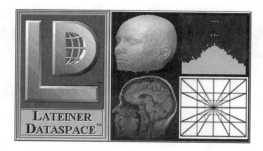

Virtual Reality at Argonne National Laboratory

URL address: **http://www.mcs.anl.gov/home/nickless/CAVE/anlcave.html**

The Mathematics and Computer Science Division at the Argonne National Laboratory presents this WWW server. It includes information on Argonne's Mathematics and Computer Science Division, which has the world's largest IBM massively parallel computer (an SP1) and is establishing a CAVE virtual reality environment.

Infrastructure and Networks

American Management Systems, Inc.

URL address: **http://www.amsinc.com/default.htm**

AMS helps commercial, government, and non-profit organizations improve performance through the use of information technology. Learn about AMS services in information technology consulting, business process reengineering, systems integration, and software design. There's also a link to financial news for investors.

AT&T—Computer Networks

URL address: **http://www.research.att.com/**

A WWW server at AT&T Bell Laboratories is available. The home page includes a link to a bibliography of about 11,000 entries covering computer networks. About one-third of these have abstracts and some entries have links to PostScript copies of the paper. Another home page link focuses on electronic publishing.

Fig. 22.8
Virtual reality is a computer-created world that enables users to experience events and environments that they can't visit in the real world, such as virtual surgery where doctors can practice surgery on patients that only exist electronically.

VI

Finding Web Resources

Fig. 22.9
This AT&T home page has a link to a bibliography of more than 11,000 documents that focus on computer networks.

An AT&T Bell Laboratories Research World-Wide Web Server

Bell Operating Companies—Modified Final Judgment

URL address: **gopher://bell.com**

The Modified Final Judgment (MFJ) Task Force, a committee of the several regional Bell operating companies that works on telecommunications issues in Washington, is now on the Internet via this WWW home page. The MFJ is the ruling that broke up the telephone monopoly.

California PUC

URL address: **gopher://brie.berkeley.edu:2234/0/Infra**

The California Public Utilities Commission (CPUC) released "Enhancing California's Competitive Strength: A Strategy for Telecommunications Infrastructure," its report to Governor Pete Wilson. This is a helpful document if you're working with your local Public Utilities Commission (PUC) to advance telecommunications in your state.

Community Networks

URL address: **http://www.cs.washington.edu/research/community-networks/**

This site provides access to information gained from community computer network surveys. If you're performing your own research, this site can provide insight into the work of others. If you're in the process of justifying telecommunications in your area, this information will be very helpful.

Computers in Networks (article)

URL address: **gopher://gopher.psg.com**

This site contains information about networking in the developing world, low-cost networking tools, and computer networking in general. This is an article that presents a general overview that will be of interest to anyone who is working with limited resources.

Global Networks
URL address: **http://santafe.edu/**

This site provides information from the Santa Fe Institute about complex systems, including global computer networks. The Santa Fe Institute is known for its approach to complex problems.

High Performance Computing
URL address: **http://www.hpcc.gov/**

The National Coordination Office for High Performance Computing and Communications (NCO/HPCC) server contains a variety of HPCC-related information, including the FY 1994 "Blue Book" titled *High Performance Computing and Communications: Towards a National Information Infrastructure.*

National Telecommunications and Information Administration
URL address: **telnet://ntiabbs.ntia.doc.gov**

This site contains information from the National Telecommunications and Information Administration (NTIA-USA). The NTIA is the group responsible for the development of the Information Superhighway in the United States.

Network Conferencing (article)
URL address: **ftp://nic.merit.edu/documents/rfc/rfc1324.txt**

This is a discussion on computer network conferencing by D. Reed. Computer network conferencing is an application that some find valuable and others find frustrating. If you want to learn more about this major application of telecommunications hardware and software, check out this site.

Online Services
The commercial online services have quickly geared up to provide both Internet and World Wide Web access to their members. If you're already a Web cruiser, you can visit the home pages of these online services to learn more about what they offer. Who knows, perhaps you'll decide to have more than one account. Here are the Web addresses for three popular services.

Online Service	Web Address
CompuServe	http://www.compuserve.com
Prodigy	http://www.astranet.com
Delphi	http://www.delphi.com

Fig. 22.10
Commercial online companies like CompuServe not only offer Web access—they have Web home pages too!

Telcos

Telephone companies also have a vested interest in maintaining an online presence as they hope to offer advanced services which may soon use the Internet/Web as a partial delivery system. You can connect to the home pages for the regional bell operating companies (RBOCS) to learn about their services. The MFJ (Modified Final Judgment) is a lobbying group sponsored by the REBOCS. The home page features information about telephone and cable TV regulation.

Company	Web Address
Ameritech	http://www.aads.net
AT&T	http://www.research.att.com
BellSouth	http://www.bst.bls.com
Bell Atlantic	http://www.ba.com
Pacific Bell	http://www.pacbell.com
Southwestern Bell	http://www.tri.sbc.com
US WEST	http://www.service.com/cm/uswest/usw1.html
MFJ Task Force	http://www.bell.com

USC Network Research

URL address: **http://cwis.usc.edu/**

The University of Southern California's (Los Angeles) Computer Networks and Distributed Systems Research Laboratory provides information about high-speed network support for multimedia traffic with real-time requirements.

U.S. Department of Commerce
URL address: **http://www.doc.gov**

The United States Department of Commerce in Washington, D.C., has a WWW server that provides access to both the National Telecommunications Information Administration (NTIA) and the National Institute for Standards and Technology (NIST). These two agencies sponsor several initiatives that impact the future of networks and computing in the U.S. You can also jump to the National Information Initiative home page.

UseNet Archives
URL address: **ftp://lcs.mit.edu/telecom-archives**

This Web site contains Telecomm archive files about telecommunications, from the UseNet group **comp.dcom.telecom**. As with most UseNet archives, some of this information is very valuable, some of it is just fun, and some of it is junk.

International

Canada—Public Works and Government Services Canada
URL address: **http://www.Pwc-Tpc.ca/**

The Experimental Public Works and Government Services Canada (PWGSC) World Wide Web server is now online. This server is being developed by members of Government Telecommunications and Informatics Services (GTIS), a special operating agency of PWGSC. They plan to provide the general public and government departments with information on PWGSC services, programs, initiatives, press releases, and documents.

▶ See "International Web Issues", p. 739

Canada—Victoria FreeNet Information
URL address: **http://freenet.victoria.bc.ca/vifa.html**

The Victoria FreeNet Association's Web server is open to all Internet users. You can access both hypertext/media magazines featuring Canadian titles and a FreeNets and Community Computer Networks home page. If you have an interest in FreeNets, which are essentially electronic towns for local and regional areas, see the FreeNets listings in Chapter 24, "Government."

▶ See "FreeNets," p. 660

VI

Finding Web Resources

Croatia

URL address: **http://tjev.tel.etf.hr/zzt/zzt.html**

This is the first WWW link to Croatia. It's the home page of the Telecommunications Department, University of Zagreb. It provides links to currently existing Net resources in Croatia.

France

URL address: **http://arctique.int-evry.fr**

This is the Web home page for the Institut National des Telecommunications, France. Also check out URL address **http://www.enst.fr/index.html**. Telecom Paris is part of a larger institution for graduate-level instruction in telecommunications.

France—INRIA

URL address: **http://zenon.inria.fr:8003**

Fig. 22.11
If you have an interest in telecommunications, you must visit France's INRIA home page, which has links to a vast amount of technical and application-related information.

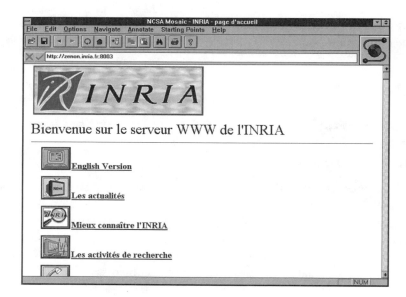

INRIA is a French research institute. You can access and keyword search a library catalog database of thousands of scientific and technical research reports. The home page also has links to news and info about INRIA and its research activities and services.

Germany—Institute for Open Communikation Systems

URL address: **http://www.fokus.gmd.de/**

This Web site is sponsored by the Institute for Open Communikation Systems FOKUS, an institute of the German National Research Center for Computer Science (GMD). You can find out about research activities that deal with the Open Application and Intercommunications Model (OAI).

Greece—Parallel Processing

URL address: **http://www.hpcl.cti.gr/**

The Athens High Performance Computing Laboratory in Athens, Greece, is a non-profit organization. The lab and the information available via this home page focus on research and development in High Performance Computing and Networking (HPCN).

Japan—Telecommunications in Japan

URL address: **http://www.crl.go.jp**

The Communications Research Laboratory (CRL) of the Ministry of Posts and Telecommunications is the only national institute responsible for the study of telecommunications technologies, radio science, and radio applications in Japan. As you would expect, Japan has expressed an extremely high degree of interest in telecommunications and this site provides the user with some insight into that country's efforts.

Switzerland—High-End Research in the Alps

URL address: **http://www.idiap.ch/**

IDIAP (Institut Dalle Molle d'Intelligence Artificielle Perceptive) is a publicly funded Swiss research institute located in the canton of Valais. It makes this WWW server available to share information on its efforts. Researchers at IDIAP work on computer vision, handwriting recognition, OCR, expert systems, neural networks, optical computing, and speech recognition.

Internet and World Wide Web Resources

CERN
URL address: **http://info.cern.ch/hypertext/WWW/TheProject.html**

Need a Web primer? Researchers at CERN created the Web, and this CERN document provides an overview of the development of the system. A link that explains the background includes an "illustrated talk" complete with viewgraphs you can download and print out. Other link choices include a bibliography of reference material, technical information, WWW newsgroups, and information about getting CERN code for the Web. Another CERN home page, **http://info.cern.ch/hypertext/WWW/LineMode/ Defaults/default.html**, is a great place to get a general overview of the Web's resources. Links break WWW sites into subject categories, servers by country, and "service types," which encompasses services such as X.500 mail gateways, FTP, and Telnet sessions.

Charm Net Personal IP Page
URL address: **http://www.charm.net/ppp.html**

This page contains lots of information and links to resources about how to obtain connection to the Internet. There are magazine articles, frequently asked questions files, comparisons of SLIP versus PPP connectivity, and, for advanced users, information on establishing an Internet/Web server.

ExpressNet
URL address: **http://www.pcxpress.com:8086/about/about.html**

This site gives you access to information on the Internet and computing, DOS and Windows-related information, software, FAQs, forums, and computer companies.

Finding People on the Internet
URL address: **http://alpha.acast.nova.edu/phone.html**

With some 30 million users, it's no small challenge to locate a single Internet user. This home page may help. It offers resources and advice on several Internet search/address systems, including Netfind (search for a user's electronic mail address), Finger (how to identify a user from their e-mail address), Phonebooks (a means of searching organizational directories), X.500 (the new standard in global mail directories), and Whois (enables you to look up details about an institution from the domain name).

Global Network Navigator Internet Help Desk

URL address: **http://gnn.interpath.net/gnn/helpdesk/index.html**

This is a very easy page to navigate. You can do online keyword searching to find what you need. Jump to the first link, "Ask the Experts," which is a weekly advice column hosted by different experts. An example of one Q&A format question fielded by an expert was, "Are Internet and UseNet the same? I hear these names used synonymously." Other home page choices include:

- *Internet Basics.* A variety of help documents and user's guides

- *Resource Guides.* A subject-based hypertext list of resources

- *Internet Tools.* E-mail, FTP, Telnet, Gopher, and more

- *Training.* Resources for Internet training

- *Access and Providers.* A list of Internet/WWW service providers

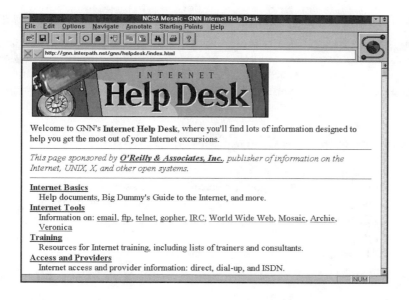

Fig. 22.12
The Internet Help Desk page provides access to much valuable Net information.

Information on WWW

URL address: **http://www.bsdi.com/server/doc/web-info.html**

This site offers an extensive array of information links, including an overview of the WWW project, hypertext terms, and starting points for Internet exploration. To help you learn about getting connected, there's a link to service providers. For hypertext authors, there are guides to the hypertext markup language (HTML) and URL information.

VI

Finding Web Resources

Matrix Information and Directory Services

URL address: **http://www.tic.com**

Fig. 22.13
Learn how to
navigate through
the systems and
resources of the
Internet and the
Web with the
links on this home
page.

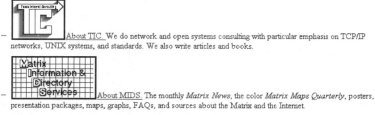

Welcome to the TIC/MIDS WWW Server

About TIC. We do network and open systems consulting with particular emphasis on TCP/IP networks, UNIX systems, and standards. We also write articles and books.

About MIDS. The monthly *Matrix News*, the color *Matrix Maps Quarterly*, posters, presentation packages, maps, graphs, FAQs, and sources about the Matrix and the Internet.

– Zilker Internet Park. An Internet access provider based in Austin, Texas.

– Bruce Sterling's agitprop.

The resources and information at this site cover the field. There are links from the home page to frequently asked questions and to maps and graphs that depict the growth of the Internet and Web. Try the link labeled "About and through WWW, Gopher, FTP and Hytelnet" to get a variety of catalogs, indexes, and resources that will help you navigate through either the Web or Internet. Another home page link, "Other interesting stuff," brings up interesting choices such as WebWeather and mailing list archives.

Netscape

URL address: **http://home.mcom.com**

◀ See "Security of
Web Transac-
tions," p. 428

This is the home page for the company that offers the Netscape browser. There's a lot of information about Netscape and links to fun and useful places on the Internet, including some development tools for creating Web pages. Follow a few links and download an evaluation copy of the Netscape browser.

Remote Sensing and Telerobotics

URL address: **http://www.eia.brad.ac.uk/mark/fave-inter.html**

This site belongs to PhD candidate Mark Cox. He offers numerous links to interactive and remote sensing devices on the Internet. You can, for example, view an aquarium or a coffee pot, check out stock in Coke machines, or operate robot arms.

Web Information

URL address: **http://loanstar.tamu.edu/~rjsparks/www.html**

Find out what transpired at the first WWW International conference, get information on different Web browsers, or learn proper etiquette for information providers. There are also tutorials for using Mosaic and WAIS and links to WWW and Internet newsgroups and search engines.

The Best of WWW Contest
URL address: **http://wings.buffalo.edu/contest/**

Brandon Plewe, Assistant Coordinator for Campus-Wide Information Services at the State University of New York at Buffalo, oversees this WWW site, which announces the winners of the "Best of the Web" contest. There are a total of 13 categories, which include "Best Educational Service," "Best Commercial Service," "Best Navigational Aid," "Best Use of Multiple Media," and "Best Document Design." In addition to a brief description of the winners in each category, there are hyperlinks to the various sites that receive the award. There's also a brief highlight and link to honorable mentions and other nominees.

Multimedia

Academic Multimedia
URL address: **http://148.100.176.70:80/prasad.htm**

The Marist College Web site represents a forum for the presentation of the work and research of students and faculty. There's a lot of experimentation, particularly in the use of multimedia technologies—and this home page will tell you about it.

Art and Multimedia
URL address: **http://cuiwww.unige.ch/Chloe/OtisCrosswire/index.html**

The CROSSWIRE collaborative art collection is available courtesy of Simon Gibbs at Centre Universitaire d'Informatique, University of Geneva. CROSSWIRE is a collaborative art project run by the OTIS digital net-gallery.

Artists and Multimedia
URL address: **http://kspace.com**

Kaleidospace provides a WWW site for promotion of independent artists, musicians, performers, CD-ROM authors, writers, animators, and filmmakers. Artists provide samples of their work, which Kaleidospace integrates into a multimedia document available via the Internet. Kaleidospace also provides placement for artists wanting to showcase their work to agents, directors, gallery owners, publishers, record labels, and other industry professionals.

Boston University Multimedia Communications Laboratory

URL address: **http://spiderman.bu.edu/**

A Web server is now up at the Multimedia Communications Laboratory at Boston University. A brief description of current lab projects and some additional information is available. Abstracts of all lab publications and some movies of the lab, the park where lab staffers eat lunch, and the Charles River are online.

Down South Multimedia

URL address: **http://sunsite.unc.edu/doug_m/pages/south/center/center.html**

The Center for the Study of the American South and SunSITE at UNC-Chapel Hill have set up the American South Internet Resource Center, a multimedia collection of resources for research and information about the south. This site is expanding quickly and welcomes any suggestions for additional links and sources.

Index to Multimedia

URL address: **http://cuiwww.unige.ch/OSG/MultimediaInfo/index.html**

See the index of multimedia information sources at CUI for a comprehensive overview of multimedia on the Internet. This is a large set of information that includes URL, Gopher, and FTP WWW sites, including several frequently asked questions (FAQ) archives.

Instruction and Multimedia

URL address: **http://library-www.scar.utoronto.ca/**

Bladen Library at Scarborough Campus, University of Toronto, invites people to visit its WWW server, which contains locally authored material by faculty, librarians, staff, and students, as well as links to other WWW servers. This server also includes a home page for the Centre for Instructional Technology Development that has information on several projects, as well as links to multimedia and instructional technology information. In addition, it provides a home page for Physical Anthropologists in Canada, with information on their activities.

Irish Multimedia

URL address: **http://www.iscm.ulst.ac.uk/**

The Interactive Systems Centre (ISC) of the University of Ulster opened its WWW server in mid-1994. The server currently contains information about the ISC and a set of links to interactive multimedia research information, which are related to the centre's research activities.

K–12 Multimedia

URL address: **http://www.nbn.com/~branson**

The Stone Soup project is an Internet multimedia cooperative for K–12 educators and students. This project is based in the Branson School, an independent high school in Ross, California.

Fig. 22.14
Appropriately named the "Stone Soup" project, this WWW site offers users images, sounds, and video produced at the Branson School in California.

Medicine and Multimedia

URL address: **http://www.nlm.nih.gov**

The National Library of Medicine offers its Web server, HyperDOC, which includes electronic access to the library's online database services (some of which require registered accounts), an interactive multimedia course on the history and uses of the Internet, several multimedia exhibits from the History of Medicine Division (HMD), and a cataloged image collection of nearly 60,000 images.

MIT Synergy Multimedia

URL address: **http://synergy.mit.edu/synhome.html**

The Synergy WWW server provides a variety of links to multimedia and graphics sources. It also allows access to a large collection of GIF images, and plans to include other multimedia formats in the future.

VI

Finding Web Resources

Multimedia Cancer Information
URL address: **http://cancer.med.upenn.edu/**

OncoLink provides multimedia information regarding all aspects of cancer and cancer therapy. This includes childhood and adult cancer, medical oncology, and radiation oncology. This server, in alliance with the University of Pennsylvania Medical Center, is to promote cancer research, to educate, and to care for patients with cancer. This WWW server is officially mandated by the Radiation Oncology Department of the University of Pennsylvania Medical Center.

Multimedia Information Sources
URL address: **http://www.clr.toronto.edu:1080/clr.html**

The Centre for Landscape Research (CLR) provides general access to its WWW server. The CLR is the research arm of the Programme in Landscape Architecture at the University of Toronto. It provides a collaborative environment for the exploration of ideas related to the design, planning, and policies of the environment. Its primary focus has been on the utilization of electronic media to foster more informed decision-making. The CLR-WWW provides information about CLR software for interactive and integrating CAD, GIS, remote sensing, multimedia and virtual worlds, teaching, publications, collaborative projects, and more. This site also serves as a major connection and resource for landscape architecture related electronic resources.

Multimedia Museum
URL address: **http://www.informatik.rwth-aachen.de/Reiff2/**

The new art association "Mehrwert e.V." is online. Its staff has established an electronic museum, which is open for all Internet users. The Museum was developed in cooperation with the Department of History of Art, the Center of Computing, and the Department of Computer Science at Aachen, Germany.

Multimedia Newsletter (online)
URL address: **http://www.hal.csuhayward.edu**

Cal State Hayward's *Mosaic Network News,* a networked multimedia newsletter, includes sample animations. Also included is a tutorial on creating multimedia. This tutorial is about picking a development platform and selecting software tools for development. Other topics include The Delta Project—Distance Learning and Beyond, and Learning about Mosaic.

Multimedia Publishing—NandoNet

URL address: **http://www.nando.net/welcome.html**

Fig. 22.15
Many of the electronic publications available via the NandoNet home page use multimedia.

The New Media Division of The News and Observer Publishing Co. maintains a World Wide Web server with a variety of publishing pieces that include *The News & Observer* (the daily newspaper for Raleigh, NC, and the Research Triangle), *The Philanthropy Journal*, *North Carolina Business*, *The Insider* (daily NC legislative updates), *Cartoons by Duane Powell*, *The North Carolina Discoveries* series (a multimedia joint effort by *The News & Observer*, WTVD [Durham, NC], and WUNC-FM [Chapel Hill, NC]), The American Dance Festival (Durham, NC) schedule and background, Unisphere (a resource for international business ventures), and NandoX (which experiments in new ways to deliver news and information).

Multimedia Tools

URL address: **http://www.cs.cmu.edu:8001/afs/cs.cmu.edu/ project/atk-ftp/web/andrew-home.html**

Andrew Consortium at Carnegie-Mellon University has a Web home page that focuses on Andrew, an extensible compound document system for UNIX systems running X-Windows. It includes a multimedia word processor, a program editor, a drawing editor, a table/spreadsheet, a font editor, and a MIME format mail/bulletin board manager. Their Web pages have more detailed descriptions of Andrew, screen snapshots, and links to an FTP archive containing the source code for their release, version 6.2.

Neuroscience Multimedia

URL address: **http://salk.edu/**

NeuroWeb, the server for the program in Neurosciences at UCSD, is open for browsing. Check out the page on the department that has information about the program, as well as faculty abstracts. Also see a fledgling "Virtual Poster Session" where actual scientific posters enter the WWW and multimedia.

VI

Finding Web Resources

Norwegian Mogul Media, Inc.
URL address: **http://www.mogul.no/**

Mogul Media offers information about multimedia, interactive television, media technology, CD-ROM publishing, and Internet services, as well as general information about the company. Information is written in Norwegian. Some articles and information are available in English.

Scripting and Prototyping for Multimedia
URL address: **http://www.cwi.nl/~guido/Python.html**

Python is an object-oriented scripting and prototyping language that some prefer over Perl, TCL, or Scheme. Python, developed in Amsterdam, is free, extensible, and runs on UNIX, DOS, and Mac. The UNIX version has optional X11 and Motif interfaces and considerable multimedia support for SGI and Sun platforms. All documentation and sources for Python are now available online via the World Wide Web, as well as via FTP at **ftp://ftp.cwi.nl/ pub/python/index.html**.

U.S. Government and Multimedia
URL address: **http://info.arc.com**

Advanced Research Corporation offers a government-related home page on the WWW. Its server provides technical reports and information on the viability of NCSA Mosaic and NCSA HTTPD to meet U.S. government information dissemination requirements. The requirements include interactive documents, multimedia, database applications, and document conversion. The server is available from 1:00 to 4:00 p.m. Eastern Time (U.S.) only.

Music

ALF MIDI
URL address: **http://alf.uib.no/People/midi/midi.html**

◀ See "Art, Music, and Entertainment," p. 467

The ALF MIDI site has a good WWW home page—the main topic is the MIDI Sample Dump Standard, but it also covers MIDI in general. The site includes documentation, programs, and sound samples.

Computer Music Journal (online publication)
URL address: **file://mitpress.mit.edu:/pub/Computer-Music-Journal**

The *Computer Music Journal* (CMJ) archive is provided for the computer music community in general. It includes the tables of contents, abstracts, editor's notes for the several volumes of CMJ, the recent bibliography, discography, and taxonomy of the field, the list of network resources for music, a number of useful related documents (such as the full MIDI and AIFF specifications), a lengthy reference list, the full text of several recent articles, and other data.

Project Gutenberg

URL address: **ftp://mrcnext.cso.uiuc.edu/etext/NEWUSER.GUT**

Project Gutenberg, a project aimed at providing copyright-cleared electronic texts, now offers computer music MIDI files. The first is Beethoven's Fifth Symphony in C-Minor.

Organizations and Associations

Cross Industry Working Team

URL address: **http://www.cnri.reston.va.us:3000/XIWT/public.html**

This site is sponsored by a multi-industry coalition of more than 40 companies committed to promoting a National Information Infrastructure through the development of technologies that cross industry boundaries.

FARNET—Networks for Research and Education

URL address: **ftp://farnet.org/farnet/farnet_info/**

This site provides information about FARNET, a non-profit corporation. The primary goal of FARNET is to advance the use of computer networks for research and education.

International Computer Science Institute

URL address: **http://http.icsi.berkeley.edu**

ICSI is a computer science research organization affiliated with the Computer Science division of the Electrical Engineering and Computer Science Department at U.C. Berkeley. ICSI connects research scientists from all over the world working together with U.C. Berkeley EECS professors and graduate students on a variety of subjects. At the ICSI WWW site, you can locate PostScript technical reports, an interface to the ICSI Gopher server, and information about the Sather and pSather languages.

International Interactive Communications Society (IICS)

URL address: **http://www.iics.org**

The IICS is an international organization that focuses on the development and application (such as education, commerce, and training) of interactive technologies (such as videodisc, CD-ROMs, and online communications). This Web site offers information about the organization and about individual chapters located around the world.

International Telecommunications Union

URL address: **gopher://info.itu.ch/**

This contains information from the International Telecommunications Union, an agency of the United Nations that attempts to set international standards for telecommunications. Also, check out the URL address **http://keskus.hut.fi** for information about the agency's telecommunications laboratory.

Internet Society

URL address: **http://info.isoc.org/home.html**

The Internet Society is an international organization that represents companies and individuals that focus on the applications and operation of the Internet. Many of the recommendations of the Internet society become the foundation for the development of technologies and policies for the Internet.

Parallel Tools Consortium—Parallel Processing

URL address: **http://www.llnl.gov/ptools/ptools.html**

The Parallel Tools Consortium offers this server to the world. It contains information on not only parallel tools, but also conferences and other parallel programming related issues.

Personal Computers and PC Software (IBM-Compatible, Macintosh)

Apple Newton

URL address: **http://www.uth.tmc.edu/newton_info/**

This WWW server provides information about the Apple Newton. It provides some insight into this device and what may be in store for the future of Personal Digital Assistants (PDAs).

IBM

URL address: **http://www.ibm.com/**

In addition to some fancy graphics and use of multimedia, this WWW server provides links to the following IBM information areas: Industry Solutions, Products and Services, Technology, More Information, News, and About IBM.

Internet Computer Index

URL address: **http://ici.proper.com**

Internet Computer Index (ICI) is an easy-to-use, free service that leads Internet users to all of the information available on the Internet relating to PCs, Macintoshes, and UNIX computers. It has a comprehensive listing of FAQ files, FTP sites, Gopher directories, newsgroups, mail lists, and online publications. You can keyword search these resources for information about specific topics or products.

Macintosh Index

URL address: **http://ici.proper.com/1/mac**
URL address: **gopher://ici.proper.com/77c/mac/.cache**

This is a searchable database of extensive information on the Internet that relates to the Macintosh. There are many Macintosh-related Gopher and WWW servers on the Internet that have interesting information. If you're primarily an e-mail user, you will find many good Macintosh mailing lists. Much of the most current information is found in UseNet newsgroups for the Macintosh.

Macintosh Information

URL address: **http://www.engr.scarolina.edu/**

The University of South Carolina's College of Engineering WWW server includes Rob's Mac Page, which has comprehensive information on the Macintosh, as well as links to WWW sites.

PC Index

URL address: **http://ici.proper.com/1/pc**

This is a searchable database of extensive information on the Internet that relates to the PC. There are many PC-related Gopher and WWW servers on the Internet that have interesting information. The files produced in the UseNet newsgroups have become the de facto repositories for PC-related information on the Internet. For more current information, you may find the online PC publications of value.

The Well Connected Mac
URL address: **http://rever.nmsu.edu/~elharo/faq/Macintosh.html**

A terrific home page for people who own Macintosh computers. Link to Macintosh Software to get a page with more than 100 other links to Web, Internet, and electronic bulletin board systems that offer commercial, shareware, and freeware products. There are also reviews of Mac hardware and software, mailing lists, newgroups, and vendor information.

Windows World (CSUSM)
URL address: **http://coyote.csusm.edu/cwis/winworld/winworld.html**

Fig. 22.16
The Windows World home page is your gateway to information and programs for Microsoft Windows.

Need new Microsoft Windows software? This Web site offers a directory and access to a variety of Windows shareware programs, which you can download. (Remember shareware is not freeware—if you use a program, you must pay a small fee to the author.) Most of the programs are compressed with the PKZip utility. The directory does list how large the program files are so you know how long it will take to download. Categories include address books, database programs, editors, games, and mail programs.

Publications, Magazines, Radio Programs, and Articles

Computer-Mediated Communication Magazine
URL address: **http://www.rpi.edu/~decemj/cmc/mag/current/toc.html**

Computer-Mediated Communication Magazine (ISSN 1076-027X) is on the Web. *Computer-Mediated Communication Magazine* is distributed for free use from the Computer-Mediated Communication Studies Center.

Cyberkind

URL address: **http://sunsite.unc.edu/shannon/ckind/title.html**

Cyberkind is a World Wide Web magazine of "Net-related fiction, nonfiction, poetry, and art." *Cyberkind* features prose and art submitted by the Internet population. All genres and subjects are included, as long as there is some connection to the Internet, cyberspace, computers, or the networked world in general. The features range from an article on writers and the Internet to a computer-related mystery, to a hyperlinked poem. The magazine also features a variety of graphic art. *Cyberkind* is always looking for submissions of prose, poetry, and art. Send submissions to **shannon@sunsite.unc.edu**.

Ericsson, Inc.

URL address: **http://www.ericsson.nl**

This server contains articles and technical information on various aspects of telecommunications. It will expand in response to reader input. Ericsson is a telecommunications supplier that assists with the mobile telecommunications infrastructure.

Gender Issues (article)

URL address: **ftp://alfred.carleton.ca/pub/freenet/93conference/ leslie_reg an_shade.txt**

"Gender Issues in Computer Networking," by Leslie Regan Shade, is an article that presents some interesting information regarding various gender-related issues with respect to telecommunications and the information age.

GlasNews

URL address: **http://solar.rtd.utk.edu/friends/news/glasnews/ master.html**

GlasNews is an online quarterly publication on East-West contacts in communications—including journalism, telecommunications, advertising, and public relations—by Art Pattison Communications Exchange Program, based in Seattle.

Journal of Computer-Mediated Communication

URL address: **http://www.huji.ac.il/www_jcmc/jcmc.html**

A scholarly publication, *The Journal of Computer-Mediated Communication* (JCMC) is a joint project of the Annenberg School for Communication, University of Southern California, and the Information Systems Division of the School of Business Administration, Hebrew University of Jerusalem.

Macmillan Computer Publishing

URL address: **http://www.mcp.com/**

Fig. 22.17

Try the Macmillan Computer Publishing Web site where you can read sample chapters of new books and order online.

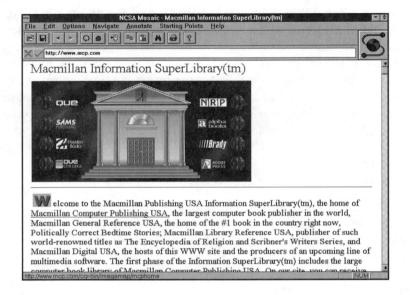

Find information on the best computer book publishers in the world. Books from Que, SAMS, New Riders, Alpha, Brady, Adobe Press, and Hayden are featured here. You can review a sample chapter or table of contents from current books. This site also contains a wealth of reference articles pulled from these leading books to answer your questions about computer software and hardware. You can order any Macmillan Computer Publishing book directly from this Web site. Download software is associated with best-selling titles.

PowerPC News

URL address: **http://power.globalnews.com/**

PowerPC News is an independent, electronic magazine published every two weeks for users and developers who want news about the IBM/Motorola/ Apple microprocessor family and the systems built upon it. The home page contains links to the full text of the magazine.

Social Issues and Cyberspace

URL address: **http://www.ics.uci.edu/~ejw/csr/cyber.html**

The *Cyberspace Report*, a public affairs radio show aired on KUCI, 88.9 FM in Irvine, California, is now available online from the Department of Information and Computer Science at the University of California, Irvine WWW server. Social issues of computing is the theme of the *Cyberspace Report*, which features interviews. Currently available shows explore the future of electronic mail, the information infrastructure in Singapore, and the future of communities on the Internet. Notable guests include Dr. Nathaniel Borenstein of Bellcore, Professor John L. King from U.C. Irvine, and Professor Phil Agre from U.C. San Diego.

Telecommunications Electronic Reviews

URL address: **gopher://info.lib.uh.edu:70/11/articles/e-journals/lita**

This is an online review of telecommunications news and activities. This is a good place to find helpful information for advanced users.

Washington Telecom Newswire

URL address: **http://wtn.com/wtn/wtn.html**

This is a daily news service devoted to telecommunications industry professionals who need news about the industry. There are links to information on federal legislation, Federal Communications Commission orders, and federal court actions. You can sample articles here, but you must pay to get all of the articles via the Web.

Worldwide Collaborative Multimedia Magazine

URL address: **http://www.trincoll.edu/homepage.html**

The Trincoll Journal is a weekly multimedia magazine available on the Web that is run by students at Trinity College in Hartford Connecticut, with all design, programming, contributions, and artwork created by people from around the world. This student project demonstrates just what can be done in terms of worldwide collaboration.

Research—Government Agencies

Telecommunications Research
URL address: **http://www-atp.llnl.gov/atp/**

This is the home page of the Advanced Telecommunications Program at the Lawrence Livermore National Labs. If you're serious about investigating telecommunications research, check out this site.

Research—Universities

Carnegie-Mellon University—Computer Vision
URL address: **http://www.cs.cmu.edu:8001/afs/cs/project/cil/ftp/html/vision.html**

A WWW home page for Computer Vision is available at Carnegie-Mellon University. It includes pointers to 20 research groups' home pages, image archives, and source code related to Robot Vision and Image Processing.

Columbia University
URL address: **http://www.ctr.columbia.edu/**

The Center for Telecommunications Research at Columbia University has just started up its WWW server. It contains pointers to other Columbia University information sources.

Cornell Theory Center Overview
URL address: **http://www.tc.cornell.edu/ctcIntro.html**

The Cornell Theory Center at Cornell University is one of four National Advanced Scientific Computing Centers supported by the National Science Foundation. From this home page, you can find out about research efforts in visualization, vectorization, and parallel processing and investigate highly parallel processing resources for the scientific community.

MIT Demonstrations
URL address: **http://www.lcs.mit.edu/**

The Massachusetts Institute of Technology Laboratory for Computer Science provides this server. It includes an index to pages and demos provided by research groups at MIT.

MIT—Telecommunications Archives

URL address: **ftp://lcs.mit.edu/telecom-archives**

The telecommunications archive at the Massachusetts Institute of Technology (MIT) site isn't for the casual user, but it contains many items of interest to engineers and developers.

University of Iowa

URL address: **gopher://iam41.arcade.uiowa.edu:2270**

The Iowa Comm Gopher server at the University of Iowa features many communications-related resources including journalism, media studies, multimedia, and telecommunications.

The University of Kansas

URL address: **http://kuhttp.cc.ukans.edu/cwis/UDK/KUhome/ KUHome.html**

The University of Kansas home page now provides easy access to locally produced services, including The Electrical Engineering & Computer Science Telecommunications & Information Sciences Laboratory at Nichols Hall (TISL). The University of Kansas provides this site for information on its work on high-speed networks, digital signal processing, simulation of communications systems, and networks. Be sure to check out the other offerings at this university.

University of Michigan College of Engineering

URL address: **http://www.engin.umich.edu/college**

The University of Michigan College of Engineering offers the Computer Aided Engineering Network's WWW server. It contains a considerable amount of online documentation, as well as network services such as the face/finger gateway.

University of Missouri

URL address: **http://www.cstp.umkc.edu/**

The University of Missouri Computer Science Telecommunications Program provides a variety of valuable computer and computer research information. If you want to be a student, or if you want to see "what's happening" there, this is the place to go.

University of Washington—Image Processing
URL address: **http://www.cs.washington.edu/research/metip/ metip.html**

The University of Washington Department of Computer Science & Engineering has created the Mathematics Experiences Through Image Processing (METIP) home page. The METIP project uses image processing techniques to create tools and activities for middle school students to motivate them in the subject of mathematics.

University of Wisconsin Computer Sciences Department
URL address: **http://www.cs.wisc.edu/~upluse/**

The Undergraduate Projects Laboratory (UPL) of the University of Wisconsin Computer Sciences Department has a home page that highlights the projects and people of the UPL. The UPL is one of the only laboratories of its kind that allows undergraduates from multiple disciplines to have access to UNIX workstations for personal independent programming projects and computer research.

Security

Computer Security
URL address: **http://mls.saic.com**

The Wateridge facility of Science Applications International Corp. (SAIC) makes its WWW Computer Security Web site available to all who are interested. Dedicated to the many facets of computer security, this site includes documents concerning current SAIC projects, security newsgroups from UseNet, and security information from around the Web.

Cryptography and Computers
URL address: **ftp://rsa.com** (login as anonymous cd pub /ciphertext)

CipherText is a newsletter (available as ASCII text) that covers ongoing issues and technologies of cryptography.

Cryptography, PGP, and Your Privacy

URL address: **http://draco.centerline.com:8080/~franl/crypto.html**

You can find volumes of information at this site with links to all types of material about computer privacy and methods of protecting it.

Supercomputing

Alabama Supercomputer Network

URL address: **http://sgisrvr.asc.edu/index.html**

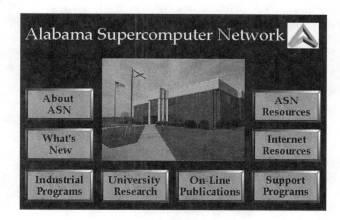

Fig. 22.18
Fast, powerful and expensive—this is the world of supercomputers which you can explore through the Alabama Supercomputer Network. Don't be shy: there's even an area for K–12 instruction.

If you haven't experienced the world of supercomputing, you should check out the Alabama Supercomputer Network. This site provides a jump-off point to other WWW servers.

Caltech—Supercomputer Sample

URL address: **http://www.ccsf.caltech.edu/ccsf.html**

The Caltech Concurrent Supercomputing Facilities (CCSF) offers this server that includes CCSF annual reports, PostScript manuals for the Intel Paragon parallel supercomputer, as well as Xmorphia: an interactive exhibition of pattern formation by a partial differential equation of reaction-diffusion type—is this how the leopard gets its spots?

Florida State University Supercomputing

URL address: **http://www.scri.fsu.edu**

The Supercomputer Computations Research Institute (SCRI) at the Florida State University in Tallahassee, Florida, is online through WWW. This server contains:

- Information on computing facilities at SCRI, and pictures and descriptions of some of the equipment.

- Recent publication information, and listings of several thousand abstracts from recently published articles.

- Information about software developed at SCRI that is available on the Internet. Notable projects include SciAn, DQS, and Dmake.

- Notes on the Tallahassee FreeNet.

Piedmont Supercomputing Center

URL address: **http://services.csp.it/welcome.html**

Fig. 22.19
Find out about supercomputing research and projects in Italy when you connect with the Piedmont Supercomputing Center home page.

Piedmont Supercomputing Center

Centro Supercalcolo Piemonte (CSP)

This is a WWW home page at the Centro Supercalcolo Piemonte, located in Turin, Italy. It is an international site for scientific computing that provides the regional scientific structures, adequate instruments, and computing resources of the most advanced level.

San Diego Supercomputer Center
URL address: **http://www.sdsc.edu/**

The San Diego Supercomputer Center is a national laboratory for computational science and engineering. It promotes research and U.S. economic competitiveness with computational tools. SDSC is affiliated with the University of California, San Diego, which is one of the nation's leading research universities. SDSC features a variety of collaborative research and educational programs, and high-performance computational and visualization tools.

From Here...

The tremendous impact that computers and computer technology have on our lives and society shows no signs of slowing down. The Web sites and resources in this chapter are good starting points for all levels of computer users. Here are a few more:

- Chapter 29, "Publications: News, Periodicals, and Books," has several Web-based publications which focus on the computer industry.

- Chapter 31, "Shopping," offers Web sites where you can purchase computer hardware and software.

VI

Finding Web Resources

Chapter 23

Education

by Bill Eager

With its origins in academia, the Internet (and now the WWW) offers tremendous resources for educators, students, and people who simply have an interest in learning. The educational resources and topics on the Web are not limited to the world of higher education. Public school districts; elementary, junior, and high schools; and even individual classes continue to develop and operate WWW servers. The home pages of these servers frequently include information about the schools (such as the school newspapers), as well as links to other educational resources.

You commonly will find requests in school home pages for other schools and classes to send e-mail to begin interschool electronic communications, in which students in different parts of the world can send letters to one another and share their experiences and knowledge. The K–12 resources are vast, ranging from the HungerWeb, a server that has an interactive hunger quiz and databases that relate to world hunger, to three-dimensional images and movies of frogs maintained at the Imaging and Distributed Computing Group of Lawrence Berkeley Laboratory.

Do you have an interest in the future of public education programs in the United States? The U.S. Department of Education maintains a server that offers details about Goals 2000, the act designed to help America reach the national education goals and to help every child realize high academic standards. Offering access to searchable databases that contain millions of records, the WWW libraries can help students achieve these goals. Many university and government WWW libraries focus on specific topics, such as agriculture, engineering, literature, or medicine. A search for information may produce text documents, photographs, or movies that you can download and use for future reference.

Universities and colleges continue to have a strong presence on the WWW. The last section of this chapter lists all the WWW addresses for educational institutions in the United States—more than 700 of them! If you like the idea of attending a school that takes advantage of cyberspace (or even cable television) to deliver fully accredited college courses, look at some of the Web home pages listed in the section titled "Distance Learning."

◀ See "Museums," p. 486

▶ See "Book and Literature Resources," p. 816

▶ See "Science Resources," p. 868

Now that you're in the mood to learn, you can find the following information in this chapter:

- Educational libraries—digital libraries where you can browse through books, often with multimedia.

- Educational resources—numerous Web sites offer resource information for educators and students. These sites are broken into traditional subject categories such as biology, computer sciences, language arts, and so on.

- Distance learning—sites that can help you get an educational degree from a college that may be thousands of miles away.

- K-12—yes, there are hundreds of Web sites at public schools around the country. Stop in and see what students are working on.

- Colleges and Universities: U.S.

- Colleges and Universities: International

- Computer Science: U.S.

- Computer Science: International

- Regional and Community Education—community and state-based educational efforts.

- The College and University List—this is a comprehensive listing of URL addresses for hundreds of U.S. educational institutions. Visit your old stomping grounds.

The Teacher Education Internet Server

URL address: **http://curry.edschool.virginia.edu/teis**

This Web site, which proves that you're never too old to learn, represents a combined effort on the part of the Society for Technology and Teacher

Education, the University of Virginia, and the University of Houston. The entire focus of the site's resources is the exploration of ways in which the Internet and Web can help teachers with their classes and programs.

Fig. 23.1
Explore the Web's educational resources as you click your way through a hypermedia image of a classroom.

The home page includes a picture of a schoolroom; the icons in the picture link to the resources. The microscope, for example, links to science information; the bookshelf links to reading resources; and the telephone links to telecommunications and networking information. If you don't have graphics capability or have difficulty with the image links, you can use the four hypertext links just below the image, which open a world of educational resources. The Whole TEIS Gopher opens doors to electronic publications such as the *Journal of Technology and Teacher Education* and *Interface*, an IBM teacher-preparation-grant school newsletter, and documents on subjects ranging from social studies to international education. Other home-page links include Special Education, Math Education and Reading, and Language Arts.

DeweyWeb

URL address: **http://ics.soe.umich.edu**

This Web server is a Sun Sparcstation 2 located at the University of Michigan School of Education. The site is an experiment that uses the WWW to facilitate communication among students and classrooms around the world. Links from the home page include the following highlighted items:

- *The ICS World Forum.* The project helps students analyze challenges from different perspectives as they role-play characters from many walks of life. Mahatma Gandhi, William Bennett, Rachel Carson, and Pope John Paul II are some of the famous people that students can pretend to be.

■ *DeweyWeb and the Journey North.* The DeweyWeb was inspired by the work of the University of Michigan ICS and by the Indiana University World School for Adventure Learning. These projects attempt to expand the classroom experience with reports from scientists and explorers, as well as by linking distant schools through telecommunications. The information in the DeweyWeb experiment is closely aligned with the World School's activities and is, therefore, called the Journey North. When you go to the Journey North, you receive the news, issues, and events that surround this Arctic adventure.

Between ICS and the World School, various telecommunications and networking technologies help serve and gather information from classrooms. DeweyWeb builds on this experience, delivering information from scientists and explorers, and giving students an opportunity to contribute their own observations and discussions.

Fig. 23.2
Designed primarily for K–12 education, the DeweyWeb home page provides access to interactive exploration of global political and scientific activities.

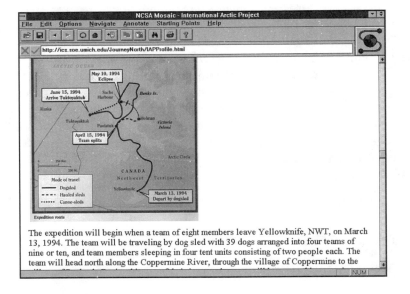

Indiana University

URL address: **http://www.indiana.edu**

Indiana University is one of the largest institutions of higher education in the United States. It serves 94,000 students, employs nearly 17,000 faculty and staff members, and has an annual budget of more than $1 billion.

Welcome to Indiana University!

- IU Presidential Inauguration & 175th Anniversary Celebration
- About Indiana University
- IU System Units and Services
- Internet Servers on all IU Campuses
- About World Wide Web

Fig. 23.3
Astronomy, law, music, and philosophy are a few of the departments to which you can connect from the Indiana University home page.

The university's WWW home page presents a variety of information about the degree programs and has links to each of the eight campuses. A good start, which gives you some idea of how large this institution is, is the link to a list of Internet servers on all IU campuses. You'll find more links here to the astronomy, computer science, law, music, philosophy, and numerous other departments and schools—even to Indiana University Press. The site is user-friendly, but be warned: you can get lost, just as you can on a real university campus. Other resources include news, weather, address books, library and research services, and access to Telnet resources.

Geography: What Do Maps Show?

URL address: **http://info.er.usgs.gov/education/teacher/what-do-maps-show/index.html**

If you've ever been lost, you know how important a good map can be. How do you read a map? What do map symbols represent? These are just a few of the topics and lesson plans that you can find on this Web site. The focus is information and resources for educators who teach upper-elementary and junior-high classes; the goal is to teach students how to use and understand maps. In addition to links for step-by-step lesson plans, the site offers an online poster and reproducible activity sheets.

The online color poster, which shows several views of Salt Lake City, is a wonderful resource. The poster includes an aerial photograph, a relief map, a road map, a topographical map, and a three-dimensional terrain map. You begin with small thumbnail images of these maps and click your way to larger images; the final images can print at 8 1/2 by 11 inches. Students learn the differences among these maps, as well as how to read the legends and keys.

VI

Finding Web Resources

From the home page, you can jump to a list of United States Geological Survey (USGS) materials that are available for educational purposes. This site represents a great WWW application.

Fig. 23.4
Good map-reading skills last a lifetime. This WWW home page provides material that teaches those skills.

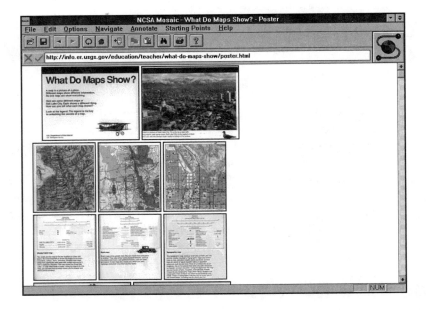

Patch American High School

URL address: **http://192.253.114.31/Home.html**

This WWW site illustrates what a motivated teacher, talented students, and a diverse educational program can accomplish. The school is located at Patch Barracks, the headquarters for the United States European Command in Vaihingen, Germany (a small section of Stuttgart); it serves the dependent children of American military personnel and civilians stationed in 19 countries.

Students and teachers at Patch share some of their European experiences on the Web. Home-page links include a picture of the school's mascot and a multimedia exhibition about the D-Day invasion of Normandy. You definitely should check out the "What's New" section; one link brings up a multimedia presentation about the Maulbronn Abbey.

Other home-page links include:

- *Student Art Galleries.* Artwork by students.

- *The Arab–Israeli Conflict.* An interactive communications course.

- *Biology Department Zoo.* Jump to a living world that includes insects, reptiles, and birds. Be sure to check out the picture of Louise, a 10-year-old boa constrictor at the zoo.

- *Music.* The World Band and recent concerts.

If you are a K–12 educator, this site may be a good place to begin an interactive classroom project. The school's e-mail address is **WWW@patch-ahs.dsi.net**.

U.S. Department of Education

URL address: **http://www.ed.gov/**

Our Mission Is to Ensure Equal *Access* to Education and to Promote Educational *Excellence* throughout the Nation.

Fig. 23.5
The U.S. Department of Education's home page has links that offer resources for K–12 and higher-education professionals.

The goals of the U.S. Department of Education include ensuring access to equal educational opportunity and improving the quality of education. If you have an interest in education in the United States, this is a good Web site. Begin with a jump to the Goals 2000 online library (**ftplink/webs/Goals_2000.web**), which provides the full text of Goals 2000, fact sheets, and other information about the act, which is designed to help America reach the National Education Goals and to move every child toward achieving high academic standards.

The home-page link titled Teacher's Guide to U.S. Department of Education brings up a new page with more than 40 links, including electronic publications, toll-free phone numbers, special technical-assistance centers, and information on drug-free schools. Another good link from the home page is Hypertext Publications, which includes a report on state higher-education profiles.

Educational Libraries

Cornell University Engineering Library
URL address: **http://www.englib.cornell.edu**

This home page has links to information about the Cornell Engineering Library and its services. The site, which provides information on several electronic-library projects, points to ICE (Internet Connections for Engineering); the Engineering Library Gopher; science and engineering journals; and general science, technology, and geology Internet resources.

National Agricultural Library
URL address: **http://probe.nalusda.gov:8000/index.html**

This server is at the U.S. Department of Agriculture's National Agricultural Library. Some of the links that this server provides are to plant-genome information, animal-genome information, an agricultural-genome Gopher, other biology servers, other WWW information, the library's phone list, and searches for projects and researchers.

National Library of Medicine
URL address: **http://www.nlm.nih.gov**

Fig. 23.6
This server offers links to documents and images that deal with health and medicine.

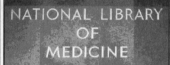

▶ See "U.S. National Health Care," p. 706

The National Library of Medicine, located on the campus of the U.S. National Institutes of Health in Bethesda, Maryland, is the world's largest library that focuses on a single scientific/professional topic. The library maintains more than 4.5 million holdings, including books, journals, reports, manuscripts, and audiovisual items. The library offers numerous online information services dealing with clinical care, toxicology and environmental health, and basic biomedical research; has research and development components, including an extramural grants program; houses a History of Medicine collection; and provides several programs designed to improve the nation's medical-library system.

North Carolina State University Webbed Library Without Walls

URL address: **http://dewey.lib.ncsu.edu**

The North Carolina State University Libraries system handles (catalog, recatalog, or withdraw) about 500 titles a week. The purpose of this server is to organize and disseminate information that relates to the research and educational needs of the students, faculty members, and staff members at NCSU. The system offers links to the information systems of the Triangle Research Libraries Network, Duke University, North Carolina State University, and the University of North Carolina at Chapel Hill. The server enables you to search the NCSU Libraries catalog, other databases and indexes, and several electronic texts.

OCLC Online Computer Library, Inc.

URL address: **http://www.oclc.org/**

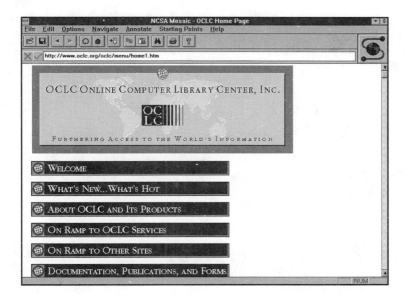

Fig. 23.7
The OCLC home page is a useful resource for professional librarians and for people who have an interest in books.

Librarians and book lovers can benefit from this Web site. The OCLC Online Computer Library Center is a not-for-profit, computer-based library service and research organization. The home page tells us, "OCLC operates the PRISM service for cataloging and resource sharing, provides online reference systems for both librarians and end users, and distributes online electronic journals." The Web site has links to news releases, product information, online information about how to use OCLC services, and access to Electronic Journals Online and the FirstSearch service (the last two are for subscribers to those reference services).

St. Joseph County Public Library
URL address: **http://sjcpl.lib.in.us**

From this Indiana library's home page, you can access the library's databases and the SJCPL online catalog, which contains more than 500,000 records and includes the holdings of three area public libraries: SJCPL, the Mishawaka–Penn Public Library, and the Plymouth Public Library. The Community Connection contains information on more than 1,200 community organizations and services.

University of Georgia Libraries
URL address: **http://scarlett.libs.uga.edu/1h/www/darchive/hargrett/wpa.html**

Take a trip on this server and examine a collection of photographs that chronicle the various Works Progress Administration (WPA) projects in Georgia, including streets, airports, schools, recreation facilities, flood-control systems, and fine-arts projects.

Virginia Tech
URL address: **http://borg.lib.vt.edu**

Electronic journal titles available at this site include the *Community Services CATALYST*, the *Journal of Counseling and Development*, the *Journal of Technology Education*, the *Journal of the International Academy of Hospitality Research*, and the *Journal of Veterinary Medical Education*.

Educational Resources

AskERIC Virtual Library
URL address: **http://eryx.syr.edu/Main.html**

What could be better than a virtual librarian who never says, "Be quiet"? The AskERIC Virtual Library is an ongoing project, building a digital library for educational information; you navigate through it as you would any real library. The site offers a narrated multimedia slide show that explains what

AskERIC is and how to use it. You can ask the virtual librarian questions through an online mail interface. Go to the reference section to search for subject-specific Infoguides, lesson plans, or AskERIC Frequently Asked Questions. This server is an extremely valuable resource for educators.

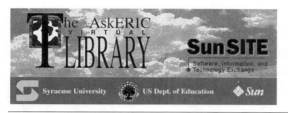

AskERIC: Key Areas

 Lesson Plans   AskERIC's Collections

 Search ERIC   Search AskERIC

Fig. 23.8
Even teachers sometimes have questions. The AskERIC Virtual Library, a repository of information for teachers, offers an online virtual librarian who can answer specific questions.

Astronomy: Mars Surveyor MENU

URL address: **http://esther.la.asu.edu/asu_tes/TES_Editor/ MsurveyorMENU.html**

NASA's Mars Surveyor program—the "next big thing" in the exploration of Mars—will begin with the launch of the Mars Global Surveyor in November 1996. The program proposes to send additional orbiters and landers to Mars every 26 months from 1996 to 2006. For now, you can access information provided by the Arizona Mars K–12 Education Program through the NASA Planetary Data System Infrared Subnode, located at Arizona State University in Tempe.

▶ See "Astronomy," p. 847

Biology: LBL Imaging and Distributed Computing Group

URL address: **http://george.lbl.gov/ITG.html**

The Imaging and Distributed Computing Group of Lawrence Berkeley Laboratory contains information about the Whole Frog project, an experiment in applying scientific imaging to education. The Whole Frog document includes images, movies, and pointers to 3-D frog-anatomy data.

Fig. 23.9
At this Web site you can try your hand at dissecting a "digital" frog.

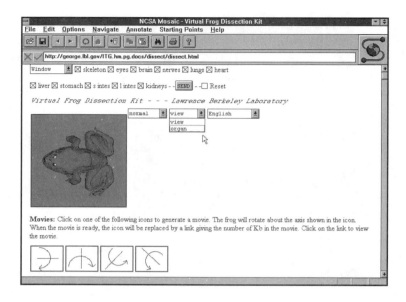

Britannica Online
URL address: **http://www.eb.com/**

Fig. 23.10
The Encyclopedia Britannica now offers online information about a world of subjects via the WWW.

The database, which is experimental on the WWW, contains the full text of the *New Encyclopedia Britannica*, 15th Edition. The automatic conversion has not been checked by the editors, so equations may be rendered incorrectly or not displayed at all. This site is fun to visit, though.

CEA Education Outreach Page
URL address: **http://cea-ftp.cea.berkeley.edu/Education/**

This Web site offers a great collection of links for educators who are just getting their feet wet in using the educational capabilities of the Internet and the WWW. Collected by the Center for EUV Astrophysics at Berkeley, California, the site offers home-page links to the broad categories of K–12 outreach, distance learning, public outreach, and undergraduate outreach, as well as links to other educational sites. You can fill out an online questionnaire to help make the site more receptive to your needs. From the distance-learning link, you can find information about how your classroom and students can connect to the Internet.

Cisco Educational Archive

URL address: **http://sunsite.unc.edu/cisco/edu-arch.html**

This educational-resource center, sponsored by Cisco Systems, Inc., provides information to help educators and schools connect with educational resources on the WWW.

Computers: Mosaic Tutorial

URL address: **http://curry.edschool.virginia.edu/murray/tutorial/ Tutorial.html**

This tutorial is designed to guide teachers in using Mosaic for the Macintosh as an instructional resource. The tutorial is divided into two main parts: "Mosaic: The Basics" and "Creating a Mosaic Document." An online reference is available for performing limited searches of these two sections.

◄ See "Internet and World Wide Web Resources," p. 568

Computers: "One Giant Leap"

URL address: **http://www.tc.cornell.edu/Edu/SQ/Gibson/**

This essay won a 1994 "Networks: Where Have You Been All My Life?" essay contest, sponsored by the U.S. Department of Education's National Center for Education Statistics, the National Science Foundation, and the National Aeronautics and Space Administration.

Computers: PCLT Exit Ramp

URL address: **http://pclt.cis.yale.edu/pclt/default.htm**

PC Lube and Tune supplies introductions, tutorials, and education on technical subjects to ordinary computer users through hypertext articles. Major articles include "Introduction to PC Hardware," "Introduction to SNA," "Introduction to TCP/IP," and "PC Serial Communications." An easy-to-install package of shareware tools is being developed for this site.

DeweyWeb: Journey North

URL address: **http://ics.soe.umich.edu/JourneyNorth/
IAPHome.html**

This site is an experiment in building a Web environment. Based on the
World School's Journey North activity, the primary feature of the experiment
is a series of maps that students can change as they enter observations of
wildlife migration.

Dictionary: English/German

URL address: **http://www.fmi.uni-passau.de/htbin/lt/lte/ltd**

Wohin wollen wir fahren? This WWW site will be a big help if you want to
translate this sentence (Where shall we go?) or learn how to say it—in German, of course. When you connect, a little entry box appears at the bottom
of your screen. Simply type a word; you get the translation. In addition, you
get a few German phrases that incorporate the word. If you type **world**, for
example, the search brings back *Welt,* as well as *ein Mann von Welt* (a man of
the world), *auf die Welt bringen* (bring into the world), and a few other useful
expressions.

Dictionary: Liz Brigman's Public WWW Page

URL address: **http://is.rice.edu:80/~liz/**

This Web site offers a variety of links to reference materials. You can
keyword-search the *Oxford English Dictionary* to find a definition of a word,
Roget's Thesaurus to get a synonym or antonym, and the *Dictionary of Computer Terms* to find out the difference between *byte* and *bit*.

Edweb/Corporation for Public Broadcasting

URL address: **http://k12.cnidr.org:90**

CPB's Edweb home page states, "The purpose of this 'hyperbook' is to present
the world of educational computing and networking in a single, easy-to-use
guide. With Edweb, you can explore online educational resources around the
world, learn about trends in education reform and the 'information highway,' examine success stories of computers in the classroom, and much
more." That sums it up nicely. The site offers many educational links for
teachers, students, and learners of all ages.

The Explorer

URL address: **http://unite.tisl.ukans.edu/xmintro.html**

Part of an effort to deliver a full range of information resources to educators and students in a simple fashion, this site has significant resources in mathematics and the natural sciences. Explorer News is an educational newsletter, published several times a month, that offers ideas for lesson plans and teaching events. One issue, for example, focuses on global change and ozone depletion; it features a unit lesson plan that includes background information on the Earth's ozone layer and hands-on activities. You can download these programs and resources to your PC for future reference or use.

Geography: Project GeoSim (Geography Education Software)

URL address: **http://geosim.cs.vt.edu/index.html**

This Web server includes detailed information about Human Population (HumPop), a multimedia tutorial program; International Population (IntlPop), a population simulation program; Migration Modeling (MigModel), a migration modeling and simulation program; and Mental Maps (MMap), a geography quiz program.

Geography: USGS Education

URL address: **http://info.er.usgs.gov/education/index.html**

Some of the links this server provides are to the U.S. Geological Survey national center tour information, the USGS library system, the GeoMedia, What's under your feet, Fact sheets, and Dinosaurs at the Museum of Paleontology, University of California at Berkeley.

▶ See "United States Geological Survey," p. 721

HungerWeb Home Page

URL address: **http://www.hunger.brown.edu/hungerweb/**

The server introduces two new facilities: an interactive hunger quiz and a gateway for sending e-mail to the president. The site is designed to be both a general education platform and a research resource. The site includes an extensive integrated database on politics, the environment, economics, and ethics relevant to hunger, as well as a broad collection of introductory material. The service encourages submissions, including research, advocacy, projects, and case and clinical studies.

VI

Finding Web Resources

InfoVid Outlet: the Educational and How-To Video Warehouse

URL address: **http://branch.com:1080/infovid/c100.html**

This server is a guide to educational, instructional, and informative videos from around the world, with more than 3,500 titles on a wide variety of subjects.

Intercultural-E-mail-Classroom-Connections

URL address: **http://www.stolaf.edu/network/iecc.html**

This Web resource is designed to help teachers who are seeking partner classrooms for international and cross-cultural electronic-mail exchanges.

Janice's K–12 Cyberspace OUTPOST

URL address: **http://k12.cnidr.org/janice_k12/k12menu.html**

The site offers a collection of resources within the K–12 Web space, as well as other things related to educational use of the Net. The site includes references to K–12 virtual libraries, National Science Foundation projects and project maps, and other "cool stuff" for kids.

JASON Project Voyage

URL address: **http://seawifs.gsfc.nasa.gov/JASON/JASON.html**

Fig. 23.11
Students and teachers can use the WWW interface to the JASON Project to look into volcanoes, tour Mayan ruins, and explore coral reefs.

This Web site puts a new spin on the class field trip. Instead of going to the pond behind the school, your students can look into the mouth of a volcano. This home page is a great way for educators and students to explore and learn about the environment. Some links include "letters" from the rain forest. Definitely worth the trip.

Language: Arabic Tutor

URL address: **http://darkwing.uoregon.edu/~alquds**

If you have a need to learn or are curious about the Arabic language, this Web site may help. You can download a Windows-based demo of software that teaches the language to beginners, featuring text (Arabic, with English explanation) and sound.

Language: Esperanto Home Page

URL address: **http://utis179.cs.utwente.nl:8001/esperanto/ hypercourse/**

Esperanto is a universal language that has been in existence for more than 100 years. The Esperanto server provides links to background information and a hypermedia tutorial on the language—so *klik hier voor de korse*.

Language: Language Bank of Swedish

URL address: **http://logos.svenska.gu.se/lbeng.html**

This site provides links to information about the Language Bank of Swedish, the Catalogue of Machine-Readable Texts and Lexical Data, the Language Bank Gopher server, the Language Bank concordance system, Scandinavian text archives, and other text archives. Text is in Swedish and English.

Language: Spanish Lessons

URL address: **http://www.willamette.edu/~tjones/Spanish/Spanish-main.html**

¿Como esta usted? (How are you?) Learn Spanish with this series of interactive Spanish lessons. If you have a sound board, you can click some audio clips and listen to them. The site offers three lessons, which also are available as PostScript files that you can download.

Literature: Electronic Text Center

URL address: **http://www.lib.virginia.edu/etext/ETC.html**

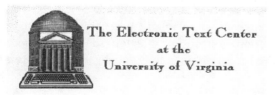

Fig. 23.12
This WWW home page is a gateway to thousands of electronic hypertext versions of great literature.

► See "Book and Literature Resources," p. 816

From the University of Virginia, this WWW site is a gateway to thousands of electronic hypertext documents and works of literature. Most of the home-page links are self-explanatory, such as British Poetry 1780–1910. When you choose Electronic Text Searchable Through the Web, you see a new menu that offers access to Middle English texts; the King James and Revised Standard Version editions of the Bible; and a 16M collection of early modern English material, including an early English dictionary.

Math and Science: The Hub
URL address: **http://hub.terc.edu/**

An Internet resource for mathematics and science education, The Hub provides services that can help you create and publish reports, curricula, projects in progress, and requests for proposals.

National Center on Adult Literacy
URL address: **gopher://litserver.literacy.upenn.edu**

Reading and writing are essential tools for living and working in the modern world. The National Center on Adult Literacy provides leadership in research and development in the field of adult literacy. This Gopher server includes information on literacy programs throughout the United States and in foreign countries. You can jump to any of four organizational units that focus on different aspects of literacy: the National Center on Adult Literacy, which engages in research and development on adult literacy in the United States; the International Literacy and Education Program, which provides a world-wide network for literacy training and development; the Penn Group on Literacy Studies, which engages in a broad range of university-based research projects; and the Literacy Technology Laboratory, which promotes the use of new technologies for learning and instruction.

Pacific Forestry Centre
URL address: **http://www.pfc.forestry.ca/**

This center is located at the Canadian Forest Service in Victoria, British Columbia. The server provides an introduction, staff profiles, recent publications, a contact list, research programs, and an advanced forest-technologies program.

Schoolnet

URL address: **http://schoolnet.carleton.ca/english**

Schoolnet represents "a cooperative initiative of Canada's provincial, territorial, and federal governments; educators, universities, and colleges; and industry." This home page has numerous links (such as educational resources organized by subject and government programs) that are useful to educators.

Science Bytes

URL address: **http://loki.ur.utk.edu/default.html**

The Science Bytes server at the University of Tennessee includes a series of illustrated articles for schoolchildren and their teachers.

UIUC Learning Resource Server

URL address: **http://www.ed.uiuc.edu**

Roam through this site's numerous links to electronic learning resources for K–12 classrooms, teachers, and educational researchers.

Xerox PARC PubWeb Server

URL address: **http://pubweb.parc.xerox.com/**

This WWW server runs at the Xerox Palo Alto Research Center in Palo Alto, California. The site includes links to the Xerox Corporation WWW server, a map viewer, PARC Research-related digital libraries, and color photos.

Distance Learning

Jones Education Networks (JEN)

URL address: **http://www.meu.edu**

How about getting a college degree by watching television or learning more about computers? JEN currently has two international cable-television channels: the Mind Extension University (ME/U) and Jones Computer Network (JCN). ME/U offers college-credit courses and degrees through well-known universities; you watch the teachers give lectures on TV. You can find out more about both of these cable channels and the degree programs through the information and links on this Web page.

VI

Finding Web Resources

The Texas Education Network (TENET)

URL address: **http://www.tenet.edu**

Fig. 23.13
The Texas
Education
Network is
nationally
recognized as a
resource for
educators—and
this Web site
proves why.

TENET is a great example of a network devoted to education. In addition to providing information and links for K–12 education, this site follows the progress of the State Networking Project, a U.S. effort on long-range planning for the application of the Internet to support the needs of the K–12 community. The site also offers some DOS, Macintosh, and Windows utilities.

Virtual Online University

URL address: **http://symnet.net/~VOU**

This site will help you attend a university that features professors from around the world. Best of all, transferable college credit is available.

K–12 Resources

Armadillo's WWW Server

URL address: **http://chico.rice.edu/armadillo/**

This Web server is a collaborative effort of the Houston Independent School District and Rice University. The site presents resources and instructional material to support an interdisciplinary course of study with a Texas theme. The material pertains mostly to K–12 education.

Glenview District 34 Schools

URL address: **http://www.ncook.k12.il.us/dist34_home_page.html**

This K–8 district in Glenview, Illinois, operates this server for several schools in this Chicago suburb. You can access the online catalogs of the district's primary libraries. The site provides other links for educators and students, including one (called Goodies) that brings up a large list of hyperlinks to education-related topics.

Hillside Elementary School

URL address: **http://hillside.coled.umn.edu/**

Hillside Elementary School

The pages of information on this World Wide Web server are being created by students at Hillside Elementary School in Cottage Grove, Minnesota. This is a joint project of Hillside Elementary School and the University of Minnesota College of Education. Our goal is to incorporate use of the resources on the Internet into the curriculum of elementary school students and to have students *participate in creating resources* that are on the Internet.

Welcome to the 1994-95 School Year

- Hillside Web Happenings
- Mrs. Collins Sixth Grade
  - Home Pages
  - The Buzz Rod Story
  - Career Interviews
  - Book Reviews
- School Information
  - Parent Teacher Association
  - School Calendar
  - School Newspaper

Fig. 23.14
Learn how sixth-graders are making an impact on the Information Superhighway when you visit this home page.

Sixth-grade students at this school develop the server, which is part of a joint project of the school and the University of Minnesota. The project focuses on integrating the Internet into elementary-level education. The goal is to have students not only look at the Internet and take information from it, but also actively participate in building it and shaping their own part of the Information Superhighway.

Illinois Mathematics and Science Academy

URL address: **http://www.imsa.edu/**

The Illinois Mathematics and Science Academy is the nation's only three-year residential public high school for talented science and mathematics students. Find out what students are learning and about other school projects.

Ithaca, Kids on Campus

URL address: **http://www.tc.cornell.edu/Kids.on.Campus/KOC94/**

This program is designed to increase computer awareness and scientific interest among Ithaca-area third-, fourth-, and fifth-grade students through hands-on activities, innovative videos, and demos. The site provides a graphical interface to a wide variety of information resources on the Internet.

VI

Finding Web Resources

K–12 Schools on the Web
URL address: **http://toons.cc.ndsu.nodak.edu/~sackmann/k12.html**

If you teachers and students think that you're alone on the Web, you're not. This site offers state-by-state hyperlinks. Click a state, and then check out the other elementary, junior-high, and senior-high school Web sites—hundreds of them.

Monta Vista High School News
URL address: **http://www.mvhs.edu/newsmenu.html**

The school is located in Cupertino, California. The site focuses on integrating the Internet in a high-school setting.

Murray Elementary School
URL address: **http://curry.edschool.virginia.edu/murray**

In collaboration with the Curry School of Education at the University of Virginia, Murray Elementary School has established a home page that has a variety of educational resources, including a Macintosh Mosaic Tutorial for K–12 educators.

NASA Langley HPCC
URL address: **http://k12mac.larc.nasa.gov/hpcck12home.html**

The home page for the High Performance Computing and Communications K–12 Program is an educational outreach program involving five high schools in the Tidewater area of Virginia. The focus of this pilot program is to investigate and develop curriculum for mathematical sciences in K–12 education.

Princeton High Schools
URL address: **http://www.prs.k12.nj.us**

Located in Princeton, New Jersey, this student-run server offers reference material and a school newspaper.

Ralph Bunche Elementary School
URL address: **http://mac94.ralphbunche.rbs.edu/**

This home page, run by a graduate of the school, offers the school newspaper, student work, and a pointer to the school's Gopher.

Smoky Mountain Field School

URL address: **http://www.ce.utk.edu/smoky.html**

The University of Tennessee's Division of Continuing Education maintains this WWW home page for the Smoky Mountain Field School. The school offers supervised wilderness adventures for people of all ages and levels of experiences. The site provides links to a current program schedule, which includes topics such as Family Hiking in the Smokies. Registration information is available online.

Virginia L. Murray Elementary School

URL address: **http://curry.edschool.Virginia.EDU:80/murray/**

The school, located in Ivy, Virginia, serves approximately 250 students in grades K–5. With funding from Albemarle County, the Parent–Teacher Organization, a local grant, and the school budget, Murray established a direct Internet connection. This home page was developed by graduate students at the Curry School of Education as part of a technology-infusion project with Albemarle County Schools.

Colleges and Universities— United States

Arizona State University: Infrared Subnode

URL address: **http://esther.la.asu.edu/asu_tes/**

Arizona State University provides the Infrared Imaging subnode, a subsidiary of the Geosciences Node of NASA's Planetary Data System. The server is located at the Thermal Emission Spectroscopy Laboratory at Arizona State University in Tempe.

Baylor College of Medicine

URL address: **http://www.bcm.tmc.edu/**

The server provides information about the Molecular Biology Computational Resource (MBCR). At this site, you can find the MBCR Guide, a hypertext manual on how to do just about anything for which a molecular biologist uses a computer. The site also provides links to several biological data-bank services on the Internet, as well as information about the Department of Human and Molecular Genetics and links of general interest to molecular biologists.

Carnegie-Mellon University: the English Server
URL address: **http://english-server.hss.cmu.edu/**

This site is a student-run cooperative that publishes humanities texts electronically at Carnegie-Mellon University. You also may want to visit the home page for Carnegie-Mellon University (**http://www.cmu.edu**), where you can learn about the university; courses and degree programs; research projects; and faculty members, staff members, and students. Home-page links go to individual departments.

Clemson University Computational Science and Engineering Resources
URL address: **http://diogenes.cs.clemson.edu/CSE/homepage.html**

Clemson University's server represents a collection of educational resources for computational science and engineering. The site provides links to servers such as Netlib, mailing lists on CSE, relevant newsgroups, and contacts for academic materials.

ECSEL Coalition
URL address: **http://echo.umd.edu/**

The Engineering Coalition of Schools for Excellence in Education and Leadership is funded by the National Science Foundation and is engaged in a five-year effort to renew undergraduate engineering education and its infrastructure. This server provides general information and links to ECSEL research projects and other engineering-education coalitions.

Ferris State University
URL address: **http://about.ferris.edu/homepage.htm**

This server offers information about Ferris State University, located in Big Rapids, Michigan; its degree programs; and the local community. The server also provides a link to the All Music Guide, a database about recorded music available on CD.

Harvard University Graduate School of Education
URL address: **http://golgi.harvard.edu/hugse**

The home page of this Web server provides information about the university and links to other education-related resources.

Fig. 23.15
If you've always
wanted to go to
Harvard, just enter
this URL address.

New Mexico State University Astronomy Department

URL address: **http://charon.nmsu.edu/**

This server offers information about the astronomy department's people, facilities, research, and educational activities. The site also provides links to images of the collision of the comet Shoemaker-Levy 9 with Jupiter.

North Carolina State University College of Engineering

URL address: **http://www.eos.ncsu.edu/coe/coe.html**

This server contains information about all aspects of the college's operations, including undergraduate and graduate programs, research programs, staffing, student activities and organizations, computer operations, and extension services. The site has links to several other departments.

Northwestern University: Learning through Collaborative Visualization

URL address: **http://www.covis.nwu.edu/**

The Web server at Northwestern University is where you'll find information about research and development of different approaches to high-school science education. Some of the projects involve networking technologies, collaborative software, and visualization tools. These educational projects are funded by the National Science Foundation and various industry partners and sponsors.

Oklahoma State University

URL address: **http://a.cs.okstate.edu/welcome.html**

This site provides information about the Department of Computer Science at Oklahoma State University in Stillwater. The server offers links to information about department resources, campus resources, and Internet resources.

VI

Finding Web Resources

Pennsylvania State University

URL address: **http://www.psu.edu**

Fig. 23.16
Penn State offers more than just the Nittany Lions; find out when you try this Web site.

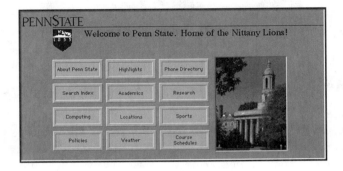

This server is the main entry point to information about Penn State. Included on this server are links to college and department Web servers, an electronic phone book, the Penn State Population Research Institute, the *Journal of Buddhist Ethics*, and other college servers. Don't forget the Nittany Lions and other Penn State sports links.

Rockefeller University

URL address: **http://www.rockefeller.edu**

From the home page, start with a link that opens a map of the campus. Then find details about the university, consult a phone directory, browse a calendar of events, or see some interesting Internet links.

University of California College of Engineering

URL address: **http://ucrengr.ucr.edu/**

Located at the University of California at Riverside, this site provides information on courses, faculty members, degree programs, and research centers. The research centers include VIS Lab, a research center for computer visualization and image processing; Systems Clinic, an opportunity for students to participate in solving industry-related problems; CE-CERT, an industry, university, and government partnership for research of air-pollution control; and U.C.M.E.P., the University of California Manufacturing Extension Program.

University of Chicago: Ancient Near East

URL address: **http://spirit.lib.uconn.edu/archnet/near_east.html**

This server is operated by the Oriental Institute of the University of Chicago. The site provides mainly Egyptological material, including announcements, the newsletter of the Archaeological Institute of America, the archives of the Ancient Near East, the newsletter of the American Schools of Oriental Research, information about the Oriental Institute, and other research on the Ancient Near East.

University of Massachusetts

URL address: **http://webserver.cogsci.umassd.edu/welcome.html**

The Computer and Information Science Department server at the University of Massachusetts in Dartmouth currently provides information on its research activities and reports, as well as on programs for graduates and undergraduates.

University of Missouri School of Journalism

URL address: **http://www.missouri.edu/~jschool**

Find out about this educational institution or jump to the *Digital Missourian*, a publication that features local (Columbia), national, and international news; sports; weather; and feature stories. The server also provides links to sections for elementary- and secondary-school students and teachers.

University of North Carolina at Chapel Hill

URL address: **http://sunsite.unc.edu/unchome.html**

This site provides information on the Sun Microsystems archives, newsgroups, and all the SunSITEs in the world.

University of Pennsylvania

URL address: **http://www.upenn.edu/**

This server offers several topics of interest and links with other Web servers on the Penn campus. The server provides gateways to PennInfo (the campuswide information system) and to Gopher servers at Penn and worldwide. Currently featured topics are engineering, educational technology services, physics, medicine, computer and information sciences, statistics, math, virtual language, cognitive science, and economics.

University of Tennessee

URL address: **http://loki.ur.utk.edu/default.html**

The Office of University Relations has developed a Web server that provides general information about the university, bicentennial information, online photographs of sculpture at the Knoxville campus, profiles of faculty members and alumni who have gained national recognition, and an official listing of the WUOT-FM radio program guide, complete with articles, images, and daily programming schedules.

University of Texas ARLUT

URL address: **http://www.arlut.utexas.edu/home.html**

The Applied Research Laboratory server at the University of Texas provides links to a variety of Web resources. Especially worthwhile is the Internet Resources Meta-Index, which you can keyword-search to locate information.

University of Washington Computer Science and Engineering

URL address: **http://www.cs.washington.edu/**

Information accessible on this server includes an overview of the department and its research, descriptions of graduate programs, research summaries, and online technical reports. The server also is the home of the WebCrawler, a WWW searcher.

Colleges and Universities— International

Australia: Australian National University

URL address: **http://coombs.anu.edu.au/CoombsHome.html**

▶ See "Education and Careers," p. 753

▶ See "Travel— Places to Go Worldwide," p. 937

Located at Australian National University in Canberra, the Coombsweb keeps track of information resources of value to researchers in the field of social sciences, humanities, and Asian studies.

Austria: University of Salzburg

URL address: **http://www.cosy.sbg.ac.at/welcome.html**

The server, located at the University of Salzburg, provides information on documents in German and English, as well a hyperlink map of Austria and Europe.

Belgium: Brussels University

URL address: **http://www.iihe.ac.be/**

This server provides information about Brussels University, the Library Information inquiry and Referral Network project, the Belgian Multimedia

Integrated Conferencing for European Researchers NSC, and gateways and search tools.

Canada: **Mount Allison University**
URL address: **http://ollc.mta.ca/tenb.html**

This server is located at Mount Allison University in Sackville, New Brunswick. The TeleEducation New Brunswick Network is used to deliver university, community-college, and other educational courses to all areas of the province of New Brunswick.

Canada: **University of Saskatchewan**
URL address: **http://www.usask.ca/**

Local information on this server is about the university, its departments, and its organizations. Canadian-based information includes links to other Canadian Web sites, including government sites.

Chile: **Universidad de Chile Departamento de Ciencias de la Computación**
URL address: **http://www.dcc.uchile.cl/**

Universidad de Chile
Facultad de Ciencias Físicas y Matemáticas
Departamento de Ciencias de la Computación

El DCC pertenece a la Facultad de Ciencias Físicas y Matemáticas de la Universidad de Chile . Es el encargado de dictar los programas de Ingeniería Civil en Computación y Magister en Ciencias mención Computación.

Fig. 23.17
This Web server gives you a sense of the types of programs that are offered in universities in foreign countries.

The server, which provides information about the University of Chile, includes links to several departments and general information about the university.

Finland: **University of Turku**
URL address: **http://www.funet.fi/resources/map.html**

This server includes a map and information from the University of Turku, the second-largest educational entity in southwestern Finland.

VI

Finding Web Resources

Germany: University of Kaiserslautern

URL address: **http://www.uni-kl.de/**

This site is located at the University of Kaiserslautern. Most of the text is presented in German. The site provides information links to the departments, the institute itself, and the servers.

Italy: Center for Advanced Studies Research and Development

URL address: **http://www.crs4.it/HTML/homecrs4.html**

From the Center for Advanced Studies, Research and Development in Sardinia, Italy, this server provides links to local-area information, selections of Italian literature (in HTML form), and annotated, political, physical, and satellite maps.

Netherlands: University of Amsterdam

URL address: **http://helios.astro.uva.nl:8888/home.html**

This server provides information about the university's astronomical institute, as well as useful links to astronomy servers, Dutch servers, and information about the Web.

Singapore: Ministry of Education

URL address: **http://www.moe.ac.sg/**

The Ministry of Education server provides information on the education system in Singapore. The site promotes education via the Internet by collating relevant educational resources and grouping them by subject.

Slovenia: University of Ljubljana

URL address: **http://www.fer.uni-lj.si/**

This site provides information from the University of Ljubljana, including links to the history of the faculty, research activities, educational programs, research labs, an e-mail address search, and an English–Slovene electronic dictionary.

Computer Science Programs— United States

Brigham Young University Computer Science

URL address: **http://www.cs.byu.edu/homepage.html**

This site provides information about the Computer Science Department at Brigham Young University, including a virtual tour of the department building and information about the department's mission, faculty, classes, resources, and laboratories.

Caltech Concurrent Supercomputing Facilities

URL address: **http://www.ccsf.caltech.edu/ccsf.html**

This server offers information about the facilities at Caltech. The server is located on the campus of the California Institute of Technology, which supports and maintains a variety of supercomputers for the Concurrent Supercomputing Consortium.

Cornell University

URL address: **http://helpdesk-www.cit.cornell.edu/ CITSHDHome.html**

Got a question? Go to an electronic help desk. This server offers information about Cornell University and a variety of links to other WWW servers that contain information about computers and computer applications. The site has links to the Free On-Line Dictionary of Computing, the Internet Computer Index, and the Global Prepress Center (a site that helps with desktop publishing).

Georgia State University Mathematics and Computer Science

URL address: **http://www.cs.gsu.edu/**

Located at Georgia State University in Atlanta, this server provides information about graduate and undergraduate courses and degrees, faculty members, research, department and university resources, other math and computer-science resources, and Internet resources, as well as information about Atlanta.

VI

Finding Web Resources

Indiana University Computer Science Department

URL address: **http://cs.indiana.edu/home-page.html**

If you want to be a computer programmer, check out the course descriptions for classes offered by this department, including Assemblers and Compilers. In addition, you can jump to documents that offer technical reports, overviews of the labs, and research projects. Advanced computer-science applications include a robotics lab and high-performance computing. The server also provides broad links to WWW resources and search tools.

Massachusetts Institute of Technology Artificial Intelligence Laboratory

URL address: **http://www.ai.mit.edu/**

Research at MIT's Artificial Intelligence Laboratory ranges from computer-based learning, vision, and robotics to development of new computers. The server provides links to these various research areas. A visit to this site will give you some insight into computer applications in the next decade, as artificial intelligence moves from science fiction to the real world.

Old Dominion University Department of Computer Science

URL address: **http://www.cs.odu.edu/index.html**

This server provides an introduction to the department, a brochure of the work in progress, a catalog of courses, lab information, and general education requirements.

Stanford University

URL address: **http://kanpai.stanford.edu/epgy/pamph/pamph.html**

Stanford University's Education Program for Gifted Youth, offered through the university's continuing-studies program, offers computer-based courses in mathematics and the mathematical sciences to bright young students. When you visit this site, you can learn about the courses and students involved in the program.

University of Florida

URL address: **http://www.cis.ufl.edu/**

This site provides information about the Computer and Information Sciences Department at the University of Florida, as well as links to departmental resources and a collection of other Web sites.

Fig. 23.18
Learn about the computer-science curriculum at the University of Florida when you visit this Web server.

University of Iowa

URL address: **http://caesar.cs.uiowa.edu/**

This server provides information from the Department of Computer Science at the University of Iowa in Iowa City. The site offers information about the computer-science department colloquia; the Iowa Virtual Tourist (a hypertext information resource for travelers); and Doctor Fun, a daily cartoon for the Internet.

University of Maryland

URL address: **http://www.umiacs.umd.edu/**

This site is located at the University of Maryland's Institute for Advanced Computer Studies. The institute was established to broaden support for computing research throughout the university system, focusing on interdisciplinary computing topics. The server provides links to information about the institute's faculty, systems staff, departments, and research.

University of Rochester

URL address: **http://www.cs.rochester.edu/**

The server provides information on the Department of Computer Science at the University of Rochester in New York state. The server provides links to the department's brochure, technical-report collection, and anonymous FTP archive, as well as a department subway map and other information about the university.

University of Washington Computer Science and Engineering

URL address: **http://www.cs.washington.edu/**

The server provides links to information on the Puget Sound region and to the university and its departments. The site also provides a summary of various research fields, including mobile computing.

VI

Finding Web Resources

University of Wisconsin Computer Sciences

URL address: **http://www.cs.wisc.edu/**

This site, located at the Computer Sciences Department of the University of Wisconsin in Madison, provides information about the Computer Systems Lab, research projects, courses, technical reports, and admission requirements.

Wesleyan University Department of Mathematics and Computer Science

URL address: **http://www.cs.wesleyan.edu/**

This server provides information about Wesleyan University, including links to information about the students and staff, local news, computing topics, islands in the Net, and Clipper encryption.

Yale University Computer Science Department Overview

URL address: **http://www.yale.edu/HTML/YaleCS-Info.html**

This server provides links to general information about the university, the Linda Group, and the Vision and Robotics interdisciplinary research group.

Computer Science Programs— International

Australia: James Cook University

URL address: **http://coral.cs.jcu.edu.au/**

This site provides information from the James Cook University Department of Computer Science. The site includes links to a department handbook, technical reports, subject information, a technical seminar series, the Australian Computer Science Academics Database, and a list of electronic libraries.

Canada: University of British Columbia Computer Science

URL address: **http://www.cs.ubc.ca/home**

This server provides information about the University of British Columbia Computer Science Department in Vancouver. You can access an online Webster's dictionary and thesaurus.

Denmark: University of Aarhus

URL address: **http://www.daimi.aau.dk/**

The home page for the University of Aarhus Department of Computer Science provides information on research activities and groups, personnel, and general information about the archives.

Germany: TU Chemnitz-Zwickau

URL address: **http://www.tu-chemnitz.de/~uer/FakInf.html**

The server provides links to all types of information about the Department of Computer Science at the Technical University of Chemnitz in Zwickau. The information is in German.

Germany: University of Erlangen-Nürnberg

URL address: **http://www.informatik.uni-erlangen.de/tree/Departments**

This server provides information about the University of Erlangen-Nürnberg and links to some of the departments at the University, including Research and Operating and Distributed Systems.

Germany: University of Hannover

URL address: **http://www.tnt.uni-hannover.de/data/info/www/tnt/welcome.html**

The Institut fuer Theoretische Nachrichtentechnik und Informaationsverarbeitung (TNT) at the University of Hannover provides information about the institute's people; research; and education on scientific topics, such as artificial intelligence, signal processing, and audio and video coding.

Greece: National Technical University of Athens

URL address: **http://www.ntua.gr/**

National Technical University of Athens (NTUA)
Department of Electrical & Computer Engineering
Computer Science Division / Software Engineering Laboratory

VI

Finding Web Resources

Fig. 23.19
In addition to computer-science information, you can view some interesting visuals created by Mandelbrot fractals at this Web site.

This server provides information from the National Technical University of Athens. Links include What's New, the Mandelbrot Explorer (exploring the Mandelbrot fractals through X Mosaic), and frequently asked questions.

Ireland: Dublin City University Centre for Software Engineering

URL address: **http://www.compapp.dcu.ie/CSE/CSE_home.html**

This server provides information about Dublin City University. The university and the WWW site help Irish software developers enhance product quality and productivity.

Ireland: Trinity College

URL address: **http://www.cs.tcd.ie:/welcome.html**

This server, located at Trinity College in Dublin, provides information about and links to the O'Reilly Institute and the University of Limerick.

Italy: University of Pisa Department of Computer Science

URL address: **http://www.di.unipi.it/welcome.html**

This home page is provided by the Department of Computer Science at the University of Pisa. The site offers information about the department, its programs, and its documentation, as well as a large icon collection.

Japan: University of Aizu

URL address: **http://www.u-aizu.ac.jp/**

The university is dedicated to research and education in computer science. The site provides a hypermedia research profile brochure and an introduction to the university and its faculty.

Netherlands: TU Delft

URL address: **http://www.twi.tudelft.nl/TWI/Overview.html**

This site offers information about TU Delft. The server provides links to information about the faculty, pure mathematics, statistics, probability theory and operations research, and applied analysis and information systems.

Norway: University of Trondheim Activities in Artificial Intelligence

URL address: **http://www.ifi.unit.no/ai.html**

This site provides information from the University of Trondheim Department of Informatics. Links are available to information on knowledge-intensive problem solving and machine learning, case-based reasoning, knowledge acquisition and modeling, and integrated architectures.

Singapore: National University of Singapore ISS Resource Guide

URL address: **http://www.iss.nus.sg/**

The Institute of Systems Science at the National University of Singapore has a home page that provides information about the institute's location, facilities, and research and educational programs.

▶ See "Singapore Online Guide," p. 742

South Africa: Rhodes University Computing Services

URL address: **http://www.ru.ac.za/**

The main campus server is located at the Computing Centre of Rhodes University in Grahamstown. The server provides Rhodes-specific information, as well as information on networking in South Africa.

Sweden: Uppsala University

URL address: **http://www.csd.uu.se/**

This home page, from the Computer Science Department at Uppsala University, provides links to local information, general information, faculty and staff members, courses, projects, and technical reports.

United Kingdom: Computational Phonology

URL address: **http://ftp.cogsci.ed.ac.uk/phonology/CompPhon.html**

This server is located at the Centre for Cognitive Science at the University of Edinburgh. The site offers documents and directories for this field and for the Association for Computational Phonology. Information includes a directory of computational phonologists around the world and past newsletters of the ACP.

United Kingdom: Imperial College Department of Computing

URL address: **http://www.doc.ic.ac.uk/**

This site provides information about the Imperial College of Science, Technology and Medicine at the University of London. The server provides links to information about the department's staff, advanced languages and architectures, distributed software engineering, logic programming, theory, and formal methods.

United Kingdom: Oxford University Computing Laboratory

URL address: **http://www.comlab.ox.ac.uk/**

This site is located at the Oxford University Computing Laboratory, which is one of the world's leading centers for the study, development, and exploitation of computing technology. The lab is responsible for all academic aspects of computing: teaching, basic research, and collaboration with industry on applied research. The server provides links to information about all aspects of the university.

United Kingdom: University of Birmingham School of Computer Science

URL address: **http://www.cs.bham.ac.uk/**

This site provides information about the computer-science Web server at the university. The server provides links to campus and regional information, the main library catalog, news, and hypertext on the object-oriented C++ programming course.

United Kingdom: University of Exeter Department of Computer Science

URL address: **http://www.dcs.exeter.ac.uk/**

This server provides information about the University of Exeter and includes links to research papers, information on postgraduate study, and personnel information.

United Kingdom: University of Manchester Computer Graphics Unit

URL address: **http://info.mcc.ac.uk/CGU/CGU-intro.html**

This server provides high-performance interactive computer-graphics facilities on a range of workstations. The CGU is part of Manchester Computing Centre, one of the regional supercomputing centers that provide facilities to the U.K. academic community.

United Kingdom: University of Wales College of Cardiff COMMA Information Server

URL address: **http://www.cm.cf.ac.uk/**

This server, located at the University of Wales College of Cardiff, provides information about the department and its research interests, lecture notes for computer-science courses, support pages for users, and recreational pages.

Regional and Community Education

Austin WWW User Group

URL address: **http://www.quadralay.com/www/Austin/ AustinOrgs/AWWWUG/AWWWUG.html**

The server of the Austin WWW User Group in Austin, Texas, provides a technical and organizational infrastructure to support the local community. The site's mission is to promote academic, commercial, and educational use of the Web.

Michigan Department of Education MDEnet

URL address: **http://web.mde.state.mi.us:1024/**

This system is designed to help arrange communication and information sharing between the Department of Education and the Michigan education community. The department is developing an internal collection strategy to locate, format, and archive popular documents and files for placement on its Gopher server.

The College and University List

This list can be an immensely valuable resource for high-school students who want to learn more about their potential choices of college degree programs. Rather than send letters to 30 colleges, asking for course information and details about the school, a student can jump on the Web and get it all in less than a day. Of course, anyone who is interested in academic subjects can find valuable information on these Web servers.

The list includes only the URL addresses; there isn't enough space to describe all the home pages. Many schools have more than one WWW home page, and some have multiple Web servers (the MIT list, for example, includes 68 addresses), each of which provides access to different information or departments.

The following example will give you some clues about where the addresses point. The listing for Georgia State University has three WWW addresses:

- **http://chara.gsu.edu**

- **http://www.cs.gsu.edu**

- **http://www.gsu.edu**

The Internet DNS address structure (described in Chapter 1, "Introduction to the World Wide Web") breaks addresses into domains. All the addresses in this section end with .edu, for education. In this example, the name to the left of .edu is .gsu, which stands for Georgia State University. The first address links to the Georgia State University Astronomy Department. You really couldn't guess this, but the acronym CHARA comes from one of the first menus in the home page that you receive, which offers the following choices:

- CHARA—The Center for High Angular Resolution Astronomy

- CHARA Array—Proposed optical imaging array

- HLCO—The Hard Labor Creek Observatory

- PEGA—The Program for Extragalactic Astronomy

- The Be Star Newsletter—The electronic journal of Be star observation

- Astronomy Graduate Study at GSU. Fill out a quick form for information by postal mail.

- GSU Astronomy FTP information

- Publications of interest to amateur and professional astronomers

- Observing forecast, current conditions, and current U.S. weather map

The second address points to the Georgia State University Mathematics and Computer Science Department's home page, which provides information about mathematics and computer science. The short address cs refers to computer science. Other common address codes include math for mathematics, psych for psychology, and eng for engineering.

In this example, the third address is the Georgia State University home page, which has links to all the other departments and resources at the university. In this home page, a prospective student can learn that GSU is the second-largest university in Georgia, that more than 22,000 students attend the school, and that approximately 50 graduate and undergraduate degrees are available in 250 areas of study through 6 colleges. You know that this URL is the university's home page because the address (**www.gsu.edu**) doesn't contain any other subdomain pointers.

Troubleshooting

I don't see my college/university on the list. Does this mean it doesn't have a Web site?

Colleges and universities are adding Web sites on a daily basis. The most common system for addressing follows the format: http://www.(name of school or abbreviation).edu. For example, if you went to Princeton you might try http://www.princeton.edu (which is the address). Or, perhaps your school has two letters like SU for Syracuse University or DU for University of Denver. Try putting those abbreviations in the middle of the www.-.edu format.

United States College and University Web Servers List (.edu Domain)

Arizona State University
http://enuxsa.eas.asu.edu
http://enws324.eas.asu.edu
http://esther.la.asu.edu
http://info.asu.edu
http://mosaic.eas.asu.edu

Boise State University
http://gozer.idbsu.edu

Boston University

http://buphy.bu.edu
http://conx.bu.edu
http://med-amsa.bu.edu
http://robotics.bu.edu
http://spiderman.bu.edu
http://web.bu.edu
http://www-busph.bu.edu

Bowling Green State University

http://hydra.bgsu.edu

Bradley University

http://bradley.bradley.edu
http://www.bradley.edu

Brandeis University

http://www.cs.brandeis.edu

Bridgewater College

http://www.bridgewater.edu

Brigham Young University

http://acm.cs.byu.edu
http://lal.cs.byu.edu
http://www.cs.byu.edu
http://www.math.byu.edu

Brown University

http://elbow.cs.brown.edu
http://ftp.brown.edu
http://garnet.geo.brown.edu
http://gopher.brown.edu
http://home.eos.brown.edu
http://home.geo.brown.edu
http://lager.geo.brown.edu
http://ns.brown.edu
http://pion.het.brown.edu
http://www.brown.edu
http://www.chem.brown.edu
http://www.cog.brown.edu

http://www.cs.brown.edu
http://www.het.brown.edu
http://www.hunger.brown.edu
http://www-geo.het.brown.edu
http://www.iris.brown.edu
http://www.physics.brown.edu
http://www.planetary.brown.edu

California Institute of Technology
http://alumni.caltech.edu
http://avalon.caltech.edu
http://brando.ipac.caltech.edu
http://ccfs.caltech.edu
http://cithe501.cithep.caltech.edu
http://cs.caltech.edu
http://electra.micro.caltech.edu
http://expet.gps.caltech.edu
http://gopher.caltech.edu
http://kaa.caltech.edu
http://robby.caltech.edu
http://www.ama.caltech.edu
http://www.caltech.edu
http://www.cco.caltech.edu
http://www.ccsf.caltech.edu
http://www.galcit.caltech.edu
http://www.gg.caltech.edu
http://www.gps.caltech.edu
http://www.ipac.caltech.edu
http://www.pcmp.caltech.edu
http://www.theory.caltech.edu
http://www.ugcs.caltech.edu

California Polytechnic State University
http://www.calpoly.edu

California State University at Chico
http://www2.ecst.csuchico.edu

California State University at Hayward
http://www.hal.csuhayward.edu
http://www.mcs.csuhayward.edu

VI

Finding Web Resources

California State University at Long Beach

http://gothic.acs.csulb.edu

Calvin College and Seminary

http://calvin.edu
http://mcmellx.calvin.edu
http://unicks.calvin.edu
http://www.calvin.edu

Carleton College

http://www.carleton.edu

Carnegie-Mellon University

http://alycia.andrew.cmu.edu
http://anther.learning.cs.cmu.edu
http://b.stat.cmu.edu
http://basisk.cimds.ri.cmu.edu
http://byron.sp.cs.cmu.edu
http://c.gp.cs.cmu.edu
http://ce.cmu.edu
http://clockwork.ws.cc.cmu.edu
http://english-server.hss.cmu.edu
http://frc.ri.cmu.edu
http://fuzine.mt.cs.cmu.edu
http://gaisberg.edrc.cmu.edu
http://gs13.sp.cs.cmu.edu
http://gs71.sp.cs.cmu.edu
http://heretic.pc.cc.cmu.edu
http://hopeless.mess.cs.cmu.edu
http://hp8.ini.cmu.edu
http://janus.brary.cmu.edu
http://legend.gwydion.cs.cmu.edu
http://logan.edrc.cmu.edu
http://mixing.sp.cs.cmu.edu
http://musashi.mt.cs.cmu.edu
http://orac.andrew.cmu.edu
http://p.gp.cs.cmu.edu
http://paneer.ndim.edrc.cmu.edu
http://porsche.boltz.cs.cmu.edu
http://robocop.modmath.cs.cmu.edu
http://sodom.mt.cs.cmu.edu
http://strauss.ce.cmu.edu

http://thule.mt.cs.cmu.edu
http://www.brary.cmu.edu
http://www.cmu.edu
http://www.contrib.andrew.cmu.edu
http://www.cs.cmu.edu
http://www.ece.cmu.edu
http://www.frc.ri.cmu.edu
http://www.mt.cs.cmu.edu

Carroll College
http://carroll1.cc.edu

Case Western Reserve University
http://biochemistry.bioc.cwru.edu
http://caisr2.caisr.cwru.edu
http://ftp.cwru.edu

Clarkson University
http://fire.clarkson.edu
http://omnigate.clarkson.edu

Clemson University
http://beast.eng.clemson.edu
http://clancy.clemson.edu
http://cmcserver.clemson.edu
http://diogenes.cs.clemson.edu
http://www.clemson.edu
http://www.cts.clemson.edu
http://www.math.clemson.edu

Cleveland State University
http://gopher.law.csuohio.edu

Colorado State University
http://www.colostate.edu

Columbia University
http://gutentag.cc.columbia.edu
http://lamont.ldgo.columbia.edu
http://lawnet.law.columbia.edu
http://rainbow.ldeo.columbia.edu

http://www.cc.columbia.edu
http://www.ctr.columbia.edu
http://www.ilt.columbia.edu
http://www.ilt.tc.columbia.edu

Cornell University

http://aruba.nysaes.cornell.edu
http://astrosun.tn.cornell.edu
http://chare.mannb.cornell.edu
http://cs-tr.cs.cornell.edu
http://dri.cornell.edu
http://fatty.law.cornell.edu
http://gopher.tc.cornell.edu:70/1
http://helpdesk-www.cit.cornell.edu
http://ibm.tc.cornell.edu
http://lylahfive.resfe.cornell.edu
http://simlab.cs.cornell.edu
http://stos-www.cit.cornell.edu
http://w4.lns.cornell.edu
http://www.cs.cornell.edu
http://www.gated.cornell.edu
http://www.law.cornell.edu
http://www.tc.cornell.edu

Creighton University

http://phoenix.creighton.edu

Dartmouth College

http://ausg.dartmouth.edu
http://cagari.dartmouth.edu
http://coos.dartmouth.edu
http://cs.dartmouth.edu
http://geminga.dartmouth.edu
http://picard.dartmouth.edu
http://www.cs.dartmouth.edu
http://www.dartmouth.edu

Dixie College

http://sci.dixie.edu
http://www.sci.dixie.edu

Embry-Riddle Aeronautical University
http://blackbird.db.erau.edu

The Exploratorium
http://isaac.exploratorium.edu
http://www.exploratorium.edu

Florida Institute of Technology
http://sci-ed.fit.edu

Florida State University
http://eucd.math.fsu.edu
http://ftp.met.fsu.edu
http://garnet.acns.fsu.edu
http://gopher.fsu.edu
http://sis.fsu.edu
http://www.fsu.edu
http://www.scri.fsu.edu

Franklin and Marshall College
http://www.fandm.edu

George Mason University
http://absolut.gmu.edu
http://www.science.gmu.edu

Georgetown University
http://gusun.georgetown.edu
http://www.georgetown.edu

Georgia Institute of Technology
http://ejc.math.gatech.edu
http://howe.ce.gatech.edu
http://isye.gatech.edu
http://mern.gatech.edu
http://moralforce.cc.gatech.edu
http://penguin.gatech.edu
http://www.gatech.edu

VI

Finding Web Resources

Georgia State Board of Regents

http://catfish.valdosta.peachnet.edu
http://k-9.oit.peachnet.edu

Georgia State University

http://chara.gsu.edu
http://www.cs.gsu.edu
http://www.gsu.edu

Gustavus Adolphus College

http://www.gac.edu

Hahnemann University

http://ubu.hahnemann.edu

Hanover College

http://www.hanover.edu

Harvard University

http://adswww.harvard.edu
http://cfa-www.harvard.edu
http://chan4.student.harvard.edu
http://cmiyagis.student.harvard.edu
http://count51.med.harvard.edu
http://courses.harvard.edu
http://egstein.student.harvard.edu
http://fas-gopher.harvard.edu
http://golgi.harvard.edu
http://gopher.dfci.harvard.edu/1
http://gopher.harvard.edu
http://hea-www.harvard.edu
http://hols.harvard.edu
http://hrl.harvard.edu
http://hsph.harvard.edu
http://huh.harvard.edu
http://huhepl.harvard.edu
http://ibhan.student.harvard.edu
http://mgelman.student.harvard.edu
http://oir-www.harvard.edu
http://phys2.harvard.edu
http://sao-www.harvard.edu

http://string.harvard.edu
http://twod.med.harvard.edu
http://weeds.mgh.harvard.edu
http://www.das.harvard.edu

Harvey Mudd College
http://www.hmc.edu

Hope College
http://smaug.cs.hope.edu

Idaho State University
http://pharmacy.isu.edu

Illinois Mathematics and Science Academy
http://gluon.imsa.edu
http://imsasun.imsa.edu
http://www.imsa.edu

Indiana University
http://astrowww.astro.indiana.edu
http://cica.indiana.edu
http://cogsci.indiana.edu
http://cs.indiana.edu
http://ftp.bio.indiana.edu
http://ftp.cica.indiana.edu
http://gopher.indiana.edu
http://infotech.indiana.edu
http://ist.indiana.edu
http://iuis.ucs.indiana.edu
http://loris.cisab.indiana.edu
http://moose.cs.indiana.edu
http://polecat.law.indiana.edu
http://scwww.ucs.indiana.edu
http://tarski.phil.indiana.edu
http://www.cica.indiana.edu
http://www.cisab.indiana.edu
http://www.cs.indiana.edu
http://www.indiana.edu
http://www-iub.indiana.edu

VI

Finding Web Resources

http://www-iub.ucs.indiana.edu
http://www.law.indiana.edu
http://www.music.indiana.edu

Indiana University-Purdue University at Indianapolis
http://chem.iupui.edu

Iowa State University
http://info.iastate.edu
http://www.b.iastate.edu
http://www.cc.iastate.edu
http://www.cs.iastate.edu
http://www.pubc.iastate.edu

Jackson State University
http://tiger.jsums.edu

Johns Hopkins University
http://muse.mse.jhu.edu
http://muse.mse.jhu.edu/spot.jhu.html
http://gopher.hs.jhu.edu
http://merlot.welch.jhu.edu

Kansas State University
http://depot.cis.ksu.edu
http://godiva.ne.ksu.edu
http://www.cis.ksu.edu
http://www.ecc.ksu.edu
http://www.eece.ksu.edu
http://www.engg.ksu.edu
http://www.ksu.edu
http://www.ksu.ksu.edu

Kent State University
http://www.mcs.kent.edu

Kestrel Research Institute
http://kestrel.edu

Lake Forest College
http://br2.lfc.edu

Louisiana State University
http://unix1.sncc.lsu.edu

Louisiana Tech University
http://aurora.latech.edu
http://info.latech.edu

Loyola College
http://www.loyola.edu

Maricopa Community College District
http://hakatai.mc.dist.maricopa.edu
http://www.emc.maricopa.edu

Marine Biological Laboratory
http://alopias.mbl.edu

Massachusetts Institute of Technology
http://ai.mit.edu
http://alecto.mit.edu
http://alexander-hamilton.mit.edu
http://amsterdam.lcs.mit.edu
http://anxiety-closet.mit.edu
http://arsenio.mit.edu
http://bresn.mit.edu
http://bronze.lcs.mit.edu
http://cag-www.lcs.mit.edu
http://clef.lcs.mit.edu
http://consult-www.mit.edu
http://cremer.mit.edu
http://debussy.media.mit.edu
http://delcano.mit.edu
http://earthcube.mit.edu
http://eddie.mit.edu
http://eecs-test.mit.edu
http://export.lcs.mit.edu
http://far.mit.edu
http://farnsworth.mit.edu
http://foundation.mit.edu
http://gopher.mit.edu

VI

Finding Web Resources

http://im.lcs.mit.edu
http://info.lcs.mit.edu
http://jack-vance.mit.edu
http://japaninfo.mit.edu
http://jazz.mit.edu
http://joet.mit.edu
http://jukebox.lcs.mit.edu
http://lancet.mit.edu
http://lcs.mit.edu
http://ltt-www.lcs.mit.edu
http://macpythia.mit.edu
http://marie.mit.edu
http://martigny.ai.mit.edu
http://medg.lcs.mit.edu
http://microworld.media.mit.edu
http://nmis03.mit.edu
http://paris.lcs.mit.edu
http://prep.ai.mit.edu
http://reading-room-www.lcs.mit.edu
http://rg.media.mit.edu
http://rtfm.mit.edu
http://sipb.mit.edu
http://sls-www.lcs.mit.edu
http://sobolev.mit.edu
http://sparta.lcs.mit.edu
http://sturgeon.mit.edu
http://synergy.mit.edu
http://the-tech.mit.edu
http://theory.lcs.mit.edu
http://timesink.mit.edu
http://tk-www.mit.edu
http://tns-www.lcs.mit.edu
http://tower.lcs.mit.edu
http://uu-gna.mit.edu
http://uu-nna.mit.edu
http://vance.mit.edu
http://web.mit.edu
http://www.ai.mit.edu
http://www-erl.mit.edu
http://www-genome.wi.mit.edu
http://www-im.lcs.mit.edu

http://www.lcs.mit.edu
http://www-ni-gateway.lcs.mit.edu
http://www-psrg.lcs.mit.edu
http://www-swiss.ai.mit.edu
http://www-techinfo.mit.edu

Memphis State University

http://www.memst.edu

Merit Computer Network

http://merit.edu
http://nic.merit.edu

MHPCC (Maui High Performance Computing Center)

http://pipene.mhpcc.edu

Miami University

http://m-media.muohio.edu

Michigan State University

http://ah3.cal.msu.edu
http://burrow.cl.msu.edu
http://esalsun10.ent.msu.edu
http://gopher.msu.edu
http://indian.cps.msu.edu
http://pads1.pa.msu.edu
http://puck.egr.msu.edu
http://re560.cl.msu.edu
http://web.cal.msu.edu
http://web.cl.msu.edu
http://web.cps.msu.edu
http://web.msu.edu
http://www.msu.edu

Mississippi State University

http://msuinfo.ur.msstate.edu
http://www.cs.msstate.edu
http://www.erc.msstate.edu
http://www.msstate.edu

Mount Wilson Observatory
http://www.mtwilson.edu

National Air and Space Museum
http://ceps.nasm.edu

National Astronomy and Ionosphere Center
http://naic.edu
http://www.naic.edu

National Radio Astronomy Observatory
http://info.aoc.nrao.edu
http://info.cv.nrao.edu
http://info.gb.nrao.edu
http://fits.cv.nrao.edu
http://fits.nrao.edu
http://fits.aoc.nrao.edu

National Supercomputing Center for Energy and the Environment
http://www.nscee.edu

New Jersey Institute of Technology
http://eies.njit.edu
http://eies2.njit.edu
http://it.njit.edu

New Mexico Institute of Mining and Technology
http://nmt.edu
http://www.nmt.edu

New Mexico State University
http://charon.nmsu.edu
http://crl.nmsu.edu
http://vitoria.nmsu.edu
http://www.apo.nmsu.edu

New York University
http://edgar.stern.nyu.edu
http://www.nyu.edu

North Carolina State University

http://dewey.b.ncsu.edu
http://ericmorgan.b.ncsu.edu
http://meawx1.nrrc.ncsu.edu
http://www.acs.ncsu.edu
http://www.catt.ncsu.edu
http://www.eos.ncsu.edu
http://www.mmrc.ncsu.edu
http://www.ncsu.edu
http://www.tx.ncsu.edu

Northeastern University

http://ftp.ccs.neu.edu
http://jh.ccs.neu.edu
http://www.ccs.neu.edu
http://www.cs.neu.edu
http://www.dac.neu.edu

Northwestern University

http://antioch.acns.nwu.edu
http://asgard.eecs.nwu.edu
http://asp.esam.nwu.edu
http://daneel.acns.nwu.edu
http://gopher.math.nwu.edu
http://holmes.astro.nwu.edu
http://hopf.math.nwu.edu
http://math.nwu.edu
http://pubweb.acns.nwu.edu
http://rossi.astro.nwu.edu
http://tup.eecs.nwu.edu
http://voltaire.mech.nwu.edu
http://words.acns.nwu.edu
http://www.acns.nwu.edu
http://www.astro.nwu.edu
http://www.brary.nwu.edu
http://www.covis.nwu.edu
http://www.eecs.nwu.edu
http://www.ils.nwu.edu
http://www.math.nwu.edu
http://www.mmss.nwu.edu

http://www.nwu.edu
http://www.psych.nwu.edu
http://www.speech.nwu.edu

Nova University
http://alpha.acast.nova.edu

Oakland University
http://gopher.acs.oakland.edu
http://mars.acs.oakland.edu
http://unix.secs.oakland.edu
http://www.acs.oakland.edu

Obern College
http://cs.obern.edu

Occidental College
http://apa.oxy.edu
http://gate.oxy.edu

Ohio State University
http://archive.cis.ohio-state.edu
http://beetle.marion.ohio-state.edu
http://hartke.b.ohio-state.edu
http://hertz.eng.ohio-state.edu
http://kirk.cgrg.ohio-state.edu
http://www.acs.ohio-state.edu
http://www.cis.ohio-state.edu
http://osc.edu
http://www.osc.edu

Oklahoma State University
http://a.cs.okstate.edu
http://ftp.math.okstate.edu
http://math.okstate.edu
http://www.okstate.edu

Old Dominion University
http://www.cs.odu
http://xanth.cs.odu

Oregon State University

http://engr.orst.edu
http://gopher.cs.orst.edu
http://www.csos.orst.edu

Pennsylvania State University

http://bjt105.rh.psu.edu
http://euler.bd.psu.edu
http://info.pop.psu.edu
http://opus.chem.psu.edu
http://random.chem.psu.edu
http://www.math.psu.edu
http://www.pop.psu.edu
http://www.psu.edu
http://www.xray.hmc.psu.edu

Pittsburgh Supercomputer Center

http://pscinfo.psc.edu

Plymouth State College

http://www.plymouth.edu

Portland State University

http://gopher.cs.pdx.edu
http://ursula.ee.pdx.edu
http://www.ee.pdx.edu

Princeton University

http://astro.princeton.edu
http://bpd.student.princeton.edu
http://princeton.edu
http://wombat.princeton.edu
http://www.princeton.edu
http://www.cs.princeton.edu

Purdue University

http://www.purdue.edu

Reed College

http://reed.edu
http://www.reed.edu

Rensselaer Polytechnic Institute

http://cs.rpi.edu
http://ftp.rpi.edu
http://wolf3.vlsc.rpi.edu
http://www.cs.rpi.edu
http://www.rpi.edu

Rice University

http://chico.rice.edu
http://es.rice.edu
http://harpo.rice.edu
http://hex.rice.edu
http://is.rice.edu
http://riceinfo.rice.edu
http://softb.rice.edu
http://vm.rice.edu

Rochester Institute of Technology

http://www.csh.rit.edu

Rockefeller University

http://pisa.rockefeller.edu

Rutgers University

http://aristarchus.rutgers.edu
http://gandalf.rutgers.edu
http://info.rutgers.edu
http://ndb.rutgers.edu
http://www-ns.rutgers.edu
http://www.rutgers.edu
http://www.usacs.rutgers.edu

Saint John's University: College of St. Benedict

http://bingen.cs.csbsju.edu

SUNY at Buffalo

http://mcbio.med.buffalo.edu
http://mirach.cs.buffalo.edu
http://www.eng.buffalo.edu
http://wings.buffalo.edu
http://www.acsu.buffalo.edu

http://www.cedar.buffalo.edu
http://www.cs.buffalo.edu
http://www.wings.buffalo.edu
http://www.geog.buffalo.edu

SUNY at Geneseo
http://mosaic.cc.geneseo.edu

SUNY at Plattsburgh
http://bio420.hawk.plattsburgh.edu

SUNY at Potsdam
http://gopher.dc.potsdam.edu

University of Alaska
http://saturn.uaamath.alaska.edu

University of Arizona
http://bozo.lpl.arizona.edu
http://info.ccit.arizona.edu
http://info-center.ccit.arizona.edu
http://lanka.ccit.arizona.edu
http://lion.ccit.arizona.edu
http://obsidian.math.arizona.edu
http://papago.rc.arizona.edu
http://seds.lpl.arizona.edu
http://www.arizona.edu
http://www.cs.arizona.edu

University of California at Berkeley
http://cea-ftp.cea.berkeley.edu
http://cs-tr.cs.berkeley.edu
http://docs34.berkeley.edu
http://ftp.cs.berkeley.edu
http://http.icsi.berkeley.edu
http://neon.cchem.berkeley.edu
http://netinfo.berkeley.edu
http://neutrino.nuc.berkeley.edu
http://www.ocf.berkeley.ed
http://remarque.berkeley.edu

VI

Finding Web Resources

http://ucmp1.berkeley.edu
http://www.berkeley.edu
http://www.cchem.berkeley.edu
http://xcf.berkeley.edu

University of Colorado

http://adswww.colorado.edu
http://bruno.cs.colorado.edu
http://cuboulder.colorado.edu
http://mcbryan.cs.colorado.edu
http://noaacdc.colorado.edu
http://piper.cs.colorado.edu
http://puppis.colorado.edu
http://refuge.colorado.edu
http://saturn.colorado.edu
http://sslab.colorado.edu
http://www.colorado.edu
http://www.cs.colorado.edu
http://www-sgc.colorado.edu

University of Denver

http://www.du.edu

University of Hawaii

http://ftp.cfht.hawaii.edu
http://gopher.hawaii.edu
http://hccadb.hcc.hawaii.edu
http://irtf.ifa.hawaii.edu
http://jach.hawaii.edu
http://kawika.hcc.hawaii.edu
http://pegasus.ed.hawaii.edu
http://pulua.hcc.hawaii.edu
http://spectra.eng.hawaii.edu
http://uhcarl.b.hawaii.edu
http://www.cfht.hawaii.edu
http://www.eng.hawaii.edu
http://www.hcc.hawaii.edu
http://www.soest.hawaii.edu

University of Maine
http://gopher.ume.maine.edu

University of Memphis
http://www.memphis.edu

University of Miami
http://iitcsun3.med.miami.edu
http://iitcsun10.med.miami.edu
http://www.ir.miami.edu
http://www.rsmas.miami.edu

University of Missouri
http://teosinte.agron.missouri.edu
http://www.phlab.missouri.edu

University of Notre Dame
http://orange-room.cc.nd.edu
http://undhe6.hep.nd.edu
http://www.nd.edu

University of Pittsburgh
http://artemis.phyast.pitt.edu
http://www.pitt.edu

University of Rochester
http://lancelot.cif.rochester.edu
http://sherman.pas.rochester.edu
http://vein.cs.rochester.edu
http://www.cs.rochester.edu

University of San Diego
http://teetot.acusd.edu

University of Southern California
http://info.broker.isi.edu
http://info.internet.isi.edu
http://venera.isi.edu
http://www.isi.edu

VI

Finding Web Resources

From Here...

In this chapter you've had a chance to visit sites that can help you exercise your brain. Now if you're either an overachiever or a AAA+ student, continue with these chapters:

- Chapter 22, "Computers," provides URLs for numerous computer-related Web sites.

- Chapter 29, "Publications: News, Periodicals, and Books," is where you'll find additional listings of electronic books in digital libraries and hypertext versions of magazine stand publications.

- Chapter 30, "Science," provides a comprehensive listing of Web sites devoted to the sciences.

Chapter 24

Government

by Bill Eager

Every year on April 15th, millions of Americans make a last minute rush to send in federal taxes. The money, of course, goes to fund the largest economic engine in the world—the U.S. government. The many different operations of the government account for approximately 11 percent of the nation's more than $5 trillion gross national product.

In theory, all of this money funds services that are of value to U.S. citizens— education, transportation, agriculture, defense. It's difficult to get a handle on the many services that are available, not to mention all of the legislative issues, government documents, and research programs. In an effort to get information out to the public, the government and various departments, agencies, divisions, and branches now use the World Wide Web system to distribute multimedia resources.

This effort begins to demystify government programs and makes it easier for ordinary citizens to "get involved" in the government decision-making process. The Department of Energy (DOE), for example, is enormous and oversees thousands of research efforts that range from the development of solar energy to testing nuclear weapons. Some of this research moves into private industry which creates commercial applications (more efficient gasoline) and new job opportunities. There are more than 20 DOE laboratories and sites across the U.S. that maintain WWW servers.

On a practical level, you can jump to a Web site that has information about efforts by the U.S. Fish and Wildlife Service to protect endangered species in your state, learn how legislation impacts social security benefits, find the phone number and address for IRS assistance, or search the Library of Congress for a specific book. State and local governments also maintain WWW servers. These provide useful resources for business people, tourists, and local residents.

FreeNets offer another mechanism for electronic access to federal, state, and local government resources and information. FreeNets began as electronic bulletin board systems (BBSs) where members of a community could use their computer to dial in and connect with a variety of local information. The first community FreeNet began in Cleveland in the mid-1980s. The name FreeNet comes from the fact that they are free of charge (except for long distance connect fees if you connect through a telephone number instead of the Web) and they use electronic networks for information delivery. FreeNets are non-profit, public service organizations. As such, these electronic towns strive to provide the members of a community with access to useful information. With their emphasis on the local community, you'll find that FreeNet databases include calendars of events for museums and town meetings, public service directories, tips on local education, health care, gardening, and many other subjects.

To reach a broad audience, many FreeNets now offer access via the Internet (usually a Telnet session) and the World Wide Web, in addition to a dial-in BBS phone number. FreeNets now exist in communities across the U.S. and Canada. Like a real town, FreeNets maintain an electronic post office, public town hall, recreation center, library, museums, and schools. When you connect with a FreeNet, you begin with a menu that resembles a city plan. Each menu selection represents a "building" that contains topical information. If you select school house, for example, you receive a series of links and documents that relate to education.

In this chapter, you learn about the following:

- Which FreeNets you can access via the Web.

- What information state and local governments offer to attract businesses to relocate to their areas, provide information to tourists, and help local citizens find answers to government-related questions.

- How the U.S. government is stepping into the Information Superhighway in a big way with Web sites for numerous federal agencies, Congress, and the White House.

FedWorld

URL address: **http://www.fedworld.gov**

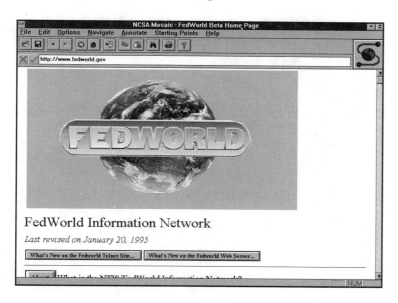

Fig. 24.1
FedWorld repre-
sents a collection
of hyperlinks to
millions of govern-
ment publications.

Have you ever read a newspaper article or listened to a radio report that cites a government study or report? This WWW site is the place to go if you want to see that report for yourself. The National Technical Information Service maintains this home page to help people deal with the challenge of accessing the vast amount of U.S. government information. How vast? NTIS provides users access to over two million documents, studies, and databases, and adds about 1300 titles each week. This WWW server is extremely popular and has been accessed more than a half a million times.

From the home page, you have three main choices. First, you can go to the FedWorld FTP site that includes information on business, health, the environment, and the White House and National Performance Review. Second, you can link to the FedWorld Telnet site that has information about 50 different agencies—you can order publications and learn about federal job opportunities. Third, you can click an alphabetical index that can help you locate and then access specific federal WWW sites. Rather than display a long list of servers, the alphabetical section has subject categories, such as Environmental Resources. When you click a category, it opens to a menu of servers that focus on that topic. This is a good starting point to jump into the U.S. government.

The White House

URL address: **http://www.whitehouse.gov**

Fig. 24.2
When you visit the White House Web site, don't forget to sign the electronic guest book.

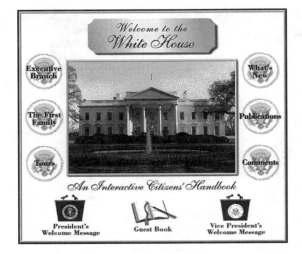

It's possible that this electronic version of the White House has received more publicity (and visits) than the real thing. The site was opened with a gala event attended by Vice President Al Gore and artist Peter Max (apparently he did some of the graphics). Mr. Gore summed up the purpose of this site when he said it's "a place on the information superhighway where people can get needed information about government services and where they can provide immediate feedback to the President."

Actually, the President doesn't read all of the e-mail that comes in through this site—but a staff member does and he passes noteworthy messages on to Mr. Clinton. The home page has graphic-based links that take you to audio messages from President Clinton, digital pictures of the first family, a tour of the White House, a map of Washington D.C., an update on Socks (the First Family's cat), information about cabinet-level agencies, and government publications. Being close to government has never been so easy.

Library of Congress

URL address: **http://lcweb.loc.gov/homepage/lchp.html**

Fig. 24.3
The Library of Congress WWW home page is your gateway to the world's largest collection of information about published works.

If your local library doesn't have the book or resource you need, take an electronic trip to the digital card catalogs and shelves at the Library of Congress WWW home page. Each week, approximately 5,000 people log in to this server. If you're looking for a specific book (by author, subject, or title), click the icon that begins a Telnet session to LOCIS (**telnet://locis.loc.gov**), the Library of Congress Information System. The menu selections at LOCIS include:

- Library of Congress Catalog
- Federal Legislation from 1973 until present
- Copyright Information
- Braille and Audio
- Organizations
- Foreign Law

▶ See "Book and Literature Resources," p. 816

Search Method	Examples
subject	browse solar energy
author	b faulkner, william
title or series	browse megatrends
partial LC call #	b call QA76.9
LC record #	loci 80-14332

The home page also sports links to some great exhibits and collections. The American Memory Project focuses on American culture and history. It catalogs items and digital reproductions, including prints and photographs. You weave your way through a few links to the collections page where you find photographs from the Civil War by Matthew Brady (1861–1865), portraits of literary figures and artists by Carl Van Vechten (1932–1964), and color photographs from the Farm Security Administration (1938–1944).

Another home page link is the Country Studies. This represents a series of documents that examine the political, social, and economic conditions in countries around the world, such as Ethiopia, Egypt, Philippines, and South Korea. If you're researching a project or paper, check out the Global Electronic Library that offers links to several WWW indexes and search tools.

United Nations

URL address: **gopher://nywork1.undp.org/**

This Gopher site is well worth the trip. Jump to different directories and documents that focus on this international organization. There are documents about U.N. conferences and council groups. You can find out what the Security Council does, and you can learn about the United Nations' important peace-keeping activities.

State of North Carolina

URL address: **http://www.sips.state.nc.us/nchome.html**

Fig. 24.4
The North Carolina WWW home page lets you access a wonderful multimedia encyclopedia that offers information about the 400-year history of the state.

What do Sir Walter Raleigh and the Wright Brothers have in common? They both played an important role in the history of North Carolina. This state takes the bull by the horns when it comes to the Information Age. From the home page, go to the FAQ document that does a good job of explaining how the state and state agencies are taking advantage of electronic communications. There's also a link to North Carolina and the Information Superhighway.

Several public agencies contributed to the resources you can access from this home page. If you want to find out what elected representatives are doing, jump to the status of bills from the North Carolina General Assembly. Other home page links include:

- Center for Geographic Information and Analysis (CGIA)
- Division of Environmental Management
- Office of State Personnel Job Vacancies
- State Library
- Cooperative Extension Service
- Institute for Transportation Research and Education (ITRE)
- Research Triangle Institute (RTI)
- Weather in North Carolina

The State Library maintains an electronic multimedia guide to the Old North State—the North Carolina Encyclopedia. This fun and easy-to-use resource for adults and children combines text and visuals to give the reader a good understanding of the state's economy, educational, and cultural assets, and the state's system of government. There are also overviews of the geography, the 100 counties, and the 400-year history of the state. It's a great tool for education, tourist promotion, and business information.

National Capital FreeNet (NCF)

URL address: **http://www.ncf.carleton.ca/**

This URL address provides WWW access to the Ottawa, Canada FreeNet. The home page has a menu that offers five selections. The first and second choices are Survival Guides for new users (#1 is in English and #2 is in French). These selections bring up menus that provide advice on topics such as Navigating Menus and Using the File System. Selection #3, NCF

VI

Finding Web Resources

Fig. 24.5
Located on a Web server in Canada, the home page for the National Capital FreeNet has links to thousands of documents and resources for both the region and the country.

Information, jumps to the NCF FreeNet main menu, where you can find approximately 18 different service areas. There aren't a lot of fancy graphics here, but you can spend days going through all of the links from this menu. A few examples include:

- *The Government Center.* Here you can weave your way to reports on Canadian national politics or to an organizational chart of the Ottawa police.

- *Professional Associations.* Find out about the Canadian Association of Journalists or other associations.

- *Schools, Colleges, and Universities.* Links here range from global education to the Ottawa Board of Education.

- *Science, Engineering, and Technology Center.* These topics range from museums to women in engineering.

From the home page, menu item #4 brings you to the NCF message of the day, which lists new services and information resources. Finally, menu item #5 brings up a hypertext GO list. This alphabetically lists all of the special interest groups (SIGS) that offer information or newsgroup messages via the NCF.

FreeNets

Cambridge Civic Network

URL address:
http://www.civic.net:2401/cambridge_civic_network/
cambridge_civic_network.html

This Web server opens the door to information about civic organizations and resources in the Cambridge, Massachusetts, area. Through exploration of the links, local residents can get involved in programs and organizations that shape the future of the community.

Denver, Colorado

URL address: **telnet://freenet.hsc.colorado.edu**

When you begin the Telnet session, login as **guest**. Some of the main menu selections include the World Futures Assembly Hall, Colorado health-care building, arts building, business and industrial park, community center and recreation area, and the courthouse and government center.

Detroit FreeNet
URL address: **http://http2.sils.umich.edu/~pegjones/ HomePage.html**

The top of this home page displays a small color image of the city of Detroit. Useful links include a map of the counties in the area and a "Meta-Index" that offers links to educational resources (including a list of schools that maintain Gopher sites), area entertainment, transportation, and weather information.

Eugene, Oregon
URL address: **http://www.efn.org/**

This Web site is home base for the Eugene FreeNet, also known as the Oregon Public Networking (OPN) Web Page. One link is to a broad-based Gopher menu (**gopher://efn.efn.org/**) where you can check a calendar that identifies dates for many local events ranging from free blood pressure checks for seniors to a Neville Brothers concert. There's also a link to Oregon Online— the state government Gopher that offers a broad range of documents, including information about current elections, candidate profiles, and ballot measures. One unique link from the home page brings up a list of other WWW home pages developed by OPN members.

Grand Rapids, Michigan
URL address: **http://www.grfn.org/**

This is a good WWW site to visit prior to your next trip to Grand Rapids. The information and links range from local weather forecasts to details about local attractions and modes of transportation.

Twin Cities FreeNet
URL address:
http://free-net.mpls-stpaul.mn.us:8000/proto_top.html

In addition to the standard FreeNet links for government, education, and recreation, the Twin Cities home page has links to a medical arts building and information about the individual neighborhoods near St. Paul and Minneapolis.

Vancouver, British Columbia

URL address: **http://freenet.vancouver.bc.ca**

This home page should be one of your first stops to an exploration of Canada and the Web. The mission statement gives some idea of the broad scope of information that you can access here:

> "The Vancouver Regional FreeNet Association is dedicated to the development, operation, and ownership of a free, publicly accessible community computer utility in the Lower Mainland of British Columbia providing the broadest possible range of information and possibilities for the exchange of experience, ideas, and wisdom."

The people who maintain the server live up to this goal by beginning with links that take you to other WWW servers and information about Vancouver (this link begins a Telnet session), British Columbia, Canada, other FreeNets in the U.S., and global WWW home pages.

Victoria, British Columbia

URL address: **http://freenet.victoria.bc.ca/vifa.html**

This home page provides a useful link to a hyperlink list of all the WWW servers in British Columbia, commercial and noncommercial. There are also links to game resources, WWW hypertext magazine collections, and gateways to other FreeNets.

Other FreeNet Addresses

FreeNets Home Page

URL address: **http://herald.usask.ca/~scottp/free.html**

This WWW resource has lists (and links) to FreeNets around the world. Peter Scott, at the University of Saskatchewan Libraries in Canada, maintains the information as a "public service." Your choices include FreeNet access via WWW, Gopher, and Telnet. There are also FreeNet mailing lists, newsgroups, reference documents, and conference schedules.

Buffalo, New York

URL address: **telnet://freenet.buffalo.edu**

Cleveland, Ohio

URL address: **telnet://freenet-in-a.cwru.edu**

Halifax, Nova Scotia
URL address: **http://www.cfn.cs.dal.ca**

Montreal, Quebec
URL address: **http//thym.remm.uqam.ca**

State and Local Government

Arizona—Phoenix
URL address: **http://www.rtd.com/arizona/phoenix/index.html**

In addition to being the state capital, Phoenix is the largest city in Arizona. This home page has numerous links to the history, cultural activities, social services, and city governments that are in the area.

California—Bay Area Governments
URL address: **http://www.abag.ca.gov/index.html**

The San Francisco Bay area encompasses a wide geographic area and several different government entities. This home page directs you to regional agencies, local governments, and a calendar of events. There's also a link to a list of state agencies, such as the California Environmental Protection Agency and the Department of Forestry and Fire Protection.

California—Palo Alto
URL address: **http://www.city.palo-alto.ca.us/home.html**

This is the heart of Silicon Valley, where computers and chips are a way of life and a means for making a living for thousands of residents. Find out about housing, visit the city library, retrieve demographic studies, learn about the schools and parks, and even visit the city council.

California—San Carlos
URL address: **http://www.abag.ca.gov/abag/local_gov/city/ san_carlos/schome.html**

This town uses its WWW site to open local government to the residents (and anyone else who has an interest). The home page has a letter from the mayor that discusses local education, and efforts and procedures by the town and citizens to ensure emergency preparedness. There is an online guide to city business, license rules and rates, news, and tips from the fire, police, parks, and recreation departments.

VI

Finding Web Resources

California—San Diego

URL address: **http://white.nosc.mil/sandiego.html**

Tourists and local residents alike can appreciate this home page. There are guides to restaurants and entertainment, specifics about disaster and emergency response procedures, and tax and local school information.

Colorado—Boulder

URL address: **http://bcn.boulder.co.us/government/boulder_city/ center.html**

Boulder has a reputation for being a city where local residents get involved in government. This home page has links to the city council members, including their phone numbers and addresses. There's detailed information about the city council agendas, city emergency preparedness, and weekly city calendars, boards, and commissions.

Illinois—Champaign County

URL address: **http://www.prairienet.org/SiliconPrairie/ccnet.html**

If you're doing business in Champaign county, or plan to relocate to the area, this WWW site has information about communities, living conditions, travel, and government resources.

Commonwealth of Kentucky

URL address: **http://www.state.ky.us**

This Web server provides access to state of Kentucky government information, tourist attractions, state parks, universities and colleges, and links to other Kentucky servers. This site also contains versions of Mosaic in case you can't get one from the NCSA site.

Massachusetts—Cambridge

URL address: **http://www.ai.mit.edu/projects/iiip/Cambridge/ homepage.html**

There are several digital maps of Cambridge here (including a subway map), a profile of the city, and links to the Civic Network and state educational resources.

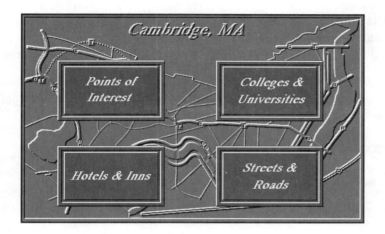

Fig. 24.6
The city of
Cambridge's
main map menu.

Minnesota

URL address: **gopher://gopher.state.mn.us/**

This site, a Gopher server, offers directories that have information on the Department of Health, Legislature, Department of Transportation, Higher Education Coordinating Board, and the Center for Arts Education.

State of Oklahoma Home Page

URL address: **http://www.oklaosf.state.ok.us**

Current information and events in the Sooner state include government, arts and recreation for tourists, application procedures for research grants, and business opportunities.

Rhode Island

URL address: **http://www.ids.net/ri/ri.html**

This is the Rhode Island state information home page with press releases and copies of the governor's speeches. You can jump to links that include artifacts at the Department of State Archives and the Department of Education. There's also a pointer to information on Providence that even includes local bus and movie schedules.

South Carolina—Greenville

URL address: **http://globalnews.globalvision.net:8001/govern.html**

Here you can retrieve the names, addresses, and phone numbers of city council members.

Texas

URL address: **http://www.texas.gov**
URL address: **file://sun.stac.dir.texas.gov/TEXAS_homepage.html**

This WWW server provides access to resources of state agencies. You can begin your tour by reading a letter from the governor. From there, jump to sites and documents from several state agencies.

Texas—Austin

URL address: **http://www.quadralay.com/www/Austin/Austin.html**

Austin is the state capital of Texas. This WWW site has more than 40 links to information about the local area and government.

Virginia

URL address: **http://www.elpress.com:80/staunton/**

Fig. 24.7
The Woodrow Wilson birthplace and museum is one of several fascinating historical sites you can visit from a link on the Virginia home page.

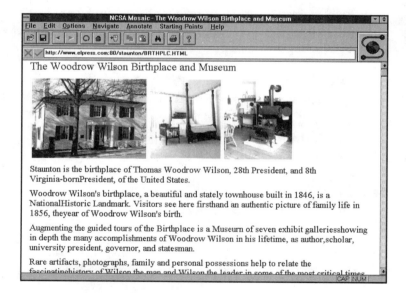

This address leads you to the home page for the "Queen City of the Shenandoah Valley." In addition to taking a virtual tour of the historic district and visiting local museums, you can jump to pages that offer details on the city government and county chamber of commerce.

U.S. Government

This section divides government WWW resources into three areas: general information, legislative, and executive branch resources. Note that this list represents only a portion of the U.S. government departments, agencies, and bureaus—many are still developing WWW servers.

▶ See, "Travel—Places to Go, United States," p. 935

General Information

Congressional Legislation—THOMAS

URL address: **http://thomas.loc.gov**

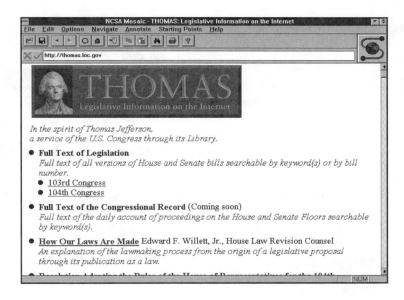

Fig. 24.8
What goes on in Congress? How are laws made? These are some of the questions the THOMAS Web site can answer.

The home page begins by saying, "In the spirit of Thomas Jefferson, a service of the U.S. Congress through its Library." At this site, you find full text of the House and Senate bills—search by keyword or bill number—and Gopher access to the House directory. Read interesting articles, such as "How Our Laws Are Made," that describes the process by which legislative proposals become law. Soon there will be a link to the full text of the Congressional record! There's also a form for sending mail to the U.S. Congress. C-SPAN, the cable network devoted to U.S. government coverage, has a link on this page with details about the program schedule.

VI

Finding Web Resources

FEDIX
URL address: **http://web.fie.com/**

Federal Information Exchange, Inc. (FEDIX) is a commercial company that provides documentation from many different government agencies. One of its goals is to connect institutions of higher education with the federal government in an effort to assist research and educational programs. FEDIX contains data from both the *Commerce Business Daily*, the *Federal Register*, and other government agencies. Try **http://www.fie.com/www/ district.htm** to get a current list of government, commercial, and educational WWW servers located in the District of Columbia.

Government Printing Office
URL address: **telnet://wais.access.gpo.gov**

This is an online service for the *Federal Register*, *Congressional Record*, and bills of the 103rd Congress databases on a WAIS server. Because this address starts a Telnet session, you need to login as **newuser** with no password.

National Information Infrastructure
URL address: **http://sunsite.unc.edu/nii/NII-Table-of-Contents.html**

Maintained at the University of North Carolina, this home page lets you review the U.S. government's proposal on the goals and development of this national communications system that will directly tie into the Internet and the World Wide Web.

National Performance Review
URL address: **http://sunsite.unc.edu/npr/nptoc.html**

This home page begins with the phrase "Creating a Government That Works Better and Costs Less." It's a hypertext version of Vice President Al Gore's proposal to improve and reinvent government, and includes a short audio message from Mr. Gore and President Clinton.

National Technology Transfer Center
URL address: **http://iridium.nttc.edu/nttc.html**

Technology transfer involves moving the technology and research that occurs in our government's facilities and government sponsored activities into the private sector where companies can apply the technology to viable commercial applications. This home page offers links to regional, state, and federal activities, as well as information on conferences, workshops, and funding that relates to technology transfer.

National Trade Data Bank

URL address: **http://www.stat-usa.gov/BEN/Services/ntdbhome.html**

National Trade Data Bank (NTDB)

You've reached the World Wide Web site of the National Trade Data Bank -- one-stop shopping for export information that is critical to today's international businesses. This WWW site provides access to the entire NTDB, which has been published on CD-ROM each month since 1990. Additions and updates to NTDB documents at this WWW site are posted as they become available.

Access to the WWW version of the NTDB is by low-cost subscription. For detailed subscription information, click here.

Free Internet access to portions of the NTDB is available for ftp and gopher users.

● Subscribers: Click here to access the NTDB

Fig. 24.9
The National Trade Data Bank Web site opens the door to more than 100 databases of information on trade.

This Web site contains trade information gathered by more than 20 federal agencies. The focus is to improve international trade and export opportunities. Topics include export opportunities by industry and product, trade statistics, how-to guides, and socioeconomic conditions. From the home page, you can search 125 trade and business databases.

North American Free Trade Agreement

URL address: **http://the-tech.mit.edu/Bulletins/nafta.html**

Here you can find more than 50 individual documents that discuss all aspects of the trade agreement between the U.S., Mexico, and Canada.

Policy Net

URL address: **http://policy.net/**

This address starts with a point-and-click graphical link (make sure your graphics option loads this) that takes you to U.S. government publications, campaigns, issues, and a guide to the U.S. Congress.

SunSITE Government Documents

URL address: **http://sunsite.unc.edu/govdocs.html**

This WWW server offers several hypertext versions of federal documents that cover a broad range of topics such as Technology for Economic Growth, The President's Progress Report, National Health Security Plan, and President Clinton's Saturday Radio Addresses (as audio files).

VI

Finding Web Resources

White House Electronic Publications
URL address: **http://www.acns.nwu.edu/us.gov.online.html**

This Web site has numerous links to documents created by the White House, such as press releases, links to databases of White House publications (such as the FTP link **ftp://cco.caltech.edu:/pub/bjmccall**), or information that addresses the White House (such as the files from the newsgroup **alt.politics.usa.misc**).

Legislative Branch

United States House of Representatives
URL address: **http://www.house.gov/**

The home page states: "The U.S. House of Representatives' World Wide Web service provides public access to legislative information as well as information about Members, Committees, and Organizations of the House and to other U.S. government information resources." There are some really interesting links to topics that include the legislative process, schedules for the legislative activity of the House, addresses and phone numbers for House members, and information about the laws of the United States. There's even a link to maps that'll help you if you're planning a visit to Capitol Hill.

United States Senate
URL address: **gopher://gopher.senate.gov:70/1**

This address takes you to a series of text files and directories. Text files include a document of FAQs about Senate Internet services and a list of all other files that this Gopher site has. There are also directories to documents distributed by members and committees. You can also do a keyword search of files.

Executive Branch

The president has direct control over the executive branch of the U.S. government. All of the departments (Agriculture, Commerce, Defense, and so on) discussed in the following sections are cabinet-level agencies that report to the president.

Department of Agriculture

USDA

URL address: **http://usda.gov**

This page is a good place to start your exploration of the United States Department of Agriculture (USDA) Internet services. The home page has links to many USDA agencies and information files.

USDA—Soil Conservation Service

URL address: **http://www.ncg.scs.ag.gov**

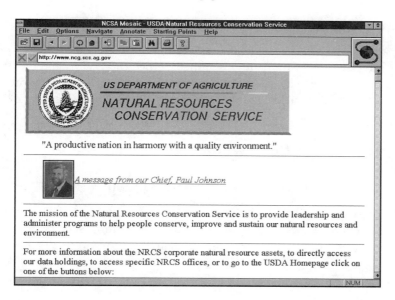

Fig. 24.10
Conservation is one of the keynotes to the resources on the U.S. Department of Agriculture home page.

The Soil Conservation Service administers programs that help people conserve and improve the country's natural resources. From this home page, you can link to comprehensive information about programs and legislative issues that relate to soil, water, air, plants, animals, and human conditions. There are also links to state, regional, and national offices.

Department of Commerce

Commerce Department

URL address: **http://www.doc.gov**

◄ See "Business
Development
and Business
Resources,"
p. 517

The Commerce Department's home page has links to documents about the department and dozens of other government-based WWW, Gopher, FTP, Telnet, and WAIS sites. You can jump to the *Commerce Business Daily*, which has a directory of federal government requests for bids on proposals; federal tax forms, which have an index of more than 700 forms that are free to download; and Senate and House sites and directories.

Information Infrastructure Task Force (IITF)

URL address: **http://iitf.doc.gov:70**

If you have an interest in the future of the Internet, the WWW, and the Information Superhighway, take a look. You'll find many interesting reports, like one on an Advanced Digital Video in the NII workshop, a calendar of events, and speeches.

National Institute of Standards and Technology (NIST)

URL address: **http://www.nist.gov/welcome.html**

NIST sponsors and conducts a variety of scientific research programs ranging from biotechnology to computer technology. Many efforts, such as the Manufacturing Extension Centers, directly help industry and small business.

National Telecommunications and Information Administration

URL address: **http://www.ntia.doc.gov/**

Organized like a book with a table of contents, the National Telecommunications and Information Administration home page has links to international activities, legislation, spectrum management, and legislative testimony.

National Oceanic and Atmospheric Administration (NOAA)

URL address: **http://www.noaa.gov**

Find out whether you need to put on sunblock 45 today. NOAA is involved with all aspects of scientific research related to the oceans and the atmosphere. For example, this agency monitors and studies the impact of the annual fires that occur in the western United States. The home page also has a link to an overview of an experimental program that provides 58 cities across the U.S. with daily information about solar ultraviolet radiation levels.

Fig. 24.11
NOAA's home page offers graphic-based links to their current research on solar ultraviolet radiation and other hot topics, such as protected species of wildlife.

National Oceanographics Data Center
URL address: **http://www.nodc.noaa.gov/index.html**

This is the home page for one of the data centers that NOAA operates. You can find out more about the center and its operations, such as how to obtain products (such as data) or submit data.

▶ See "Meteorology," p. 861

U.S. Bureau of the Census
URL address: **http://www.census.gov**

U.S. Bureau of the Census

Welcome Message from Our Director

NEWS FLASH: U.S. Population Totals 261.7M as 1995 Begins.

Fig. 24.12
The Bureau of the Census home page connects you with volumes of reports, statistics, and data about the population of the United States.

VI

Finding Web Resources

The role of the U.S. Bureau of the Census is to constantly collect data about the people and economy of the U.S. It then takes this data and produces volumes of reports. This home page is easy to use and incorporates a lot of small icons for areas like Center for Economic Studies, Financial Data, International Programs, and Statistical Briefs—lots of data here. Also try the Census Phone List (URL address **http://gopher.census.gov:70/1m/Bureau/ Who/who**), a Who's Who list that contains phone numbers for many different services that relate to census information including census customer service; regional offices; and agriculture, construction, government, housing, and state and local data centers.

U.S. Patent and Trademark Office
URL address: **http://www.uspto.gov**

Here you'll find a variety of information about patents and intellectual property, which brings to light interesting issues about patents as they relate to information and data on computer networks. You can also take a look at information on public hearings of software patent protection.

Department of Defense

The following Department of Defense (DOD) sites are open to the public. However, there are many DOD WWW sites that contain information of a more secure nature and to which access is limited to military personnel only.

ARPA
URL address: **http://ftp.arpa.mil**

This information server is an FTP site that provides some information about the activities and programs of the Advanced Research Projects Agency (ARPA)—the group that got the Internet started back in the 1960s. It contains information provided by the Computing Systems Technology Office (CSTO). There are details about the High Performance Computing and Communications Program, and links to research and solicitation for government projects. In its goal to become a completely electronic-based program, this WWW server will become a central entry point for all ARPA electronic information services.

The Air Force

Air Force
URL address: **http://www.hq.af.mil/USAF/USAF.html**

Fly high when you start with this home page for the U.S. Air Force. You can jump to the Headquarters for the Air Force, learn about Air Force Reserves and education, or read about pilot training efforts.

Fig. 24.13
A wealth of hot
links on the Air
Force home page
provide you with
more information
on this service
branch than you
imagined possible.

The Army

U.S. Army
URL address: **http://white.nosc.mil/army.html**

This WWW home page for the Army has a variety of links to education and
research efforts. There's even one to the U.S. Military Academy at West Point.

Army Corps of Engineers
URL address: **http://www.usace.mil/cespd.html**

This is the WWW site for the South Pacific Division of the Army Corps of
Engineers. You can access bid documents for current projects, public archives,
and geographic maps.

Army Research Laboratory
URL address: **http://info.arl.army.mil**

The purpose of this WWW site is to enable scientists from government,
academia, and industry to discover information about ARL, including facilities and research projects.

Defense Information Systems Agency's Center for Engineering
URL address: **http://disa11.disa.atd.net**

A very specialized server with information on "technology insertion activities
for information systems in the Department of Defense." The focus is on IS
technologies, such as wireless and ATM—Asynchronous Transfer Mode,
which is a high-speed switching/transmission technology for delivery of
broadband voice, video, and data. For the general public, there's a test video
of the Clementine Moon Shot (455K) and a sound clip from Neil Armstrong.
Don't forget to sign the visitors book.

The Navy

U.S. Naval Observatory

URL address: **http://www.usno.navy.mil**

Here there is information on the observatory, star catalogs, earth orientation, precise time and time interval, and the directorate of astrometry.

Navy Online

URL address: **http://www.ncts.navy.mil**

This is your electronic gateway to the Department of Navy online resources. You'll find fact sheets and public affairs information.

David Taylor Model Basin, Communications & Information Systems Department

URL address: **http://navysgml.dt.navy.mil**

This is another home page for computer enthusiasts. The Communications & Information Systems Department provides the Navy with expertise in the CALS and SGML initiatives, both of which deal with the implementation of electronic documentation and electronic purchase orders.

Naval Research Laboratory

URL address: **http://www.nrl.navy.mil**

This is the Navy's research and development lab that was created in 1923 by Congress. The research focuses on the naval environments—the sea, sky, and space. You'll find an organizational directory and information about specific research efforts.

Department of Education

U.S. Department of Education

URL address: **http://www.ed.gov**

◀ See "U.S. Department of Education," p. 597

Established in 1980, the Department of Education focuses on providing access to equal educational opportunities for all individuals. The department sponsors programs that are designed to improve the quality of the U.S. educational system. From the home page, you can jump to information about the

National Education Goals, teacher's and researcher's guides to the USDOE, staff, offices, newsletters, and other educational resources.

Department of Energy

Energy Sciences Network—ESnet

URL address: **http://www.es.net**

The Energy Sciences Network is a nationwide computer data communications network managed and funded by the U.S. Department of Energy (DOE) Office of Energy Research (ER). ESnet enhances energy research by connecting the U.S. energy research community, which consists of the DOE national laboratories and DOE-funded, to U.S. universities. ESnet facilitates access to scientific facilities, provides information dissemination among scientific collaborators throughout all ER programs, and provides access to ER supercomputer facilities. You can download contact information, an electronic brochure, the ESnet Steering Committee, a map of the network backbone, and individual sites and statistics on network usage. There's also an electronic white pages that has approximately 130,000 entries.

Fermi National Accelerator Laboratory

URL address: **http://fnnews.fnal.gov**

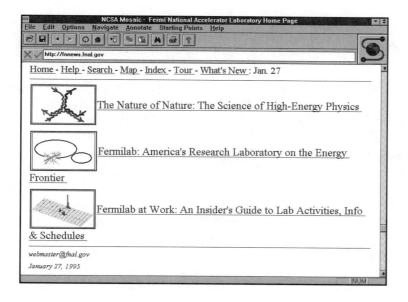

Fig. 24.14
The Fermilab home page offers you information on one of the most advanced research centers in the world.

This server includes information for the general public on Fermilab, which studies high-energy physics—the fundamental particles and forces of nature. It includes information for physicists and other technical professionals in related subjects. Descriptions of education programs are also online.

Office of Environment, Safety, and Health

URL address: **http://apollo.osti.gov/eh/eh_home.html**

There's not a lot here. The office focuses on issues of safety and health for DOE facilities.

Office of Science Education and Technical Information

URL address: **http://apollo.osti.gov/home.html**

This WWW site offers a broad overview of the Department of Energy's efforts with news information, directory of DOE servers, and People, Places, and Organizations links. There's an unfinished (in construction) link to a national DOE telephone directory.

Office of Energy Research

URL address: **http://www.acl.lanl.gov/DOE/OER.html**

This is a good overview page for the different types of energy research such as fusion, nuclear, and basic energy.

Superconducting Super Collider

URL address: **http://www.ssc.gov**

The Superconducting Super Collider is not being built; however, this home page does offer links to information about the project, including a rather sad link entitled "A chronicle of events up to the fatal vote."

Laboratories of the Department of Energy

Argonne National Laboratory
URL address: **http://www.anl.gov**

Located near Chicago, Argonne employs almost 5,000 people who research various aspects of energy. The home page has both audio links and links to documents about the Lab's research.

Brookhaven National Laboratory

URL address: **http://suntid.bnl.gov:8080/bnl.html**

Here there are overviews of scientific research programs that examine energy, such as the "Relativistic Heavy Ion Collider."

Lawrence Berkeley Laboratory

URL address: **http://www.lbl.gov/LBL.html**

Nine Nobel prize winners have worked at LBL. Start with an Introduction to the Lab and then work your way into research news, scientific programs, technology transfer (science that moves into private industry), and educational programs.

Lawrence Livermore National Laboratory

URL address: **http://www.llnl.gov**

This government research and development lab has many different projects. From the WWW home page, learn about high-performance computing, advanced sensors, and energy technologies.

Los Alamos National Laboratory

URL address: **http://www.lanl.gov/welcome.html**

This home page gives you links to a variety of documents on energy and nuclear weapons research.

National Energy Research Supercomputer Center

URL address: **http://www.nersc.gov**

Located at the Lawrence Livermore National Laboratory, this center is the home base for supplying high-performance computer and networking services to the nationwide energy research community. From the home page, jump to newsletters and newsgroups to find out more specifics, retrieve an introductory brochure, or (if you're a qualified user) request computer and storage allocations.

National Renewable Energy Laboratory

URL address: **http://www.nrel.gov**

NREL's server provides information on renewable energy research, development, and applications including technology transfer of renewable energy research to the private sector, accumulated energy data and resource maps, publications, and business and job opportunities.

VI

Finding Web Resources

Oak Ridge National Laboratory
URL address: **http://www.ornl.gov**

This server provides information on subjects about the laboratory including basic and applied research, media releases, ORNL publications, and educational opportunities.

Pacific Northwest Laboratory
URL address: **http://www.pnl.gov:2080**

There aren't a lot of links here. The home page describes activities of the lab: "A major part of PNL's activities is specifically focused on resolving environmental issues, such as waste cleanup at Hanford and global climate change."

Princeton Plasma Physics Laboratory
URL address: **http://www.pppl.gov**

Energy research, technology transfer, and lab resources are some of the documents you can read online at this site.

Sandia National Laboratory
URL address: **http://www.sandia.gov**

The home page is a long list of links to information about Sandia, such as capabilities, facilities, news and events, and a phone book. There's also a link to New Mexico weather.

Department of Health and Human Services

U.S. Department of Health and Human Services
URL address: **http://www.os.dhhs.gov**

The U.S. Department of Health and Human Services (HHS) is a cabinet agency that focuses on a variety of tasks to maintain and improve the health and well-being of the nation's population. With an emphasis on children, the elderly, persons with disabilities, the poor, and others who are most vulnerable, HHS is the principal government agency responsible for protecting health and for providing human services to Americans. This WWW home page has a multitude of links for information on the mission, programs, organization, initiatives, activities, and the impact of this agency.

FDA Center for Food Safety & Applied Nutrition

URL address: **http://vm.cfsan.fda.gov/index.html**

This site is a very valuable source of information about food safety and nutrition. Here you can find out about food labeling, the seafood hotline, food-borne illness education, cosmetics labeling, and other useful data.

National Institute of Health

URL address: **http://www.nih.gov**

The National Institute of Health Web server links you with a variety of information about U.S. health programs, resources, and research activities. The home page offers NIH Grants and Contracts, Research Opportunities, and topics of Molecular Biology and Molecular Modeling.

Social Security Administration

URL address: **http://www.ssa.gov/SSA_Home.html**

Information here is available in English and Spanish. You can find social security news, benefit information (including disability, survivors, and so on), a social security handbook (a summary of all benefits and policies), speeches, and legislative data.

Department of the Interior

United States Fish and Wildlife Service

URL address: **http://www.fws.gov/**

If you enjoy the great outdoors, you'll enjoy this WWW site. It links to information about the National Wildlife Refugee System, saving endangered species, conserving migratory birds, restoring fisheries, and enforcing wildlife laws.

United States Geological Survey

URL address: **http://www.usgs.gov**

Start your visit to this home page with an audio or video message. The USGS is a "fact-finding and research organization" that deals specifically with the earth sciences. Many people know about the USGS because of the topographical maps they create. There are many links available here.

Assistant Secretary for Territorial and International Affairs

URL address: **http://info.er.usgs.gov/doi/territorial-International-Affairs.html**

▶ See "United States Geological Survey," p. 721

This department helps with issues related to federal policy in Guam, the U.S. Virgin Islands, American Samoa, and other territories.

Bureau of Indian Affairs

URL address: **http://info.er.usgs.gov/doi/bureau-indian-affairs.html**

This agency works with Indian tribal governments and Native Alaskan village communities. There aren't a lot of links here, just basic information.

Bureau of Land Management

URL address: **http://info.er.usgs.gov/doi/bureau-land-management.html**

The BLM manages almost 272 million acres or one-eighth of the nation's land resources. You find detailed information about programs and state-by-state contact addresses. You can also jump to the BLM FTP site (**ftp://dsc.blm.gov**).

Bureau of Mines

URL address: **http://www.usbm.gov**

This home page has links to history, organizational structure, lists of new publications (such as annual state reports), and Internet-accessible services.

Bureau of Reclamation

URL address: **http://info.er.usgs.gov/doi/bureau-of-reclamation.html**

The Bureau of Reclamation is known for its large dams and power plant projects. This page tells you a bit more.

Minerals Management Service

URL address: **http://info.er.usgs.gov/doi/minerals-management-service.html**

This service manages most of the mineral resources on the nation's outer continental shelf. You find news releases, state contacts, and an FTP link to more information.

National Park Service

URL address: **http://info.er.usgs.gov/doi/national-park-service.html**

Our first national park was Yellowstone, which was created in 1872. This WWW document gives you information about the service and its regional offices.

Department of Justice

Federal Bureau of Investigation

URL address: **http://naic.nasa.gov/fbi/FBI_homepage.html**

This home page begins with a $1 million reward for information about 14 unsolved bombings—jump in to learn more.

Department of Transportation

U.S. Department of Transportation

URL address: **http://www.dot.gov**

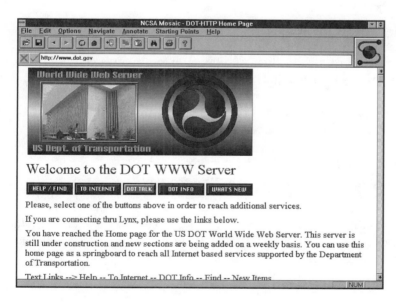

Fig. 24.15
Whether you own a bicycle, car, or semi, the information in the Department of Transportation home page may be of interest.

When you're driving down the highway, you probably aren't thinking about this Web site. But if you need to learn about USDOT programs, find someone who works at USDOT, or find out about procurement and grant management, check this out.

Independent Agencies and Institutions

Center for Earth and Planetary Studies
URL address: **http://ceps.nasm.edu:2020/homepage.html**

This Regional Planetary Images Facility (RPIF) is a reference library for people who want to view the collection of images from various space missions. There are approximately 300,000 digital images of planets available.

IRS
URL address: **http://www.ustreas.gov/treasury/bureaus/irs/ irs.html**

Now, instead of worrying about getting a call from the IRS, you can knock on their door. The home page has four main links, which include:

- Tax forms and instructions

- Frequently asked questions

- Where to file

- Where to get help

Choose the first link to either see a list of all forms or search through the forms. In link two, you find out how to check the status of your return. Link three is a state-by-state list of where you file, and the last link provides a series of phone numbers for help for individuals, small business, and the handicapped.

Small Business Administration
URL address: **http://www.sbaonline.sba.gov/**

This is the one-stop shopping source for small business owners. The home page has three main links that bring up information for assistance in starting, financing, and expanding a business. There are also more than 100 field offices. You can retrieve information about your regional contacts and local events via a graphical map.

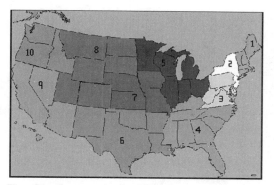

Please click on the state or colored location that represents your region.

Fig. 24.16
The SBA WWW region map will link you to information about field offices around the country.

National Aeronautics and Space Administration (NASA)

NASA Home Page

URL address: **http://www.gsfc.nasa.gov/NASA_homepage.html**

This WWW site connects you to every resource that deals with NASA, national space labs and facilities, research information, and space missions.

▶ See "National Aeronautics and Space Administration (NASA)," p. 838

NASA Affiliated Institutions

Ames Research Center

URL address: **http://www.arc.nasa.gov**

Located in California, Ames performs a variety of research programs and has the world's most sophisticated wind tunnel.

Dryden Flight Research Center

URL address: **http://www.dfrf.nasa.gov/dryden.html**

This center focuses on high-performance flight research and testing.

Goddard Space Flight Center

URL address: **http://www.gsfc.nasa.gov/GSFC_homepage.html**

The mission of the Goddard Space Flight Center is "to expand knowledge of the Earth and its environment, the solar system, and the universe through observations from space." The home page also has a link to an X.500 address directory which provides e-mail addresses for people who work at Goddard.

GSFC SeaWiFS Project

URL address: **http://seawifs.gsfc.nasa.gov/SEAWIFS.html**

This is the home page for NASA's global ocean color monitoring mission that uses information gathered by satellites to examine the conditions of the Earth's oceans.

Jet Propulsion Laboratory

URL address: **http://www.jpl.nasa.gov**

This is a fun WWW site. You can jump to an extensive list of space images, such as the Magellan mission topographic map of the surface of Venus, and then view the GIF images.

Johnson Space Center

URL address: **http://www.jsc.nasa.gov/JSC_homepage.html**

The Johnson Space Center plays a major role in space missions. The home page has links to very technical subjects, such as the Robotics Systems Technology Branch and the Mechanical Design and Analysis Branch.

Kennedy Space Center Home Page

URL address: **http://www.ksc.nasa.gov/ksc.html**

Fig. 24.17
The Kennedy Space Center logo on their home page proudly displays an artistic look at the center and a space shuttle launch.

Built in the 1960s, this is where the majority of the space shuttle launches occur today. The home page lets you jump to historical archives, space shuttle mission overviews, and a list of upcoming events.

Langley

URL address: **http://www.larc.nasa.gov/larc.html**

Langley's mission is broad and ambitious: "To be the world leader in pioneering science and innovative technology to ensure U.S. aeronautical and space preeminence." Find out more from this WWW site.

Scientific & Technical Information Program

URL address: **http://www.sti.nasa.gov**

This Web site provides documents that explain NASA programs, as well as a comprehensive NASA thesaurus that lets you know, for example, that Argon-Oxygen atmosphere is another term for cabin atmosphere.

Government Consortia

Army High Performance Computing Research Center

URL address: **http://www.arc.umn.edu/html/ahpcrc.html**

This is a university-based research and development consortium that focuses on computing.

National Center for Atmospheric Research

URL address: **http://http.ucar.edu/metapage.html**

NCAR uses supercomputers to learn about the atmosphere and weather. For skiers, the home page has a link to a Colorado ski report.

National Consortium for High Performance Computing

URL address: **http://www.nchpc.lcs.mit.edu/**

Learn all about the meetings, conferences, courses, workshops, and member institutions in this consortia for computing.

VI

Finding Web Resources

More Federal Information— Government Gophers

The following are U.S. Government Gopher sites that offer documents (many of them are compressed) that you can view online or download.

Congressional Information from Library of Congress

URL address: **gopher://gopher.loc.gov:70/11/congress**

Environmental Protection Agency (EPA)

URL address: **gopher://futures.wic.epa.gov:70/1**

Extension Service USDA Information

URL address: **gopher://zeus.esusda.gov:70/1**

Federal Communications Commission (FCC)

URL address: **gopher://gopher.fcc.gov:70/1**

Federal Government Information from Library of Congress

URL address: **gopher://gopher.loc.gov:70/11/federal**

Federal Networking Council Advisory Committee

URL address: **gopher://fncac.fnc.gov:70/1**

National Center for Education Statistics

URL address: **gopher://gopher.ed.gov:10000/1**

United States Budget 1995

URL address: **gopher://gopher.esa.doc.gov:70/11/BUDGETFY95**

White House Information Service

URL address: **gopher://gopher.tamu.edu:70/11/.dir/president.dir**

From Here...

This chapter has provided a lot of Web addresses that will get you to information resources provided by local, state, and national government entities. If you are still hungry for more information in this vein, try the following chapters:

- Chapter 27, "International Web Resources," takes you to the Web sites for other countries (and governments) around the world.

- Chapter 32, "Sports, Hobbies, Travel, Cooking, and Recreation," lists some sites sponsored by local goverments (in the U.S. and abroad) that are designed to help tourists.

VI

Finding Web Resources

Chapter 25

Health and Medicine

by Bill Eager

Health and medicine are subjects that affect every man, woman, and child. The topic is important and controversial. With a national health bill that exceeds $900 billion and approximately 37 million uninsured Americans, the U.S. health-care system faces tremendous challenges as government, health-care providers, employers, and employees look for positive changes in the quality, cost structure, and coverage of medical care. Conference proceedings, proposals, statistics, and opinions on the issue of health care exist on many WWW servers.

Debates about medical care often are heated, because health is an extremely personal topic.

Millions of people live with medical conditions ranging from allergies to diabetes to migraine headaches. Medical institutions and commercial firms conduct a never-ending quest for cures, medication, and fitness programs that will help people live longer, happier, healthier lives.

The resources in this section are listed in categories that help you find the information that fits your specific medical interest or requirement. The section "General Health Resources by Topic" categorizes Web home pages that relate to general health themes, such as allergies and family medicine. "Health Centers" lists institutions that focus on a very specific area of medical research or information, such as the Center of Food Safety and Applied Nutrition. "Medical Education" lists institutions that have programs that train individuals to provide medical care, and the "Research" section lists organizations that focus on the research aspects of medical science. In this chapter you will find numerous Web sites that offer medical resources for:

- Specific diseases (such as AIDS)

- Conditions (such as pregnancy)

- Emergencies (such as poisons)

- Good health practices (exercise programs and nutrition)

- Medical research and development activities

Abdominal Training FAQ

URL address: **http://clix.aarnet.edu.au/misc.fitness/abdominal-training.html**

If you want to keep your abdominal area in tip-top shape or simply want to eliminate a spare tire, this is the WWW address for you! From the University of Queensland in Australia, this series of frequently asked questions is an introduction to the basic principles of training the abdominal area. The creation of this set of WWW documents was motivated by frequent questions on the topic in the newsgroup **misc.fitness**. The table of contents has links to documents that provide advice on common questions about midsection exercise. These questions include the following:

- Question 4: How do I exercise the abs?

- Question 5: What's wrong with situps?

- Question 6: What are good ab exercises?

- Question 7: Is there a specific order I should do exercises in?

HealthNet

URL address: **http://debra.dgbt.doc.ca/~mike/healthnet**

Fig. 25.1
The hyperlinks on the HealthNet home page take you to government agencies and educational institutions around the world.

HealthNet should be one of your first destinations in your exploration of health and medicine on the Web. Developed by the Communications Development Directorate of Industry Canada, the project is designed to raise awareness about health-care applications for the Information Superhighway. HealthNet uses the WWW to educate health-care providers, governments, private groups, and people who are interested in health care about the electronic health services that are currently available and about the future developments that may be feasible.

The HealthNet WWW Demonstration Project accomplishes this education in two ways. First, the project provides a comprehensive set of hypertext links to medical and health-care resources on the Internet/World Wide Web. Second, the project provides an interactive hands-on resource for demonstrating future medical and health-care applications for the Information Superhighway.

HealthNet hyperlinks take you to the following categories of health-related information:

- Biotechnology initiatives and health-care human-resource planning
- Clinical and administrative applications
- Government health-care sites
- Health-care applications for the electronic highway
- Hypertext list of Internet health-care resources and contact information
- Medical and health research applications
- Medical education and community health applications

The HealthNet WWW Demonstration Project is an international collaborative effort. Available publicly via the Internet, the project welcomes participation from anyone who wants to contribute ideas, materials, or comments.

U.S. Department of Health and Human Services

URL address: **http://www.os.dhhs.gov**

Fig. 25.2
This Web server provides access to a vast amount of information on U.S.-government documents and programs related to health.

A Cabinet agency, the U.S. Department of Health and Human Services (HHS) focuses on programs that maintain and improve the health and well-being of the nation's population. The agency emphasizes programs that help children, the elderly, persons with disabilities, and the poor. The department administers Social Security benefits; oversees government programs which attempt to prevent and control disease, alcohol abuse, and drug abuse; conducts and supports medical and biomedical research; promotes child development; and ensures the safety and efficacy of drugs. HHS administers nearly 300 grant programs that directly serve or assist one of every five Americans.

The purpose of this WWW server is to provide information on the mission, programs, organization, initiatives, and activities of the HHS. From the top of the home page, you can jump to an alphabetized listing of specific programs, beginning with "AIDS Related Information" and ending with "Social Security Statistics." The server provides a link to the Catalog of Federal Domestic Assistance Programs (**http://www.sura.net/gsa.html**), which the General Services Administration maintains. From this server, you can perform searches for information about financial and nonfinancial assistance programs.

The HHS home page also provides links to information and resources made available by the various organizations that comprise HHS and other health-related agencies. The following table lists a few of these resources:

Health Organization	Internet/WWW Address
Centers for Disease Control FTP	**file://ftp.cdc.gov**
Food and Drug Administration	**telnet://fdabbs.fda.gov**
National Center for Food Safety and Applied Nutrition	**http://vm.cfsan.fda.gov/index.html**
National Center for Toxicological Research Gopher	**gopher://gopher.nctr.fda.gov**
National Institutes of Health	**http://www.nih.gov**
National Institute of Allergy and Infectious Diseases Gopher	**gopher://gopher.niaid.nih.gov**
National Institute of Mental Health Gopher	**gopher://gopher.nimh.nih.gov**
National Institute of Environmental Health Sciences Gopher	**gopher://gopher.niehs.nih.gov**
National Library of Medicine	**http://www.nlm.nih.gov**

Healing Methods

URL address: **http://zeta.cs.adfa.oz.au/Spirit/healing.html**

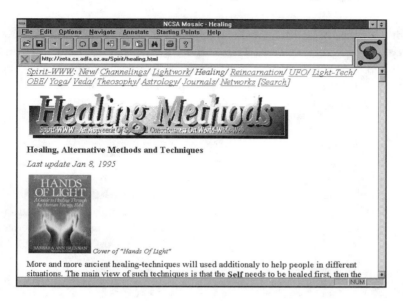

Fig. 25.3
Find out about numerous forms of alternative medicine at the Healing Methods home page.

This site provides interesting articles about auras, chakras, homeopathy, herbs, and more. The home page states, "More and more ancient healing-techniques will [be] used additionaly [sic] to help people in different situations. The main view of such techniques is that the **Self** needs to be healed first, then the **Body** will be well too."

The information and articles are divided into material for scholars and basic knowledge. About half a dozen interesting JPEG images are available, including a chart of the foot reflex zones. Other resource links take you to Web sites that focus on vegetarianism, Internet Relay Chats on healing, mailing lists about self-awareness, and newsgroup articles on alternative medicine and healthy eating. Live long and healthy.

Palo Alto Medical Foundation

URL address: **http://www.service.com/PAMF/home.html**

A not-for-profit organization, the Palo Alto Medical Foundation encompasses a research institute and health-care and education divisions. At the facility, approximately 160 physicians provide medical care for more than 110,000 people. Scientists conduct research in the areas of human health concerns,

VI

Finding Web Resources

including immunology and infectious diseases, cholesterol metabolism, heart and cardiovascular dynamics, and cancer-cell biology. Instructors in the health-care division teach classes in a variety of areas related to health promotion, including early diagnosis and prevention.

From the home page, you can access the monthly publication HealthNews (**http://www.service.com/PAMF/healthnews/home.html**), which is published by the Palo Alto Medical Clinic/Health Care Division of the Palo Alto Medical Foundation for Health Care, Research and Education. Other links include a community health calendar and health education/support groups.

Rapid changes are occurring in the U.S. health-care system. The quality of care, rising costs, and benefits are some of the important issues that face companies, medical providers, and private citizens. The hypertext link "The Symposium—Can Managed Care Heal America?" (**http://www.service.com/PAMF/symposium.html**) takes you to documentation on this conference, which was a follow-up on five separate conferences that addressed the costs and administration of health care.

Stanford University Medical Center

URL address: **http://med-www.Stanford.EDU/MedCenter/welcome.html**

Fig. 25.4
When you jump to this home page, you access the information resources of the oldest medical center in the western United States.

The Stanford University Medical Center (SUMC) is internationally recognized for its outstanding achievements in teaching, research, and patient care. From the home page, you can jump to a page of phone numbers for the departments in the medical center; numerous links to other biomedical resources are available. You also can follow links to detailed information about the facilities and services of the following entities, which are part of SUMC:

- *Stanford University School of Medicine.* Through its educational programs, the school conducts extensive research in many areas of medicine.

- *Stanford University Clinic.* The Stanford University Clinic is made up of more than 100 outpatient clinics, where members of the medical school faculty focus their activities in medical practice and medical education.

- *Stanford University Hospital.* The hospital is a university-owned, not-for-profit organization that provides acute and tertiary care to local, national, and international patients.

- *Lucille Salter Packard Children's Hospital at Stanford.* The hospital is an independent, not-for-profit, pediatric teaching hospital that provides acute and tertiary care exclusively for children.

General Health Resources by Topic

All you have to do is walk into a pharmacy and look across rows and rows of over-the-counter medicines and ointments to realize that health, like the human body, is a very diverse area. The following WWW sites are broken down into broad categories that relate to specific health resources and subjects, including the following:

AIDS	Exercise and Rehabilitation
Allergies	Family Medicine
Alternative Healing	Genetic Disorders
Alzheimer's Disease	Insurance
Cancer	Lyme Disease
Clinical Alerts	Mental Health
Cosmetics	Nutrition
Dentistry	Poisons
Diabetes	Substance Abuse
Disabilities	U.S. National Health Care

AIDS Issues

AIDS

URL address: **gopher://odie.niaid.nih.gov/11/aids**

This site provides links to a great deal of information about AIDS, including study recruitment, nursing for HIV/AIDS patients, the National Commission on AIDS, and U.S. and international AIDS resources.

AIDS Information

URL address: **http://nearnet.gnn.com/wic/health.03.html**

The National Institute of Allergy and Infectious Disease maintains a special section of its Gopher for AIDS information. The institute also provides an online newsletter on the treatment of AIDS.

Condom Country

URL address: **http://www.ag.com/condom/country**

Fig. 25.5
At this home page you can find out everything you want to know about condoms—and more.

This site provides information on condoms and other sexual items, as well as government statistics on AIDS, instructions for condom use, and a hypertext history of the condom.

Allergies

Clark County (Nevada) Pollen/Spore Reports

URL address: **http://www.unlv.edu/CCHD/pollen/**

You can find out about pollen and spore reports in two areas. Available are the Roto-rod, which provides weekly pollen counts for various places around the Las Vegas valley, and the Burkhard Spore Trap, which gives daily pollen counts sampled at Sunset Park. The reports are maintained by the Clark County Health District POCD.

National Institute of Allergy and Infectious Diseases (NIAID) Gopher
URL address: **gopher://gopher.niaid.nih.gov**

These documents contain a variety of information about allergies.

Alternative Healing

Alternative Medicine
URL address: **http://werple.mira.net.au/sumeria/**

This site has it all. Follow links to articles about oxygen, cosmology, the immune system, cancer, and books about alternative medicine.

Good Medicine
URL address: **http://none.coolware.com/health/good_med/ ThisIssue.html**

Good Medicine is a terrific electronic magazine for people who are interested in alternative health. The magazine provides links to feature articles on topics including massage, visualization in fitness and rehabilitation, and herbology. A new issue is posted every two months.

Homeopathy
URL address: **http://www.dungeon.com/home/cam/homeo.html**

The Homeopathy home page includes links to FAQs, books, a list of organizations in the United States and United Kingdom (complete with phone numbers and addresses), and mailing lists and newsgroups on the subject.

Alzheimer's Disease

Alzheimer Web
URL address: **http://werple.mira.net.au/~dhs/ad.html**

This home page provides links to documents such as "What Is Alzheimer's Disease?" and "What Is the Cause of Alzheimer's Disease?" The site also offers information about diagnosis, pathology, and research laboratories that focus on cures.

Cancer

Breast Cancer Information Clearinghouse

URL address: **http://nysernet.org/breast/Default.html**

Fig. 25.6
The Breast Cancer Information Clearinghouse has useful information and contacts on research, issues, and treatment of breast cancer.

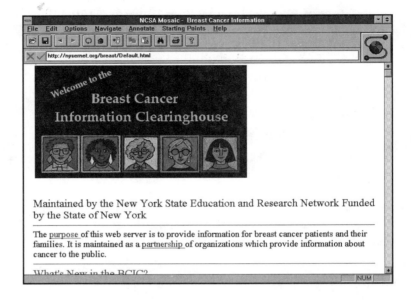

This Internet-accessible resource provides information on breast cancer from many organizations. Current sources represent government health agencies, hospitals, libraries, hospices, and not-for-profit agencies.

CancerNet (NCI International Cancer Information Center)

URL address: **http://nearnet.gnn.com/wic/med.11.html**

The National Cancer Institute's Gopher and WWW server offers information for both physicians and patients.

Japan Access to National Cancer Center

URL address: **http://www.ncc.go.jp/**

This home page, for the Japanese National Cancer Center, provides a link to the list of all the PDQ statements available on CancerNet. For most diseases, two statements are provided for each diagnosis: one for physicians, and the other for patients.

University of Pennsylvania OncoLink
URL address: **http://cancer.med.upenn.edu/**

This cancer-oriented server is directed to physicians, health-care personnel, social workers, patients, and patients' supporters. Topics include medical oncology, radiation oncology, pediatric oncology, surgical oncology, medical physics, psychosocial support for oncology patients' families, and links to other resources. The information is updated frequently.

Cosmetics

Cosmetics in CFSAN
URL address: **http://vm.cfsan.fda.gov/cosmetic.html**

At this site, you can find a tremendous amount of information on decoding the labels on cosmetics. Even though cosmetics labels are chemistry-oriented, you can learn to read them and make purchases wisely.

Dentistry

Dental Net
URL address: **http://www.pencom.com/dentalweb/**

Check out some great tips on maintaining good teeth. Other links include dental-health options. You can even make an appointment with the dentists who maintain this server (it's in Austin, Texas).

United Medical and Dental School
URL address: **http://www.umds.ac.uk/**

Find out about dental-materials science or read the *Journal of Medical Imaging* at this site. This server is more for dentists than for patients.

Diabetes

Diabetes Knowledgebase
URL address: **http://islet.medsch.wisc.edu/**

This site is designed and maintained by the University of Wisconsin Medical School to provide diabetes-related information to the world community. The goal is to enhance the lives of people who have diabetes. Current and future links offer details on diabetic supplies; insulin pumps; biochemistry; recipes; the American, Canadian, and British diabetes associations; traveling with diabetes; exercise; and a detailed glossary of diabetes terms.

VI

Finding Web Resources

Disabilities

American with Disabilities Act
URL address: **gopher://wiretap.spies.com/00/Gov/disable.act**

Be patient—this 150K-plus document is the entire text of the 1990 act. Great information for employers and the disabled.

Disability Page
URL address: **http://www.eskimo.com/~dempt/disability.html**

This site provide links to more than 50 disability-related Web sites, including polio references, the National Rehabilitation Information Center, the national library service for the blind and physically handicapped, the deaf Gopher site, and ADA (Americans with Disabilities Act) regulations.

Handicap News
URL address: **ftp://handicap.shel.isc-br.com**

This server provides a variety of information for disabled people, including legal, medical, and social-service resources.

Exercise and Rehabilitation

Barry's Periodized Workout Plans
URL address: **http://bigdipper.umd.edu/health-fitness/periodization.html**

Weightlifter Barry Merriman shares his weight-training routine, which he used to gain substantial size and strength. He delves into issues of nutrition, supplements, steroids, and training.

Stretching
URL address: **http://archie.ac.il/papers/rma/stretching_1.html**

We all know that stretching is good for us. This server provides information about flexibility, types of stretches, ranges of joint motion, and the physiology of stretching.

Typing Injuries
URL address: **http://www.cis.ohio-state.edu/hypertext/faq/usenet/typing-injury-faq/top.html**

You could get cramps just typing this URL address. Typing-related injuries are no joke, though. This site offers a series of frequently asked questions about repetitive stress injuries, carpal tunnel syndrome, keyboards, and so on.

Family Medicine

Family Medicine Sites
URL address: **http://mir.med.ucalgary.ca:70/1/family**

This site provides links to information about family medicine. Because such an abundant amount of information is available, this site is a good place to start your quest for medical answers.

Medicine Servers
URL address: **http://white.nosc.mil/med.html**

The medicine servers listed at this site are Health and Medical, The Virtual Hospital, EINet Galaxy, North Carolina State University Study Carrel Server, Stanford University Yahoo Server, and Rice University Information Server.

Virtual Hospital
URL address: **http://vh.radiology.uiowa.edu**

The Virtual Hospital™ **The Virtual Hospital(TM)**

Fig. 25.7
The Virtual Hospital encompasses a variety of hypermedia books that focus on medical issues.

Presented by the Electric Differential Multimedia Laboratory in the Department of Radiology at the University of Iowa College of Medicine, this Web server provides a digital medical and health-sciences library. This library encompasses a series of hypermedia text books. For example, when you click Iowa Health Book, you jump to a page where you can learn about heart attacks and strokes. The UIHC Medical Museum is another interesting link, with choices including the history of microscopes and a virtual-hospital demonstration, in which you move through a series of hypertext documents that tell you how people can take advantage of computer-based health information. This server is both fun and educational.

Genetic Disorders

On-Line Mendelian Inheritance in Man
URL address: **http://gdbwww.gdb.org/omimdoc/omimtop.html**

This server, maintained by Johns Hopkins University, is a comprehensive source of information on genetic disorders.

Insurance

Insurance Research Network
URL address: **http://mmink.cts.com/mmink/dossiers/irn.html**

Want insurance information without the hassle of dealing with an insurance salesperson? This site offers a free health-insurance quote, which can be mailed or faxed to you.

Lyme Disease
URL address: **gopher://gopher.lymenet.org/**

This site provides many documents and directories about court cases, medical information, publications, resource guides, and support groups.

Mental Health

Florida Mental Health Institute
URL address: **http://hal.fmhi.usf.edu/**

Fig. 25.8
Although the Florida Mental Health Institute Web site focuses on Florida mental-health issues, any user will find useful information about the broad topic of mental health.

Mental health, which encompasses ailments and conditions ranging from depression to Alzheimer's disease, is as important as our blood pressure or cholesterol level. The Florida Mental Health Institute focuses on helping state residents maintain and improve their mental health through research, education, and demonstration programs.

From this home page, you can jump to information about the four departments that comprise FMHI: Aging and Mental Health, Child and Family Studies, Community Mental Health, and the Department of Mental Health Law and Policy. Each department provides information about its specific topic. You also can jump to a list of scholarly publications.

Nutrition

Department of Food Science and Nutrition
URL address: **http://fscn1.fsci.umn.edu/fscn.htm**

The University of Minnesota's Department of Food Science and Nutrition, where this server is located, offers undergraduate and graduate programs in nutrition and in food science, preparing students for careers related to food and health. The server provides information on the school and on studies of nutrition and food science.

Poisons

Poisons Information Database (Singapore)
URL address: **http://biomed.nus.sg/PID/PID.html**

This database provides links to information on plant, snake, and animal toxins, as well as directories of venom antidotes, toxicologists, and poison-control centers around the world. Information is available in English and Chinese.

Substance Abuse

Alcoholism Research Database
URL address: **http://nearnet.gnn.com/wic/med.02.html**
URL address: **lib.dartmouth.edu**

This server offers a database of articles and information about alcoholism and other forms of substance abuse.

Smoking and Smoking Cessation
URL address: **http://128.196.106.42/smoking.html**

Whether you light up every day, are trying to quit, are helping someone else quit, or are a secondhand smoker, this page has information for you. The first series of links takes you to one of the Web searchers, opening a search for the most recent Web resources. You also may be interested in the link to the Stop Smoking Handout from Rice University or the link to the University of Pennsylvania's smoking, tobacco, and cancer documents. These files may not make you break the habit, but they'll help.

Travel and Health
URL address: **http://www.who.ch/TravelAndHealth/TravelAndHealth_Home.html**

The World Health Organization in Geneva, Switzerland, provides information on diseases, immunizations, and disease prevention through this server. Be sure to check this resource well in advance of your travel dates.

U.S. National Health Care

History of Medicine
URL address: **http://www.nlm.nih.gov:8002/**

The On-Line Images from the History of Medicine service provide access to nearly 60,000 color and black-and-white images (photographs, artwork, and printed texts) drawn from the collection of the History of Medicine Division at the U.S. National Library of Medicine. The eclectic collection includes a photograph of a Greek vase from the 4th century B.C., showing a bandaging scene; a picture of Abraham Lincoln visiting soldiers' graves at Bull Run; and a scene of American nurses escorting a group of refugee orphans on the beach at Etretat, France, during World War II.

Interfaith Health Program of the Carter Center
URL address: **http://www.interaccess.com/ihpnet**

The International Network for Interfaith Health Practices is an electronic forum for dialogue and resource sharing among people of all religious traditions. This site focuses on information about the relationship between spirituality and health. The site provides links to text archives on the subject and links to other Web health resources.

National Health Security Plan
URL address: **http://sunsite.unc.edu/nhs/NHS-T-o-C.html**

This server contains a summary of the need for health-care reform and support documents that have been released to the public to date. Documents include the full text of the Health Security Act, President Clinton's address to the joint session of Congress (as written and as delivered), the president's announcement of the formation of the Task Force on National Health Care Reform.

National Institutes of Health
URL address: **http://www.nih.gov/**

This National Institutes of Health server, maintained by the Division of Computer Research and Technology, provides biomedical information related to health issues and clinical protocols, NIH grants and contracts, research opportunities at NIH from the NIH Office of Education, and information on molecular biology and molecular modeling.

National Library of Medicine
URL address: **http://www.nlm.nih.gov/**

Fig. 25.9
"What's Up, HyperDOC?" is a hypertext document that gives you information about new services on the National Library of Medicine Web computer.

A multimedia/hypertext resource of the U.S. National Library of Medicine, this server maintains more than 4.5 million records, including books, reports, and audiovisual materials. The home page provides information about this service, including "What's Up, HyperDOC?" and "About the NLM," visitor information, current events at the library, contact people at the NLM, online information services, and research and development activities. From the home page, you also can jump to GIF maps of the library building.

Health Centers

Arizona Health Sciences Center
URL address: **http://128.196.106.42/nutrition.html**

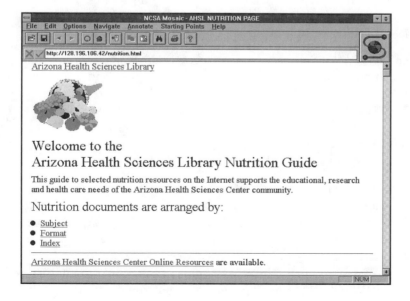

Fig. 25.10
The Arizona Health Sciences Center offers a comprehensive series of links to Web documents and sites about nutrition.

VI

Finding Web Resources

This site will remind you that you are what you eat. The WWW server provides a terrific hypertext guide to selected nutrition resources on the Internet/WWW; it also supports the educational, research, and health-care needs of the Arizona Health Sciences Center community. You have several options for sorting and viewing the resources, which range from medical-based clip art to a food and nutrition newsletter.

Center for Biomedical and Biophysical Technologies
URL address: **http://citbb.unige.it**

This server provides information resources from the Center for Biomedical and Biophysical Technologies and the Biophysical Institute Laboratories at the University of Genoa. The server provides references to information sources on biology, chemistry, cognitive science, mathematics, medicine, physics, and nanotechnology.

Center for Food Safety and Applied Nutrition
URL address: **http://vm.cfsan.fda.gov/list.html**

Did you know that you spend 25 cents of every dollar on products that are regulated by the U.S. Food and Drug Administration? Of this amount, 75 percent is spent on food. The Center for Food Safety and Applied Nutrition promotes and protects the public health by ensuring that the food supply is safe, nutritious, wholesome, and honest, and that cosmetics are safe and properly labeled.

From this WWW home page, you can assess a variety of useful consumer information. Links are available to information on food and cosmetics labels, a seafood hotline, a list of brochures that you can order from the FDA, and an online FDA phone book that has more than 10,000 entries.

Center for Health Law Studies
URL address: **http://lawlib.slu.edu/centers/hlthlaw**

The St. Louis University School of Law recognizes public concern about health-care issues, health-care reform, and the impact of law on health-care delivery. The Center for Health Law Studies represents the school's commitment to increase contributions to education; research; policy analysis; publications; and services for law students, practicing health lawyers, and health-care professionals. This WWW home page has links to information about the school's educational programs, alumni, publications, and research activities.

Center for Neuroscience

URL address: **http://www.uchc.edu/**

This home page is from the University of Connecticut at Farmington. The server provides information on the Center for Neuroscience.

Historical Center for the Health Sciences

URL address: **http://http2.sils.umich.edu/HCHS/**

The University of Michigan Historical Center for the Health Sciences offers an electronic clearinghouse for information on resources in the history of health care and the health sciences. The site is designed for use primarily by historians, educators, policy makers, archivists, librarians, and manuscript and museum curators.

Lawson Research Institute

URL address: **http://earthcube.mit.edu/uwo/lri_home.html**

Learn about the St. Joseph's Hospital, Lawson Research Institute's research programs. A few of the divisions of this Institute include maternal and newborn health, adult respiratory distress syndrome, behavioral neurology and neuropsychology research group, Centre for Activity and Aging/Gerontology Group, and Gastroenterology/GI Surgery Group.

Lister Hill National Center for Biomedical Communications

URL address: **http://www.nlm.nih.gov/lhc.dir/lhncbc.html**

Computers are almost as common as stethoscopes in the world of medicine. This home page is for a research-and-development division of the National Library of Medicine in Bethesda, Maryland. Among the principal activities of the division (and hyperlinks on the home page) are development of the Unified Medical Language System Project, work on scientific visualization and virtual reality, medical-expert systems, natural-language processing, computer-aided instruction, machine learning, and the biomedical applications of high-speed communication techniques.

National Center for Biotechnology Information

URL address: **http://www.ncbi.nlm.nih.gov**

This server provides information from the National Institutes of Health's GenBank Genetic Sequence Database, which contains a collection of all known DNA sequences.

University of Bonn Medical Center
URL address: **http://imsdd.meb.uni-bonn.de/welcome.en.html**

This home page, from the University of Bonn Medical Center, leads you to links about AIDS, cancer, dentistry, nursing, nutrition, occupational medicine, pharmacy topics, physics, psychobiology, and telemedicine.

Health-Care Employment

MedSearch America
URL address: **http://www.medsearch.com:9001/**

They may not be the most underemployed sector of the work force, but doctors, nurses, pharmacists, and internists do need jobs. MedSearch America provides access to health-care recruiting information. Whether you are a health-care professional looking for a job or a health-care employer looking to fill a position, MedSearch America can be a valuable resource.

You can search job listings, resume´ postings, and resource services at any time via this WWW site. One day, for example, the site had job listings for a physical therapist in Troy, New York; for a clinical dietitian in Aberdeen, Washington; and for a director of surgical services in Plantation, Florida.

Medical Education

Advanced Laboratory Workstation Project
URL address: **http://www.alw.nih.gov**

Fig. 25.11
From this extremely specialized home page, users can learn about molecular modeling and DNA sequencing.

Advanced Laboratory Workstation Project at NIH

"No Matter Where you Go .. There You Are"

The Advanced Laboratory Workstation Project at the National Institutes of Health provides an Andrew File System-based and distributed administration and computing project. Some of the applications for the computer technology include molecular graphics and modeling, medical-image processing, gel analysis, DNA and protein sequencing and searching, statistical analysis, and laboratory-data acquisition.

Association for Experiential Education

URL address: **http://www.princeton.edu/~rcurtis/aee.html**

Association for Experiential Education Home Page (AEE)

Fig. 25.12
If you are involved in medical education, you will enjoy learning about the Association for Experiential Education.

With more than 2,000 members, AEE is a broad-based not-for-profit organization that includes people who work in education, mental health, and outdoor education. The focus of the group (and the home page) is experiential-educational programs that emphasize health and well-being (experience is a great teacher). You can find out more about the organization when you jump to a description of the annual convention.

Baylor College of Medicine

URL address: **http://www.bcm.tmc.edu/**

The college is located in Houston, and the home page has links to information on the college, the Houston area, the Molecular Biology Computational Resource Guide, the Department of Human and Molecular Genetics, and the Systems Support Center.

Boston University School of Public Health

URL address: **http://www-busph.bu.edu/**

This site is sponsored by the school's library and maintained by resident students. The server provides information about library services, staff members, student announcements, job opportunities, and medical specialties, as well as links to groups at the Boston University School of Medicine.

Edinburgh Chemical Engineering Department
URL address: **http://www.chemeng.ed.ac.uk/**

This site provides links to information about the university and the department (mostly regarding bioreactors and medical devices).

Educational Technology Branch
URL address: **http://wwwetb.nlm.nih.gov/**

This server provides information related to educational technology in the health profession, the branch's research programs, and branch personnel. Also provided are details about the ETB's Learning Center for Interactive Technology.

Emory University
URL address: **http://www.cc.emory.edu/welcome.html**

Located in Atlanta, this server provides information on the university's School of Medicine and the Division of Geriatrics, as well as other subjects.

Indiana University Department of Radiology
URL address: **http://foyt.indyrad.iupui.edu/HomePage.html**

The server provides links to information on radiology events, the division, medical resources on the Internet, and funding sources for radiologists.

University of Geneva Faculty of Medicine School of Dentistry Orthodontics
URL address: **http://www.unige.ch/smd/orthotr.html**

This university server is dedicated to the dissemination of basic and therapeutic knowledge on dentofacial trauma and intends to become a forum on experimental and clinical data.

University of Oklahoma
URL address: **http://157.142.72.77/ouhsc/ouhscokc.html**

The University of Oklahoma is located in Oklahoma City. Its Health Sciences Center houses the schools of allied health, dentistry, medicine, nursing, pharmacy, public health, and graduate college. Included on this page are the phone numbers for each of the schools. Other links take you to health resources for the entire state of Oklahoma—such as hospitals and the state department of health.

University of Texas at Houston
URL address: **http://www.uth.tmc.edu/**

This server contains information about the university's Health Science Center, including information on students, employees, policies, and procedures.

University of Virginia Health Sciences
URL address: **http://www.med.virginia.edu/**

The top of this home page displays a picture of doctors in surgery and a wide shot of the university, which is located in Charlottesville, in the foothills of the Blue Ridge Mountains. The home page has links to information about the Health Sciences Center library, as well as to the schools of medicine and nursing. A link to the topic of education brings up further links to subjects including "Cell Injury and Death" and "Circulatory Disturbances."

U.S. College of Pharmacy
URL address: **http://157.142.72.77/pharmacy/uscop.html**

What this site offers is a state-by-state listing of pharmacy schools. It includes the name of the school, address, and phone and fax numbers. It should be very helpful for a person who wants to either research an education in pharmacy or get the phone number for the school from which they graduated.

WelchWeb (William H. Welch Medical Library)
URL address: **http://www.welch.jhu.edu/**

Designed by the Welch Medical Library at Johns Hopkins University to help the institution's affiliates identify and use Welch resources and services, the server provides information about access to Welch databases, library services, instructional opportunities, and publishing assistance.

Yale University School of Medicine Image Processing and Analysis Group
URL address: **http://noodle.med.yale.edu/**

This server is operated by the School of Medicine at Yale University. Links are available to an assortment of information about the group, the university, and the local area (New Haven, Connecticut).

Research

Anesthesiology

URL address: **http://gasnet.med.nyu.edu/HomePage.html**

If you are an anesthesiologist this is the site for you! There are links to hypertext textbooks about procedures and emergencies, a bibliography, online journals, and other Web sites that focus on this important practice.

Biological Imaging and Visualization Lab

URL address: **http://bioviz.biol.trinity.edu/**

Trinity University Biological Imaging and Visualization Lab maintains this Web server, which provides information about Trinity University and about the BioViz lab for dynamic visualization and three-dimensional reconstruction of biological images.

Brigham and Women's Hospital, Department of Radiology

URL address: **http://count51.med.harvard.edu/BWH/BWHRad.html**

Fig. 25.13
This Web site is interesting because several online educational programs are under development.

This teaching hospital is affiliated with Harvard University Medical School. The Department of Radiology is committed to clinical and laboratory research. You can jump to links that describe programs on patient care, training, research, and faculty. Other links tell you about educational programs and medical conferences. In an effort to use computer-based media for education, the server provides a link to a nuclear medicine electronic teaching file.

Brookhaven Protein Data Bank

URL address: **http://www.nih.gov/htbin/pdb**

You can browse search and view the molecular-structure data in the Brookhaven Protein Data Bank.

Fujita Health University

URL address: **http://pathy.fujita-hu.ac.jp/pathy.html**

This is Pathy WWW for medical information. This medical information resource is under continuous development. For help, questions, or comments, please send electronic mail to pathy@fujita-hu.ac.jp.

Use entirely at your own risk - no warranty is expressed or implied.

Pathy project Contributors

Fig. 25.14
Much of the information available via this home page is in Japanese. Topics include leukemia, chemotherapy, and hematology.

This server provides medical information from the Fujita Health University. Some text on Pathy WWW is in Japanese, including the Textbook of Leuke-mia, a chemotherapy database, online case reports, and medical archives. The Pathology Gallery of Hematology also is available.

Genome Database

URL address: **http://gdbwww.gdb.org/**

The Genome Database supports biomedical research, clinical medicine, and professional and scientific education. The database (and this Web site) pro-vide for the storage and distribution of data about genes and other DNA markers, genetic disease, as well as bibliographic information.

Lawrence Livermore National Laboratory

URL address: **http://www.llnl.gov**

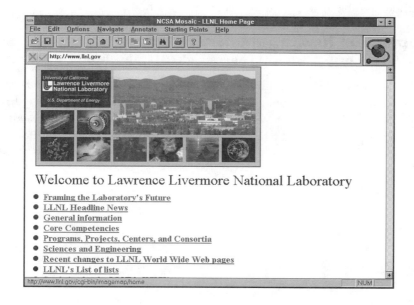

Fig. 25.15
A U.S. government facility, the Lawrence Livermore National Labora-tory provides a variety of informa-tion about general health and biomedicine.

Located in Livermore, California, Lawrence Livermore National Laboratory conducts a variety of research programs, including a few that focus on health and biomedicine. The home page has links to information on the research programs. If you have the right equipment (an audio board and speakers), you can begin your tour of this site by listening to a short message from the director of public affairs.

Or, choose Headline News, which takes you to a visitor center. Then you can perform a keyword search on LLNL press releases. A search for *medical*, for example, produces several releases, including one that describes efforts by LLNL and a manufacturing firm to reduce the cost of hip replacements.

Institute for Molecular Virology at the University of Wisconsin-Madison
URL address: **http://www.bocklabs.wisc.edu**

The server provides computer-generated animated images of viruses, topographical maps, digitized electron micrographs of viruses, and tutorial information on selected virology topics.

NIH Molecular Modeling
URL address: **http://www.nih.gov/molecular_modeling/ mmhome.html**

This site offers the National Institutes of Health's hypertext primer on molecular modeling methods, software, and applications. The site provides a central source of information about the major aspects of molecular modeling methods and biological applications of these methods.

Population Health Summary System
URL address: **http://www.ihi.aber.ac.uk/IHI/phss.html**

This site is an example of a very specific Web resource. The Population Health Summary System is developing a summary of the health careers of the entire population of Wales, which will be made available to all health-care practitioners in the principality. The home page has links that describe these efforts.

From Here...

In this chapter you've learned about Web sites that offer practical information about health and medicine. Other sources can be found in:

■ Chapter 28, "Issues, Politics, Religion, and World Events," lists sites that focus on the medical issues of the day—such as AIDS and abortion.

■ Chapter 29, "Publications: News, Periodicals, and Books," has several Web publications devoted specifically to medical research and family medical issues.

■ Chapter 30, "Science," includes government and company sites which focus on the research side of medicine.

Chapter 26

History and Geography

by Bill Eager

Whether it's Julius Caesar's expansion of the Roman Empire, the signing of the American Declaration of Independence, or the enactment of the Chinese Cultural Revolution, bold actions and events in history have a profound effect on our lives today and influence the decisions we make about the future. The World Wide Web is about as close as you can get to a time machine. Jump to a Web server in England to read about and view artifacts from an archaeological exploration of a Roman fort in Scotland, or take an interactive tour of Texas history and see what the Alamo looked like before the famous battle.

From the thick, wet rain forests of Latin America to the dry, sandy dunes of Northern Africa, geography and geology play an equally important role in determining how millions of people live, work, and play. You also find maps showing legal borders as well as the natural contour of the landscape. You can find and explore both types of maps on the WWW.

Try, for example, an interactive global map sponsored by Xerox (URL address **http://pubweb.parc.xerox.com/map**), where you can zoom into different parts of the world. Or, you can travel to a Canadian Web site (URL address **http://www.emr.ca**), where you can view maps and photographs displaying the country's tremendous natural resources.

The Web transforms history and geography from dull, academic subjects into exciting, important areas of research and exploration. The resources in this chapter are divided into the following categories:

- History by continent and country
- Archaeology

- History of the Greeks and Romans
- Geography and maps

Scrolls from the Dead Sea

URL address: **http://sunsite.unc.edu/expo/deadsea.scrolls.exhibit/ intro.html**

Fig. 26.1
Scientists and archaeologists unravel the mysteries of the Dead Sea Scrolls— find out how when you visit this interactive exhibit.

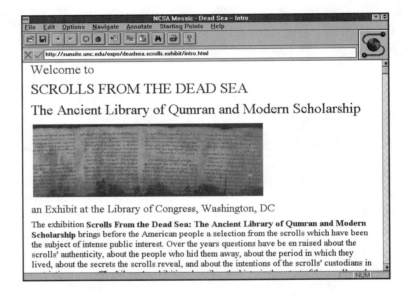

The Ancient Library of Qumran and Modern Scholarship sponsors this exhibit. The physical exhibit is located at the Library of Congress in Washington, D.C.; the WWW server is at the University of North Carolina. Many questions about these mysterious scrolls abound. Are they indeed authentic? Who were the people who wrote and then carefully hid them? What was the world like when they were written?

This interactive, multimedia exhibit describes the historical context of the scrolls and the Qumran community where they may have been produced. You can read about and relive the story of their discovery—2,000 years after they were hidden. The exhibit encourages viewers to learn about the challenges and activities of archaeology and scroll research.

United States Geological Survey (USGS)

URL address: **http://www.usgs.gov**

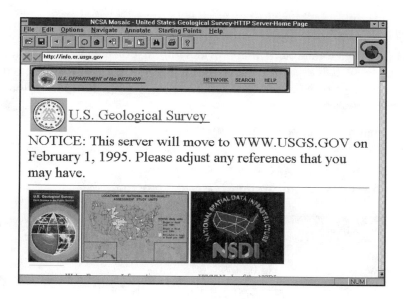

Fig. 26.2
This WWW home site gives you a new perspective on land and natural resources in the United States.

This site uses the multimedia aspects of the Web as a powerful tool for education and exploration. Everywhere you turn you find another clickable image, icon, map, or link. The home page opens with a short introduction that tells you the USGS was established by an act of Congress in 1879 as an agency of the Department of the Interior.

Three large inline images are on-screen—a color picture of a USGS brochure, a color map of the United States, and a contour map. Each of these images is a clickable link to other resources. The brochure links to:

> National Earth Science Issues
>
> Overview of USGS Services and Activities
>
> Fact Sheets

The color map brings you to information about U.S. water resources, and the contour map links to information about mapping. Some of the other areas you can visit include:

- Education—the USGS library system, the largest earth-science library in the world. Find out what individual collections offer (including maps).

- A list of publications and fact sheets, such as Geology and Human Activity in the Florida Keys or the International Strategic Minerals Inventory report series. Many of these publications are free or have a small fee—you learn how to get them.

- The Digital Data Series that provides information about USGS electronic data, such as a geologic map of the sea floor of Western Massachusetts Bay constructed from digital sonar images, photographs, and sediment samples. These data sources are available as CD-ROMs.

- Employment opportunities with the USGS.

World Map—Xerox PARC Map Viewer
URL address: **http://pubweb.parc.xerox.com/map**

Fig. 26.3
Zoom and pan around the world with this interactive global map.

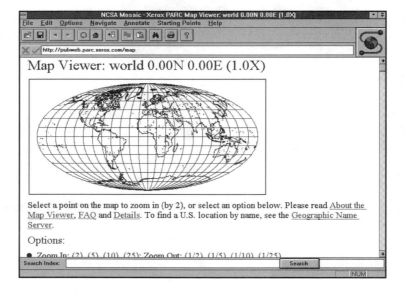

▶ See "Travel—Places to Go, Worldwide," p. 937

Sponsored by Xerox PARC, this hypermedia world map viewer is custommade for the WWW. The home page presents a global map. Position your mouse on a section of the map and click. You zoom in by a factor of two; but don't stop, total zoom-in/zoom-out parameters let you go up to a factor of 25. Utility features allow you to show country borders and rivers.

The project was initially created in June of 1993 and improvements are constantly made. Links embedded in the HTML (hypertext markup language) map are controls that change the map rendering. As a result, you can pan or zoom into an area of the map.

Canadian Geographical Name Server

URL address: **http://www-nais.ccm.emr.ca/cgndb/geonames.html**

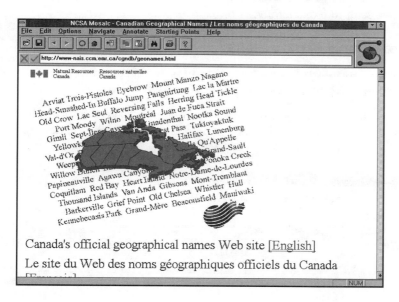

Fig. 26.4
Check out the database on this server to see whether there's a Canadian town with your last name.

This "Geo-Names" home page offers a variety of information including a forms-based search of some 500,000 Canadian official geographical names—areas and cities. You can query this database with your own last name to see whether a town or region is named after you! Available in both English and French, the home page also offers links to geographic publications and databases of digital data.

History

Africa—African Art

URL address: **http://www.lib.virginia.edu/dic/exhib/93.ray.aa/African.html**

This is an exhibition of African Art. From the home page jump to an introduction, elements of the African Aesthetic, or the exhibition, where you can see and read about the Sowei Mask worn over the head of female dancers, a wooden sculpture of a family, or other artifacts.

Europe and Russia

Ireland—Thesaurus Linguarum Hiberniae

URL address: **http://curia.ucc.ie/curia/menu.html**

A fancy name for a project that makes computer-based copies of mediaeval Irish texts. You can browse through a selection of these texts including the *Dream of Oengus*.

Italy—Museum of Early Instruments

URL address: **http://hpl33.na.infn.it**

Fig. 26.5
The home page of the Museum of Physics in Italy features images that lead to historical information.

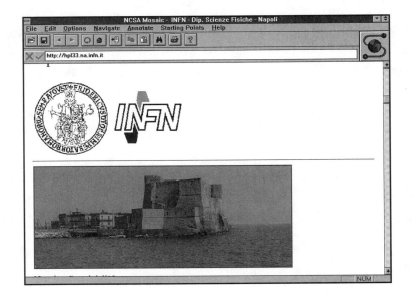

This Web site offers information about the early instruments at the Institute of Physics located in Naples, Italy. The collection includes 400 physics-based scientific items dating back to 1645, including an antique lens made in Florence. The home page has links to an introduction about the museum, as well as links to the history and description of items in the categories of optics, heat, and electromagnetism. You also can take a self-guided tour of this electronic museum.

Russia—Virtual Exhibits

URL address: **http://www.kiae.su/www/wtr/exhibits.html**

This site explores virtual exhibitions from Russia. You can jump among the Kremlin, the Contemporary Fine Arts Center, the Paleontology Institute, and the Soviet Archives. The Russian WWW servers are all under development, but are worth a visit.

Middle East

Egypt—Archaeological Survey in the Eastern Desert of Egypt

URL address: **http://rome.classics.lsa.umich.edu/projects/coptos/desert.ht ml**

This is a report on a research project that focuses on questions about trade routes, particularly the trans-desert routes, between the Nile Valley and the Red Sea. These routes linked the civilizations of the Mediterranean with those of the Indian Ocean between 300 B.C. and A.D. 400.

Shikhin

URL address: **http://www.colby.edu/rel/Shikhin.html**

A WWW exploration of the location and identification of Ancient Shikhin in Israel. This is a hypermedia overview of the history and archaeology of this ancient site, complete with images.

Turkey

URL address: **http://www.ege.edu.tr/Turkiye**

This site covers the Black Sea to the city of Istanbul. Browse through the classical architecture and sculpture, the Greek and Roman cities of western Turkey, or get an illustrated tour with Michael Greenhalh of the Department of Art History at the Australian National University.

Asia

Oriental Institute
URL address: **http://www-oi.uchicago.edu/oi/ default.html**

Fig. 26.6
View ancient artifacts when you visit the many links on the home page of the Oriental Institute.

You will find more links than text on this home page. The Oriental Institute is both a museum and research organization focusing on the study of the ancient Near East. You can explore the museum, archaeology, and philology projects.

Start with the first link, the museum, and then go to the highlights of the collection where you can choose regions of the world such as Cyprus, Egypt, Iran, Mesopotamia, and Syria. You can then move into descriptions and digital images of individual items. For example, the Egyptian collection has the Book of the Dead, a Model of a Butcher Shop, and a Mud Brick Stamped with a Cartouch of Ramses II.

United States

ArchNet—University of Connecticut Anthropology Department
URL address: **http://spirit.lib.uconn.edu/archnet/archnet-ascii.html**

This WWW server is a resource for northeastern archaeology history and preservation. Access the University of Connecticut Archaeology Archives or take a virtual tour of the Connecticut State Natural History Museum.

California—Palo Alto Historical Association
URL address: **http://www.commerce.digital.com:80/palo-alto/ historical-assoc/home.html**

Did you know that Palo Alto, Spanish for "tall tree," was the name given to the California town because of a large twin redwood tree found on the banks of the San Franciaquito Creek? You learn other interesting details about the history of Palo Alto at this Web site.

D-Day
URL address: **http://192.253.114.31/D-Day/**
Table_of_contents.html

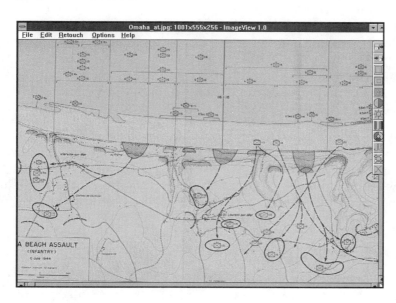

Fig. 26.7
Relive the important campaigns of World War II at the D-Day home page. This image shows the Allied assault plan.

High school students have created this interesting page of links to the history of D-Day with an emphasis on U.S. involvement. Here, you find an archive of Army and Navy newsreels, the *Stars & Stripes* newspaper, famous speeches from the National Archives, and a collection of maps and battle plans from the Center for Military History.

Oneida Indian Nation
URL address: **http://nysernet.org:80/oneida/**

The Web site explains the history of the Oneida Indians, overviews Oneida customs, and details the story of the sovereign nation agreement between the Oneidas and the United States. Check out a sound sample of the Oneida language or go on a photographic tour.

Oregon—World War II Farming
URL address: **http://arcweb.sos.state.or.us/osuhomepage.html**

Not all Americans fought on the front lines during World War II. This is a Web interactive exhibit maintained at the Oregon State University Archives on the subject "Fighters on the Farm Front: Oregon's Emergency Farm Labor

◀ See "State and Local Government," p. 663

Service, 1943–1947." The exhibit commemorates the state's Emergency Farm Labor Service, a program sponsored by the Oregon State College Extension Service to ensure an adequate farm labor supply during and immediately after World War II. This site provides two links, one to information about the exhibit and the other to the actual exhibit. There are 67 images that include photos, posters, and printed documents.

Texas—The Alamo
URL address: **http://www.lib.utexas.edu/Libs/CAH/ texas/cah_texas1.html**

The Center for American History has a collection containing books, maps, and other documents that detail the history of Texas from Spanish colonization to the present day. Wind your way through pages in this interactive exhibit of Texas history. View Santa Anna's battle map for the assault on the Alamo or view the oldest photograph taken in Texas—an 1849 daguerreotype that shows the front of the Alamo chapel.

World

History Archives
URL address: **http://history.cc.ukans.edu/history/subject_tree/ index.html**

This home page for the Heidelberg history archives categorizes history resources into two areas. First, there are epochs including Antiquity, Middle Ages, Early Modern, and 19th and 20th Century. Second, you can search for historical resources by continent, including Europe, North and South America, Asia, Africa, and Australia.

Historical Documents
URL address: **gopher://gopher.tntech.edu:70/ 11gopher_root%3a%5bcampus.as.hist%5d**

From the University of Tennessee, this site connects you to a vast warehouse of historical documents that are of significance to countries around the world—from Lincoln's first inaugural address to Clinton's State of the Union address to the manifesto of the Communist party.

◀ See "Internet and World Wide Web Resources," p. 568

History of Computing
URL address: **http://ei.cs.vt.edu/~history/**

Some people might argue that computing hasn't been around long enough to deserve a "history." Well, this site may prove them wrong with links to people who have shaped that history. You can also check out images of the ENIAC computer or a computer in a Buddhist temple.

History of Mathematics

URL address: **http://aleph0.clarku.edu/~djoyce/mathhist/ mathhist.html**

This site is sort of a who's who in the history of mathematics. Jump to information about the use of math in ancient China, or find out how Galileo and Francis Bacon contributed to this science.

History of Science

URL address: **http://nearnet.gnn.com:80/wic/histsci.toc.html**

From the Global Network Navigator, this page has two useful links. One is to the History of Science server, which opens a gateway to a Gopher that, as the GNN page states, is "an attempt to collect and catalog the writings and papers of respected scientists in a single place." The other link takes you to HOST, which stands for the History and Philosophy of Science and Technology, an academic journal focusing on scientific history.

International History

URL address:
http://heiwww.unige.ch/iuhei/history/

Welcome to the International History and Politics section

Fig. 26.8
You find a variety of historical documents, exhibits, and newsgroups at the International History and Politics Web site.

This WWW site contains links to an assortment of historical resources including the Charter of the United Nations, history newsgroups, the multimedia Soviet Archive, and 1492 exhibits.

This Day in History

URL address: **http://www.cm.cf.ac.uk/M/on-this-day**

This site is a lot of fun. On any given day, the server tells you what famous people in history were born that day. You can then hyperlink to a short biography of that person. Find out whether you share a birthday with Janis Joplin or Edgar Allen Poe.

◄ See "Cardiff's Movie Database," p. 468

VI

Finding Web Resources

United States Holocaust Memorial Museum
URL address: **http://www.ushmm.org**

Located in Washington D.C., this museum (and the Web site) focus on the history and memory of the Holocaust. You find links to general information about the museum, educational programs (including a brief history and frequently asked questions), and guidelines for teaching about the subject. There also are links to the Research Institute, which offers archival information for researchers, and to the association of Holocaust organizations, a network of organizations.

Vietnam
URL address: **ftp://ftp.msstate.edu/docs/history/USA/Vietnam/**

Download documents from this FTP site about the records from the National Archives, combat casualties, and even songs.

Greek and Roman

Catalogi Codicum Montis Athonis
URL address: **http://abacus.bates.edu/~rallison/**

▶ See "Anthropology," p. 847 Learn about Greek manuscripts of the Philotheou Monastery. Search through an electronic catalog of materials maintained at Bates College.

Classics and Mediterranean Archaeology Home Page
URL address: **http://rome.classics.lsa.umich.edu/welcome.html**

Links here to field projects, courses, exhibits, atlases, and bibliographies provide a good starting point for a journey into past civilizations.

Leptiminus Archaeological Project
URL address: **http://rome.classics.lsa.umich.edu/projects/lepti/lepti.html**

This is a multimedia report on the site of Leptiminus and fieldwork from 1990–1993 by Dr. Nejib Ben Lazreg, Institut National du Patrimoine; and Dr. John H. Humphre, Sebastian Heath, and David Stone, University of Michigan. GIF images support the text report.

Fig. 26.9
At nearly 200K, this GIF of an unearthed aqueduct takes a while to download at 14.4 Kbps but it is worth the wait.

Newstead Project
URL address: **http://www.brad.ac.uk/acad/archsci/field_proj/ newstead/newstead.html**

This project investigates the region around the Roman fort of Trimontium, which is near Newstead in the Borders region of southern Scotland. It describes a number of Roman artifacts ranging from wooden tent pegs to military parade helmets.

Pompeii Forum
URL address: **http://jefferson.village.virginia.edu/pompeii/page-1.html**

In A.D. 79, a great volcanic eruption of Mt. Vesuvius devastated the city of Pompeii. This project focuses on the urban center of Pompeii where the main religious, civic, and commercial activities occurred. From the home page, go to the forum map that opens a list of specific buildings in the city, such as the Imperial Cult Building. Click a building name and jump to a variety of pictures.

Archaeology

Archaeological Fieldwork Server
URL address: **http://durendal.cit.cornell.edu/TestPit.html**

Do you enjoy "a dig"? This server provides links to fieldwork opportunities including positions for volunteers, contract work, and field schools. Links on the home page are broken down into Europe, Middle East, and North America.

VI

Finding Web Resources

Archaeology

URL address: **http://spirit.lib.uconn.edu/archaeology.html**

This home page has links to other documents and servers of interest to archaeologists. Selections include the Museum of Cagliari, a survey in the eastern desert of Egypt, Northeastern archaeology, Mediterranean archaeology, the Leptiminus Archaeological Project in Tunisia, the Dead Sea Scrolls exhibit at the University of North Carolina, and the national archaeological database from the U.S. National Park Service.

Classics and Mediterranean Archaeology

URL address: **http://rome.classics.lsa.umich.edu/welcome.html**

This WWW server collects links to Internet resources of interest to Mediterranean archaeologists. Included are links to field projects, texts and journals, museums, atlases, newsgroups, and mailing lists.

Geography and Maps

Antarctica—Maps of Antarctica

URL address: **http://www.hmc.edu/www/people/teverett/antarctica/Maps.html**

Fig. 26.10
The Maps of Antarctica Web server shows how specific locations on this continent relate to other areas of the world.

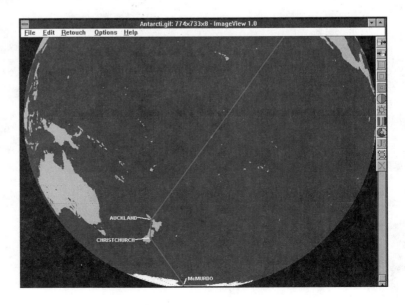

Here, you find a nice selection of color graphic maps of Antarctica that show the relationship between locations on this continent to the rest of the world with highlighted lines. Specific areas include McMurdo Station and its vicinity, Taylor Valley, and McMurdo Dome. All the maps are GIF images and load fairly quickly.

Boston

URL address: **http://www.bu.edu/images/metromap.gif**

This is the actual URL address for a GIF file depicting a map of metropolitan Boston.

Department of Geography

URL address: **http://lorax.geog.scarolina.edu**

This University of South Carolina site has information about the department's graduate programs, faculty and student directories, an alumni registry, and links to other sources of geographic information. Also, a link to a geographic map of South Carolina and the newsletter of the AAG GIS Specialty Group is included.

Digital D.C.

URL address: **http://www.c3.lanl.gov/~cjhamil/Browse/main.html**

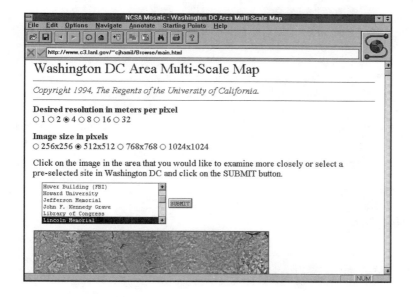

Fig. 26.11
At this site, you can pick various famous monuments in the Washington D.C. area and then retrieve images and maps.

Never been to Washington D.C.? Well, this site lets you explore it by "zooming" down from outer space into different areas of the city. You choose a site, such as the Lincoln Memorial, from a list. You also pick resolution and image size for display. Then you get the picture. The images were gathered by satellite photography.

Digital Shaded Relief Map of the U.S.

URL address: **http://www.zilker.net/~hal/apl-us//**

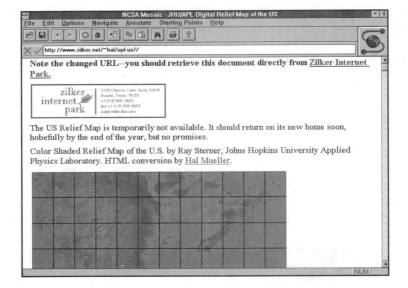

Fig. 26.12
The Shaded Relief Map of the U.S. Web server offers a topographical map view of the country.

This is an on-again, off-again resource—but well worth the visit when it's up. You begin with a home page image of the U.S. divided into a grid. When you click a specific grid area, you get two-color, shaded relief maps of the area. One shows coastlines, boundaries, and rivers and the other has a topographical view. You can then select one of these maps to continue to "zoom" into the specific area you want to view.

The overall map coverage area ranges from 65 to 125 degrees west longitude and 25 to 50 degrees north latitude. The server also has high-resolution images of the state of Wyoming.

Geographic Name Information System

URL address: **gopher://mudhoney.micro.umn.edu:4324/ 7geo%20search**

Use this WWW interface to a Gopher server that looks up the names of towns and cities across the U.S. Enter New York, for example, and you find more than one "Big Apple." New Mexico, Florida, Texas, Iowa, and Kentucky all have towns with the name New York. Click one of these towns to get detailed information about telephone area codes, population, latitude, longitude, elevation, ZIP codes, and counties in the area.

Geography—Indexes and WWW Resources

URL address: **http://honor.uc.wlu.edu:1020/-ge**

This site is an extensive list of WWW servers by geographic location—first all 50 states, and then country by country. When you select a state or country, you get a new list of servers in that area, many of which provide information on the geography and history of the area.

Map Collection

URL address: **http://www.lib.utexas.edu/Libs/PCL/Map_collection/ Map_collection.html**

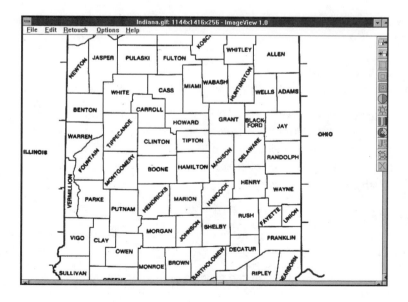

Fig. 26.13
All of the maps here may not be the most aesthetically pleasing, but with over 200,000 maps including this census map of Indiana (blown up to show central Indiana—home of Macmillan Computer Publishing and Que), you are bound to find a map that suits your needs.

This address connects you with information about the Perry-Castaneda Library Map Collection (some 200,000+ maps) at the University of Texas at Austin. You can weave your way through links to different parts of the world. For example, start with Maps of Africa, and then select Botswana to retrieve the map. Many of the maps were created by the Central Intelligence Agency.

Mars Atlas

URL address: **http://fi-www.arc.nasa.gov/fia/projects/bayes-group/Atlas/Mars/**

If you enjoy out-of-this-world geography, travel to this Web server, which offers a browsable, zoomable, scrollable atlas of Mars. The project is a spin-off of an "image super-resolution project" at NASA Ames Artificial Intelligence Research Branch. It shows the locations (footprints) of thousands of high-resolution Viking Orbiter images. You begin with a high (1440×740 pixels) or low resolution (600×300 pixels) image of Mars and then you select specific areas for further exploration. You also find links to images of Jupiter, Saturn, Uranus, and Neptune.

Peru—Red Cientifica Peruana

URL address: **http://www.rcp.net.pe/rcp_ingles.html**

This WWW server represents the central point for the Internet network in this country. It provides a neat overview of this Latin American country with maps, descriptions of the land, the economy, and government.

Project GeoSim

URL address: **http://geosim.cs.vt.edu/index.html**

Project GeoSim has a WWW server that distributes Geography Education software developed by the Departments of Geography and Computer Science at Virginia Tech. The software runs on MS-DOS, Macintosh, and DECstations running X-Windows. The Gopher address, **gopher://geosim.cs.vt.edu/1**, is also available.

Railroad Maps

URL address: **http://www-cse.ucsd.edu/users/bowdidge/railroad/rail-maps.html**

Some of the featured maps you can access via this server include the London Underground, San Francisco Bay Area Rapid Transit (BART), Long Island Railroad, Paris Metro, and Tokyo and Cambridge, Massachusetts train systems.

Rare Maps

URL address: **http://scarlett.libs.uga.edu/1h/www/darchive/ hargrett/maps.html**

View rare maps from the period 1600–1880 such as the Americae Nova Tabula by Joan Blaeu (1596–1674). The home page explains, "This sample represents our efforts to digitize over 850 rare maps produced from about 1600 to 1870. These maps were scanned from microfilm negatives at 2400dpi; they are very large files. The average TIFF file size is 2 1/2M and the average JPEG size is 500K."

Rwanda

URL address: **http://www.intac.com/PubService/rwanda/images/**

Here you'll find color and black-and-white maps of Rwanda and the cities in this country.

Space Remote Sensing

URL address: **http://ma.itd.com:8000/welcome.html**

According to its home page description, "The Institute for Technology Development/Space Remote Sensing Center (ITD/SRSC) is a not-for-profit organization dedicated to the development and commercialization of remote sensing (satellite imagery) and Geographic Information System technologies into the private and public sectors." The research from this organization helps create new maps and improve farm-management techniques.

The JASON Project

URL address: **http://seawifs.gsfc.nasa.gov/scripts/JASON.html**

This is an educational program that helps school students learn more about our planet's geography and environmental issues. Dr. Robert D. Ballard started the project in 1989 after he received thousands of letters from children who were interested in how he found the RMS *Titanic*.

The program uses computer and video technology to describe explorations. Teachers can access ideas for educational curricula that accompany the project. From the home page, you can jump into a voyage to the volcanoes of Hawaii or a journey to the rain forests of Belize.

VI

Finding Web Resources

Fig. 26.14
This map of Belize is just one of the many geographic resources available via The JASON Project Web site.

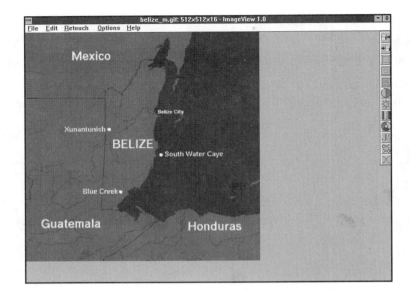

From Here...

It can be mesmerizing to sit in front of your PC and click links that transport you around the world and through the history of humankind. If your thirst for exploration hasn't been quenched, then try the sites in these chapters:

- Chapter 20, "Art, Music, and Entertainment," lists digital museums that offer a look at history from a cultural perspective.

- Chapter 27, "International Web Resources," consists of information that will let you continue globetrotting by visiting sites from around the world.

- Chapter 28, "Issues, Politics, Religion, and World Events," provides listings of Web sites that take a global perspective of important social issues.

Chapter 27

International Web Resources

by Bill Eager

From a user's point-of-view, the most exciting aspect of the World Wide Web is that you can read, view, and listen to the thoughts of people around the globe from the comfort of your study or living room. With a few clicks of the mouse, you can jump between 10 or 20 countries in less than an hour. Learn about cultures and traditions; plan a vacation or business trip; understand the legal and economic systems; discover the latest scientific activities in international research centers; or find out about organizations or associations that relate to your own interests or professional pursuits. These are a few of the thrilling, educational, and useful activities that you can perform via the global WWW.

As you leap from continent to continent, you will notice that most Web sites either have English as their official language or offer both a native language and English. However, there are still many WWW servers that have information only in a native tongue. This fact, too, is part of the special international flavor of the medium, and if you know a foreign language, are learning a foreign language, or simply have an interest in looking at information written in a foreign language, you will enjoy visiting these servers. Some countries, like Japan and Russia, provide advice on how to obtain a WWW browser that displays information in its unique character set (Japanese or Russian).

In this chapter, you find the following:

- Good starting places to access quickly a variety of information about international information, ranging from tips for tourists to business opportunities

■ International resources listed by specific category, such as art, cuisine, education, travel, and scientific research

■ An alphabetical listing of WWW servers in countries in all regions of the world

Gateway to Antarctica

URL address: **http://icair.iac.org.nz/**

◄ See "Dewey-
Web," p. 593

Covered by 90 percent of the world's ice, which has an average thickness of about 2,000 meters, most people consider the continent of Antarctica to be a cold and mysterious place. Now, thanks to sponsorship by the National Science Foundation, you can visit the South Pole without getting frostbite. This WWW server links you with interesting information about the geological history of the continent, the impact that Antarctica has on the world's environment, opportunities to travel to the continent (physically), and Antarctica gifts.

Fig. 27.1
Did you know that less than 5 percent of Antarctica's land is without permanent ice or snow? This is one of the many interesting facts you learn when you visit Gateway to Antarctica.

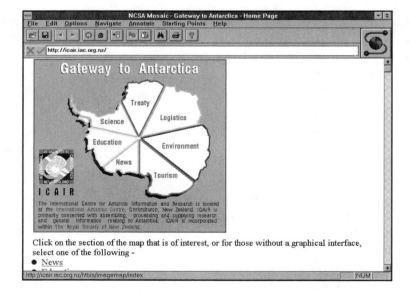

You learn that the climate for most of Antarctica is that of a cold desert. In the region of the South Pole, about seven centimeters of snow accumulates annually and it has an annual mean temperature of -49°C. As the ice sheet reflects most of the sun's heat back into the atmosphere, it collects almost no heat and significantly influences world weather patterns.

Antarctica received tremendous media attention when it was discovered that ozone depletion, known as the Ozone Hole, was getting larger over the South Pole. This WWW server contains annual program reports for several nations involved in experiments on the continent.

If you're even more adventurous, there are links to help you take the next step—a trip to Antarctica. Learn about Southern Heritage Expeditions, a company specializing in expedition cruises to Antarctica and Subantarctic Islands, and Arctic Adventures, a Norwegian Company that specializes in Arctic tours. Or order a free copy of the Antarctic Gift Shop Catalog.

New Zealand

URL address: **http://www.cs.cmu.edu:8001/Web/People/mjw/NZ/ MainPage.html**

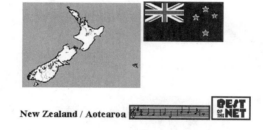

New Zealand / Aotearoa

Fig. 27.2
Special tips on hitchhiking and sightseeing are a few of the many useful tidbits you get when you visit the New Zealand WWW home page.

When you visit this home page, you increase your knowledge of this country as you learn that New Zealand is situated the same distance east of Australia as Moscow is from London, and that it is bigger than Connecticut but smaller than Canada. These facts just scratch the surface of the many interesting and useful things you learn about New Zealand. Sports enthusiasts can find out about windsurfing and water-skiing in the beautiful waters surrounding the country. Hikers can receive detailed information about "tramping," the art of walking in the outdoors.

If you are involved in international trade, or simply want to buy a new sweater, you learn that wool is one of the major exports. And, if you enjoy dabbling in international cooking, you can jump to various recipes, including this one for Pavlovas:

3 egg whites	1 teaspoon vinegar
3 tablespoons cold water	1 teaspoon vanilla essence
1 cup castor sugar	3 teaspoons cornflour

Beat egg whites until stiff, add cold water, and beat again. Add castor sugar gradually while still beating. Slow beater and add vinegar, vanilla, and cornflour. Place on greased paper on greased tray and bake at 150° C (300° F) for 45 minutes, and then leave to cool in the oven.

Other home page links bring you to subdocuments, which offer yet more links to information about New Zealand, such as:

New Zealand News Stories

Travel and Tourist Information

Physical Environment: Geography, Natural History, Environment

History, People, Language, and Culture

Recreation, Entertainment, and Sports

Government and Public Affairs

Singapore Online Guide

URL address: **http://www.ncb.gov.sg/sog/sog.html**

Fig. 27.3
This WWW resource provides an interactive tourist information guide complete with an electronic tour agent.

A travel agent might have a difficult time pulling together this much information about Singapore. This electronic version of the Singapore Official Guide is issued by the Singapore Tourist Promotion Board (STPB) and is free to all tourists and travelers. The first edition is a prototype being developed by the Digital Media Center (DMC) of the National Computer Board.

The hyperlinks on the home page very closely represent the type of information that you find in a good travel guide: places to visit, hotels, shopping, and more. To make your journey even more interesting, an interactive tour agent gives you a customized minitour of Singapore. And if you don't see what you need, you can keyword search articles about Singapore to get more specific information. When you have finished visiting this WWW server, you'll be ready to pack your bags. Here are some of the main selections and topics you can jump to from the home page:

Nippon Telephone and Telegraph Corporation

URL address: **http://www.ntt.jp**

NIPPON TELEGRAPH AND TELEPHONE
CORPORATION
日本電信電話株式会社

Fig. 27.4
Learn about the
Nippon Telephone
and Telegraph
Company and
jump to a variety
of interesting
Japanese resources.

Nippon Telephone and Telegraph Company and its subsidiaries provide a broad range of telecommunication services in Japan, including telephone, telegraph, leased circuit, data communication, and miscellaneous services. NTT also sells terminal equipment.

In addition to providing general information about its overseas offices and NTT service information, this home page provides links to the following 12 laboratories that are part of its R&D department:

Basic Research Laboratories

Software Laboratories

Communication Switching Laboratories

Telecommunications Networks Laboratories

Network Information Systems Laboratories

Human Interface Laboratories

Transmission Systems Laboratories

Radio Communication Systems Laboratories

LSI Laboratories

Opto-Electronics Laboratories

Interdisciplinary Research Laboratories

Communication Science Laboratories

A unique feature of the NTT WWW information is the way it provides Japanese documents. It refers to five browsers that present information in Japanese (all in a UNIX environment).

Window-to-Russia

URL address: **http://www.kiae.su/www/wtr/**

Window-to-Russia is a Moscow-based project created by Relcom Corporation, initiated to give the worldwide network community a means of WWW access to a variety of information resources from and about Russia. Some resources are in Russian. (To view these Russian texts, you need to install KOI-8 Cyrillic fonts.) Main menu links offer the following resources:

Arts, Culture, History, and Human Sciences

Business Opportunities

Science, Technology, Computers, and Software

Other Russian Web servers

Russian-Related Sources Outside Russia

Art and Entertainment

Dublin Pub Review
URL address: **http://www.dsg.cs.tcd.ie:/dsg_people/czimmerm/ pubs.html**

This site includes the most complete descriptions of Dublin's venues on the Internet. It is divided into two sections: pubs and nightclubs. Each entry comes with a short review and an address.

International Shakespeare Globe Centre in Germany

URL address: **http://www.rrz.uni-koeln.de/phil-fak/englisch/ SHAKESPEARE/engl/indexe.html**

Learn about this organization and its involvement in the reconstruction of Shakespeare's Globe Theater, as well as links to performances, workshops, and other Web sites devoted to Shakespeare.

Kylie Minogue

URL address: **http://www.eia.brad.ac.uk/kylie/index.html**

The site provides hypertext about the Australian singer Kylie Minogue. The discography has links to samples from each of the songs and pictures from album and single covers, as well as other related areas like fan mail and newsletters.

Nando.Net

URL address: **http://www.nando.net/welcome.html**

This site includes samples of many newspapers, journals, cartoons, schedules, games, stories, and statistics. Daily updates.

Ohio State University at Newark, Art Gallery

URL address: **http://www.cgrg.ohio-state.edu/mkruse/osu.html**

Art Gallery exhibits the work of local, national, and international artists. Exhibitions are available to the public.

Pablov International

URL address: **http://www.twics.com/~TOKUMARU/home.html**

This site has information on art from Japan. Specifically, the home page has links to a gallery of art and information about cinema.

Associations and Organizations

Association for Experiential Education

URL address: **http://www.princeton.edu/~rcurtis/aee.html**

AEE is a nonprofit, international membership organization with roots in adventure education. It is committed to the development, practice, and evaluation of experiential learning in all settings. With more than 2,000 members in over 20 countries, AEE's membership consists of individuals and organizations with affiliations in education, recreation, outdoor adventure programming, mental health, youth service, physical education, management development training, corrections, programming for people with disabilities, and environmental education.

ATM Forum

URL address: **http://www.atmforum.com/**

ATM is an international non-profit organization formed with the objective of accelerating the use of ATM (Asynchronous Transfer Mode) telecommunications products and services through a rapid convergence of interoperability specifications. In addition, the forum promotes industry cooperation and awareness. Currently, the ATM Forum consists of over 500 member companies, and it remains open to any organization interested in accelerating the availability of ATM-based solutions.

Bay Area Model Mugging

URL address: **http://www.ugcs.caltech.edu/~rachel/bamm.html**

This organization is a worldwide self-defense organization for women. Learn about the various individual and corporate classes which this San Francisco organization puts on.

Graduate Institute of International Studies

URL address: **http://heiwww.unige.ch/**

Explore Internet history and politics, economics, law, art galleries, music, and more.

Global Fund for Women

URL address: **http://www.ai.mit.edu/people/ellens/gfw.html**

▶ See "Not-for-Profit Organizations," p. 790

This is an international grant-funding organization that supports groups committed to women's well-being and full participation in society.

Hostelling International

URL address: **http://cyber.cclims.com/comp/ayh/ayh.html**

The home page tells us that hostelling is designed to "...help all people, but especially young people, gain a greater understanding of the world and its people." This is the site for the Golden Gate Council, which is part of the

International Hostel Organization. Members can visit more than 6,000 hostels in 70 countries. You can visit links that tell you about hostels and the organization, and you can fill in a form to get more information.

International Association of Open Systems Professionals

URL address: **http://www.uniforum.org/**

The International Association of Open Systems Professionals has announced its World Wide Web server. It contains information about the association, its programs, and services.

International Commission on Illumination

URL address: **http://www.hike.te.chiba-u.ac.jp/ikeda/CIE/ home.html**

The International Commission on Illumination, CIE from its French title Commission Internationale de l'Eclairage, is an organization devoted to international teamwork and the exchange of information among its member countries on matters relating to the science and art of lighting. Its publications and disks are available from the CIE National Committees and the CIE Central Bureau in Vienna.

International Organization for Plant Information

URL address: **http://life.anu.edu.au/biodiversity/iopi/iopi.html**

This Web site contains links to hypermedia taxonomic information—fancy way of saying databases on plant information. IOPI came into being in 1991 at a meeting hosted by the Australian Biological Resources Study. Forty-nine botanists from 11 countries participated, and an idea was born to consider the establishment of a global plant species information system. Proceed to learn more information through the links from this site.

International Society for Optical Engineering

URL address: **http://www.spie.org/**

This non-profit professional association—the International Society for Optical Engineering—is dedicated to advancing research and applications in the optical sciences. This site provides many links to information relevant to the topic.

Rotary

URL address: **http://www.tecc.co.uk/public/PaulHarris/**

Fig. 27.5
A browser is provided lots of links to information about the global Rotary organization and its chapters.

With some 26,000 Rotary clubs around the world, the Rotary organization is indeed a global effort. There is much information for the casual browser, as well as for those who are interested in details of joining or creating a local Rotary chapter. One link will provide you with a list of Rotary BBS and Internet connections. The Rotary effort is dedicated to alleviating suffering around the world.

Southampton University Astronomy Group

URL address: **http://sousun1.phys.soton.ac.uk/**

The group provides an index of recent International Astronomical Union telegrams. To avoid breaching the copyright on the circulars, the full text of the telegrams is available only locally. If you have your own legitimate source for these documents, this search tool tells you in which telegrams to look for news on certain astronomical objects and events.

Business and Legal

Cleveland State University

URL address: **http://www.law.csuohio.edu/**

The home page for the Joseph W. Bartunek III Law Library in Ohio links to legal Internet resources, OhioLINK, and other library Telnet sites, the technical and computer information center, and experimental CGI gateways.

Electronic Industries Association of Japan

URL address: **http://fuji.stanford.edu/orgs/UCOM.html**

Established by the Electronic Industries Association of Japan (EIAJ), UCOM California promotes the import of semiconductors while contributing to the development and maintenance of free international trade. There is information about UCOM California's purpose, activities, and services provided to U.S. semiconductor chip manufacturers.

Employee Ownership

URL address: **http://www.fed.org/fed/**

You can get information and strategies on international developments in employee ownership and equity compensation methods. You also can have access to the latest research and statistics from case studies of successful employee-owned firms.

Social Security Administration

URL address: **http://www.ssa.gov/SSA_Home.html**

This site offers public information about retirement, survivors, disability, and other Social Security Administration programs, the status of the SSA Trust Fund, and legislation affecting SSA. Do you have employees in other countries? International Agreement information is available.

► See "Law and Legal Resources," p. 788

Trade Law

URL address: **http://ananse.irv.uit.no/trade_law/nav/trade.html**

This server contains various international trade treaties, conventions, laws and rules, and other trade instruments.

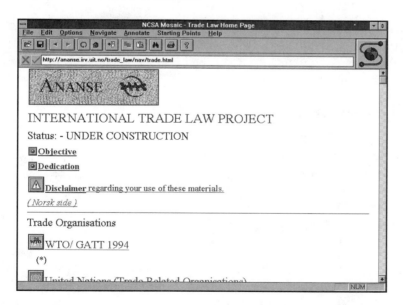

Fig. 27.6
This is the place to visit if you need to learn about the sale or carriage of goods, insurance, or other matters of international law.

VI

Finding Web Resources

Uruguay Round—Final Act (24-May-1994)

URL address: **http://heiwww.unige.ch/gatt/final_act/**

This server contains the results of the Uruguay Round of multilateral trade negotiations and is available at the Graduate Institute of International Studies.

Washington College of Law

URL address: **http://sray.wcl.american.edu/pub/wcl.html**

This server is for the Washington College of Law at the American University. It focuses mainly on the European Community, United Nations, and other international law documents. You can view a list of links to international materials, U.S. legal documents, and help in other areas.

Computer Technology

Institut Dalle Molle d'Intelligence Artificelle Perceptive (IDIAP)

URL address: **http://www.idiap.ch/**

◀ See "Computers," p. 545

The IDIAP is a publicly funded research institute located in the Le Valais region of Switzerland. Researchers at the institute work on computer vision, handwriting recognition and OCR, expert systems, neural networks, optical computing, and speech recognition.

University of Aizu

URL address: **http://www.u-aizu.ac.jp/**

The University of Aizu was established in 1993 to provide education and research in computer science. The hypermedia research profile brochure is People Advancing Knowledge for Humanity.

Upsilon Pi Epsilon Honor Society

URL address: **http://www.cs.purdue.edu/upe/upe-main.html**

This honor society is the first and only international honor society for the Computing Sciences. It was founded to recognize scholarly activities and professionalism. Many chapters honor faculty as well as students with membership. The home page has a listing of all chapters.

Stony Brook

URL address: **http://www.sunysb.edu/**

This site includes research information focusing on math, chemistry, earth space sciences, electrical engineering, and theoretical and x-ray physics. It also provides links to research-related and economic development opportunities.

Conferences

Association for Computing Machinery

URL address: **http://info.acm.org/**

The information available through ACM's Internet services provides you with details on a range of subjects, including conferences, calls for papers, ACM periodicals and books, ACM special interest groups, members' services, chapters, technical outreach programs, and the ACM International Collegiate Programming Contest.

Departamento de Ciencias de la Computacion

URL address: **http://www.dcc.uchile.cl/**

As the first WWW server in Chile, it provides information about the Department of Computer Science and includes a map of WWW/Gopher servers in Chile. It also includes information about the 20th International Conference on Very Large Databases.

First WWW Conference

URL address: **http://www1.cern.ch/WWW94/Welcome.html**

At this first conference, the Best of the Web '94 awards were announced in 12 categories and a WWW Hall of Fame was created. The exhibit should serve as an example for the rest of the Web.

Management Briefing Seminars

URL address: **http://ott22.engin.umich.edu/mbs/mbsdoc.html**

This is an international conference held annually at the Grand Traverse Resort of Michigan's Grand Traverse Bay. It keeps you up to date on issues facing the automotive industry, manufacturing, and quality assurance.

VI

Finding Web Resources

UIAH Entrypoint

URL address: **http://www.uiah.fi/**

The University of Art and Design Helsinki provides information on the International Symposium on Electronic Art (ISEA) and the International Conference on Colour Education.

▶ See "Cooking, Dining, and Beverages," p. 910

Cooking, Food, and International Cuisine

Boston Restaurant List

URL address: **http://www.osf.org:8001/boston-food/boston-food.html**

In addition to detailed reviews of recommended restaurants in and around Boston, there's also an online forum for submitting new or updated restaurant reviews.

Grapevine

URL address: **http://www.opal.com/grapevine**

This Web-accessible magazine is dedicated to wine lovers. It carries reviews and information about wines and vineyards from all over the world.

Italian Recipes from the University of Minnesota

URL address: **gopher://spinaltap.micro.umn.edu/11/fun/Recipes/Italian**

This site provides a list of links to several types of dishes and how many of the individual recipes are available. Everything from carbonara (3) to spaghetti sauce (6). The users who submit the recipe usually tell from where they got it, and may include a few other interesting details.

Oriental Recipes from the University of Minnesota

URL address: **gopher://spinaltap.micro.umn.edu/11/fun/Recipes/Oriental**

This site includes a list of links to recipes for several types of dishes. Some of them include barmi-goregn, Chinese spaghetti, potstickers, sagh, sambal-bajak, sambal-lilang, shu-mei, sukiyaki, and tofu-meat. Included with the recipe is a note from the provider about where it is from.

Tex-Mex Recipes from the University of Minnesota

URL address: **gopher://spinaltap.micro.umn.edu/11/fun/Recipes/ TexMex**

A list of links to recipes for foods that will make your mouth (and eyes) water. There are chalupas, enchiladas, fajitas, quiches, salads, salsa, tex-mex beans, refried beans, tacos, tortilla-cass, and tucson-tostadas. There is a bit of information about the origin of the recipe included.

Education and Careers

College of Textiles

URL address: **http://www.tx.ncsu.edu/**

The North Carolina State University College of Textiles is the largest of its kind in the United States. It offers one of only two accredited Textile Engineering programs in the country, and produces more than half of the textile graduates in the U.S. each year.

◀ See "Colleges and Universities—International," p. 618

Fig. 27.7
From carpets to drapes, the textile industry plays an important role in our everyday life. Visit this server and find out about the industry and one of the nation's largest textile schools.

Griffith University

URL address: **http://www.gu.edu.au/**

Here, you find information about the university, its structure, work, and people. It is located in the Brisbane-Gold Coast corridor of Australia.

Lakemedelsstatistik

URL address: **http://www.ls.se/**

This is a medical information system, located in Stockholm, called MedLink. It distributes medical information via the Web to all the doctors and nurses in Sweden.

Norsk Regnesentral

URL address: **http://www.nr.no/**

The Norwegian Computing Center is a research institute dedicated to studies of information technology and applied statistics. Information is presented in Norwegian and English. The center is located in Oslo.

University of Montreal
URL address: **http://www.droit.umontreal.ca/english.html**

The server of the Centre de Recherche en Droit Public and the Faculty of Law at the University of Montreal is experimental. It allows links to information on Canadian and Quebec law, as well as to other legal sources in the world.

University of Saarland, Germany
URL address: **http://www.jura.uni-sb.de/indexengl.html**

Most of the information at this law-related server site is in German. There are links to codes and sources of law, news bulletins, exemplary cases, and the Internet virtual library.

XFIND Index of CERN
URL address: **http://crnvmc.cern.ch:80/FIND/DICTIONARY?**

This server provides a dictionary that combines the Free Online Dictionary of Computing and a natural English dictionary. Its files were preprocessed at CERN. If you incorrectly spell the word you want to define, it gives you correctly spelled words that it thinks you meant to enter. You may choose the correct one from there. It will then go on to give the definition and other related information.

Environmental

Center for Atmospheric Science
URL address: **http://www.atm.ch.cam.ac.uk/**

Located at the University of Cambridge, UK, this server provides information such as degrees offered, seminars, and information about the UK Universities Global Atmospheric Modelling Programme (UGAMP).

EcoWeb
URL address: **http://ecosys.drdr.virginia.edu/EcoWeb.html**

EcoWeb is an environmental WWW server that provides and connects users to environmental information on the local, state, regional, and global level. Telnet and dial-up access are also available.

Forensic Science

URL address: **http://ash.lab.r1.fws.gov/**

The USFWS Forensic Laboratory is a part of the U.S. Fish and Wildlife Service Division of Law Enforcement. Its mission is to provide forensic support to federal, state, and international wildlife agencies.

Geological Survey of Finland

URL address: **http://www.gsf.fi/**

The server contains information on research activities and international services. The GSF, which was established in 1885, is a government-funded agency responsible to the Ministry of Trade and Industry.

ICE House—Information Center for the Environment

URL address: **http://ice.ucdavis.edu**

The center is a cooperative effort between environmental scientists at the University of California and a variety of state, federal, and international organizations that focuses on environmental protection. The home page has links to information about a wide variety of environmental organizations, events, and documents, such as "Man and the Biosphere" and the "California Rivers Assessment." Jump to the John Muir (of Sierra Club fame) exhibit and find out everything there is to know about this important historical figure in the environmental movement.

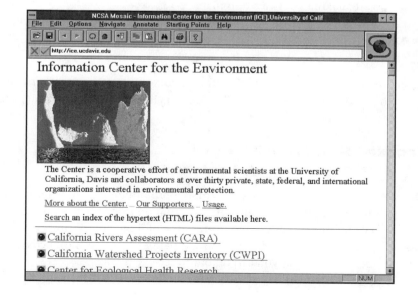

Fig. 27.8
Saving the environment is a task that requires the efforts of many people and organizations. This home page points you toward some of the key players in this important endeavor.

VI

Finding Web Resources

Ocean Research Institute
URL address: **http://www.ori.u-tokyo.ac.jp/**

Server for the Ocean Research Institute at the University of Tokyo. It has links to an outline of the university, research units and facilities, other oceanographic institutions and data centers, research vessels, and other services at ORI.

School of Ocean and Earth Science and Technology
URL address: **http://www.soest.hawaii.edu/**

This server comes from the University of Hawaii at Manoa. It consists of a list of organizations, academic programs, facilities, and research programs. There are even old, spectacular images of hurricanes that might be of interest.

► See "Travel—Places to Go, Worldwide," p. 937

Interesting Sites and National Travel Guides

Australia
URL address: **http://www.csu.edu.au/education/australia.html**

This site is a guide to information resources about Australia to distribute via the WWW. It contains links to facts and figures, maps, travel information, government and history, and much more. This guide can be a great help while you are making your vacation plans.

Brazil
URL address: **http://www.rnp.br**

This is a WWW server maintained by the National Research Network in Rio de Janeiro. It offers links to other WWW servers in Brazil and Latin America. All information is in Portuguese.

Canada—New Brunswick
URL address: **http://www.csi.nb.ca/econ-dev**

This site is sponsored by the government as a promotion for doing business in New Brunswick. There is detailed information on labor costs, weather, recreational facilities, vacation opportunities, building and housing. There's a link to a hypertext-based economic journal that describes business activity and a forms interface that you can fill out to receive hardcopy.

Canadian Communities Atlas

URL address: **http://ellesmere.ccm.emr.ca/ourhome/communit/
ourhome/introduc.html**

This Web site is a digital atlas, providing an overview of 10 Canadian communities. The atlas reflects the views of elementary and high school students
about their communities using text, maps, photographs, and drawings. There
are links to a community in each province in Canada, and text is in both
English and French.

Cambodia

URL address: **http://none.coolware.com/entmt/cambodia/
cambodia.html**

From the temples of Angkor Wat to the Killing Fields outside of Phnom Penh,
this Web site has a collection of pictures and a short diary that provides a
digital tour of Cambodia.

ESTONIA!

URL address: **http://www.eenet.ee/english.html**

This server provides a map of Estonia and links to the following: Where is
Estonia?; Estonia; World; About Estonia; EENet WHOIS, and also NetFind.
You can access this information in Estonian.

Europe

URL address: **http://s700.uminho.pt/europa.html**

If you haven't taken a European trip yet this year, you must check out this
terrific WWW home page—from it you can jump to many countries in
Europe (see fig. 27.9). When you click a flag for a particular country on the
hypermedia map, you jump to a server in that country.

France

URL address: **http://web.urec.fr/france/france.html**

This is a great site for visiting France. If you have inline images turned on,
there is a large interactive map of France. Click a region of the map, and
you'll get a new map of that region. Or, if one of the towns is in a red rect-
angle, you can click it and receive more information about the town.

Fig. 27.9
Use this
Web server's
hypermedia map
of Europe to jump
quickly to one of
the European
countries.

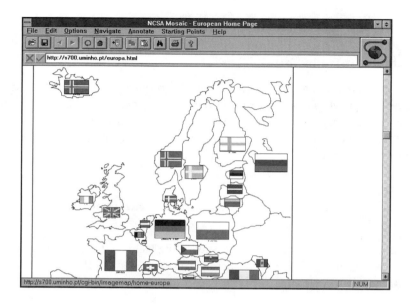

Global Network Navigator—Travelers' Center

URL address: **http://gnn.interpath.net/gnn/meta/travel/
index.html**

Before you plan your next trip, be sure to visit the GNN Travelers' Center.
You can get a quick update on the editor's notes, visit a specific region, country, state, or city guide for help, and receive information on staying healthy
in several of the countries you may want to visit. This one is packed with
information, so plan to spend some time browsing.

Iran

URL address: **http://tehran.stanford.edu**

Information about the culture, people, language, art, and literature from Iran.
There are GIF images and audio files that you can download.

Ireland: The Internet Collection

URL address: **http://itdsrv1.ul.ie/Information/Ireland.html**

This server contains links to various sources that contain information on
Ireland (see fig. 27.10). A few of the areas include maps, the virtual tourist
guide to Ireland, photos from the weather satellites, and genealogical research
in Ireland.

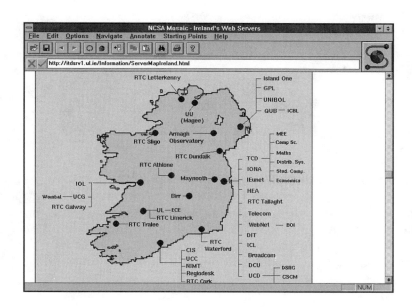

Fig. 27.10
You can find everything from Irish pubs to Irish music via this home page, which presents an interactive map of Ireland.

Jerusalem Mosaic

URL address: **http://www1.huji.ac.il/jeru/jerusalem.html**

With a recorded history of some 4,000 years, Jerusalem is of interest to many people. This server links to a lot of information and maps. You can even sign the Visitors Book!

Museums of Paris

URL address: **http://mistral.enst.fr/~pioch/louvre/museums.html**

This server contains presentations about the three major art museums in Paris, each dedicated to a certain period. Featured are the Louvre, the Le Musée d'Orsay, and the Centre Georges Pompidou (Beaubourg)—the oldest museum in Paris. You will find the history of the museum and the master-pieces most intriguing.

◄ See "Museums," p. 486

New Zealand

URL address: **http://www.cs.cmu.edu:8001/Web/People/mjw/NZ/MainPage.html**

The home page has links to information about travel and tourist information of New Zealand. Connections include environment, history, language and culture, universities, recreation, and entertainment.

VI

Finding Web Resources

Peru

URL address: **http://www.rcp.net.pe/rcp_ingles.html**

Fig. 27.11
If you want to learn Spanish or learn about the Spanish culture in Peru, this WWW home page can help.

Ceremonial Mask of Señor of Sipán.

Are you learning Spanish? One of the hyperlinks on this home page brings up a Spanish language tutorial. There are also several sources of information links about Peru, its system, and the networks of Latin America and the Caribbean at this site. The RCP, which is the Internet Network of Peru, reaches 23 of the 24 provinces that make up that country. It functions as the center of the 200 affiliated institutions.

Portugal

URL address: **http://s700.uminho.pt/Portugal/portugal.html**

This home page brings you to an assortment of useful tourist information about Portugal.

Russian Academy of Science

URL address: **http://ucmp1.berkeley.edu/pin.html**

The Paleontological Institute of the Russian Academy of Science in Moscow, Russia, is the world's largest paleontological institute. The museum, run by the institute, is open to the public and has "loaned" some of its exhibits for use on the WWW Virtual Library because it does not have an Internet line of its own.

Russian and East European Studies

URL address: **http://www.pitt.edu/~cjp/rees.html**

This is a directory of Internet resources listed by discipline. There are links to language, literature, music, art, culture, government and public affairs, education, business, history, geography, and so on. There are also links to national home pages and other major sites.

Russia—Moscow Kremlin Online Excursion

URL address: **http://www.kiae.su/www/wtr/kremlin/begin.html**

This online excursion was organized jointly by State Museums of the Moscow Kremlin, COMINFO Ltd., and Relcom Corp. It begins by letting you select links that you want to visit, such as Red Square or Cathedral Square, and goes from there. These materials are part of an on-going project to put Moscow Kremlin on CD-ROM.

Singapore

URL address: **http://www.ncb.gov.sg/sif/issues.html**

This newsletter is a publication of the Singapore International Foundation dedicated to increase and improve the interaction of Singapore and Singaporeans with the world. It covers lifestyle, events, and culture.

Slovakia—Cavern Stary Hrad

URL address: **http://www.tuke.sk/sh/sh-a.html**

This server allows you to go spelunking in the Caverns of Stary Hrad in Kosice, Slovakia. They were discovered in 1967 and are still bringing forth new discoveries. During this tour, you can almost feel what it's like to be in the caverns.

Slovenija

URL address: **http://www.ijs.si/slo.html**

The presentation of Slovenia is now spread over the J. Stefan Institute and the University of Maribor servers. Both now jointly offer general geographical, cultural, tourist, and other information about Slovenia and some hints about Slovenian wine and food recipes. Links to other WWW and Gopher servers in Slovenia, as well as links to online information and library services, are provided.

Turkey

URL address: **http://www.metu.edu.tr**

Located close to Ankara, the Middle East Technical University sponsors this WWW information and server. You find information about the university, as well as links to other resources in Turkey (most of the information is in Turkish).

Vatican Exhibit

URL address: **http://sunsite.unc.edu/expo/vatican.exhibit/ Vatican.exhibit.html**

Millions of pilgrims and tourists come to Rome every year. It holds treasures of architecture, art, and history. The Vatican Exhibit provides a connection to several links, a few of which include the Vatican library, archaeology, humanism, and orientation to Rome.

International Communication

International Marine Signal Flags

URL address: **http://155.187.10.12:80/flags/signal-flags.html**

Try the international marine signal flags character set to send useful messages. Strung end-to-end and hung from bow to stern from the rigging, they are also used to decorate the ship for festivities and ceremonies. The home page has GIF images of each flag.

People and Cultures

Aboriginal Studies Register

URL address: **http://coombs.anu.edu.au/WWWVL-Aboriginal.html**

This provider keeps track of information facilities of value and significance to researchers in the field of Aboriginal and Indigenous Peoples studies. It is sponsored via the Australian National University's Coombsweb.

Judaism and Jewish Resources

URL address: **http://www.acm.uiuc.edu/signet/JHSI/judaism.html**

This site has a rich source of links to information about Jewish resources. A few of them are a sensitive map (this is a visual interface to all the WWW and Gopher servers in Israel), the Shamash Project, Jerusalem One, the Hebrew calendar, Dead Sea Scrolls, and an introduction to Judaism.

Latin American Studies

URL address: **http://lanic.utexas.edu/las.html**

Visit this home page for links to studies of Latin America in general, Latin America related services, Argentina, Brazil, Bolivia, Chile, Colombia, Costa Rica, Ecuador, Mexico, Peru, Uruguay, and Venezuela. When you click a country name, you get a list of several servers/WWW documents that are either in the country or have information about the country.

Obituary Page

URL address: **http://catless.ncl.ac.uk/Obituary/README.html**

This site is a register of the names, dates, cause of death, and what they are well-known for, of people around the world who have died. You can register a death via this site or mail details for entry. Most of the names are provided by readers.

Vikings Home Page

URL address: **http://control.chalmers.se/vikings/viking.html**

This site contains lots of information about the Viking Age (793–1050), its native Vikings and culture, and a small Swedish-Viking-English dictionary. There are also links to information about the Vikings of Russia.

Publications

Complexity International

URL address: **http://life.anu.edu.au:80/ci/ci.html**

This is a research journal with an intent to make the publication entirely Web-based hypermedia. Contributions are invited.

▶ See "International Literature," p. 820

IKEDA Lab

URL address: **http://www.hike.te.chiba-u.ac.jp/**

Hirokai Ikeda and Yasuhiko Higaki announce a shared electronic publication of the IEC Standard 417 to the Internet on a trial basis, with permission of the Central Office of the International Electrotechnical Commission (IEC). The original paper-based publication from the IEC in Geneva has been reproduced as a hypertext with graphics in the Ikeda Laboratory. The standard is for graphical symbols for use on equipment. It has been maintained and will continue to be maintained and supplemented by the IEC SC3C, in accordance with the needs in the fields of electrotechnology.

International Teletimes

URL address: **http://www.wimsey.com/teletimes.root/ teletimes_home_page.html**

This site is a general interest magazine, published in Vancouver, Canada, and distributed all over the world. It covers a wide variety of subjects.

Mother Jones

URL address: **http://www.mojones.com/**

This magazine has grants available for documentary photographers. Check the classifieds, travel opportunities, surveys, internship opportunities, letters to the editor, views on politics, and more (see fig. 27.12).

VI

Finding Web Resources

Fig. 27.12
You can explore electronic versions of internationally focused Mother Jones dating back to 1993.

Science and Research

Athens High Performance Computing Laboratory
URL address: **http://www.hpcl.cti.gr/**

AHPCL is in Athens, Greece. It is a non-profit organization formed by the University of Athens, the National Technical University of Athens, and the Computer Technology Institute of the University of Patras, to do research and development in High Performance Computing and Networking (HPCN). The laboratory is the owner of a Parsytec GCel 3/512 massively parallel, 512-node computer, and this server focuses mainly on issues involving this machine and work done on it.

Australian National University Bioinformatics
URL address: **http://life.anu.edu.au:80/**

ANU's Bioinformatics facility provides hypermedia information on the Internet in a number of themes, including biodiversity, bioinformation, biomathematics, and complex systems.

Daresbury Laboratory
URL address: **http://www.dl.ac.uk/**

The Daresbury Laboratory is based near Warrington in northwest England. Its research facilities in 2 Ge V synchrotron radiation source; advanced computing facilities, including parallel computers; and RUSTI, the Research Unit for Surfaces, Transforms and Interfaces are made available to users from the UK and other countries.

Gemini 8m Telescopes Project
URL address: **http://www.gemini.edu/**

The project's goal is to build two telescopes, one on Mauna Kea, Hawaii, the other on Cerro Pachon, Chile. The scientific goal of these telescopes is to produce near-diffraction-limited images at infrared wavelengths. If that doesn't tell you enough, try some of the links to the "Scientific Specifications" or a "Gemini Newsletter." This is a great resource if you have an interest in telescopes.

Marine Research
URL address: **file://ua.nrb.ac.uk/pub/rvshome.html**

The purpose of Research Vessel Services is to provide support for marine research undertaken by the Natural Environment Research Council (NERC) supported scientists. This service is located in Barry, South Wales, and has links to several other sites, including the RVS mission statement, organization, resources, current research cruises, and other sites and images.

SRI International
URL address: **http://www.sri.com/**

Welcome to SRI International's WWW Server.

Fig. 27.13
SRI International is one of the largest research firms in the world. This home page can tell you more about the organization and its programs.

SRI International, formerly the Stanford Research Institute, has links to the following:

The Artificial Intelligence Center (AIC)

The Collaborative Environment for Concurrent Engineering Design (CECED) project

The Computer Science Laboratory (CSL)

The Virtual Perception Program

With more than 3,000 employees, offices in countries around the world, and revenues that exceed $300 million, SRI is one of the world's largest contract research firms. Its main operating groups are engineering research, science and technology, business and policy, and the David Sarnoff Research Center.

Sports and Recreation

Footbag Club
URL address: **http://gregorio.stanford.edu/footbag/**

This home page provides information on the international sport of footbag. Pick up information on events, festivals, tournaments, demos, and regular meetings.

> **Note**
>
> You find a more comprehensive list of sports-related Web sites in Chapter 32.

World Wide Web Server Summary

Following is a summary of some of the WWW servers located in countries around the world. The URL addresses represent computers/home pages that are good starting points for each country, although it should be noted that most countries have many more WWW servers and home pages than those listed here.

Many of these servers present information in the language of the nation, such as Japanese, Portugese, Norwegian, and so on. So prepare yourself for some of the same challenges that might present themselves if you were to travel to these countries.

> **Note**
>
> A listing after a URL address that states "(sensitive map)" is *not* part of the address. This is only a note to let you know that the server provides a graphic, hypermedia map of the country that has links to other WWW resources in the country.

Many of these pages have *sensitive maps*. There are three types of sensitive maps. One allows you to click any area of the map, at which point you go to a server or document that has information about that region. The map of Greece is an example of this type (see fig. 27.14).

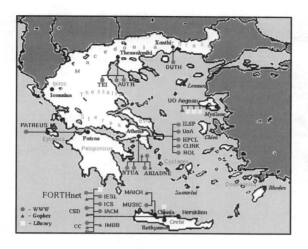

Fig. 27.14
This is the home page for the WWW sensitive map of Greece. When you click a specific area, such as the island of Crete, you travel to information about that location.

A second type of map brings up a map along with icons of general areas of interest, such as tourism or the economy, which take you again to a server or document that highlights those areas of interest. The sensitive map of Chile is an example (see fig. 27.15).

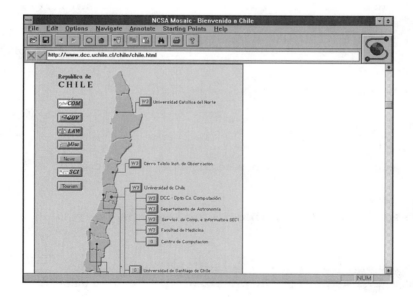

Fig 27.15
With this sensitive map of Chile you select an area of interest, such as Tourism, to learn about what the country has to offer.

VI

Finding Web Resources

A third type of map highlights and has links to specific WWW or Gopher servers at specific locations, such as a university or government office. The sensitive map of Israel provides an example (see fig. 27.16).

Fig. 27.16

The sensitive map of Israel lets you click areas that represent WWW or Gopher servers for specific institutions, such as the Tel-Aviv University.

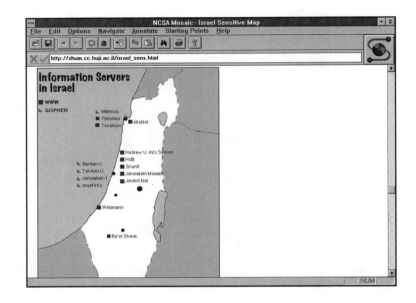

Africa

URL address: **http://osprey.unisa.ac.za/0/docs/south-africa/html**
URL address: **http://www.ru.ac.za**
URL address: **http://www.und.ac.za/prg/prg.html**

Antarctica

URL address: **http://icair.iac.org.nz**

Asia

China

URL address: **http://www.ihep.ac.cn/china_www.html**

Hong Kong

URL address: **http://www.cuhk.hk/hkwww.htm**

Japan

URL address: **http://www.ntt.jp/SQUARE/www-in-JP.html**
URL address: **http://www.ntt.jp/japan/map** (sensitive map)

Taiwan

URL address: **http://peacock.tnjc.edu.tw/ROC_sites.html**

Thailand (List of Web Sites)

URL address: **http://www.chiangmai.ac.th/Servers-th.html**

Australia and New Zealand

Australia

URL address: **http://www.csu.edu.au/education/australia.html**

New Zealand

URL address: **http://www.cs.cmu.edu:8001/Web/People/mjw/NZ/ MainPage.html**

Canada

URL address: **http://www.sal.ists.ca/services/w3_can/ www_index.html**

URL address: **http://www.sal.ists.ca/services/w3_can/ geographical.html**

Europe

Europe Overall

URL address: **http://s700.uminho.pt/europa.html**

Austria

URL address: **http://www.ifs.univie.ac.at/austria.html**

Belgium

URL address: **http://info1.vub.ac.be:8080/Belgium_map/index.html**

Croatia

URL address: **http://tjev.tel.etf.hr/hrvatska/prijava.html**

Czech Republic

URL address: **http://www.cesnet.cz:81/cesnet/cesnet-map.html**

Denmark

URL address: **http://www.dd.dk/Denmark**

URL address: **http://info.denet.dk/dk-infoservers.html**

URL address: **http://www.daimi.aau.dk/denmark.html**

Finland

URL address: **http://www.funet.fi/resources/map.html**

URL address: **http://www.cs.hut.fi/finland.html**

VI

Finding Web Resources

France

URL address: **http://web.urec.fr/docs/www_list_fr.html**

URL address: **http://web.urec.fr/france/france.html** (sensitive map)

Germany

URL address: **http://www.chemie.fu-berlin.de/outerspace/www-german.html**

Greece

URL address: **http://www.forthnet.gr/hellas/hellas.html** (sensitive map)

Hungary

URL address: **http://www.fsz.bme.hu/hu-infoservers.html**

Iceland

URL address: **http://www.rfisk.is/english/sites.html**

URL address: **http://www.isnet.is/WWW/servers.html**

Ireland

URL address: **http://itdsrv1.ul.ie/Information/IrishServerList.html**

Italy

URL address: **http://www.mi.cnr.it/NIR-IT/NIR-list.html** (by city)

URL address: **http://www.mi.cnr.it/NIR-IT/NIR-map.html** (sensitive map)

Netherlands

URL address: **http://www.eeb.ele.tue.nl/map/netherlands.html** (sensitive map)

Norway

URL address: **http://www.ii.uib.no/~magnus/norway.html**

URL address: **http://www.service.uit.no/homepage-no** (sensitive map)

Poland

URL address: **http://info.fuw.edu.pl/pl/servers-list.html**

URL address: **http://info.fuw.edu.pl/poland.html** (sensitive map)

Portugal

URL address: **http://s700.uminho.pt/Portugal/all-pt.html**

Slovakia

URL address: **http://www.tuzvo.sk/list.html**

Slovenia

URL address: **http://www.ijs.si/slo.html** (sensitive map)

Spain

URL address: **http://www.gae.unican.es/general/es-servers.html**
URL address: **http://www.uji.es/spain_www.html**

Sweden

URL address: **http://www.sunet.se/map/sweden.html** (sensitive map)

Switzerland

URL address: **http://www.math.ethz.ch/~zari/admin/chw3.html**
URL address: **http://heiwww.unige.ch/switzerland/** (sensitive map)

United Kingdom

URL address: **http://src.doc.ic.ac.uk/all-uk.html**
URL address: **http://www.cs.ucl.ac.uk/misc/uk/intro.html**

The Middle East

Israel

URL address: **http://shum.cc.huji.ac.il/israel_sens.html** (sensitive map)

Turkey

URL address: **http://www.bilkent.edu.tr/turkiye.html**
URL address: **http://www.metu.edu.tr/Turkey**

Mexico and Central America

Costa Rica

URL address: **http://ns.cr**

Mexico

URL address: **http://info.pue.udlap.mx/mexico.html**
URL address: **http://info.pue.udlap.mx/www-mex-eng.html** (sensitive map)

Russia and the Countries of the Former Soviet Union

Estonia
URL address: **http://www.eenet.ee/english.html**

Russia
URL address: **http://www.kiae.su/www/wtr/kremlin/begin.html**

South America

Argentina
URL address: **http://www.ar:70**

Brazil
URL address: **http://www.rnp.br/cern.html**

Chile
URL address: **http://www.dcc.uchile.cl/servers.html**
URL address: **http://www.dcc.uchile.cl/chile/chile.html** (sensitive map)

Equador
URL address: **http://mail.usfq.edu.ec/root.htm**

Peru
URL address: **http://www.rcp.net.pe/rcp.html**

United States of America
The Virtual Tourist: hypermedia map of the U.S. with links on individual states.

North America
URL address: **http://wings.buffalo.edu/world/na.html**

Alaska
URL address: **http://info.alaska.edu:70/1s/Alaska**

Hawaii
URL address: **http://www.eng.hawaii.edu/hawaiisvc.html**

From Here...

This chapter is a great starting place for your international electronic journeys. Many times, the sites for specific countries will open a "pot of gold" in terms of unexplored sites in that country or region of the world.

If you are planning a vacation or have other international interests, you might also want to reference the following chapters:

- Chapter 21, "Business and Finance," shows you where there are reviews of international sites which focus on business opportunities.

- Chapter 26, "History and Geography," contains sites about many different places and regions from around the world.

- Chapter 28, "Issues, Politics, Religion, and World Events," lists various interesting sites with an international focus.

- Chapter 29, "Publications: News, Periodicals, and Books," shows you where to find URL addresses for articles, books and newspapers that contain valuable information about foreign countries—and may be published in other countries.

- In Chapter 32, "Sports, Games, Hobbies, Travel, Cooking, and Recreation," you can check out some of the interactive travel guides in the travel section.

VI

Finding Web Resources

Chapter 28

Issues, Politics, Religion, and World Events

by Bill Eager

This chapter lists WWW resources that provide information about organizations, services, and events of a social nature. Perhaps the most noble use of communication technology is as an instrument of social change, whereby electronic data is transformed from bits and bytes to information that touches people's hearts and moves them to take action to improve the lives of other people—people who may live across the street or across the globe.

There is justifiable concern that only the well-to-do—those who can afford powerful computers and Internet connections—will take advantage of the technology and applications of a system like the World Wide Web, and that we will see the creation of a society of information haves and have-nots. Another scenario, however, envisions a different situation: information about organizations that help the have-nots reaches people who pitch in to help; and technology that reaches a broad audience through outlets such as libraries, schools, government facilities, and public information kiosks.

Several organizations focus their efforts on ensuring the useful development of communications technology. The Electronic Frontier Foundation, for example, lobbies for legislation that will ensure that individual rights mandated by the U.S. Constitution and Bill of Rights are protected with respect to new communications technologies and infrastructures.

The potential for the WWW to have a positive impact on the lives of individual citizens and on society in general is real. You can connect to a database at Columbia University to search for employment opportunities, jump to the Amnesty International home page and find out about human-rights conditions and issues in hundreds of countries (and how you can help), search through online images of missing children sponsored by the National Center for Missing and Exploited Children, or get practical environmental tips from the electronic version of *The Citizen's Handbook* on a Web site at the University of North Carolina.

Religion and religious organizations also have a presence on the Web. These home pages offer links to a variety of educational resources and social services.

Specific resources in this chapter are in the following categories:

- Children: resources for children and parents

- Crime: what's being done to reduce or prevent crime

- Employment: using the Web to get a job or improve your career

- Environmental Issues: organizations and information related to the environment

- Human Sexuality and Marriage: how to have safe sex and improve a marriage

- Law and Legal Resources: explaining the letter of the law from corporate mergers to copyrights

- Not-for-Profit Organizations: organizations that focus on helping people and improving society

- Philosophy: articles by and about famous philosophers

- Politics and Political Issues: topics ranging from the Clinton administration to politics in the United Kingdom

- Public Policy and World Events: international topics including food, education, and human rights

- Publications: electronic magazines that focus on international issues

- Religion: resources that focus on religious beliefs

Amnesty International

URL address: **http://www.igc.apc.org/igc/amnesty.html**
URL address: **gopher://gopher.igc.apc.org:70/11/orgs/ai**

Amnesty International

Fig. 28.1
The Amnesty
International
home page takes
you to resources
that focus on
global human
rights.

The famous Amnesty International logo—a candle wrapped in barbed wire—tells you a lot about this organization. Founded in 1961, Amnesty International focuses on issues and events that examine and improve human rights around the world. This Web and Gopher site offers links that provide information about the organization and its goals. You can get fact sheets, obtain an introductory brochure, or learn how to join the organization.

Other links and files take you to the specific information for which the organization is known, such as the Urgent Action Network, which issues calls to action when a person's life is in danger or when someone has disappeared, is being tortured, or is not receiving proper medical care. Click the link to Amnesty International Printed Reports and Documentation to bring up a searchable list of all documents, including country reports, the annual report, and reports on regions or issues. You can order any of these reports. The site also provides an electronic directory of Amnesty International offices and contact people around the world.

Legal Information Institute

URL address: **http://www.law.cornell.edu/lii.table.html**

The Legal Information Institute

Cornell Law School

Fig. 28.2
This home page is
a great resource if
you need to find
information about
the legal profes-
sion or specific
legal rulings.

VI

Finding Web Resources

You will enjoy this home page if you are in the legal profession, have ever used a lawyer, or simply are interested in the major legal rulings of our time. The Legal Information Institute connects the resources of the Cornell University Law School with the legal profession, other law schools, and the world via the Internet. All LII publications are electronic, and the LII created and owns the copyright on the Cello WWW browser.

From the home page, links go to a variety of hypertext documents, including Supreme Court decisions, issues related to civil rights, the U.S. Patent and Copyright acts, legal proceedings in U.S. and international cases, an e-mail directory of the faculty of all U.S. law schools, and links to international legal resources. You can perform keyword searches on many of the archives.

Click the Search U.S. Supreme Court Syllabi link to get an index that allows you to search all Supreme Court decisions archived at the Case Western Reserve FTP site (**ftp://ftp.cwru.edu**). The result of a search is a hypertext document that contains links to all the opinions in cases that relate to your search. If you search on the word *gun*, for example, you get a list of several cases, one being *Harold E. Staples, III, Petitioner v. United States* (May 23, 1994). You can learn that Justice Clarence Thomas delivered the opinion of the court, which states that the National Firearms Act makes it unlawful for any person to possess a machine gun that is not properly registered with the federal government.

You also can jump to other interesting legal resources, such as "German Legal Materials from the Juristisches Internetprojekt" (in German) and "South African Politics (including Constitution, Interim Flag, and Ballot)."

Jerusalem Mosaic

URL address: **http://www1.huji.ac.il/jeru/jerusalem.html**

Fig. 28.3
When you jump to this home page, you can take an interactive tour of the sights and sounds of Jerusalem.

Travel to Israel and take this wonderful guided tour of Jewish history and religion, which dates back some 4,000 years. Jerusalem Mosaic is a guided tour that gives you the impression that you are actually visiting this great city, the capital of the state of Israel. Many monuments here are associated with great biblical figures.

From this home page, you can see the site of the mystic hill city (Jerusalem) founded in the third millennium B.C., as well as the Urusalim, which appears in pottery inscriptions at the beginning of the second millennium. You also can listen to the "Song of Jerusalem" or view maps, paintings, and photographs of the city.

The tour combines many forms of media in an interactive tour. You travel through an assortment of gates to look at and read about different parts of the city. The gates offer categories of images, including faces, maps, paintings, and views. Several aerial photographs give you a unique perspective. This passage describes the type of images that you will view: "We peek into the different neighborhoods and observe the roofs, squares, streets, and gardens, along with the numerous historical buildings which beautify the city."

Other home-page links connect you with information on major events in the history of Jerusalem, more information about the city, and other Web servers in Israel.

Jobnet

URL address: **http://sun.cc.westga.edu:80/~coop/localhome.html**

Getting a job can be a little easier with the help of this WWW server. The home page represents a collection of employment resources and job leads collected from the WWW, UseNet news, and list servers. You can access information about employment trends, statistics, and career opportunities.

Jobnet also provides links to several employment services and organizations that list jobs, such as Academe This Week from the *Chronicle of Higher Education*, the Academic Position Network, the On-Line Career Center, and government databases that list federal employment opportunities. Frequently, the links connect with Gopher servers, which you then navigate through submenus until you find specific descriptions of job openings.

Children

Adolescence

URL address: **http://galaxy.einet.net/galaxy/Community/The-Family/Adolescence.html**

Having difficulty communicating with your teenager? Or are you a teenager? This WWW site offers information on the subject of parenting teenagers, as well as links to information for teenagers.

Children and Education
URL address: **http://galaxy.einet.net/galaxy/Community/
The-Family/Children.html**

◀ See "Educa-
tional Re-
sources,"
p. 600

This Web home page has links to information about a variety of aspects of
childhood. For educational purposes, the site offers poems, stories, songs, and
activities. Also available is information about the problem of child abuse.

Florida Health Baby Hotline
URL address: **http://freenet3.scri.fsu.edu:81/ht-free/fhbaby.html**

Whether you are about to become a parent for the first time or are having a
second or third child, this WWW site offers useful information. The site provides links to information about prenatal care, breast-feeding, and keeping
babies healthy.

GEMS: Missing Kids
URL address: **http://www.gems.com/kids/index.html**

This server allows you to view images from the Missing Children Database. If
you discover information about any of these children, you can contact the
National Center for Missing and Exploited Children at (800) THE-LOST.

Home Schooling
URL address: **http://www.armory.com/~jon/hs/HomeSchool.html**

If you have a living room, you have a classroom. Home schooling is becoming a popular method of educating children. From this home page, you can
access home-schooling resource lists by state and special interest, historical
documents, and electronic books. The site also has links to ERIC (the Educational Resources Information Center) and OERI INet, a Gopher run by the
U.S. Department of Education that offers information and free educational
software.

Infants
URL address:**http://galaxy.einet.net/galaxy/Community/
The-Family/Infants.html**

The information on this Web page begins with material on prenatal care. You
can access links to resources and documents on issues of infant care, such as
the dangers of pesticides and lead poisoning, as well as advice on nutrition
and day care.

Missing Children Database and Forum

URL address: **http://www.scubed.com:8001/public_service/missing.html**

Now on the Internet, this database contains information about and pictures of children who are missing. The database is maintained by the National Center for Missing and Exploited Children.

Phone Friend

URL address: **http://freenet3.scri.fsu.edu:81/ht-free/phfriend.html**

Does your child get lonely, scared, or bored when he or she is home alone after school? This Web site has information about a telephone service that is a companion to children who live in the Tallahassee area. Parents will be happy to learn that Phone Friend supports and makes children feel confident about taking care of themselves when they must be alone.

Plugged In

URL address: **http://www.pluggedin.org**

Fig. 28.4
The Plugged In page offers information and tips on educational opportunities in low-income communities.

The home page explains, "Plugged In is a non-profit group dedicated to bringing the educational opportunities created by new technologies to children and families from low-income communities." The links help teachers and community workers by providing overviews of educational projects and resources.

Teaching Parenting

URL address: **http://joe.uwex.edu/joe/1993fall/iw5.html**

This WWW home page describes a program that distributes educational materials to parents of young children. The program, supported by McDonald's restaurants, is in effect in several Ohio counties. The information at this site may inspire other communities to begin similar programs.

Crime

Center for Innovative Computer Applications

URL address: **http://www.cica.indiana.edu/projects/Police/index.html**

This Web site offers information about how computers help the Indiana State Police solve crimes. Learn how photographic images taken at the crime scene are digitized and enhanced with computer technology.

Center to Prevent Handgun Violence

URL address: **http://www.psych.nwu.edu/biancaTroll/lolla/politics/handguns/handgun.html**

This not-for-profit organization is dedicated to the prevention of gun violence. The organization works with as many resources as possible to prevent further bloodshed. This page has several links, including one that jumps to a letter from Sarah Brady.

Employment

CareerMosaic

URL address: **http://www.careermosaic.com/cm/home.html**

Fig. 28.5
CareerMosaic can help you find a new job or learn skills for a better job.

If you need a job or a career, this site may provide assistance. *PC Week's Lab* magazine voted CareerMosaic one of the best commercial sites on the Web. You can access an indexed, searchable database of job opportunities. Some of the job listings come from 22 UseNet .jobs newsgroups. A search for *television*, for example, produced 32 job opportunities in the field of broadcasting. Another link takes you to a library with text files that offer advice on career management and job hunting.

Employment Opportunities and Resume Postings
URL address: **http://galaxy.einet.net/GJ/employment.html**

This server provides a comprehensive list of links to educational, government, and private-sector job opportunities. Most of the sites listed are Gopher sites with documents that describe positions.

Employment Resources
URL address: **http://alpha.acast.nova.edu/employment.html**

This Web page has links to the following resources, which focus on employment opportunities: Academic Position Network, *Chronicle of Higher Education*, Employment Opportunities (EINet Galaxy), ESPAN's Interactive Employment Network, MedSearch America, Online Career Center, Job Banks (University of Texas at Austin), Job Banks (Latino network), and Jobs in Federal Government.

Engineering Employment Expo
URL address: **http://stimpy.cen.uiuc.edu/comm/expo/**

Fig. 28.6
This Web site provides information about an annual job fair in which more than 100 companies provide information about employment opportunities.

Sponsored by students in the Engineering Council of the University of Illinois (Urbana–Champaign), this job fair allows students and members of the community to meet with representatives of more than 100 companies to obtain information about summer and permanent employment opportunities. Links on the home page tell you how to get involved. The site also provides a list of companies that attend the job fair; some of the company names are links to the Web servers of those companies.

ESPAN
URL address: **http://www.espan.com**

ESPAN is the home page for the interactive employment network. Use the links to view a salary guide, visit a career fair, or post your résumé for the world to see. The site also provides useful tips for job seekers on writing résumés and conducting interviews.

Interest Groups
URL address: **http://alpha.acast.nova.edu/cgi-bin/news-lists.pl/jobs**

This site offers the network mailing lists of several UseNet newsgroups. Get the latest scoop about jobs in Israel; American jobs and grants; openings in specific areas, such as libraries, physics, and television; classes and seminars; volunteers; and employment issues.

International Employment Listings
URL address: **gopher://sun.cc.westga.edu:70/1/coop/JobNet/**

You can search this server for international jobs by subject area, including corporate, education, government, science, and social services.

Job Board
URL address: **http://www.io.org/~jwsmith/jobs.html**

This site provides a daily listing of jobs that are represented by recruiters. Most of the jobs are international and in the computer and information-sciences fields.

Monster Board
URL address: **http://www.monster.com**

Great name for a job resource right? This site has job announcements for people with computer and technical backgrounds. There are profiles of jobs and of the companies that offer them. You can fill out a form and include your résumé, and the staff of the Monster Board will pass them on to the recruiters at the companies. Typically there are more than 500 jobs available.

Résumé Server

URL address: **http://ibd.ar.com/Resume/**

This site provides a long list of hypertext résumés. There is no charge to list and read these résumés, which generally are a couple of pages long and include a date stamp that tells you when the person put his or her résumé on the system.

Environmental Issues

Center for Renewable Energy and Sustainable Technology

URL address: **http://solstice.crest.org/common/crestinfo.html**

This Web server provides links to documents, exhibits, and resources about renewable energy, energy efficiency, and energy issues. The site offers files about the use of photovoltaics in Switzerland and Indonesia, an illustrated report on nonmotorized vehicles, and a quarterly newsletter.

▶ See "Environmental Sciences," p. 858

Citizen's Handbook of North Carolina's Environmental Information Sources

URL address: **http://sunsite.unc.edu/nc/nc_env_handbook/ home.html**

The Citizen's Handbook is an electronic version of a guide which addresses a wide range of environmental issues that affect the state. Topics covered in this electronic version of the handbook include agriculture, soil, air-quality, resources, energy, and hazardous materials. Learn how to dispose of pesticides, where to purchase organic farming supplies, and what the dangers of radon are. The hypertext document (also available in hard-copy form) also lists governmental and nongovernmental information sources.

Cygnus Group

URL address: **http://garnet.msen.com:70/1/vendor/cygnus/ULS**

This environmental and educational Web server includes the ULS (Use Less Stuff) newsletter, which contains articles about product packaging, waste reduction and recycling, laser-printer cartridges, compact fluorescent light bulbs, and other topics. Pointers go to other environmental and educational Web databases.

Energy Efficient Housing in Canada

URL address: **http://web.cs.ualberta.ca/~art/house/**

If only we could build our homes in such a manner that they take full advantage of the sun's heat during the cold season and the cooling shade of trees when it's hot outdoors. This site provides links to information about energy-efficient home construction. This information is useful for people who are building new homes and for people who are remodeling existing structures.

Environmental Resource Center

URL address: **http://ftp.clearlake.ibm.com/ERC/HomePage.html**

This Web site offers information for consumers who are interested in environmentalism. The center, which is a cooperative effort between private industry and government, focuses on the collection and distribution of information about environmentally positive activities.

The EnviroWeb

URL address: **http://envirolink.org/start_web.html**

Fig. 28.7
Visit the EnviroWeb home page if you want to learn about "green" companies or to get ideas about environmental efforts for your own home.

This Web site provides several links to sources of information on the environment, as well as methods of adding new documentation to the EnviroWeb. You can, for example, go to the EnviroProducts Directory for a list of "green" products, services, and businesses, or you can jump to the Virtual Environmental Library, which the home page describes as being "the most comprehensive clearinghouse of environmental information available in electronic format."

The EnviroLink Network's staff not only gathers information from other online resources, but also works with organizations, governments, and private citizens to put useful information and ideas on the Internet.

Jalan Hijau: 40 Tips To Go Green

URL address: **http://www.ncb.gov.sg/jkj/env/greentips.html**

Jalan Hijau is a Singapore-based environmental group. This site is an electronic version of a flier, "40 Tips to Go Green," which the group initially distributed during Earth Day 1992. The publication contains tips for use at home, on the road, while you're shopping, and at work, as well as an address to which you can write for more information.

National Environmental Scorecard

URL address: **http://www.econet.apc.org/lcv/scorecard.html**

This Web site provides information about the environmental voting records of U.S. senators and representatives. One link displays the changes brought about in environmental politics and describes the work that remains to be done.

Rocky Mountain Institute

URL address: **http://www.infosphere.com/aspen/rockymtn/ rmi_Homepage.html**

Learn about this non-profit institute which focuses on seven different areas (and there are links to each), including energy, water, economic renewal, agriculture, global security, green development, and transportation.

Sierra Club

URL address: **http://www.sierraclub.org/**

Fig. 28.8
The Sierra Club home page offers links to information about the organization as well as to other Web sites that focus on the environment.

This is the home page for this international organization devoted to the environment. It includes links to the history, local club chapters, member information and an application form, and a hypertext version of *The Planet*, the Sierra Club news magazine.

Human Sexuality and Marriage

Marriage

URL address: **http://galaxy.einet.net/galaxy/Community/
The-Family/Marriage.html**

Just what is marriage, and how does it relate to the family? This site provides
links to information about the history of marriage, separation and divorce,
child custody, same-sex marriages, and related topics.

Mortality Attributable to HIV Infection

URL address: **http://herbst7.his.ucsf.edu/Issue1/
AIDSmort1992.html**

This site offers updated data from the National Vital Statistics System that
was obtained from death certificates filed in all 50 states and the District of
Columbia.

Preventing HIV and AIDS

URL address: **http://bianca.com/lolla/politics/aids/**

◀ See "AIDS
Issues,"
p. 698
This site provides extensive links to information related to HIV and AIDS.
Much of the information is from the U.S. Center for Disease Control. The site
also provides a link to the AIDS Parlor, where you can add your own comments and read what other users wrote.

Queer Resources Directory

URL address: **http://vector.casti.com/QRD/.html/
QRD-home-page.html**

This resource page for gays and lesbians includes newsletters from chapters of
the Gay and Lesbian Alliance Against Defamation, information about the Gay
Games, and other information on such issues as gays in the military and
religion.

Law and Legal Resources

Copyright

URL address: **gopher://wiretap.spies.com/11/Gov/Copyright**

This Gopher site offers several documents that explain how U.S. copyright
law works.

Corporate Law

URL address: **http://www.law.uc.edu/CCL**

The Center for Corporate Law at the University of Cincinnati's College of Law maintains this WWW server, which contains data that assists lawyers in the practice of corporate and securities law. You can, for example, learn about the Public Utilities Holding Company Act of 1935 or the Securities Investor Protection Act of 1970.

Federal Communications Law Journal

URL address: **http://www.law.indiana.edu/fclj/fclj.html**

The Indiana University School of Law maintains this home page, which allows you to perform a full text search of all back issues. You also can read the publication online.

Federal Crime Control Bill

URL address: **http://broadway.vera.org/pub/crimebill/cb.html**

You may recall the news coverage of this bill when it was passed in 1994. This site offers links to information about all 33 titles of the bill.

Merger Policy

URL address: **http://www.vanderbilt.edu/Owen/froeb/merger/ hmpp.html**

A merger is two big companies getting together. This site explains the concept of mergers in much greater detail. Links are available to information on merger cases, guidelines, statutory merger law, mergers in the news, and research issues.

Patent Law

URL address: **http://town.hall.org/patent/patent.html**

If you invent something, you may want to protect your rights with a patent. This site provides links to material that explains U.S. patent law. You can even search a patent database to see whether your idea has already been patented.

Self-Help Law

URL address: **http://www.digital.com/gnn/bus/nolo/**

This site provides some interesting articles, reports, and even jokes to help people who want (or need) to deal with legal issues without legal representation.

Westlaw

URL address: **gopher://wld.westlaw.com**

Westlaw is a searchable database of more than 675,000 law firms, branch offices, and specific lawyers across the nation. You can get addresses, phone numbers, and contact names from this database. Be as specific as possible in your search; a search for *Denver*, for example, retrieves 200 listings.

Not-for-Profit Organizations

ACLU (American Civil Liberties Union)

URL address: **gopher://pipeline.com:70/11/society/aclu**

The American Civil Liberties Union fights for individuals' rights and regularly litigates cases that relate to First Amendment rights and other issues. The Gopher site offers newsletters, speeches, legislative alerts, and Supreme Court rulings. The site also tells you how to order ACLU publications and how to join the organization.

Computer Professionals for Social Responsibility

URL address: **http://www.cpsr.org/home**

This public-interest organization focuses on the effects of computers on society, covering topics that involve computers, freedom, and privacy. You can browse through reports and publications. Hot topics include technologies such as Caller ID and the Clipper chip security system.

Electronic Frontier Foundation

URL address: **http://www.eff.org**

The Electronic Frontier Foundation focuses on ensuring that individual rights mandated by the U.S. Constitution and Bill of Rights are protected with respect to new communications technologies and infrastructures. This home page provides information about the organization and its activities.

Florida Mental Health Institute

URL address: **http://hal.fmhi.usf.edu**

This home page provides information on the institute's research, training, and demonstration programs in Florida. The site provides links to publications (such as "An Overview of Judicial Enforcement of the Fair Housing Amendments Act of 1988") and other resources.

Foundation for National Progress

URL address: **http://www.mojones.com/masthead.html**

Founded in 1975, this organization focuses on educating and empowering people for progressive change. FNP publishes *Mother Jones* magazine and administers Mother Jones reporting internships.

Global Fund for Women

URL address: **http://www.ai.mit.edu/people/ellens/gfw.html**

The Global Fund for Women is an international grant-making organization with the mission "to provide funds to seed, strengthen, and link groups that are committed to women's well-being...." This home page has links that fill you in on the activities of this non-profit organization. You might start with a link to a set of frequently asked questions. And there is a link to information about applying for a grant.

GURUKUL: The Teacher's Family

URL address: **http://www.acsu.buffalo.edu/~naras-r/gurukul.html**

This home page is operated by GURUKUL, an organization founded by a group of students. The server and the organization promote rural education in India and the Third World. The focus on education begins with literacy and housing issues.

INFACT's Tobacco Industry Campaign

URL address: **http://sunsite.unc.edu/boutell/infact/infact.html**

The smoking issue seems to have only two sides: for and against. This Web site helps you learn the answers to questions such as, "What are the effects of secondhand smoke?" and "Why are certain tobacco companies being boycotted?" The focus is on reducing the marketing of tobacco to children and young people around the world.

Mother Jones: Mojo Interactive

URL address: **http://www.mojones.com/mojo_interactive/
mojo_interactive.html**

This page is part of the Mother Jones Web site. It provides links to articles and information on important social issues like creating economic opportunity, curbing violence in America, and making democracy work. Further links take you directly to non-profit organizations that deal with these issues.

National Charities Information Bureau Standards

URL address: **http://www.ai.mit.edu/people/ellens/Non/ncib.html**

The links on this WWW home page can help you evaluate the governance, policy, and program fundamentals of various national charities.

National Child Rights Alliance

URL address: **http://www.ai.mit.edu/people/ellens/NCRA/ncra.html**

NCRA is the only national organization directed entirely by child and adult survivors of abuse and neglect. Child abuse involves not only physical abuse, rape, and murder, but also deprivation of safety, food, medical care, and shelter by society at large. This home page provides links to documents and resources on these topics.

National Rifle Association

URL address: **http://www.nra.org**

The National Rifle Association provides information about gun ownership, safety, and legislative issues.

Philosophy

American Philosophical Gopher

URL address: **gopher://apa.oxy.edu**

This site provides information on the association, a philosophical calendar, grants, calls for papers, books, and images.

File Room

URL address: **http://fileroom.aaup.uic.edu/FileRoom/documents/homepage.html**

Produced by the Randolph Street Gallery in Chicago, this home page offers an illustrated archive on censorship. You'll find everything from a definition of censorship to case studies to anticensorship resources.

Philosophy on the Web
URL address: **http://www.phil.ruu.nl/philosophy-sites.html**

The title of this page says it all. There's nothing fancy here—just about 150 links to Web sites, Gopher sites, electronic journals, and college departments that focus on philosophy.

Philosophy: The American Philosophical Association
URL address: **http://english-server.hss.cmu.edu/Philosophy.html**

This server is a definitive resource for people who are interested in philosophy. You can find out about the American Philosophical Association or read articles by or about great philosophers: Aristotle, Bacon, Descartes, Kant, Locke, and Nietzsche, to name a few. The files are large, so you'll want to download them to your hard drive to read later.

Politics and Political Issues

Anarchy List
URL address: **http://www.cwi.nl/cwi/people/Jack.Jansen/**
anarchy/anarchy.html

the Anarchy List

Fig. 28.9
Anarchy—the word itself almost sounds dangerous. Go to this home page to find out more.

This site offers a mailing list and archive of postings regarding anarchy as a structure for society.

Central Intelligence Agency
URL address: **http://www.ic.gov**

No secrets here. Browse through links that tell you about CIA personnel, the history of the organization (including activities such as involvement in the Cuban Missile Crisis), and an aerial photograph of CIA headquarters.

◀ See "Department of Justice," p. 683

VI

Finding Web Resources

Electronic Democracy Information Network

URL address: **gopher://garnet.berkeley.edu:1250/11**

Information at this Gopher site is designed to increase awareness of events and resources that will have a positive effect on everything from revitalization of inner-city communities to the creation of a global peacetime economy.

Government, Law, and Society

URL address: **http://english-server.hss.cmu.edu/Govt.html**

How does the world of politics affect our everyday lives? Visit this server and find out. The site provides everything from an overview of Democratic and Republican party platforms to information about Ross Perot's book *United We Stand*. Read speeches, campaign stories, and political documents that tie the efforts of politicians to education, jobs, the environment, and feminist issues.

Political Participation Project

URL address: **http://www.ai.mit.edu/projects/ppp/home.html**

From the Massachusetts Institute of Technology, this page is designed to help cybersurfers get involved. Jump to a summary of political activity on the Net, a directory of grassroots organizations, and articles about the political process.

Politics in the U.K.

URL address: **http://ah.soas.ac.uk/LD/Home.html**

This page shows that politics is not strictly an American phenomena. Read election leaflets or find out about European elections.

rec.guns

URL address: **http://sal.cs.uiuc.edu/rec.guns/**

Links on this home page take you to information about types of guns; gun safety, terminology, and acronyms; the National Rifle Association; and the constitutional right to keep and bear arms. Visit this site if you are thinking about buying a gun either for sport or safety. You will learn both your rights and responsibilities as a gun owner. Much of the information is collected from gun newsgroups.

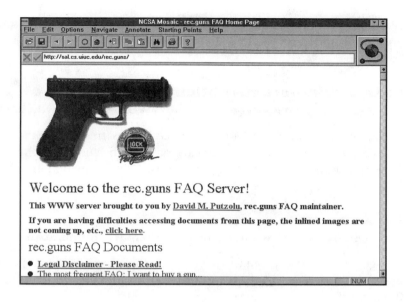

Fig. 28.10
The large icon of a gun on this home page tells you immediately that the site provides links to information about owning and using guns.

Right Side of the Web

URL address: **http://www.clark.net/pub/jeffd/index.html**

This page is for anyone who is—or wants to be—conservative. For starters, try the links to the Contract with America, the Rush Limbaugh information pages, and the Newt Gingrich fan club.

Public Policy and World Events

Crisis in Rwanda

URL address: **http://www.intac.com/PubService/rwanda/**

A plane crash on April 6, 1994 that killed the presidents of Rwanda and Burundi began the now tragic, bloody civil war. This Web site contains information and documents about relief organizations, war statistics, and human-rights issues, as well as maps of the vicinity and reports on current activities.

Food Gatherers

URL address: **http://garnet.msen.com:70/1/causes/fgs**

Food Gatherers, a food service serving Washtenaw County, Michigan, provides hunger-related and food-rescue information at this site. Information

VI

Finding Web Resources

available includes the text of *Keeping It out of the Dump*, which includes some history of food resources if you're interested in starting or joining a food-rescue group.

Fourth World Documentation Project

URL address: **ftp://ftp.halcyon.com/pub/FWDP/WWW/fwdp.html**

Organized by the Center for World Indigenous Studies, this FTP site maintains archives of more than 300 documents on "Fourth World" nations (countries with the very lowest living standards). The information includes essays, position papers, United Nations documents, and speeches.

Global Change

URL address: **http://www.ciesin.org/TG/thematic-home.html**

This page provides links to guides that focus on the human aspect of global change. These reference materials are organized in subject areas such as agriculture, health, land use, ozone depletion, and politics.

Graduate Institute of International Studies

URL address: **http://heiwww.unige.ch:80/**

This site provides information on subjects that include international history and politics, economics, and law. The site also offers a variety of interesting publications, such as *Ten Years of Turbulence: The Chinese Cultural Revolution* and *World Financial Markets*.

Human Dimensions Research Programs and Global Environmental Change

URL address: **http://www.ciesin.org/TG/HDP/HDP-home.html**

The name of this server is a mouthful, but the resources that it provides are timely and global. The focus is on information and research efforts that help people understand and make positive changes in the global condition, in terms of environmental, social, and political issues.

Human Rights

URL address: **http://www.idt.unit.no/~isfit/human.rights.html**

The site contains links to an enormous amount of information about human rights and related issues. Speeches about peace and human rights by the Dalai Lama and Taslima Nasrin are available. There is also a link to the U.S. State Department's 1994 Annual Report on Human Rights.

HumPop and IntlPop

URL address: **http://geosim.cs.vt.edu/huip.html**

This Web site offers two multimedia tutorial programs: HumPop, which enables you to interact with a population-change simulation program; and IntlPop, which allows you to simulate population growth.

HungerWeb

URL address: **http://www.hunger.brown.edu/hungerweb/**

The home page begins, "In the 5 minutes you spend surfing through the HungerWeb more than 120 children will die because of hunger....What are we going to do about it?" This site offers several links to information that addresses the seemingly insurmountable issue of hunger, which plagues about one-fifth of the people on this planet.

Institute for Global Communications

URL address: **http://www.igc.apc.org/**

The header on the home page accurately describes this site: "Your one-stop guide to progressive organizations and resources." There are links which clearly organize social issues. One link to "the issues" brings up a new page with links to everything from animal rights to water issues. The publications link opens a page that offers further links to Web sites that have articles about social issues. Finally, a link to a directory of organizations brings up a huge hypertext list of non-profit groups.

Institute for Social Studies

URL address: **http://andante.iss.uw.edu.pl/issgen.html**

Located at the University of Warsaw in Poland, this WWW server focuses on social topics and provides both English and Polish documents. One example is a *Warsaw Voice* article called "Foxes and Hedgehogs," which addresses the effect of age, sex, marital status, and residence on the psychological condition of Poles. You'll be amazed to learn that in most Western countries, age accounts for 4 percent of cases of depression, whereas in Poland, the figure is as high as 43 percent.

International Institute for Sustainable Development

URL address: **http://www.iisd.ca/linkages/index.html**

The IISD publishes the Earth Negotiations Bulletin. This home page is a clearinghouse for information on international meetings related to the global environment and development. You can jump to resources about the International Conference on Population Development in Cairo, a gallery of photos, and the Earth Negotiations Bulletin.

PeaceNet Home Page

URL address: **http://www.igc.apc.org/igc/pn.html**

This not-for-profit organization's Web site deals with human rights. The organization collects current information about related issues and assists in the effective communication and cooperation of human-rights communities throughout the world.

Planet Earth

URL address: **http://white.nosc.mil/info.html**

This site is a monster! The home page provides links to many WWW resources; if you don't have a lot of RAM, load the text version or disable inline graphics. The Community Resource links are quite good. You can, for example, get a listing of the environmental voting records for legislators by state (the National Environmental Scorecard).

Population Research Institute

URL address: **http://info.pop.psu.edu**

The Population Research Institute supports population research at Pennsylvania State University. The server offers working papers from the Association of Population Centers, rural-center bibliographies, information on North Carolina's rural-aging program, and information on Penn State's Center on Aging and Health in Rural America.

Population Studies Center

URL address: **http://www.psc.lsa.umich.edu/**

Fig. 28.11
How does global population affect society? Visit the Population Studies Center home page to find out.

Population Studies Center - *University of Michigan*

The PSC sponsors research and training programs. From the University of Michigan, this home page points to global demographic information, such as health, fertility, labor-force characteristics, and migration. You can browse through abstracts of publications on these and other subjects.

Public Policy Education

URL address: **http://joe.uwex.edu/joe/1993winter/tp1.html**

This site provides a short article about public policy called "The Need of an Informed Populace to Make Wise Public Policy."

Social Science Information Gateway

URL address: **http://sosig.esrc.bris.ac.uk/**

Located at the University of Bristol in the United Kingdom, this server enables you to search for specific social-science resources on the WWW. The topics are broad, ranging from feminism to politics to social welfare. Each topic takes you to more documents. If you select feminism, for example, you can open a file that contains biographies of 500 famous women.

World Summit for Social Development

URL address: **http://www.iisd.ca/linkages/topics/10topice.html**

This home page provides details about preparations for and events of the annual World Summit for Social Development, which was created by United Nations Resolution 47/92. The goal is to alleviate and reduce poverty, expand employment, and enhance social integration on a global scale.

Publications

American Employment Weekly

URL address: **http://branch.com:1080**

This Web site features information about the publication *American Employment Weekly,* which contains help-wanted ads in job categories that include accounting, banking, data processing, engineering, human resources, manufacturing, and sales.

ANSWERS

URL address: **http://www.service.com/answers/cover.html**

Subtitled *The Magazine for Adult Children of Aging Parents,* this publication is written for anyone who faces questions, issues, and concerns related to having an aging parent. The magazine covers aspects of taking care of an elderly parent, including how to deal with the emotional aspects and where to get help if you need it. The Web site offers sample articles and a subscription form.

VI

Finding Web Resources

Fig. 28.12
This is the home page for ANSWERS, a magazine for people who have aging parents.

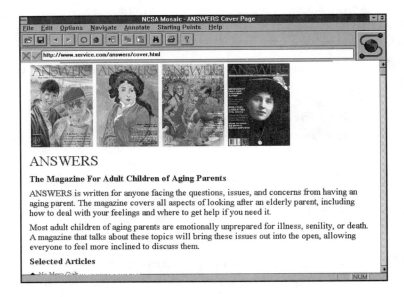

National Health Security Plan Table of Contents
URL address: **http://sunsite.unc.edu/nhs/NHS-T-o-C.html**

This site provides the complete executive summary and all supporting documents of the National Health Security Plan.

Prison Legal News
URL address: **http://www.ai.mit.edu/people/ellens/PLN/pln.html**

This site provides an electronic version of a monthly newsletter published and edited by prisoners in Washington state. The publication's motto, "Working to Extend Democracy to All," speaks of the prisoners' desire to uphold their rights in the judicial system. A sample copy and subscriptions are available.

Taxing Times 1995
URL address: **http://www.scubed.com:8001/tax/tax.html**

This Taxing Times information server now has more than 450 of the 750 Internal Revenue Service tax forms, instructions, and publications online. State forms for California and New Jersey also are available. Many of the forms are available as PostScript and TIFF files, and all the forms are free.

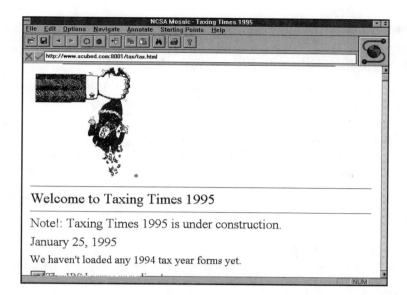

Fig. 28.13
Doing your taxes
is never easy, but
this Web site offers
online information
and tax forms that
may make the
process a little less
painful.

Religion

Baha'i Faith

URL address: **http://herald.usask.ca/~maton/bahai.html**

Information about The Baha'i Faith

Select any of the items below...

Fig. 28.14
The Baha'i faith is
one of the world's
major religions,
and this Web page
offers links to
information for
education and
worship.

Although a large percentage of Americans don't know about the Baha'i faith, it is one of the world's major religions. This home page provides background information and resources for study and worship.

Bethany Christian Services

URL address: **http://www.bethany.org/bethany/what_we_do.html**

This home page provides information on a variety of social services, with a focus on Christianity.

VI

Finding Web Resources

Bhagavad Gita

URL address: **http://www.cc.gatech.edu/gvu/people/Phd/ Rakesh.Mullick/gita/gita.html**

This server provides the complete hypertext version of this important religious document.

Catholic Resources

URL address: **http://www.cs.cmu.edu:8001/Web/People/spok/ catholic.html**

This home page provides a list of hyperlinks to other Catholic resources on the Web.

Christian Musicians

URL address: **http://csclub.uwaterloo.ca/u/gjhurlbu/ccm.html**

This large Web page offers GIF images of many Christian musicians and some information about their work.

Christian Resource List

URL address: **http://saturn.colorado.edu:8080/Christian/list.html**

This home page has numerous pointers to Christian resources and organizations, as well as four online Bibles, devotionals, history and culture, documents, and newsgroups.

Global Jewish Networking

URL address: **http://www.huji.ac.il/www_jewishn/www/t01.html**

This home page offers a tremendous number of Jewish resources, including libraries, catalogs, WWW servers, reading lists, information about the Holocaust, conferences, and software resources.

Judaism and Jewish Resources

URL address: **http://sleepless.acm.uiuc.edu/signet/JHSI/ judaism.html**

You'll find a variety of interesting Jewish resources at this site, including a link to the Israel touch-screen map—a visual interface to all WWW and Gopher servers in Israel, Jewish mailing lists, and newsgroups. The site also provides links to companies that provide Jewish goods and services.

Orthodox Christian Page in America

URL address: **http://www.york.ac.uk/~em101/Orthodox.html**

URL address: **http://nikon.ssl.berkeley.edu/~dv/orthodox/Orthodox.html**

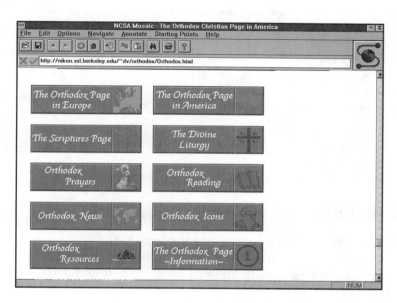

Fig. 28.15
Orthodox Christians can find many resources at this home page.

This Web site offers numerous resources for orthodox Christians ranging from the Mount Athhos Greek Manuscripts Catalog to icons, prayers, songs, and the Divine Liturgy.

Religion Database

URL address: **http://schiller.wustl.edu/DACLOD/daclod/id=00076.dcl**

This site is a true smorgasbord of hyperlinks to religious information, offering links to Jewish music and art, the Baha'i faith, Islam, Mormonism, and even a horoscope system.

Religion Page

URL address: **http://hakatai.mcli.dist.maricopa.edu/smc/ml/religion.html**

This home page is a great resource for people who are interested in learning about many religions. Links are available to documents, books, bibliographies, and other WWW religion servers that include information on

Buddhism, Christianity, Confucianism, Hinduism, Islam, Judaism, Native American religions, Taoism, shamanism, and religions of India.

Religious Society of Friends

URL address: **http://www.uidaho.edu:80/~norum933/quaker/**

This site is the home page for the Society of Friends, commonly known as the Quakers. The page contains information about the society and its meetings.

Taoism

URL address: **htt://www.cnu.edu/~patrick/taoism.html**

This site offers a great deal of information about Taoism, including electronic versions of the *Tao Te Ching* translations, a copy of Sun Tzu's *The Art of War,* and pointers to other WWW resources on Taoism.

From Here...

The social issues of the world are broad and complex. The WWW now offers a unique opportunity for private citizens and organizations to get involved in making the world a better place. You may want to follow up your studies by reading the following chapters:

■ Chapter 27, "International Web Resources," lists links to hundreds of Web sites in other countries.

■ Chapter 29, "Publications: News, Periodicals, and Books," offers a comprehensive listing of magazines, newspapers, and college publications that frequently address social issues.

Chapter 29

Publications: News, Periodicals, and Books

by Bill Eager

Digital ink—it allows writers, editors, and publishers to distribute articles, stories, and books on the Web, and it enable users to enjoy a rich tapestry of multimedia information. Electronic publications have several advantages over their hard-copy cousins. For one, the impact and power of news relies on rapid distribution. An electronic news story can move from the event through the communications process and on to a WWW server in less than an hour—even television has a hard time competing with this type of instant publication.

Besides speed to market, electronic publications have a second unique quality: anyone who has access to a WWW server can be a writer and publisher. This capability has had a profound impact on the scientific and academic communities. Several years ago, after a researcher or academic professional wrote an article, a rather lengthy peer-review and publishing process meant that it could take more than six months for the material to be available to the public. Now, by self-publishing on the Web, the same people can bring their ideas, theories, and research results to market much faster. Likewise, young authors who want to publish articles or stories can find a WWW outlet that will get their words out to the world via electronic magazines, which cost less than five dollars to create and distribute.

This shouldn't suggest that all scientists and all writers are madly throwing vast quantities of unqualified manuscripts on to the WWW. Indeed, many electronic journals still require peer review, and commercial electronic magazines have editors who rework copy and reject manuscripts. As you weave your way through the resources in this chapter, however, you will come across works that probably would not have been published in the mainstream system that produces hardcopy reading material—and some of the electronic material is very good!

Electronic publications come in the same flavors that appear in hard copy: books, magazines, journals, newspapers, and newsletters. A phenomenal quantity of electronic books is available via the WWW, including plenty of classics; the complete works of William Shakespeare, for example, reside on a server at the Massachusetts Institute of Technology. Many new publications are available, too, such as the electronic version of the *Big Island of Hawaii Handbook,* a guide for travelers. Authors who write with the intention of publishing on the Web often include hypertext and hypermedia links in their manuscripts.

Magazines usually have a broad audience and are published on a weekly or monthly schedule. Journals and newsletters normally focus on a specific subject for a narrow audience; they publish weekly, monthly, or quarterly. Because there is no cost for paper, printing, or distribution, all these electronic publications can incorporate graphics, photographs, audio, and (in the case of the Global Network Navigator) even video. These publications truly are multimedia.

All these publications use hypertext to enable readers to jump from chapter to chapter; from front page to story; or from an icon to an image, audio, or video clip. You'll find that many of the commercial electronic publications, which are digital versions of the hard-copy issues, offer only a few articles; they really are teasers designed to get you to subscribe to the "real thing." Another trend on the Web is that some publications actually ask you to subscribe (yes, with your credit card) to gain access to their Web pages—which may be complete versions of their hardcopy publication.

Electronic publishing also offers benefits for you, the reader. Using the WWW, you can find an article or story on just about any subject that you can think of. You can read publications that you might not normally subscribe to or have access to. And because the WWW is global, you can jump to newspapers and publications in Russia, Italy, or other countries without worrying about postage or timeliness. So sit back, get a cup of tea or coffee, and enjoy reading global electronic publications.

This chapter lists resources in the following categories:

- *Authors*—Web sites devoted to the works of authors including Lewis Carroll and J.R.R. Tolkien

- *Books and Brochures*—electronic texts, often complete with images

- *Book and Literature Resources*—bibliographies, articles, and online books

- *College Publications*—Web periodicals written and produced by college students

- *International Literature*—delve into literature from Spain or China

- *Journals*—mostly scholarly and professional publications

- *Magazines and Newsletters*—resources that enable you to bypass that huge rack of magazines in the grocery store

- *Newspapers*—resources that give you the daily news, even from a town that's thousands of miles away

Gazette Telegraph

URL address: **http://usa.net/gazette/today/Gazette.html**

You subscribe (online) to get this publication, just as you would to a "real" newspaper. From the full-color masthead to the icons for different sections, the home page is a great example of an electronic newspaper. Under the banner, you find the current weather conditions and a headline for the top story of the day, with a one-paragraph teaser designed to make you want to jump to the story. Next come a few more headlines, followed by icons for weather, local, nation, sports, world, business, and arts and entertainment.

You can leave mail for the *Gazette* staff. Clicking an icon opens a form in which you can enter your name, your e-mail address, and your message. You can join a reader discussion area, where you can read comments by other readers, as you would in a newsgroup, or leave your own message for other readers. Even though the *Gazette* is a daily publication, you can jump to an archive of the preceding week's issues.

Project Gutenberg

URL address: **http://www.cs.cmu.edu:8001/Web/booktitles.html**

URL address: **ftp://mrcnext.cso.uiuc.edu/etext/NEWUSER.GUT**

Fig. 29.1
Project Gutenberg
is a Web site that
offers the
complete text of
classic works of
literature.

Entries last updated for month of: **February, 1995**

We are now clocking in at approx. 150 accesses per day! Keep spreading the word!

1 General Project Information
  — About this Web server
  — The history of the project
  — How to donate Etexts
  — How to join the project
  — How to prepare Etexts
  — Newgroup discussion (**bit.listserv.gutnberg**)

If you enjoy literature, especially the classics, you will love this WWW server. Project Gutenberg began in 1971, when Michael Hart began to enter the text of famous books into electronic files stored in the mainframe of the Materials Research Lab at the University of Illinois. Since 1971, more than 100 texts have been added to the collection, and the texts have been "mirrored" or duplicated at several Web sites.

The books stored at this site have two significant features. First, the books are stored as ASCII text, which means that you can read and download them to any type of computer system. Second, all the books are in the public domain, which means that you don't have to worry about copyright issues when you download and use the books. Authors represented in the collection include Emily Brontë, Edgar Rice Burroughs, Charles Dickens, Nathaniel Hawthorne, Herman Melville, William Shakespeare, Mary Shelley, Henry David Thoreau, Mark Twain, and Jules Verne.

Electronic Newsstand

URL address: **gopher://gopher.enews.com:70/11**

The Electronic Newsstand was founded in July 1993 to provide Internet users a means of accessing information created by magazine (hard-copy) publishers. As you would at a traditional newsstand, you can browse these publications at no charge. A few of the publications that you will find here are *Animals, Business Week, Inc. Magazine, Computer World, Canoe & Kayak, Fiber Optics News,* and *Federal Employees News Digest*.

The subjects cover every area of interest, including computers, technology, science, business, economics, foreign affairs, arts, sports, and travel. Each publisher provides an online table of contents and a few articles from a current issue. You also can keyword-search the archives of specific publications for articles. These articles actually are teasers, which the publishers hope will encourage you to order a single copy or a subscription via the newsstand's e-mail address or 800 number.

▶ See "Books and Maps," p. 879

Macmillan Computer Publishing

URL address: **http://www.mcp.com/**

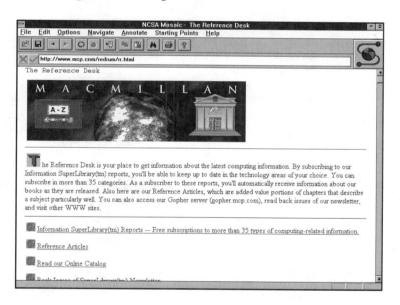

Fig. 29.2
Macmillan Computer Publishing maintains a Web site that offers useful reference information and sample chapters of computer books.

Find information on the best computer book publishers in the world. Books from Que, Sams, New Riders, Alpha, Brady, and Hayden are featured at this site. You can review sample chapters or tables of contents from current books. This site also offers a wealth of reference articles pulled from these books to answer your questions about computer software and hardware. You can order any Macmillan Computer Publishing book directly from this Web site and download software associated with best-selling titles.

Center for the Study of Southern Culture

URL address: **http://imp.cssc.olemiss.edu**

Fig. 29.3
At this home page, you'll find a variety of electronic publications that focus on the American South.

Welcome To The Center For the Study of Southern Culture's World Wide Web Server

For more than 16 years, the Center for the Study of Southern Culture at the University of Mississippi has sponsored educational and research programs about the American South. The center offers B.A. and M.A. degrees in Southern Studies. This WWW home page provides an outlet for information about the cultural activities of the region. From the home page, you can jump to lists of events in each state in the region.

The center also publishes several periodicals that you can peruse from the home page, including the following:

- *Southern Culture Catalog*—contains videos, sound recordings, and periodicals

- *The Southern Register*—a newsletter of the Center for the Study of Southern Culture, containing updates on current activities (such as the study of the culture of a 28,000-acre quail-hunting reserve)

- *Living Blues*—a journal of the African-American blues tradition

- *Living Blues: Blues Directory*—a guide to the blues-music industry

- *Reckon*—a magazine of Southern culture

- *Rejoice!*—a gospel-music magazine

- *Old Time Country*—a source for traditional country music

Authors

Asimov, Isaac

URL address: **http://www.lightside.com/SpecialInterest/asimov/
asimov-faq.html**

This site has got to be the definitive Q&A about Isaac Asimov, including answers to questions such as "Where was he born?" and "What books have
been written about him?"

Carroll, Lewis

URL address: **http://www.cs.indiana.edu/metastuff/dir.html**

This Web server offers electronic versions of *Alice in Wonderland* and *Through
the Looking-Glass*. (Carroll would have loved hypertext.)

Cervantes, Miguel de

URL address: **http://158.122.3.3/servicio.html**

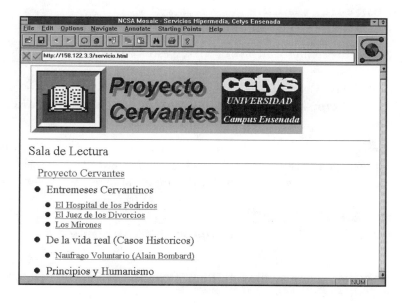

Fig. 29.4
If you enjoy
reading literature
in its original
language, try the
Cervantes Web
site.

This site offers an archive of Miguel de Cervantes texts—in Spanish. Offerings
include *Entremeses Cervantinos: El Hospital de los Podridos, El Juez de los
Divorcios*, and *Los Mirones*.

Clarke, Arthur C.

URL address: **http://www.hotwired.com**

Go through *Wired* magazine's home page to access this 1993 interview with Clarke.

Dickens, Charles

URL address: **http://www.wonderland.org/Works/Charles-Dickens/christmas-carol/**

This page has hypertext to Dickens classics such as *A Christmas Carol*.

Jordan, Robert

URL address: **http://faser.cs.olemiss.edu/jordan/jordan.html**

This home page includes Robert Jordan frequently asked questions, plus fan material related to the author's *Wheel of Time* series. The information was collected from discussions on UseNet.

Shakespeare, William

URL address: **http://the-tech.mit.edu/Shakespeare.html**

This site has the complete archive of Shakespeare's works.

Stoker, Bram: *Dracula*

URL address: **http://www.cs.cmu.edu:8001/Web/People/rgs/drac-table.html**

This home page is a hypertext version of Bram Stoker's horror novel, *Dracula*. Start with Chapter 1, "Jonathan Harker's Journal," and weave your way to Chapter 27, "Mina Harker's Journal," with a lot of vampire bites in between.

Stross, Charles

URL address: **http://www.lysator.liu.se/sf_archive/sub/Charles_Stross/index.html**

This site offers a collection of short stories, from *Interzone* and other sources, by U.K. author Charles Stross.

Tolkien, J.R.R.

URL address: **http://csclub.uwaterloo.ca/u/relipper/tolkien/rootpage.html**

This site provides a resource guide and index of Internet resources related to Tolkien and his fiction: clubs, newsgroups, and dictionaries.

Twain, Mark

URL address: **http://hydor.colorado.edu/twain/**

This site provides links to Twain's short stories and essays, his novels, and other Web sites that devote attention to this master of words.

Wordsworth, William

URL address: **http://www.cc.columbia.edu/~svl2/wordsworth/ index.html**

This home page will bring you to the complete poetical works of William Wordsworth. Choose a link to a chronological listing and then pick your poem!

Books and Brochures

Adventures of Sherlock Holmes

URL address: **http://www.cs.cmu.edu:8001/afs/andrew.cmu.edu/ acs/library/etexts/namedsubject/literature/A.C.Doyle.dir/ holmes/The_Adventures_of_Sherlock_Holmes.dir/**

Now this address deserves some detective work to figure it out. If, however, you can accurately type it into your browser, you will get to a page that contains about a dozen links to different Sherlock Holmes mysteries.

ANIMA

URL address: **http://www.wimsey.com/anima/ ARTWORLDhome.html**

Find out what's going on in the art world. This site provides reviews and listings of visual, performing, literary, and video arts. Choose an art form, and then weave down to specific documents, such as the Fine Art Forum, which students at Griffith University in Australia produce to discuss art and technology.

Bible—King James Version

URL address: **gopher://ccat.sas.upenn.edu:3333/11/Religious/ Biblical/KJVBible**

This site contains the complete text of the King James version of The Bible. One of the nice features is a link to keyword searching—type in a word in a dialog box, press Enter, and you'll get a complete rundown of all references to that word in the Bible.

Citizen's Handbook of North Carolina's Environmental Information Sources

URL address: **http://sunsite.unc.edu/nc/nc_env_handbook/ R_Table_of_Contents.html**

◀ See "Public Policy and World Events," p. 795

Learn how to be good to the environment. Compiled by Susan E. Hass, this electronic environmental guide offers 11 chapters, which are arranged into alphabetical listings of government and nongovernment sources for information and publications. Many of the documents and "green tips" are simple things that everyone can do to help preserve environmental resources and reduce pollution.

The Doomsday Brunette

URL address: **http://zeb.nysaes.cornell.edu/CGI/ddb/demo.cgi**

This electronic sci-fi novel is set in 2056. Unfortunately, you don't get the entire book for free, but check it out.

For Sale By Owner

URL address: **http://www.human.com/mkt/fsbo/fsbo.html**

Fig. 29.5
If you are looking to buy or sell a home, this publication is a unique new resource.

This electronic publication is for California home buyers and home sellers who want to check out listings or place ads. A hard-copy version is distributed in Santa Cruz, Santa Clara, and Monterey counties.

Hacker Crackdown

URL address: **http://www.scrg.cs.tcd.ie/scrg/u/bos/hacker/ hacker.html**

This site is an electronic version of *The Hacker Crackdown* by Bruce Sterling. Sections include "Crashing the System," "The Digital Underground," "Law and Order," and "The Civil Libertarians."

Moon Publications

URL address: **http://bookweb.cwis.uci.edu:8042/Books/Moon/hawaii.html**

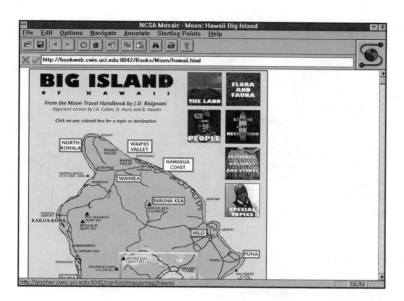

Fig. 29.6
The *Big Island of Hawaii Handbook* uses all the multimedia aspects of the WWW to enable you to explore Hawaii in an exciting, interactive manner.

This site offers a hypertext travel guide based on J.D. Bisignani's *Big Island of Hawaii Handbook*. The site uses the multimedia capabilities of the WWW, presenting text, maps, photos, and audio to tell you about the Big Island's land, culture, history, and recreational opportunities.

Samples of Electronic Publishing: Electric Press Inc.

URL address: **http://www.elpress.com/samples/samples.html**

This commercial WWW server demonstrates a variety of electronic publications that use hypermedia. Examples include an electronic catalog for direct-mail purposes, an electronic newsletter with photographs, and a product brochure.

Fig. 29.7
If you are planning an online publication, this site is an excellent place to look for samples and examples.

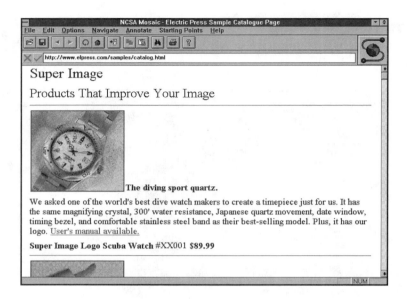

Book and Literature Resources

Association des Bibliophiles Universels
URL address: **http://web.cnam.fr/ABU/**

Founded in 1993, the Association des Bibliophiles Universels (ABU) offers online texts of French public-domain literature. The site also includes some information about the organization (in French).

Banned Books Online
URL address: **http://www.cs.cmu.edu:8001/Web/People/spok/ banned-books.html**

This site represents a "special exhibit of books that have been the objects of censorship or censorship attempts." The books featured at this site range from *Ulysses* to *Little Red Riding Hood*.

Best-Quality Audio Web Poems
URL address: **http://www.cs.brown.edu/fun/bawp**

Get your cup of cappuccino, then browse through and listen to a collection of recordings of poetry readings and spoken performances. This site may be the closest thing to the old outdoor cafes in Paris. Files are in MPEG-2 audio format.

Bryn Mawr Classical Review

URL address: **//gopher.lib.Virginia.EDU:70/11/alpha/bmcr**

This site is a review of classical literature distributed over the Internet.

Christian Classics Ethereal Library

URL address: **http://www.cs.pitt.edu/~planting/books**

This site offers a huge collection of classic Christian books, sermons, devotionals, and other documents. As the home page states: "There is enough good reading material here to last you a lifetime." It's true; the text and articles date back to several years after the birth of Christ.

Clearinghouse for Subject-Oriented Internet Resource Guides

URL address: **http://http2.sils.umich.edu/~lou/chhome.html**

From the University of Michigan's University Library (School of Information and Library Science), this WWW site offers a searchable resource for publications on the humanities, social sciences, science, and other subjects.

The Global Network Navigator

URL address: **http://nearnet.gnn.com**

The Global Network Navigator combines a variety of the WWW resources in icons on the home page. The site provides links to news and periodicals, including overviews of the *Lonely Planet* books and guides—a series of paperback books which describe remote and interesting travel destinations.

Global Population Publications

URL address: **http://www.pop.psu.edu:70/1m/library/catalog**

This site provides an extensive hypertext list of library-catalog titles that deal with issues of global population growth and world demographics. Sample publication titles include *Adolescent Mothers in Later Life* and *Population Factors in Development Planning in the Middle East*. When you click the title of a publication, you get information about the author, the publisher, the publication date, and the library call number.

Indexes of Online Books

URL address: **http://nearnet.gnn.com/wic/lit.18.html**

Published fiction usually is available on the Internet only if it is out of copyright. This site is the home page for the Global Network Navigator Indexes of Online Books, many of which are very recent or have not even been published in hard copy.

Fig. 29.8

The Global Network Navigator WWW site provides one-stop shopping for many electronic news and publications.

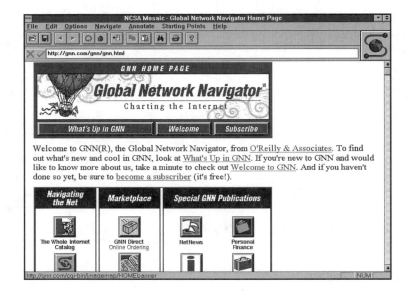

Information Arcade

URL address: **http://www.arcade.uiowa.edu**

Located at the University of Iowa (in the library), the Information Arcade is a facility that provides UI students, faculty, and staff members access to information sources on the Internet.

Internet Book Information Center

URL address: **http://sunsite.unc.edu/ibic/IBIC-homepage.html**

This site is a hypertext guide to information about books on the Internet. The WWW Virtual Library literature is maintained by the Internet Book Information Center. The server is provided courtesy of SunSITE, a joint project of Sun Microsystems and the University of North Carolina at Chapel Hill. The IBIC's mission is to provide Internet-based access to useful, interesting information about books.

Internet Poetry Archive
URL address: **http://sunsite.unc.edu/dykki/poetry/home.html**

This Web poetry archive makes available poems by contemporary poets in several languages. You will find links to the texts of the poems, pictures of the poets, the voices of the poets reading the poems, and a bibliography.

Lysator Computer Society
URL address: **http://www.lysator.liu.se**

Lysator is an association for computer-interested students at Linköping University in Sweden. Lysator manages its own machines and provides links to three interesting art and literature sections: The Science Fiction/Fantasy Archive, which collects sci-fi and fantasy reviews, bibliographies, news lists, electronic magazines, and artwork; Project Runeberg, which publishes electronic texts in Scandinavian languages; and Anime and Manga, which are Japanese comics and animations that are enjoying a growing cult status.

Online Books
URL address: **http://www.cs.indiana.edu/metastuff/bookfaq.html**

This online directory of electronic books that you can find on the Internet is a good place to start your search for a particular title.

Science and Magic
URL address: **http://www.lysator.liu.se/sf_archive/sftexts/lists/Science_and_Magic**

This server has information about books that bridge the gap between science fiction and fantasy.

College Publications

Aviation and Aerospace Newspaper
URL address: **http://avion.db.erau.edu**

Avion Online is Embry-Riddle Aeronautical University's college newspaper. The site provides links to current and past issues, with articles ranging from the space shuttle to mergers in the commercial aerospace industry.

◀ See "Colleges and Universities—United States," p. 613

The Bucknellian

URL address: **http://www.bucknell.edu/bucknellian**

Fig. 29.9
The Bucknellian is
an example of a
student-run
university
newspaper on the
WWW.

This site is the WWW home page for the student-run newspaper of Bucknell University, located in Lewisburg, Pennsylvania. The site offers articles about the arts, social and political issues, and university events.

Georgetown Gonzo

URL address: **http://sunsite.unc.edu/martin/gonzo.html**

This site is a satirical Georgetown University publication that, as the home page states, is "unofficial, unsponsored, and underground." Article titles include "Enter the Duck: A Kung Fu Play in One Act" and "Hamlet Was a College Student."

The Tech

URL address: **http://the-tech.mit.edu/The-Tech**

This site is the electronic version of the oldest (since 1881) and largest newspaper of the Massachusetts Institute of Technology. Articles in each issue focus on the world and nation. Other sections of the paper include columns, arts, and sports. You can send a letter to the editor via a special Comment button in every issue.

International Literature

British Comedy Pages

URL address: **http://cathouse.org:8000/BritishComedy**

You've heard of the British sense of humor. Look through a collection of pages and links that cover all aspects of British comedy. You know about Monty Python, which is listed here; check out other humorous shows, such as the radio series "The Goons."

China News Digest

URL address: **http://www.cnd.org:80/**

This home page provides links to current news and to classic Chinese novels.

◄ See "Interesting Sites and National Travel Guides," p. 756

Ireland: CURIA Irish Manuscript Project

URL address: **http://curia.ucc.ie**
URL address: **http://curia.ucc.ie/curia/menu.html**

The Irish literature archive, known as the Thesaurus Linguarum Hiberniae, collects and puts online Irish literature dating from 600 to 1600 A.D. The site is somewhat hard to go through, but many interesting Irish texts are available.

Russian and East European Studies

URL address: **http://www.pitt.edu/~cjp/rslang.html**

At this site, you will find links to Russian literature and historical information.

Swedish Language Bank

URL address: **http://logos.svenska.gu.se/**

The Language Bank of Swedish, a text archive at Gloumteborg University's Department of Swedish, consists of approximately 30 million words of fiction, legal texts, and newspapers. This Web server provides information about the collection, as well as a Telnet connection to the Language Bank's online concordance system.

Journals

Chronicle of Higher Education

URL address: **http://chronicle.merit.edu**
URL address: **gopher://chronicle.merit.edu:70/1**

This publication focuses on issues of importance to people who work in higher education. A typical article title is "What They're Reading on College Campuses." The publication contains articles and listings of employment opportunities (usually, hundreds) for teachers and administrators.

Complexity International

URL address: **http://life.anu.edu.au:80/ci/ci.html**

◄ See "Resources for Musicians," p. 496

This publication is a journal of scientific papers about complex systems, including artificial life, chaos theory, and genetic algorithms.

Computer Music Journal

URL address: **file://mitpress.mit.edu:/pub/Computer-Music-Journal/ CMJ.html**

The *Computer Music Journal* archive is provided for readers of the publication and the computer-music community. The archive includes a table of contents, abstracts, and editor's notes for several volumes of *CMJ*, including the recent bibliography and discography of the field, as well as the list of network resources for music. The site also offers related documents, such as the complete MIDI and AIFF specifications, a reference list, and the text of recent articles.

Conservation Ecology

URL address: **http://journal.biology.carleton.ca**

This publication is an "in-construction" scientific journal that focuses on research in ecosystems, landscapes, park management, and endangered species.

Cultronix

URL address: **http://english-server.hss.cmu.edu/cultronix.html**

This cultural-studies journal uses multimedia to discuss a variety of cultural topics, such as the medical industry and the effects of machine culture.

English Server (Carnegie-Mellon University)

URL address: **http://english-server.hss.cmu.edu**

The CMU English Department sponsors this server, which is run by graduate students, for distribution of research, criticism, novels, and hypertexts. The site also offers science-fiction-related texts on film and television.

Federal Communications Law Journal

URL address: **http://www.law.indiana.edu:80/fclj/fclj.html**

◄ See "Law and Legal Resources," p. 788

Communications law is big business as it relates to cable and broadcast television, radio, and now computer communications. This journal comes from the Indiana University School of Law.

Government Information in Canada
URL address: **http://www.usask.ca/library/gic/index.html**

This quarterly electronic journal focuses on articles that relate to the provinces and the Canadian government. One example is "Parliamentary Papers: Change Is the Name of the Game," an article by Brian Land. Some of the information, such as the editorial, is written in French.

Internaut
URL address: **http://www.astro.nwu.edu:80/lentz/**

This journal contains timely articles and FAQs (frequently asked questions) about space, as well as General Astronomy Information leaflets; The Nine Planets, a solar-system reference; and links to other space resources.

Journal of Buddhist Ethics
URL address: **http://www.psu.edu/jbe/jbe.html**

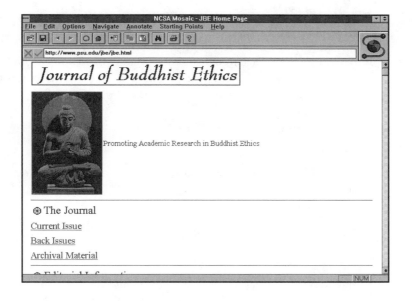

Fig. 29.10
Like many electronic journals on the Web, the *Journal of Buddhist Ethics* offers timely articles, essays, and a calendar of events.

This electronic academic journal addresses Buddhism through articles such as "Kraft's Inner Peace, World Peace: Essays on Buddhism and Nonviolence." Bulletins mention different timely topics, such as employment opportunities in religious studies and seminars on Buddhism.

Learned InfoNet

URL address: **http://info.learned.co.uk**

This Web site is sponsored by Learned Information, Ltd., a publishing and conference-organizing company that focuses on information industries. The LI NewsWire link offers abstracts and news about the world of online information. Titles include "Europe Acts on Superhighways" and "Electronic Libraries: Visions of the Future." The site also provides a link to information about conferences on online information.

NASDAQ Financial Executive Journal

URL address: **http://www.law.cornell.edu/nasdaq/nasdtoc.html**

This publication, a joint project of the Legal Information Institute at Cornell Law School and the NASDAQ^{SM} Stock Exchange, contains in-depth articles and interviews such as "Disclosure from the Analyst's Perspective."

Psycoloquy

URL address: **http://info.cern.ch/hypertext/DataSources/bySubject/Psychology/Psycoloquy.html**

Sponsored by the American Psychological Association, this electronic publication now has 20,000 readers. The interdisciplinary journal contains features on psychology, philosophy, behaviorism, and artificial intelligence.

Scholarly Communications Project

URL address: **http://borg.lib.vt.edu**

This home page links you to several scholarly journals, including *The Journal of Fluids Engineering DATABANK, The Journal of Technology Education*, and *The Journal of Veterinary Medical Education*.

Secular Web

URL address: **http://freethought.tamu.edu**

This site addresses secular issues, including atheism, agnosticism, humanism, and skepticism. The site also maintains an archive of free-thought literature called "The Freethought Web."

Telektronikk

URL address: **http://www.nta.no/telektronikk/4.93.html**

This site offers a huge collection of interesting articles about electronic communications, such as "Coordination: Challenge of the Nineties: Multimedia as a Coordinating Technology." You can perform a full-text search of the articles. The site truly is an international collaboration.

Tree Physiology
URL address: **http://sol.uvic.ca/treephys**

This monthly publication is distributed in more than 60 countries. The electronic version includes reviews, reports, and papers about tree physiology, such as the impact of air pollutants on trees, tree growth, and reproduction.

Magazines and Newsletters

AM/FM
URL address: **http://www.tecc.co.uk/public/tqm/amfm**

This WWW site is a monthly newsletter that features events and personalities in the United Kingdom radio industry. This electronic publication includes back issues that date from July 1992. Few images are available here, but you will find solid reports about the business.

ANSWERS
URL address: **http://www.service.com/answers/cover.html**

Answers: the Magazine for Adult Children of Aging Parents, is written for anyone who faces questions, issues, and concerns that relate to having an aging parent. The magazine covers aspects of taking care of an elderly parent, including how to deal with the emotional impact and where to get help if you need it. Sample articles and a subscription form are available electronically.

◀ See "Human Sexuality and Marriage," p. 788

Big Dreams
URL address: **http://www.wimsey.com/~duncans/**

This electronic newsletter is devoted to personal development and starting a business. Each month brings a new hypertext issue.

Boardwatch
URL address: **http://www.boardwatch.com**

Boardwatch is an international trade magazine devoted to online communications and BBS systems. This site offers an electronic, hypertext version of the publication, and information about online systems. It also reviews and overviews the latest activities on the Web. You can also find a forms-based page where you can send e-mail or letters to the editor and staff of the magazine.

VI

Finding Web Resources

Cambridge University Science Fiction Society

URL address: **http://myrddin.chu.cam.ac.uk/cusfs/ttba**

This Web site provides the magazine of the Cambridge University Science Fiction Society, which contains fiction, reviews, poetry, and artwork.

Capacity Index

URL address: **http://www.wimsey.com/Capacity/**

At this Web site, you'll find an art-and-culture publication that features poetry and other artistic endeavors from Canada.

COLOQUIO

URL address: **http://www.clark.net/pub/jgbustam/coloquio/ coloquio.html**

This Spanish-cultural magazine is published monthly for Spanish speakers, teachers, professors of the Spanish language, and other interested people. Hard-copy circulation is in the Washington, D.C., and Baltimore areas.

Cyberkind

URL address: **http://sunsite.unc.edu/shannon/ckind/title.html**

Fig. 29.11
The *Cyberkind* WWW site illustrates the type of new writing that is available on the Web.

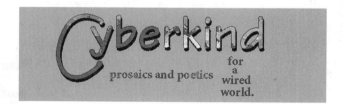

A WWW magazine of Net-related fiction, nonfiction, poetry, and art, *Cyberkind* features prose and art submitted by the Internet population. All genres and subjects are included, with the condition that they have some connection with the Internet, cyberspace, computers, or the networked world. Features range from articles about writers and the Internet to computer-related mysteries to hyperlinked poems. A variety of graphic art also is available.

Fashion Page

URL address: **http://www.charm.net/~jakec**

Fashion Page is a Web magazine that focuses on the ever-volatile world of fashion. Read about menswear, womenswear, styles, fashion trends, and how to care for fashions. If you're interested in modeling, you may want to read the detailed list of modeling agencies.

Informationweek

URL address: **http://techweb.cmp.com/iwk**

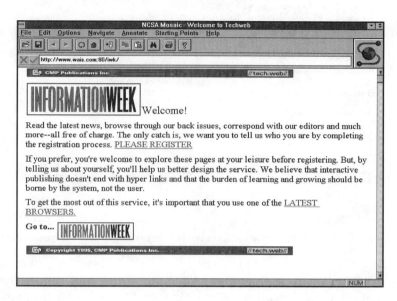

Fig. 29.12
Informationweek maintains a Web site that provides access to back issues.

Try this digital version of *Informationweek*, a leading trade magazine for the computer industry. The site offers articles, audio, video, and games. You can browse through back issues and send e-mail to the editors.

International Teletimes

URL address: **http://www.wimsey.com/teletimes/
teletimes_home_page.html**

From a WWW server in Vancouver, Canada, *International Teletimes* is a general-interest electronic publication—and there really is something for everyone. Each monthly issue focuses on a topic, such as history or TV and film. One issue that focuses on travel, for example, contains articles including "Hawaii Pubcrawl," by Ken Eisner, and "Toronto to Vancouver by Train," by Paul Gribble.

Fig. 29.13
International Teletimes is a monthly WWW publication that contains articles on subjects ranging from travel to film.

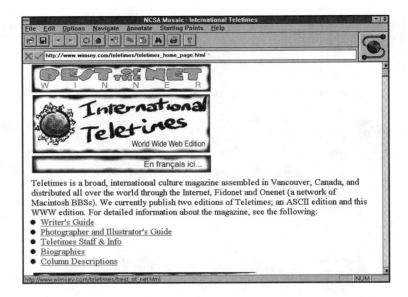

Internet World

URL address: **http://www.mecklerweb.com/mags/iw/iwhome.htm**

This site is the home page for MecklerWeb, a WWW information gathering place sponsored by Mecklermedia. In addition to *Internet World*, an electronic version of a monthly magazine for Internet users, MecklerWeb helps companies put information about their products and services on the Web.

Interserve Magazine

URL address: **http://www.interserv.com**

Start with your graphics settings *on* for this home page; it contains only icons. This site really is an electronic connecting station, with links (and instructions) that enable you to access Internet newsgroups via Mosaic and other services.

InterText Magazine

URL address: **http://ftp.etext.org/Zines/InterText/intertext.html**

This publication is an electronic magazine of fiction and nonfiction articles. More than 20 issues are online, providing a great deal of good reading.

Mogul Media

URL address: **http://www.mogul.no/mogul/artikler/artikler.html**

From Norway, *Mogul Media* contains a variety of research articles that focus on new media, such as "The Effect of the Media User Interface on Interactivity and Content," by Terje Norderhaug. Some articles are in English, but it wouldn't hurt to brush up on your Norwegian.

Morpo Review

URL address: **http://morpo.creighton.edu/morpo**

This publication is a nice, bimonthly collection of stories and poetry, and it is color-coded; a white bullet indicates a story, and a green bullet indicates poetry. Each page has a forward and a backward icon for easy navigation.

Mother Jones

URL address: **http://www.mojones.com/motherjones.html**

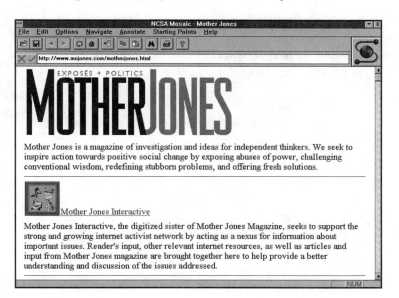

Fig. 29.14
Did you miss Woodstock '94? You can read all about it in *Mother Jones*.

This international magazine contains exposés and progressive political commentary. The magazine contains articles about topics such as specific legislators, political races, U.S. foreign policy, political activists, and education. A great deal of hypermedia (especially images) is available at this WWW site.

NCSA Access

URL address: **http://www.ncsa.uiuc.edu/Pubs/access/accessDir.html**

From the National Center for Supercomputing Applications, this magazine contains articles about the issues and research that NCSA deals with, such as "Enhancing Reality with VR" and "Supercomputing and the Environment."

PC Magazine

URL address: **http://www.ziff.com/~pcmag**

Fig. 29.15
This electronic version of *PC Magazine* offers computer-related stories and links to other computer resources.

Published by Ziff-Davis Publishing Company, *PC Magazine* (the hardcopy) provides PC product evaluations, such as reviews of CD-ROMs, to more than a million readers. This site is an electronic version of the publication. Also check out the address **http://www.ziff.com/~pcweek/ best_news.html**, which lists some other electronic publications.

Postmodern Culture

URL address: **http://jefferson.village.virginia.edu/pmc/ contents.all.html**

This publication is a joint project of North Carolina State University, Oxford University Press, and the University of Virginia's Institute for Advanced Technology in the Humanities. The site provides links to fiction stories, poetry, articles, and reviews. The articles usually are esoteric but deal with interesting subjects, such as Ann Larabee's "Remembering the Shuttle, Forgetting the Loom: Interpreting the Challenger Disaster." You can keyword-search these archives.

PowerPC News

URL address: **http://power.globalnews.com/**

This WWW electronic magazine is published twice a month. The target audience is users and developers who are interested in news and information about the IBM/Motorola/Apple microprocessors.

Time **Magazine**
URL address: **http://www.timeinc.com**

This site is the home page for several publications created by Time, Inc. "On this page, you'll find a compass to some of the world's greatest writing and photography and a whole lot of other Internet goodies. Click on any of the blue underlined words to explore the stories featured here, on any logo to visit a home page, or to TIMELINE to see today's news from TIME, Money, and Entertainment Weekly." The site offers reviews of books, movies and TV shows; samples of articles; copy from cover stories; and a series of special-interest bulletin boards that cover subjects ranging from health and medicine to Washington, D.C.

TwentyNothing
URL address: **http://www.mit.edu:8001/afs/athena.mit.edu/user/t/ h/thomasc/Public/twenty/intro.html**

Fig. 29.16
The graphic of a kayaker on the home page suggests that you will find fast action in this magazine.

This quarterly hypertext magazine is written by people in their twenties. This site offers only two issues, but those issues contain interesting articles such as "Plainly, Change Comes to Spain," which examines some of the economic changes that have occurred in that country. Or check out "The Bachelor Gourmet"—the title says it all.

Verbiage Magazine
URL address: **http://sunsite.unc.edu/boutell/verbiage/index.html**

This WWW magazine showcases short fiction. Jump from the home page to an index for each issue; then select a story that sounds interesting. You also can submit fiction (up to 3,000 words) to this WWW site.

Washington Weekly

URL address: **http://dolphin.gulf.net**

This electronic newsmagazine focuses on national politics, news, and opinion. There is a catch, though: you have to subscribe (yes, money is involved) to get access to the Web pages.

Webster's Weekly

URL address: **http://www.awa.com/w2**

This WWW-only publication comes out every Wednesday. Topics are broad, ranging from music and movies to politics and sex.

HotWired **Magazine**

URL address: **http://www.wired.com**

Fig. 29.17
If you can't get enough of the printed version of *Wired*, this site presents some material that's available only electronically.

This is the electronic version of *Wired* magazine. To gain access (which is currently free), you must register as a user via an on-screen form. Kind of a New Wave, hip-hop, cyber magazine, *HotWired* contains a variety of interesting computer-related articles. The site provides links to back issues, a mailing-list archive, a Clipper chip archive, and a promotional video (2M in QuickTime).

Workplace Labor Update

URL address: **http://venable.com/wlu/wlu3.htm**

This WWW newsletter, published by a law firm, addresses issues of employment law. Links on the home page provide up-to-date news about violence in the workplace, retroactivity of the 1991 Civil Rights Act, alcohol and drug use, company downsizing, and COBRA health insurance.

Newspapers

Gazeta Online

URL address: **http://info.fuw.edu.pl/gw/0/gazeta.html**

This site is the WWW electronic version of Poland's largest daily newspaper, *Gazeta Wyborcza*. Unfortunately, unless your Polish is pretty good, you won't be able to read much of the news.

Georgia Newspaper Project

URL address: **http://scarlett.libs.uga.edu:70/1h/www/darchive/ aboutgnp.html**

This site contains information about a microfilm archive of some 1,200 public and private Georgia newspapers. One fun feature is a link from the home page that takes you to a set of icons that represent the mastheads of Georgia newspapers; click a masthead to get a description of the newspaper.

News-Observer

URL address: **http://www.nando.net/nando.html**

This publication is the daily newspaper of Raleigh, North Carolina.

Palo Alto Weekly

URL address: **http://www.service.com/PAW/home.html**

This site is the electronic version of a California newspaper that has a weekly circulation of 50,000. This version comes out twice a week. The site provides a home-page link to "Palo Alto: the First 100 Years," as well as links to articles about child care, education, the community, and housing.

VI

Finding Web Resources

St. Petersburg Press

URL address: **http://www.spb.su/sppress/index.html**

Fig. 29.18
This WWW site provides articles from the *St. Petersburg Press*, a weekly Russian newspaper (written in English).

Live from Russia, this site is an HTML version of the weekly, English-language newspaper. Major article categories include business, culture, and news. Articles, such as "Local Police Help Smash Million-Dollar Nuclear Crime Gang," have somewhat sensational titles. Be sure to check out the classified section, which includes listings such as "20-year-old English, Russian-speaking nice lady from Finland is looking for friend from St. Petersburg...."

Star-Tribune

URL address: **http://www.trib.com/trib_home.html**

This WWW daily newspaper is provided by the Casper, Wyoming, *Star-Tribune*. The site also provides links to other WWW resources.

Today's News

URL address: **http://www.cfn.cs.dal.ca/Media/TodaysNews/ TodaysNews.html**

Although this Web site does not offer a complete transcript of *The Daily News* from Halifax, Nova Scotia, you will find a story of the day; local and national news summaries; a daily listing of metro activities; sports and business news; and "Mou's Cartoon," a daily cartoon that is in GIF image format.

L'Unione Sarda

URL address: **http://www.crs4.it/~ruggiero/unione.html**

This site is an online version of the Italian newspaper. The site offers hundreds of articles and back issues, but you need to be able to read Italian.

USA Today

URL address: **http://alpha.acast.nova.edu/usatoday.html**
URL address: **telnet://spacemet.phast.umass.edu**

These links open Telnet sessions that bring you daily summaries of *USA Today* reports. Log on as **guest**.

The Virginian-Pilot

URL address: **http://www.infi.net/pilot/tvp.html**

From this home page, you can jump to news (newsgroup information), classified, community news, arts and entertainment, and travel sections.

Additional Electronic Publications via Gopher

When you connect with the following Gopher sites, you get an on-screen display of icons that represent individual files, which are documents and articles. The file name usually provides a good clue about the information that you will find if you click the icon.

Austin Daily Texan

URL address: **gopher://ftp.cc.utexas.edu:3003/1/microlib/info/texan/today**

Citations for Serial Literature

URL address: **gopher://dewey.lib.ncsu.edu/11/library/stacks/csl**

The Nation

URL address: **gopher://gopher.igc.apc.org/11/pubs/nation.gopher**

Review of Early English Drama

URL address: **gopher://vm.utcs.utoronto.ca/11/listserv/reed-l**

From Here...

Reading all these electronic publications could take a lifetime—and as you read, new publications come online. If you are an avid reader and want hard-copy editions, however, read the following chapters:

- Chapter 20, "Art, Music, and Entertainment," shows you Web sites that have publications which focus on the arts.

- Chapter 28, "Issues, Politics, Religion, and World Events," shows you where there are Web publications that focus on social and political issues that face individuals and society at large.

- Chapter 31, "Shopping," provides the Web addresses of additional bookstores where you can purchase books online.

Chapter 30

Science

by Bill Eager

From botany to zoology, the WWW has information about every category of science. Perhaps one reason for this is that computers enhance scientific research. Scientists use computers to record and analyze data from experiments, model images of phenomena not visible to the human eye (such as a 3D image of protein structure or a graphic representation of weather conditions), and store databases that range from catalogs of animal species to dinosaur fossils. The WWW was originally created to assist scientists who work in the area of high-energy physics and, as a result, a number of institutions that focus on this complex science have a presence on the Web. But you don't have to have a Ph.D. in nuclear science to enjoy and use the scientific information. WWW servers can help you grow roses, locate the Big Dipper, or develop a lesson plan for a sixth grade biology class. The broad categories of resources in this chapter include:

- Agricultural (botany) and animal sciences

- Anthropology

- Astronomy

- Biology

- Chemistry

- Complex systems

- Engineering

- Environmental sciences

- Meteorology

- Museums

- Physics

- Resources

- Telecommunications

National Aeronautics and Space Administration (NASA)

URL address: **http://hypatia.gsfc.nasa.gov/NASA_homepage.html**
URL address: **telnet://spacelink.msfc.nasa.gov/**

Fig. 30.1
The NASA home page is the definitive source of information and links to other resources about space science, technology, and flights.

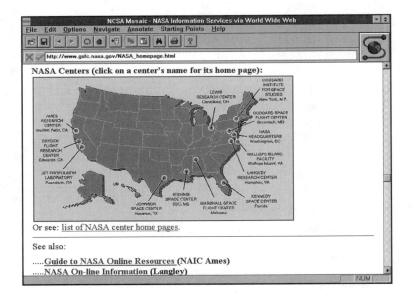

◀ See "U.S. Government," p. 667

NASA, the United States National Aeronautics and Space Administration, is the undisputed world leader in the exploration of space. The NASA mission statement located at the WWW home page declares, "As explorers, pioneers, and innovators, we boldly expand frontiers in air and space to inspire and serve America and to benefit the quality of life on Earth.... We explore the universe to enrich human life by stimulating intellectual curiosity, opening new worlds of opportunity, and uniting nations of the world in this quest."

Because it is federally funded, NASA makes information about its programs available to the public. Many of the NASA materials are designed for use by educators and students who access information about NASA's scientific projects, space missions, educational programs, and newsletters. NASA Spacelink, which is a Telnet site, provides lesson plans, GIF digital images, educational software, and schedules for NASA Select TV—a television channel that NASA makes available to cable companies and others who have access to a satellite downlink system.

Delving into NASA's resources on the Web is similar to exploring outer space—it is enormous, and one destination quickly opens up new avenues for discovery. NASA's WWW home page contains a map of the United States that highlights the primary NASA-connected institutions. Each of the "hot buttons" for the locations on the map links users to these institutions.

Here are a few of the WWW sites available from the NASA home page. You can also go to them directly.

◄ See "Laboratories of the Department of Energy," p. 678

- NASA Jet Propulsion Laboratory

    URL address: **http://www.jpl.nasa.gov**

- NASA Langley Research Center Home Page

    URL address: **http://mosaic.larc.nasa.gov/larc.html**

- NASA Spacelink (interactive session). This is probably the site most used by public school teachers and students.

    URL address: **telnet://spacelink.msfc.nasa.gov/**

- NASA Headline News

    URL address: **http://www.cs.indiana.edu/finger/gateway/ nasanewsespace.mit.edu**

- NASA Kennedy Space Center Home Page

    URL address: **http://www.ksc.nasa.gov/ksc.html**

VI

Finding Web Resources

Dinosaurs—Honolulu Community College

URL address: **http://www.hcc.hawaii.edu/dinos/dinos.1.html**

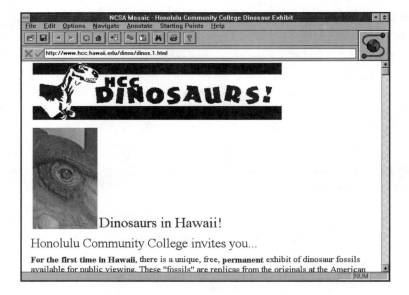

Dinosaurs are everywhere—movies, television programs, T-shirts—and now on the Web. Did you know that the triceratops lived 70 million years ago, grew to 30 feet long, and weighed 7 tons? Take this wonderful trip to the WWW server at Honolulu Community College where you can learn (or teach) about dinosaurs. There are some terrific images of these prehistoric creatures, and the exhibits in this electronic museum contain artifacts from around the world.

From the home page you begin a guided tour, which you can either read or hear (by clicking the audio icon). You get the feeling that a real guide stands beside you as a voice says, "We could not afford nor did we have the space for the full tyrannosaurus rex skeleton, so we did also purchase, here on the right, a full tyrannosaurus rex hind leg. It stands 12 to 13 feet tall as you can see there; and as you look at this leg, the bones of the feet and the leg, you can see very much the connection with birds...."

Australian National Botanic Gardens

URL address: **http://155.187.10.12:80/index.html**

Fig. 30.3
Go "down under"
and learn about
the thousands of
plants that grow in
Australia.

Australia has much more to offer than kangaroos and beer. The logo for this WWW home page, a Banksia branch with one flowering and one fruiting inflorescence superimposed over a map of the Australian continent, gives you some idea about the topic—plant life in Australia. This WWW site is a valuable resource for both the serious gardener and the professional botanist.

Located in Canberra, the Australian National Botanic Gardens maintains a collection of some 90,000 native plants from all parts of the continent. Learn about the science and the gardening requirements for flowers, plants, and trees. The Flower of the Week link provides information about a specific flower that is in bloom at the Gardens. You can almost smell the aroma as you read the descriptions—"The perfume of golden wattles pervades throughout the gardens, whilst banksias, grevilleas, and hakeas continue to flower." Other home page links bring you to:

- ANBG Integrated Botanical Information System (IBIS)
- Bibliography of plant identification
- A selection of botanical glossaries
- Australian Nature Conservation Agency Libraries
- Centre for Plant Biodiversity Research (CPBR)
- Australian Biological Resources Study (ABRS)
- Australian Network for Plant Conservation (ANPC)

National Renewable Energy Laboratory

URL address: **http://www.nrel.gov**

Fig. 30.4
Wind power, photovoltaics, biofuels—these are some of the renewable energy technologies that you find at the NREL home page.

Scientific research plays an important role in the understanding and application of resources and technologies that simultaneously provide energy and improve the environment. NREL, a national laboratory of the United States Department of Energy, is renowned for its research activities in renewable energy.

NREL's WWW server provides information about the laboratory and research activities, which encompass photovoltaics, wind energy, biofuels, biomass power, fuels utilization, solar industrial and building technologies, and solar thermal electric and waste management. From the home page, you can access information about this research, commercial and experimental applications, energy resource maps, publications, business partnerships—even job opportunities at the lab.

Acoustics

Acoustics Lecture

URL address: **http://www.isi.ee.ethz.ch/~schmid/work/akustik/**

The home page tells us, "These are the lecture notes for a lecture given by Prof. Eric Rathe at the Swiss Federal Institute of Technology." The text is also available as PostScript files and is written in German.

Acoustic and Vibration Group of Sherbrooke University

URL address: **http://www-gaus.gme.usherb.ca/gaus_ang.html**

This is the home page for a Canadian research group that works exclusively in the study of acoustics and vibrations. There are links here to research papers and overviews of projects.

International Lung Sounds Association

URL address: **http://www.umanitoba.ca/Medicine/Pediatrics/ILSA/
index.html**

This organization focuses on respiration acoustics, and the links bring you to
abstracts, bibliographies, tools, and techniques.

Agricultural (Botany) and Animal Sciences

Agricultural Information Links

URL address: **http://www.cs.indiana.edu/internet/agri.html**

This home page offers links to a variety of agricultural information including
livestock reports and market prices. Main links include agricultural information at Penn State, CSU Fresno, Clemson, Purdue, and Cornell.

Agricultural Genome World Wide Web Server

URL address: **http://probe.nalusda.gov:8000/about.html**
URL address: **http://probe.nalusda.gov:8000/animal/index.html**

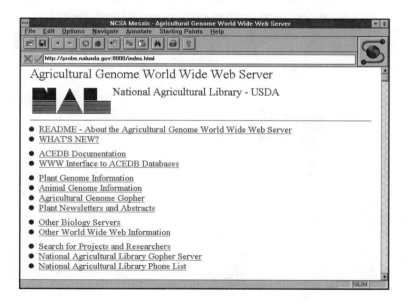

Fig. 30.5
You can access a
wealth of useful
plant, animal, and
biology informa-
tion from this
page.

VI

Finding Web Resources

The Agricultural Genome WWW server is a service provided by the USDA and the National Agricultural Library in Beltsville, Maryland. This information is useful to farmers or to anyone who may have an interest in plants, animals, or biology. There is even a link to a National Agricultural Library telephone list.

Animal Sounds

URL address: **http://info.fuw.edu.pl/multimedia/sounds.animals**

Do you want to hear a bat? A cow? A donkey? This server maintains an enormous collection of animal noises. Download and play these short sound bites.

FDA Animal Drug Database

URL address: **http://borg.lib.vt.edu/ejournals/vetfda.html**

The Generic Animal Drug and Patent Restoration Act of 1988 requires that a list of all FDA-approved animal drug products be made available to the public. This information is available via the Veterinary Medical Informatics Laboratory server at Virginia Polytechnic Institute and University.

Insects—CSU Gillette Entomology Club

URL address: **http://www.colostate.edu/Depts/Entomology/ ent.html**

Fig. 30.6
Neat bug pictures and more infest this site.

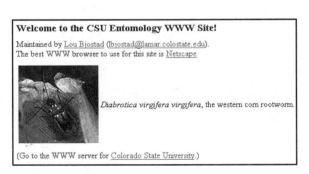

> **Welcome to the CSU Entomology WWW Site!**
>
> Maintained by Lou Bjostad (lbjostad@lamar.colostate.edu).
> The best WWW browser to use for this site is Netscape.
>
> *Diabrotica virgifera virgifera*, the western corn rootworm.
>
> (Go to the WWW server for Colorado State University.)

Fascinated by the world of insects? Take a peek at slide 281, a close-up of *Vanessa cardui* (painted lady butterfly), or slide 364, a visually stunning image of *Agrosoma placetis* (adult leafhopper on chili leaf). The Gillette Entomology Club at Colorado State University offers a large collection of insect slides for sale, including comprehensive lists of insects that are pests.

Japanese Dairy Cattle Improvement Program

URL address: **http://ws4.niai.affrc.go.jp/dairy/dairy.html**

This site provides an overview of several Japanese Dairy Cattle Improvement Programs including genetic evaluation, dairy bull progeny testing, and a dairy herd improvement program.

Fig. 30.7
Moo. This site provides an overview of several Japanese dairy cattle improvement programs.

Mammal Species of the World

URL address: **gopher://nmnhgoph.si.edu/00/.docs/mammals_info/ about**

This checklist contains the names of the 4,629 known species of mammals. They are categorized in a taxonomic hierarchy that includes order, family, subfamily, and genus. Caution—be sure to include the period before the word "docs" in the URL address!

Meat Animal Research Center

URL address: **http://sol.marc.usda.gov**

This is the home page for the USDA Meat Animal Research Center located in Clay Center, Nebraska.

New York State Agricultural Experiment Station

URL address: **http://aruba.nysaes.cornell.edu:8000/about.htm**

The New York State Agricultural Experiment Station is part of the New York State College of Agriculture and Life Sciences. Here, you can access information on a variety of animal sciences including pest management, plant genetics, and horticultural sciences.

Plant Genome Information

URL address: **http://probe.nalusda.gov:8300**

The data contained in the Plant Genome server comes from collaborators who collect, organize, and evaluate data for individual specimens.

Prescription Farming
URL address: **http://ma.itd.com:8000/p-farming.html**

The Space Remote Sensing Center sponsors this WWW server. By using satellite and computer technology, farmers can detect trouble spots, such as bug infestations, and customize fertilizer use in specific sections of a field.

University of Delaware College of Agricultural Sciences
URL address: **gopher://bluehen.ags.udel.edu:71/hh/.recruit/ AgriculturalSci.html**

This site provides complete information on this school, which has a greenhouse laboratory and a 350-acre teaching and research complex that maintains beef cattle, sheep, swine, horses, poultry, and a herd of dairy cows.

Veterinary Medicine Educational Network
URL address: **http://www.vetnet.ucdavis.edu**

This server contains academic program information and links to other veterinary medicine schools and colleges.

Fig. 30.8
The Veterinary Medicine Educational Network.

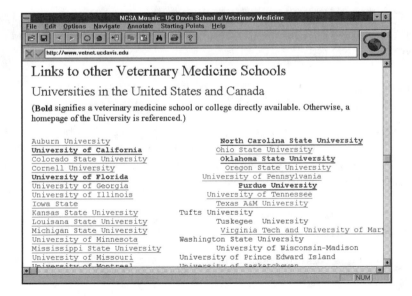

W.M. Keck Center for Genome Information
URL address: **http://keck.tamu.edu/cgi/goals/goals.html**

This center provides computer hardware and software to support the study of plant and animal genomes of agricultural and biomedical interest. The site houses information of interest to both the agricultural and the biomedical communities, and promotes interaction and exchange of information between these communities.

Anthropology

Anthropology Laboratory
URL address: **http://www.usc.edu/dept/v-lib/anthropology.html**

This home page is a powerful tool for anthropologists who are involved in fieldwork, research, publication, and education. You can jump to documents that use the WWW as a tool for anthropology, including a version of a Mambila transcript with digitized recordings and noun classification in Swahili.

A large number of the World Wide Web's available anthropology resources are also indexed through this site, making it a pointer to such important sources as the Anthropology and Culture Archives at Rice University, Yale University's Peabody Museum of Natural History, the Bishop Museum in Honolulu, and the Center for World Indigenous Studies' Fourth World Documentation Project. This is a rich resource.

Astronomy

Aurora Borealis
URL address: **ftp://xi.uleth.ca/pub/solar/Aurora/Images**

If you enjoy seeing images of auroral activity, here is an FTP site that houses a great many of them. You can download them to your own computer.

American Astronomical Society

URL address: **http://blackhole.aas.org/AAS-homepage.html**

This WWW address takes you to the American Astronomical Society home page. From here, you can learn about the society and meeting schedules or jump into a wide array of options.

Astronomy

URL address: **http://info.cern.ch/hypertext/DataSources/bySubject/astro/astro.html**

Fig. 30.9
See the stars and more from this page.

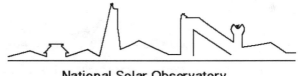

National Solar Observatory

When you connect with this home page, you are at "T minus 10," about to head to other worlds. Check out indexes at NASA, the XXII General Assembly of the International Astronomical Union, the Sloan Digital Sky Survey, the STELAR project, the Space Telescope Electronic Information System, or the Astrophysics Data System project. The National Solar Observatory home page (**http://argo.tuc.noao.edu**) is also available through CERN's Astronomy home page.

Companies

URL address: **ftp://furmint.nectar.cs.cmu.edu/usr2/anon/space-companies**

This FTP site provides a list of companies related to the space industry. Whether you are looking for a job or just interested in seeing who is involved, this is a good point of information.

Italian National Telescope Galileo

URL address: **http://www.pd.astro.it/TNG/TNG.html**

Astronomy fans learn about this telescope facility, which serves all of Italy. You can also view images on the development of this project.

Magellan Mission to Venus

URL address: **http://newproducts.jpl.nasa.gov/magellan**

NASA's Jet Propulsion Lab offers this site about the Magellan mission to Venus, which ended with a dramatic plunge of the satellite into the atmosphere of Venus. Check out a comprehensive gallery of images and information from the five-year mission.

Northern Lights Planetarium

URL address: **http://www.uit.no/npt/homepage-npt.en.html**

From Norway, this site focuses on spreading knowledge about nature's gigantic lightshow known as Aurora Borealis. In addition to the information about the Northern Lights, the server contains documents about the Northern Lights Planetarium and links to other Web sites in Norway.

Planetary Information

URL address: **http://astrosun.tn.cornell.edu/Home.html**

This is the WWW server home page on astronomy information from Cornell University. It includes the archives of *Icarus*, the international journal of solar system exploration, among other resources.

Space Flights

URL address: **ftp://archive.afit.af.mil/pub/space**
URL address: **ftp://kilroy.jpl.nasa.gov/pub/space**

The Orbital Element Sets from NASA, and others, are available at these FTP sites. For individuals trying to track space flights, this is valuable information.

Space Students

URL address: **http://seds.lpl.arizona.edu/**

This WWW server is offered by the Students for the Exploration and Development of Space, based in Arizona. If you are a student and want to find others who are serious about space, check this out.

VI

Finding Web Resources

Fig. 30.10
The space students page has links to information that will help students gain a better understanding of astronomy.

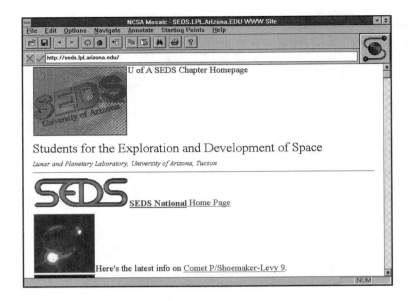

Biology

Biosciences

URL address: **http://golgi.harvard.edu/biopages/all.html**

This home page may take longer than usual to load, not because there are a lot of fancy graphics, but because of the vast number of hyperlinks here—perhaps more than 100 and many that relate to biology and the sciences. The hyperlinks to information are categorized first by provider and then by subject, and cover the areas of anthropology, archaeology, evolution, biological journals, biological molecules, Internet resources, biological software and data FTP archives, and molecular evolution. You could spend a day going back and forth from this home page!

Marine Biological Laboratory

URL address: **http://alopias.mbl.edu/Default.html**

Founded in 1888, MBL, located in Woods Hole, Massachusetts, is America's oldest marine lab. This server offers in-depth information about the lab and biological sciences that relate to marine life. You can learn about research and education programs, browse through the Women of Science project files, or reference an online catalog of marine flora and fauna specimens.

Optometry—The VizWiz Server

URL address: **http://research.opt.indiana.edu/VizWiz.html**

This page has a link to a database of clinical information and procedures about optometry collected from several institutions. There's also an online slide show about how to use the database.

Parasite Page

URL address: **http://www.umich.edu/~cardtris/cardtris.htm**

If you've ever been scared in 6th grade by the thought of a tapeworm slowly eating you from inside, you'll enjoy this site. There are links to information about biological parasites and some "related" links to short stories and government activities that are considered parasitic.

Proteins and Enzymes—Johns Hopkins Bioinformatics

URL address: **http://www.gdb.org/hopkins.html**

This site represents a set of links that connect to different protein databases around the world.

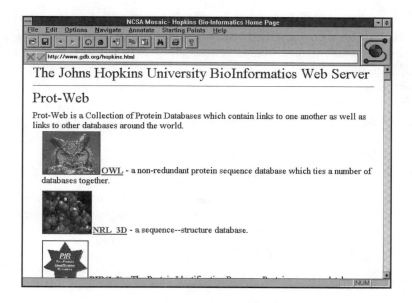

Fig. 30.11
Proteins and enzymes—the building blocks of life—are features at this WWW home site. The protein database, which Johns Hopkins maintains, is a collection of protein sequences and structures.

Protein Science
URL address: **http://www.prosci.uci.edu**

This is an electronic version of a journal devoted to the science of proteins. Links are also available to images and other sites on the Web devoted to scientists and researchers involved in this unique area of science.

Shark Images
URL address: **http://ucmp1.berkeley.edu/Doug/shark.html**

The shark is one of the oldest living organisms on the planet, with a history that dates back some 400 million years. If you have a fascination with this creature, or want to take a close-up look at the Great White shark, this Web site will oblige. In all, this site has 14 separate images of sharks.

Chemistry

Crystallographic Data Centre
URL address: **http://www.chem.ucla.edu/chempointers.html**

This home page has links to a variety of chemistry sites and documents that focus on the study of crystals. These include the Cambridge Crystallographic Data Centre, the Chemistry Server at the Center for Scientific Computing (Finland), the Chemical Physics Preprint Database, the Computer Center Institute for Molecular Science, the Department of Applied Molecular Science (SOUKAN), Crystallography in Europe, and the chemistry departments at major universities and institutes worldwide.

Chemical Physics Preprint Database
URL address: **http://www.chem.brown.edu/chem-ph.html**

This is a joint chemical/physics database maintained by the Department of Chemistry at Brown University and the Theoretical Chemistry and Molecular Physics Group at the Los Alamos National Laboratory. The target audience is the international theoretical chemistry community.

Crystals
URL address: **http://www.unige.ch/**

Link to the Geneva University server and then choose Crystallography to find information regarding crystallography in Europe on a WWW server maintained by the European Crystallographic Committee.

Pacific Forestry Center

URL address: **http://pine.pfc.forestry.ca**

A description of the Canadian Advanced Forest Technologies Program, this WWW server takes you into the field of wood and wood product research. This is a great home page if you want to get involved in advanced forestry.

Fig. 30.12
Visit this home page and the next time you "knock on wood," you'll think about the science behind the material.

Periodic Table

URL address: **http://www.cchem.berkeley.edu/Table/index.html**

The Periodic Table is available online from this server at Berkeley. It is clickable! When you click an element's symbol, you see a full explanation (see fig. 30.13).

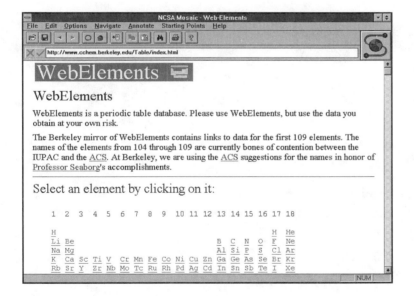

Fig. 30.13
The periodic table was never so much fun in school.

Complex Systems

Complex systems represents a field of scientific study that has become popular in the past decade. It should come as no surprise that the world we live in is "complex"—events, animals, and plants all interact constantly. Hence, the study of these interrelationships is termed *complex systems*. The specific areas of scientific study include artificial life, biocomplexity, cellular automata, chaos, criticality, fractals, learning systems, neural networks, nonlinear dynamics, parallel computation, and self-organization. These areas of scientific research represent a new paradigm for scientists as research begins to cut across traditional disciplines such as biology and chemistry.

Artificial Intelligence

Gopher address: **gopher://life.anu.edu.au:70/11/complex_systems/ai**

Of course, if scientists are studying artificial life, certainly they are studying artificial intelligence! This Gopher site at the Australian National University is a good one.

Artificial Life Online

URL address: **http://alife.santafe.edu/**

Fig. 30.14
Explore the science behind artificial life via Artificial Life Online.

Check out this WWW server on artificial life from the Santa Fe Institute. This is a good place to start looking at the study of complex systems.

Cellular Automata—Tutorial for Beginners

URL address: **http://life.anu.edu.au:80/complex_systems/ tutorial1.html**

This WWW server in Australia provides a hypermedia tutorial on cellular automata.

Complexity International

URL address: **http://life.anu.edu.au/ci/ci.html**

The hypermedia journal *Complexity International* publishes papers of original, previously unpublished work in the field of complex systems.

Complex Systems Information on the Internet

URL address: **http://www.seas.upenn.edu/~ale/cplxsys.html**

Head towards this WWW server to find a guide to Internet resources on complex systems.

Fractals—Fractal Microscope

URL address: **http://www.ncsa.uiuc.edu/Edu/Fractal/Fractal_Home.html**

The Fractal Microscope

A Distributed Computing Approach to Mathematics in Education

Fig. 30.15
The Fractal Microscope page is designed to help scientists understand more about complex systems.

The Fractal Microscope is of major interest to scientists working with complex systems. This WWW server is a home page and can take the visitor to many other resources.

Fractals—Images

URL address: **http://www.cnam.fr/fractals.html**

This WWW server in France offers numerous images of fractals.

Fractals—Mandelbrot Set

URL address: **gopher://life.anu.edu.au:70/I9/.WWW/complex_systems/mandel1.gif**

To download the basic Mandelbrot set shown in GIF format, go to this site.

Fractals—Tutorial

URL address: **http://life.anu.edu.au:80/complex_systems/tutorial3.html**

This home page provides a hypermedia tutorial on fractals and scale.

VI

Finding Web Resources

Fuzzy Logic—Tutorial

URL address: **http://life.anu.edu.au:80/complex_systems/fuzzy.html**

This WWW server in Australia provides a hypermedia tutorial on fuzzy logic.

Engineering

Chemical Engineering

URL address: **http://www.che.ufl.edu/WWW-CHE/index.html**

Chemical engineering information from a variety of sources is indexed here. This index provides WWW jump points to chemistry departments at the University of Florida, Edinburgh University, Rensselaer Polytechnic Institute, the University of California (Riverside), Virginia Polytechnic Institute and State University, Kansas State University, and the Cornell University School of Chemical Engineering.

Civil Engineering at Georgia Tech

URL address: **http://howe.ce.gatech.edu/WWW-CE/home.html**

Take the WWW route to Georgia Tech's home page to learn more about the institution and its work in the field of civil engineering.

Cornell's Engineering Library

URL address: **http://www.englib.cornell.edu**

If you are on the hunt for information regarding engineering, check out this WWW server at Cornell's Engineering Library.

Electrical Engineering

URL address: **http://epims1.gsfc.nasa.gov/engineering/ee.html**

If you want to know what NASA has to do with electrical engineering, check out this WWW server.

Engineering Case Study Library

URL address: **http://www.civeng.carleton.ca/cgi-bin/ecl-query/ ECL/abstracts.db/html-url=1**

This catalog lists cases available from the ASEE Engineering Case Program, which are currently distributed by the Rose-Hulman Institute of Technology.

The cases are accounts of real engineering work written for use in engineering education, and cover most engineering disciplines. A small number of cases are available electronically.

Industrial Engineering

URL address: **http://isye.gatech.edu/www-ie/**

Georgia Tech offers information on industrial engineering via its WWW server. Naturally, you'll also find out about the university while visiting this site.

Materials Engineering

URL address: **http://m_struct.mie.clarkson.edu/VLmae.html**

Clarkson University hosts this WWW site and maintains information regarding materials, engineering, and its university programs.

Mechanical Engineering

URL address: **http://CDR.stanford.edu/html/WWW-ME/home.html**

This Stanford WWW home page takes you well into the world of mechanical engineering. This site has lots of jump points and information.

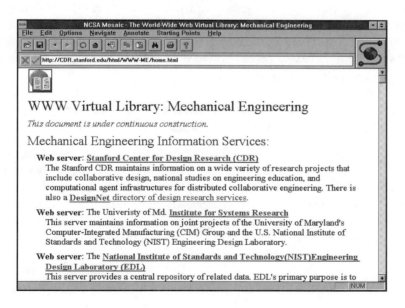

Fig. 30.16
The mechanical engineering section in the Virtual Library.

VI

Finding Web Resources

Nuclear Engineering

URL address: **http://neutrino.nuc.berkeley.edu/NEadm.html**

This frequently updated site is in Berkeley and serves as the WWW Virtual Library for nuclear engineering. Many WWW sites are accessible from here, including the Chernobyl database and a nuclear safety site.

UIUC Student Engineering Council

URL address: **http://stimpy.cen.uiuc.edu/**

The University of Illinois Urbana-Champaign is home to one of the most active Student Engineering Councils in the country. Every year, they sponsor many student-run events for student engineering societies, the College of Engineering, and the community. Two of the largest events are the Engineering Employment EXPO and the UIUC Engineering Open House.

Environmental Sciences

Climate—Centre for Atmospheric Science

URL Address: **http://www.atm.ch.cam.ac.uk/**

Located at the University of Cambridge, UK, this site offers information on the Center itself, such as degrees offered and seminars, as well as information about the UK Universities Global Atmospheric Modeling Programme (UGAMP). This includes a connection to the UGAMP FTP server, which offers software and publications.

Climate—German Climate Computer Center

URL address: **http://www.dkrz.de/index-eng.html**

This is the WWW server of the German Climate Computer Center. The English part of this server is still under construction, but is definitely worth checking out. The German Climate Computer Center is a supercomputing center for climate research and is charged with providing the German climate research community with computational, archival, and post processing resources. Here you find information about the German Climate Computer Center, climate research, conferences, and workshops.

Environmental Research Institute of Michigan (ERIM)

URL address: **http://www.erim.org**

(Last Update: 12/21/94)

Fig. 30.17
Remote sensing
and image
processing are two
of the areas of
research that ERIM
performs.

ERIM is a non-profit, high-technology organization that performs research
and development and related services for its sponsors. They have expertise in
the areas of remote sensing techniques and applications, image and signal
processing, and technology transfer.

Landscape and Environments

URL address: **http://life.anu.edu.au/landscape_ecology/
landscape.html**

At this Australian site, you find abstracts that relate to landscape ecology,
biogeography, paleoenvironments, paleoclimates, pollen, fire, and weather.

National Oceanic and Atmospheric Administration (NOAA)

URL address: **telnet://NOAADIR@nodc.nodc.noaa.gov**

This is an interactive connection to the National Oceanic and Atmospheric
Administration database.

National Water Condition Report

URL address: **http://nwcwww.er.usgs.gov:8080**

Water, water everywhere. This is the electronic version of the United States
Geological summary on surface water, ground water, and reservoir conditions
from across the United States and Canada. Find out about recent rainfall,
historical flooding, and water conditions.

VI

Finding Web Resources

Ocean Research Institute (ORI), University of Tokyo
URL address: **http://www.ori.u-tokyo.ac.jp**

The Ocean Research Institute at the University of Tokyo promotes research about the marine sciences. You'll find out about ORI, including the five-year cruise plans for the Institute's research vessels, reports from past cruises, and pointers to other oceanographic Web sites.

United States Fish and Wildlife Service
URL address: **http://bluegoose.arw.r9.fws.gov**

◀ See "Depart-
ment of the
Interior,"
p. 681

This WWW server provides information about the National Wildlife Refuge System and topics of interest for wildlife and natural resources management.

Geology

Canada—Natural Resources
URL address: **http://www.emr.ca**

This Web site is similar to the USGS site in the United States. Maintained by the Canadian Forest Service, this site provides links to government departments and resources in energy, geomatics, and minerals.

Canada—The Model Forest Program
URL address: **http://NCR157.NCR.Forestry.CA/MF.HTM**

Fig. 30.18
One of the slides
in this presenta-
tion is a map
showing the
make-up of the
Canadian forest by
type of vegetation.

Here is an excellent example of the merging of two technologies. This page contains an interactive photo presentation from Photo CD on Canada's forests. Don't miss this!

Finland—Geological Survey

URL address: **http://www.gsf.fi**

This government-run WWW site is responsible for acquiring and making data available (on the Web) about geological information and natural resources in Finland.

MIT Earth Resources Lab

URL address: **http://www-erl.mit.edu/**

This high-end home page describes the ERL as "primarily concerned with applied geophysics as it relates to tectonophysics, seismology (especially seismic exploration), environmental engineering, and parallel computing."

Volcanoes

URL address: **http://www.geo.mtu.edu/eos/**

Get ready to explode! At this home page, you find information about NASA projects that investigate volcanoes, the type of sensing equipment that scientists use, the data that they collect, and images of volcanoes.

Meteorology

Current Weather Maps and Movies

URL address: **http://rs560.cl.msu.edu/weather**

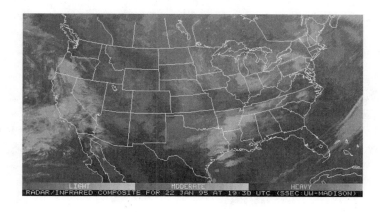

Fig. 30.19
The Michigan State University WWW Weather server offers both still images and movies that depict current weather conditions.

This weather database receives weather information from around and above the globe, including the Department of Meteorology at the University of

Edinburgh, Scotland and NASA readings. Every hour, maps in this database are updated so that you can see weather patterns as they are happening—it's almost as good as TV weather. In addition to still images, you can view weather movies, if you have viewing software that handles the MPEG format.

Kochi University—Weather Index

URL address: **http://www.is.kochi-u.ac.jp/weather/index.en.html**

Going to the Far East? Located in Japan, this WWW home page offers a collection of images about the Earth's environment and weather information. Specific images of weather conditions in Japan, the Asian area, and southern hemisphere are provided. Retrieve JPEG, GIF, and MPEG animation (15 frames per second).

MIT Radar Lab

URL address: **http://graupel.mit.edu/Radar_Lab.html**

This unique collection of weather information includes a weather gallery, a list of frequently asked questions, a hypertext glossary of weather terminology, and a history of radar at MIT. The lab maintains an archive that contains 20 years of observations of storm systems.

NCAR Data Support

URL address: **http://www.ucar.edu/metapage.html**

The National Center for Atmospheric Research (NCAR) supervises research programs and maintains databases of information that relate to meteorology. This WWW home page offers links to some of these resources.

Purdue Weather Processor

URL address: **http://thunder.atms.purdue.edu**

This WWW server uses a software program called WXP to create "weather visualization" for current and past meteorological data. The result is a variety of digital weather maps produced from satellite, surface, air, and radar readings. Weather forecasts range from 48 hours to 7 days—this will help you plan that vacation.

Space Environment Lab

URL address: **http://www.sel.bldrdoc.gov/today.html**

Weather is not limited to events on Earth. When you visit this server, located at the National Oceanic and Atmospheric Administration (NOAA), you can see the "weather" conditions in space and on the sun. A variety of images of the sun show current conditions on the sun's surface and solar radiation patterns.

Museums

Conservation OnLine

URL address: **http://palimpsest.stanford.edu/**

Conservation OnLine (CoOL) is devoted to information concerning the conservation of museum, library, and archives information. What is science without museums, libraries, and archives?

Dinosaurs—The Berkeley Hall of Dinosaurs

URL address: **http://ucmp1.berkeley.edu/exhibittext/ cladecham.html**

The Hall of Dinosaurs has exhibits from around the world. This museum offers a hypermedia tour of the science of paleontology. The graphics are very good, and the "hot buttons" provide an effective method of touring the place.

Discovery Center

URL address: **http://www.cfn.cs.dal.ca/Science/DiscCentre/ DC_Home.html**

Based in Nova Scotia, Canada, this museum is devoted to educating students and the general public about science and technology. The home page has links to a weather forecasting exhibit, a hypertext newsletter, information about the museum, and other Web sites that focus on science.

Gems & Minerals—Smithsonian

URL address: **http://galaxy.einet.net/images/gems/gems-icons.html**

This is from the Smithsonian Gem & Mineral Collection. It takes about two minutes (at 14.4 Kbps) to load this home page—but it's worth the wait. A beautiful display of gems and minerals ranging from the brilliant blue azurite to a 68-carat diamond (46 different color images in all) appears on the home page (see fig. 30.20). Click the name of a gem for further information.

Fig. 30.20
Although you might not be able to buy the 68-carat diamond illustrated on a later screen of this home page, you will enjoy the overview of gems and minerals.

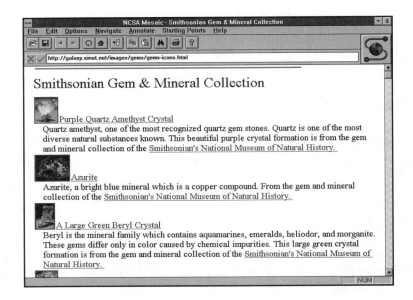

Natural History in London
URL address: **http://www.nhm.ac.uk/**

This site is from the Natural History Museum, London. The history of the natural sciences is one of the broadest fields of scientific study—learn about our planet and the animals that inhabit Earth.

Ontario Science Center
URL address: **http://www.osc.on.ca/**

Fun for all ages. This is the site of the electronic version of this very real museum devoted to exploration of science. You can jump to a floor plan of the museum and then click areas to visit exhibits. Some of the other home page links offer a "Young Person's Guide to the Internet," an exhibit of the human body, a newsletter, and articles from the magazine *Newscience*.

Physics Instruments Museum
URL address: **http://hpl33.na.infn.it/Museum/Museum.html**

This site displays early instruments of the Institute of Physics of Naples. If you use current physics instruments, you will enjoy touring the exhibits of gadgetry once used by scientists and students to learn of our world.

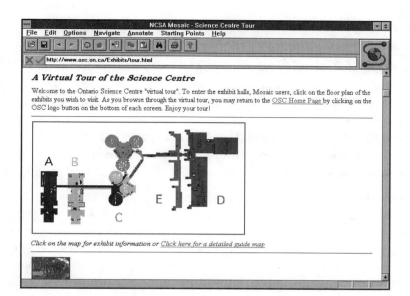

Fig. 30.21
The Ontario Science Center offers an interactive Web site where you take a virtual tour of the museum.

San Francisco Exploratorium

URL address: **http://www.exploratorium.edu/**

An all-time favorite for science buffs in its nonelectronic version, this WWW server includes online exhibits.

University of California Museum of Paleontology

URL address: **http://ucmp1.berkeley.edu/noinline.html**

Located on the campus of the University of California at Berkeley, the UCMP is responsible for the conservation of paleontological materials, collections development, and research and instructional support. The Museum's collections, rated fourth in size for all collections in America, include protists, plants, invertebrates, and vertebrates.

Physics

Astrophysics—Abstracts

URL address: **http://adswww.harvard.edu/abs_doc/abstract_service.html**

This Web server is for researchers, writers, students, and anyone interested in space physics. It connects you to the Astrophysics Data System Abstract Service.

VI

Finding Web Resources

Astrophysics—European Space Information System
URL address: **http://mesis.esrin.esa.it/html/esis.html**

This WWW server comes from the European Space Information System (ESIS), which is the European equivalent to the United States' NASA program. This site leads you to explore many other servers around the world.

Astrophysics—Frequently Asked Questions
URL address: **ftp://rtfm.mit.edu/pub/usenet-by-group/ sci.space.news**

This site provides answers to Frequently Asked Questions (FAQs) on the **sci.space news** newsgroup. The purpose of an FAQ site is to reduce the amount of needless question-asking on the newsgroup. It is always a good idea to check out the related FAQ prior to asking general questions on the newsgroup. If you move up one directory, you can access many other science newsgroups.

Astrophysics—Space Images
URL address: **ftp://iris1.ucis.dal.ca/pub/gif**

This FTP site is available on the Web. Here you will find GIF images from Voyager, Hubble, and other sources of space images.

Astrophysics—Space Telescope
URL address: **telnet://STARCAT@stesis.hq.eso.org/**

This site offers an interactive session in the Space Telescope–European Coordinating Facility STARCAT archive. Look into this searchable database for more information about how the European telescope community works.

Astrophysics—Space Telescope Science Institute
URL address: **http://stsci.edu/top.html**

This is the WWW server offered by the Space Telescope Science Institute's electronic information service. Space telescopes are more electronic than optical these days, which means that many, many, digital images are being created and stored. This is one place to learn more about this field of science.

Atomic and Solid State Physics (LASSP)
URL address: **http://www.lassp.cornell.edu/sethna/sethna.html**

This is the home page for the LASSP World Wide Web server, located at Cornell University. Entertaining science is done here!

High Energy Physics

URL address: **http://heplibw3.slac.stanford.edu/FIND/ FHMAIN.HTML**

This Stanford University WWW server provides a free guide to high energy physics software. If you are active in the study of high energy physics, you will find this server very useful.

High Energy Physics

URL address: **http://wwwcn.cern.ch/hepix/overview.html**

This server provides general information about high energy physics. As an overview site, it provides a terrific place from which to jump to more specific information. CERN is also the home of the World Wide Web.

High Energy Physics

URL address: **http://info.desy.de/user/projects/Lattice.html**

Lattice field theory is one area of high energy physics that warrants a server dedicated to describing the various projects going on. This one is located in Germany.

High Energy Physics

URL address: **http://www.cern.ch/Physics/PhysSoc.html**

CERN offers this directory of physics societies on its WWW server. This is a good starting point if you want to locate a physics society for general information, to join, or to subscribe to various print or electronic publications.

High Energy Physics

URL address: **http://slacvm.slac.stanford.edu/find/explist.html**

This Stanford server presents a compilation of experiments' home pages. If you want to keep track of various experiments in progress, try this server.

High Energy Physics Newsletters

URL address: **http://www.hep.net/documents/newsletters/ newsletters.html**

This WWW server presents a compilation of physics newsletters. This is an extremely valuable tool for individuals who seek more information about high energy physics than they can possibly absorb!

Low Temperature Laboratory

URL address: **http://www.hut.fi/English/HUT/Units/Separate/
LowTemperature/**

This address takes you to Finland where you can find out what's happening
where it is really cold!

Physics

URL address: **http://info.cern.ch/hypertext/DataSources/bySubject/
Physics/ Overview.html**

This server provides a hypertext directory of physics resources. Its links lead
to a mind-boggling array of physics research and information sources.

Resources

BEST North America

URL address: **http://medoc.gdb.org/best.html**

Identify and locate researchers with interests and expertise that match
yours—assuming that you are a researcher. This site has an online inventory
of researchers, inventions, and facilities at U.S. and Canadian universities and
other organizations. In all, there are 40,000 records of individuals, 5,000
inventions, and 2,000 facilities.

Canada Institute for Scientific and Technical Information

URL address: **http://www.cisti.nrc.ca/cisti/cisti.html**

CISTI is a supplier of scientific, technical, engineering, and medical information. It is also the library of the National Research Council of Canada. The
information on this site covers CISTI products and services, bibliographic and
scientific databases, and research journals and books. The link to SwetScan
lets you search the table of contents of 14,000 scientific journals! It is available in both English and French.

Innovator Newsletter

URL address: **http://succeed.che.ufl.edu/SUCCEED/pubs/innovator/**

This newsletter provides information on the education research activities and developments of the Southeastern University and College Coalition for Engineering Education. Also included are publication lists, conference announcements, and relevant information on other initiatives in undergraduate engineering education improvement.

Knowledge Sharing Effort (KSE)

URL address: **http://www-ksl.stanford.edu/knowledge-sharing/ README.html**

The Knowledge Sharing Effort (KSE) public library is a public directory for information and software related to the ARPA Knowledge Sharing Effort.

The National Institute of Standards and Technology (NIST)

URL address: **http://www.nist.gov/welcome.html**

NIST sponsors and conducts a variety of scientific research programs ranging from biotechnology to computer technology. Many efforts, such as the Manufacturing Extension Centers, directly help industry and small business.

Search for Projects and Researchers

URL address: **http://probe.nalusda.gov:8300/projects.html**

A list of indexes of funded research proposals is provided to allow the user to search for people or topics. The areas covered are the National Institute of Health, the Department of Energy, the National Science Foundation, and the United States Department of Agriculture.

Telecommunications

Amateur Radio (aka Ham Radio)

URL address: **http://buarc.bradley.edu/**

This site provides general information such as: What is Amateur Radio?, Amateur Radio Information, Shortwave/Radio Catalog, University of Hawaii/Amateur Radio Information, Shuttle Amateur Radio Experiment, the US & Canada Callbook, Amateur Radio Clubs, and UseNet newsgroups.

From Here...

Science is a topic that has few boundaries—either political or imaginative. The sites in this chapter should get you well on your way to understanding the mysteries of the universe. If you need more, try these chapters:

- Chapter 23, "Education," describes many Web sites devoted to helping people learn about the sciences.

- Chapter 25, "Health and Medicine," offers Web sites that deal with the use of science to solve medical conditions.

- Chapter 31, "Shopping," covers Web sites that sell scientific products.

Chapter 31

Shopping

by Bill Eager

Would you like to shop in a mall where there are never any parking hassles? Where the stores are never out-of-stock, new merchandise appears on a regular basis, and you are always the first in line? If this appeals to you, explore some of the electronic shopping malls and stores on the World Wide Web. A number of service providers and companies now operate malls where a home page is simultaneously a front door and a directory for many different specialty stores.

Taking full advantage of the multimedia aspects of the WWW, these cyberspace stores offer digital images and sound clips that describe their products and services. If you like the merchandise, you often can fill out an online order form and receive the product the next day! Window shopping takes on a new dimension with the global nature of the WWW. Now, it's as easy to visit an exotic or specialty store that's 8,000 miles away as it is to drive downtown. Or, you may want to plan your next visit to a foreign shopping center. Countries like Japan and cities like Singapore have World Wide Web home pages that offer tips on converting sizes for clothing from United States to foreign standards, or color maps that identify streets and individual shops. From a compact disc of classical music to a bottle of rare Slovenian wine to a high-powered motorboat, there is probably a WWW store that will satisfy your shopping needs.

The resources in this chapter focus on WWW home pages and companies that directly sell products or services. The stores in this chapter are in the following categories:

- Arts—From paintings to earrings.

- Books—Books for science fiction readers and computer book readers.

- Computers—Hard drives, CD-ROMS, and PCs are a few of your choices.

- Electronic Malls—These digital malls have many different stores and companies in them.

- Hobbies and recreation—Whether you bike, hike, or like to play card games, these sites offer what you want.

- Gifts and products—Browse through electronic flower shops, auto dealer lots, even food stores.

- Services—From resumes to on-location photography.

Internet Shopping Network

URL address: **http://shop.internet.net**

Fig. 31.1
You can search through and purchase 20,000 computer-related products from the Internet Shopping Network's WWW site.

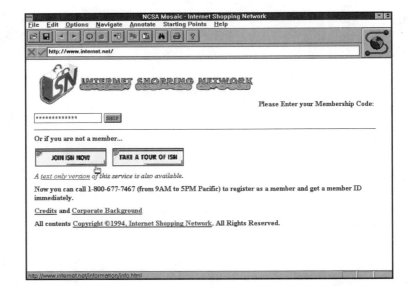

The Internet Shopping Network (ISN) began online operation in 1994. The major purpose of this electronic mall is global merchandising. The Internet Shopping Network (ISN) online catalog contains products from more than 800 high-technology companies. 31 Membership, which is free, means that you have the privilege of ordering, downloading demos, or accessing reviews. Nonmembers can only window-shop and take a tour of the service. There is an online form for membership, but you must fill it out and fax it back to the company. This is a security measure to protect your credit card information.

Because this service is graphics-intensive, you may want to disable your inline images when you browse. The merchandise in the various stores consists of approximately 20,000 computer hardware and software-related products. When you enter the service, a series of product category icons appears, such as Macintosh products or modems. Jump into a category and begin a search for individual products. It doesn't take long to find the product you're looking for, complete with the ISN price.

Slovenian Wine Shops

URL address: **http://www.ijs.si/vinoteke.html**

Vinoteka is the Slovene word for wine, and this home page is a fantastic guide for information about where you can sample and purchase wines in Slovenia. Learn about Vinoteka Bradesko, a store located at the City Fairground in Ljubljana, which offers the largest selection of wines in Slovenia and will let you taste wines. If you get a bit tipsy, try the in-store restaurant.

In addition to reviews of wine stores, there is a database, called the *wine archives*, that provides information about the country's best wineries and wines. For example, the Wine Tabernacle in Maribore sports a collection of almost all post-1945 Slovenia vintages—some bottles that can't be found anywhere else. You may want to remember that the Master Cellarer keeps a secret mini-tabernacle with 50 of the most precious bottles. Click on the name of this or any other highlighted winery, and you get a JPEG image of the vineyards, wine cellar, or some other aspect of wine production. The home page also has links to information about wholesale depots and wine specialty shops.

Downtown Anywhere

URL address: **http://awa.com**

Downtown Anywhere provides a good example of an electronic town. A bit of amusing self-promotion begins at the home page, which states: "Conveniently located in central cyberspace, Downtown Anywhere is a great place to browse, earn, share, and trade. Everything you can think of is available; just think of making it available. We offer choice real estate and all the amenities to anyone seeking a virtual office, a virtual showroom, or a virtual laboratory in the heart of the new marketplace of ideas."

Fig. 31.3
The Downtown Anywhere home page has the look and feel of a real town. Do some window shopping!

Like a "real town," Downtown Anywhere has icons that bring you to different locations in the cybertown. For example, you can go to real estate to learn how to sell services and products in this village. This "town" has a library, a financial district, museums, and Main Street with many shops and services. The jump to Main Street opens the door to a variety of stores, which you can then select to go to their home pages and begin your online shopping. For music lovers, there is CDnow!, which claims to have "The largest selection of music CDs on the Internet." If you need to upgrade your computer, try Compusource International—a discount supplier of computer products. If you want to help save the planet, there are at least 140 products in the catalog by Environmentally Sound Products, Inc. And if you just want to make a fashion statement, try T-shirts by Mighty Dog Designs.

Shopping in Singapore

URL address: **http://www.ncb.gov.sg/sog/6.shop.html**

Before you plan your next shopping trip to Singapore, check out this home page. Singapore is a duty-free port and shopping is a major activity. Products range from hand-crafted Asian carpets and jewelry to cameras and electronic goods. There are outdoor bazaars and indoor shopping centers, with most establishments open 12 hours every day. If you are looking for an interesting gift, jump from the home page to the section on Singapore Handicrafts. This describes the Singapore Handicraft Center at Chinatown Point, which has more than 60 shops that specialize in oriental treasures like scroll paintings, jade carvings, and embroidered quilts.

Here is an example of the in-depth descriptions that you can access: "Orchard Road, so-called because of the fruit trees and spice gardens growing here in former days, is the Fifth Avenue, the Champs Elysees, the Via Veneto of

Singapore. For sheer volume, quality, and choice, it can rival any one of them. Every shopping center along the stretch from Tanglin Road to Orchard Road to Marina Bay is filled with a myriad of goods from around the world." In addition to inline images of the shops and shopping districts, you can click on little icons to bring up full-screen JPEG maps of the shopping areas. Individual stores are highlighted.

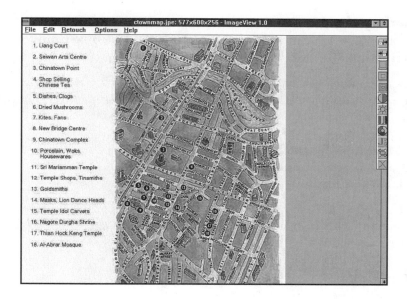

Fig. 31.4
Exotic jewelry, hand-made rugs, and spices are a few of the offerings you can sample via the Singapore Shops Web site.

BizWeb

URL address: **http://www.bizweb.com**

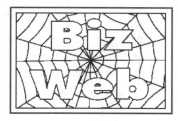

Fig. 31.5
The BizWeb site helps you become an informed buyer as you jump between Web pages for companies that offer similar products and services.

VI

Finding Web Resources

This Web site is perfect for comparison shoppers. The home page offers a directory of products that is all-inclusive—finance, food, publishing, flowers, clothing. Select a category, and from here jump to a hypertext list of companies that offer these products and—here's the beautiful part—you can then jump to *their* home page on the Web. This means that you can quickly do competitive shopping between companies that offer the same product or service. More than 500 different companies are represented.

Apparel and Accessories

Earrings by Lisa

URL address: **http://mmink.cts.com/mmink/kiosks/earrings/ earrings.html**

View a selection of earrings from Multimedia Ink Designs in Poway, California. Earrings are made of materials such as turquoise, sterling silver, 14K gold, real rock materials, glass, clay, plastic, and non-precious metal objects.

Footware—Rope Sandals

URL address: **http://mmink.cts.com/mmink/kiosks/sandals/ ropesandals.html**

It doesn't have to be summer to enjoy a nice pair of sandals. This home page offers many selections, including six- and two-strap versions in several materials.

HeadFirst!

URL address: **http://www.headfirst.com/**

If you're into snowboarding, this is the site for you. You can find t-shirts, sweats, headgear, stickers, and order forms at this site.

Nine Lives

URL address: **http://chezhal.slip.netcom.com/index.html**

This is the site for a women's clothing consignment store. You can jump to a forms page where you can enter your preferences for clothing (size, price range, and manufacturer) and then search the current inventory. You can purchase online as well.

Noir Leather

URL address: **http://www.w2.com/noirleather.html**

A complete collection of leather goods and jewelry—boots, clothing, boot accessories, and some bondage items—are found here. You can order online with your credit card.

Shirts—Appellation Spring

URL address: **http://www.wilder.com/winery.html**

Fig. 31.6
This WWW site helps you locate and order t-shirts that display logos and artwork of California wineries.

This home page, Appellation Spring, is the WWW source for t-shirts from California wineries. You can click the names of the various wineries to jump to a short description of the wines and small pictures of the t-shirts (these pictures can be enlarged). You can order shirts via the telephone or e-mail.

Shirts—Mighty Dog Designs

URL address: **http://sashimi.wwa.com/~notime/mdd/Index.html**

The owners of this Web service will design a t-shirt for you, even if you are a Net Surfer or Web Walker. Now you can be the first in your neighborhood or Web circle to wear the styles of the Internet.

Shirts from STUFF

URL address: **http://www.stuff.com:80/cgi-bin/ display_file?filename=/catalog.html&session_id=cu5bpe.6d5**

A long WWW address gets you to this home page with clickable images of t-shirts. Examples include a dragon, wizard, space top, and parachuting bears.

Art

Artists and Works

URL address: **http://lydia.bradley.edu/exhibit/artists.html**

This server provides titles of artwork, descriptions of the piece, medium, size (with and without matting), price, artist name, and address of the gallery where the art is located (physically).

◀ See "Artists," p. 476

Colorburst Studios

URL address: **http://www.teleport.com/~paulec/catalog.html**

Niobium jewelry is colorful metal-based jewelry. If you're looking for unusual accessories, check out this home page.

Eagle Aerie Gallery

URL address: **http://www.advantage.com/EAG/EAG.html**

Located in Tofino, British Columbia, this gallery features the art of Roy Henry Vickers. The home page provides information about individual pieces, as well as sales information.

ImageMaker—Artistic Gifts for Dog Lovers

URL address: **http://fender.onramp.net:80/imagemaker/**

Artist Monique Akar is online with her pen-and-ink drawings of approximately 156 dog breeds. She creatively captures the essence of each breed and will imprint your selection on quilts, aprons, umbrellas, photo albums, or just about anything you want for your enjoyment or gift giving. She also has a large selection of porcelain items to choose from.

Pearl Street Online Gallery

URL address: **http://antics.com/pearl.html**

Fig. 31.7
You will find images of wildflowers and Southwestern scenes at this WWW gallery.

This electronic gallery is located in Boulder, Colorado. The server provides digital images of photographic and computer-enhanced art, such as hand-colored pictures of the Southwest. There is also information about how to send submissions of works to the gallery and how to obtain prints.

Books and Maps

Alternative Textbooks

URL address: **http://www.internex.net/TEXTBOOKS/home.html**

If you're in the market for new and used textbooks, this is the Web site for you. You can link to Stanford Texts, which is a book exchange. Some non-book items include World Cup soccer memorabilia such as t-shirts, polo shirts, souvenirs, and caps.

◀ See "Book and Literature Resources," p. 816

Computer Softpro Books

URL address: **http://storefront.xor.com/softpro/index.html**

This home page is an extension of Softpro Books—the retail computer book-store. They are currently in Boston and Denver, but they have the goal to be the best computer book store anywhere. They have line-listings and a catalog for online use.

Computer Bookstore

URL address: **http://www.nstn.ns.ca/cybermall/roswell/roswell.html**

Located in Halifax, Nova Scotia, Canada, Roswell Electronic Computer Book-store sponsors this home page. Their WWW database has more than 7,000 titles, which you can search online.

Future Fantasy

URL address: **http://www.commerce.digital.com/palo-alto/FutureFantasy/home.html**

This bookstore specializes in science fiction, fantasy, mystery, and horror. You can look through an electronic catalog and place orders via an electronic order form on the WWW. There is also a newsletter.

International—E.J. Brill, Publishers (Netherlands)

URL address: **gopher://infx.infor.com:4900**

This home page enables you to search for publications by using several different methods; the links provide ordering information.

Fig. 31.8
The world of fantasy is thoroughly explored at this Web site, where you can order books electronically.

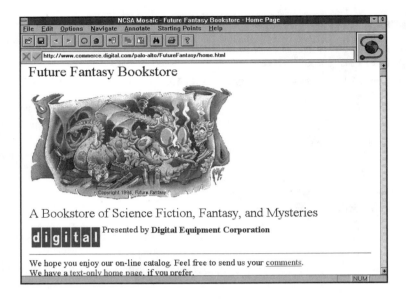

Macmillan Computer Publishing
URL address: **http://www.mcp.com/**

Find information on the best computer book publishers in the world. Books from Que, Sams, New Riders, Alpha, Brady, and Hayden are featured at this site. You can review sample chapters or tables of contents from current books. This site also offers a wealth of reference articles pulled from these books to answer your questions about computer software and hardware. You can order any Macmillan Computer Publishing book directly from this Web site and download software associated with best-selling titles.

Maps—DeLorme Mapping Order Information
URL address: **http://www.delorme.com/orders/orders.htm**

This electronic store has all kinds of maps. You can link to information about *Street Atlas USA*, *Global Explorer*, *MapExpert*, *GPS MapKit*, *XMap Professional*, and *The Paper Atlas* and *Gazetteer* series.

Nautical Bookshelf
URL address: **gopher://gopher.nautical.com:2550/1**

This is the list for everyone interested in anything that would be covered in nautical books. There are references to online services, a free book guide, ordering information, discounts, and boating tips.

Online Bookstores

URL address: **http://thule.mt.cs.cmu.edu:8001/jrrl-space/bookstores.html**

This is a list of book publishers, catalogs, and bookstores that you can connect to via the Internet.

Scholastic, Inc.

URL address: **http://scholastic.com:2005**

Fig. 31.9
Jump through the links on this home page to find educational books, toys, or games for your children.

Scholastic is a publisher and distributor of children's educational materials, including books, magazines, and now electronic products. Through a link to the Ultimate Education Store—an online catalog—you can learn about the various products. An electronic Scholastic Newsletter also provides curriculum ideas and a discussion of trends in education.

Spanish Bookstore

URL address: **http://www.fundesco.es**

This electronic bookstore (based in Spain) offers a searchable database of titles in the Spanish language. Most of the books relate to the social impact of computer communications. Online ordering is available.

Tor Books

URL address: **http://sunsite.unc.edu/ibic/Tor-homepage.html**

Tor Books, an imprint of Tom Doherty Associates, Inc., is a New York-based publisher of hard- and soft-cover books. Tor focuses on science fiction and fantasy literature. The home page offers listings of recent and forthcoming books, a newsletter, and pointers to other science fiction resources.

VI

Finding Web Resources

United States Judaica Catalog

URL address: **http://tig.com/USJ/index.html**

This Web address links you to an electronic catalog of books on Judaism—it actually starts with a Web site that then opens a second Gopher site. Links to other resources on Judaism are also available.

Computer

Anchiano Computer Eyewear

URL address: **http://www.branch.com/eyewear/eyewear.html**

Worried about computer monitor eyestrain? Find out about glasses with a rotating lens that may reduce headaches, dry eyes, and other monitor-related discomforts. An online order form is provided.

CD-ROMs—JF Lehmanns Fachbuchhandlung

URL address: **http://www.germany.eu.net:80/shop/jfl/jfl_kat.html**

This WWW home page has links to online CD-ROM and book catalogs.

Cybersource

URL address: **http://software.net**

Even though your hard drive could never hold them all, this site offers links where you can find out about and purchase more than 7,500 software products for DOS, Windows, Macintosh, and UNIX.

Dell Computer Home Page

URL address: **http://www.us.dell.com/**

◀ See "Computer Hardware," p. 553

Online shopping for computers, hardware, software, parts, and support is available at this site. The links on this page make it easy to get information or to order a paper copy of the catalog.

DVAL Visualization Tools

URL address: **http://dval-www.larc.nasa.gov/software/overview.html**

Links are available to information about software on the SGI and SUN platforms and to other visualization tools.

Equipment and Software (by Manufacturer)

URL address: **http://gn.update.uu.se:70/1/chp/mf**

This WWW server provides links to several different vendors and manufacturers, including Digital Equipment Corporation, Infocom, International Business Machines, and the XKL Systems Corporation.

Fintronic Linux Systems

URL address: **http://www.fintronic.com/linux/catalog.html**

If you are looking for a PC that runs a version of UNIX, this company offers PC systems with *Linux* pre-installed. Linux is a UNIX-like operating system.

Software for UNIX Workstations

URL address: **http://www.math.ethz.ch/~www/unix/software.html**

This home page has information about four different categories of software: text processing, calculation, general purpose programs (such as graphics, editors, and utilities), and programming (language compilers and development tool kits).

Electronic Malls

The following electronic mall home pages open doors to other vendors and home pages of companies that sell products and services. Depending upon the vendor, there are several ways you can actually make a purchase when you see a product you want to buy. Most purchases are made with credit cards and the methods to place an order include the following:

- Calling a phone number to place an order

- Calling the mall or vendor first to establish "membership," whereby you give them your credit card information for future purchases (this helps secure your credit card information) and then shop online

- Shopping online and entering credit card information via a WWW form box

- Sending electronic mail to the company with an order

Adverts Search Engine

URL address: **http://apollo.co.uk/**

Fig. 31.10

If you want to shop around the world via the Internet, try this home page, pick a country, and then pick a vendor.

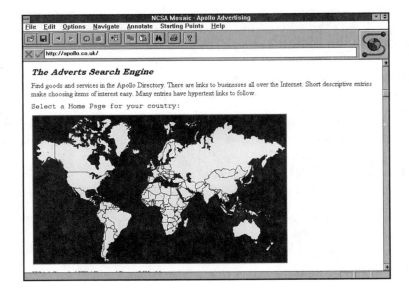

There's nothing quite like one-stop global shopping. This home page loads with a map of the world—a global mall. You click any part of the globe you want to shop in and bingo!—you "go" to Europe or Australia or South America. Actually you get a new page full of different Internet companies who operate from the four corners of the world. It's fun, it's fast, and it's easy to spend money.

Branch Information Services

URL address: **http://branch.com:1080/**

Did you ever think of getting a Bonsai tree or buying clothing from a place that will donate 5 percent of the sale to AIDS-related causes? You will find links to unusual and hard-to-find items such as Russian fine art, ergonomic workstation chairs, tuxedos, and gourmet popcorn. Most links just offer product descriptions with some GIF images and phone numbers for ordering.

CommerceNet

URL address: **http://www.commerce.net**

From marketing and selling products to transmitting electronic orders and payments, Silicon Valley-based CommerceNet focuses on the business applications of the WWW.

Commercial Sites on the Web
URL address: **http://tns-www.lcs.mit.edu/commerce.html**

This Web site regularly lists links to commercial sites on the WWW—there are malls, stores, and businesses. You can find the perfect gift or product for that someone special.

CTSNET Marketplace
URL address: **http://www.cts.com:80/cts/market/**

You find an interesting collection of merchants at this WWW page, including those that offer rare coins, health and beauty products, and computer equipment.

CyberMall
URL address: **http://www.nstn.ns.ca/cybermall/cybermall.html**

This Web server, which is from Canada, is a storefront for a variety of Canadian vendors. Products and services are broken into four broad categories that include bookstores, disability services, real estate, and telecommunications.

DASH
URL address: **http://www.dash.com/netro/das/das.html**

The Denver Area Super Highway offers Netropolis, a virtual city that has digital exhibits for different seasons with decorations and games. For example, Glint's Haunted House is the Halloween exhibit. Also, Denver and Colorado-based weather forecasts are provided.

Index of Services
URL address: **http://www.shore.net/~adfx/1.html**

This Web site offers an extensive list of shopping links you can access from this page. More than 125 links are available to catalogs, services, products, travel ideas, food, spices, and offers for free promotional items.

Internet Business Directory
URL address: **http://ibd.ar.com**

This is a home page to more than 200 businesses. Start with the link to Catalogs, where you can get a list of individual companies. For ease of browsing, large catalogs are subdivided with links. For example, Trophies by Edco, Inc. has links to A: Medals; B: Trophies; C: Wooden Plaques; and D: Corporate Overview. The home page also has a link to the Internet Better Business Bureau.

Internet Shopkeeper—A WWW Mall

URL address: **http://www.ip.net:80/shops.html**

People and small businesses from around the world can set up and manage their own shops in this electronic mall. The home page has links to rates and setup information.

Fig. 31.11
The Internet Shopkeeper electronic mall opens doors to businesses from around the world.

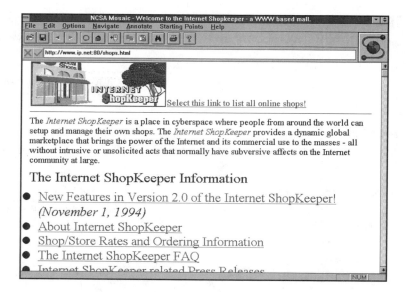

Los Angeles Internet Group

URL address: **http://www.primenet.com/~laig**

The LAIG home page has several valuable links for Internet surfers. You can find out about Internet-related resources, jump to the Information Showcase where several businesses have set up shop, browse the CD-ROM Network, which connects you to several publishers of CD-ROMs, or try the Seminars link to learn about the Internet.

Made in America

URL address: **http://www.icw.com/america/made.html**

This mall features three separate mini-malls which offer products and services made in America. Choose home page links to Adirondack Mountain Specialties, American Way, or Country Store Goods from Vermont. Each of these links opens a series of new stores. In many cases you can order online.

MarketPlace.com

URL address: **http://marketplace.com**

The home page says it all, "Our mission with MarketPlace.com is to offer the Internet community a convenient and useful online shopping environment full of information, entertainment, and tools. Many of the items listed are available for purchase here using VISA, Master Card, or American Express."

Marktplatz

URL address: **http://www.marktplatz.ch/**

This "mall" is in Switzerland (as are a lot of the vendors). English, French, German, and Italian is spoken (written actually) here. Jump from the home page to a listing of product and service categories that include commerce, tourism, arts and culture, sports, entertainment, education, and science. From here you'll get a listing of companies that fit these categories. There aren't a whole lot of purchasing opportunities here, but there's plenty of good information about the companies.

NetMarket

URL address: **http://www.netmarket.com**

Links from this home page provide access to several good gift stores that sell flowers, music, and discount books.

Oneworld

URL address: **http://oneworld.wa.com**

From Seattle, Washington, this Web server offers links to companies and organizations in the Northwest. There is Wilson WindowWare, a software company where you can even download some Mosaic shareware during a session, the Asia-Pacific Chamber of Commerce, and a real estate agent who offers properties in the area.

Quadralay MarketPlace

URL address: **http://www.quadralay.com/www/Cyb_Pot/ index.html**

This home page is for shops and vendors primarily in the Austin, Texas area. There are also links to information about the city of Austin and Quadralay's own software products.

SPRY World Wide Web Services
URL address: **http://www.freerange.com**

SPRY, the folks who offer Internet In a Box, maintains this home page, which points to a number of interesting services, including an electronic mall.

Stanford Shopping Center
URL address: **http://netmedia.com/ims/ssc/ssc.html**

This Web site provides an electronic overview of a *real* mall—the Stanford Shopping Center. There are links to a map of the center, directions, shops by name and type, and links to send messages to the center. The links to individual store names, such as Athlete's Foot and The Gap, bring up a phone number for the store.

Tag Online Mall
URL address: **http://www.tagsys.com**

This Web home page divides company services into useful categories, which are your first links. These include Personal, Business, Retail, Travel, and Miscellaneous Services. An example of a retail store is Unique Jewelry by Diana Kane; examples of travel services include tours of New York City and guides to healthy restaurants in NYC; and an example of a personal service is a directory of accountants.

The Internet Plaza
URL address: **http://plaza.xor.com**

Books, computer network services, software, and cartoons are a few of the offerings on this Internet/WWW mall.

UWI Catalogue
URL address: **http://kzsu.stanford.edu/uwi/maul.html**

An eclectic collection of "stores" is at this home page. Record labels like Bulb and Choke, Inc. that sell compact discs, and magazines like *Synergy* are available.

Sell-It on the WWW
URL address: **http://xmission.com/~wwwads**

This site provides advertising on the Web. More than 20 companies are in this electronic mall whose products range from baseball cards to arts and crafts to computer hardware and software to gourmet coffee to publications to computer consulting—you get the idea.

Shopping In

URL address: **http://www.onramp.net/shopping_in**

Products in this mall include apparel, books, art, and decorative accessories. You can even order and have products shipped overnight. Also, a variety of bargains can be found at a "sister" site **http://www.onramp.net/goodstuf**—such as "three hundred dollar luggage for seventy-five bucks." Finally, a design studio for the Internet is at **http://www.onramp.net/product**.

Village Mall

URL address: **http://crusher.bev.net/mall/index.html**

This site features shopping in the Blacksburg, Virginia, area for local residents and browsers on the Internet. A few of the links you can select are grocery stores, carpentry, bookstores, restaurants, entertainment, and services.

WebScope

URL address: **http://stelcom.com/webscope/customers.html**

You find a collection of services and products in this electronic mall. Examples include PC FISHelp, PC software for commercial fishing; Global Leasing Services, equipment leasing; On Target Marketing, a direct marketing company; and ARTrageous!, computer clip art. Online ordering is an option with some vendors.

Food and Beverages

Cafe MAM—Organically Grown Coffee

URL address: **http://mmink.cts.com/mmink/dossiers/cafemam.html**

Tired of staring at your monitor? Take a coffee break. This is the Web server for coffee beans and a small selection of advertisement t-shirts and mugs. If you place your order before noon Pacific Time, they will roast the beans and ship your selection the same day.

▶ See "Cooking, Dining, and Beverages," p. 910

Chocolate Factory

URL address: **http://mmink.cts.com/mmink/dossiers/choco.html**

Chocolate lovers now have a place to hang out. Check out the various good-ies and gift baskets and then place your order.

Fruit Baskets from Pemberton Orchards

URL address: **gopher://ftp.std.com:70/11/vendors/fruit.baskets**

Now, electronic merchants offer 100 percent satisfaction-guaranteed service. This firm has fruit baskets for personal and corporate occasions, and you can order via the telephone, fax, or electronic mail with overnight delivery. Men-tion "Shop on the World" for a 10 percent discount.

Honey Bee Hams

URL address: **http://mail.eskimo.com/~jeffpolo/**

Ninety-three percent fat free—what could be better? You can find out about these hams and order online.

Hot Sauce

URL address: **http://www.presence.com/hot/**

Welcome to Hot Hot Hot, the Net's coolest hot sauce shop!

Your mouth feels like it's on fire, and you're loving it. This Pasadena, Califor-nia specialty hot sauce shop offers selections of hot food and spices from around the world. Choose from the likes of Dave's Insanity Sauce, Pure Hell, Scorned Woman Hot Sauce, and over 100 other HOT sauces.

Todd & Holland Teas
URL address: **http://rare-teas.com/teas/teas.html**

The home page informs you that, "Todd & Holland are merchants of choice, rare loose leaf teas to serious tea drinkers worldwide." There are detailed descriptions of dozens of rare teas (like the $160 a pound Mystic India and Ceylon tea).

Virginia Diner Catalog
URL address: **http://www.infi.net/vadiner/catalog.html**

Move over Jimmy Carter—no disrespect intended. This gourmet peanut and gift catalog offers peanutty selections and other goodies. The Virginia Diner in Wakefield, Virginia offers a peanut recipe of the month online (at this writing, it was Southern Peanut Pie).

Hobbies and Recreation

Antique Shops
URL address: **http://www.elpress.com:80/staunton/ANTQS.HTML**

If you are an antique buff, you won't be able to resist the temptation to spend some time at this server—home page for the Staunton Antique Shops. Most of the shops listed are in Staunton, Virginia, but several are listed for the surrounding area as well. Addresses, phone numbers, and business hours are also given. Happy hunting!

Bikes—Climbing High
URL address: **http://ike.engr.washington.edu/aixcell/climb.html**

This is the home page for the Los Gatos Cyclery, a mountain bike shop that sells Specialized, Trek, and Bridgestone bikes, as well as a wide variety of cycling gear and other sport accessories.

Camping—Guide to the Gear
URL address: **http://io.datasys.swri.edu/Gear.html**

This hypertext guide has links to and evaluations of many kinds of gear. Directions for making homemade stoves and fire starters—which come in handy at the campsite—are available.

Cards—Non-Sport Cards Page

URL address: **http://empire.umd.edu/**

This WWW server specializes in the art of card collecting. The home page has links that deal with comics, science fiction, and all types of trading cards (including sports related). There's also a list of card companies with addresses and phone numbers.

Crafts, Hobbies & Home Arts—InfoVid Outlet

URL address: **http://branch.com:1080/infovid/c313.html**

This is a comprehensive list of educational and "how-to" videos for learning about crafts, hobbies, and home arts. A description of the subject, name of the instructor, and price for the tapes, which are presented by Digitalis Television Productions, are provided.

Climbing Hardware

URL address: **http://www.dtek.chalmers.se/Climbing/Hardware/index.html**

▶ See "Recreational Sports," p. 920

For all rock-climbing enthusiasts, this home page has information about specific hardware and shops that will help you get up those cliffs.

FISHNET—Global Shopping Network

URL address: **http://www.gsn.com/**

Fig. 31.14
The FISHNET Web site offers information and products for recreational and professional fishermen and women.

You jump from this page into what is really a department store for fishermen (and women). You will find areas for fishing, boating, sailing, clubs, shows, and events. From these areas you fine-tune your search (there's also a search feature). For example, fishing will open fly fishing and a salt water pro tackle shop.

Games—Sundragon Games

URL address: **http://www.sundragon.com/sundragon/home.html**

Do you enjoy games? This home page helps you find and order any of 15,000 strategy, role playing, card, board, or any other type of game you can think of.

Welcome to Sundragon Games...

...The Internet's Neighborhood Game Club

Fig. 31.15
Checkers, Risk, or
Mortal Kombat?
This home page
focuses on games.

Marine Supplies—Sailorman

URL address: **gopher://gopher.gate.net/11/marketplace**

Sailorman specializes in new and used marine gear. Inventory constantly changes, and an area is available for consignment items. Located in Ft. Lauderdale, Florida, the company also produces special orders—if it is made, they can probably get it.

Running Page

URL address: **http://polar.pica.army.mil/people/drears/running/
running.html**

This WWW home page contains links to running-related products and magazines, as well as volumes of information about the sport itself.

Sports Cards

URL address: **http://www.icw.com/sports/sports.html**

Are you searching for a particular card that is almost impossible to find? This WWW home page can help you locate sports cards and other collectibles with access to items categorized in the areas of football, basketball, baseball, and hockey. Cards are available in multiples or singles by using the online order form.

Tennis—The Racquet Workshop

URL address: **http://arganet.tenagra.com/Racquet_Workshop/
Workshop.html**

If you enjoy the game of tennis, you must get to this site and get there fast! It is brand new and will fill all your tennis needs, whether for yourself or a gift for someone else. Links are provided to racquets, racquet extras, shoes and socks, tennis apparel, and accessories.

VI

Finding Web Resources

Westminster Supply
URL address: **http://www.icw.com/westminster/medical.html**

While working on crafts, you might want to use the type of multipurpose latex gloves that medical personnel have been using for years. This product has so many uses! Keep your hands and nails clean while doing mechanical work in your garage or enjoying your favorite hobby. Use these disposable gloves whenever you want to protect your hands.

Windsurfing Sports
URL address: **http://www.sccsi.com/Windsurfing/shop.html**

Fill all your windsurfing needs either in the area of Houston, Texas, or online. Take lessons at Mud Lake and use the WhySail Mail-order Catalog to buy or rent all the equipment you need to enjoy the sport for many years to come.

Music and Video

Compact Disc Connection
URL address: **telnet://cdconnection.com**

This would be a good place to start looking for new music; the online catalog has about 80,000 titles.

Noteworthy Music
URL address: **http://www.netmarket.com/noteworthy/bin/main/ :st=z11pf0v43n|3**

or perhaps easier access via the NetMarket Mall at **http://www.netmarket.com**

This electronic store features a selection of more than 17,000 compact discs. You can browse or do searches for specific titles, artists, or songs. Digital images of CD covers are also provided.

Picture Palace
URL address: **http://www.tagsys.com/Ads/PicPal/**

This site includes a complete line of action, adventure, sports films, and videos. You can find even some collector's items such as a rare Bruce Lee interview. You can view video clips from the home page and jump to online ordering.

Science Television

URL address: **http://www.service.com/stv/home.html**

Do you have a desire or need to learn about the chaos theory? Scientists and students are the target market for the videotapes in this collection.

Video Disc International

URL address: **http://www.thesphere.com/VDI/VDI.html**

Before CD-ROMs, there were videodiscs. Browse through a searchable catalog (keyword by title) of laser disc offerings. Video Disc International carries over 2,000 laser disc titles.

Products and Gifts

Autos—Cars, Cars, Cars

URL address: **http://www.netpart.com:80/jacob/**

Now you can buy any make, model, or year of car from Jacob Goldman in Huntington Beach, California. Links are provided to information about specific cars, so jump to this home page and get that antique or classic you have always wanted.

Autos—DealerNet

URL address: **http://www.dealernet.com/**

Fig. 31.16
Even auto dealers and manufacturers have a presence on the Web.

VI

Finding Web Resources

DealerNet is one-stop shopping for your auto needs. You can jump to links to manufacturers and dealers or find out information about insurance or auto accessories.

Autos—Webfoot's Silicon Valley Used Car Lot

URL address: **http://pond.cso.uiuc.edu/ducky/cars/sfbay/ sfbay.car.lot.html**

This is interactive commerce at its best. You can read and post ads (using a fill-in form) for cars wanted or for sale. Categories such as autos, trucks, classics, and bicycles make it easy to find what you want. Links are also provided to other San Francisco Bay-Area Web sites (mostly transportation-related) and a California driving FAQ.

China and Crystal GiftNET

URL address:
http://www.netmarket.com/giftnet/bin/main/:st=mer7es3zck|3

This page has links that take you to information on china, crystal, flatware, and other gifts. All the products come from national manufacturers. You get a very long list of individual sets with prices and just click the [order] link if you want to order something.

Flowers—Absolutely Fresh Flowers

URL address: **http://www.cts.com:80/~flowers**

This home page reminds you that flowers are great for birthdays, anniversaries, thank yous, get wells, congratulations, and, of course, I love you's.

Flowers—Buning the Florist

URL address: **http://www.satelnet.org/flowers/**

Located in Ft. Lauderdale, Florida, this florist has been serving its customers since 1925. It is now online and also can be reached by regular mail, e-mail, or 800 number. Whatever the occasion, a gift of flowers is always appropriate.

Flowers—Grant's FTD

URL address: **gopher://branch.com/11s/florist/**

This may be easier than ordering flowers through the phone book. The server allows you to select and view floral arrangements and fruit baskets. You can order for delivery anywhere in the United States and Canada.

Hello Direct

URL address: **http://www.hello-direct.com/hd/home.html**

Even with the great resources available on the WWW, the telephone remains an important tool for communications. Hello Direct sells every type of telephone and phone accessory you can imagine—cordless, callerID, and digital answering machines. Check it out.

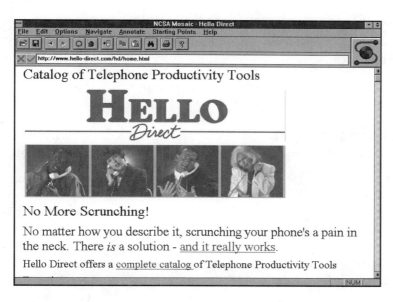

Fig. 31.17
The Hello Direct home page points you to every type of telephone and phone accessory you may ever need.

Marilyn Monroe Postage Stamps

URL address: **http://www.kiosk.net/marilyn**

The island nation of St. Vincent has issued a limited edition set of nine different postage stamps commemorating the star's life and career. The stamps are displayed on this site in actual size and color. Links to little known facts about Marilyn are provided, and you can even order a set of the stamps online.

Office Furniture Express Direct

URL address: **http://ofx.com/ofx/**

Examine (online) a complete selection of office furniture designed to help you organize your office. There's even a buyer's guide to help you make your selections.

San Francisco Music Box

URL address: **http://www.shopping2000.com/shopping2000/music_box/**

Paperweights, figurines, and music boxes are some of the selections you can read about (and see) via hyperlinks on this home page. Ordering information is available.

Shopping in Australia—Glass Wings

URL address: **http://www.aus.xanadu.com/GlassWings/welcome.html**

From Australia, this hyper-mall has a variety of products, services, and resources that range from art to games to restaurant reviews.

Shopping in Japan

URL address: **http://www.ntt.jp/japan/TCJ/SHOPPING/00.html**

◄ See "Interesting Sites and National Travel Guides," p. 756

If you're planning a trip to Japan, stop here first. You can get general information such as shopping hours, tax-free shopping tips, a directory for converting sizes, and a list of weights and measures. Also, jump to resources on where and what to buy.

Shopping in Norway

URL address: **http://www.oslonett.no/html/adv/advertisers.html**

This is an electronic storefront for several companies in Norway. This hodge-podge of products and services includes books, software, consulting, music copyrights, adventure travel, and company profiles.

Solar Panel Power

URL address: **http://www.wilder.com/solar.html**

◄ See "National Renewable Energy Laboratory," p. 842

Solar panels capture the energy of the sun and convert it into electricity. This Web site tells you about a portable solar panel product that you can use to play radios and other small items. A link to an explanation about how the product works is provided. You can order via e-mail or the telephone.

Stork Delivers

URL address: **http://www.stork.com/sd.html**

When the newborn arrives, you should visit this site. Take a hypertext stroll through several "baskets," which include toys and clothing for babies.

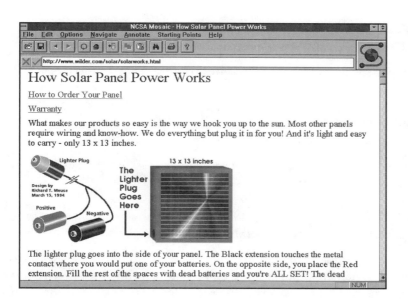

Fig. 31.18
Visit this site and you'll learn about a product that captures the energy of the sun and transforms it into electricity you can use for small appliances.

Tech Museum Store

URL address: **http://www.thetech.org/techstore.html**

If you want an unusual gift, start here. Like what? Find out about silicon jewelry, laser holograms, puzzles, science labs kits, and robots.

Services and Supplies

Americans with Disabilities—Access Media

URL address: **http://www.human.com/mkt/access/index.html**

The Americans with Disabilities Act requires that employers, schools, and government agencies provide architectural access to their premises and alternative aids and services for people with disabilities. Access Media is a nonprofit organization that provides important documents relating to the special needs of millions of Americans.

BusinessCards Online

URL Address: **http://drogheda.nuance.com:80/businesscard/**

Now here's an original idea. This company can help you take your business card and transform it into a digital card that can be seen by Internet travelers. People who visit this site can then keyword search to locate the talent they need.

Business Media

URL address: **http://www.infoanalytic.com/bmi/index.html**

This page includes a complete hypertext listing of video projectors to attach to computers. Learn about features, usage, and pricing.

Company Corporation

URL address: **http://incorporate.com/tcc/home.html**

Jump to this home page if you own a small business and you want help with incorporation. Everything can be done online.

DIALOG

URL Address: **http://www.dialog.com/**

This Knight-Ridder Information company maintains huge databases of articles from numerous publications and businesses. From the home page you can search first for the database that will help you the most, then for information within a database. This site is a dream page for researchers or librarians.

Document Center

URL address: **http://www.service.com/doccenter/home.html**

This company and its home page specialize in documents. You can order publications about government and industry specifications and standards.

Graphics—Michele-Shine Media

URL address: **http://www.internex.com/MSM/home.html**

Michele-Shine Media creates logos, graphics, and icons for presentations— including online presentations.

Internet Company

URL address: **http://enews.com**

Based in Massachusetts, this company/Web site is a gateway to both the Electronic Newsstand, which offers electronic magazines via the Web, and Counterpoint Publishing, which offers government documents via the Web. Annually, the Internet Company helps reply to 10 million inquiries for the Electronic Newsstand and deliver 5 million documents per year via the Internet for Counterpoint Publishing, which specializes in electronic versions of federal information.

Nottingham Arabidopsis Stock Center

URL address: **http://nasc.life.nott.ac.uk/description.html**

Learn about the services and organizational structure of the Nottingham Arabidopsis Stock Center (NASC). Based at the University of Nottingham, UK, NASC distributes seed free of charge to Europe, Australia, and Africa. The Arabidopsis Biological Resource Centre (ABRC) at Ohio State University (USA) distributes seed to North America and Canada.

Photography—Craig Stewart Studio

URL address: **http://www.sccsi.com/Stewart/craig_stewart.html**

This is the Web page of a commercial photography studio in the Houston, Texas area. The studio specializes in studio illustration.

Photography—Enrico Ferorelli Enterprises

URL address: **http://branch.com:1080/enrico/enrico.html**

For your corporate photography needs or annual reports, portraits, and advertising, this site directs you to the talents of an international photographer.

Photography—Mary and Michael's Wedding

URL address: **http://www.commerce.digital.com/palo-alto/ WeddingPhoto/home.html**

Capture those special moments with the help of Mary and Michael Wedding Photography. Located in Palo Alto, California, this home page has many links to photos and information about the business.

UNIX Security Topics

URL address: **http://ausg.dartmouth.edu/security.html**

This home page has links to 13 sources of information regarding security issues.

From Here...

Hopefully, you haven't gone beyond your credit limit during your exploration of these sites. A few other businesses can be found in the following chapters:

VI

Finding Web Resources

- Chapter 21, "Business and Finance," lists firms such as IBM and Federal Express, which are more business oriented.

- Chapter 32, "Sports, Games, Hobbies, Travel, Cooking, and Recreation," has some useful addresses for people who like to travel—including lodging and hotel sites where you can book a room online.

Chapter 32

Sports, Games, Hobbies, Travel, Cooking, and Recreation

by Bill Eager

Sports and computers? You might not immediately think that the world of modems and disk drives has a connection with the world of athletics, hobbies, or travel—the World Wide Web makes the connection. When it comes to spectator sports, like baseball or soccer, WWW sites offer daily reports on the outcome of games. And, to prepare for an event, you can access schedules and statistics of the teams and players. After browsing through a couple of these home pages, you will know more than the television commentators with their fancy computer systems.

Perhaps, rather than watching other people get their exercise, you enjoy making your own muscles work. You may get a rush from competition on the golf course or the ski slopes. There is a WWW server that meets your needs. Do you relish the satisfaction of climbing to the peak of a vertical rise or love feeling the wind as you speed down a tall mountain on your bicycle? Again, there are WWW home pages that focus on these activities. You can learn new tricks and tips that will give you that competitive edge, find out about local and national clubs, and retrieve maps and photographs that point towards unexplored territory.

Web resources also are available that can improve your skills and pique your interest in a hobby. There are home pages for chefs, bird watchers, and model enthusiasts. You can find a new French recipe or locate advice on how to train your new puppy. The ultimate in recreation may be adventure travel, where you visit a new country or city and explore the land, culture, and people. WWW resources can help you plan and book that next exciting trip, whether it's to a Louisiana bayou or the Himalayan mountains. The resources in this chapter lead the way. This chapter covers the following categories:

- Cooking, dining, and beverages

- Games

- Hobbies

- Home improvement

- Recreational sports

- Spectator sports

- Travel—Resources, hotels, and travel agencies

- Travel—Places to go in the United States

- Travel—Places to go worldwide

Professional Football Server

URL address: **http://www.netgen.com/sis/NFL/NFL.html**

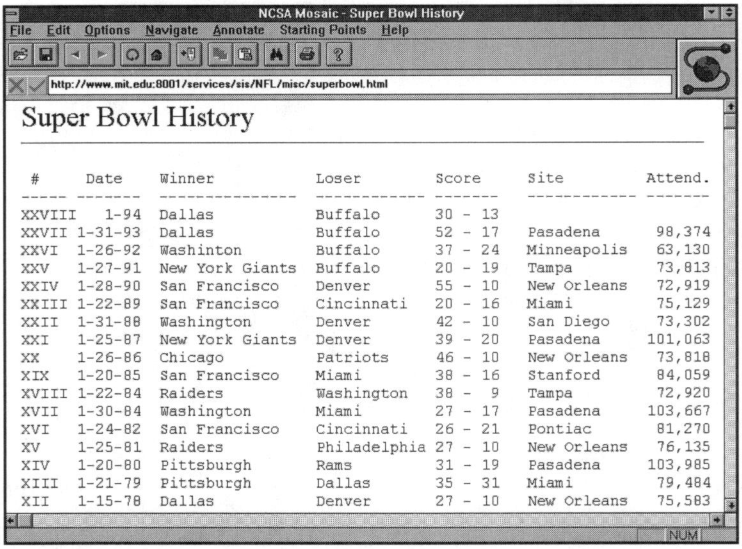

Fig. 32.1
Interested in team-by-team NFL schedules or any other football information? This is the definitive Web site on football.

```
                        NCSA Mosaic - Super Bowl History
 File  Edit  Options  Navigate  Annotate  Starting Points  Help

 http://www.mit.edu:8001/services/sis/NFL/misc/superbowl.html

 Super Bowl History
 _____

 #       Date    Winner          Loser        Score    Site          Attend.
 -----   ------- --------------  ------------ -------   ------------  -------
 XXVIII   1-94   Dallas          Buffalo      30 - 13
 XXVII  1-31-93  Dallas          Buffalo      52 - 17   Pasadena       98,374
 XXVI   1-26-92  Washinton       Buffalo      37 - 24   Minneapolis    63,130
 XXV    1-27-91  New York Giants Buffalo      20 - 19   Tampa          73,813
 XXIV   1-28-90  San Francisco   Denver       55 - 10   New Orleans    72,919
 XXIII  1-22-89  San Francisco   Cincinnati   20 - 16   Miami          75,129
 XXII   1-31-88  Washington      Denver       42 - 10   San Diego      73,302
 XXI    1-25-87  New York Giants Denver       39 - 20   Pasadena      101,063
 XX     1-26-86  Chicago         Patriots     46 - 10   New Orleans    73,818
 XIX    1-20-85  San Francisco   Miami        38 - 16   Stanford       84,059
 XVIII  1-22-84  Raiders         Washington   38 -  9   Tampa          72,920
 XVII   1-30-84  Washington      Miami        27 - 17   Pasadena      103,667
 XVI    1-24-82  San Francisco   Cincinnati   26 - 21   Pontiac        81,270
 XV     1-25-81  Raiders         Philadelphia 27 - 10   New Orleans    76,135
 XIV    1-20-80  Pittsburgh      Rams         31 - 19   Pasadena      103,985
 XIII   1-21-79  Pittsburgh      Dallas       35 - 31   Miami          79,484
 XII    1-15-78  Dallas          Denver       27 - 10   New Orleans    75,583
```

It's third down and four to go. From this home page, by Eric Richard, you can get enough NFL information to become a sports commentator. In fact, the WWW Sports Information system (of which this is part) won the 1994 Best of the Web Contest for "Best Entertainment Site." Divided into conferences, this site gives team-by-team schedules, round-by-round draft selections, and information on proposed NFL realignments. You can quickly look up statistics from years gone by. Choose from the following:

- *Super Bowl History.* Remember Super Bowl XIII when Pittsburgh beat Dallas 35 to 31?

- *Super Bowl Standings by Team.* The Kansas City Chiefs are 1 and 1.

- *Team History and Information.* The Buffalo Bills Rich Stadium can handle a screaming crowd of 80,290.

Or, try the Year-by-Year NFL Awards to see a listing of Heisman Trophy winners dating back to 1935, when Jay Berwanger, a Chicago halfback, took honors. If you like football, you'll love this Web site. (Note that the NFL has no connection with this service.)

Games Domain

URL address: **http://wcl-rs.bham.ac.uk/GamesDomain**

Want to know the difference between a Cheat and a Crack in the game Crusaders of the Dark Savant? Popular is an understatement for this WWW site. In one month, some 55,727 requests for different HTML documents were made—the equivalent of about 151 requests every hour! This server has more than 140 game-related links.

Not only is Games Domain huge, it's also an easy site to navigate. It has helpful features, like a What's New section that instantly tells you about new resources or links that have been added, and color-coded bullets in front of menu selections that tell you if there are further submenus. If you start your visit by jumping to UseNet, GamesFAQs will give you basic Q&As for all sorts of games (many of these documents use hypertext).

Fig. 32.2
From Checkers to Samurai Showdown, the Games Domain server has information about the rules, clubs, and contests for every game imaginable.

For the next stop, jump to the games-related link; there was at least 50 links to other specific WWW game home pages—from titles like The World At War: Operation Crusader to Othello (possibly helpful if you play the Microsoft Windows game Reversi). There is also a large selection of games-related FTP links. So if you're into board games, get onto this Web site!

United States Travel and Tourism Information Network

URL address: **http://www.colorado.edu/USTTIN/**

Fig. 32.3
Whether you're going somewhere on business or pleasure, the USTTIN home page offers links to Web sites and services that can make your journey more enjoyable.

The USTTIN home page is a traveler's dream come true. Start with a large graphic that has image-based links to Maps, Traveler Services, Attractions/Recreation, and Conventions. If you choose Maps, another page appears with a clickable picture of the United States. You can then choose any state you may be interested in traveling to. New pages offer information about the Tourism Office, specific details about the sites to see and places to stay in that state, and even more maps.

The Attractions/Recreation link takes you to a list of links that includes Arts, Museums, and Cities. The Cities one is quite good; it opens a page that offers information about cities in all the states. Special events, such as New Orleans' Mardi Gras, are highlighted. Choose Traveler Services to get a clickable list of sites that focus on lodging, transportation, and visitor information. The Conventions link opens doors to information about conventions across the United States. You may never go home again after you visit this Web site.

Grand Canyon National Park

URL address: **http://www.kbt.com/gc/gc_home.html**

Fig. 32.4
Everyone has a sense of awe when it comes to the Grand Canyon— this Web site relays that sense.

Every year, almost five million people visit this geologic wonder where you can stand at the edge of the canyon and stare straight down some 4,000 feet. This Web site makes your trip to the Park much more enjoyable. Home page links include:

- *A brief history of the Grand Canyon.* Major events from 10,000 years ago until today.

- *Locator and trail map.* Links to maps.

- *Backcountry trail description.* Details about the trails that lead down into the canyon.

- *Images.* Links to more than a dozen digital pictures of the area and wildlife.

- *Services at the park.* What the Park Service offers—both camping and a nice hotel.

- *Books and guides.* A bibliography of guides.

- *Other things to do in the area.* Links to other parks in the area, area museums, and interesting towns.

VI

Finding Web Resources

Golf Links

URL address: **http://www.gdol.com/golf.links.html**

GolfData is the sponsor of this WWW site. It offers great hyperlinks to golf courses and resources on the Web, and around the world. In addition, there are links to many other pages (see additional sites later in this chapter).

Fig. 32.5
Visit the Golf Links page to find challenging golf courses around the world or simply get pointers from the pros.

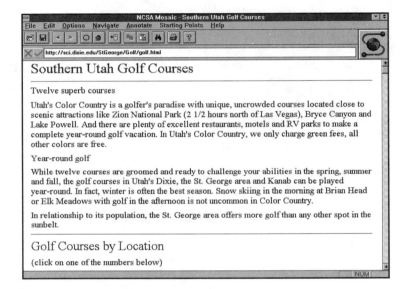

Railroads

URL address: **http://www-cse.ucsd.edu/users/bowdidge/railroad/rail-home.html**

Fig. 32.6
Whether you enjoy traveling by train, have an interest in old railroad lines, or want to build a model railroad, this Web site will serve your needs.

Railroad-related Internet Resources

This WWW server provides pointers to interesting and important railroad-related information sources on the Internet. Some model-railroading information is also included. The original list of resources were compiled by Matthew Mitchell (mmitchell@asrr.arsusda.gov) for his FAQ for rec.railroad. The information here was derived from that FAQ. Robert Bowdidge(bowdidge@cs.ucsd.edu) created this hypertext version of the FAQ in order to provide an easy-to-use central connection point for accessible rail-related information. Any thank-yous for this compilation should go to Matthew; however, typos and complaints about the style should go to Robert.

From single gauge trains of old to modern passenger trains to information about model railroads, this Web site has it all. The home page offers 17 different areas for exploration. Here is a brief summary of several of the links and some examples of the resources they may open for you:

- *Link of the Week.* As it states, a new link each week that, for example, may connect to a JPEG image of a model railroad in Australia.

- *What's New.* Recent additions to the Internet/WWW—possibly a list of hotels that are next to railroad tracks (who needs sleep?).

- *Mailing Lists.* Like the Transit Issues Discussion List.

- *Commercial Online Services.* Like CompuServe's TrainNet or GEnie's Travel by Rail.

- *Databases.* A database of existing diesels or steam locomotive rosters for Canadian railroads.

- *Railroad Maps.* JPEG, GIF, and PostScript images of the French Metro or the San Francisco BART system.

Rec.Travel Library

URL address: **ftp://ftp.cc.umanitoba.ca/rec-travel/README.html**

If you are planning a trip, this is a great resource. The site maintains a library of documents for travelers and tourists. Brian Lucas, at the University of Manitoba in Canada, operates the site. Links at the home page offer access to more than 15M of travel information; you can find a file on just about any country in the world. Useful information on airfare, cruise reviews, tour operators, and travel agents is available, as well as an electronic newsletter on Caribbean travel. Or, click on the Tourism Offices link and access a database of more than 680 tourist offices worldwide. You can perform a keyword search by entering a company name, and the database retrieves the address and phone number of the tourist offices in that country.

Cooking, Dining, and Beverages

Coffee Houses in Seattle

URL address: **http://www.halcyon.com/zipgun/mothercity/mothercity.html**

Fig. 32.7
Learn about the best coffees and coffee houses in Seattle, Washington at this Web site.

Links at this home page offer reviews of coffee houses, as well as coffee brands in Seattle—where more coffee is consumed per capita than in any other United States city.

Cooking—News Group Recipes

URL address: **http://www.vuw.ac.nz/non-local/recipes-archive/recipe-archive.html**

◄ See "Cooking, Food, and International Cuisine," p. 752

Online cookbooks are a great resource when you have simply run out of ideas for dinner. This home page is an archive of recipes that collect in the newsgroup **rec.food.recipes**.

Cooking—Gourmet Food and Recipes

URL address: **http://www.ip.net/tu/home.html**

Browse through a selection of international gourmet foods or check out recipes that come from the best chefs in the world. You can find gifts for yourself or friends, or bone up on the latest cooking techniques.

Cooking—Web Sites

URL address: **http://www.vuw.ac.nz/who/Amy.Gale/other-sites.html**

This page has well over 100 links to Web sites that focus on the fine art of cooking and eating. The links are carefully broken down into areas such as recipes, commercial sites, ethnic food, restaurants, and more. On the same server, you might want to try the Cooking-FAQ (URL address: **http://www.vuw.ac.nz/who/Amy.Gale/cooking-faq**). Slightly over 60K, this is a detailed (text-based—there are no links) list of questions, answers, and information. Cooking terms and addresses for newsgroups and Gopher sites also are included.

Gate's Food Page

URL address: **http://sfgate.com/fun/food/**

The next time you're in Washington, D.C., try Mark Miller's Red Sage restaurant; or when in Palo Alto, try the Country Fare. From the *San Francisco Chronicle* and *San Francisco Examiner* food pages, this site offers links to restaurant pages that represent most large cities. Many reviews of eating establishments are also offered.

Gumbo Pages

URL address: **http://www.webcom.com/~gumbo/welcome.html**

The home page tells visitors, "The Gumbo Pages are a musical, culinary, and cultural information source about New Orleans and French Louisiana, with essential information for the visitor to New Orleans and Acadiana (or "Cajun country"), intended to maximize your good time there. An initial caveat—if you're going there, forget about sleep, and quit worrying about your waistline." Jump from the home page into a nice list of Cajun and Gumbo recipes that'll light your mouth up.

La Comida Mexicana

URL address: **http://www.udg.mx/Cocina/menu.html**

Several interesting recipes for Mexican dishes are here. Just a note—the information is in Spanish!

Over the Coffee

URL address: **http://www.infonet.net/showcase/coffee/**

Everything you ever wanted to know about coffee. There are many links here to magazines (some online), organizations (yes, organizations), equipment manufacturers—you name it. And if you have any questions about coffee blends or specialty drinks, there are links to books and frequently asked questions—there's even a glossary of coffee terms. So, get a "buzz."

Recipe Folder

URL address: **http://english-server.hss.cmu.edu/Recipes.html**

This is an extensive list of home page links to all sorts of recipe documents. The three main categories are: vegetarian; dead animals (which encompasses beef, chicken, pork, and seafood); and an area that includes desserts, salads, drinks, and regional dishes.

Russian Cookbook

URL address: **http://solar.rtd.utk.edu/friends/life/cookbooks/ russian/master.html**

Hey, you don't have to live in Russia to enjoy Russian food. This Web page has links to many different categories of dishes—fish, breads, salads, snacks, and so on. People from around the world contribute their own Russian recipes to this electronic cookbook.

Spencer's Beer Page

URL address: **http://guraldi.itn.med.umich.edu/Beer/**

Beer lovers rejoice. There are many home page links to information on beer labels, recipes for homebrew, beer lists, beer tasting, beer clubs, beer songs, and frequently asked questions. Not a whole lot of time left for drinking.

Vegetarian

URL address: **gopher://ftp.std.com/11/nonprofits/veg-info**

◀ See "General Health Resources by Topic," p. 697

There are lots of files and directories here for people who don't like to eat meat. Find recipes, information on protein, and vegetarian ethics.

Games

Atomic Cafe

URL address: **http://atomic.neosoft.com/Atomic.html**

This home page tells you about the World At War computer game series produced by Avalon Hills and Atomic Games. In addition to a detailed description of the individual games, there are some graphic images and a few historical facts about WWII.

Welcome to the Atomic Games Home Page

Our latest game:

The World At War: OPERATION CRUSADER

Fig. 32.8
Learn about the
World At War
game series at this
WWW home page.

Billiards

URL address: **http://nickel.ucs.indiana.edu/~fulton/PoolFAQ.html**

This Web page only has one text file about billiards; however, it is fairly comprehensive. You can learn about games (such as Cut-throat or Eight Ball). This site also has terms, a bibliography, and addresses for billiard supply houses.

Birthday Server

URL address: **http://sunsite.unc.edu/btbin/birthday**

Another year older? This site gives you a list of other people who share your birthday, and it may offer a link to their home page so you can wish them well. Also, you can register your birthday—you may get more cards than you expect!

Blackjack Server

URL address: **http://www.ua.com/blackjack/bj.html**

From a company called Universal Access, this is a fun, interactive site. It will play blackjack with you—and it even gives you some fake digital money to play with. Can you beat the dealer?

VI

Finding Web Resources

Game Bytes

URL address: **http://sunsite.unc.edu/GameBytes**

Perhaps you'd like to read about a computer or video game before you plunk down your money. *Game Bytes* is an electronic magazine that offers both reviews and images of many different games on the market.

Backgammon/Stephen's WWW Backgammon

URL address: **http://www.statslab.cam.ac.uk/~sret1/backgammon/main.html**

Double sixes—a good roll. This WWW site helps the uninitiated learn how to play the game. There are rules, books, and newsgroups. Advanced players can jump in and actually play Backgammon on the Internet.

Bridge on The Web

URL address: **http://www.cs.vu.nl/~sater/bridge/bridge-on-the-web.html**

This is the home page for people who love the game of Bridge. You can jump to lists of tournaments, read bridge newsgroups, or connect with either the Stanford University Bridge Club or the University of Warwick Bridge Society. One great link is to OKbridge (**http://www.cts.com/~clegg**)—a unique WWW computer site/program that allows four people, anywhere in the world, to play a game of bridge in real time. At any one time, there could be hundreds of people playing OKbridge—professionals and novices.

Chess—The Internet Chess Library

URL address: **http://nic.onenet.net:80/chess/**

◄ See "Journals," p. 821

Checkmate! This site is for the serious chess player. There are links to databases of master games, which you can load into computer chess games, links to text files about the game, and lists of the 1,000 best and worst rated players in the world. Finally, if you want to see some chess pictures, there is an extensive collection of GIF images of chess boards and chess playing celebrities.

Mind Games

URL address: **http://weber.u.washington.edu/~jlks/mindgame.html**

Here are some interactive head games. You can play the "Pick a Number Game," "The Math Game," or "The Grammar Game" links. It's fun and it may blow your mind. For example, when you try to pick a number, there's a very good chance that this site will be able to "read your mind." Try it.

Puzzle Archives

URL address: **http://alpha.acast.nova.edu/puzzles.html**

If you like puzzles and brain teasers, visit this site. Both puzzles and their solutions are provided.

Scrabble FAQ

URL address: **http://http.cs.berkeley.edu/~stevena/faq.html**

It's all here. A large Scrabble FAQ file, a link to the North American tournaments, rules, and a club roster (who would have guessed that the Cabo San Lucas Scrabble Club in Mexico meets every Thursday?).

The Game Cabinet

URL address: **http://web.kaleida.com/u/tidwell/GameCabinet.html**

This site offers an assortment of board game and non-board game rules and information from around the world. The information on this Web site covers not only game rules, but also game histories, clubs to join, and reviews of the games.

TrekMUSE!

URL address: **http://grimmy.cnidr.org/trek.html**

"Make it so" might be the motto of this Web site. Find out how to play the interactive Internet game TrekMUSE!, complete with an MPEG video of Star Trek, which you can download and view.

Video Games—Cardiff's Video Game Database Browser

URL address: **http://www.cm.cf.ac.uk/Games**

Video games from Sega, 3DO, and Atari are a few of the products reviewed in an extensive list of 1,300 titles that you can access via this Web site. Other links include video game magazine information, newsgroups, and frequently asked questions.

Hobbies

Beer Brewing

URL address: **http://guraldi.itn.med.umich.edu/Beer**

What is the difference between beer and ale? How do you turn hops into a tasty treat? If you'd like the answers to these questions, or some good recipes for your own homebrew, check out this WWW site.

HAM Radio—Bradley University Amateur Radio Club

URL address: **http://buarc.bradley.edu/**

The club is from Bradley University, in Peoria, IL. Many of the links are to local happenings, but there is a link to the Amateur Radio page that helps you to learn about amateur radio, visit other club home pages, and search for hams on the Internet. Also check out the following sites for more information including call signs, letters from amateur radio newsgroups, and FCC regulations:

> **http://www.mit.edu:8001/callsign**
> **http://www.acs.ncsu.edu/HamRadio**
> **http://www.mcc.ac.uk/OtherPages/AmateurRadio.html**

Birding

URL address: **http://compstat.wharton.upenn.edu:8001/~siler/birding.html**

Fig. 32.9
If you like to feed or watch birds, this WWW home page contains many resources.

Birding on the Web

This WWW site is a great resource for birders with newsletters, exhibits, books, and "bird chat." Be prepared for a slow load time, though, because about 20 bird images and logos are on the home page.

Birds

URL address: **http://www.abdn.ac.uk/~nhi019/intro.html**

These Web pages focus on our feathered friends and provide useful links to sightings, conferences, ornithological research, bird clubs, and bird art.

Beekeeping

URL address: **http://weber.u.washington.edu/~jlks/bee.html**

You are invited to learn the ancient art of beekeeping and to explore files, photos, and advice on this hobby and business.

Coaster Compendium

URL address: **http://sunsite.unc.edu/darlene/coaster/coaster.html**

It's true—many people make a hobby out of roller coasters, and this Web page is here to help. Do an online search for a particular coaster, jump to the **rec.roller-coaster** newsgroup, check out FAQs, and browse through a hyper-list of coasters by state. Lots of specifics here—such as the fact that the "Corkscrew" at Cedar Point Amusement Park in Ohio has a height of 78 feet, goes 40 miles per hour, and has 3 inversions. Start screaming.

Dog Information on the Web

URL address: **http://www.sce.carleton.ca/comm/wilf/ doggy_info.html**

You may not be able to teach old dogs new tricks, but you can learn a few things about dogs at this Web site. Lots of links include FAQ (frequently asked question) files on all sorts of breeds, digital photos of Labs, novels about dogs, and companies that sell dog gifts.

Fish Information Service

URL address: **http://www.actwin.com/fish/index.html**

This is an archive of information about aquariums. It covers freshwater, marine, tropical, and temperate fish.

Genealogy

URL address: **http://www.xmission.com/~jayhall/**

We all have relatives. Sponsored by Everton Publishers, this site offers links to more than 200 genealogical resources on the Internet. The links are organized in a series of subject-headed pages such as Beginning Your Search, Genealogical Archives and Libraries, United States Genealogical Resources, Non-United States Resources, Special Genealogical Resources, and Genealogical Software Archives. Connect today and start your search for your great-great-great ancestors.

Pets

URL address: **ftp://quartz.rutgers.edu (directory pub/pets)**

Although this is not a WWW server, you can find many frequently asked questions about animals, mostly dogs.

Photography—Minolta Users Group

URL address: **http://tronic.rit.edu/Minolta**

This site is dedicated to discussion of Minolta products, including cameras (there's a lot on the Maxxum series), binoculars, and other optical gear. It is also a repository for the Minolta Internet Mailing List archives—sometimes there are letters that offer advice to Minolta.

Quilting

URL address: **http://ttsw.com/MainQuiltingPage.html**

Welcome to the World Wide Quilting Page

Fig. 32.10
Quilt history, supply stores, and patterns are a few of the resources available at this Web site.

If you have boxes and boxes of fabric scraps and just can't bear the thought of tossing them away, this may be a good time to develop your quilting skills. At this site, you'll learn that the word "quilt" can be applied not only to a type of bed coverlet or blanket, but also to the ornamental padding and stitching of fabrics for placemats, Christmas stockings, and so on.

Radio Control Sailing

URL address: **http://honeybee.helsinki.fi/surcp/rcsail.htm**

The radio control sailors of Finland share this sailing information with the rest of the Web. They provide descriptions and pictures, along with the Finnish Competition Schedule, which includes results of Finnish and international competitions.

Stamp Collectors

URL address: **http://www.mbnet.mb.ca/~lampi/stamps.html**

This page is essentially a jumping off point to many different Web sites for stamp collectors. You can, for example, see stamps of Finland, learn about trading stamps with other collectors, or find out about clubs. Another useful Web site for stamp collectors is the U.S. Postal Service Web site at URL address **http://www.usps.gov**.

Textiles

URL address: **http://palver.foundation.tricon.com/crafts/
index.html**

Do you know what *Tvaandstickning* is? In English, it's twined knitting! For all
you knitters and stitchers, this site, maintained by Diana Lane, provides links
to a good selection of patterns, supplies, events, and tips.

World Wide Cats

URL address: **http://www.xs4all.nl/~dmuller/wwc.html**

This is a unique site. Visitors are asked to e-mail a digital photo of their beloved cat. The site has a "cat of the week" image on the home page. If your
photo is chosen, your cat could be seen by millions! There are lots of other
links to cat Web sites that offer useful information about care, breeding, and
playing.

Home Improvement and Gardening

Books That Work

URL address: **http://www.btw.com**

This is the site for Books That Work. Homeowners, turn on your PCs! This
site has a large amount of information related to gardening, landscaping,
home improvement, and other related activities. Find out about more than
500 different gardening products; view a glossary of terms or a directory of
useful toll-free phone numbers of manufacturers; and get access to a set of
URLs to other home and garden Web sites.

Partnet

URL address: **http://part.net/**

You may not need all the parts in this searchable database—they range from
motors to electrical to gears—but you never know.

Rec.woodworking

URL address: **http://www.cs.rochester.edu/u/roche/wood.html**

If you like wood and you like to work with wood, this is your site. Links take
you to information about woodworking tools, safety, how to create beautiful
wooden furniture, and how to bend wood, and images of furniture.

The Time Life Complete Gardener Encyclopedia

URL address: **http://www.timeinc.com/vg/TimeLife/CG/ vg-search.html**

The home page states, "Looking for a plant, tree, or shrub? This searchable database will eventually contain more than 2,000 species selected for general use in North American horticultural practice."

Venamy Orchids

URL address: **http://www.shopping2000.com/shopping2000/ venamy/**

This provides a comprehensive description of how to plant and grow orchids.

Wirenet

URL address: **http://www.deltanet.com/wirenet/**

You'll find this site useful whether you are putting in a new light fixture or rewiring your entire home. This site offers links to tips about wiring, a glossary of terms, and descriptions of products for sale.

Recreational Sports

Aviation Bulletin Board

URL address: **gopher://venus.hyperk.com:2100/**

This site is for serious flyers. It offers directories and files of the "Airman's Information Manual," a pilot and controller glossary, and links to weather conditions all around the world.

Badminton

URL address: **http://mid1.external.hp.com/stanb/badminton.html**

It's all here. Jump to links about the rules, international organizations, tournaments, places to play, and vendors that sell equipment.

Bicycle—California Mountain Biking

URL address: **http://xenon.stanford.edu/~rsf/mtn-bike.html**

This site provides general information on mountain biking and information on trails in the San Francisco and Northern California areas.

Fig. 32.11
If you like to mountain bike and live in or are visiting California, check out this site.

Bicycle—Colorado Front Range Cycling

URL address: **http://www.lance.colostate.edu/~ja740467/bike/frbike.html**

This site discusses mountain biking in Colorado, providing extensive information on clubs and trails.

Boating

URL address: **http://www.recreation.com:80/boats/**

Ahoy mate! This WWW server contains a lot of boating information, e-mail lists, links to other boating sites, the Charter boat directory, and boat classifieds.

Boating—Paddling

URL address: **http://www.recreation.com:80/paddling**

Learn how to prevent the canoe from tipping over! This is the page for a server that contains information on canoeing, kayaking, and rafting. Find out about clubs and associations, manufacturers, outfitters and guides, and publications.

Climbing Archive

URL address: **http://www.dtek.chalmers.se/Climbing/index.html**

This is a compilation of climbing material and information for people who enjoy the sport of rock climbing. It includes a daily newsflash, upcoming events, exercise programs, and hardware information.

Fencing

URL address: **http://www.ii.uib.no/~arild/fencing.html**

Touché! Those interested in the art of fencing can find books, drawings, clubs, events, and even the Internet fencing encyclopedia at this site. Information is mostly from Europe, Japan, and the United States.

Fishing

URL address: **http://www.geo.mtu.edu/~jsuchosk/fish/fishpage**

Perhaps you'd like to compare your fish stories to those of other people? The Fishing home page offers pictures of fish and a link to the anonymous FTP sites that house the fish GIFS from the FLYFISH LISTSERV.

Frisbee—George Ferguson's Ultimate Frisbee

URL address: **http://www.cs.rochester.edu/u/ferguson/ultimate/**

This is the WWW server for Ultimate Frisbee fanatics. It is loaded with links to rules, games, and tournament information.

Golfing—Alberta

URL address: **http://bear.ras.ucalgary.ca/brads_home_page/ CUUG/golf.html**

If you're planning a golf trip to Alberta, Canada, this WWW site has detailed descriptions of many courses such as the Kananaskis course—it has the Rocky Mountains for a backdrop and consists of two 18-hole championship courses.

Golfing—Princeton Golf Archives

URL address: **http://dunkin.princeton.edu/.golf/**

A site for the serious golfer, this archive has documents that tell you how to design a club or calculate slope and handicaps. It also has GIF and BMP images.

Golfing—Southern Utah Golf Courses

URL address: **http://sci.dixie.edu/StGeorge/Golf/golf.html**

If you never thought of Utah as a golf paradise, this server will change your mind. Many fine courses are located near areas of incredible natural beauty, such as Zion National Park, Bryce Canyon, and Lake Powell. The home page has a fantastic color map of the area with courses indicated. You can click on a course to get more information.

Golfing—The 19th Hole

URL address: **http://www.tr-rises.panam.edu/golf/19thhole.html**

There's lots of good golf information here—equipment sources, a golf digest record book, golf associations, and—if you don't already know them—the rules of golf.

Gymn Forum

URL address: **http://www.rmii.com/~rachele/gymnhome.html**

There are lots of links on this page—gymnastics mailing lists, archives of FAQs, a calendar for meets, collegiate rankings, and information on magazines devoted to the sport.

Hang Gliding Mosaic Picture Server

URL address: **http://cougar.stanford.edu:7878/ HGMPSHomePage.html**

The Hang Gliding Picture Server is a WWW server that contains hang gliding and paragliding related material, including a collection of hang gliding photos and movies, the hang gliding FAQ, archived issues of a mailing list, and programs related to hang gliding.

Fig. 32.12
This is just one of the many great hang gliding photos you can access at this Web site.

Hiking and Camping—Backcountry

URL address: **http://io.datasys.swri.edu**

You don't have to be a Boy Scout to enjoy getting out into the wilderness. This WWW home page offers links to information about hiking clubs, reviews of outdoor gear, trip reports, and some hypermedia maps.

Kite Flying—Jason's Web Kite Site

URL address: **http://www.latrobe.edu.au/Glenn/KiteSite/Kites.html**

Next time someone tells you to go fly a kite, connect to this WWW home page. Here you'll find JPEG images of single, dual, and quadline kites. There also are kite plans, newsletters, and other assorted kite flying activities.

Martial Arts

URL address: **http://www.nesc.k12.ar.us/ph_stuff/PracticeHall_Homepage.html**

This is a monthly online magazine that provides stories and advice for people involved in martial arts.

Motorcycles

URL address: **http://www.halcyon.com/moto/rec_moto.html**

How's your Hog? If you think this refers to a farm animal, check out the agricultural listings—this site has reviews of motorcycles, safety and training, motorcycle images, and racing information.

Fig. 32.13
You can find pictures of all sorts of classic motorcycles at this home page.

Outdoor Action Program

URL address: **http://www.princeton.edu/~rcurtis/oa.html**

This site is maintained by members of the Outdoor Action Program at Princeton University, and much of the information is related to outdoor activities in that area. There are other links to outdoor equipment, rock climbing, paddling, clubs, skiing, and caving.

Running Page

URL address: **http://polar.pica.army.mil/running.real/ running.html**

Millions of people love to run—for exercise and sport. This page has lots of good links to running clubs, races, the U.S. Track and Field organizations, publications, running products (even software), and, of course, a listing of marathon races.

Sailing and Boating

URL address: **http://www.aladdin.co.uk/sihe/**

Just hope the wind is going in the direction you want. Here you'll find links to everything from the latest on this year's America's Cup to the Sail Training Association page, various yacht clubs and associations, and other sites that focus on various forms of boating.

Scuba—Aquanaut

URL address: **http://www.opal.com/aquanaut**

Aquanaut is a WWW magazine dedicated to recreational and technical scuba diving. It provides links to reviews of dive gear and equipment, dive destinations, a database of divable shipwrecks, underwater pictures, and weather maps. Check out the fish pictures!

Skiing—Alaska Alpine Club

URL address: **http://info.alaska.edu:70/0/Alaska/rec/aac/class1**

The Alaska Alpine Club offers instruction in ski-mountaineering and climbing every spring at the University of Alaska, Fairbanks campus.

VI

Finding Web Resources

Fig. 32.14
The world of scuba diving awaits you at this Web server—learn about dive gear and discover terrific underwater locations.

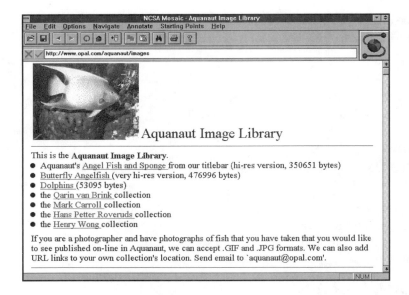

Skiing—Powder Hound Ski Report

URL address: **http://www.icw.com/skireport.html**

If you are in the mood to get out on the slopes and would like to learn about snow and weather conditions, check out this server.

Skiing—Ski Web

URL address: **http://www.sierra.net/SkiWeb**

Fig. 32.15
Catch some of the world's great slopes on the Ski Web.

The subtitle to this page says it all: "Your guide to the world of skiing by skiers (and snowboarders too)!" The home page has links to ski information by area. Like swooshing down a black run, you can leap from ski resorts in California to Utah to Vermont. And, if you've got enough money for the airfare, find out about skiing in Europe. Everything you need is here. You'll find links to information about transportation, packages, and rentals; and details on elevations, distance of runs, types of lifts, and rates. Cross-country enthusiasts are not left out.

Skiing—World

URL address: **http://www.cs.colorado.edu/homes/mcbryan/ public_html/bb/ski/ski.html**

This site provides bulletin boards to report world skiing conditions for both Alpine and Nordic (backcountry).

Skydiving

URL address: **http://www.cis.ufl.edu/skydive**

If you want a taste of this sport without leaving the ground, start with a trip to this home page. You can see pictures and read descriptions about this high-flying sport.

Spelunking

URL address: **http://speleology.cs.yale.edu/**

Spelunking is, in plain English, cave exploration. Spend some time at this site and find out about societies and associations devoted to this sport, equipment, events, and programs. There are also links to photos and cartoons.

Squash Player's Association

URL address: **http://www.ncl.ac.uk/~npb**

If you play squash—or want to—this place is fun. This site provides links from the home page to rules, clubs, newsletters, tournaments, and more.

Swimming

URL address: **http://alf2.tcd.ie/~redmondd/swim/header.html**

Here you'll find a set of links to current world records, workout and training procedures, advice for swimming injuries, and current competitions.

Tennis

URL address: **http://arganet.tenagra.com/Racquet_Workshop/ Tennis.html**

"Encouraging tennis players everywhere to GO TO THE 'NET for tennis information and sporting goods." This page offers you links to player news, equipment tips, tennis news, other WWW tennis resources, and the Racquet Workshop—an online tennis shop.

Unicycling

URL address: **http://nimitz.mcs.kent.edu/~bkonarsk**

You know that funny, yet difficult, sport where people ride a bicycle with only one wheel? This home page offers frequently asked questions (how many can there be?), information about unicycle games, and "Red's Nightmare," a 3.6M MPEG animation of a red unicycle.

Windsurfing

URL address: **http://www.dsg.cs.tcd.ie/dsg_people/afcondon/ windsurf/windsurf_home.html**

If you have a fine sense of balance and like the water, try this sport—but first check out this home page.

Fig. 32.16
Surf's up! This Web server offers windsurfing locations, images, and videos from around the world.

Spectator Sports

Autoracing Archive

URL address: **http://www.eng.hawaii.edu/Contribs/carina/ ra.home.page.html**

This service is provided for the racing enthusiasts of the Internet. You find information here on Formula One, IndyCar, and NASCAR racing. It links to race results, schedules, point standings, and other information.

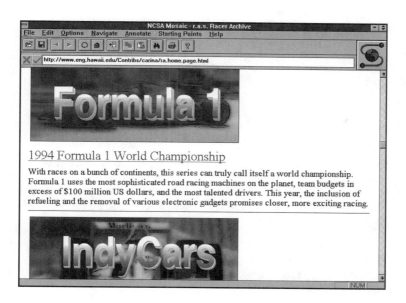

Fig. 32.17
This site contains
many pictures of
racing greats,
along with a
wealth of
other racing
information.

Baseball Information Center

URL address: **http://www.gems.com/ibic/**

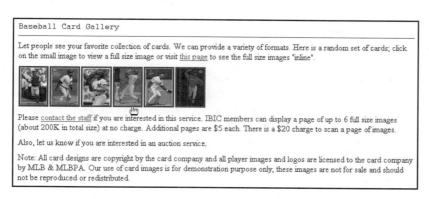

Fig. 32.18
The baseball card
gallery is one of
the features of the
Baseball Informa-
tion Center.

The Internet Baseball Information Center provides access to statistics, fantasy leagues, and discussion groups. An annual membership fee of $25 is used to help cover the costs of using a commercial stats service—some of the features are only available to members. Links include:

- General Information and frequently asked questions

- Player Statistics

- League Reports

VI

Finding Web Resources

- Fantasy Leagues
- Baseball Card Gallery
- Professional Baseball
- Hall of Fame

Baseball Server—Nando X

URL address: **http://www.nando.net/baseball/bbmain.html**

There is more to baseball than beer and box scores. The Baseball Server's columnists, Bill Arnold and Mark Camps, give you the inside scoop with "Beyond the Box Score."

Basketball—NBA

URL address: **http://tns-www.lcs.mit.edu/cgi-bin/sports/nba/schedule**

URL address: **http://www.netgen.com/sis/sports.html**

This site provides highlights of games played during the NBA season, NBA schedules, and an NBA sports server.

British Society of Sports History

URL address: **http://info.mcc.ac.uk/UMIST_Sport/bssh.html**

As the home page states, the aims of the Society are: "to promote, stimulate, and encourage discussion, study, research, and publication on the history of sport and physical education." Jump to the Sports Historian, and you'll quickly realize that American football has not been the only game in town as you read articles like "Crowd and Player Violence in Edwardian Cricket" or "English Editors of German Sporting Journals at the Turn of the Century."

European Championships in Athletics

URL address: **http://helsinki94.eunet.fi/**

In addition to voting for your favorite athletes, you can jump to documents that show results of competitions, pictures, and other information about the championships and the town of Helsinki.

Goodwill Games

URL address: **http://www.com/goodwill/index.html**

This site provides many features about the 1994 Goodwill Games, including information about the organization and history, as well as the games' sponsors. St. Petersburg is well represented with a bulletin and gallery.

Female Bodybuilders

URL address: **http://www.ama.caltech.edu/~mrm/body.html**

At the very least, this is a unique site in the Web universe. The page has links to pictures of female bodybuilders, statistics on their measurements, bios, results of contests, and addresses for fan mail.

Hockey—Jamaican Bobsledders

URL address: **http://www.mit.edu:8001/afs/athena.mit.edu/user/ j/b/jbreiden/hockey/internet/top.html**

This is the home page for the Jamaican Bobsledders, a team of spirited ice hockey players at the Massachusetts Institute of Technology. The links lead to information about the Bobsledders, game announcements, the roster, team archives, and inspirational material.

Hockey—NHL Schedule

URL address: **http://www.cs.ubc.ca/nhl**

This provides schedules and other information about the 26 teams that make up the National Hockey League. You can get to the action quickly by linking to a site called Playing Today. You also can link to games for particular dates. Other links provide information about your favorite team and ways of following games between divisions.

Hockey—Professional Hockey Server

URL address: **http://maxwell.uhh.hawaii.edu/hockey/nhl94/ playoff94.html**

This site provides links to so much information it will boggle even the sharpest sports mind. It includes National Hockey League results of the 1993–94 Stanley Cup Playoffs.

Rowing

URL address: **http://www.comlab.ox.ac.uk/archive/other/rowing.html**

This is the home page for information about the sport of rowing. You can jump to information about individuals located in various parts of the world, Regatta results such as the U.K. National Championships, and straightforward definitions and rules. There are even photographs and a link to the River and Rowing Museum.

Rugby

URL address: **http://rugby.phys.uidaho.edu/rugby.html**

This WWW server provides access to information about the rules and competitive events in the world of Rugby.

Satchel Sports

URL address: **http://www.starwave.com/SatchelSports.html**

Sports fans alert! This site contains scores, stats, features, columns, news, and photos—all updated daily—of both professional and college sports. There's also a sports quiz that'll test your sports IQ.

Soccer

URL address: **http://iamwww.unibe.ch/~ftiwww/Sonstiges/Tabellen/Eindex.html**

This site offers standings, statistics, and scores throughout the world, including a large archive file. You can learn about soccer clubs, Internet soccer newsgroups, and the 1995 European Cup.

Soccer—World Cup USA '94

URL address: **http://sunsite.sut.ac.jp/wc94/index.html**

The level of excitement was high as the United States geared up to host the event, and the rest of the world was in tune while they prepared to participate. You find links to game sites and schedules, host city information, participating teams, World Cup information, and a good selection of game highlight photos.

Travel—Resources, Hotels, and Travel Agencies

Avid Explorer

URL address: **http://www.explore.com/**

Take the guesswork out of planning your cruise or land expedition with the vast amount of travel information at your fingertips. There are links to special packages for exceptional values, maps, and weather reports.

GNN Travelers' Center

URL address: **http://nearnet.gnn.com/mkt/travel/center.html**

This is a comprehensive travel center; you can get tips on how to plan and where to go for your next excursion. Links to other WWW travel resources are also provided.

Himalayan Expeditions

URL address: **http://www.netpart.com/che/brochure.html**

How about a trip up some of the tallest mountains in the world? Check out this home page before you buy your climbing gear. There are also adventure trips to other places—like Africa.

Hospitality

URL address: **http://www.tele.fi/~hospitality**

This site is beneficial not only to travelers, but also to companies and individuals that are part of the international hospitality industry. Links are provided to a variety of Web pages relating to travel, such as hotels and travel agencies, marketing tips for hotels, and the International Diary of all trade fairs around the world.

Hyatt Hotels

URL address: **http://www.travelweb.com/thisco/common/ hyatt.html**

This Web site for Hyatt Hotels takes you on electronic mini-vacations at 16 resort hotels in the United States and Caribbean. You can view pictures of these high-end resorts, and go to links that contain local attractions, maps of the area, current weather conditions, rates, restaurants, and meeting spaces. You can check out vacancies and book a hotel room.

The Rec.Travel Library

URL address: **http://www.digimark.net/rec-travel**

If you like to travel, start here. This is the archive site and FAQ library for the rec.travel.* newsgroups. There are documents about traveling, tourist destinations, tour operators, and pointers to other travel collections.

Matterhorn Travel Wholesalers

URL address: **http://www.explore.com/mat/matterhorn.html**

Find out about unique travel opportunities. This site links to information on sailing on a yacht with captain and crew in the Virgin Islands; an England pub and theatre weekend; or St. Patrick's Day in Ireland.

Travel Advisories

URL address: **http://www.stolaf.edu/network/travel-advisories.html**

From the U.S. State Department, these advisories provide reports about the safety hazards that may be involved in traveling to foreign countries. You can also subscribe to an Internet mailing list to receive advisories.

Travelers' Checklist

URL address: **http://www.ag.com/travelers/checklist**

◀ See "Services and Supplies," p. 899

You can pack your bags *after* you visit this Web page. This online catalog contains various travel-related products, including voltage converters, adapters, money belts, and currency conversion calculators. There are also travel tips about foreign electricity and travel safety.

Travel Web

URL address: **http://www.travelweb.com**

Fig. 32.19
Travel Web offers direct links to some of the world's largest hotel chains.

THISCO (The Hotel Industry Switching Company), a company owned by the lodging industry, maintains this travel-related site. THISCO is the organization that links the reservation systems of 20 of the largest hotel chains with the world's airline computer systems. Web travelers can use Travel Web to make hotel reservations at some participating chains, including Best Western, Clarion, Econo Lodge, Ramada, and Four Seasons Hotels.

Travel—Places to Go, United States

Center for the Study of Southern Culture
URL address: **http://imp.cssc.olemiss.edu/**

The Center for the Study of Southern Culture provides links to sources of information on country, gospel, and blues music; a magazine of Southern culture; and cultural events for the Southern states region. Get ready for good Southern hospitality.

Florida—Orlando
URL address: **http://florida.com/orlando/orlando1.htm**

Here you'll find everything you need for your next trip to the Orlando area. Yes, there are links to Disney World information plus many more, such as the Orlando Science Center, Sea World, dining, and places to stay. If you want to learn more about Disney specifically, you might also try the Disney Web site (URL address: **http://www.disney.com**).

Louisiana—The Barrow House Inn
URL address: **http://sparky.cyberzine.org/html/Inn/innpage.html**

Touted as "The most recommended inn of Audubon's beloved English Louisiana Plantation Country," the inn is located in the heart of St. Francisville, Louisiana.

Missouri Botanical Garden
URL address: **http://straylight.tamu.edu/MoBot/welcome.html**

A 79-acre garden of flora and fauna is here for your sightseeing pleasure. Links take you to information on plants in bloom, educational programs, flora of China, Mesoamericana, and North America. Don't miss the tour—it begins whenever you're ready.

New England Travel
URL address: **http://www.std.com/NE/netrav.html**

See the beautiful New England states like never before when you visit this Web site. Find out what individual states in New England have to offer for touring, and get tips on lodging and dining.

VI

Finding Web Resources

New York—Buffalo Restaurant Guide

URL address: **http://www.cs.buffalo.edu/pub/WWW/ restaurant.guide/restaurant.guide.html**

You may know that Buffalo, New York has cold weather and a football team, but did you know that it has a lot of good restaurants? This site tells you about them. Links organize restaurants by category, cuisine, and location. After you find a restaurant, a short review discusses the food and provides price, location, and phone number.

Northern California Spiderweb

URL address: **http://www.spiderweb.com/swhome.html**

This is a hypertext directory of the culture, commerce, and community services of Northern California's Sonoma and Marin Counties. There are also links to other communities around the United States.

Virginia—Arlington County

URL address: **http://www.co.arlington.va.us/**

Fig. 32.20
Across the river from Washington, D.C., Arlington has much to offer residents and visitors.

Whether you live in Arlington County or simply plan to visit, this server helps you access information about the area. Home page icons and links bring you to information about the famous Iwo Jima statue, Arlington Cemetery, the Pentagon, the D.C. area, and a regional map. Other resources include tourism, shopping, and restaurants.

Virginia, Staunton

URL address: **http://www.elpress.com/staunton**

Staunton, Virginia is just a few hours from Washington, D.C. It is a vacation spot for travelers who have an interest in historic sites, museums, or the great outdoors.

Washington—Seattle Online Entertainment Guide

URL address: **http://useattle.uspan.com**

The United States Performing Arts Network sponsors this page, which encompasses a comprehensive listing of what's happening in Seattle. You'll find movie listings, dining, the music scene, laser shows, and listings of auditions for performers.

Travel—Places to Go, Worldwide

Austria—Salzburg

URL address: **http://www.tcs.co.at/fvp.html**

This site provides MPEG videos and documents of Salzburg and the surrounding areas (most of the text is in German).

Canada—Calgary, Alberta

URL address: **http://bear.ras.ucalgary.ca/brads_home_page/CUUG/calgary.html**

Find out about the Stampede and learn about the sports teams, parks, accommodations, and hobby clubs that this northern city offers.

Canada—Intelligent Information Systems of Canada

URL address: **http://www.iisys.com/iishome.htm**

Try this online travel guide for cities in the United States and Canada. Links describe many of the attractions and services in the areas.

Canada—Prince Edward Island

URL address: **http://www.crafts-council.pe.ca/vg/index.html**

Prince Edward Island is Canada's smallest province, located off the eastern coast of North America. This site offers information about vacationing on Prince Edward Island.

Germany—Railroading in Germany

URL address: **http://rzstud1.rz.uni-karlsruhe.de/~ule3/ info-trn.html**

This WWW site lets you in on all the secrets for enjoying travel in Germany by railroad. There are tips, rail fares, descriptions of different types of trains (with pictures), and an overview of overnight travel on the rail.

India

URL address: **http://www.cs.clemson.edu/~nandu/india.html**

Fig. 32.21
In addition to travel information, this is a valuable site for researching the history and culture of India.

With 25 states that cover more than nine million square miles of land, India offers a lot of exploration. This home page offers links that tell you about the languages, religions, and music. Information about travel agents that book trips to India and an "adventure summary" of a traveler's trip are also available.

Moon Travel Handbooks

URL address: **http://www.moon.com:7000**

This site offers a variety of travel-related Internet exhibits and text. Areas of the world covered include Asia, Latin America, Africa, and Hawaii. Check out the first installment of *Road Trip USA*—a travel-guide work-in-progress whose chapters will be added to the server, route-by-route, prior to the publication of a paperback edition in the fall of 1995. The first route is Route 50, which spans the United States.

North Atlantic Cruises

URL address: **http://www.centrum.is/com/vinland.html**

Adventure cruising in the North-Atlantic with on-board Internet access.

Fig. 32.22
From the relaxation of a pleasure cruise to the excitement of deep water sea angling, this Web site can get you there.

Vinland Limited offers adventure cruises in the North Atlantic. Try a marine salvage operation, sea angling, or a more relaxing pleasure cruise. This site links to descriptions of the cruises.

Virtual Tourist

URL address: **http://wings.buffalo.edu/world**

Want to be a world traveler? This home page links you with tourist guides for many foreign locations, including Japan and New Zealand.

◀ See "Interesting Sites and National Travel Guides," p. 756

From Here...

The Web resources in this chapter should help you fill up whatever spare time you may have left—either at the end of the day or during a vacation. You might also try the following chapters:

■ Chapter 29, "Publications: News, Periodicals, and Books," offers several Web magazines that focus on extra-curricular activities, sports, and travel.

■ Chapter 31, "Shopping," has a variety of guides to international shopping and stores that sell games and sports-related gear.

VI

Finding Web Resources

Chapter 33

Hot FTP and Gopher Sites

by Bill Eager

Thousands of FTP sites are on the Internet, and they have extensive collections of software, images, and documents just waiting to be downloaded to your PC. Gopher sites also contain a wonderful assortment of resources—maps, documents, photographs, and sound files. In fact, both FTP and Gopher sites are so popular that they often become overloaded during peak hours (9:00 a.m. to 5:00 p.m. EST). If a site has too many visitors, you won't be able to connect.

In this chapter, you find both FTP and Gopher sites, in that order. The sites are listed in the following general categories:

- Arts and music
- Computers
- Government
- Health
- International
- Publications
- Science
- Sports and recreation

> **Note**
>
> You can connect to *all* these FTP and Gopher sites via the World Wide Web! Enter the URL address into your browser address field with this format: gopher://<*address of Gopher*>. If there is a path, just enter it right after the address. Here's an example for the Project Gutenberg electronic books site:
>
> **gopher://spinaltap.micro.umn.edu/1/Ebooks**.
>
> For FTP sites the format is ftp://<*address of ftp site/resource*>.

Hot FTP Sites

◄ See "Locating the FTP Information You Want," p. 147

◄ See "Connecting to an Anonymous FTP Server," p. 154

◄ See "Retrieving a File from an Anonymous FTP Server," p. 159

The following list of hot FTP sites provides an excellent introduction to the world of online files. Although these FTP sites are organized by various subject categories, you'll find that most sites contain all types of files, including software programs you can run on your PC. Also, many FTP sites are mirrored, which means that other FTP sites have the same files.

Arts and Music

Online Digitized Music

FTP address: **ftp.luth.se**
Subdirectory: /pub/sounds/songs

This site contains the San Diego State University sound archives. From Abba to ZZ Top, this is a comprehensive index of songs, many with audio sound clips.

Dance

FTP address: **ftp.std.com**
Subdirectory: /pub/dance

This site has extensive information on global dance resources including the countries of Brazil, Ireland, Spain, Venezuela, and Yugoslavia. This site also contains documents on dance styles such as ballroom, swing, and tango. The /pub directory has many other resources as well—check out the clip art.

Music Lyrics

FTP address: **ftp.nevada.edu**
Subdirectory: pub/guitar

Need lyrics to a song? You'll find them at this site. This subdirectory has files of lyrics with chords for artists and groups from A to Z. Under E, for example, you'll find the Eurythmics right between Enya and the Everly Brothers.

Photographs
FTP address: **wuarchive.wustl.edu**

Maintained by Washington University at St. Louis, this is one of the biggest FTP sites on the Net. Among the treasures are hundreds, possibly thousands of downloadable image files—formats include GIF and JPEG. Be sure to read the index if you want to know what's what.

Computers

Apple Software Applications
FTP address: **mac.archive.umich.edu**
Subdirectory: /mac

This University of Michigan site has freeware and shareware applications for many different Apple products.

Compression Utilities
FTP address: **pit-manager.mit.edu**
Subdirectory: /pub

Massachusetts Institute of Technology maintains this server where you'll find compression applications, UseNet newsgroup information, and some electronic publications.

Compression Utilities
FTP address: **ftp.cso.uiuc.edu**

Compression and decompression programs for most computer platforms are available at this site.

Computer Resources
FTP address: **brolga.cc.uq.oz.au**

This University of Queensland computer has files of information about Microsoft Windows, the Internet RFCs (request for comments in which people discuss technology trends on the Internet), and newsgroup postings.

VI

Finding Web Resources

FARNET—Networks for Research and Education
FTP address: **ftp.cerf.net**
Subdirectory: /farnet/farnet_info/

This site provides information about FARNET, a non-profit corporation. The primary goal of FARNET is to advance the use of computer networks for research and education.

Frequently Asked Questions
FTP address: **rtfm.mit.edu**

This site holds the archives of all the FAQ (frequently asked questions) lists.

Internet
FTP address: **ds.internic.net**

This site is run by InterNIC; you'll find a variety of Internet-related documents and information here.

Macmillan Computer Publishing
FTP address: **ftp.mcp.com**

Macmillan Computer Publishing maintains this FTP site that offers many useful Internet and computer resources and shareware programs.

Microsoft
FTP address: **ftp.microsoft.com**

You can access and download a variety of Microsoft utilities and some games (including Win32s), and find out about Microsoft products.

National Center for Supercomputing Applications
FTP address: **ftp.NCSA.uiuc.edu**
Subdirectory: /PC/Windows/Mosaic
Subdirectory: /Web/Mosaic/Windows

Try both of these subdirectories at the NCSA site to get the latest information about the World Wide Web browser NCSA Mosaic for Windows.

Newsgroup Newsreader—WinTrump
FTP address: **ftp.trumpet.com.au**
Subdirectory: /pub/pc/wintrump

If you want to try another Windows newsreader besides WinVN, download the WinTrump newsreader from this directory.

Newsgroup Newsreader—WinVN and Updates
FTP address: **titan.ksc.nasa.gov**
Subdirectory: /pub/win3/winvn

This is one of NASA's computers, where you can download the latest updates to the WinVN newsreader software.

Newsgroups
FTP address: **ftp.cs.bham.ac.uk**
Subdirectory: /pub/usenet

This comes from the University of Birmingham, School of Computer Science, in the United Kingdom. You can view the archives of UseNet newsgroups. Other areas on this server include research papers and software programs.

Newsgroup Info
FTP address: **turbo.bio.net**

This is the **news.announce.newgroups** archive.

Security
FTP address: **watmath.waterloo.edu**

This site provides lots of stuff, including some programs that help to ensure security with electronic communications.

Software—All Types
FTP address: **oak.oakland.edu**

This is a major mirror site that maintains copies of software programs from other Net sites.

Software—Microsoft Windows
FTP address: **ftp.cica.indiana.edu**
Subdirectory: pub/pc/win3

Indiana University is a central site for Microsoft Windows applications. This site is mirrored at FTP **archive.orst.edu** in subdirectory /pub/mirrors/ftp.cica.indiana.edu.

UseNet Archives

FTP address: **lcs.mit.edu**

Subdirectory: /telecom-archives

This site contains Telecomm Archives files about telecommunications, from the UseNet group **comp.dcom.telecom**. As with most UseNet archives, some of this information is very valuable, some of it is just fun, and some of it is junk.

Viruses

FTP address: **cert.org**

Subdirectory: pub/virus-l/docs/vtc

This archive lists computer viruses.

Government

Bureau of Land Management

FTP address: **dsc.blm.gov**

The BLM manages almost 272 million acres or one-eighth of the nation's land resources. You'll find detailed information about programs and state-by-state contact addresses.

Electronic Frontier Foundation

FTP address: **ftp.eff.org**

Explore the legal aspects of communication via the Internet.

Legal Information Institute and Cello Web Browser

FTP address: **ftp.law.cornell.edu**

Subdirectory: pub/LII/Cello

This is the home site for the Legal Information Institute at Cornell University. Download the latest version of the Cello Web browser, or go up a directory or two to find information about legal issues. You can even explore a directory called /humor if you need a good lawyer joke.

United States Constitution

FTP address: **archive.nevada.edu**

From the University of Nevada, you'll be able to find the United States Constitution as well as a variety of religious texts including the Bible.

White House Publications
FTP address: **cco.caltech.edu**
Subdirectory: /pub/bjmccall

This site contains searchable databases of White House publications.

Health

Abdominal Training FAQ
FTP address: **rtfm.mit.edu**
Subdirectory: /pub/usenet/misc.fitness/Abdominal_Training_FAQ

If you want to keep your abdominal area in tip-top shape, or simply eliminate a "spare tire," this is the FTP site for you! The creation of this set of documents was motivated by frequent questions on the topic in the newsgroup **misc.fitness**.

Centers for Disease Control (CDC)
FTP address: **ftp.cdc.gov**

Find out about the major diseases and current research and prevention efforts.

Home and Leisure

Pets
FTP address: **rtfm.mit.edu**
Subdirectory: /pub/usenet/rec.pets

This is a collection of UseNet articles about pets. You'll also find FAQs (frequently asked questions) about birds, cats, and ferrets—yes, ferrets.

Recipes
FTP address: **gatekeeper.dec.com**
Subdirectory: /pub/recipes

This is from Digital Equipment Corp. in Palo Alto. Go to the /pub directory, and you'll find games, graphic files, multimedia, and a directory called /recipes containing detailed instructions for more than 200 recipes culled from UseNet newsgroups, including African stew, swordfish, and pecan pie.

International

Israel
FTP address: **israel.nysernet.org**
Subdirectory: /israel

You can find a variety of information about current and historical events relating to Israel. This site contains an electronic journal, information about the Holocaust, Israel projects, and politics.

Publications

Electronic Smorgasbord
FTP address: **wiretap.spies.com**

This contains a collection of interesting documents.

Handicap News
FTP address: **handicap.shel.isc-br.com**

A variety of information for disabled individuals including legal, medical, and social service resources is available at this address.

Project Gutenberg
FTP address: **mrcnext.cso.uiuc.edu**
Subdirectory: pub/etext

If you enjoy literature, especially the classics, then you will love this server. More than a hundred electronic versions of classic books are in this collection. Some of the authors represented include Emily Bronte, Edgar Rice Burroughs, Charles Dickens, Nathaniel Hawthorne, Herman Melville, William Shakespeare, Mary Shelley, Henry David Thoreau, Mark Twain, and Jules Verne.

InterText Magazine
FTP address: **ftp.etext.org**
Subdirectory: Zines/InterText/intertext.html

This is an electronic magazine of fiction stories and articles. More than 20 issues are online, which provide lots of good reading.

Science Fiction

FTP address: **ftp.lysator.liu.se**

Linkoping University offers a variety of science fiction files.

Television and Movies

FTP address: **quartz.rutgers.edu**
Subdirectory: pub/television

You can find many frequently asked questions about television. If movies are more your thing, try the /tv+movies subdirectory, which has files on both television and movies. The /pub directory has a variety of other subjects including Disney, economics, food, humor, and sex.

Twin Peaks and NASA

FTP address: **audrey.levels.unisa.edu.au**

You connect with the University of South Australia at this site. There's a directory for *Twin Peaks* (the TV show) that has scripts, sounds, pictures, and reviews. Also, NASA space flight information—manifests, launch times, images, and historical documents—is available.

Science

Agriculture

FTP address: **ftp.sura.net**
Subdirectory: pub/nic/

Download the file agricultural.list for a file of agricultural lists.

Aurora Borealis

FTP address: **xi.uleth.ca**
Subdirectory: /pub/solar/Aurora/Images

If you enjoy seeing images of auroral activity, here is an FTP site that houses a great many of them. You can download them to your own computer.

Biology—United States National Institute of Health

FTP address: **ncbi.nlm.nih.gov**

A "heavy" site that contains files of interest to the molecular biology community. The NCBI/GenBank is responsible for building, maintaining, and distributing GenBank, the NIH genetic sequence database that collects all known DNA sequences from scientists worldwide.

Sports and Recreation

Football—College
FTP address: **ubvms.cc.buffalo.edu**

The /collfootball directory contains information and statistics on—guess what? Other directories on this computer worth exploring include /gopher/gifs (where you can find a variety of image files including Batman and the world—there's probably some connection) and /newsletters (which has several electronic publications).

Football—Professional
FTP address: **ftp.vnet.net**
Subdirectory: pub/football

Fourth down and three to go. You'll find it all here—Fantasy Football, football software programs, and files of images (BMP, GIF, and JPEG) of famous football heroes doing their thing.

Games
FTP address: **ftp.uwp.edu**
Subdirectory: /pub/msdos/games

This site contains a large collection of computer games and demos of games that you can download and play.

Photography
FTP address: **ftp.nevada.edu**
Subdirectory: pub/photo

Professional and amateur photographers will enjoy files that offer tips for better photography, using light meters, and how to shoot wedding pictures.

Scuba and Space
FTP address: **ames.arc.nasa.gov**

With the files at this site, you can either explore the space above the atmosphere (that is—outer space) or the space below the surface of the ocean. Many files on NASA activities and scuba diving are available.

Hot Gopher Sites

Here are a few tips that can make Gopher travel more enjoyable. When you access a Gopher main menu, check to see if there is a document file (usually it's the first choice) titled "About the ___ Gopher," where the blank is the name of the Gopher. This document tells you a little about the organization that maintains the site, as well as the resources you're likely to find. It's a good place to start.

Most of the Gopher addresses on this hotlist are straightforward—you enter the address, and it opens the main menu for the site. Some, however, move you directly to submenus; some to documents. There can be three elements to connect to a Gopher site:

- The name of the host (computer)
- The port
- The path

Here, for example, is the Gopher address for the NASA Goddard Space Flight Center: **gopher.gsfc.nasa.gov**—enter the address and away you go. Here's the address for Project Vote Smart, a Gopher site that offers information about political races and bills that are up for a vote: **gopher.neu.edu:1112**. Notice the number 1112 after the address. This indicates that you connect to a specific port on the computer. Some Windows-based Gopher software asks you to enter this port number separately from the address of the computer. If you are using a dial-in terminal emulation, just type it after the address. 99.9% of the time the port is 70, which is a common default. Unless otherwise noted here, the port is 70.

Finally, if you're connecting to a specific Gopher submenu or document, you may need to enter the "path" that gets you there. For example, here is the address for a Gopher site that has information on Chicago area galleries and museums: **nuinfo.nwu.edu/1/entertainment/galleries**. Again, depending on which software program you use to connect to this Gopher, you may have to enter the path (which is everything after the first forward slash /).

◀ See "Connecting to a Gopher Server," p. 163

◀ See "Locating Gopher Information," p. 164

◀ See "Saving Files from a Gopher Server," p. 175

VI

Finding Web Resources

If for some reason you have trouble connecting to a site that has a long path, just enter the first part of the address (before the first slash); then you can go through a couple of menus to get to the resource. Unless noted, there is no additional path to the Gophers on this list.

Art and Music

Barbershop Quartet
Gopher address: **timc.pop.upenn.edu**

This site offers resources for the barbershop community—not the people who cut hair. Guides to organizations, quartet information, recordings, an a cappella newsgroup, and more are available here.

ECHO Gopher
Gopher address: **echonyc.com**

This site has a music calendar, reviews of new musical works, music organizations, music festivals, and more, more, more.

FineArt Forum
Gopher address: **gopher.msstate.edu**

This is a monthly electronic newsletter of the Art, Science, and Technology Network (ASTN). Topics are art and technology.

Project Bartleby
Gopher address: **gopher.cc.columbia.edu**

From Columbia University, avid readers (or high school students who want a supplement to Monarch Notes) will enjoy this site! Start with an 1857 translation of the *Odyssey* of Homer. Inaugural addresses of the United States presidents and poetry by John Keats, William Wordsworth, and many more are available.

The WELLgopher
Gopher address: **gopher.well.sf.ca.us**

If your artistic tastes run from the music of the Grateful Dead to the poetry of William S. Burroughs, this site has it all. Some of the Gopher choices include Art, Music, Film, Authors, Cyberpunk, and the *Whole Earth Review* (the magazine).

Business, Finance, and Employment

Monetary Statistics
Gopher address: **una.hh.lib.umich.edu**
Path: 1/ebb/monetary

This is for the serious investor! Start with foreign exchange rates and work your way down to daily state and local bond rates and treasury saving bond sales. More than 100 different documents that deal with finance and money are available.

Online Career Center
Gopher address: **garnet.msen.com**

Select the Online Career Center (OCC) from the bottom of this Gopher menu. You can browse the OCC either by job location or keyword search.

United States Patents
Gopher address: **summit.ece.ucsb.edu**
Path: 1/Resources/ENGR/Patents

A *patent* is the legal equivalent of a deed for property—except that the property is an invention or product. You can search patent applications from the United States Patent Office or delve into an archive of computer patents.

Westlaw
Gopher address: **wld.westlaw.com**

This Gopher lets you access a searchable database of more than 675,000 law firms, branch offices, and specific lawyers across the nation. You'll get addresses, phone numbers, and contact names. Be as specific as possible in your search; a search for "Denver" retrieves 200 listings.

Computers

Bell Operating Companies—Modified Final Judgment
Gopher address: **bell.com**

The Modified Final Judgment (MFJ) Task Force, a committee of the several regional Bell operating companies that works on telecommunications issues in Washington, is now on the Internet. The MFJ is the ruling that broke up the telephone monopoly.

VI

Finding Web Resources

Computers in Networks (article)
Gopher address: **gopher.psg.com**

Information about networking in the developing world, low-cost networking tools, and computer networking in general are provided here. This is an article that presents a general overview of interest to anyone working with limited resources.

Electronic Frontier Foundation
Gopher address: **gopher.eff.org**

The Electronic Frontier Foundation (EFF) focuses on ensuring that individual rights mandated by the United States Constitution and Bill of Rights are protected with respect to new communications technologies and infrastructures. This Gopher is also a good resource for general Internet information.

International Telecommunications Union
Gopher address: **info.itu.ch**

This Gopher contains information from the International Telecommunications Union, an agency of the United Nations that attempts to set international standards for telecommunications.

Internet Network Information Center—InterNIC
Gopher address: **gopher.internic.net**

Established by the National Science Foundation, InterNIC offers many resources for people and companies that use the Internet. You can use this Gopher to access and search the AT&T-maintained InterNIC Directory to look for other people on the Internet. If you've got an Internet question, start here!

National Center for Supercomputing Applications
Gopher address: **gopher.ncsa.uiuc.edu**

This is the Gopher site for the organization that created the Mosaic World Wide Web browser. Lots of Internet resources are at this site.

Education

Apple Computer Higher Education Gopher
Gopher address: **info.hed.apple.com**

This is a combination PR site to promote new Apple products. Try the menu selection Higher Education Info, which opens up resources about conferences, events, programs, and "media centers." This site also provides connections to other Gopher educational sites.

AskERIC
Gopher address: **ericir.syr.edu**

If you're a teacher, you need to know about—and explore—AskERIC. This site has numerous resources (like documents, ideas for curriculum, and teacher Q&As) for educators.

Chronicle of Higher Education
Gopher address: **chronicle.merit.edu**

This is the publication for educators who work in higher education. There are articles about what universities around the world are doing, reviews of federal policy that has an impact on teaching, and a significant positions-available section.

Higher Education Resources
Gopher address: **gopher.digimark.net**

A broad selection of resources divided into elementary and higher education are available here.

K–12 Resources
Gopher address: **k12.cnidr.org**

This site has an extensive collection of links to other Gopher sites that focus on educational resources for K–12 teachers. If you have any trouble with this address, try the numerical address: **128.109.179.45**. Try either Janice's K12 Gopher or the Global Schoolhouse Gopher to access local, state, and federal files and programs that enhance the educational process.

KIDLINK
Gopher address: **kids.duq.edu**

This is a source of global networking for children ages 10 to 15. They can find out how other children around the world are using the Internet and tap into a variety of educational resources. If you're an adult, you'll also enjoy this site!

Library of Congress (LOC)
Gopher address: **marvel.loc.gov**

This is a tremendous Gopher with information on many different subjects. You can search the library for specific documents and resources; connect to many Internet services (like other Gopher and FTP sites); find out about events at the LOC; and access a treasure trove of government publications.

Mathematics
Gopher address: **archives.math.utk.edu**

Find a variety of teaching tools, including software, that focus on the subject of mathematics. This also links to other math Gopher sites.

National Center for Education Statistics
Gopher address: **gopher.ed.gov**

This United States Department of Education Gopher server has databases and files that contain "information aimed at improving teaching and learning." You can get lost here with documents that explain things like the Goals 2000 Educate America Act, grant programs, publications, and much more.

National Center on Adult Literacy (NCAL)
Gopher address: **litserver.literacy.upenn.edu**

This Gopher server includes information on literacy programs throughout the United States and in foreign countries.

What's Happening in Your State?
Gopher address: **digital.cosn.org**
Path: 1/State and Local Network Projects/State Networks

This is a terrific resource for educators who want to be on the Information Superhighway. State-by-state menus open documents that highlight current educational initiatives to get classrooms plugged in.

Gopher Super Sites
These two Gophers, both at large universities, have menus that can get you to just about any other Gopher in the world. They provide many submenus and a lot of information.

University of Minnesota
Gopher address: **gopher.micro.umn.edu**

A terrific collection of Gopher menus is available here. You'll find discussion groups, phone books, fun and games, and the ever-popular All the Gopher Servers In the World directory—where you can weave your way around the globe.

University of Iowa
Gopher address: **panda.uiowa.edu**

This site provides not only general information about the university and Iowa City, but also great menu selections to Gopherspace. Open the Online information menu to access a world of libraries, perform FTP searches via Archie, and check out the Song Lyric Server.

Government
The following are United States Government Gopher sites that offer documents (many of them are compressed) that you can either view online or download.

American Political Science Association
Gopher address: **apsa.trenton.edu**

If you think politics just means dropping in your ballot once every four years, then this Gopher will open your eyes to a new world. Areas include international relations, political theory, public policy, and even an e-mail directory of political scientists.

Census Information
Gopher address: **gopher.census.gov**

Once every decade, the people in the United States get counted. This Gopher has information about population statistics, county business patterns, top city rankings, demographics, and a "Who's Who at the Census Bureau." So jump in and see how big your city, state, and nation really are.

Corporation of National Research Initiatives
Gopher address: **ietf.CNRI.Reston.Va.US**

Operated by CNRI, this Gopher lets you access a lot of information, such as e-mail addresses of people in Congress and at the White House, the White House press release service, and, for some strange reason, national weather forecasts.

Consumer Product Safety Commission
Gopher address: **cpsc.gov**

Product safety is part of everyday life—from cars and lawn mowers to children's products. The Consumer Product Safety Commission Gopher provides resources to help you understand the nature of "safe" products.

Environmental Protection Agency
Gopher address: **futures.wic.epa.gov**

This Gopher site tells you all about the federal agency charged with keeping America beautiful. Learn about programs, read newsletters, and participate in a "virtual workshop on environmental technology."

Federal Communications Commission (FCC)
Gopher address: **gopher.fcc.gov**

The FCC has the rather awesome task of regulating broadcasting industries and allocating "spectrum" for radio, cable, cellular phones, and other wireless technologies, even high-definition television. Find out what's going on.

Federal Information Exchange (FEDIX)
Gopher address: **fedix.fie.com**

Federal Information Exchange, Inc. (FEDIX) is a commercial company that provides documentation from many different government agencies. FEDIX contains data and documents from the *Commerce Business Daily*, the *Federal Register*, and other government agencies.

Project Vote Smart
Gopher address: **gopher.neu.edu**
Port: 1112

The reason many people don't get involved in the political process is because it's hard to. Project Vote Smart brings you information about political candidates and bills in Congress, and tells you what the votes are for specific bills.

United States Budget 1995
Gopher address: **gopher.esa.doc.gov**

The last menu item in this Gopher is for the 1995 Fiscal Budget of the United States Government. See if there's anything left to fix those pot holes.

United States Senate Gopher
Gopher address: **gopher.senate.gov**

This contains documents distributed by members and committees; you can do a full text search on all the files to find what you're looking for. Another useful Gopher is the United States House of Representatives at **gopher.house.gov**.

Various United States Government Agencies
Gopher address: **gopher.state.mn.us**

A Gopher server, this page offers directories that have information on the Department of Health, the Legislature, Department of Transportation, Higher Education Coordinating Board, and the Center for Arts Education.

Health

Disability
Gopher address: **val-dor.cc.buffalo.edu**

This site provides resources for individuals who have a disability or are in the process of rehabilitation.

National Institute of Allergy and Infectious Diseases (NIAID) Gopher
Gopher address: **gopher.niaid.nih.gov**

These documents contain a variety of information about both allergies and infectious diseases. An AIDS information directory contains fact sheets and press releases about the disease.

National Cancer Center—Tokyo
Gopher address: **gopher.ncc.go.jp**

If you or someone you know has cancer, this Gopher provides a variety of documents and links to other Gophers that focus on the research, remediation, and cure of cancer.

National Institute of Mental Health (NIMH) Gopher
Gopher address: **gopher.nimh.nih.gov**

Learn more about mental health and some of the programs available.

National Library of Medicine
Gopher address: **gopher.nlm.nih.gov**

This site has extensive holdings, so be prepared to stay a while. Fact sheets and newsletters about medical programs, AIDS information, resource lists, and bibliographies are available here. Information about many different areas of medicine and medical conditions are also available.

Nursing
Gopher address: **nightingale.con.utk.edu**

Nurses play an important role in helping patients deal with and recover from illness. This Gopher provides some resources to help nurses help you.

Stanford University Medical Center
Gopher address: **med-gopher.stanford.edu**

The Stanford University Medical Center (SUMC) is internationally recognized for its outstanding achievements in teaching, research, and patient care. This Gopher site helps you explore some of the resources at the center.

World Health Organization
Gopher address: **gopher.who.ch**

The World Health Organization, at Geneva, provides information regarding diseases, immunizations, and prevention.

Home and Leisure

Cooking
Gopher address: **spinaltap.micro.umn.edu**
Path: 1/fun/Recipes

Italian, Oriental, Mexican—you name it; if you need a recipe for tonight's dinner, connect to this Gopher site. To access recipes, first choose the menu selection Fun, and then Recipes. You'll be cooking up great spaghetti sauce, sambal-lilang, or fajitas.

Gardening
Gopher address: **leviathan.tamu.edu**

Gardening not only produces a delicious variety of healthy vegetables and beautiful flowers, it's also a good form of exercise and stress therapy. This is the site of the Texas Agricultural Extension Services Gopher. When you select Master Gardener from the main menu, you have access to documents on many different plants such as fruits and nuts, flowering plants, vegetables, grasses, and trees. You can search this database to locate the specific topic or plant you're working with.

International and Travel

Amtrak Train Schedules
Gopher address: **gwis.circ.gwu.edu**
Path: 1/General Information/Train Schedules/Amtrak Train Schedules

All Aboard! This Gopher at George Washington University maintains a collection of files that have the schedules of Amtrak trains across the United States. Submenus are organized by geographic location. If you need to know when the Sunset Limited leaves Los Angeles and arrives in Miami, make your first stop this Gopher.

Finland
Gopher address: **gopher.funet.fi**

You can learn a lot from the Finnish Forest Research Institute, Helsinki University of Technology.

Germany
Gopher address: **solaris.rz.tu-clausthal.de**

This is your one-stop shopping place for all the Gophers (at least many of them) in Germany.

India
Gopher address: **soochak.ncst.ernet.in**
Path: 1s/mtdc

If you're traveling to India for business or pleasure, this Gopher collection provides useful tips. Browse through a city-by-city menu that opens up a text file telling you about the town; how to get there by air, rail, or road; sightseeing opportunities; and local accommodations.

Scotland
Gopher address: **gopher.almac.co.uk**

It's hard to resist a menu selection titled Everything about Scotland. That's what you'll get—history, Scottish clans, the Dalriada Celtic Heritage Society, poetry, festivals, and the list just keeps on going.

Singapore
Gopher address: **gopher.technet.sg**

Travel to Singapore; read local news; learn about the island, city, and state; get the local time; or jump to other Gopher sites in Singapore all through this site.

South Africa
Gopher address: **gopher.up.ac.za**

This is a great gateway to information about South Africa with connections to the *South Africa Watch Magazine* (actually from Canada), the African National Congress, and other Gopher sites at universities across the continent.

United Kingdom—Railroad Timetables
Gopher address: **gopher.cam.ac.uk**
Path: 1/Misc/BR

Access a list of timetables, phone numbers, and locations of rail stations, and general notes about rail service through this site. Unfortunately, this information doesn't ensure that trains will run on time!

Museums

Chicago Area Galleries and Museums
Gopher address: **nuinfo.nwu.edu**
Path: 1/entertainment/galleries

This provides a calendar of exhibits and a guide to the Dittmar and Mary and Leigh Block galleries.

Museums Galore
Gopher address: **ithaki.servicenet.ariadne-t.gr**
Path: 1/HELLENIC_CIVILIZATION/MUSEUMS

Not only is this a long Gopher address, it will take you a long time to get through all the resources. Take your pick of art galleries or museums of Cyprus, maritime, natural history, science and technology, and theatrical.

National Archives
Gopher address: **gopher.nara.gov**

The National Archives holds all sorts of important historical information. You can find out about current exhibits, or search through the holdings to find what you're looking for.

The Exploratorium
Gopher address: **gopher.exploratorium.edu**

This is an electronic version of the museum in San Francisco. An all-time favorite for science buffs, this Web server includes online exhibits that explain science in plain English.

Media: Publications, Movies, and Television

C-SPAN Gopher
Gopher address: **c-span.org**

If you have cable television, you've probably seen C-SPAN (perhaps by accident). It's the 24-hour-a-day channel devoted to government activities. This Gopher tells you about the television network, provides a program schedule, tells you what C-SPAN is doing with classrooms, and provides links to other government resources.

Bryn Mawr Classical Review
Gopher address: **gopher.lib.Virginia.EDU**

A variety of current electronic publications as well as copies of historical books and novels are available here. Some of the menu items, like the *Grolier Academic American Encyclopedia*, cannot be accessed without clearance.

Electronic Newsstand
Gopher address: **gopher.enews.com**

The Electronic Newsstand is your one-stop shopping place for publications. This Gopher site lets you read articles from many different magazines. Like a traditional newsstand, you can browse at no charge through these publications. Subjects cover every area of interest—computers, technology, science, business, economics, foreign affairs, arts, sports, and travel. Each publisher

VI

Finding Web Resources

provides an online table of contents and a few articles pulled from a current issue. These articles are really teasers to encourage you to order copies of or subscriptions to the publications. A few of the publications that you find here include *Animals*, *Business Week*, *Inc. Magazine*, *Computerworld*, *Canoe & Kayak*, *Fiber Optics News*, and *Federal Employees News Digest*.

Movies
Gopher address: **spinaltap.micro.umn.edu**
Path: 1/fun/Movies

Take your pick of science fiction, action adventure, or pure romance. Access month-by-month reviews of Hollywood's latest endeavors as well as flicks dating back to 1987.

Online Books—Project Gutenberg
Gopher address: **spinaltap.micro.umn.edu**
Path: 1/Ebooks

Project Gutenberg is an on-going project that creates electronic versions of classic and public-domain works of literature. Search by author, call letter, or title. You can either read the books online or download them to your PC. Quite an extensive collection is available already; begin with *Aesop's Fables*, browse the *King James Bible*, tear through *The Scarlet Letter*, and finish *The War of the Worlds*.

Television News
Gopher address: **tvnews.vanderbilt.edu**

Every day TV news tells us what's happening around the world. This Gopher maintains an archive of documents about television news. Menu choices include evening news abstracts, special reports (like coverage of the Persian Gulf War or the coup attempt in the USSR); you can even order videotapes of programs.

Science

Agriculture—PENpages—Penn State University
Gopher address: **penpages.psu.edu**

This Gopher offers variety of agricultural information, including livestock reports and market prices. Resources for teachers are also available.

Biology
Gopher address: **nmnhgoph.si.edu**

This address connects you to some of the biology and natural history collections and resources at the Smithsonian Institute. It's a great resource for teachers, students, and scientists.

Biology at Harvard
Gopher address: **huh.harvard.edu**

This is pretty much for the serious biologist. You can browse through the Harvard biological collection catalog, or read the Mycological Society of America bulletin board. It may be better than counting sheep.

Botany—Australian National Botanical Gardens
Gopher address: **osprey.erin.gov.au**

Direct from "down under," this Gopher tells you everything you need to know about plant life in Australia.

Botany—Missouri Botanical Gardens
Gopher address: **gopher.mobot.org**

This is a wide collection that includes flora of North America, a manual on plants in Costa Rica, and the ever-popular moss database. If you select Plants In Bloom from the main menu, you can do a keyword search for gardens, apparently around the world, that have displays of certain flowers and plants.

Chemistry
Gopher address: **acsinfo.acs.org**

If you enjoy laboratory experiments where you mix chemicals, or you need to know the atomic weight of hydrogen, then this Gopher, sponsored by the American Chemical Society, is for you!

Environment—EcoGopher
Gopher address: **ecosys.drdr.virginia.edu**

All sorts of informational goodies about the environment are provided here. Environmental groups, mailing lists, a library, an environmental chat area, and a link to EcoLynx—a World Wide Web interface to this information—are available.

VI

Finding Web Resources

Geology—United States Geological Survey
Gopher address: **info.er.usgs.gov**

This Gopher site gives you a new perspective on the land and natural resources in the United States. Information about maps, earth sciences, and USGS fact sheets that overview the work of the agency are available here.

Oceanography
Gopher address: **gopher.esdim.noaa.gov**

The National Oceanic and Atmospheric Administration (NOAA) is a government agency involved with all aspects of scientific research related to the oceans and the atmosphere. For example, this agency monitors and studies the impact of the annual fires that occur in the United States. Links to weather information, as well as satellite images, are also provided here.

Space
Gopher address: **gopher.gsfc.nasa.gov**

This is the Gopher server for the Goddard Space Flight Center, one of NASA's centers. You can download space images from the Hubble space telescope, learn about Goddard and NASA space research, and find out why the space shuttle makes sense.

Shopping

Books—International
Gopher address: **infx.infor.com**
Port: 4900

This site enables you to search for publications by several different methods (title/author), and the menus provide ordering information.

Books—Nautical
Gopher address: **gopher.nautical.com**
Path: 1/

The list for everyone interested in anything that would be covered in nautical books. References to online services, a free book guide, ordering, discounts, and boating tips are offered here.

CyberGate
Gopher address: **gopher.gate.net**

CyberGate is an electronic mall. Go into the Marketplace from the main menu to search for publications, boating supplies, a credit bureau, and much more.

CyberMall
Gopher address: **gopher.nstn.ca**

There is a lot of shopping here. Bookstores, computer equipment, and an electronic record store with 3,500 compact disc titles are available through this site.

Flowers—Grant's FTD
Gopher address: **branch.com**
Path: 1s/florist/

This may be easier than ordering flowers through the phone book. The server allows you to select and view floral arrangements and fruit baskets. You can order for delivery anywhere in the United States and Canada.

Weather

University of Illinois Weather Machine
Gopher address: **wx.atmos.uiuc.edu**

Will it rain on your picnic? Check out avalanche forecasts, earthquake bulletins, flood warnings, and weather maps from around the world. You can jump into a state-by-state menu that provides local conditions and forecasts.

From Here...

Even though it's tempting to use only the Web to travel to Web sites, FTP and Gopher sites represent rich resources for Web travelers and should not be ignored. To find more information about these important Internet systems and how to best use Mosaic to get information and files from these sites, refer to the following chapters:

■ Chapter 1, "Introduction to the World Wide Web," explains how the FTP and Gopher systems work.

VI

Finding Web Resources

- Chapter 8, "FTP and Mosaic," tells you how to browse through and download from FTP sites using the Mosaic browser.

- Chapter 9, "Gopher and Mosaic," shows you useful techniques for navigating through Gopherspace with NCSA Mosaic.

Part VII

WebCD

34 What's on WebCD

Chapter 34

What's on WebCD

by Jim Minatel

If you've read other chapters in this book, you probably read about a program or utility that you are ready to install. Or, if you're like many users, you turned to this chapter first because you want to see what's on WebCD and then dive right in. Regardless of whether you read the book from front to back or are starting at the back, this chapter should help you find the software that you need to make the most of the Net.

You can find a wide variety of software on WebCD for use with the World Wide Web and the rest of the Internet. We spent scores of online hours over the past few months gathering the best freeware, shareware, and public-domain software available. I hope these efforts will save you a significant amount of online time and money.

In addition to software that is freely available on the Net, special arrangements were made to bring you several commercial products, including a special version of Mosaic and software that can connect you to several major Internet service providers. In some cases, this software just can't be obtained for free anywhere other than on WebCD. In other cases, the software may be free but not easy to get.

Finally, a large collection of useful documents about the Internet is included on WebCD. You can find all the RFCs, STDs, and FYIs on WebCD.

So drop WebCD into your CD-ROM drive and get ready to load the best collection of Web and Net utilities anywhere.

This chapter covers the following topics:

- What shareware is
- How to get new versions of software on WebCD
- How to install programs from WebCD
- Software for connecting to the Net
- World Wide Web and HTML software
- Graphics and multimedia viewers for use with Mosaic and other Web browsers
- Software for UseNet news, FTP, Archie, Gopher, Internet Relay Chat, Telnet, and many other Internet applications and utilities
- Internet documents

What Is Shareware?

Much of the software on WebCD is shareware. Shareware is software that you can try before you buy; it's not free software, but it is a neat idea.

Shareware software is written by talented and creative people. Quite often, the software provides the same power as programs that you can purchase at your local computer or software store. You have the advantage, however, of knowing what you are getting before you buy it.

> **Note**
>
> In the case of the Internet, shareware often was the only choice before traditional retail software vendors recognized the large market for products. Shareware software was part of the large driving force in opening the Internet for your use.

All shareware software on WebCD comes with a text file (or instructions in the software itself) that tells you how to register the software. You are obligated to register any shareware software that you plan to use regularly.

What benefits do you gain by registering the shareware? First, you have a clean conscience, knowing that you have paid the author for the many hours he or she spent in creating such a useful program.

Second, registering the software can give you additional benefits, such as technical support from the author, a printed manual, or additional features that are available only to registered users. Consult the individual programs for details about what bonuses you may receive for registering.

Third registering your shareware usually puts you on the author's mailing list. Registration enables the author to keep you up to date about new versions of the software, bug fixes, compatibility issues, and so on. Again, the benefits of registration vary from product to product. Some authors even include in the cost of registration a free update to the next version.

Finally, if the license agreement states that you must pay to continue using the software, you are violating the license if you don't pay. In some cases, unregistered use may be a criminal offense. Although an individual user is not likely to be arrested or sued for failing to pay registration for shareware, the small possibility of repercussions is no excuse for violating the license. Wise corporations and businesses register shareware to avoid any chance of legal problems.

> **Note**
>
> Several of the authors and companies that provided software for WebCD asked that a notice of their copyright, shareware agreement, or license information be included in this book. The lack of such a statement printed in this book does not mean that the software is not copyrighted or does not have a license agreement. Please see the text or help files for any program for which you need copyright or licensing information.

Getting Updates for Software on WebCD

The advantage is simple. Putting all this great software on WebCD saves you many hours of looking for and downloading the software yourself. The only downside is that as new versions of software become available, WebCD stays the same.

As a result, a special FTP site was created to enable users of this book to get new versions of the software on WebCD. As soon as an update is received, it will be posted on the FTP site. You can download by anonymous FTP. The FTP address for this site is **ftp.mcp.com**. (MCP stands for Macmillan Computer Publishing, the company that owns Que, which is the publisher of this book.) The directory for software in this book is /pub/que/net-cd. Any time you want, you can log on to this FTP site and look for new software.

What if you want to be told when new software is posted? Your time will be wasted if you look and find nothing new that interests you. Well, Que thought about that, too. You can subscribe to the WebCD mailing list by sending an e-mail message to **subscribe@misl.mcp.com**. The body of the message should be subscribe webcd.

> **Note**
>
> You also can subscribe to the WebCD mailing list by visiting the MCP World Wide Web site at **http://www.mcp.com**. From there, choose the Reference Desk; then click Information Super Library Reports. Enter your name, e-mail address, and company name. Select WebCD. Then click Send.

The Macmillan site and mailing list are not the only ways to keep up to date. Many of the programs on WebCD are regularly updated at several of the major software FTP sites. Sites (and directories) to check out for Windows Internet software include the following:

ftp.cica.indiana.edu in the directory /pub/pc/win3/winsock

archive.orst.edu in the directory /pub/mirrors/ftp.cica.indiana.edu

ftp.ncsa.uiuc.edu in the directory /Web

oak.oakland.edu in the directory /SimTel/win3/winsock

> **Note**
>
> Many of the authors and companies asked that an e-mail or postal address where they can be contacted be included in this book. If you don't find a specific e-mail address listed here, you can find an e-mail address for nearly every program on WebCD in the documentation that comes with the program or in the program (often by choosing **H**elp, **A**bout).

Installing Software from WebCD

Before using any of the software on WebCD, you need to install it. Many of the programs come with their own installation program. If a program includes an installation program, the description of it in this chapter gives you the directions you need to get it installed.

For programs that don't have an installation program, the installation process is straightforward. To install a program that doesn't have an installer, follow these steps:

1. Create a directory on your hard drive for the software.

> **Note**
>
> It's a good idea to create one main directory in the root of your hard drive for all your Web software (such as, c:\web) and then create subdirectories for individual programs in that directory. This keeps the root directory of your hard drive less cluttered.

2. Copy all the files and subdirectories from the program's directory on WebCD to the directory you created on your hard drive. The easiest way to do this in Windows is to select all the files and subdirectories to copy in File Manager and drag them from the window for your CD to the directory on your hard drive. This is shown in figure 34.1.

> **Note**
>
> A directory name appears after the name of each program in this chapter. The directory name is where you can find the software on WebCD.

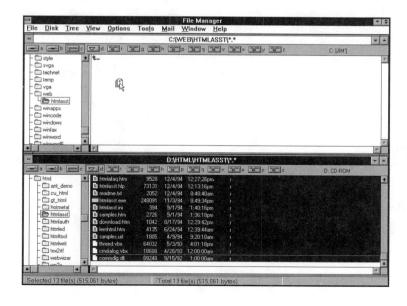

Fig. 34.1
If you are copying subdirectories, be sure to answer yes when prompted if you want to create the new subdirectories.

3. If you used File Manager to copy the files, you need to turn off the Read Only attribute. To do this, select all the files in the directory you copied them to and then choose **F**ile, Proper**t**ies. In the dialog box shown in figure 34.2, deselect **R**ead Only and then choose OK.

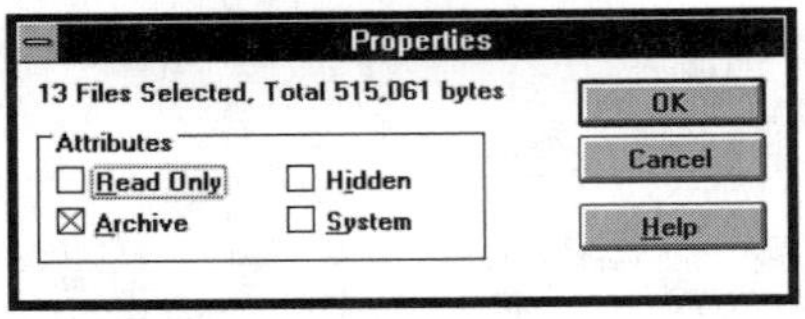

Fig. 34.2
Click the Read Only box so that no X or shading appears. When you choose OK, the Read Only attribute will be turned off for all files.

4. After all the files are copied, create an icon to run the program from Program Manager for each program you plan to run in Windows. The easiest way to do this is to drag the program file from the directory on your hard drive in File Manager to Program Manager and drop it in the program group where you want the icon. This is shown in figure 34.3.

Fig. 34.3
Dragging a file from File Manager to Program Manager doesn't move it, it just creates a program icon in Program Manager.

Tip
It's a good idea to create a new program group to hold all your Web software program icons. In Program Manager, choose **F**ile, **N**ew and then click Program **G**roup.

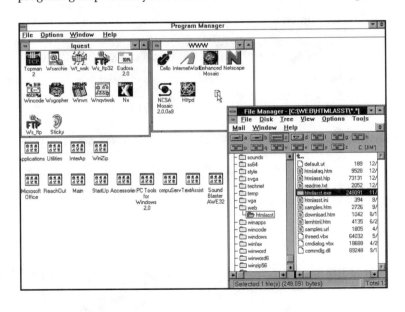

That's all there is to it. Repeat these steps for any software you want to install.

Luckman Interactive Enhanced Mosaic

\luckman\disk1

Luckman Interactive Enhanced Mosaic is a commercial version of Mosaic. Enhanced Mosaic is discussed in detail in Chapter 12. The program includes TCP/IP software to allow you to connect to the Internet. If you do not already have an Internet connection, this software is preconfigured to connect to the Portal service provider. A special offer from Portal for Luckman Interactive Enhanced Mosaic users is included. (See the file portal.wri for details on this offer.) Alternatively, you can configure the software to work with an existing Internet account; however, doing so requires in-depth knowledge of your service provider's login process and TCP/IP setup.

> **Note**
>
> Que licensed this software for purchasers of this book. Luckman Interactive Enhanced Mosaic is *not* shareware, public-domain software, or freeware; it may not be copied or redistributed by any means.

To install the software, change to the \luckman\disk1 directory on WebCD, and run setup.exe. Then follow the on-screen directions to set up the software to use Portal or your current service provider. If you choose to use Portal, you have to send them some application information, and they will send you an account number. The quickest way to do this is by fax. They try to get your account set up in a day or two.

> **Note**
>
> Enhanced Mosaic requires Win32. The setup program reminds you to install this program from the accompanying Win32 disk. The version of Win32s required is the version on this CD. If you do not have Win32 installed, see the section "Win32s" later in this chapter.

The TCP/IP connection software is Distinct's TCP/IP for Windows. If you do not use Portal, you need to run Quick Config after running the setup program to configure your connection to work with Console.

Luckman Interactive Enhanced Mosaic is an enhanced version of NCSA Mosaic. You can use Enhanced Mosaic with any Winsock TCP/IP software, not just the Distinct software.

Win32s

\win32s

◄ See "Installing the Windows 32-bit Libraries," p. 69

Several programs on WebCD require Win32 to run. If you are running Windows 3.1, Windows 3.11, or Windows for Workgroups 3.11, you need to install Win32s to make these programs run. The version here is Win32s 1.20 with OLE 2.02, which is the correct version to use with NCSA Mosaic version 2 Alpha 9. Other programs that require Win32 also work with this version. Complete installation directions for installing Win32s appear in Chapter 4, "Getting Mosaic Running in Windows."

> **Note**
>
> You may not redistribute Win32s without the permission of Microsoft.

All-in-One Suites

If you are looking for a quick-and-easy solution to most of your Internet software needs, one of these suites may be exactly what you need. Both of these suites include connection software and tools for Web browsing, email, and other Internet services.

Internet Chameleon with Instant Internet

\suites\chameleo

Internet Chameleon v4.1 is a complete Internet Windows-based application. Chameleon supports FTP transfer, Telnet logins to remote computers over the Internet or standard TCP/IP connections, e-mail sending and receiving, remote pinging of Internet servers, and World Wide Web browsing.

Before installing Chamelon, close any other applications you are using. You have to close Windows and restart your machine before using the software after it is installed because it does modify your autoexec.bat file. To begin the installation, run setup.exe (in Windows) in the \suites\chameleo\disk1 directory. (When you are prompted for disks 2 and 3 during installation, enter the path name for these directories on WebCD.)

After you run the installation, you still have to register this software before you can use it. The software registration process is automated and sets up the software immediately. You have the option of registering to use the software for a 30-day trial period, which is free, or you can purchase a full license to use the software when you register. You can also set it up to work with an existing service provider's account or to register for a new account with one of several providers that have joined with NetManage to provide instant access. Some of these providers offer free trials, others don't. Read the information for each provider before proceeding if you are interested.

> **Note**
>
> To register the software, you must provide a credit card number, even if you are just registering for the trial time period. The registration takes place over phone lines, not over the Internet, so you should not worry at all about the safety of your credit card number. If you don't provide a valid card number, you can't use the software.

For complete directions on completing the installation and registering the software, see the file inetcham.wri in the \disk1 subdirectory.

> **Note**
>
> If you have used an older version of the NetManage Chameleon Sampler, you will notice some major differences in this version. First, the software now includes all the features of the retail version. Second, you can use this trial version for only 30 days. To continue using the software after 30 days, you must register and purchase the full retail version. Finally, this software cannot be installed over the older sampler.

Pipeline

\suites\pipeline

This software connects you to The Pipeline, a custom service provider. The Pipeline software provides access to e-mail, Gopher, WWW, FTP, and UseNet news through The Pipeline's service. In addition to providing access to the Internet, The Pipeline also allows its users to create Web pages on its system and provides software for doing this. To install the software, run the program setup.exe from the \suites\pipeline directory. The version included on WebCD is version 2.07. (If you get a message that threed.ubx is an old version when you run Pipeline, delete that file from your \windows\system directory and reinstall Pipeline.

Software for Connecting to the Internet (TCP/IP)

If you want to connect to the Internet, you need software. Whether you use a modem to dial up a SLIP or PPP account, connect from your Windows LAN at work, or connect from DOS, the software here can make the connection.

Core Internet-Connect 2.0 Trial Version

\tcpip\inetcon2

This program, which provides Winsock and TCP/IP for networks, is designed to help end users connect; it also is designed for developers who want to build other TCP/IP applications based on it.

To run the automatic installation, run setup.exe (in Windows) in the \tcpip\inetcon2 directory.

> **Note**
>
> This package contains the Internet-Connect© Trial Copy program. Internet-Connect is a registered trademark of Core Systems. Internet-Connect is developed and marketed by Core Systems, 245 Firestone Drive, Walnut Creek, CA 94598, (510) 943-5765.

Crynwr Packet Drivers

\tcpip\crynwr\pktd11, \tcpip\crynwr\pktd11a, \tcpip\crynwr\pktd11b, \tcpip\crynwr\pktd11c, \tcpip\crynwr\exp16116

This collection of drivers is required by most DOS-based (and some Windows-based) Internet applications. The collection serves as an interface between established network software and packet-based Internet connections. A wide range of drivers is included in these archive files for most popular network packages, such as Novell's NetWare and Artisoft's LANtastic. The source code for each driver is also included. If you are experienced enough to alter the code for a driver, you can reassemble these drivers to function differently or better than they do in their current form.

To install the Crynwr Packet Drivers, copy only the files that you need. You'll find all the documentation for these drivers in the \pktd11 subdirectory. Please read the documentation for this and your applications to determine which files you need.

NetDial

\tcpip\netdial

NetDial is an Internet dial-up program with many features. NetDial can call, connect to your Internet host, log you in, and run your TCP/IP program at the click of a mouse. Other features include baud-rate support to 256K baud, up to 99 redial attempts, automatic dialing on startup, sound support, up to five separate configurations, cumulative timer window (tracks all time online), built-in call log viewer/editor, up to five startup programs on startup, and additional modem support.

To install NetDial, run \tcpip\netdial\setup.exe in Windows. For more information about the program and installation, see the files read.me and install.txt.

Slipper/CSlipper

\tcpip\slippr

Slipper/CSlipper version 1.5 is a DOS-based replacement application for SLIP8250. Slipper and CSlipper were written to provide Internet connections through a packet-driver interface. Both applications are very small and command-line-driven. For information about using Slipper or Cslipper and their options, see slipper.doc.

Trumpet Winsock

\tcpip\twsk20b

Trumpet Winsock is the most widely used shareware Winsock package. The software supports modem and network connections. At the time of this writing, twsk20b.zip is the officially released, working version. This version, which was recently released, includes new features such as firewall support, improved scripting, and routing capabilities. Trumpet also has fixed the minor problems in version 1 and a bug with PPP in the first release of version 2.

After copying this program to your hard drive, you need to provide IP address information. If you are using this program over a modem, you need to modify login.cmd to work with your service provider. You also may need to add the directory that contains Trumpet to your path statement in autoexec.bat. The file install.doc contains installation and configuration information.

> **Note**
>
> The Trumpet Winsock is currently distributed as shareware. You may use the Trumpet Winsock for 30 days to evaluate its usefulness. If at the end of that time you are satisfied with the Trumpet Winsock as a product, you should register it.
>
> Trumpet Winsock Version 2.0b has a "Send Registration" option that automatically posts encrypted credit card details to Trumpet Software International. Choose **F**ile, **R**egister to take advantage of this feature.

World Wide Web

It is amazing how much software is available for use with the World Wide Web. Even though WWW is one of the newest developments on the Internet, there is an abundance of good software relating to it. Dig in and enjoy.

Launcher

\www\launcher

This freeware program is a neat utility that allows you to launch a Windows application from a link in a Web browser such as Mosaic. This feature allows you to open an application (such as WordPerfect or Excel) without having to create a link to a particular document. Source code is supplied; for directions on using it, see the file readme.

Lynx

\www\lynx

This program is a WWW client for DOS machines. Lynx is an alpha release and does not support forms at present. On the positive side, each URL you access is opened in a separate window so that you can have several documents open at once. It also has support for displaying inline images. See the readme.txt file for information on configuring DOS Lynx to work with your Internet connection.

SlipKnot

\www\slipknot

SlipKnot is a graphical World Wide Web browser specifically designed for Microsoft Windows users who have UNIX shell accounts with their service providers. SlipKnot's primary feature is that it does not require SLIP or PPP or

TCP/IP services. It also allows background retrieval of multiple documents and storage of complete documents on users' local hard disks.

To install SlipKnot, run \www\slipknot\setup.exe in Windows and follow the directions on-screen. After completing the installation, copy the snterm.exe, snweb.exe, and slipknot.ini files from the \snot105b subdirectory on WebCD to the directory where you installed this on your hard drive. (Be sure to turn off the **R**ead Only attribute as described in "Installing Software from WebCD.") Copying these files upgrades the software to the latest version. The read.me file contains some information about possible installation glitches should you encounter trouble.

Web4ham
\www\web4ham

Web4ham is a World Wide Web server for Windows. The program enables your Windows PC to act like a WWW site that other WWW users can access with any Web client software.

Windows httpd 1.4
\www\whttpd

If you're setting up your own Web server in Windows based on the directions in Chapter 18 of this book, this is the software you'll be using. Please note that earlier versions of this software were freeware, but that this version is shareware and requires a payment after a 30-day trial period for continued use. See index.htm for details of this agreement.

For installation instructions, see Chapter 18.

URL Grabber Demo
\www\grabdemo

Have you ever read an article in a UseNet newsgroup or an e-mail message and seen a URL that you wanted to save for further reference? Sure, you can copy and paste the URL into a browser and then save it in a hotlist or book-mark, but this handy little utility makes this process even easier. The URL Grabber toolbar enables you to grab a URL from documents as you read them and then save a collection of addresses as HTML documents that you can open in any WWW browser. You then have a Web document that contains all the links to the URL addresses that you saved, enabling you to jump to those URLs quickly and easily.

In this demo version, you are limited to grabbing three addresses each time you run the program. For information about ordering the full version, which doesn't have this limit, see the help file.

HTML

HTML documents are at the heart of the Web. Whether you're creating a Web site for a major corporation or just putting up a few personal pages, you need an HTML editor or translator (unless you plan on hiring someone else to do the work for you). This area has seen a flood of good programs and we've got most of them here for you.

ANT_HTML
\html\ant_demo

◀ See "The ANT Template for Word," p. 392

ANT_DEMO.DOT is a template designed to work in Word for Windows 6 and Word for Mac 6 to facilitate the creation of hypertext documents. You can insert HTML codes into any new or existing Word document or into any ASCII document. ANT_DEMO is a demonstration version of the ANT_PLUS conversion utility and the ANT_HTML package. Both ANT_HTML and ANT_PLUS work in all international versions of Word 6.

For directions for installation and use, see Chapter 17.

> **Note**
>
> ANT_HTML.DOT and ANT_DEMO.DOC are copyright © 1994 by Jill Swift. For more information, contact Jill Swift, P.O. Box 213, Montgomery, TX 77356, **jswift@freenet.fsu.edu**.

CU_HTML
\html\cu_html

◀ See "CU_HTML," p. 397

This template enables you to write hypertext (HTML) documents in Word for Windows 2 and 6. The version included here is version 1.5. This package is described in some detail in Chapter 17 along with installation directions.

> **Note**
>
> CU_HTML was developed by Kenneth Wong Y.P. and Anton Lam S.Y. of the Computer Services Centre of the Chinese University of Hong Kong. The package can be distributed freely, except in conjunction with any commercial or for-fee product. You must obtain permission from the authors if the package is to be included in any commercial or for-fee product, and you must distribute this copyright notice with the software.
>
> The software is provided as is. Currently, no warranty exists, and no support in any form will be entertained. You use this software at your own risk. You can, however, send comments and wish lists to **anton-lam@cuhk.hk**.

GT_HTML

\html\gt_html

This is another Word 6 template for creating HTML documents. Only a small number of HTML tags are currently supported, but the ones that are included are the most common tags and should be useful for many basic HTML documents.

◀ See "GT_HTML Template for Word," p. 399

For installation instructions and a more complete description, please see Chapter 17.

HTML Assistant for Windows

\html\htmlasst

This program is a simple shareware HTML document editor. Most commands are implemented via a huge toolbar. The program is a good editor for small documents, but this version limits file size to 32K file. (A pro version that loads larger documents is available; see the help file for order information.) One neat feature of note is the program's capability to convert files that contain URLs (for example, Cello bookmarks and Mosaic .ini files) to HTML documents that can be read with any Web browser.

◀ See "HTML Assistant," p. 400

For installation instructions and a more complete description, please see Chapter 17.

HTML Author

\html\htmlauth

This is another template for creating HTML documents in Word 6 for Windows. To use HTML Author, copy all the files from this directory to a directory on your hard drive as explained in "Installing Windows or DOS Software on WebCD." and then copy the htmlauth.dot template into your Microsoft Word for Windows templates directory. (This will usually be the directory c:/winword/template.) To create an HTML source document, just start up Microsoft Word for Windows and create a new document, selecting htmlauth.dot as the template. For more complete directions, see the manual that is included in Word and HTML formats.

> **Note**
>
> The HTML Author software and its associated manual are Copyright © 1995 Grahame S. Cooper. You may copy and use them provided you do not modify them (other than to change the paragraph styles).
>
> The HTML Author software is provided AS IS without warranty or guarantee. Neither Grahame S. Cooper nor the University of Salford accept any liability for errors or faults in the software or any damage arising from the use of the software.
>
> New versions and updates of the software may be obtained from the University of Salford at the following World Wide Web address: **http://www.salford.ac.uk/docs/depts/iti/staff/gsc/htmlauth/summary.html**.

HTMLed
\html\htmled

◀ See "HTMLed," p. 402

HTMLed is a powerful shareware HTML document editor. The interface features a toolbar for ease of use, and the abundant and clear menus make it easy to find the features that you need.

For installation instructions and a more complete description, please see Chapter 17.

RTF To HTML
\html\rtf2html

This is a utility for converting documents from the RTF format to HTML. RTF (Rich Text Format) is a format that many word processors, including Word for Windows, can import and export. The package also includes a Word 2 for Windows template for writing HTML.

After copying this program from WebCD to a directory on your hard drive, move rtftohm.dll to somewhere in your path. The best place for it is your \windows directory. html.dot should be moved to your Word template directory, usually \winword\template. You can then open a new document in WinWord using html.dot as the template.

HTML Writer

\html\htmlwrit

HTML Writer is a stand-alone HTML authoring program. Most HTML tags can be inserted via an extensive set of menu choices. It has a nice toolbar for implementing many HTML tags. Another good feature is the support of templates. You can use templates to help design and create HTML documents with a consistent look and feel.

SoftQuad HoTMetaL

\www\hotmetal

This freeware program is a full-featured, professional-quality HTML editor for Windows. With this program, you can edit multiple documents at the same time, use templates to ensure consistency between documents, and use the powerful word-processor-like features to do such things as search and replace.

◀ See "HoTMetaL," p. 406

For installation instructions and a more complete description, please see Chapter 17.

Note

The commercial version, HoTMetaL PRO, includes the following new features:

- A clean-up filter called TIDY for any invalid legacy HTML files

- Bit-mapped graphics inline in your documents

- Macros to automate repetitive tasks and reduce errors

- Rules checking and validation to ensure correct HTML markup

- Built-in graphical table editor

- Capability to fix invalid HTML documents and import them (with the Interpret Document command)

- URL editor

- Full table and forms support

- Macro creation and editing support

- Document-validation commands

- Support for Microsoft Windows help

- Printed manual and access to support personnel

- Home-page templates

- Editing tools

- Spell checking

- Thesaurus

- Full, context-sensitive search and replace capability

You can order a copy of HoTMetaL PRO from SoftQuad; the price is $195.

Tex2RTF

\html\tex2rtf

This utility is a handy way to convert LaTeX files to HTML in Windows. (It also converts LaTeX to Windows Help file format if you need that capability.) LaTeX is a format that is very popular for files created in print and online, and is also a common language use for technical documents. This program has a very good help system that you should read through to help you make the most of it.

WebWizard

\html\webwiza

This is another HTML authoring system that works as a template in Word 6 for Windows. It adds a new toolbar with some HTML commands and a new WebWizard menu to the Word 6 menu bar when loaded.

To install WebWizard, run the \html\webwiza\setup.exe file in Windows and follow the directions on-screen. Once WebWizard is loaded, you can use it by opening a new file and selecting web.wiz (which should be in the Word templates directory) as the template. Note that since this template name does not end with a .dot extension, you'll have to select to show all files in the Attach Templates dialog box to see this in the list.

The documentation provided here (in the \html\webwiza\doc directory on WebCD) is for a larger commercial version of this called SGML TagWizard but the two products function in the same way. HTML is a subset of the SGML markup language, so WebWizard is a subset of the SGML product. If you need an SGML document creator, see the readme.txt file for information about contacting the creator of this product.

Viewers

If you frequently download graphics or sound files, you need software to view or listen to these files. Although a commercial graphics program may have more power and versatility than the programs listed here, you sometimes prefer to use a smaller, simpler program.

In addition to programs for graphics and sound, the following sections list text editors and other file-viewing programs. For directions on setting up Mosaic to use these (or other) viewers, see Chapter 5.

While no one is likely to use all these programs, we have included those with similar features to give more choices. What is right in one situation may not be right in others.

Media Blastoff

\viewers\blastoff

This viewer provides support for several popular graphics formats as well as sound and movies. The file formats that will probably be of most use to you with the Internet are GIF, AVI, and WAV.

To install it, run \viewers\blastoff\setup.exe in Windows and follow the directions on-screen.

GrabIt Pro

\viewers\grabpro

This is a Windows screen capture utility. If you are putting Web pages together for software documentation, you'll find this an invaluable aid in creating pages with embedded screen shots. (It does not save files in GIF format, so if you want to use saved images as inline images, you need to convert them using one of the other utilities discussed here.) There is a Windows 3.1 and Windows NT version, both of which are included here.

To install this, run the gpsetup.exe program in Windows from either the win31 or winnt directory and follow the directions on-screen.

Image'n'Bits

\viewers\ima

This is a graphics manipulation and conversion utility. Among the formats support are BMP and GIF. Some of the special effects it includes are dithering, pixelize, and solarize, just to name a few. If you are working with artistic images or photographs as Web images, this program is very useful.

To install this program, run \viewers\ima\setup.exe in Windows and follow the directions on-screen.

GhostView

\install1\viewers\gsview

GhostView v1.0, a Windows 3.1 application, can be used to view printer files that conform to GhostScript 2.6 or later standards. GhostScript is an interpreter for the PostScript page-description language used by many laser printers. GhostView also can be used to print GhostScript embedded documents. Source code for this application is part of the archive. GhostView is the interpreter that NCSA recommends for use with Mosaic for viewing PostScript files with GhostScript. See gsview.doc for installation and setup directions. (You also need the GhostScript 2.61 files, which are on WebCD in the directory \viewers\gsview\gscript. See use.doc for installation and setup directions.)

Jasc Media Center

\viewers\jascmedi

If you have a large collection of multimedia files you have collected from the Web, you will find this utility useful for keeping them organized. It supports 37 file formats including GIF, JPEG, MIDI, WAV, and AVI. Formats that aren't supported can still be used if you have an external file filter for them.

To install Jasc Media Center, run \viewers\jascmedi\setup.exe in Windows.

LView

\viewers\lview

◀ See "Using Viewers," p. 95

This is one of the best all-around graphics viewers and utilities. NCSA recommends this viewer for both GIF and JPEG images with Mosaic. It also supports TIFF, PCX, and several other image formats. In addition to viewing these files, you can retouch images by adjusting their color balance, contrast, and many other attributes.

MegaEdit

\viewers\megaedit

MegaEdit version 2.08 is a Windows text file editor that has many of the standard features that you might find in a DOS-based text editor. This application works for multiple or large files. MegaEdit provides internal support for the original IBM OEM (original equipment manufacturer) font set. This support means that MegaEdit has the capability to correctly display extended IBM characters, such as the line sets with which other Windows-based editors have problems.

> **Note**
>
> This version of MegaEdit is a shareware version that is limited to files of 5,000 lines or less. The full version has no file-size limit except for the limits placed on it by the amount of virtual memory that you have in Windows.

Murals

\viewers\murals

What are you going to do with all the JPEG and GIF images that you download from the Internet? How about using them as Windows wallpaper? Murals enables you to use JPEG and GIF images as wallpaper directly without converting them to BMP format; this capability saves you a great deal of disk space.

MPEGPLAY

\viewers\mpegwin

This is an MPEG movie player for Windows. The current version requires Win32 to run. MPEGPLAY is the viewer recommended by NCSA for use with Mosaic. This latest version adds a Save As feature so that there is now a way to save movies downloaded by Mosaic. If you've used older versions of this with Mosaic, you'll appreciate this new feature. This is an unregistered shareware version and will not play files larger than 1M. This limitation is removed if you register.

◀ See "Installing the Windows 32-bit Libraries," p. 69

◀ See "Using Viewers," p. 95

To install it, run \viewers\mpegwin\setup.exe in Windows and follow the directions on screen.

Paint Shop Pro

\viewers\paintshp

This is a powerful graphics viewing and editing utility. It supports about 20 different graphics file formats including the common GIF and GPEG formats found on the Web. It has a host of features for editing and manipulating graphics, and rivals commercial packages with the number and variety of filters and special effects. It also includes a screen capture program.

To install it, run \viewers\paintshp\setup.exe in Windows and follow the directions on-screen.

PlayWave
\viewers\playwav

PlayWave is a simple Windows application for playing WAV sound files. The program requires fewer mouse clicks for playing waves and can be set to loop a wave file continuously. The author states that this application may not work on all systems. To use it, just use the File Manager to "associate" .WAV files with PlayWave, not the Sound Recorder. Then, when you double-click on .WAV file names, PlayWave will come up, not the Sound Recorder. To use it with Mosaic, designate it as the viewer for WAV files and when you down-load a WAV format sound it will start.

Video Audio Viewer
\viewers\vaview

This is a viewer for Microsoft Video for Windows (AVI) and WAV files. It requires the Microsoft video for Windows runtime files, which are discussed later in this chapter. This viewer is designed to work with Mosaic. To install it, copy the file vsetup.exe to your hard drive, turn off the read only attribute, and then run it. This setup will not run directly WebCD from CD.

Video for Windows
\viewers\vid4win

This is the Microsoft Video for Windows runtime version that you need to view Video for Windows (AVI) files. This is the latest version, 1.1d. Even if you have Video for Windows installed, you should check the version to see if it is older. This newer version runs significantly faster and better than some older versions.

The installation program restarts Windows when done, so save anything you are working on and exit all applications before starting. To install Video for Windows, run \viewers\vid4win\setup.exe in Windows and follow the directions on-screen.

VuePrint
\viewers\vueprint

Here's a useful combination if you get a lot of UUEncoded graphics from the internet. VuePrint is a graphics viewer that opens, saves, and prints graphics in JPEG and GIF formats, as well as several other popular formats. It includes a screen saver that displays collections of these file formats. It also has a built-in UUEncoder and UUDecoder. This makes it pretty much an all-in-one graphics solution for most of your Internet graphics needs.

To install this, just copy the files from either the \win31 or \winnt directory to your hard drive as described earlier in this chapter in "Installing Software from WebCD." The first time you run this, it installs the screen saver for you. There are also menu options for uninstalling and reinstalling the screen saver.

WinJPEG
\viewers\winjpg

WinJPEG is a Windows-based graphics-file viewer and converter. You can read and save TIFF, GIF, JPG, TGA, BMP, and PCX file formats with this viewer/converter. WinJPEG has several color-enhancement and dithering features that allow the user to alter a graphics file slightly. The program also supports batch conversions and screen captures.

WinECJ
\viewers\winecj

WinECJ is a fast JPEG viewer. The program has the capability to open multiple files and has a slide-show-presentation mode.

WinLab
\viewers\winlab

This is a powerful graphics viewer and editor. In addition to the image processing features, it has built-in twain and network support and a Winsock compliant application for sending and receiving images.

WPlany
\viewers\wplany

This sound utility plays sound files through a Windows Wave output device (like a SoundBlaster card). NCSA recommends WPlany for use with Mosaic. The program supports several sound-file formats (including most formats that are used on the Net) and is very easy to use.

E-Mail

E-mail is one of the most popular applications on the Internet. A freeware version of Eudora and several other popular programs are included on WebCD.

Eudora

\email\eudora

Tip
For detailed exploration of this product and Internet e-mail see Que's *Using Eudora*.

Eudora version 1.4.4 is an e-mail package that offers many features. Eudora supports private mailboxes, reply functions, periodic mail checking, and many more features that make this software one of the best mail packages on the market.

> **Note**
>
> You can get information about Eudora 2, the commercial version, on the Web page for Qualcomm's QUEST group. The URL is **http://www.qualcomm.com/quest/ QuestMain.html**. Alternatively, you can get information about the commercial version by sending e-mail to **eudora-sales@qualcomm.com** or by calling (800) 2-EUDORA—that is, (800) 238-3672. You can find the latest version of the freeware version at **ftp.qualcomm.com** in the directory quest/eudora/windows/1.4.

Pegasus Mail

\email\pegasus

Pegasus Mail is a powerful, easy to use e-mail program. Several add-ins for Pegasus make it easier to send attachments of popular document types, such as Ami Pro and Word for Windows. One of these add-ins, Mercury (a mail transport system), is included in the install2\email\pegasus\mercury directory. Pegasus is free software that can be used without restriction.

RFD MAIL

\email\rfdmail

RFD MAIL is a Windows offline mail reader that supports many online services, including CompuServe, Delphi, GEnie, MCI Mail, World UNIX, the Direct Connection, MV Communications, Panix, the Well, the Portal System, NETCOM, CRL, INS, and the Internet Access Company. The program's other features include support for scripts; an address book; folders with drag, drop, and search capability; backup and restore capability; polling; and multiple signature blocks.

Registration grants you the code to unlock the shareware version, a free update, and technical support via e-mail.

To install the program, run \email\rfdmail\install.exe in Windows.

Transfer Pro

\email\xferpro

Transfer Pro is a Windows-based shareware tool that allows you to send text, application data, messages, images, audio, video, executable files, and other data types via e-mail, using the latest MIME 1.0 standards according to RFC1341. The program supports UU and XX encoding and decoding.

To install the program, run \email\xferpro\setup.exe in Windows.

UseNet News

If you plan to read UseNet news on a regular basis, you'll want to use one of the excellent newsreaders listed in this section. Although most of the Web browsers discussed throughout this book include some newsreader functions, you'll probably find that for frequent news reading, you need a dedicated newsreading program. Newsreaders are available for both Windows and DOS.

◀ See "Using Mosaic to Access UseNet Newsgroups," p. 185

NewsXpress

\news\nxpress

This is one of the newest Windows newsreaders, but it is quickly becoming very popular. It has all the features found in the traditional leaders in this category and adds a more pleasant interface.

Trumpet News Reader

\news\wt_wsk

This program is a full-featured shareware Winsock newsreader for Windows. You can use this program to perform all the expected functions, such as reading, posting, and replying (as a follow-up post or by e-mail). You also can save messages and decode attached files.

After copying this to your hard drive, you have to provide information about your news server and your Internet account the first time that you run it. (This is the same information that you need to use the News feature in Mosaic, as discussed in Chapter 10.)

> **Note**
>
> Three other versions of this software are available for other types of Internet connections:
>
> - WT_LWP requires Novell LWP DOS/Windows and is located in the directory \news\wt_lwp.
>
> - WT_ABI requires the Trumpet TSR TCP stack and is located in the directory \news\wt_abi.
>
> - WT_PKT works with a direct-to-packet driver (internal TCP stack) and is located in the directory \news\wt_pkt.
>
> All these versions are similar in function to the Winsock version.

WinVN Newsreader

\news\winvn16

Tip
WinVN and UseNet are discussed in detail in Que's *Using UseNet Newsgroups*.

This program is a full-featured, public-domain Winsock newsreader for Windows. Like the Trumpet program, this program provides all the expected features. You need to provide information about your news server and Internet account the first time you run it.

> **Note**
>
> You'll find new versions of this program at **ftp.ksc.nasa.gov** in the /pub/win3/ winvn directory. New releases are posted at that site rather frequently.

Gopher

Several good Gopher clients are available, offering varying degrees of features and varying degrees of complexity. You are sure to find a program that suits your needs. (Unfortunately for us, some of the popular free Gopher clients have recently been commercialized, and we can't include them here although they are still freely available on the Net.)

Although you can access all of Gopherspace through the World Wide Web with a Web browser, you'll want to use a dedicated Gopher application if you send a lot of time gophering.

Gopher for Windows
\gopher\wgopher

The Chinese University of Hong Kong created this simple little Gopher client. If you are looking for something fancy, this program may not be the ticket for you. If you want something fast and simple, though, this program is the perfect Gopher client.

FTP and Archie

If you plan to perform many file transfers on the Internet, you want to find an FTP client that you like. You also need a good Archie client to help you find the files that you want to transfer. Although you can use just about any Web browser for FTP, and although some Web pages perform Archie searches, an Archie program and an FTP client are must-haves if you download many files.

WSArchie
\install2\ftp\wsarchie

WSArchie is a Winsock-compliant Archie program that allows you to connect to an Archie server and search for a file by using the familiar Windows interface. The program comes preconfigured with the locations of several Archie servers. You can configure WSArchie to transfer files directly from the list of found files so that you don't have to open your FTP client manually and then reenter the address and directory information. This software doesn't work this way, however, with the current version of WS_FTP32.

◄ See "Using Archie from Telnet," p. 182

WS_FTP
\ftp\ws_ftp16

This is the popular WS_FTP FTP freeware client for Windows. WS_FTP makes it very easy use FTP in a Windows point-and-click fashion that is as easy to understand as File Manager. It comes with configurations for connection to several popular FTP sites and you can add more to the list. It also has support for advanced features such as firewalls. There is also a 32-bit version in the \ftp\ws_ftp32 directory.

◄ See "Where to Get Mosaic for Windows and Associated Software," p. 64

WinFTP

\ftp\winftp

If you have used WS_FTP, you'll recognize WinFTP; the author based his work on the source code from WS_FTP, and for the most part, the operation is the same. WinFTP offers a few nice additional features. With the history dialog box, you can select a directory that you have already visited, without having to traverse the entire directory tree. There are filters to allow you to look for specific file types, such as *.txt, or *.zip, in the local and remote hosts, and many other features. This directory contains a 16-bit and 32-bit version.

Internet Relay Chat

Internet Relay Chat is a real-time way to carry on a conversation with one person or several people via computer over the Internet. Whatever you type, everyone else sees. Little software is available for the PC for IRC, but the program included in this section is very good.

WSIRC

\irc\wsirc

This product comes in several styles: a freeware version, a shareware version that provides more functions when it is registered, and retail versions for personal and corporate use. The author also can custom-design an IRC client for special needs. The freeware and shareware versions are both included on WebCD. In this release, the shareware version has all the features enabled, but only for a limited time; after 30 days, you must register the shareware version to continue using it. The freeware version has no such limitations.

Other Internet Applications and Useful Utilities

All the main categories were covered in this book, but a great deal of software doesn't fit any of the major categories. The following sections cover the programs that just didn't fit anywhere else.

ArcMaster

\other\arcmastr

This is a handy utility for compressing and decompressing files using many popular compression formats. Support formats include ZIP, LHZ, and ARJ. You need to have the file compression/decompression utilities for each of these as this is just a front-end to make it easier to use the DOS utilities. It supports drag and drop, allows you to conveniently manipulate compressed files, and converts files from one compression format to another.

ArcShell

\other\arcshell

ArcShell is a Windows shell for ZIP, LHZ, ARC, and ARJ compression files. You need to have the file compression/decompression utilities for each of these as this is just a front-end to make it easier to use the DOS utilities.

Batch UUD for DOS

\other\batchuud

As the name implies, this program is a batch UUDecoder that runs in DOS. With UUD, all you have to do is run UUD *.* in DOS or with the Windows command File, **R**un, and all saved files in UUEncoded format are decoded. The program is smart, as well: by alphabetizing all entries, UUD can make a logical guess at the order of split files.

> **Note**
>
> UUEncoding is performed to convert binary files (programs and archives) to text so that they can be transmitted over the Internet via messages. After receipt, the message files must be converted back to their original binary form.

COMt

\other\comt

COMt is a shareware program that allows a standard Windows-based communication program to act as a Telnet client in a TCP/IP environment. It allows you to use the more powerful features of your communication program in a Telnet session.

Run \other\comt\install.exe (in Windows) to run the automatic installation or read readme.txt to install the program manually.

Crip for Windows
\other\cripwin

This is a Windows-based text encryption program. It was designed for use over the Internet and has options for dealing with PC linefeeds in files that will be sent over the Internet. (See the readme file for information on this.)

Drag And Zip
\other\dragzip

Drag And Zip is a set of utilities that makes Windows 3.1 File Manager into a file manager for creating and managing ZIP, LZH, and GZ files. With its built-in routines to zip and unzip files, Drag And Zip makes it very easy to compress files into ZIP files and to extract files from ZIP files from any Windows File Manager that supports drag and drop. Drag And Zip also supports use of copies of PKZIP, LHA and GUNZIP, to manage compressed files. Drag And Zip has a built-in virus scanner that you can use to scan the files in the compressed file for possible viruses.

To install Drag And Zip, run \other\dragzip\dzsetup.exe in Windows and follow the directions on-screen.

Enigma for Windows
\other\enigma

This is a file encryption program that supports the DES encryption standard used by many U.S. government agencies. While it isn't designed for sending encrypted messages via Internet e-mail, you can use it for transferring files through any protocol that supports binary transfer. So, you can encrypt files on an FTP site, you can send encrypted files as attachments to e-mail using UUEncode or MIME, or you can make encrypted files available via the WWW as links from an HTML document. This is not a public key system, so the same password is used to encode and decode files. This does limit its security for Internet usage since anyone who would be receiving a file would need your password.

To install this, run \other\enigma\install.exe in Windows.

EWAN—Emulator Without A good Name

\other\ewan

Although this emulator does not have a good name, it is a good product. In a typical setting, this program is used primarily for Telnet; you can save configurations for several different Telnet sites. The program supports a capture log, and you can perform the usual copy and paste operations from the text to the capture log.

EWAN is not installed by WebCD; to install it, run \install1\other\ewan\ install.exe.

Extract

\other\extract

Extract version 3.04 is a Windows application for encoding and decoding UU-embedded files.

> **Note**
>
> The documentation with this software is slightly out of date. The author requests that e-mail regarding the product be sent to **dpenner@msi.cuug.ab.ca**. His surface mail address is Eau Claire Place II, 650, 521 - 3rd Avenue S.W., Calgary, Alberta, T2P 3T3.

Finger 1.0

\other\finger10

Finger 1.0 is a simple but functional Finger client. Enter a host and user name, and the program reports information about the user, as determined by the host. (This feature is useful for finding e-mail addresses and other information at a given host computer.)

IP Manager

\other\ipmgr

Do you have trouble keeping track of IP addresses? If so, IP Manager is the solution. It helps you keep track of IP addresses, ensures that you don't have duplicate addresses, and even launches FTP and Telnet sessions.

This trial version is limited to only 25 devices. You may try IP Manager for 21 days. If at the end of the trial period you decide not to purchase IP Manager, it should be deleted.

Name Server Lookup Utility
\other\nslookup

This program is a simple but powerful little utility for looking up information about a specific machine or domain on the Internet. The program reports the numeric IP address and other information for the site or machine name.

Sticky
\other\sticky

This interesting application enables you to post little "sticky notes" on other users' computers via the Internet. You can create a small database of other users to send these notes to.

To install Sticky, run \other\sticky\sticky.exe in Windows to begin the installation.

TekTel
\other\tektel

TekTel is a simple Telnet application with Textronix T4010 and VT100 emulation. The program, which is written in Visual Basic, still is a little rough around the edges. The source code is included.

Time Sync
\other\tsync

Time Sync version 1.4 is a Windows-based application that is designed to synchronize your PC's clock with the time on a UNIX host. This program, which relies on an established WinSock connection, is written in Visual Basic.

To install Time Sync, run \other\tsync\setup.exe in Windows.

U2D
\other\u2d

This handy program converts UNIX text file line endings to DOS text file format. All you have to do is drag a file (or files) from File Manager to the U2D icon to process them.

UUCode

\other\uucode

UUCode is a Windows-based application used to decode UUEncoded files sent over the Internet in messages. This application also encodes a binary file in UUCode so that it can be inserted into a message and sent over the Internet in this manner. The program's configuration options include file overwriting, default file names, and status messages.

To install UUCode, run \other\uucode\setup.exe in Windows.

Visual Basic Run Time DLLs

\other\vbrun

Many of the Windows programs included on WebCD are written in Visual Basic and require one of these files to run. Most of the time, these files will be installed by the program or will have been installed by something else. But, if you ever get an error message that says something like `Cannot run, cannot find vbrunx00.dll`, just copy the missing VB Run Time file from here to your \windows\system directory.

VoiceChat

\other\ivc

VoiceChat is a great example of a cutting-edge Internet application. This program enables two users connected to the Internet to talk to each other via their PCs. The program requires both PCs to have sound cards, microphones, and speakers.

The current version of IVC does not transmit the conversation in real time. It waits for a pause (such as the pause at the end of a sentence) and transmits the whole phrase at once. Audio quality is not affected by a SLIP connection, but you can choose a lower sampling rate to speed transmission. Even so, the sound should be telephone-quality or better. If you use Trumpet Winsock, be sure to upgrade to version 2.0b because IVC is not compatible with earlier versions. See the ivc.faq file for more information about using this interesting application.

If you register this program, you get additional features, such as answering-machine and fax modes. See the file readme.now for installation directions.

WinCode

\other\wincode

WinCode is a great utility for UUEncoding and UUDecoding files. A couple of really nice features are the way that the program handles multiple files (effortlessly) and its capability to tie its menus to other programs. The program decodes many poorly encoded files that other decoders can't handle.

To install WinCode, run the \other\wincode\install.exe in Windows

Windows Sockets Host

\other\wshost

Windows Sockets Host is a simple utility that determines a host computer's name based on a numeric IP address, or vice versa.

Windows Sockets Net Watch

\other\ws_watch

This program makes active checks on Internet hosts that are listed in its database file. This is useful for monitoring a host to see if it is functioning. This program is designed to work on any Winsock DLL, but the documentation has some notes on which Winsocks it works well on and which it has problems with.

Windows Sockets Ping

\other\ws_ping

Ping is an uncomplicated Windows application used to test an Internet connection. The author wrote the program to test whether his two computers were connected on the Internet; you can use it to do the same thing. The source code is included in the archive, and the author grants you permission to alter it, if necessary. Windows 3.1 and Windows NT versions are included.

> **Note**
>
> Because Ping uses nonstandard Winsock calls, this application may not run on every Winsock stack.

WinWHOIS

\other\winwhois

WinWHOIS is a good Windows-based, WHOIS search front-end application. The program keeps a log of responses, so you can copy and paste an address if you find what you are looking for. The program is very easy to use.

WinZip

\other\winzip

WinZip version 5.6 is a fantastic Windows ZIP archive-managing program that no Internet user should be without. This application provides a pleasant graphical interface for managing many archive-file formats, such as ZIP, ARJ, ARC, and LZH. WinZip allows you to open text files from an archive directly to the screen, so that you can read a file in an archive without actually extracting it. Another feature in this version enables you to uninstall a program soon after you install it.

Version 5.6 has added support of archives that use the GZIP, TAR, and Z formats that are very common on the Internet. You can now manage these files just as easily as ZIP files. It is common to find files on the Internet that have been stored as TAR files and then compressed with GZIP or Z. WinZip handles these multiple formats with no problems. This support is unique among the other ZIP file utilities discussed in this chapter.

WinZip is shareware and well worth the $29 registration fee for an individual user.

To install WinZip, run \other\winzip\setup.exe in Windows.

YAWTELNET

\other\yawtel

YAWTELNET (Yet Another Windows Socket Telnet) is a freeware Telnet client designed specifically to work well with Mosaic. Many of the menu commands are not functional, but you can select text in the active window and copy it to another application.

> **Note**
>
> YAWTELNET is copyright © 1994, Hans van Oostrom. Refer to license.txt in the yawtel directory for complete copyright information.

Zip Master

\other\zipmastr

ZMW is a standalone Windows 3.1 ZIP utility. PKZIP and PKUNZIP are not required to use this, which sets it apart from most other Windows based ZIP utilities. You can use it to add to, freshen, or update existing ZIP files, create new ZIP files, extract from or test existing ZIP files, view existing ZIP file contents, and many other functions.

Zip Manager

\other\zipmgr

This is another Windows ZIP utility that doesn't require you to also have PKZIP or PKUNZIP. It is 100-percent PKZIP 2.04 compatible and the compression utilities are designed especially for windows. ZMZIP and ZMUNZIP are built-in to Zip Manager.

To install it, run \other\zipmgr\zmsetup.exe in Program Manager.

> **Note**
>
> You must run the ZMSETUP program to expand all the files before the program can be used. You must run msetup.exe from the Windows Program Manager. Other shells like the Norton Desktop or PC Tools for Windows are not 100-percent compatible with our setup program and may cause it to fail when attempting to create the Zip Manager Group.

Examples from *Special Edition Using the World Wide Web and Mosaic*

\html\examples

Throughout Chapters 15 and 16, which discuss HTML, you'll see examples of HTML code. All the longer examples and code that was used for figures is included in this directory. You'll also find some HTML documents with links to many of the pages listed throughout the book.

Internet Documents

The final group of files on WebCD is a large collection of documents about the Internet. I hope that you find having all this information at your finger-tips useful. Any documents that were zipped are now expanded; you can read them in a text viewer or word processor directly from WebCD, or you can copy them.

Internet Provider Lists

\docs\lists\provider

This directory contains several text files that list many companies and provid-ers on the Internet that supply a constant Internet connection. Many of the sites listed in this text file also have dial-up access to the Internet; others do not. Information such as contact name, phone number, Internet address, and system information is listed for each site in the provider lists, which are ar-ranged by region. The lists are compiled and maintained by InterNIC.

RFCs

\docs\rfc

More than 1,000 RFCs (Request for Comments) are available on WebCD. These RFCs—the working notes of the committees that develop the protocols and standards for the Internet—are numbered in the order in which they were released. (Zeros were added to the beginning of the number part of the file names for the ones numbered below 1,000 so that they display in numeri-cal order in File Manager. For example, rfc3 was changed to rfc0003.) Some numbers are skipped. These numbers represent RFCs that are outdated or that have been replaced by newer ones.

STDs

\docs\std

If an RFC becomes fully accepted, it becomes a standard and is designated an STD (Internet Activities Board Standards). STDs tend to be technical.

FYIs
\docs\fyi

FYIs (For Your Information) are a subset of RFCs; they tend to be more informative and less technical.

From Here...

If this chapter didn't provide enough information and you're hungry for more, I suggest that you read the following chapters:

- Chapter 8, "FTP and Mosaic," discusses the Internet File Transfer Protocol and how to transfer files by using FTP with Mosaic. With this knowledge, you can download even more software and files.

- Chapter 19, "Web Searching," helps find things that you need that are not on WebCD.

- Chapter 33, "Hot FTP and Gopher Sites," points you to some of the best sites for finding software, Internet documents, and more.

Index

F

M

O

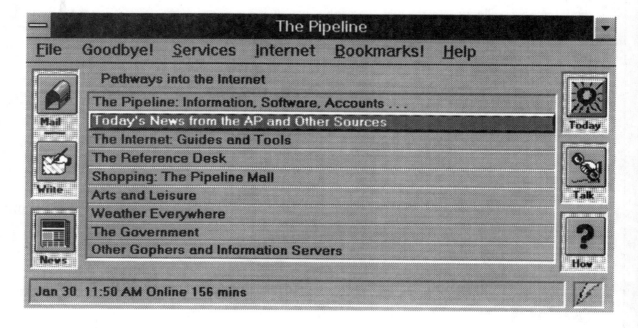

SoftQuad
HoTMetaL PRO™

Create and publish Web pages faster and more easily with the first commercial quality HTML word processor for Windows, Mac and Unix.

Powerful Word Processing Features

- Spell-checker, thesaurus, and dictionary
- Built-in graphical table editor and table support
- Home Page and other useful templates
- Forms support
- In-line graphics display

Easy-to-use Markup Tools

- Insert Element: Choose from a list of only-valid elements
- Edit Links & Attributes: Add hypertext links easily
- Rules Checking & Validation: Ensure correct HTML markup
- TIDY: Import any HTML document, including an invalid document

"A serious product for creating high quality HTML pages ... With HoTMetaL, it's almost certain you'll get your HTML document correct on the first try."
PC Computing

"... leading-edge technology."
PC Magazine

"The current Windows HTML editor of choice."
Boardwatch Magazine

"SoftQuad...has created a set of software applications that connect today's pre-press world to the virtual press of tomorrow's Web page publishing."
Graphic Exchange Magazine

SoftQuad
Panorama PRO

View the Wider World of SGML on the World Wide Web

Introducing SoftQuad Panorama PRO, the first SGML browser for the World Wide Web. By putting SGML on the Web, SoftQuad Panorama PRO gives users and publishers access to longer and more complex documents than are currently available, finer control of their display, more powerful searching, broader presentation and style features, and enhanced linking capabilities.

Order your copy of HoTMetaL PRO ($195 US) or Panorama PRO ($139 US) today. Complete this form, then return it by fax or mail. Or, place your order directly from SoftQuad's Web site or by email.

Please place my order for:

☐ HoTMetaL PRO ☐ Panorama PRO

Platform: _____
Operating System: _____
Name: _____
Title: _____
Company: _____
Address: _____
_____
Phone#: _____
Fax#: _____
PO# or Credit Card#: _____

Tel: (416) 239-4801 Toll Free in US: 800-387-2777 Fax: (416) 239-7105
email: sales@sq.com Web Site: http://www.sq.com

SoftQuad

WebWizard™

The World-Wide Web authoring system that works with your word processor

If you've spent more time learning editing commands than developing new Web documents, WebWizard is for you. WebWizard is an HTML authoring system that works as an add-on to Microsoft Word for Windows 6.0. It lets you insert tags, convert graphics, and format documents by pointing and clicking—all from within the friendly confines of Word 6.0.

WebWizard delivers these features and benefits:

★ Creates fully-formatted HTML and Word documents in a single file

WebWizard uses standard Word files, letting you insert HTML tags that can be hidden. Now you can create documents that can be viewed on the Web and formatted and printed like any other Word files.

★ Provides "Assisted Tagging"

When you click to insert HTML tags, WebWizard provides a dialog box that shows which tags can be inserted in that specific context. Tags are clearly distinguishable, and you have full access to all HTML attributes.

★ Automatically works with any HTML DTD

Because WebWizard has a full SGML parser built in, you can use any HTML DTD. So when standards change, or when companies like NetScape™ extend the standards, WebWizard continues to work uninterrupted.

★ Automatically translates any graphic to GIF format

With WebWizard, any graphic that can be pasted into Word can be converted to GIF format simply by pointing and clicking.

Here's what the experts have to say:

"For those authoring HTML, it takes away the guesswork associated with filtering files from Microsoft Word."
The Seybold Report, July 1994

"NICE Technologies' Word for Windows add-on...has a simple yet well-designed toolbar that will help you build error-free HTML Level 2 compliant documents."
PC Magazine, February 1995

For more information, or to order WebWizard, contact:

NICE Technologies
2121 41st Avenue, Suite 303
Capitola, CA 95010
Phone: (408) 476-7850
Fax: (408) 476-0910
Email: nicetech@netcom.com

WebWizard and NICE Technologies are trademarks of NICE Technologies.
All other trademarks are the properties of their respective owners.

15 Hour Free Trial*

Internet access doesn't have to be expensive or difficult. Now you can enjoy **professional quality access** to the Internet for a **reasonable price.** We staff our network site **24 hours a day**, 7 days a week, 365 days a year, to keep the network up and running.

We also have put together a collection of shareware programs for our Windows users to make getting started on the Internet a breeze. You'll get all the software you need and installation instructions when you subscribe.

Options for Every User

- Shell and SLIP accounts starting at $10.00 per month, with 120 hours per month included.

- Dedicated 14.4, 28.8, and 56K connections available.

- Dedicated T1 and T3 service available.

High Speed Lines

All of our modems are 14.4 Kbps or faster. No waiting for a slow 9600 baud connection. We also have new 28.8K V.34 modem lines for the ultimate in SLIP/PPP speed. ISDN service is also available. Call for details.

To Get an Account Now:

Call (317) 259-5050 or (800) 844-8649 and tell us you saw our ad in *Special Edition Using the World Wide Web and Mosaic.*

We'll set up your account immediately and send you all the information and software you need so that you have your Internet access working with no hassles and no delays.

*Some restrictions apply. Call for details.

Before using any of the software on this disc, you need to install the software you plan to use. See Chapter 34 for directions on installing this software correctly. If you have problems with WebCD, please contact Macmillan Technical Support at (317) 581-3833. We can be reached by e-mail at **support@mcp.com** or on CompuServe at GO QUEBOOKS.